CAMBRIDGE GREEK TESTAMENT FOR
SCHOOLS AND COLLEGES

GENERAL EDITOR :—J. J. S. PEROWNE, D.D.
BISHOP OF WORCESTER.

THE ACTS

OF

THE APOSTLES

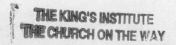

London: C. J. CLAY AND SONS,
CAMBRIDGE UNIVERSITY PRESS WAREHOUSE,
AVE MARIA LANE.

Glasgow: 50, WELLINGTON STREET.

Leipzig: F. A. BROCKHAUS.
New York: THE MACMILLAN COMPANY.
Bombay & Calcutta: MACMILLAN & CO. Ltd.

THE ACTS

OF

THE APOSTLES

WITH MAPS, NOTES AND INTRODUCTION

By

J. RAWSON LUMBY, D.D.

CAMBRIDGE:
At the University Press
1904

First Edition, 1885.
Reprinted 1887, 1891, 1894, 1899, 1904.

PREFACE
BY THE GENERAL EDITOR.

THE General Editor of *The Cambridge Bible for Schools* thinks it right to say that he does not hold himself responsible either for the interpretation of particular passages which the Editors of the several Books have adopted, or for any opinion on points of doctrine that they may have expressed. In the New Testament more especially questions arise of the deepest theological import, on which the ablest and most conscientious interpreters have differed and always will differ. His aim has been in all such cases to leave each Contributor to the unfettered exercise of his own judgment, only taking care that mere controversy should as far as possible be avoided. He has contented himself chiefly with a careful revision of the notes, with pointing out omissions, with suggesting occasionally a reconsideration of some question, or a fuller treatment of difficult passages, and the like.

Beyond this he has not attempted to interfere, feeling it better that each Commentary should have its own individual character, and being convinced that freshness and variety of treatment are more than a compensation for any lack of uniformity in the Series.

ON THE GREEK TEXT.

In undertaking an edition of the Greek text of the New Testament with English notes for the use of Schools, the Syndics of the Cambridge University Press have not thought it desirable to reprint the text in common use*. To have done this would have been to set aside all the materials that have since been accumulated towards the formation of a correct text, and to disregard the results of textual criticism in its application to MSS., Versions and Fathers. It was felt that a text more in accordance with the present state of our knowledge was desirable. On the other hand the Syndics were unable to adopt one of the more recent critical texts, and they were not disposed to make themselves responsible for the preparation of an

* The form of this text most used in England, and adopted in Dr Scrivener's edition, is that of the third edition of Robert Stephens (1550). The name "Received Text" is popularly given to the Elzevir edition of 1633, which is based on this edition of Stephens, and the name is borrowed from a phrase in the Preface, "Textum ergo habes nunc ab omnibus receptum."

entirely new and independent text: at the same time it would have been obviously impossible to leave it to the judgment of each individual contributor to frame his own text, as this would have been fatal to anything like uniformity or consistency. They believed however that a good text might be constructed by simply taking the consent of the two most recent critical editions, those of Tischendorf and Tregelles, as a basis. The same principle of consent could be applied to places where the two critical editions were at variance, by allowing a determining voice to the text of Stephens where it agreed with either of their readings, and to a third critical text, that of Lachmann, where the text of Stephens differed from both. In this manner readings peculiar to one or other of the two editions would be passed over as not being supported by sufficient critical consent; while readings having the double authority would be treated as possessing an adequate title to confidence.

A few words will suffice to explain the manner in which this design has been carried out.

In the *Acts*, the *Epistles*, and the *Revelation*, wherever the texts of Tischendorf and Tregelles agree, their joint readings are followed without any deviation. Where they differ from each other, but neither of them agrees with the text of Stephens as printed in Dr Scrivener's edition, the consensus of Lachmann with either is taken in preference to the text of Stephens. In all other cases the text of Stephens as represented in Dr Scrivener's edition has been followed.

In the *Gospels*, a single modification of this plan has been rendered necessary by the importance of the Sinai MS. (א), which was discovered too late to be used by Tregelles except in the last chapter of St John's Gospel and in the following books. Accordingly, if a reading which Tregelles has put in his margin agrees with א, it is considered as of the same authority as a reading which he has adopted in his text; and if any words which Tregelles has bracketed are omitted by א, these words are here dealt with as if rejected from his text.

In order to secure uniformity, the spelling and the accentuation of Tischendorf have been adopted where he differs from other Editors. His practice has likewise been followed as regards the insertion or omission of Iota subscript in infinitives (as ζῆν, ἐπιτιμᾶν), and adverbs (as κρυφῇ, λάθρα), and the mode of printing such composite forms as διαπαντός, διατί, τουτέστι, and the like.

The punctuation of Tischendorf in his eighth edition has usually been adopted : where it is departed from, the deviation, together with the reasons that have led to it, will be found mentioned in the Notes. Quotations are indicated by a capital letter at the beginning of the sentence. Where a whole verse is omitted, its omission is noted in the margin (*e.g.* Matt. xvii. 21 ; xxiii. 12).

The text is printed in paragraphs corresponding to those of the English Edition.

Although it was necessary that the text of all the portions of the New Testament should be uniformly constructed in accordance with these general rules, each editor has been left at perfect liberty to express his preference for other readings in the Notes.

It is hoped that a text formed on these principles will fairly represent the results of modern criticism, and will at least be accepted as preferable to "the Received Text" for use in Schools.

J. J. STEWART PEROWNE.

CONTENTS.

INTRODUCTION.

I. DESIGN OF THE AUTHOR.

THE writer of the Acts of the Apostles sets forth, in his introductory sentences, that the book is meant to be a continuation of a 'former treatise.' It is addressed to a certain 'Theophilus,' and since, among the other books of the New Testament, the third Gospel is written to a person of the same name, it is not unnatural to take these compositions to be the work of the same author. Hence the unvarying tradition of antiquity (see pp. xx. xxi.) has ascribed both works to St Luke. We will however leave for the present the consideration of this tradition, and turn to the contents of the books. We find that the author describes the earlier work as a 'treatise of all that Jesus *began* both to do and teach until the day in which He was taken up' (Acts i. 1, 2). This description accords exactly with the character and contents of St Luke's Gospel. We find also that the opening sentences of the Acts are an expansion and explanation of the closing sentences of that Gospel. They define more completely the 'power from on high' there mentioned (Luke xxiv. 49), they tell us how long the risen Jesus remained with His disciples, they describe the character of His communications during the forty days, and they make clear to us, what otherwise would have been difficult to understand, viz. how it came to pass that the disciples, when their Master had been taken from them, 'returned to Jerusalem *with great joy*' (Luke xxiv. 52). When we read in the Acts of two men in white apparel who testified to the desolate gazers that the departed Jesus was to come again as He had been seen to go into heaven, we can comprehend that they would recall His words (John xiv. 28),

'I go away and come again unto you. If ye loved me ye would *rejoice* because I said, I go unto the Father,' and that they would be strengthened to act upon them.

Thus, from the way in which this second account of the Ascension supplements and explains the former brief notice in the Gospel, it seems reasonable to accept the Acts as a narrative written with the purpose of continuing the history of the Christian Church after Christ's ascension, in the same manner in which the history of Christ's own deeds had been set forth in the Gospel. Now the writer declares that his object in the first work had been to explain what 'Jesus *began* to do and teach.' He had not, any more than the other Evangelists, aimed at giving a complete life of Jesus. He set forth only an explanation of those *principles* of His teaching, and those great acts in His life, on which the *foundations* of the new society were to be laid. If then the second book be meant to carry on the history in the same spirit in which it had been commenced, we shall expect to find in it no more than what the disciples *began* to do and teach when Jesus was gone away from them. And such unity of purpose, and consequently of treatment, will be all the more to be looked for because both books are addressed to the same person.

That the Acts of the Apostles is a work of this character, a history of *beginnings* only, will be apparent from a very brief examination of its contents. We are told by the writer that Christ, before His ascension, marked out the course which should be taken in the publication of the Gospel. 'Ye shall be witnesses unto me both in Jerusalem, and in all Judaea, and in Samaria, and unto the uttermost parts of the earth.' Taking these words for his theme the author directs his labour to shew in what manner the teaching of the Apostles was *begun* in each of these appointed fields of labour. And he does no more. He mentions the eleven Apostles by name at the outset, implying thereby that each one took his due share in the work of evangelization. But of many of them we hear no more. It did not come within the historian's purpose to describe their portion of the work. With like brevity he relates how the Apostolic band was completed by the election of Matthias into the place

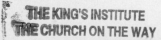

of Judas. This done, he turns to his proper theme, which is what Jesus did from heaven through the Spirit after His ascension, and this work he exemplifies in the history of a series of *beginnings* of Christian congregations in various places. He tells us how the disciples, filled with the Holy Ghost, preached in Jerusalem until it was declared by the lips of their adversaries (Acts v. 28) that the city was filled with their doctrine. After this *commencement* we hear but little of the work done in Jerusalem.

The author's next step is to relate how from the Holy City the mission of the disciples was extended into Judaea and Samaria. To make this intelligible it is found needful to describe with some detail the events which led to the death of Stephen, and before that to point out the position which the first martyr held in the new society. And as the defence which Stephen made before the Jewish rulers forms what may be called the Apology to the Jews for the universalism of Christianity, we have the argument of that speech given at some length. The time had arrived when the Gospel was to be published to others than Jews, and we can see from the charges laid against Stephen that this further spread of their labours had been dwelt upon in the addresses of the Christian teachers. 'Blasphemous words' spoken 'against the Temple and the Law' would be but a vague accusation were it not explained by the defence which was made in reply to it. From this defence we see what the provocation was which had roused the Jews against Stephen. It was the doctrine that God was the God not of the Jews only, but also of the Gentiles, and that His worship was no longer to be restricted to any particular locality as heretofore. To prove to his hearers that this was shewn in their own history and taught by their own prophets, Stephen points out that it was not in the Holy Land, to which they attached such sanctity, that God first appeared to Abraham, but in Mesopotamia; that God was with him also in Haran, and that when He had brought 'the father of the faithful' into Canaan, He gave no permanent possession therein either to him or to his descendants for many generations. Yet though the people of Israel were for a long time strangers in Egypt God was with them there. He blessed them so that they multiplied exceedingly, and manifested His constant care of them in their slavery until at last He sent them a deliverer in Moses. This prophet God had trained first in Pharaoh's court and then in the land of Midian, and had manifested His presence to him in a special manner in the wilderness of Mount Sinai, and all these tokens of God's care of His people had been shewn without any preference on the part of Jehovah for one place above another.

The mention of Moses leads the speaker into a brief digression, in which he compares the rebellious behaviour of the Israelites towards their deliverer, with the hostile disposition of the Jews towards Jesus. But he soon resumes the thread of his argument, and points out that the Tabernacle, and with it the visible sign of God's presence among His chosen people, was moving from place to place for forty years in the wilderness, and that when the people came into Canaan there was no thought of a fixed abode for the Tabernacle until the days of David : that then God did not at once permit the building of the Temple which that king designed to raise, and when Solomon was at length allowed to build God's house, the voice of their prophets, as Stephen reminds his hearers, still testified that the Most High did not dwell in temples made with hands, but sat in heaven, while earth was as His footstool, and that He was the Maker and Preserver not of one race, but of all men. This language, enforcing, from a review of their own history and prophecies, the position which Stephen had taken up in the defence of the new doctrine, and rather going beyond, than defending himself against, the accusation of his opponents, roused their indignation. Apparently perceiving this, the speaker concludes his defence not with a peroration, but with a solemn rebuke, in which he says that, with all their zeal for the Law they have not kept the true spirit of that heaven-sent deposit of which they had been made the guardians. Provoked still more by such a declaration the crowd broke out into a furious rage, and by stoning Stephen and persecuting all who adhered to his cause, endeavoured to stop the spread of the Christian doctrines, but these persecutions

became the cause of a still wider propagation of the new teaching and effected the very object to which the Jews were so
strongly opposed.

Stephen's defence is the longest speech contained in the Acts,
and the great prominence given to it by the author seems to
harmonize with what we judge to be his general design. For
this address was the *first ἀπολογία* for the wider extension of the
preaching of the disciples, and on such initiatory stages of the
movement it is after the author's manner to dwell.

He next proceeds with the history of the propagation of
Christ's doctrine in Judæa and Samaria. And as if to indicate at
once that the message was now to be spread to the farthest
corners of the earth, Philip's mission to the Ethiopian eunuch
is mentioned. Thus we are informed concerning the firstfruits
of the faith in Africa, but the story is carried no farther, nor have
we any after-record concerning Philip, except the notice (xxi. 8)
which seems to imply that he made his home for the future
in Caesarea, where the population would be mainly Gentiles.

Saul's conversion and Peter's visit to Cornelius may be called
companion pictures. They seem meant to display the two lines of
activity by which the conversion of the Gentiles was to be brought
about. The one mission, initiated by St Peter, was to those
among the heathen who, like the centurion of Caesarea, had been
already led to some partial knowledge of God, through the study
of the Jewish Scriptures. On the other hand the great Apostle of
the Gentiles was sent forth to his allotted work among those who
were to be turned (Acts xiv. 15) 'from their vanities to serve
the living God which made heaven and earth and all things
therein.'

As soon as Peter's share in the *beginning* of his mission is
concluded, and he has twice testified concerning it (xi. 4—17,
xv. 7—11) that his action had been prompted by a Divine
revelation, and that the propriety of what he had done was
confirmed by the witness of the Holy Spirit, our historian dis-
misses him, the most energetic of the original twelve, from his
narrative, because the other *beginnings* of Gospel-preaching
among the heathen can be better explained by following the

career of St Paul, the chief pioneer of the Christian faith as it spread to the ends of the earth. Still through the whole of what is related concerning the labours of that Apostle, we learn only of the *founding* of Churches and societies, and of the *initial* steps of the Christian work in those places which he visited. We are indeed told that St Paul proposed, some time after the completion of their first missionary journey (xv. 36), that he and Barnabas should go and visit those cities in which they had already preached the word of the Lord. But that proposal came to nought. The Apostle with Silas subsequently visited only Lystra and Derbe, and that apparently for the sole purpose of taking Timothy as a companion in his further labours. After this visit, the account of which is summed up in three verses, the whole of the second journey was made over new ground. Troas, Philippi, Thessalonica, Athens and Corinth were visited, and probably in all these places, and in others unnamed, the *beginnings* of a Christian society were established. We know that it was so in three of these cities. In returning by sea to Jerusalem the Apostle touched at Ephesus, but remained there so short a time that his real work in that metropolis can hardly be dated from this visit. We are only told that he entered into the Synagogue and reasoned with the Jews (xviii. 19), no mention being made of what was his special work, the mission to the Gentiles. But on his third journey, as though he had foreseen how 'great a door and effectual' was opened to him in Ephesus, he chose that city as the first scene of his settled labours. There he continued for the greater part of three years, and became in that time, we cannot doubt, the founder of the Asiatic Churches of the Apocalypse. From thence he passed over to Macedonia, but though this journey is noticed there is no word told us concerning the Churches which had been founded there by St Paul and his companions on the previous visit, nor concerning his labours in Greece whither he afterwards went. Nay even though he made a special halt on his homeward voyage at Philippi, where was a congregation which above all others was a deep joy to the Apostle, we have no detail recorded of the condition in which he found the brethren whom he so much

loved. Very little had been said concerning the results of the
former stay at Troas (xvi. 8—11) to indicate whether any Christian brotherhood had been established there; and it may be that
the missionaries were forbidden of the Spirit at that time to preach
in Troas as in the rest of Asia. For this reason, it seems, the
historian dwells more at length (xx. 6—12) on the residence of
St Paul in that city during his third journey, in such wise as to
make clear to us that here too the work of Christ was now *begun*.
After that, during the whole course of the voyage, with the ex-
ception of the invitation of the Ephesian elders to Miletus and the
solemn parting address given to them there, in which we hear
repeated echoes of the language of St Paul's Epistles, there
is no mention of any stay at places where the work of Evangelization had already commenced. And when Jerusalem is
reached the imprisonment speedily follows, and the writer
afterwards records merely those stages in the Apostle's history
which led up to his visit to Rome. He might have told us
much of the two years passed in Cæsarea, during which St
Paul's friends were not forbidden 'to minister or to come unto
him.' He might have told us much of those two other years
of the Roman imprisonment, of which he knew the termination.
But this entered not into his plan of writing. He has made
no attempt to write a history of St Paul, any more than of
St Peter. As soon as we have heard that the message of the
Gospel was published first to the Jews and then to the
Gentiles in the empire-city of the world in that age, the author
pauses from his labour. He had completed the task which he
undertook: he had described what Jesus, through His messengers, *began* to do and teach, after His ascension into heaven, for
in reaching Rome the message of the Gospel had potentially
come 'to the uttermost parts of the earth.'

II.   THE TITLE.

It will be clear from what has been already said of its contents
that the title, by which the book is known to us, can hardly have
been given to it by its author. The work is certainly not '*The*

Acts of *the* Apostles.' It contains no detailed account of the work of any of the Apostles except Peter and Paul. John is mentioned on three occasions, but he appears rather as the companion of Peter than as the doer of any special act by himself. Of James the son of Zebedee we have no notice except of his execution by Herod, while much more space is devoted to Stephen and Philip, who were not Apostles, than to him. The same remark applies to the notices of Timothy and Silas. We may conclude then that the title, as we now have it, was a later addition. The author (Acts i. 1) calls the Gospel 'a treatise' (λόγος), a term the most general that could be used; and if that work were styled by him 'the first treatise,' the Acts would most naturally receive the name of 'the second treatise.' Or it may be that the form of title given in the *Cod. Sinaiticus* was its first appellation. There the book is called simply (πράξεις) 'Acts,' and for a while that designation may have been sufficient to distinguish it from other books. But it was not long before treatises came into circulation concerning the doings of individual Apostles and Bishops, and these were known by such titles as 'The Acts of Peter and Paul,' 'The Acts of Timothy,' 'The Acts of Paul and Thecla,' &c. It would become necessary, as such literature increased and was circulated, to enlarge the title of this original volume of 'Acts,' and from such exigency we find in various MSS. different titles given to it, such as 'Acts of the Apostles,' 'Acting of Apostles,' 'Acts of all the Apostles,' 'Acts of the Holy Apostles,' with still longer additions in MSS. of later date.

III.   THE AUTHOR.

All the traditions of the early Church ascribe the authorship of the Acts to the writer of the third Gospel, and Eusebius (*Hist. Eccl.* II. 11) says, 'Luke, by race a native of Antioch and by profession a physician, having associated mainly with Paul and having companied with the rest of the Apostles less closely, has left us examples of that healing of souls which he acquired from them in two inspired books, the Gospel and the Acts of the Apostles.' Eusebius lived about 325 A.D. Before his time Tertullian, A.D. 200, speaks (*De jejuniis*, 10) of the descent of the Holy Ghost upon the Apostles and of Peter going up to the housetop to pray, as facts mentioned in the commentary of Luke. Also (*De baptismo*, 10) he says, 'We find in the Acts of the Apostles that they who had received the baptism of John had not received the Holy Ghost, of which indeed they had not even heard.' Similar quotations could be drawn from Clement of Alexandria, a little anterior to Tertullian, and also from Irenaeus, who wrote about A.D. 190. The earliest clear quotation from the Acts is contained in a letter preserved in Eusebius (*H. E.* v. 2) sent by the Churches in the south of Gaul to the Christians of Asia and Phrygia and written A.D. 177, concerning the persecutions of the Church in Gaul. Alluding to some who had been martyred there, the writers say, "They prayed for those who ordered their torture as did Stephen, that perfect martyr, 'Lord, lay not this sin to their charge.'" In still earlier writings there are found words which may well be allusions to 'the Acts,' yet they are not sufficiently distinct to warrant their insertion as quotations. But in the scarcity of writings at this early period we need not be surprised if a century elapsed after the writing of the book before we can discover traces of its general circulation. It was probably completed, as we shall see, between A.D. 60—70, and if in a hundred years from that time the Christians of Europe could quote from it as a book well known to their brethren in Asia we may feel quite sure that it had been in circulation, and generally known among Christians, for a large portion of the intervening century. Modern critics have doubted the existence of 'the Acts' at the date when this letter of the Churches of Vienne and Lyons was written, and have argued thus: "The tradition of St Stephen's martyrdom, and the memory of his noble sayings, may well have remained in the Church, or have been recorded in writings then current, from one of which indeed eminent critics conjecture that the author of Acts derived his materials[1]."

[1] *Supernatural Religion*, III. 25.

As if it were easier to admit on conjecture the existence of writings for which no particle of evidence is forthcoming, than to allow, in agreement with most ancient tradition, that 'the Acts' was composed at the date to which, on the face of his work, the writer lays claim.

In his book the author makes no mention of himself by name, though in the latter part of his narrative he very frequently employs the pronoun 'we,' intimating thereby that he was present at the events which in that portion of his work he is describing. The passages in which this pronoun is found (xvi. 10—17; xx. 5—38; xxi. 1—18; xxvii.; xxviii.) deserve special notice. The author of 'the Acts,' by alluding in the opening words to his 'former treatise,' leads us to the belief that in this second work he is about again to use material which he gathered from those who had been eyewitnesses and ministers in the scenes which he describes. Much of this material he has clearly cast into such a shape as fitted his purpose, and much which was no doubt at hand for him he did not use because of the special aim which in his treatise he had in view. It is very difficult to believe that an author who has in other parts systematically shaped other men's communications, many of which would naturally be made to him in the first person, into a strictly historical narrative, should in four places of his work have forgotten to do this, and have left standing the 'we' of those persons from whom he received his information. It seems much more natural to infer that the passages in question are really the contributions of the writer himself, and that, on the occasions to which they refer, he was himself a companion of St Paul. For whoever the writer may have been he was neither neglectful nor ignorant of the rules of literary composition, as may be seen by the opening words both of the Gospel and 'the Acts.'

But it has been alleged that anyone who had been the companion of St Paul at those times, to which reference is made in the passages we are considering, would have had much more and greater things to tell us than the writer of 'the Acts' has here set down. This would be quite true if the author had set out with the intention of writing a life of St Paul. But, as has been observed before, this is exactly what he did not do. His book is a description of the *beginnings* of Christianity. And bearing this in mind we can see that the matters on which he dwells are exactly those which we should expect him to notice. In the first passage (xvi. 10—17) he describes the events which were connected with the *planting of the first Christian Church* in Europe at Philippi, and though the word 'we' only occurs in the verses cited above, it would be ridiculous to suppose that he, who wrote those words implying a personal share in what was done, was not a witness of all that took place while Paul and Silas remained in Philippi. A like remark applies to the second passage (xx. 5—38). Here too the word 'we' is not found after verse 15, where we read 'we came to Miletus.' But surely having been with St Paul up to this point, there can be no reason for thinking that the writer was absent at the time of that earnest address which the Apostle gave to the Ephesian elders whom he summoned to Miletus to meet him; an address which is exactly in the style that we should, from his Epistles, expect St Paul to have used, and which we may therefore judge the writer of 'the Acts' to have heard from the Apostle's lips, and in substance to have faithfully reported.

The next 'we' passage (xxi. 1—18) brings the voyagers to Jerusalem, and there the writer represents himself as one who went with St Paul to meet James and the Christian elders when the Apostle was about to give an account of his ministry among the Gentiles. But though after that the story falls again, as a history should, into the third person, have we any right to conclude from this that the writer who had come so far with his friend, left him after he had reached the Holy City? It seems much more natural to suppose that he remained near at hand, and that we have in his further narrative the results of his personal observation and enquiry, especially as when the pronoun 'we' again appears in the document it is (xxvii. 1) to say 'it was determined that *we* should sail into Italy.' The writer who had been the companion of St Paul to Jerusalem is at his side when he is to be sent to Rome. The events intervening had been such that there was no place for the historian to speak in his own person, but the moment when he is allowed again to become St Paul's companion in travel, the personal feature reappears, and the writer continues to be eye-witness of all that was done till Rome was reached, and perhaps even till the Apostle was set free, for he notes carefully the length of time that the imprisonment lasted.

That the writer of 'the Acts' does not mention St Paul's Epistles is what we should expect. He was with St Paul, and not with any of those congregations to which the Epistles were addressed, while as we have said, the *planting* of the Church, and not the further edification thereof was what he set before him to be recorded in 'the Acts.' Moreover we are not to look upon St Luke as with St Paul in the same capacity as Timothy, Silas, or Aristarchus. He was for the Apostle 'the beloved physician'; a Christian brother it is true, but abiding with St Paul because of his physical needs rather than as a prominent sharer in his missionary labours.

The passages in question seem to give us one piece of definite information about their writer. They shew us that he accompanied St Paul from Troas as far as Philippi, and there they leave him. But they further shew that it was exactly in the same region that the Apostle, when returning to Asia for the last time, renewed the interrupted companionship, which thenceforward till St Paul's arrival in Rome seems only to have been interrupted while the Apostle was under the charge of the Roman authorities. If we suppose, as the title given to him warrants us in doing, that Theophilus was some official, perhaps in Roman employ; that he lived (and his name is Greek) in the region of Macedonia; then the third Gospel may very well have been written for his use by St Luke while he remained in Macedonia, and 'the Acts' subsequently when St Paul had been set free. In this case when addressing Theophilus, who would know how the writer came to Macedonia with St Paul, and how he went away again as that Apostle's companion, the places in which the author has allowed 'we' to stand in his narrative are exactly those in which the facts would dictate its retention.

Nor is this personal portion of the writer's narrative so unimportant as has been alleged by some critics. The founding of the Church at Philippi may be called the recorded birthday of European Christendom. And for the writer of 'the Acts' it was not unimportant to tell us that a Christian Church was established at Troas, seeing that he had said in an earlier place that on a former visit they were forbidden of the Spirit to preach the word in Asia. Who moreover can reckon the address at Miletus an unimportant document in early Church history? Does it not shew us how the prescient mind of the Apostle saw the signs of the times, the germs of those heretical opinions which he lived to find more fully developed, and against which he afterwards had to warn Timothy and Titus, against which too almost all the letters of the other Apostles are more or less directed? And how the 'Apostle of the Gentiles' was brought to Rome was a subject which could not but find full place in a history of the *beginnings* of the Gospel. For though the writer of 'the Acts' fully acknowledges the existence of a Christian Church in Rome before St Paul's arrival, it was a part of his purpose to shew us how that Church was *for the first time* strengthened by the personal guidance and direction of one of the Apostles.

The letters of St Paul bear their witness to St Luke's presence with the Apostle when he was a prisoner in Rome; for in the Epistle to Philemon, written from Rome during his first imprisonment, the writer sends to Philemon the salutation of Luke (ver. 24) as one of his fellow-labourers, and in the Epistle to the Colossians (iv. 14) he is also mentioned as 'Luke the beloved physician.' Indeed it seems very probable that St Luke afterwards continued to be the companion of St Paul, for in a later Epistle (2 Tim. iv. 11) we find him saying, 'Only Luke is with me.'

That 'the beloved physician' was the writer both of the Gospel and of 'the Acts' may perhaps also be inferred from the use which the author makes of technical medical terms in his description of diseases, as in the account of Simon's wife's mother (Luke iv. 38), in the story of the woman with the issue of blood (viii. 43, 44), and in his narration of the agony of Christ

(xxii. 44). Also in the description of the cripple at the Temple gate (Acts iii. 7), in the notice of the death of Herod Agrippa (xii. 23), and when he writes of the blindness of Elymas (xiii. 11), and of the sickness of the father of Publius in Melita (xxviii. 8). A comparison of the Greek phraseology of the Gospel and of 'the Acts' leads also to the conclusion that the two books are from the same hand. It should further be noticed that there are more than fifty words used in the Gospel and also in 'the Acts' which are not found elsewhere in the New Testament.

This work, as well as the Gospel, being anonymous, attempts have been made to refer the authorship to some other person than St Luke, seeing that it is only assigned to him by tradition, and that his name never appears in the story as do the names of other actors in the work. Some critics have suggested that Timothy was the author of those sections in which the plural pronoun 'we' occurs, because in the letters addressed to the Corinthians, Thessalonians and Philippians, St Paul mentions Timothy with great affection as his fellow-preacher. It is argued that whoever wrote the narrative of the Acts must have been in very close relation to St Paul at the time when he visited Corinth and Thessalonica and Philippi, and that the name of such a man would not have been omitted, at all events, from the opening greetings of all these Epistles. But we can see from Acts xx. 4—5 that there was an intimate companion of St Paul, who for some reason remained at his side when the others could leave him, and who there states expressly that he was with the Apostle when Timothy had gone away. And the suggestion of those who think that Luke the physician was taken with him by St Paul because of the bodily infirmities under which the Apostle laboured, and that it is in this capacity, rather than as a fellow-preacher, that St Luke was in such close attendance during the missionary journeys, is worthy of consideration. If this were so, Luke, though the writer of the diary, yet would not come so prominently before the Churches in the various cities which were visited, as those companions of St Paul who were fellow-missionaries, and this would explain why he is omitted in the greetings of the letters afterwards written by St Paul to the newly-founded congregations. Moreover, the physician would be the one person who would naturally remain in attendance, when the fellow-preachers had gone forth on their several ways.

Nor is there any better ground for supposing, as some have done, that Silas is the narrator who writes in the first person. We have only to look at Acts xv. 22, where, in the portion of the narrative which, according to this hypothesis, must have been written by Silas, he is spoken of as a 'chief man among the brethren,' to see that Silas could not be the writer of such a notice concerning himself.

And the argument which would make Silas (i.e. *Silvanus*), and Luke (i.e. *Lucanus*), two names belonging to one and the same person, because the one is derived from *silva* = a wood, and the other from *lucus* = a grove, and so their sense is cognate, does not merit much consideration. It is said in support of this view that Silas and Luke are never mentioned together. But it is plain from the story of the preaching and arrest of Paul and Silas at Philippi, that the writer who there speaks in the first person plural was a different person from Silas (cf. Acts xvi. 16—19). And with regard to the cognate significa-tion of the two names it should be borne in mind that when such double appellations were given to the same person they were not derived from the same language. *Cephas* and *Thomas* are Aramaic, while *Peter* and *Didymus* are Greek. But *Silvanus* and *Lucanus* have both a Latin origin.

With still less ground has it been suggested that Titus was the author of these personal sections and that some later writer incorporated them in his work. Titus was with St Paul in his missionary journeys, as we know from the second Epistle to the Corinthians, but to accept him as author of 'the Acts' would be to prefer a theory of modern invention before the tradition which, though not capable of exact verification, has the voice of long antiquity in its favour. We are therefore inclined to give the weight which it deserves to the ancient opinion, and to accept the traditional view of the origin of both the Gospel and 'the Acts,' rather than any of the modern suppositions, which are very difficult to be reconciled with the statements in 'the Acts' and the Epistles, and which are the mere offspring of critical imaginations.

IV. DATE OF THE WORK.

That the writer was one who lived amid the events with which he deals will be clear to any one who will consider how he connects his narrative with contemporary history, and that in no case can he be proved to have fallen into error. We find him speaking of Gamaliel (Acts v. 34) exactly as what we know from other sources about that doctor of the Law would lead us to expect a contemporary to speak. In the same place he deals with historical events in connection with Theudas and Judas, and it has been shewn in the notes that there is great probability that all he says is correct; for he speaks of the latter of these rebels with more exactness than is found in Josephus, while the former has probably been unnamed by that writer, because the rebellion in which Theudas was concerned was comprised under the general description that he gives of the numerous outbreaks with which Judaea was at that time disturbed.

Again, the writer of 'the Acts' brings Caesarea before us exactly in the condition in which we know it to have been under Roman government, in the period before the destruction of Jerusalem. He alludes (xi. 28) to the famine in the days of Claudius Cæsar, in language which only one who had personal knowledge of the event would have used. He gives a notice of Herod Agrippa which accords with Josephus in most minute details, and which shews that the writer of the description was most intimately acquainted with the circumstances which attended that monarch's death. In his mention of Cyprus he makes it clear, by the designation which he uses for the Roman governor of that island, that he was conversant with all the circumstances of its government, which had but recently undergone a change, as is pointed out in the notes on St Paul's visit to Cyprus. Of the same character is his very precise notice of the magisterial titles in Thessalonica and Malta. He employs in his narrative about these places no general expression, signifying 'ruler' or 'chief man,' but gives the special names of the officials there, using words far from common, and which modern investigations have proved to be of that precision which bespeaks a personal acquaintance with the condition of the districts to which the writer refers.

It is noteworthy also that he introduces at Ephesus the burning of the books of magic exactly at that place where, almost above any city in the whole of Asia, such acts were held in the greatest repute. So too the whole dialogue which he records when Paul was rescued by the chief captain in Jerusalem is full of incidental allusions to the tumults and disorders with which Judaea was afflicted at the time, allusions which would hardly have been made, and certainly not so naturally and without all comment, by a writer who put together the story of the Acts at a time long after the Apostles were dead. The mention of the large force told off to convey Paul to Caesarea is just one of those notices which a later writer would never have invented. A body-guard of *four hundred and seventy* men for the conveyance of a single prisoner would have seemed out of all proportion except to one who when he wrote knew that the whole land was infested with bands of outlaws, and that these desperadoes could be hired for any outrage at the shortest notice.

In the same way Felix, Festus and Agrippa are brought before us in exact harmony with what we learn of their history and characters from other sources, and with none of that description which a late writer would have been sure to introduce, while a contemporary would know it to be unnecessary. Even the speech of Tertullus before Felix, both by what it says and what it omits, in its words of flattery, is evidence that we are dealing with the writing of one who lived through the events of which he has given us the history.

But it is in the frequent notices of Jerusalem that the most cogent evidence is to be found for the date of the writer. That city was destroyed by the Romans A.D. 70, but in the whole of the Acts there is no single word to indicate that the author of this book knew anything of that event or even of the causes whose operation brought it about. The city is always mentioned as still in its grandeur; the Temple services and sacrifices continue to be observed; at the great feasts the crowds of strangers assemble as the Law enjoined, and among its population the Scribes and Pharisees and Sadducees act the same parts which they do in the Gospel histories; localities such as Solomon's porch, and the field Akeldama, the tower of Antonia and its near neighbourhood to the Temple, are spoken of as though still existing and as well-marked spots; the synagogues erected in the city for the foreign Jews are mentioned, and the writer speaks of them as places which would be well known to his readers. Annas and Caiaphas and Ananias are to him no characters removed by long years of past history, but recent holders of office in the city which was still standing in all security. These features, so many and so various, of contemporary knowledge mark the Acts as a book which must have been written before the overthrow of Jerusalem, and as the narrative terminates about the year 63 A.D., we conclude that its composition must have been completed very soon after that date, and probably not later than A.D. 66. About the latter year St Paul was martyred at Rome, and had the writer of the Acts known of that event it is very difficult to imagine that he would have made no allusion to it in such passages as those in which the Apostle declares his expectation of death and his readiness to suffer in the cause of Christ.

But not only does the writer of the Acts move easily in his narrative as if amid contemporary history, and give notices of persons and places as one would do to whom actual experience in what he writes about makes his footing sure, he has also left an undesigned testimony to the date at which he wrote in the character of his narrative. We know that before the end of the first century the Christian Church was troubled by the rise of much false doctrine. In the New Testament we have a few allusions to false teachers, as when it is said of Hymenaeus and Alexander (1 Tim. i. 19, 20) that they 'have made shipwreck concerning the faith,' and (2 Tim. ii. 17, 18) of Hymenaeus and Philetus, that they 'have erred concerning the truth.' But from

other sources we learn much more than from Holy Writ concerning these first heretical teachers. The earliest and most
prominent among them were the Gnostics, who derived their
name from the pretensions which they made to superior knowledge (γνῶσις). This knowledge, as they taught, distinguished the
more elevated among mankind from the vulgar, for whom faith
and traditional opinion were said to be sufficient. These teachers
also perverted the Scriptures by great license in the use of
allegorical explanation; they held that from God had emanated
generations of spiritual beings, whom they named *Aeons* (αἰῶνες),
and who, from the description given of them, are seen to be im-
personations of the Divine attributes. By the Gnostics matter
was declared to be evil, but superior knowledge could enable men
either by asceticism to become superior to it, or if they indulged
in excesses, to do so without harm. These heretics also denied
the resurrection of the body. One of their number, Cerinthus,
taught that Christ was one of the Aeons, and that he descended
upon the man Jesus at His baptism, and gave Him the power of
working miracles, but departed from Him before His crucifixion.
There were many other forms assumed by their various heretical
doctrines, but what has been said will be a sufficient notice of
their character for us to see how free from all knowledge of such
speculations was the writer of the Acts. He mentions the
opposition of the Judaizing Christians, those of the Circumcision,
and he records in many places the violent assaults made on the
first missionaries by those sections of the heathen population
who saw that the spread of Christianity would interfere with
their sources of gain, but of Gnosticism in any of its phases he
has never a word, though that kind of teaching was widely
spread before the end of the first century. It is therefore to be
believed that his history was composed before such heretical
teaching had spread, or even made itself much known, otherwise
we must suppose that the writer, though aware of the existence
of all these errors, has yet been able to compile a narrative of
the early years of the Church without giving us a hint of what
had been developed within her at the time when he wrote. He
has brought forward St Paul speaking at Miletus (xx. 29, 30),

'I know that after my departing shall grievous wolves enter in among you, not sparing the flock. Also of your own selves shall men arise, speaking perverse things, to draw away disciples after them;' and yet on such a passage he has given no sign that the words of the Apostle had been exactly verified. To suppose that the writer could thus compose his book and never shew that he knew of the later course of the history of the Church, if he did know of it, is quite as difficult as to conceive that he was aware of the overthrow of the Holy City, and yet, though making mention of Jerusalem in almost every chapter, he has never let fall a word to intimate his knowledge that the city no longer existed. The only safe conclusion to which a consideration of these characteristics of the Acts can lead us is that the author wrote as he has done because, at the time when he was writing, Gnosticism had not been spread abroad, nor was Jerusalem destroyed.

The absence of any allusions to the writings of St Paul in the Acts is a piece of the same kind of evidence for the early date of its composition. Many of the Pauline Epistles were no doubt written and in the possession of those Churches to which they were addressed before the composition of the Acts, but they had not yet been widely circulated, and so were probably unknown to St Luke. There are, however, some points in the history, which he has given us, that derive support from the Epistles. Thus the provision for widows, alluded to Acts vi. 1, was a new feature of social obligation introduced by Christianity. In the narrative of St Luke we are shewn that this was one of the earliest cares of the infant Church, and that it even took precedence of all that we now embrace under the name of public worship. Consonant with this part of the early Christian organization are the regulations given by St Paul to Timothy (1 Tim. v. 9) concerning provision for the widows in the Church over which he was to preside. Again the historian gives in several places the account of Saul's conversion after he had been a persecutor of the Christians; in entire accord with this the Apostle speaks of himself (1 Tim. i. 13) as 'a blasphemer, and a persecutor, and injurious,' but as having 'obtained mercy because he did it ignorantly in unbelief.' St Paul tells of his escape from Damascus (2 Cor. xi. 32) in language which agrees with what we read in the Acts (ix. 23—25). In like manner he makes mention (Gal. i. 18) of his visit to Jerusalem to see Peter and James exactly as St Luke mentions it in the history (Acts ix. 28). We learn from the Acts (xii. 17) that James was president of the Church in Jerusalem, and with that agrees the testimony of St Paul (Gal. ii. 9), while the persecutions which the Apostle underwent in Lystra, Antioch and Iconium, of which the historian speaks at some length (Acts xiii., xiv.), are mentioned by St Paul when he is writing to Timothy, a native of Lystra (2 Tim. iii. 10, 11), as matters about which the latter had full knowledge. So too the letters of St Paul confirm the history in the Acts with reference to the sufferings endured by the Apostle in his mission to Macedonia. Speaking of these sufferings he reminds the Philippians (i. 30) that their conflict is of the same kind as they had seen him endure. He alludes also (ii. 22) to their knowledge of the character of Timothy whom St Luke mentions as one of St Paul's companions in that journey. And at an earlier period when writing to the Thessalonians (1 Thess. i. 6) he makes mention of the great affliction under which they had received the word of the Gospel, and specially names (ii. 2) the shameful treatment to which he and his companions had been subjected at Philippi. Then the teaching recorded at Athens in which the Apostle points out how men from natural religion should be led to 'seek the Lord if haply they may feel after Him and find Him' has its counterpart in what is said in the opening of the Epistle to the Romans. There too St Paul declares that the invisible things of God, even His eternal power and Godhead, are clearly seen, being understood by the things that are made, so that men are without excuse. While the quotation from Aratus in that same speech on Mars' Hill is exactly in the style of St Paul, as may be seen from similar quotations made by him 1 Cor. xv. 33 and Titus i. 12, while no other N.T. writer is found quoting from the works of heathen authors.

Again both history and letters shew us how St Paul laboured with his own hands for the support not only of himself but of those who were with him. St Luke mentions the working with Aquila and Priscilla at Corinth (xviii. 3) and puts a reference to the like conduct at Ephesus into the Apostle's mouth (xx. 34) when he is speaking to the elders at Miletus. The passages which confirm this narrative in the Epistles will be found in 1 Cor. iv. 12; 2 Cor. xi. 8—10; 1 Thess. ii. 9; 2 Thess. iii. 8; while from Rom. xvi. 4 and 2 Tim. iv. 19 we have evidence that these persons whom St Luke tells us were fellow-workers with the Apostle as tent-makers were really friends whom he valued highly as brethren in Christ.

On another point we have similar confirmation of one document by the others. We know from the Acts how St Paul encouraged the Gentiles to aid with their substance the poor Christians in Judaea, and he mentions (Acts xxiv. 17) that it was to bring some of the alms collected in answer to his appeals that he had come to Jerusalem when he was attacked in the Temple. Writing to the Romans (xv. 25) the Apostle says 'Now I go unto Jerusalem to minister unto the saints' and in the next verse mentions the 'contributions' of Macedonia and Achaia. We have also a proof (1 Cor. xvi. 1) that such collections were directed to be made in the churches of Galatia as well as at Corinth, and the same subject is mentioned 2 Cor. viii. 1—4.

In Acts xix. 21, the historian tells us of St Paul's intention to visit Rome, and to the Christians there the Apostle writes (Rom. i. 13) 'I would not have you ignorant that oftentimes I have purposed to come unto you.' We know from the Acts very incidentally (xxvii. 2) that Aristarchus went with St Paul when he was carried prisoner to Rome. This is confirmed by the language which the Apostle uses in a letter written during that imprisonment (Col. iv. 10) where he speaks of Aristarchus as his fellow-prisoner, a term which might well be used figuratively by him to express the devotion of the friend who gave up his own liberty that he might minister to the venerable Apostle.

Such coincidences of testimony in works written independently of each other are of the highest value, and could only be found in writings produced by those who wrote from direct personal knowledge. So that we are in this way brought to the conclusion that the narrative of the Acts was composed before the time when the Epistles of St Paul had been brought into circulation. For there is in the history no notice of the letters, and yet the details betoken the same freshness, and closeness to the events of which they speak, as is seen in the confessedly contemporary allusions made by St Paul in his Epistles. There can, therefore, be no great difference in their date of composition between those Epistles of St Paul from which we have quoted and St Luke's account in the Acts of the Apostles.

A consideration of these various features of the Acts,—that the writer makes mention of contemporary secular history as one who was living among the events of which he speaks; that in his work we find no indication that he knew of the fall of Jerusalem; that he displays no acquaintaince with the heretical tenets which were rife before the end of the first century; that he makes no reference to any of St Paul's Epistles, though writing as one fully conversant with the missionary-travels of that Apostle,—forces us to the conclusion that the work was written at some time between A.D. 63 and A.D. 70, and most probably about midway between these dates.

V.   THE SOURCES OF THE NARRATIVE.

In the preface to the Gospel of St Luke the writer states definitely that the information which he is about to record for Theophilus was derived from those 'which from the beginning were eye-witnesses and ministers of the word.' And as he himself was certainly not a disciple of Christ from the first, it was necessary that in the earlier treatise he should consult others, and it may have been needful to do so for the greater portion of what he has there written. But in the later book the sources of his information are not necessarily of exactly the same kind as for the Gospel. So that the preface of the Gospel need not be taken as having reference to the Acts likewise; and it is manifest from the passages in which the author in the Acts speaks in the first person plural that he meant to imply that he was himself an eye-witness of the events which he is there describing. What has been said in the notes on iii. 8 about the graphic character of the language there used, and of its similarity in style to the Gospel of St Mark, the vivid narratives of which have much in common with the acknowledged language of St Peter, it seems not improbable that the account of the events at and after the Ascension and of the spread of the Gospel in Jerusalem (Acts i.—v.) may have been drawn directly or indirectly from that Apostle's information. We may also ascribe to the same source all those portions of the narrative in which St Peter plays a conspicuous part, and of which the language is markedly of one character. Such portions would include ix. 32—xi. 18 and also xii. 1—19, much of which could have come in the first instance from no other lips than those of Peter himself. From some member of the Hellenistic party, of whom St Luke would meet many during his travels with St Paul, (just as we know (xxi. 8) that he dwelt with Philip the Evangelist many days at Caesarea,) our author probably drew the whole of that portion of his narrative which relates to the appointment of the deacons and the accusation, defence and death of Stephen (vi.—vii.), as well as those notices of the after movements of the Hellenistic missionaries (viii. 1—40, xi. 19—30, xii. 25) which are found at intervals in the history.

The narrative of Saul's conversion (ix. 1—30) must have been told by St Paul himself, and after xiii. 1 the remainder of the book deals exclusively with the labours of that Apostle, and as the writer had abundant opportunities while journeying with St Paul of hearing all the history of his life before he became his companion, we cannot suppose that he has recorded anything in that part of his narrative except what was derived from the information of the Apostle or his fellow-labourers.

There remain the two historic notices (1) of the rest experienced by the Churches of Judaea and Galilee and Samaria (ix. 31) and (2) of the death of Herod Agrippa (xii. 20—23); but of these, if, as we have endeavoured to shew, he were living amidst the events of which he writes, the author would be aware from his personal knowledge; and the natural manner in which both these incidents are introduced indicates how well the writer knew that for his Christian readers as well as for himself a slight hint would recall the bypast trials of Christ's Church.

VI. ON SOME ALLEGED DIFFICULTIES IN THE CHARACTER OF THE NARRATIVE IN THE ACTS.

It has been said in recent criticism on the Acts that the book represents the Gospel as intended not for Jews only but for all mankind, in a manner at variance with the teaching of the Gospels. Those who put forward this objection would assign the teaching of the universality of the Gospel message to St Paul alone and would set it down as his development of what was meant at first to be only a modification of Judaism.

That in the Acts the preaching of the Gospel is represented as for all nations is certainly true. St Peter says (ii. 39) 'The promise is unto you and to your children and to *all that are afar off*, even as many as the Lord our God shall call.' The accusation laid against Stephen (vi. 14) was that he had said 'Jesus of Nazareth shall destroy this place and *change the customs which Moses delivered us*' and his whole defence shews that he had preached that not the Jews nor Jerusalem were any longer to be God's special care, but that all men were now to be embraced in His covenant, while the whole of St Paul's labours are directed to make of Jews and Gentiles one worldwide Church of Christ. But the student of the Gospels need surely find no stumblingblock here. For if we take that which is on all hands accepted as the most Jewish of the Gospels, that of St Matthew, we can see that the universalism of the Acts is therein foreshadowed from the first, and spoken of definitely before the close. To God's ancient people His offers of mercy were made first, and in accordance with this is the conduct of all the preaching of the Acts, but Gentiles are no longer excluded when once Christ has been born. To lay the foundations of the Christian Church firmly in the short space of the ministerial life of its Founder it was needful that the labours both of Himself and His disciples should be confined within a limited range, and directed to a people prepared by the Old Testament revelation and among whom some were likely to be ready to hear the words of the Gospel message. But while the infant Jesus is in His cradle we see *wise men from the East* brought to be His earliest worshippers. The voice of His herald proclaims that not the natural seed of Abraham shall of necessity be heirs of the promises, but that God is able of the very stones (and if so, much more from among the rest of mankind) to raise up children unto Abraham. When the ministry of Christ is begun and He takes up His abode in the border land of the Gentiles, we are reminded that it had been made known of old that 'the people which sat in darkness were to see great light, and that light is sprung up for them that sat in the region and shadow of death.' Then what can be more universal than the benedictions with which the Sermon on the Mount begins? The poor in spirit, the mourners, the meek, the pure, the merciful, these are not restricted to the Jewish race, and on these it is that Jesus utters His first blessings. How often too does He shew that the customs of the Jews were to be done away, the ceremonial law, the fastings and the sabbaths to be disregarded, while the moral law was to be widened and deepened so that all men should learn that they were neighbours one of another! How often does He select the Samaritans to illustrate His teaching, and place them before us as those with whom He was well pleased, while He points out (Matt. viii. 10) that in the Roman centurion there was faith manifested beyond what He had found in Israel! It is true that when Jesus first sent out the twelve (Matt. x. 5) He said unto them 'Go not into the way of the Gentiles' but this was in the same spirit in which all the teaching of Christianity had its commencement among the Jews. Yet the Lord, who gave the injunction that this should be so, knew that those to whom the message was first sent would largely refuse to hear. For He adds to his commission the warning that His ministers are going as 'sheep among wolves,' and foretells that they should be persecuted from one city to another (Matt. x. 16—23), and goes on to say that His message is to be published far and wide, yea even proclaimed, as it were, from the housetops. When He speaks afterwards (Matt. xii. 18—21) of His own work in the language of Isaiah He quotes 'He shall shew judgment to *the Gentiles*...and in His name shall *the Gentiles* trust' and before the close of that same address He adds those words which proclaim that not only the ties of race but even those of family and kindred are to be disregarded in comparison with the unity of all men in Him 'Whosoever shall do the will of my Father which is in heaven, the same is my brother and sister and mother.'

Think too how he figures the kingdom of God. It is a tree (Matt. xiii. 32) in whose branches the birds of the air from all quarters shall come and find a home: it is a net cast into the wide sea of the world and gathers (xiii. 47) of every kind of fish; while the field in which God's seed is to be sown is not Judæa nor Palestine nor any limited region, but in His own gracious exposition (xiii. 38) 'The field is the world.' He makes known (Matt. xviii. 11) that His mission is not to save one race only but to seek and save that which is lost, and says to the professedly, but only outwardly, religious among His own people (xxi. 31) 'The publicans and harlots go into the kingdom of God before you,' and adds the solemn warning afterwards (xxi. 43) 'The kingdom of God shall be taken from you, and given to a nation bringing forth the fruits thereof.'

And as the end of His life drew near Jesus spake even more plainly. Thus He says (Matt. xxiv. 14) 'This Gospel of the kingdom shall be preached in *all the world* for a witness unto *all nations*,' and His final commission (xxviii. 19) bids His disciples do what St Luke tells us in the Acts they did: 'Go ye therefore and teach *all nations* baptizing them...and teaching them to observe all things whatsoever I have commanded you.'

When in one Gospel we find so many evidences of what the character of the Christian preaching was meant to be, we need not examine farther to see with how little ground it is asserted that in the Acts St Luke paints Christianity in different colours from anything that was known to the writers of the Gospels or set forth in the life and teaching of Jesus. As the angels proclaimed at the birth of the Lord, 'the tidings of great joy' were to be 'unto all people,' and the new-born King while 'the glory of God's people Israel' was also heralded from the first as to be 'a light to lighten the Gentiles.'

Another objection to the narrative in the Acts is that the book marks no rupture with Judaism. To bring this objection into prominence much stress is laid, by those who use it, on the severity with which St Paul speaks of the Judaizers in some parts of his letters, notably in the Epistle to the Galatians. From the language there used it is argued that the Apostle had broken altogether with Judaism, and that the picture of his life and labours as we have received it in the Acts is untrustworthy. Now first of all it is extremely unlikely that the preachers of Christ's Gospel, with His example before them, would sever themselves from their Jewish brethren until circumstances arose which forced them to do so. Our Lord had been a devout Jew while rebuking without measure what was deserving of rebuke in Pharisaic Judaism. And what we have set before us in the Acts, first in the doings of the twelve, and then in the story of St Paul, is in natural sequence to the Gospel history. Peter and John going up to the Temple at the hour of prayer is the link which binds one history to the other, and it is a link which would not lightly be broken, for who could be so powerfully appealed to by the first Evangelists as those who had the ancient scriptures already in their hands?

And in St Paul's case a distinction should be made between Judaism and Judaizers. He knew that Judaism must pass away, yet how tenderly, lovingly he deals in his letters with the devout Jew. The Judaizers, who were of set purpose an obstacle and hindrance to the work of the Gospel, he cannot away with. They are the men who desire merely 'to make a fair shew in the flesh,' who preach 'another Gospel,' and therefore are to the Apostle anathema. But he could still see constantly in the Law the pædagogue appointed to bring men to Christ; and how near his heart his own people were we can discern from that Moses-like language of his written to the Romans at the very same time that he wrote in his severest strain to the misleading Judaizers among the Galatians. In what a truly tender light St Paul regarded all that was Jewish is seen from his words to the Romans (Rom. ix. 1—5) 'I say the truth in Christ, I lie not, my conscience bearing witness with me in the Holy Ghost, that I have great sorrow and unceasing pain in my heart. For I could wish that I myself were anathema from Christ for my brethren's sake, my kinsmen according to the flesh: who are Israelites; whose is the adoption, and the glory, and the covenants, and the giving of the law, and the service *of God*, and the promises; whose are the fathers, and of whom is Christ as concerning the flesh, who is over all, God blessed for ever.' Now this very same feeling is shewn to us in the Acts. There to the Jews he becomes a Jew that he may gain them for the Gospel. He follows the advice of the brethren in Jerusalem and takes on him the Nazirite vow, and in his speech before the Council he shrinks not from saying 'I am a Pharisee, a son of Pharisees,' exactly in accord with the spirit which dictates again his argument to the Romans (xi. 1) 'Did God cast off His people? God forbid. For I also am an Israelite.' And those whom God had not cast off we may rest sure St Paul had not cast off, nor made with them such a breach as is suggested by those who argue from some expressions in his Epistles that the behaviour described in the Acts is not such as St Paul would have shewn to the other disciples nor they to him.

Again it is said that in the Acts Peter is represented as Pauline in all he says and does and Paul's conduct is pictured as in complete harmony with Peter's. But to those who believe that these two were both Apostles of the same Jesus, both preachers of the same Evangel, both guided by the same Holy Spirit, there is nothing but what is natural in this. The historian brings both before us as labouring for the same work, the extension of the Gospel according to Christ's command from Jerusalem to the ends of the earth. He gives us only short abstracts of what either preacher said, and is it not to be supposed that there would be great similarity in the drift of their addresses? Their main theme must be the Resurrection as a proof of the Divinity and the Messiahship of Jesus. Their chief exhortation 'Repent and be baptized in the name of Jesus Christ for the remission of your sins.'

But this figment of a Pauline and a Petrine party never entered into the thoughts of either Luke or Paul or Peter. There were partizans of Paul and of Peter at Corinth, it is true, but we know how they were rebuked by Paul himself, who bade them remember that Christ was not divided. Nor is there any evidence worth the name that His Apostles were divided. Paul tells us how he rebuked Peter because he stood condemned by the inconsistency of his own actions. But it was the rebuke of a friend and not of an opponent, for in the same chapter he speaks of Peter as one who had been entrusted by the Spirit with the Gospel of the circumcision, and who had given to him and Barnabas the right hand of fellowship, as labourers in a common cause though in different fields. But neither in the Acts nor in the Epistles have we any warrant for that opinion which is so prominent in the Clementine fictions of the second century. There, without being named, St Paul is alluded to by Peter 'as the man who is mine enemy,' and under the guise of Simon Magus is attacked for reproving Peter at Antioch. These writings are a most worthless ground on which to base any argument at all. Their author, whoever he may have been, durst not mention St Paul by name, so doubtful is he of the acceptance which his work will meet with; and yet it is of these works that writers who deny the fidelity of the New Testament documents assert 'there is scarcely a single writing which is of so great importance for the history of Christianity in its first stage.' It is out of these fictions that the Petrine and Pauline parties have been evolved. The writings of Justin Martyr, who knew the sentiments of Christians in the Holy Land at the beginning of the second century, have no trace of these parties, neither is there a trace to be found in what is left us of the writings of that Judæo-Christian Hegesippus. And if these men, who were in the position to know most about it, have no word of the matter, we can only conclude that the opposition so much dwelt on did not exist, but that, just as in the Acts we have it set before us, the preaching of Peter and Paul was in entire harmony. For them Christ was not divided, nor did their doctrine differ except so far as was made necessary by the condition of the audiences which they addressed. For a fuller discussion of this subject than is here possible, and for demonstration that there was no antagonism between Paul and the rest of the Apostles, the reader is referred to Dr Lightfoot's Essay on 'St Paul and the Three' in his Edition of the Epistle to the Galatians.

In the notes on various readings the text of the Vulgate has been compared throughout and it will be found that that version supports to a remarkable degree the readings given in the earliest MSS.

The language of the Acts, and in part the grammar, has been illustrated, where it is possible, from the Septuagint (and especially from the Greek of the Apocryphal Books), since to that version we are indebted in the main for the New Testament diction.

As will be seen from the Index, a considerable number of extracts from the Homilies of Chrysostom on the Acts have been given in the notes. The study of patristic commentaries is now encouraged by some of the University examinations. It therefore seemed worth while to draw the attention of the student from the first to such commentaries, and no more attractive writer than Chrysostom could be found with whom to begin an acquaintance with patristic Greek.

Where the recently published 'Teaching of the Twelve Apostles' offers any matter illustrative of St Luke's history it has been noticed, and in the same manner reference will be found not unfrequently made to the various portions of the Apocryphal Acts.

For grammatical reference *Winer-Moulton* has been quoted where the student might wish for a fuller discussion of any point than could be given in the notes.

ΠΡΑΞΕΙΣ ΑΠΟΣΤΟΛΩΝ

1 ¹ Τὸν μὲν πρῶτον λόγον ἐποιησάμην περὶ πάντων, ὦ Θεόφιλε, ὧν ἤρξατο ὁ Ἰησοῦς ποιεῖν τε καὶ διδάσκειν, ² ἄχρι ἧς ἡμέρας ἐντειλάμενος τοῖς ἀποστόλοις
διὰ πνεύματος ἁγίου οὓς ἐξελέξατο ἀνελήμφθη. ³ οἷς
καὶ παρέστησεν ἑαυτὸν ζῶντα μετὰ τὸ παθεῖν αὐτὸν ἐν
πολλοῖς τεκμηρίοις, δι᾽ ἡμερῶν τεσσεράκοντα ὀπτανόμενος αὐτοῖς καὶ λέγων τὰ περὶ τῆς βασιλείας τοῦ
θεοῦ· ⁴ καὶ συναλιζόμενος παρήγγειλεν αὐτοῖς ἀπὸ
Ἱεροσολύμων μὴ χωρίζεσθαι, ἀλλὰ περιμένειν τὴν
ἐπαγγελίαν τοῦ πατρὸς ἣν ἠκούσατέ μου ⁵ ὅτι Ἰωάννης
μὲν ἐβάπτισεν ὕδατι, ὑμεῖς δὲ ἐν πνεύματι βαπτισθήσεσθε ἁγίῳ οὐ μετὰ πολλὰς ταύτας ἡμέρας. ⁶ οἱ μὲν
οὖν συνελθόντες ἠρώτων αὐτὸν λέγοντες, Κύριε, εἰ ἐν
τῷ χρόνῳ τούτῳ ἀποκαθιστάνεις τὴν βασιλείαν τῷ
Ἰσραήλ; ⁷ εἶπεν πρὸς αὐτούς, Οὐχ ὑμῶν ἐστιν γνῶναι
χρόνους ἢ καιροὺς οὓς ὁ πατὴρ ἔθετο ἐν τῇ ἰδίᾳ ἐξουσίᾳ,
⁸ ἀλλὰ λήμψεσθε δύναμιν ἐπελθόντος τοῦ ἁγίου πνεύματος ἐφ᾽ ὑμᾶς, καὶ ἔσεσθέ μου μάρτυρες ἔν τε Ἱερουσαλὴμ καὶ ἐν πάσῃ τῇ Ἰουδαίᾳ καὶ Σαμαρείᾳ καὶ ἕως
ἐσχάτου τῆς γῆς. ⁹ καὶ ταῦτα εἰπὼν βλεπόντων αὐτῶν
ἐπήρθη, καὶ νεφέλη ὑπέλαβεν αὐτὸν ἀπὸ τῶν ὀφθαλμῶν
αὐτῶν. ¹⁰ καὶ ὡς ἀτενίζοντες ἦσαν εἰς τὸν οὐρανὸν

πορευομένου αὐτοῦ, καὶ ἰδοὺ ἄνδρες δύο παρειστήκεισαν
αὐτοῖς ἐν ἐσθήσεσι λευκαῖς, [11] οἳ καὶ εἶπαν, Ἄνδρες
Γαλιλαῖοι, τί ἑστήκατε βλέποντες εἰς τὸν οὐρανόν;
οὗτος ὁ Ἰησοῦς ὁ ἀναλημφθεὶς ἀφ' ὑμῶν εἰς τὸν οὐρανὸν
οὕτως ἐλεύσεται ὃν τρόπον ἐθεάσασθε αὐτὸν πορευό-
μενον εἰς τὸν οὐρανόν. [12] τότε ὑπέστρεψαν εἰς Ἱερουσαλὴμ ἀπὸ ὄρους τοῦ καλουμένου Ἐλαιῶνος, ὅ ἐστιν
ἐγγὺς Ἱερουσαλὴμ σαββάτου ἔχον ὁδόν. [13] καὶ ὅτε
εἰσῆλθον, εἰς τὸ ὑπερῷον ἀνέβησαν οὗ ἦσαν καταμένοντες, ὅ τε Πέτρος καὶ Ἰωάννης καὶ Ἰάκωβος καὶ
Ἀνδρέας, Φίλιππος καὶ Θωμᾶς, Βαρθολομαῖος καὶ
Μαθθαῖος, Ἰάκωβος Ἀλφαίου καὶ Σίμων ὁ Ζηλωτὴς
καὶ Ἰούδας Ἰακώβου. [14] οὗτοι πάντες ἦσαν προσκαρτεροῦντες ὁμοθυμαδὸν τῇ προσευχῇ σὺν γυναιξὶν καὶ
Μαριὰμ τῇ μητρὶ τοῦ Ἰησοῦ καὶ τοῖς ἀδελφοῖς αὐτοῦ.

[15] Καὶ ἐν ταῖς ἡμέραις ταύταις ἀναστὰς Πέτρος ἐν
μέσῳ τῶν ἀδελφῶν εἶπεν· ἦν τε ὄχλος ὀνομάτων ἐπὶ
τὸ αὐτὸ ὡς ἑκατὸν εἴκοσιν· [16] Ἄνδρες ἀδελφοί, ἔδει
πληρωθῆναι τὴν γραφὴν ἣν προεῖπεν τὸ πνεῦμα τὸ ἅγιον
διὰ στόματος Δαυεὶδ περὶ Ἰούδα τοῦ γενομένου ὁδηγοῦ
τοῖς συλλαβοῦσιν Ἰησοῦν, [17] ὅτι κατηριθμημένος ἦν ἐν
ἡμῖν καὶ ἔλαχεν τὸν κλῆρον τῆς διακονίας ταύτης.
[18] οὗτος μὲν οὖν ἐκτήσατο χωρίον ἐκ μισθοῦ τῆς ἀδικίας,
καὶ πρηνὴς γενόμενος ἐλάκησεν μέσος, καὶ ἐξεχύθη
πάντα τὰ σπλάγχνα αὐτοῦ· [19] καὶ γνωστὸν ἐγένετο
πᾶσι τοῖς κατοικοῦσιν Ἱερουσαλήμ, ὥστε κληθῆναι τὸ
χωρίον ἐκεῖνο τῇ ἰδίᾳ διαλέκτῳ αὐτῶν Ἀχελδαμάχ,
τοῦτ' ἔστιν χωρίον αἵματος. [20] γέγραπται γὰρ ἐν βίβλῳ
ψαλμῶν, Γενηθήτω ἡ ἔπαυλις αὐτοῦ ἔρημος καὶ μὴ
ἔστω ὁ κατοικῶν ἐν αὐτῇ, καί, Τὴν ἐπισκοπὴν αὐτοῦ
λαβέτω ἕτερος. [21] δεῖ οὖν τῶν συνελθόντων ἡμῖν ἀνδρῶν

ἐν παντὶ χρόνῳ ᾧ εἰσῆλθεν καὶ ἐξῆλθεν ἐφ᾿ ἡμᾶς ὁ κύριος Ἰησοῦς, ²² ἀρξάμενος ἀπὸ τοῦ βαπτίσματος Ἰωάννου ἕως τῆς ἡμέρας ἧς ἀνελήμφθη ἀφ᾿ ἡμῶν, μάρτυρα τῆς ἀναστάσεως αὐτοῦ σὺν ἡμῖν γενέσθαι ἕνα τούτων. ²³ καὶ ἔστησαν δύο, Ἰωσὴφ τὸν καλούμενον Βαρσαββᾶν, ὃς ἐπεκλήθη Ἰοῦστος, καὶ Μαθθίαν. ²⁴ καὶ προσευξάμενοι εἶπαν, Σὺ κύριε καρδιογνῶστα πάντων, ἀνάδειξον ὃν ἐξελέξω ἐκ τούτων τῶν δύο ἕνα ²⁵ λαβεῖν τὸν τόπον τῆς διακονίας ταύτης καὶ ἀποστολῆς, ἀφ᾿ ἧς παρέβη Ἰούδας πορευθῆναι εἰς τὸν τόπον τὸν ἴδιον. ²⁶ καὶ ἔδωκαν κλήρους αὐτοῖς, καὶ ἔπεσεν ὁ κλῆρος ἐπὶ Μαθθίαν, καὶ συγκατεψηφίσθη μετὰ τῶν ἕνδεκα ἀποστόλων.

2 ¹ Καὶ ἐν τῷ συμπληροῦσθαι τὴν ἡμέραν τῆς Πεντηκοστῆς ἦσαν πάντες ὁμοῦ ἐπὶ τὸ αὐτό. ² καὶ ἐγένετο ἄφνω ἐκ τοῦ οὐρανοῦ ἦχος ὥσπερ φερομένης πνοῆς βιαίας καὶ ἐπλήρωσεν ὅλον τὸν οἶκον οὗ ἦσαν καθήμενοι, ³ καὶ ὤφθησαν αὐτοῖς διαμεριζόμεναι γλῶσσαι ὡσεὶ πυρός, καὶ ἐκάθισεν ἐφ᾿ ἕνα ἕκαστον αὐτῶν, ⁴ καὶ ἐπλήσθησαν πάντες πνεύματος ἁγίου, καὶ ἤρξαντο λαλεῖν ἑτέραις γλώσσαις καθὼς τὸ πνεῦμα ἐδίδου ἀποφθέγγεσθαι αὐτοῖς. ⁵ ἦσαν δὲ ἐν Ἱερουσαλὴμ κατοικοῦντες Ἰουδαῖοι, ἄνδρες εὐλαβεῖς ἀπὸ παντὸς ἔθνους τῶν ὑπὸ τὸν οὐρανόν· ⁶ γενομένης δὲ τῆς φωνῆς ταύτης συνῆλθεν τὸ πλῆθος καὶ συνεχύθη, ὅτι ἤκουον εἷς ἕκαστος τῇ ἰδίᾳ διαλέκτῳ λαλούντων αὐτῶν. ⁷ ἐξίσταντο δὲ πάντες καὶ ἐθαύμαζον λέγοντες, Οὐχ ἰδοὺ πάντες οὗτοί εἰσιν οἱ λαλοῦντες Γαλιλαῖοι; ⁸ καὶ πῶς ἡμεῖς ἀκούομεν ἕκαστος τῇ ἰδίᾳ διαλέκτῳ ἡμῶν ἐν ᾗ ἐγεννήθημεν, ⁹ Πάρθοι καὶ Μῆδοι καὶ Ἐλαμῖται, καὶ οἱ κατοικοῦντες τὴν Μεσοποταμίαν, Ἰουδαίαν τε καὶ Καπ-

παδοκίαν, Πόντον καὶ τὴν Ἀσίαν, ¹⁰ Φρυγίαν τε καὶ
Παμφυλίαν, Αἴγυπτον καὶ τὰ μέρη τῆς Λιβύης τῆς
κατὰ Κυρήνην, καὶ οἱ ἐπιδημοῦντες Ῥωμαῖοι, Ἰουδαῖοί
τε καὶ προσήλυτοι, ¹¹ Κρῆτες καὶ Ἄραβες, ἀκούομεν
λαλούντων αὐτῶν ταῖς ἡμετέραις γλώσσαις τὰ μεγαλεῖα
τοῦ θεοῦ. ¹² ἐξίσταντο δὲ πάντες καὶ διηπόρουντο, ἄλλος
πρὸς ἄλλον λέγοντες, Τί θέλει τοῦτο εἶναι; ¹³ ἕτεροι
δὲ διαχλευάζοντες ἔλεγον ὅτι Γλεύκους μεμεστωμένοι
εἰσίν.

¹⁴ Σταθεὶς δὲ ὁ Πέτρος σὺν τοῖς ἕνδεκα ἐπῆρεν τὴν
φωνὴν αὐτοῦ καὶ ἀπεφθέγξατο αὐτοῖς, Ἄνδρες Ἰουδαῖοι
καὶ οἱ κατοικοῦντες Ἱερουσαλὴμ πάντες, τοῦτο ὑμῖν
γνωστὸν ἔστω, καὶ ἐνωτίσασθε τὰ ῥήματά μου. ¹⁵ οὐ
γὰρ ὡς ὑμεῖς ὑπολαμβάνετε οὗτοι μεθύουσιν, ἔστιν γὰρ
ὥρα τρίτη τῆς ἡμέρας, ¹⁶ ἀλλὰ τοῦτό ἐστιν τὸ εἰρημένον
διὰ τοῦ προφήτου Ἰωήλ, ¹⁷ Καὶ ἔσται ἐν ταῖς ἐσχάταις
ἡμέραις, λέγει ὁ θεός, ἐκχεῶ ἀπὸ τοῦ πνεύματός μου
ἐπὶ πᾶσαν σάρκα, καὶ προφητεύσουσιν οἱ υἱοὶ ὑμῶν καὶ
αἱ θυγατέρες ὑμῶν, καὶ οἱ νεανίσκοι ὑμῶν ὁράσεις ὄψον-
ται, καὶ οἱ πρεσβύτεροι ὑμῶν ἐνυπνίοις ἐνυπνιασθήσον-
ται· ¹⁸ καί γε ἐπὶ τοὺς δούλους μου καὶ ἐπὶ τὰς δούλας
μου ἐν ταῖς ἡμέραις ἐκείναις ἐκχεῶ ἀπὸ τοῦ πνεύματός
μου, καὶ προφητεύσουσιν. ¹⁹ καὶ δώσω τέρατα ἐν τῷ
οὐρανῷ ἄνω καὶ σημεῖα ἐπὶ τῆς γῆς κάτω, αἷμα καὶ πῦρ
καὶ ἀτμίδα καπνοῦ. ²⁰ ὁ ἥλιος μεταστραφήσεται εἰς
σκότος καὶ ἡ σελήνη εἰς αἷμα, πρὶν ἐλθεῖν ἡμέραν
κυρίου τὴν μεγάλην καὶ ἐπιφανῆ. ²¹ καὶ ἔσται πᾶς ὃς
ἂν ἐπικαλέσηται τὸ ὄνομα κυρίου σωθήσεται.

²² Ἄνδρες Ἰσραηλῖται, ἀκούσατε τοὺς λόγους τούτους·
Ἰησοῦν τὸν Ναζωραῖον, ἄνδρα ἀποδεδειγμένον ἀπὸ τοῦ
θεοῦ εἰς ὑμᾶς δυνάμεσι καὶ τέρασι καὶ σημείοις, οἷς ἐποί-

ησεν δι᾽ αὐτοῦ ὁ θεὸς ἐν μέσῳ ὑμῶν, καθὼς αὐτοὶ οἴδατε, 23 τοῦτον τῇ ὡρισμένῃ βουλῇ καὶ προγνώσει τοῦ θεοῦ ἔκδοτον διὰ χειρὸς ἀνόμων προσπήξαντες ἀνείλατε, 24 ὃν ὁ θεὸς ἀνέστησεν λύσας τὰς ὠδῖνας τοῦ θανάτου, καθότι οὐκ ἦν δυνατὸν κρατεῖσθαι αὐτὸν ὑπ᾽ αὐτοῦ. 25 Δαυεὶδ γὰρ λέγει εἰς αὐτόν, Προορώμην τὸν κύριον ἐνώπιόν μου διὰ παντός, ὅτι ἐκ δεξιῶν μου ἐστίν, ἵνα μὴ σαλευθῶ· 26 διὰ τοῦτο ηὐφράνθη μου ἡ καρδία καὶ ἠγαλλιάσατο ἡ γλῶσσά μου, ἔτι δὲ καὶ ἡ σάρξ μου κατασκηνώσει ἐφ᾽ ἐλπίδι, 27 ὅτι οὐκ ἐγκαταλείψεις τὴν ψυχήν μου εἰς ᾅδην οὐδὲ δώσεις τὸν ὅσιόν σου ἰδεῖν διαφθοράν. 28 ἐγνώρισάς μοι ὁδοὺς ζωῆς, πληρώσεις με εὐφροσύνης μετὰ τοῦ προσώπου σου. 29 ἄνδρες ἀδελφοί, ἐξὸν εἰπεῖν μετὰ παρρησίας πρὸς ὑμᾶς περὶ τοῦ πατριάρχου Δαυείδ, ὅτι καὶ ἐτελεύτησεν καὶ ἐτάφη, καὶ τὸ μνῆμα αὐτοῦ ἔστιν ἐν ἡμῖν ἄχρι τῆς ἡμέρας ταύτης. 30 προφήτης οὖν ὑπάρχων καὶ εἰδὼς ὅτι ὅρκῳ ὤμοσεν αὐτῷ ὁ θεὸς ἐκ καρποῦ τῆς ὀσφύος αὐτοῦ καθίσαι ἐπὶ τὸν θρόνον αὐτοῦ, 31 προϊδὼν ἐλάλησεν περὶ τῆς ἀναστάσεως τοῦ Χριστοῦ, ὅτι οὔτε ἐγκατελείφθη εἰς ᾅδου οὔτε ἡ σάρξ αὐτοῦ εἶδεν διαφθοράν. 32 τοῦτον τὸν Ἰησοῦν ἀνέστησεν ὁ θεός, οὗ πάντες ἡμεῖς ἐσμὲν μάρτυρες. 33 τῇ δεξιᾷ οὖν τοῦ θεοῦ ὑψωθεὶς τήν τε ἐπαγγελίαν πνεύματος τοῦ ἁγίου λαβὼν παρὰ τοῦ πατρὸς ἐξέχεεν τοῦτο ὃ ὑμεῖς βλέπετε καὶ ἀκούετε. 34 οὐ γὰρ Δαυεὶδ ἀνέβη εἰς τοὺς οὐρανούς, λέγει δὲ αὐτός, Εἶπεν κύριος τῷ κυρίῳ μου, κάθου ἐκ δεξιῶν μου, 35 ἕως ἂν θῶ τοὺς ἐχθρούς σου ὑποπόδιον τῶν ποδῶν σου. 36 ἀσφαλῶς οὖν γινωσκέτω πᾶς οἶκος Ἰσραὴλ ὅτι καὶ κύριον αὐτὸν καὶ Χριστὸν ὁ θεὸς ἐποίησεν, τοῦτον τὸν Ἰησοῦν ὃν ὑμεῖς ἐσταυρώσατε.

37 Ἀκούσαντες δὲ κατενύγησαν τὴν καρδίαν, εἶπόν

τε πρὸς τὸν Πέτρον καὶ τοὺς λοιποὺς ἀποστόλους, Τί
ποιήσωμεν, ἄνδρες ἀδελφοί; ³⁸ Πέτρος δὲ πρὸς αὐτούς,
Μετανοήσατε, καὶ βαπτισθήτω ἕκαστος ὑμῶν ἐπὶ τῷ
ὀνόματι Ἰησοῦ Χριστοῦ εἰς ἄφεσιν τῶν ἁμαρτιῶν ὑμῶν,
καὶ λήμψεσθε τὴν δωρεὰν τοῦ ἁγίου πνεύματος. ³⁹ ὑμῖν
γάρ ἐστιν ἡ ἐπαγγελία καὶ τοῖς τέκνοις ὑμῶν καὶ πᾶσιν
τοῖς εἰς μακράν, οὓς ἂν προσκαλέσηται κύριος ὁ θεὸς
ἡμῶν. ⁴⁰ ἑτέροις τε λόγοις πλείοσιν διεμαρτύρατο, καὶ
παρεκάλει αὐτοὺς λέγων, Σώθητε ἀπὸ τῆς γενεᾶς τῆς
σκολιᾶς ταύτης.

⁴¹ Οἱ μὲν οὖν ἀποδεξάμενοι τὸν λόγον αὐτοῦ ἐβαπτί-
σθησαν, καὶ προσετέθησαν ἐν τῇ ἡμέρᾳ ἐκείνῃ ψυχαὶ
ὡσεὶ τρισχίλιαι. ⁴² ἦσαν δὲ προσκαρτεροῦντες τῇ διδαχῇ τῶν ἀποστόλων καὶ τῇ κοινωνίᾳ, τῇ κλάσει τοῦ
ἄρτου καὶ ταῖς προσευχαῖς. ⁴³ ἐγίνετο δὲ πάσῃ ψυχῇ
φόβος· πολλά τε τέρατα καὶ σημεῖα διὰ τῶν ἀποστόλων
ἐγίνετο. ⁴⁴ πάντες δὲ οἱ πιστεύοντες ἦσαν ἐπὶ τὸ αὐτὸ
καὶ εἶχον ἅπαντα κοινά, ⁴⁵ καὶ τὰ κτήματα καὶ τὰς
ὑπάρξεις ἐπίπρασκον καὶ διεμέριζον αὐτὰ πᾶσιν, καθότι
ἄν τις χρείαν εἶχεν· ⁴⁶ καθ᾽ ἡμέραν τε προσκαρτεροῦντες
ὁμοθυμαδὸν ἐν τῷ ἱερῷ, κλῶντές τε κατ᾽ οἶκον ἄρτον,
μετελάμβανον τροφῆς ἐν ἀγαλλιάσει καὶ ἀφελότητι
καρδίας, ⁴⁷ αἰνοῦντες τὸν θεὸν καὶ ἔχοντες χάριν πρὸς
ὅλον τὸν λαόν. ὁ δὲ κύριος προσετίθει τοὺς σωζομένους
καθ᾽ ἡμέραν ἐπὶ τὸ αὐτό.

3 ¹ Πέτρος δὲ καὶ Ἰωάννης ἀνέβαινον εἰς τὸ ἱερὸν
ἐπὶ τὴν ὥραν τῆς προσευχῆς τὴν ἐνάτην. ² καί τις ἀνὴρ
χωλὸς ἐκ κοιλίας μητρὸς αὐτοῦ ὑπάρχων ἐβαστάζετο·
ὃν ἐτίθουν καθ᾽ ἡμέραν πρὸς τὴν θύραν τοῦ ἱεροῦ τὴν
λεγομένην ὡραίαν τοῦ αἰτεῖν ἐλεημοσύνην παρὰ τῶν
εἰσπορευομένων εἰς τὸ ἱερόν· ³ ὃς ἰδὼν Πέτρον καὶ Ἰωάν-

νην μέλλοντας εἰσιέναι εἰς τὸ ἱερὸν ἠρώτα ἐλεημοσύνην
λαβεῖν. ⁴ἀτενίσας δὲ Πέτρος εἰς αὐτὸν σὺν τῷ Ἰωάννῃ
εἶπεν, Βλέψον εἰς ἡμᾶς. ⁵ὁ δὲ ἐπεῖχεν αὐτοῖς προσδοκῶν τι παρ' αὐτῶν λαβεῖν. ⁶εἶπεν δὲ Πέτρος, Ἀργύριον
καὶ χρυσίον οὐχ ὑπάρχει μοι· ὃ δὲ ἔχω, τοῦτό σοι
δίδωμι· ἐν τῷ ὀνόματι Ἰησοῦ Χριστοῦ τοῦ Ναζωραίου
ἔγειρε καὶ περιπάτει. ⁷καὶ πιάσας αὐτὸν τῆς δεξιᾶς
χειρὸς ἤγειρεν αὐτόν. παραχρῆμα δὲ ἐστερεώθησαν αἱ
βάσεις αὐτοῦ καὶ τὰ σφυρά, ⁸καὶ ἐξαλλόμενος ἔστη, καὶ
περιεπάτει, καὶ εἰσῆλθεν σὺν αὐτοῖς εἰς τὸ ἱερὸν περι-
πατῶν καὶ ἁλλόμενος καὶ αἰνῶν τὸν θεόν. ⁹καὶ εἶδεν
πᾶς ὁ λαὸς αὐτὸν περιπατοῦντα καὶ αἰνοῦντα τὸν θεόν·
¹⁰ἐπεγίνωσκον δὲ αὐτόν, ὅτι οὗτος ἦν ὁ πρὸς τὴν ἐλεημοσύνην καθήμενος ἐπὶ τῇ ὡραίᾳ πύλῃ τοῦ ἱεροῦ· καὶ
ἐπλήσθησαν θάμβους καὶ ἐκστάσεως ἐπὶ τῷ συμβεβη-
κότι αὐτῷ.

¹¹Κρατοῦντος δὲ αὐτοῦ τὸν Πέτρον καὶ τὸν Ἰωάννην
συνέδραμεν πᾶς ὁ λαὸς πρὸς αὐτοὺς ἐπὶ τῇ στοᾷ τῇ
καλουμένῃ Σολομῶντος ἔκθαμβοι. ¹²ἰδὼν δὲ ὁ Πέτρος
ἀπεκρίνατο πρὸς τὸν λαόν, Ἄνδρες Ἰσραηλῖται, τί θαυμάζετε ἐπὶ τούτῳ, ἢ ἡμῖν τί ἀτενίζετε ὡς ἰδίᾳ δυνάμει
ἢ εὐσεβείᾳ πεποιηκόσιν τοῦ περιπατεῖν αὐτόν; ¹³ὁ θεὸς
Ἀβραὰμ καὶ Ἰσαὰκ καὶ Ἰακώβ, ὁ θεὸς τῶν πατέρων
ἡμῶν, ἐδόξασεν τὸν παῖδα αὐτοῦ Ἰησοῦν, ὃν ὑμεῖς μὲν
παρεδώκατε καὶ ἠρνήσασθε κατὰ πρόσωπον Πιλάτου,
κρίναντος ἐκείνου ἀπολύειν· ¹⁴ὑμεῖς δὲ τὸν ἅγιον καὶ
δίκαιον ἠρνήσασθε, καὶ ᾐτήσασθε ἄνδρα φονέα χαρισ-
θῆναι ὑμῖν, ¹⁵τὸν δὲ ἀρχηγὸν τῆς ζωῆς ἀπεκτείνατε, ὃν
ὁ θεὸς ἤγειρεν ἐκ νεκρῶν, οὗ ἡμεῖς μάρτυρές ἐσμεν
¹⁶καὶ ἐπὶ τῇ πίστει τοῦ ὀνόματος αὐτοῦ τοῦτον, ὃν
θεωρεῖτε καὶ οἴδατε, ἐστερέωσεν τὸ ὄνομα αὐτοῦ, καὶ

ἡ πίστις ἡ δι᾽ αὐτοῦ ἔδωκεν αὐτῷ τὴν ὁλοκληρίαν ταύτην ἀπέναντι πάντων ὑμῶν. ¹⁷ καὶ νῦν, ἀδελφοί, οἶδα ὅτι κατὰ ἄγνοιαν ἐπράξατε, ὥσπερ καὶ οἱ ἄρχοντες ὑμῶν· ¹⁸ ὁ δὲ θεὸς ἃ προκατήγγειλεν διὰ στόματος πάντων τῶν προφητῶν, παθεῖν τὸν Χριστὸν αὐτοῦ, ἐπλήρωσεν οὕτως. ¹⁹ μετανοήσατε οὖν καὶ ἐπιστρέψατε εἰς τὸ ἐξαλειφθῆναι ὑμῶν τὰς ἁμαρτίας, ὅπως ἂν ἔλθωσιν καιροὶ ἀναψύξεως ἀπὸ προσώπου τοῦ κυρίου ²⁰ καὶ ἀποστείλῃ τὸν προκεχειρισμένον ὑμῖν Χριστὸν Ἰησοῦν, ²¹ ὃν δεῖ οὐρανὸν μὲν δέξασθαι ἄχρι χρόνων ἀποκαταστάσεως πάντων ὧν ἐλάλησεν ὁ θεὸς διὰ στόματος τῶν ἁγίων ἀπ᾽ αἰῶνος αὐτοῦ προφητῶν. ²² Μωϋσῆς μὲν εἶπεν ὅτι Προφήτην ὑμῖν ἀναστήσει κύριος ὁ θεὸς ὑμῶν ἐκ τῶν ἀδελφῶν ὑμῶν ὡς ἐμέ· αὐτοῦ ἀκούσεσθε κατὰ πάντα ὅσα ἂν λαλήσῃ πρὸς ὑμᾶς. ²³ ἔσται δὲ πᾶσα ψυχὴ ἥτις ἂν μὴ ἀκούσῃ τοῦ προφήτου ἐκείνου ἐξολεθρευθήσεται ἐκ τοῦ λαοῦ. ²⁴ καὶ πάντες δὲ οἱ προφῆται ἀπὸ Σαμουὴλ καὶ τῶν καθεξῆς ὅσοι ἐλάλησαν, καὶ κατήγγειλαν τὰς ἡμέρας ταύτας. ²⁵ ὑμεῖς ἐστε οἱ υἱοὶ τῶν προφητῶν καὶ τῆς διαθήκης ἧς διέθετο ὁ θεὸς πρὸς τοὺς πατέρας ἡμῶν, λέγων πρὸς Ἀβραάμ, Καὶ ἐν τῷ σπέρματί σου ἐνευλογηθήσονται πᾶσαι αἱ πατριαὶ τῆς γῆς. ²⁶ ὑμῖν πρῶτον ὁ θεὸς ἀναστήσας τὸν παῖδα αὐτοῦ ἀπέστειλεν αὐτὸν εὐλογοῦντα ὑμᾶς ἐν τῷ ἀποστρέφειν ἕκαστον ἀπὸ τῶν πονηριῶν ὑμῶν.

4 ¹ Λαλούντων δὲ αὐτῶν πρὸς τὸν λαόν, ἐπέστησαν αὐτοῖς οἱ ἱερεῖς καὶ ὁ στρατηγὸς τοῦ ἱεροῦ καὶ οἱ Σαδδουκαῖοι, ² διαπονούμενοι διὰ τὸ διδάσκειν αὐτοὺς τὸν λαὸν καὶ καταγγέλλειν ἐν τῷ Ἰησοῦ τὴν ἀνάστασιν τὴν ἐκ νεκρῶν, ³ καὶ ἐπέβαλον αὐτοῖς τὰς χεῖρας καὶ ἔθεντο εἰς τήρησιν εἰς τὴν αὔριον· ἦν γὰρ ἑσπέρα ἤδη.

⁴ πολλοὶ δὲ τῶν ἀκουσάντων τὸν λόγον ἐπίστευσαν, καὶ
ἐγενήθη ἀριθμὸς τῶν ἀνδρῶν ὡσεὶ χιλιάδες πέντε.
⁵ ἐγένετο δὲ ἐπὶ τὴν αὔριον συναχθῆναι αὐτῶν τοὺς
ἄρχοντας καὶ τοὺς πρεσβυτέρους καὶ τοὺς γραμματεῖς
ἐν Ἱερουσαλήμ, ⁶ καὶ Ἄννας ὁ ἀρχιερεὺς καὶ Καϊάφας
καὶ Ἰωάννης καὶ Ἀλέξανδρος καὶ ὅσοι ἦσαν ἐκ γένους
ἀρχιερατικοῦ. ⁷ καὶ στήσαντες αὐτοὺς ἐν τῷ μέσῳ
ἐπυνθάνοντο, Ἐν ποίᾳ δυνάμει ἢ ἐν ποίῳ ὀνόματι ἐποιήσατε τοῦτο ὑμεῖς; ⁸ τότε Πέτρος πλησθεὶς πνεύματος
ἁγίου εἶπεν πρὸς αὐτούς, Ἄρχοντες τοῦ λαοῦ καὶ πρεσβύτεροι, ⁹ εἰ ἡμεῖς σήμερον ἀνακρινόμεθα ἐπὶ εὐεργεσίᾳ
ἀνθρώπου ἀσθενοῦς, ἐν τίνι οὗτος σέσωσται, ¹⁰ γνωστὸν
ἔστω πᾶσιν ὑμῖν καὶ παντὶ τῷ λαῷ Ἰσραήλ, ὅτι ἐν
τῷ ὀνόματι Ἰησοῦ Χριστοῦ τοῦ Ναζωραίου, ὃν ὑμεῖς
ἐσταυρώσατε, ὃν ὁ θεὸς ἤγειρεν ἐκ νεκρῶν, ἐν τούτῳ
οὗτος παρέστηκεν ἐνώπιον ὑμῶν ὑγιής. ¹¹ οὗτός ἐστιν
ὁ λίθος ὁ ἐξουθενηθεὶς ὑφ᾽ ὑμῶν τῶν οἰκοδόμων, ὁ γενόμενος εἰς κεφαλὴν γωνίας. ¹² καὶ οὐκ ἔστιν ἐν ἄλλῳ
οὐδενὶ ἡ σωτηρία· οὐδὲ γὰρ ὄνομά ἐστιν ἕτερον ὑπὸ
τὸν οὐρανὸν τὸ δεδομένον ἐν ἀνθρώποις ἐν ᾧ δεῖ σωθῆναι
ἡμᾶς.
¹³ Θεωροῦντες δὲ τὴν τοῦ Πέτρου παρρησίαν καὶ
Ἰωάννου, καὶ καταλαβόμενοι ὅτι ἄνθρωποι ἀγράμματοί
εἰσιν καὶ ἰδιῶται, ἐθαύμαζον, ἐπεγίνωσκόν τε αὐτοὺς ὅτι
σὺν τῷ Ἰησοῦ ἦσαν, ¹⁴ τόν τε ἄνθρωπον βλέποντες σὺν
αὐτοῖς ἑστῶτα τὸν τεθεραπευμένον, οὐδὲν εἶχον ἀντει-
πεῖν. ¹⁵ κελεύσαντες δὲ αὐτοὺς ἔξω τοῦ συνεδρίου ἀπελθεῖν, συνέβαλλον πρὸς ἀλλήλους ¹⁶ λέγοντες, Τί ποιήσωμεν τοῖς ἀνθρώποις τούτοις; ὅτι μὲν γὰρ γνωστὸν
σημεῖον γέγονεν δι᾽ αὐτῶν, πᾶσιν τοῖς κατοικοῦσιν Ἱερουσαλὴμ φανερόν, καὶ οὐ δυνάμεθα ἀρνεῖσθαι· ¹⁷ ἀλλ᾽ ἵνα

μὴ ἐπὶ πλεῖον διανεμηθῇ εἰς τὸν λαόν, ἀπειλησώμεθα
αὐτοῖς μηκέτι λαλεῖν ἐπὶ τῷ ὀνόματι τούτῳ μηδενὶ
ἀνθρώπων. ¹⁸ καὶ καλέσαντες αὐτοὺς παρήγγειλαν τὸ
καθόλου μὴ φθέγγεσθαι μηδὲ διδάσκειν ἐπὶ τῷ ὀνόματι
τοῦ Ἰησοῦ. ¹⁹ ὁ δὲ Πέτρος καὶ Ἰωάννης ἀποκριθέντες
εἶπον πρὸς αὐτούς, Εἰ δίκαιόν ἐστιν ἐνώπιον τοῦ θεοῦ,
ὑμῶν ἀκούειν μᾶλλον ἢ τοῦ θεοῦ, κρίνατε· ²⁰ οὐ δυνάμεθα γὰρ ἡμεῖς ἃ εἴδαμεν καὶ ἠκούσαμεν μὴ λαλεῖν.
²¹ οἱ δὲ προσαπειλησάμενοι ἀπέλυσαν αὐτούς, μηδὲν
εὑρίσκοντες τὸ πῶς κολάσωνται αὐτούς, διὰ τὸν λαόν,
ὅτι πάντες ἐδόξαζον τὸν θεὸν ἐπὶ τῷ γεγονότι. ²² ἐτῶν
γὰρ ἦν πλειόνων τεσσεράκοντα ὁ ἄνθρωπος ἐφ' ὃν γεγόνει τὸ σημεῖον τοῦτο τῆς ἰάσεως.

²³ Ἀπολυθέντες δὲ ἦλθον πρὸς τοὺς ἰδίους καὶ ἀπήγγειλαν ὅσα πρὸς αὐτοὺς οἱ ἀρχιερεῖς καὶ οἱ πρεσβύτεροι
εἶπαν. ²⁴ οἱ δὲ ἀκούσαντες ὁμοθυμαδὸν ἦραν φωνὴν
πρὸς τὸν θεὸν καὶ εἶπαν, Δέσποτα, σὺ ὁ ποιήσας τὸν
οὐρανὸν καὶ τὴν γῆν καὶ τὴν θάλασσαν καὶ πάντα τὰ ἐν
αὐτοῖς, ²⁵ ὁ τοῦ πατρὸς ἡμῶν διὰ πνεύματος ἁγίου στόματος Δαυεὶδ παιδός σου εἰπών, ἱνατί ἐφρύαξαν ἔθνη
καὶ λαοὶ ἐμελέτησαν κενά; ²⁶ παρέστησαν οἱ βασιλεῖς
τῆς γῆς καὶ οἱ ἄρχοντες συνήχθησαν ἐπὶ τὸ αὐτὸ κατὰ
τοῦ κυρίου, καὶ κατὰ τοῦ Χριστοῦ αὐτοῦ. ²⁷ συνήχθησαν γὰρ ἐπ' ἀληθείας ἐν τῇ πόλει ταύτῃ ἐπὶ τὸν
ἅγιον παῖδά σου Ἰησοῦν, ὃν ἔχρισας, Ἡρώδης τε καὶ
Πόντιος Πιλᾶτος σὺν ἔθνεσιν καὶ λαοῖς Ἰσραήλ, ²⁸ ποιῆσαι ὅσα ἡ χείρ σου καὶ ἡ βουλή σου προώρισεν γενέσθαι.
²⁹ καὶ τὰ νῦν, κύριε, ἔπιδε ἐπὶ τὰς ἀπειλὰς αὐτῶν, καὶ
δὸς τοῖς δούλοις σου μετὰ παρρησίας πάσης λαλεῖν τὸν
λόγον σου ³⁰ ἐν τῷ τὴν χεῖρά σου ἐκτείνειν σε εἰς ἴασιν
καὶ σημεῖα καὶ τέρατα γίνεσθαι διὰ τοῦ ὀνόματος τοῦ

ἁγίου παιδός σου Ἰησοῦ. ³¹ καὶ δεηθέντων αὐτῶν ἐσαλεύθη ὁ τόπος ἐν ᾧ ἦσαν συνηγμένοι, καὶ ἐπλήσθησαν
ἅπαντες τοῦ ἁγίου πνεύματος, καὶ ἐλάλουν τὸν λόγον
τοῦ θεοῦ μετὰ παρρησίας.

³² Τοῦ δὲ πλήθους τῶν πιστευσάντων ἦν καρδία καὶ
ψυχὴ μία, καὶ οὐδὲ εἷς τι τῶν ὑπαρχόντων αὐτῷ ἔλεγεν
ἴδιον εἶναι, ἀλλ᾽ ἦν αὐτοῖς ἅπαντα κοινά. ³³ καὶ δυνάμει
μεγάλῃ ἀπεδίδουν τὸ μαρτύριον οἱ ἀπόστολοι τῆς ἀναστάσεως τοῦ κυρίου Ἰησοῦ, χάρις τε μεγάλη ἦν ἐπὶ
πάντας αὐτούς. ³⁴ οὐδὲ γὰρ ἐνδεής τις ἦν ἐν αὐτοῖς·
ὅσοι γὰρ κτήτορες χωρίων ἢ οἰκιῶν ὑπῆρχον, πωλοῦντες
ἔφερον τὰς τιμὰς τῶν πιπρασκομένων ³⁵ καὶ ἐτίθουν παρὰ
τοὺς πόδας τῶν ἀποστόλων· διεδίδετο δὲ ἑκάστῳ καθότι
ἄν τις χρείαν εἶχεν. ³⁶ Ἰωσὴφ δὲ ὁ ἐπικληθεὶς Βαρνάβας ἀπὸ τῶν ἀποστόλων, ὅ ἐστιν μεθερμηνευόμενον υἱὸς
παρακλήσεως, Λευΐτης, Κύπριος τῷ γένει, ³⁷ ὑπάρχοντος
αὐτῷ ἀγροῦ, πωλήσας ἤνεγκεν τὸ χρῆμα καὶ ἔθηκεν
παρὰ τοὺς πόδας τῶν ἀποστόλων.

5 ¹ Ἀνὴρ δέ τις Ἀνανίας ὀνόματι σὺν Σαπφείρῃ τῇ
γυναικὶ αὐτοῦ ἐπώλησεν κτῆμα, ² καὶ ἐνοσφίσατο ἀπὸ
τῆς τιμῆς, συνειδυίης καὶ τῆς γυναικός, καὶ ἐνέγκας
μέρος τι παρὰ τοὺς πόδας τῶν ἀποστόλων ἔθηκεν.
³ εἶπεν δὲ ὁ Πέτρος, Ἀνανία, διατί ἐπλήρωσεν ὁ σατανᾶς
τὴν καρδίαν σου, ψεύσασθαί σε τὸ πνεῦμα τὸ ἅγιον καὶ
νοσφίσασθαι ἀπὸ τῆς τιμῆς τοῦ χωρίου; ⁴ οὐχὶ μένον
σοὶ ἔμενεν καὶ πραθὲν ἐν τῇ σῇ ἐξουσίᾳ ὑπῆρχεν; τί ὅτι
ἔθου ἐν τῇ καρδίᾳ σου τὸ πρᾶγμα τοῦτο; οὐκ ἐψεύσω
ἀνθρώποις ἀλλὰ τῷ θεῷ. ⁵ ἀκούων δὲ ὁ Ἀνανίας τοὺς
λόγους τούτους, πεσὼν ἐξέψυξεν· καὶ ἐγένετο φόβος
μέγας ἐπὶ πάντας τοὺς ἀκούοντας· ⁶ ἀναστάντες δὲ οἱ
νεώτεροι συνέστειλαν αὐτὸν καὶ ἐξενέγκαντες ἔθαψαν.

⁷ ἐγένετο δὲ ὡς ὡρῶν τριῶν διάστημα καὶ ἡ γυνὴ αὐτοῦ μὴ εἰδυῖα τὸ γεγονὸς εἰσῆλθεν. ⁸ ἀπεκρίθη δὲ πρὸς αὐτὴν Πέτρος, Εἰπέ μοι, εἰ τοσούτου τὸ χωρίον ἀπέδοσθε; ἡ δὲ εἶπεν, Ναί, τοσούτου. ⁹ ὁ δὲ Πέτρος πρὸς αὐτήν, Τί ὅτι συνεφωνήθη ὑμῖν πειράσαι τὸ πνεῦμα κυρίου; ἰδοὺ οἱ πόδες τῶν θαψάντων τὸν ἄνδρα σου ἐπὶ τῇ θύρᾳ, καὶ ἐξοίσουσίν σε. ¹⁰ ἔπεσεν δὲ παραχρῆμα πρὸς τοὺς πόδας αὐτοῦ, καὶ ἐξέψυξεν· εἰσελθόντες δὲ οἱ νεανίσκοι εὗρον αὐτὴν νεκράν, καὶ ἐξενέγκαντες ἔθαψαν πρὸς τὸν ἄνδρα αὐτῆς. ¹¹ καὶ ἐγένετο φόβος μέγας ἐφ᾽ ὅλην τὴν ἐκκλησίαν καὶ ἐπὶ πάντας τοὺς ἀκούοντας ταῦτα.

¹² Διὰ δὲ τῶν χειρῶν τῶν ἀποστόλων ἐγίνετο σημεῖα καὶ τέρατα πολλὰ ἐν τῷ λαῷ· καὶ ἦσαν ὁμοθυμαδὸν ἅπαντες ἐν τῇ στοᾷ Σολομῶντος· ¹³ τῶν δὲ λοιπῶν οὐδεὶς ἐτόλμα κολλᾶσθαι αὐτοῖς, ἀλλ᾽ ἐμεγάλυνεν αὐτοὺς ὁ λαός· ¹⁴ μᾶλλον δὲ προσετίθεντο πιστεύοντες τῷ κυρίῳ, πλήθη ἀνδρῶν τε καὶ γυναικῶν, ¹⁵ ὥστε καὶ εἰς τὰς πλατείας ἐκφέρειν τοὺς ἀσθενεῖς καὶ τιθέναι ἐπὶ κλιναρίων καὶ κραβάττων, ἵνα ἐρχομένου Πέτρου κἂν ἡ σκιὰ ἐπισκιάσῃ τινὶ αὐτῶν. ¹⁶ συνήρχετο δὲ καὶ τὸ πλῆθος τῶν πέριξ πόλεων Ἰερουσαλήμ, φέροντες ἀσθενεῖς καὶ ὀχλουμένους ὑπὸ πνευμάτων ἀκαθάρτων, οἵτινες ἐθεραπεύοντο ἅπαντες.

¹⁷ Ἀναστὰς δὲ ὁ ἀρχιερεὺς καὶ πάντες οἱ σὺν αὐτῷ, ἡ οὖσα αἵρεσις τῶν Σαδδουκαίων, ἐπλήσθησαν ζήλου ¹⁸ καὶ ἐπέβαλον τὰς χεῖρας ἐπὶ τοὺς ἀποστόλους, καὶ ἔθεντο αὐτοὺς ἐν τηρήσει δημοσίᾳ. ¹⁹ ἄγγελος δὲ κυρίου διὰ νυκτὸς ἤνοιξεν τὰς θύρας τῆς φυλακῆς ἐξαγαγών τε αὐτοὺς εἶπεν, ²⁰ Πορεύεσθε καὶ σταθέντες λαλεῖτε ἐν τῷ ἱερῷ τῷ λαῷ πάντα τὰ ῥήματα τῆς ζωῆς ταύτης.

²¹ ἀκούσαντες δὲ εἰσῆλθον ὑπὸ τὸν ὄρθρον εἰς τὸ ἱερὸν καὶ ἐδίδασκον. παραγενόμενος δὲ ὁ ἀρχιερεὺς καὶ οἱ σὺν αὐτῷ συνεκάλεσαν τὸ συνέδριον καὶ πᾶσαν τὴν γερουσίαν τῶν υἱῶν Ἰσραήλ, καὶ ἀπέστειλαν εἰς τὸ δεσμωτήριον ἀχθῆναι αὐτούς. ²² οἱ δὲ παραγενόμενοι ὑπηρέται οὐχ εὗρον αὐτοὺς ἐν τῇ φυλακῇ· ἀναστρέψαντες δὲ ἀπήγγειλαν ²³ λέγοντες ὅτι Τὸ δεσμωτήριον εὕρομεν κεκλεισμένον ἐν πάσῃ ἀσφαλείᾳ καὶ τοὺς φύλακας ἑστῶτας ἐπὶ τῶν θυρῶν, ἀνοίξαντες δὲ ἔσω οὐδένα εὕρομεν. ²⁴ ὡς δὲ ἤκουσαν τοὺς λόγους τούτους ὅ τε στρατηγὸς τοῦ ἱεροῦ καὶ οἱ ἀρχιερεῖς, διηπόρουν περὶ αὐτῶν, τί ἂν γένοιτο τοῦτο. ²⁵ παραγενόμενος δέ τις ἀπήγγειλεν αὐτοῖς ὅτι Ἰδοὺ οἱ ἄνδρες οὓς ἔθεσθε ἐν τῇ φυλακῇ εἰσὶν ἐν τῷ ἱερῷ ἑστῶτες καὶ διδάσκοντες τὸν λαόν. ²⁶ τότε ἀπελθὼν ὁ στρατηγὸς σὺν τοῖς ὑπηρέταις ἦγεν αὐτούς, οὐ μετὰ βίας, ἐφοβοῦντο γὰρ τὸν λαόν, μὴ λιθασθῶσιν· ²⁷ ἀγαγόντες δὲ αὐτοὺς ἔστησαν ἐν τῷ συνεδρίῳ. καὶ ἐπηρώτησεν αὐτοὺς ὁ ἀρχιερεὺς ²⁸ λέγων, Παραγγελίᾳ παρηγγείλαμεν ὑμῖν μὴ διδάσκειν ἐπὶ τῷ ὀνόματι τούτῳ, καὶ ἰδοὺ πεπληρώκατε τὴν Ἰερουσαλὴμ τῆς διδαχῆς ὑμῶν, καὶ βούλεσθε ἐπαγαγεῖν ἐφ᾽ ἡμᾶς τὸ αἷμα τοῦ ἀνθρώπου τούτου. ²⁹ ἀποκριθεὶς δὲ Πέτρος καὶ οἱ ἀπόστολοι εἶπαν, Πειθαρχεῖν δεῖ θεῷ μᾶλλον ἢ ἀνθρώποις. ³⁰ ὁ θεὸς τῶν πατέρων ἡμῶν ἤγειρεν Ἰησοῦν, ὃν ὑμεῖς διεχειρίσασθε κρεμάσαντες ἐπὶ ξύλου· ³¹ τοῦτον ὁ θεὸς ἀρχηγὸν καὶ σωτῆρα ὕψωσεν τῇ δεξιᾷ αὐτοῦ δοῦναι μετάνοιαν τῷ Ἰσραὴλ καὶ ἄφεσιν ἁμαρτιῶν. ³² καὶ ἡμεῖς ἐσμὲν μάρτυρες τῶν ῥημάτων τούτων, καὶ τὸ πνεῦμα τὸ ἅγιον ὃ ἔδωκεν ὁ θεὸς τοῖς πειθαρχοῦσιν αὐτῷ.

³³ Οἱ δὲ ἀκούσαντες διεπρίοντο καὶ ἐβουλεύοντο ἀνε-

λεῖν αὐτούς. ³⁴ ἀναστὰς δέ τις ἐν τῷ συνεδρίῳ Φαρισαῖος ὀνόματι Γαμαλιήλ, νομοδιδάσκαλος τίμιος παντὶ
τῷ λαῷ, ἐκέλευσεν ἔξω βραχύ τι τοὺς ἀνθρώπους
ποιῆσαι, ³⁵ εἶπέν τε πρὸς αὐτούς, Ἄνδρες Ἰσραηλῖται,
προσέχετε ἑαυτοῖς ἐπὶ τοῖς ἀνθρώποις τούτοις, τί μέλ-
λετε πράσσειν. ³⁶ πρὸ γὰρ τούτων τῶν ἡμερῶν ἀνέστη
Θευδᾶς, λέγων εἶναί τινα ἑαυτόν, ᾧ προσεκλίθη ἀνδρῶν
ἀριθμὸς ὡς τετρακοσίων, ὃς ἀνῃρέθη, καὶ πάντες ὅσοι
ἐπείθοντο αὐτῷ διελύθησαν καὶ ἐγένοντο εἰς οὐδέν.
³⁷ μετὰ τοῦτον ἀνέστη Ἰούδας ὁ Γαλιλαῖος ἐν ταῖς ἡμέ-
ραις τῆς ἀπογραφῆς καὶ ἀπέστησεν λαὸν ὀπίσω αὐτοῦ·
κἀκεῖνος ἀπώλετο, καὶ πάντες ὅσοι ἐπείθοντο αὐτῷ
διεσκορπίσθησαν. ³⁸ καὶ τὰ νῦν λέγω ὑμῖν, ἀπόστητε
ἀπὸ τῶν ἀνθρώπων τούτων καὶ ἄφετε αὐτούς· ὅτι ἐὰν
ᾖ ἐξ ἀνθρώπων ἡ βουλὴ αὕτη ἢ τὸ ἔργον τοῦτο, κατα-
λυθήσεται· ³⁹ εἰ δὲ ἐκ θεοῦ ἐστίν, οὐ δυνήσεσθε καταλῦσαι αὐτούς, μήποτε καὶ θεομάχοι εὑρεθῆτε. ⁴⁰ ἐπείσθησαν δὲ αὐτῷ, καὶ προσκαλεσάμενοι τοὺς ἀποστόλους
δείραντες παρήγγειλαν μὴ λαλεῖν ἐπὶ τῷ ὀνόματι τοῦ
Ἰησοῦ, καὶ ἀπέλυσαν. ⁴¹ Οἱ μὲν οὖν ἐπορεύοντο χαίροντες ἀπὸ προσώπου τοῦ συνεδρίου, ὅτι κατηξιώθησαν
ὑπὲρ τοῦ ὀνόματος ἀτιμασθῆναι· ⁴² πᾶσάν τε ἡμέραν
ἐν τῷ ἱερῷ καὶ κατ’ οἶκον οὐκ ἐπαύοντο διδάσκοντες
καὶ εὐαγγελιζόμενοι τὸν Χριστὸν Ἰησοῦν.

6 ¹ Ἐν δὲ ταῖς ἡμέραις ταύταις πληθυνόντων τῶν
μαθητῶν ἐγένετο γογγυσμὸς τῶν Ἑλληνιστῶν πρὸς
τοὺς Ἑβραίους, ὅτι παρεθεωροῦντο ἐν τῇ διακονίᾳ τῇ
καθημερινῇ αἱ χῆραι αὐτῶν. ² προσκαλεσάμενοι δὲ οἱ
δώδεκα τὸ πλῆθος τῶν μαθητῶν εἶπαν, Οὐκ ἀρεστόν
ἐστιν ἡμᾶς καταλείψαντας τὸν λόγον τοῦ θεοῦ διακονεῖν
τραπέζαις. ³ ἐπισκέψασθε οὖν, ἀδελφοί, ἄνδρας ἐξ ὑμῶν

μαρτυρουμένους ἑπτὰ πλήρεις πνεύματος καὶ σοφίας,
οὓς καταστήσομεν ἐπὶ τῆς χρείας ταύτης· ⁴ ἡμεῖς δὲ τῇ
προσευχῇ καὶ τῇ διακονίᾳ τοῦ λόγου προσκαρτερήσομεν. ⁵ καὶ ἤρεσεν ὁ λόγος ἐνώπιον παντὸς τοῦ πλήθους,
καὶ ἐξελέξαντο Στέφανον, ἄνδρα πλήρη πίστεως καὶ
πνεύματος ἁγίου, καὶ Φίλιππον καὶ Πρόχορον καὶ Νικά-
νορα καὶ Τίμωνα καὶ Παρμενᾶν καὶ Νικόλαον προσήλυτον Ἀντιοχέα, ⁶ οὓς ἔστησαν ἐνώπιον τῶν ἀποστόλων,
καὶ προσευξάμενοι ἐπέθηκαν αὐτοῖς τὰς χεῖρας. ⁷ καὶ
ὁ λόγος τοῦ θεοῦ ηὔξανεν, καὶ ἐπληθύνετο ὁ ἀριθμὸς
τῶν μαθητῶν ἐν Ἰερουσαλὴμ σφόδρα, πολύς τε ὄχλος
τῶν ἱερέων ὑπήκουον τῇ πίστει.

⁸ Στέφανος δὲ πλήρης χάριτος καὶ δυνάμεως ἐποίει
τέρατα καὶ σημεῖα μεγάλα ἐν τῷ λαῷ. ⁹ ἀνέστησαν δέ
τινες τῶν ἐκ τῆς συναγωγῆς τῆς λεγομένης Λιβερτίνων
καὶ Κυρηναίων καὶ Ἀλεξανδρέων καὶ τῶν ἀπὸ Κιλικίας
καὶ Ἀσίας συνζητοῦντες τῷ Στεφάνῳ, ¹⁰ καὶ οὐκ ἴσχυον
ἀντιστῆναι τῇ σοφίᾳ καὶ τῷ πνεύματι ᾧ ἐλάλει. ¹¹ τότε
ὑπέβαλον ἄνδρας λέγοντας ὅτι Ἀκηκόαμεν αὐτοῦ λαλοῦντος ῥήματα βλάσφημα εἰς Μωϋσῆν καὶ τὸν θεόν.
¹² συνεκίνησάν τε τὸν λαὸν καὶ τοὺς πρεσβυτέρους καὶ
τοὺς γραμματεῖς, καὶ ἐπιστάντες συνήρπασαν αὐτὸν
καὶ ἤγαγον εἰς τὸ συνέδριον, ¹³ ἔστησάν τε μάρτυρας
ψευδεῖς λέγοντας, Ὁ ἄνθρωπος οὗτος οὐ παύεται λαλῶν
ῥήματα κατὰ τοῦ τόπου τοῦ ἁγίου καὶ τοῦ νόμου· ¹⁴ ἀκηκόαμεν γὰρ αὐτοῦ λέγοντος ὅτι Ἰησοῦς ὁ Ναζωραῖος
οὗτος καταλύσει τὸν τόπον τοῦτον, καὶ ἀλλάξει τὰ ἔθη
ἃ παρέδωκεν ἡμῖν Μωϋσῆς. ¹⁵ καὶ ἀτενίσαντες εἰς
αὐτὸν πάντες οἱ καθεζόμενοι ἐν τῷ συνεδρίῳ, εἶδον τὸ
πρόσωπον αὐτοῦ ὡσεὶ πρόσωπον ἀγγέλου.

7 ¹ Εἶπεν δὲ ὁ ἀρχιερεύς, Εἰ ταῦτα οὕτως ἔχει; ² ὁ

δὲ ἔφη, Ἄνδρες ἀδελφοὶ καὶ πατέρες, ἀκούσατε. ὁ θεὸς
τῆς δόξης ὤφθη τῷ πατρὶ ἡμῶν Ἀβραὰμ ὄντι ἐν τῇ
Μεσοποταμίᾳ πρὶν ἢ κατοικῆσαι αὐτὸν ἐν Χαρράν, [3] καὶ
εἶπεν πρὸς αὐτόν, Ἔξελθε ἐκ τῆς γῆς σου καὶ ἐκ τῆς
συγγενείας σου, καὶ δεῦρο εἰς τὴν γῆν ἣν ἄν σοι δείξω.
[4] τότε ἐξελθὼν ἐκ γῆς Χαλδαίων κατῴκησεν ἐν Χαρράν.
κἀκεῖθεν μετὰ τὸ ἀποθανεῖν τὸν πατέρα αὐτοῦ μετῴκισεν αὐτὸν εἰς τὴν γῆν ταύτην εἰς ἣν ὑμεῖς νῦν κατοι-
κεῖτε, [5] καὶ οὐκ ἔδωκεν αὐτῷ κληρονομίαν ἐν αὐτῇ οὐδὲ
βῆμα ποδός, καὶ ἐπηγγείλατο δοῦναι αὐτῷ εἰς κατά-
σχεσιν αὐτὴν καὶ τῷ σπέρματι αὐτοῦ μετ᾽ αὐτόν, οὐκ
ὄντος αὐτῷ τέκνου. [6] ἐλάλησεν δὲ οὕτως ὁ θεὸς ὅτι
Ἔσται τὸ σπέρμα αὐτοῦ πάροικον ἐν γῇ ἀλλοτρίᾳ, καὶ
δουλώσουσιν αὐτὸ καὶ κακώσουσιν ἔτη τετρακόσια.
[7] καὶ τὸ ἔθνος ᾧ ἐὰν δουλεύσουσιν, κρινῶ ἐγώ, ὁ θεὸς
εἶπεν, καὶ μετὰ ταῦτα ἐξελεύσονται καὶ λατρεύσουσίν
μοι ἐν τῷ τόπῳ τούτῳ. [8] καὶ ἔδωκεν αὐτῷ διαθήκην
περιτομῆς· καὶ οὕτως ἐγέννησεν τὸν Ἰσαὰκ καὶ περιέτεμεν αὐτὸν τῇ ἡμέρᾳ τῇ ὀγδόῃ, καὶ Ἰσαὰκ τὸν Ἰακώβ,
καὶ Ἰακὼβ τοὺς δώδεκα πατριάρχας. [9] καὶ οἱ πατρι-
άρχαι ζηλώσαντες τὸν Ἰωσὴφ ἀπέδοντο εἰς Αἴγυπτον·
καὶ ἦν ὁ θεὸς μετ᾽ αὐτοῦ, [10] καὶ ἐξείλατο αὐτὸν ἐκ πασῶν
τῶν θλίψεων αὐτοῦ, καὶ ἔδωκεν αὐτῷ χάριν καὶ σοφίαν
ἐναντίον Φαραὼ βασιλέως Αἰγύπτου, καὶ κατέστησεν
αὐτὸν ἡγούμενον ἐπ᾽ Αἴγυπτον καὶ ὅλον τὸν οἶκον αὐτοῦ.
[11] ἦλθεν δὲ λιμὸς ἐφ᾽ ὅλην τὴν Αἴγυπτον καὶ Χαναὰν καὶ
θλῖψις μεγάλη, καὶ οὐχ εὕρισκον χορτάσματα οἱ πατέρες ἡμῶν. [12] ἀκούσας δὲ Ἰακὼβ ὄντα σιτία εἰς Αἴγυπτον ἐξαπέστειλεν τοὺς πατέρας ἡμῶν πρῶτον· [13] καὶ ἐν
τῷ δευτέρῳ ἀνεγνωρίσθη Ἰωσὴφ τοῖς ἀδελφοῖς αὐτοῦ,
καὶ φανερὸν ἐγένετο τῷ Φαραὼ τὸ γένος Ἰωσήφ. [14] ἀπο-

στείλας δὲ Ἰωσὴφ μετεκαλέσατο Ἰακὼβ τὸν πατέρα
αὐτοῦ καὶ πᾶσαν τὴν συγγένειαν ἐν ψυχαῖς ἑβδομήκοντα πέντε. ¹⁵ καὶ κατέβη Ἰακὼβ εἰς Αἴγυπτον, καὶ
ἐτελεύτησεν αὐτὸς καὶ οἱ πατέρες ἡμῶν, ¹⁶ καὶ μετετέθη-
σαν εἰς Συχὲμ καὶ ἐτέθησαν ἐν τῷ μνήματι ᾧ ὠνήσατο
Ἀβραὰμ τιμῆς ἀργυρίου παρὰ τῶν υἱῶν Ἐμμὼρ ἐν
Συχέμ. ¹⁷ καθὼς δὲ ἤγγιζεν ὁ χρόνος τῆς ἐπαγγελίας
ἧς ὡμολόγησεν ὁ θεὸς τῷ Ἀβραάμ, ηὔξησεν ὁ λαὸς
καὶ ἐπληθύνθη ἐν Αἰγύπτῳ, ¹⁸ ἄχρι οὗ ἀνέστη βασιλεὺς
ἕτερος ἐπ᾽ Αἴγυπτον, ὃς οὐκ ᾔδει τὸν Ἰωσήφ. ¹⁹ οὗτος
κατασοφισάμενος τὸ γένος ἡμῶν ἐκάκωσεν τοὺς πατέρας
τοῦ ποιεῖν τὰ βρέφη ἔκθετα αὐτῶν εἰς τὸ μὴ ζωογονεῖσθαι. ²⁰ ἐν ᾧ καιρῷ ἐγεννήθη Μωϋσῆς, καὶ ἦν ἀστεῖος
τῷ θεῷ. ὃς ἀνετράφη μῆνας τρεῖς ἐν τῷ οἴκῳ τοῦ
πατρός. ²¹ ἐκτεθέντος δὲ αὐτοῦ ἀνείλατο αὐτὸν ἡ θυγά-
τηρ Φαραὼ καὶ ἀνεθρέψατο αὐτὸν ἑαυτῇ εἰς υἱόν. ²² καὶ
ἐπαιδεύθη Μωϋσῆς ἐν πάσῃ σοφίᾳ Αἰγυπτίων· ἦν δὲ
δυνατὸς ἐν λόγοις καὶ ἔργοις αὐτοῦ. ²³ ὡς δὲ ἐπληροῦτο
αὐτῷ τεσσερακονταετὴς χρόνος, ἀνέβη ἐπὶ τὴν καρδίαν
αὐτοῦ ἐπισκέψασθαι τοὺς ἀδελφοὺς αὐτοῦ τοὺς υἱοὺς
Ἰσραήλ. ²⁴ καὶ ἰδών τινα ἀδικούμενον ἠμύνατο, καὶ
ἐποίησεν ἐκδίκησιν τῷ καταπονουμένῳ πατάξας τὸν
Αἰγύπτιον. ²⁵ ἐνόμιζεν δὲ συνιέναι τοὺς ἀδελφοὺς ὅτι
ὁ θεὸς διὰ χειρὸς αὐτοῦ δίδωσιν σωτηρίαν αὐτοῖς· ²⁶ οἱ
δὲ οὐ συνῆκαν. τῇ τε ἐπιούσῃ ἡμέρᾳ ὤφθη αὐτοῖς μαχομένοις, καὶ συνήλλασσεν αὐτοὺς εἰς εἰρήνην εἰπών,
Ἄνδρες, ἀδελφοί ἐστε· ἱνατί ἀδικεῖτε ἀλλήλους; ²⁷ ὁ δὲ
ἀδικῶν τὸν πλησίον ἀπώσατο αὐτὸν εἰπών, Τίς σε
κατέστησεν ἄρχοντα καὶ δικαστὴν ἐφ᾽ ἡμῶν; ²⁸ μὴ ἀνελεῖν με σὺ θέλεις, ὃν τρόπον ἀνεῖλες ἐχθὲς τὸν Αἰγύπτιον; ²⁹ ἔφυγεν δὲ Μωϋσῆς ἐν τῷ λόγῳ τούτῳ, καὶ

ἐγένετο πάροικος ἐν γῇ Μαδιάμ, οὗ ἐγέννησεν υἱοὺς δύο.
³⁰ καὶ πληρωθέντων ἐτῶν τεσσεράκοντα ὤφθη αὐτῷ ἐν
τῇ ἐρήμῳ τοῦ ὄρους Σινᾶ ἄγγελος ἐν φλογὶ πυρὸς βά-
του. ³¹ ὁ δὲ Μωϋσῆς ἰδὼν ἐθαύμασεν τὸ ὅραμα· προσερ-
χομένου δὲ αὐτοῦ κατανοῆσαι ἐγένετο φωνὴ κυρίου,
³² Ἐγὼ ὁ θεὸς τῶν πατέρων σου, ὁ θεὸς Ἀβραὰμ καὶ
Ἰσαὰκ καὶ Ἰακώβ. ἔντρομος δὲ γενόμενος Μωϋσῆς
οὐκ ἐτόλμα κατανοῆσαι. ³³ εἶπεν δὲ αὐτῷ ὁ κύριος,
Λῦσον τὸ ὑπόδημα τῶν ποδῶν σου· ὁ γὰρ τόπος ἐφ᾽
ᾧ ἔστηκας γῆ ἁγία ἐστίν. ³⁴ ἰδὼν εἶδον τὴν κάκωσιν
τοῦ λαοῦ μου τοῦ ἐν Αἰγύπτῳ, καὶ τοῦ στεναγμοῦ
αὐτῶν ἤκουσα, καὶ κατέβην ἐξελέσθαι αὐτούς· καὶ νῦν
δεῦρο ἀποστείλω σε εἰς Αἴγυπτον. ³⁵ τοῦτον τὸν Μωϋσῆν, ὃν ἠρνήσαντο εἰπόντες, Τίς σε κατέστησεν ἄρχοντα
καὶ δικαστήν; τοῦτον ὁ θεὸς καὶ ἄρχοντα καὶ λυτρωτὴν
ἀπέσταλκεν σὺν χειρὶ ἀγγέλου τοῦ ὀφθέντος αὐτῷ ἐν
τῇ βάτῳ. ³⁶ οὗτος ἐξήγαγεν αὐτοὺς ποιήσας τέρατα
καὶ σημεῖα ἐν γῇ Αἰγύπτῳ καὶ ἐν ἐρυθρᾷ θαλάσσῃ καὶ
ἐν τῇ ἐρήμῳ ἔτη τεσσεράκοντα. ³⁷ οὗτός ἐστιν ὁ Μωϋσῆς ὁ εἴπας τοῖς υἱοῖς Ἰσραήλ, Προφήτην ὑμῖν ἀναστήσει ὁ θεὸς ἐκ τῶν ἀδελφῶν ὑμῶν ὡς ἐμέ. ³⁸ οὗτός
ἐστιν ὁ γενόμενος ἐν τῇ ἐκκλησίᾳ ἐν τῇ ἐρήμῳ μετὰ τοῦ
ἀγγέλου τοῦ λαλοῦντος αὐτῷ ἐν τῷ ὄρει Σινᾶ καὶ τῶν
πατέρων ἡμῶν, ὃς ἐδέξατο λόγια ζῶντα δοῦναι ἡμῖν,
³⁹ ᾧ οὐκ ἠθέλησαν ὑπήκοοι γενέσθαι οἱ πατέρες ἡμῶν,
ἀλλὰ ἀπώσαντο καὶ ἐστράφησαν ἐν ταῖς καρδίαις αὐτῶν εἰς Αἴγυπτον, ⁴⁰ εἰπόντες τῷ Ἀαρών, Ποίησον ἡμῖν
θεοὺς οἳ προπορεύσονται ἡμῶν· ὁ γὰρ Μωϋσῆς οὗτος,
ὃς ἐξήγαγεν ἡμᾶς ἐκ γῆς Αἰγύπτου, οὐκ οἴδαμεν τί
ἐγένετο αὐτῷ. ⁴¹ καὶ ἐμοσχοποίησαν ἐν ταῖς ἡμέραις
ἐκείναις καὶ ἀνήγαγον θυσίαν τῷ εἰδώλῳ, καὶ εὐφραί-

νοντο ἐν τοῖς ἔργοις τῶν χειρῶν αὐτῶν. ⁴²ἔστρεψεν
δὲ ὁ θεὸς καὶ παρέδωκεν αὐτοὺς λατρεύειν τῇ στρατιᾷ
τοῦ οὐρανοῦ, καθὼς γέγραπται ἐν βίβλῳ τῶν προφητῶν,
Μὴ σφάγια καὶ θυσίας προσηνέγκατέ μοι ἔτη τεσσεράκοντα ἐν τῇ ἐρήμῳ, οἶκος Ἰσραήλ, ⁴³καὶ ἀνελάβετε τὴν
σκηνὴν τοῦ Μολὸχ καὶ τὸ ἄστρον τοῦ θεοῦ Ῥεφάν, τοὺς
τύπους οὓς ἐποιήσατε προσκυνεῖν αὐτοῖς; καὶ μετοικιῶ
ὑμᾶς ἐπέκεινα Βαβυλῶνος. ⁴⁴ἡ σκηνὴ τοῦ μαρτυρίου
ἦν τοῖς πατράσιν ἡμῶν ἐν τῇ ἐρήμῳ, καθὼς διετάξατο
ὁ λαλῶν τῷ Μωϋσῇ ποιῆσαι αὐτὴν κατὰ τὸν τύπον
ὃν ἑωράκει· ⁴⁵ἣν καὶ εἰσήγαγον διαδεξάμενοι οἱ πατέρες ἡμῶν μετὰ Ἰησοῦ ἐν τῇ κατασχέσει τῶν ἐθνῶν, ὧν
ἔξωσεν ὁ θεὸς ἀπὸ προσώπου τῶν πατέρων ἡμῶν, ἕως
τῶν ἡμερῶν Δαυείδ, ⁴⁶ὃς εὗρεν χάριν ἐνώπιον τοῦ θεοῦ
καὶ ᾐτήσατο εὑρεῖν σκήνωμα τῷ οἴκῳ Ἰακώβ. ⁴⁷Σολο-
μῶν δὲ ᾠκοδόμησεν αὐτῷ οἶκον. ⁴⁸ἀλλ᾽ οὐχ ὁ ὕψιστος
ἐν χειροποιήτοις κατοικεῖ, καθὼς ὁ προφήτης λέγει, ⁴⁹Ὁ
οὐρανός μοι θρόνος, ἡ δὲ γῆ ὑποπόδιον τῶν ποδῶν μου·
ποῖον οἶκον οἰκοδομήσετέ μοι, λέγει κύριος, ἢ τίς τόπος
τῆς καταπαύσεώς μου; ⁵⁰οὐχὶ ἡ χείρ μου ἐποίησεν
ταῦτα πάντα; ⁵¹σκληροτράχηλοι καὶ ἀπερίτμητοι καρδίαις καὶ τοῖς ὠσίν, ὑμεῖς ἀεὶ τῷ πνεύματι τῷ ἁγίῳ
ἀντιπίπτετε, ὡς οἱ πατέρες ὑμῶν καὶ ὑμεῖς. ⁵²τίνα τῶν
προφητῶν οὐκ ἐδίωξαν οἱ πατέρες ὑμῶν; καὶ ἀπέκτειναν τοὺς προκαταγγείλαντας περὶ τῆς ἐλεύσεως τοῦ
δικαίου, οὗ νῦν ὑμεῖς προδόται καὶ φονεῖς ἐγένεσθε,
⁵³οἵτινες ἐλάβετε τὸν νόμον εἰς διαταγὰς ἀγγέλων, καὶ
οὐκ ἐφυλάξατε.

⁵⁴Ἀκούοντες δὲ ταῦτα διεπρίοντο ταῖς καρδίαις αὐτῶν καὶ ἔβρυχον τοὺς ὀδόντας ἐπ᾽ αὐτον. ⁵⁵ὑπάρχων
δὲ πλήρης πνεύματος ἁγίου, ἀτενίσας εἰς τὸν οὐρανὸν

εἶδεν δόξαν θεοῦ καὶ Ἰησοῦν ἑστῶτα ἐκ δεξιῶν τοῦ θεοῦ, [56] καὶ εἶπεν, Ἰδοὺ θεωρῶ τοὺς οὐρανοὺς διηνοιγμένους καὶ τὸν υἱὸν τοῦ ἀνθρώπου ἐκ δεξιῶν ἑστῶτα τοῦ θεοῦ. [57] κράξαντες δὲ φωνῇ μεγάλῃ συνέσχον τὰ ὦτα αὐτῶν καὶ ὥρμησαν ὁμοθυμαδὸν ἐπ' αὐτόν, [58] καὶ ἐκβαλόντες ἔξω τῆς πόλεως ἐλιθοβόλουν. καὶ οἱ μάρτυρες ἀπέθεντο τὰ ἱμάτια αὐτῶν παρὰ τοὺς πόδας νεανίου καλουμένου Σαύλου, [59] καὶ ἐλιθοβόλουν τὸν Στέφανον, ἐπικαλούμενον καὶ λέγοντα, Κύριε Ἰησοῦ, δέξαι τὸ πνεῦμά μου. [60] θεὶς δὲ τὰ γόνατα ἔκραξεν φωνῇ μεγάλῃ, Κύριε, μὴ στήσῃς αὐτοῖς τὴν ἁμαρτίαν ταύτην. καὶ τοῦτο εἰπὼν ἐκοιμήθη.

8 [1] Σαῦλος δὲ ἦν συνευδοκῶν τῇ ἀναιρέσει αὐτοῦ. Ἐγένετο δὲ ἐν ἐκείνῃ τῇ ἡμέρᾳ διωγμὸς μέγας ἐπὶ τὴν ἐκκλησίαν τὴν ἐν Ἱεροσολύμοις· πάντες δὲ διεσπάρησαν κατὰ τὰς χώρας τῆς Ἰουδαίας καὶ Σαμαρείας πλὴν τῶν ἀποστόλων. [2] συνεκόμισαν δὲ τὸν Στέφανον ἄνδρες εὐλαβεῖς καὶ ἐποίησαν κοπετὸν μέγαν ἐπ' αὐτῷ. [3] Σαῦλος δὲ ἐλυμαίνετο τὴν ἐκκλησίαν, κατὰ τοὺς οἴκους εἰσπορευόμενος, σύρων τε ἄνδρας καὶ γυναῖκας παρεδίδου εἰς φυλακήν. [4] οἱ μὲν οὖν διασπαρέντες διῆλθον εὐαγγελιζόμενοι τὸν λόγον.

[5] Φίλιππος δὲ κατελθὼν εἰς τὴν πόλιν τῆς Σαμαρείας ἐκήρυσσεν αὐτοῖς τὸν Χριστόν. [6] προσεῖχον δὲ οἱ ὄχλοι τοῖς λεγομένοις ὑπὸ τοῦ Φιλίππου ὁμοθυμαδὸν ἐν τῷ ἀκούειν αὐτοὺς καὶ βλέπειν τὰ σημεῖα ἃ ἐποίει. [7] πολλοὶ γὰρ τῶν ἐχόντων πνεύματα ἀκάθαρτα, βοῶντα φωνῇ μεγάλῃ ἐξήρχοντο· πολλοὶ δὲ παραλελυμένοι καὶ χωλοὶ ἐθεραπεύθησαν· [8] ἐγένετο δὲ πολλὴ χαρὰ ἐν τῇ πόλει ἐκείνῃ. [9] ἀνὴρ δέ τις ὀνόματι Σίμων προῦπῆρχεν ἐν τῇ πόλει μαγεύων καὶ ἐξιστάνων τὸ ἔθνος τῆς Σαμαρείας, λέγων εἶναί τινα ἑαυτὸν μέγαν, [10] ᾧ προσεῖχον

πάντες ἀπὸ μικροῦ ἕως μεγάλου λέγοντες, Οὗτός ἐστιν
ἡ δύναμις τοῦ θεοῦ ἡ καλουμένη μεγάλη. ¹¹προσεῖχον
δὲ αὐτῷ διὰ τὸ ἱκανῷ χρόνῳ ταῖς μαγείαις ἐξεστακέναι
αὐτούς. ¹²ὅτε δὲ ἐπίστευσαν τῷ Φιλίππῳ εὐαγγελιζομένῳ περὶ τῆς βασιλείας τοῦ θεοῦ καὶ τοῦ ὀνόματος
Ἰησοῦ Χριστοῦ, ἐβαπτίζοντο ἄνδρες τε καὶ γυναῖκες.
¹³ὁ δὲ Σίμων καὶ αὐτὸς ἐπίστευσεν, καὶ βαπτισθεὶς ἦν
προσκαρτερῶν τῷ Φιλίππῳ, θεωρῶν τε σημεῖα καὶ
δυνάμεις μεγάλας γινομένας ἐξίστατο.

¹⁴Ἀκούσαντες δὲ οἱ ἐν Ἱεροσολύμοις ἀπόστολοι ὅτι
δέδεκται ἡ Σαμάρεια τὸν λόγον τοῦ θεοῦ, ἀπέστειλαν
πρὸς αὐτοὺς Πέτρον καὶ Ἰωάννην, ¹⁵οἵτινες καταβάντες
προσηύξαντο περὶ αὐτῶν ὅπως λάβωσι πνεῦμα ἅγιον.
¹⁶οὐδέπω γὰρ ἦν ἐπ᾽ οὐδενὶ αὐτῶν ἐπιπεπτωκός, μόνον
δὲ βεβαπτισμένοι ὑπῆρχον εἰς τὸ ὄνομα τοῦ κυρίου
Ἰησοῦ. ¹⁷τότε ἐπετίθεσαν τὰς χεῖρας ἐπ᾽ αὐτούς, καὶ
ἐλάμβανον πνεῦμα ἅγιον. ¹⁸ἰδὼν δὲ ὁ Σίμων ὅτι διὰ
τῆς ἐπιθέσεως τῶν χειρῶν τῶν ἀποστόλων δίδοται τὸ
πνεῦμα, προσήνεγκεν αὐτοῖς χρήματα ¹⁹λέγων, Δότε
κἀμοὶ τὴν ἐξουσίαν ταύτην, ἵνα ᾧ ἐὰν ἐπιθῶ τὰς
χεῖρας λαμβάνῃ πνεῦμα ἅγιον. ²⁰Πέτρος δὲ εἶπεν πρὸς
αὐτόν, Τὸ ἀργύριόν σου σὺν σοὶ εἴη εἰς ἀπώλειαν, ὅτι
τὴν δωρεὰν τοῦ θεοῦ ἐνόμισας διὰ χρημάτων κτᾶσθαι.
²¹οὐκ ἔστι σοι μερὶς οὐδὲ κλῆρος ἐν τῷ λόγῳ τούτῳ·
ἡ γὰρ καρδία σου οὐκ ἔστιν εὐθεῖα ἔναντι τοῦ θεοῦ.
²²μετανόησον οὖν ἀπὸ τῆς κακίας σου ταύτης, καὶ δεήθητι τοῦ κυρίου εἰ ἄρα ἀφεθήσεταί σοι ἡ ἐπίνοια τῆς
καρδίας σου· ²³εἰς γὰρ χολὴν πικρίας καὶ σύνδεσμον
ἀδικίας ὁρῶ σε ὄντα. ²⁴ἀποκριθεὶς δὲ ὁ Σίμων εἶπεν,
Δεήθητε ὑμεῖς ὑπὲρ ἐμοῦ πρὸς τὸν κύριον, ὅπως μηδὲν
ἐπέλθῃ ἐπ᾽ ἐμὲ ὧν εἰρήκατε. ²⁵οἱ μὲν οὖν διαμαρτυρά-

μενοι καὶ λαλήσαντες τὸν λόγον τοῦ κυρίου ὑπέστρεφον εἰς Ἱεροσόλυμα, πολλάς τε κώμας τῶν Σαμαρειτῶν εὐηγγελίζοντο.

²⁶ Ἄγγελος δὲ κυρίου ἐλάλησεν πρὸς Φίλιππον λέγων, Ἀνάστηθι καὶ πορεύου κατὰ μεσημβρίαν ἐπὶ τὴν ὁδὸν τὴν καταβαίνουσαν ἀπὸ Ἱερουσαλὴμ εἰς Γάζαν· αὕτη ἐστὶν ἔρημος. ²⁷ καὶ ἀναστὰς ἐπορεύθη. καὶ ἰδοὺ ἀνὴρ Αἰθίοψ εὐνοῦχος δυνάστης Κανδάκης βασιλίσσης Αἰθιόπων, ὃς ἦν ἐπὶ πάσης τῆς γάζης αὐτῆς, ἐληλύθει προσκυνήσων εἰς Ἱερουσαλήμ, ²⁸ ἦν τε ὑποστρέφων, καὶ καθήμενος ἐπὶ τοῦ ἅρματος αὐτοῦ καὶ ἀνεγίνωσκεν τὸν προφήτην Ἡσαΐαν. ²⁹ εἶπεν δὲ τὸ πνεῦμα τῷ Φιλίππῳ, Πρόσελθε καὶ κολλήθητι τῷ ἅρματι τούτῳ. ³⁰ προσδραμὼν δὲ ὁ Φίλιππος ἤκουσεν αὐτοῦ ἀναγινώσκοντος Ἡσαΐαν τὸν προφήτην, καὶ εἶπεν, Ἆρά γε γινώσκεις ἃ ἀναγινώσκεις; ³¹ ὁ δὲ εἶπεν, Πῶς γὰρ ἂν δυναίμην ἐὰν μή τις ὁδηγήσει με; παρεκάλεσέν τε τὸν Φίλιππον ἀναβάντα καθίσαι σὺν αὐτῷ. ³² ἡ δὲ περιοχὴ τῆς γραφῆς ἣν ἀνεγίνωσκεν ἦν αὕτη· Ὡς πρόβατον ἐπὶ σφαγὴν ἤχθη, καὶ ὡς ἀμνὸς ἐναντίον τοῦ κείροντος αὐτὸν ἄφωνος, οὕτως οὐκ ἀνοίγει τὸ στόμα αὐτοῦ. ³³ ἐν τῇ ταπεινώσει ἡ κρίσις αὐτοῦ ἤρθη· τὴν γενεὰν αὐτοῦ τίς διηγήσεται; ὅτι αἴρεται ἀπὸ τῆς γῆς ἡ ζωὴ αὐτοῦ. ³⁴ ἀποκριθεὶς δὲ ὁ εὐνοῦχος τῷ Φιλίππῳ εἶπεν, Δέομαί σου, περὶ τίνος ὁ προφήτης λέγει τοῦτο; περὶ ἑαυτοῦ ἢ περὶ ἑτέρου τινός; ³⁵ ἀνοίξας δὲ ὁ Φίλιππος τὸ στόμα αὐτοῦ καὶ ἀρξάμενος ἀπὸ τῆς γραφῆς ταύτης εὐηγγελίσατο αὐτῷ τὸν Ἰησοῦν. ³⁶ ὡς δὲ ἐπορεύοντο κατὰ τὴν ὁδόν, ἦλθον ἐπί τι ὕδωρ, καί φησιν ὁ εὐνοῦχος, Ἰδοὺ ὕδωρ· τί κωλύει με βαπτισθῆναι; ³⁸ καὶ ἐκέλευσεν στῆναι τὸ ἅρμα, καὶ κατέβησαν ἀμφότεροι εἰς τὸ ὕδωρ,

ὅ τε Φίλιππος καὶ ὁ εὐνοῦχος, καὶ ἐβάπτισεν αὐτόν. ³⁹ὅτε δὲ ἀνέβησαν ἐκ τοῦ ὕδατος, πνεῦμα κυρίου ἥρπασεν· τὸν Φίλιππον, καὶ οὐκ εἶδεν αὐτὸν οὐκέτι ὁ εὐνοῦχος· ἐπορεύετο γὰρ τὴν ὁδὸν αὐτοῦ χαίρων. ⁴⁰Φίλιππος δὲ εὑρέθη εἰς Ἄζωτον, καὶ διερχόμενος εὐηγγελίζετο τὰς πόλεις πάσας ἕως τοῦ ἐλθεῖν αὐτὸν εἰς Καισάρειαν.

9 ¹Ὁ δὲ Σαῦλος ἔτι ἐμπνέων ἀπειλῆς καὶ φόνου εἰς τοὺς μαθητὰς τοῦ κυρίου, προσελθὼν τῷ ἀρχιερεῖ ²ᾐτήσατο παρ' αὐτοῦ ἐπιστολὰς εἰς Δαμασκὸν πρὸς τὰς συναγωγάς, ὅπως ἐάν τινας εὕρῃ τῆς ὁδοῦ ὄντας, ἄνδρας τε καὶ γυναῖκας, δεδεμένους ἀγάγῃ εἰς Ἱερουσαλήμ. ³ἐν δὲ τῷ πορεύεσθαι ἐγένετο αὐτὸν ἐγγίζειν τῇ Δαμασκῷ, ἐξαίφνης τε αὐτὸν περιήστραψεν φῶς ἐκ τοῦ οὐρανοῦ, ⁴καὶ πεσὼν ἐπὶ τὴν γῆν ἤκουσεν φωνὴν λέγουσαν αὐτῷ, Σαοὺλ Σαούλ, τί με διώκεις; ⁵εἶπεν δέ, Τίς εἶ, κύριε; ὁ δέ, Ἐγώ εἰμι Ἰησοῦς, ὃν σὺ διώκεις. ⁶ἀλλὰ ἀνάστηθι καὶ εἴσελθε εἰς τὴν πόλιν, καὶ λαληθήσεταί σοι ὅ τι σε δεῖ ποιεῖν. ⁷οἱ δὲ ἄνδρες οἱ συνοδεύοντες αὐτῷ εἱστήκεισαν ἐνεοί, ἀκούοντες μὲν τῆς φωνῆς, μηδένα δὲ θεωροῦντες. ⁸ἠγέρθη δὲ Σαῦλος ἀπὸ τῆς γῆς, ἀνεῳγμένων δὲ τῶν ὀφθαλμῶν αὐτοῦ οὐδὲν ἔβλεπεν· χειραγωγοῦντες δὲ αὐτὸν εἰσήγαγον εἰς Δαμασκόν. ⁹καὶ ἦν ἡμέρας τρεῖς μὴ βλέπων, καὶ οὐκ ἔφαγεν οὐδὲ ἔπιεν.

¹⁰Ἦν δέ τις μαθητὴς ἐν Δαμασκῷ ὀνόματι Ἀνανίας, καὶ εἶπεν πρὸς αὐτὸν ἐν ὁράματι ὁ κύριος, Ἀνανία. ὁ δὲ εἶπεν, Ἰδοὺ ἐγώ, κύριε. ¹¹ὁ δὲ κύριος πρὸς αὐτόν, Ἀναστὰς πορεύθητι ἐπὶ τὴν ῥύμην τὴν καλουμένην εὐθεῖαν καὶ ζήτησον ἐν οἰκίᾳ Ἰούδα Σαῦλον ὀνόματι Ταρσέα. ἰδοὺ γὰρ προσεύχεται, ¹²καὶ εἶδεν ἄνδρα Ἀνανίαν ὀνόματι εἰσελθόντα καὶ ἐπιθέντα αὐτῷ χεῖρας,

ὅπως ἀναβλέψῃ. ¹³ ἀπεκρίθη δὲ Ἀνανίας, Κύριε,
ἤκουσα ἀπὸ πολλῶν περὶ τοῦ ἀνδρὸς τούτου, ὅσα
κακὰ τοῖς ἁγίοις σου ἐποίησεν ἐν Ἱερουσαλήμ· ¹⁴ καὶ
ὧδε ἔχει ἐξουσίαν παρὰ τῶν ἀρχιερέων δῆσαι πάντας
τοὺς ἐπικαλουμένους τὸ ὄνομά σου. ¹⁵ εἶπεν δὲ πρὸς
αὐτὸν ὁ κύριος, Πορεύου, ὅτι σκεῦος ἐκλογῆς ἐστίν μοι
οὗτος τοῦ βαστάσαι τὸ ὄνομά μου ἐνώπιον ἐθνῶν τε
καὶ βασιλέων υἱῶν τε Ἰσραήλ· ¹⁶ ἐγὼ γὰρ ὑποδείξω
αὐτῷ ὅσα δεῖ αὐτὸν ὑπὲρ τοῦ ὀνόματός μου παθεῖν.
¹⁷ ἀπῆλθε δὲ Ἀνανίας καὶ εἰσῆλθεν εἰς τὴν οἰκίαν, καὶ
ἐπιθεὶς ἐπ᾽ αὐτὸν τὰς χεῖρας εἶπεν, Σαοὺλ ἀδελφέ, ὁ
κύριος ἀπέσταλκέν με, Ἰησοῦς ὁ ὀφθείς σοι ἐν τῇ ὁδῷ ᾗ
ἤρχου, ὅπως ἀναβλέψῃς καὶ πλησθῇς πνεύματος ἁγίου.
¹⁸ καὶ εὐθέως ἀπέπεσαν αὐτοῦ ἀπὸ τῶν ὀφθαλμῶν ὡς
λεπίδες, ἀνέβλεψέν τε, καὶ ἀναστὰς ἐβαπτίσθη, ¹⁹ καὶ
λαβὼν τροφὴν ἐνίσχυσεν· ἐγένετο δὲ μετὰ τῶν ἐν Δαμασκῷ μαθητῶν ἡμέρας τινάς, ²⁰ καὶ εὐθέως ἐν ταῖς
συναγωγαῖς ἐκήρυσσεν τὸν Ἰησοῦν, ὅτι οὗτός ἐστιν ὁ
υἱὸς τοῦ θεοῦ. ²¹ ἐξίσταντο δὲ πάντες οἱ ἀκούοντες καὶ
ἔλεγον, Οὐχ οὗτός ἐστιν ὁ πορθήσας ἐν Ἱερουσαλὴμ
τοὺς ἐπικαλουμένους τὸ ὄνομα τοῦτο, καὶ ὧδε εἰς τοῦτο
ἐληλύθει, ἵνα δεδεμένους αὐτοὺς ἀγάγῃ ἐπὶ τοὺς ἀρχιερεῖς; ²² Σαῦλος δὲ μᾶλλον ἐνεδυναμοῦτο καὶ συνέχυνεν
τοὺς Ἰουδαίους τοὺς κατοικοῦντας ἐν Δαμασκῷ, συμβιβάζων ὅτι οὗτός ἐστιν ὁ Χριστός.

²³ Ὡς δὲ ἐπληροῦντο ἡμέραι ἱκαναί, συνεβουλεύσαντο
οἱ Ἰουδαῖοι ἀνελεῖν αὐτόν· ²⁴ ἐγνώσθη δὲ τῷ Σαύλῳ ἡ
ἐπιβουλὴ αὐτῶν. παρετηροῦντο δὲ καὶ τὰς πύλας
ἡμέρας τε καὶ νυκτός, ὅπως αὐτὸν ἀνέλωσιν· ²⁵ λαβόντες
δὲ οἱ μαθηταὶ αὐτοῦ νυκτὸς διὰ τοῦ τείχους καθῆκαν
αὐτὸν χαλάσαντες ἐν σπυρίδι.

²⁶Παραγενόμενος δὲ εἰς Ἰερουσαλὴμ ἐπείραζεν κολλᾶσθαι τοῖς μαθηταῖς· καὶ πάντες ἐφοβοῦντο αὐτόν, μὴ πιστεύοντες ὅτι ἐστὶ μαθητής. ²⁷Βαρνάβας δὲ ἐπιλαβόμενος αὐτὸν ἤγαγεν πρὸς τοὺς ἀποστόλους, καὶ διηγήσατο αὐτοῖς πῶς ἐν τῇ ὁδῷ εἶδεν τὸν κύριον καὶ ὅτι ἐλάλησεν αὐτῷ, καὶ πῶς ἐν Δαμασκῷ ἐπαρρησιάσατο ἐν τῷ ὀνόματι Ἰησοῦ. ²⁸καὶ ἦν μετ᾽ αὐτῶν εἰσπορευόμενος καὶ ἐκπορευόμενος εἰς Ἰερουσαλήμ, ²⁹παρρησιαζόμενος ἐν τῷ ὀνόματι τοῦ κυρίου, ἐλάλει τε καὶ συνεζήτει πρὸς τοὺς Ἑλληνιστάς· οἱ δὲ ἐπεχείρουν ἀνελεῖν αὐτόν. ³⁰ἐπιγνόντες δὲ οἱ ἀδελφοὶ κατήγαγον αὐτὸν εἰς Καισάρειαν καὶ ἐξαπέστειλαν αὐτὸν εἰς Ταρσόν. ³¹ἡ μὲν οὖν ἐκκλησία καθ᾽ ὅλης τῆς Ἰουδαίας καὶ Γαλιλαίας καὶ Σαμαρείας εἶχεν εἰρήνην, οἰκοδομουμένη καὶ πορευομένη τῷ φόβῳ τοῦ κυρίου, καὶ τῇ παρακλήσει τοῦ ἁγίου πνεύματος ἐπληθύνετο.

³²Ἐγένετο δὲ Πέτρον διερχόμενον διὰ πάντων κατελθεῖν καὶ πρὸς τοὺς ἁγίους τοὺς κατοικοῦντας Λύδδα. ³³εὗρεν δὲ ἐκεῖ ἄνθρωπόν τινα ὀνόματι Αἰνέαν ἐξ ἐτῶν ὀκτὼ κατακείμενον ἐπὶ κραβάττου, ὃς ἦν παραλελυμένος. ³⁴καὶ εἶπεν αὐτῷ ὁ Πέτρος, Αἰνέα, ἰᾶταί σε Ἰησοῦς Χριστός· ἀνάστηθι καὶ στρῶσον σεαυτῷ. ³⁵καὶ εὐθέως ἀνέστη. καὶ εἶδαν αὐτὸν πάντες οἱ κατοικοῦντες Λύδδα καὶ τὸν Σάρωνα, οἵτινες ἐπέστρεψαν ἐπὶ τὸν κύριον.

³⁶Ἐν Ἰόππῃ δέ τις ἦν μαθήτρια ὀνόματι Ταβιθά, ἣ διερμηνευομένη λέγεται Δορκάς. αὕτη ἦν πλήρης ἀγαθῶν ἔργων καὶ ἐλεημοσυνῶν ὧν ἐποίει. ³⁷ἐγένετο δὲ ἐν ταῖς ἡμέραις ἐκείναις ἀσθενήσασαν αὐτὴν ἀποθανεῖν· λούσαντες δὲ ἔθηκαν αὐτὴν ἐν ὑπερῴῳ. ³⁸ἐγγὺς δὲ οὔσης Λύδδας τῇ Ἰόππῃ οἱ μαθηταὶ ἀκούσαντες ὅτι Πέτρος ἐστὶν ἐν αὐτῇ, ἀπέστειλαν δύο ἄνδρας πρὸς

αὐτὸν παρακαλοῦντες, Μὴ ὀκνήσῃς διελθεῖν ἕως ἡμῶν.
[39] ἀναστὰς δὲ Πέτρος συνῆλθεν αὐτοῖς· ὃν παραγενό-
μενον ἀνήγαγον εἰς τὸ ὑπερῷον, καὶ παρέστησαν αὐτῷ
πᾶσαι αἱ χῆραι κλαίουσαι καὶ ἐπιδεικνύμεναι χιτῶνας
καὶ ἱμάτια, ὅσα ἐποίει μετ᾽ αὐτῶν οὖσα ἡ Δορκάς.
[40] ἐκβαλὼν δὲ ἔξω πάντας ὁ Πέτρος καὶ θεὶς τὰ γόνατα
προσηύξατο, καὶ ἐπιστρέψας πρὸς τὸ σῶμα εἶπεν,
Ταβιθὰ ἀνάστηθι. ἡ δὲ ἤνοιξεν τοὺς ὀφθαλμοὺς αὐτῆς,
καὶ ἰδοῦσα τὸν Πέτρον ἀνεκάθισεν. [41] δοὺς δὲ αὐτῇ χεῖρα
ἀνέστησεν αὐτήν· φωνήσας δὲ τοὺς ἁγίους καὶ τὰς
χήρας παρέστησεν αὐτὴν ζῶσαν. [42] γνωστὸν δὲ ἐγένετο
καθ᾽ ὅλης τῆς Ἰόππης, καὶ ἐπίστευσαν πολλοὶ ἐπὶ τὸν
κύριον· [43] ἐγένετο δὲ αὐτὸν ἡμέρας ἱκανὰς μεῖναι ἐν
Ἰόππῃ παρά τινι Σίμωνι βυρσεῖ.

10 [1] Ἀνὴρ δέ τις ἐν Καισαρείᾳ ὀνόματι Κορνήλιος,
ἑκατοντάρχης ἐκ σπείρης τῆς καλουμένης Ἰταλικῆς,
[2] εὐσεβὴς καὶ φοβούμενος τὸν θεὸν σὺν παντὶ τῷ οἴκῳ
αὐτοῦ, ποιῶν ἐλεημοσύνας πολλὰς τῷ λαῷ καὶ δεόμενος
τοῦ θεοῦ διαπαντός, [3] εἶδεν ἐν ὁράματι φανερῶς, ὡσεὶ
περὶ ὥραν ἐνάτην τῆς ἡμέρας, ἄγγελον τοῦ θεοῦ εἰσελ-
θόντα πρὸς αὐτὸν καὶ εἰπόντα αὐτῷ, Κορνήλιε. [4] ὁ δὲ
ἀτενίσας αὐτῷ καὶ ἔμφοβος γενόμενος εἶπεν, Τί ἐστιν,
κύριε; εἶπεν δὲ αὐτῷ, Αἱ προσευχαί σου καὶ αἱ ἐλεημοσύναι σου ἀνέβησαν εἰς μνημόσυνον ἔμπροσθεν τοῦ
θεοῦ. [5] καὶ νῦν πέμψον ἄνδρας εἰς Ἰόππην καὶ μετάπεμψαι Σίμωνά τινα ὃς ἐπικαλεῖται Πέτρος· [6] οὗτος
ξενίζεται παρά τινι Σίμωνι βυρσεῖ, ᾧ ἐστιν οἰκία παρὰ
θάλασσαν. [7] ὡς δὲ ἀπῆλθεν ὁ ἄγγελος ὁ λαλῶν αὐτῷ,
φωνήσας δύο τῶν οἰκετῶν καὶ στρατιώτην εὐσεβῆ τῶν
προσκαρτερούντων αὐτῷ, [8] καὶ ἐξηγησάμενος ἅπαντα
αὐτοῖς ἀπέστειλεν αὐτοὺς εἰς τὴν Ἰόππην.

⁹ Τῇ δὲ ἐπαύριον ὁδοιπορούντων ἐκείνων καὶ τῇ πόλει ἐγγιζόντων ἀνέβη Πέτρος ἐπὶ τὸ δῶμα προσεύξασθαι περὶ ὥραν ἕκτην. ¹⁰ ἐγένετο δὲ πρόσπεινος καὶ ἤθελεν γεύσασθαι· παρασκευαζόντων δὲ αὐτῶν ἐγένετο ἐπ' αὐτὸν ἔκστασις, ¹¹ καὶ θεωρεῖ τὸν οὐρανὸν ἀνεῳγμένον καὶ καταβαῖνον σκεῦός τι ὡς ὀθόνην μεγάλην, τέσσαρσιν ἀρχαῖς καθιέμενον ἐπὶ τῆς γῆς, ¹² ἐν ᾧ ὑπῆρχεν πάντα τὰ τετράποδα καὶ ἑρπετὰ τῆς γῆς καὶ πετεινὰ τοῦ οὐρανοῦ. ¹³ καὶ ἐγένετο φωνὴ πρὸς αὐτόν, Ἀναστὰς Πέτρε θῦσον καὶ φάγε. ¹⁴ ὁ δὲ Πέτρος εἶπεν, Μηδαμῶς, κύριε, ὅτι οὐδέποτε ἔφαγον πᾶν κοινὸν καὶ ἀκάθαρτον. ¹⁵ καὶ φωνὴ πάλιν ἐκ δευτέρου πρὸς αὐτόν, Ἃ ὁ θεὸς ἐκαθάρισεν σὺ μὴ κοίνου. ¹⁶ τοῦτο δὲ ἐγένετο ἐπὶ τρίς, καὶ εὐθὺς ἀνελήμφθη τὸ σκεῦος εἰς τὸν οὐρανόν.

¹⁷ Ὡς δὲ ἐν ἑαυτῷ διηπόρει ὁ Πέτρος, τί ἂν εἴη τὸ ὅραμα ὃ εἶδεν, ἰδοὺ οἱ ἄνδρες οἱ ἀπεσταλμένοι ἀπὸ τοῦ Κορνηλίου διερωτήσαντες τὴν οἰκίαν τοῦ Σίμωνος ἐπέστησαν ἐπὶ τὸν πυλῶνα, ¹⁸ καὶ φωνήσαντες ἐπυνθάνοντο εἰ Σίμων ὁ ἐπικαλούμενος Πέτρος ἐνθάδε ξενίζεται. ¹⁹ τοῦ δὲ Πέτρου διενθυμουμένου περὶ τοῦ ὁράματος εἶπεν τὸ πνεῦμα αὐτῷ, Ἰδοὺ ἄνδρες τρεῖς ζητοῦσί σε· ²⁰ ἀλλὰ ἀναστὰς κατάβηθι, καὶ πορεύου σὺν αὐτοῖς μηδὲν διακρινόμενος, ὅτι ἐγὼ ἀπέσταλκα αὐτούς. ²¹ καταβὰς δὲ Πέτρος πρὸς τοὺς ἄνδρας εἶπεν, Ἰδοὺ ἐγώ εἰμι ὃν ζητεῖτε· τίς ἡ αἰτία δι' ἣν πάρεστε; ²² οἱ δὲ εἶπαν, Κορνήλιος ἑκατοντάρχης, ἀνὴρ δίκαιος καὶ φοβούμενος τὸν θεόν, μαρτυρούμενός τε ὑπὸ ὅλου τοῦ ἔθνους τῶν Ἰουδαίων, ἐχρηματίσθη ὑπὸ ἀγγέλου ἁγίου μεταπέμψασθαί σε εἰς τὸν οἶκον αὐτοῦ καὶ ἀκοῦσαι ῥήματα παρὰ σοῦ. ²³ εἰσκαλεσάμενος οὖν αὐτοὺς ἐξένισεν. τῇ δὲ ἐπαύριον ἀναστὰς ἐξῆλθεν σὺν αὐτοῖς, καί τινες τῶν ἀδελφῶν τῶν

ἀπὸ Ἰόππης συνῆλθον αὐτῷ. ²⁴ τῇ δὲ ἐπαύριον εἰσῆλθαν εἰς τὴν Καισάρειαν· ὁ δὲ Κορνήλιος ἦν προσδοκῶν αὐτούς, συγκαλεσάμενος τοὺς συγγενεῖς αὐτοῦ καὶ τοὺς ἀναγκαίους φίλους.

²⁵ Ὡς δὲ ἐγένετο τοῦ εἰσελθεῖν τὸν Πέτρον, συναντήσας αὐτῷ ὁ Κορνήλιος πεσὼν ἐπὶ τοὺς πόδας προσεκύνησεν. ²⁶ ὁ δὲ Πέτρος ἤγειρεν αὐτὸν λέγων, Ἀνάστηθι· καὶ ἐγὼ αὐτὸς ἄνθρωπός εἰμι. ²⁷ καὶ συνομιλῶν αὐτῷ εἰσῆλθεν, καὶ εὑρίσκει συνεληλυθότας πολλούς, ἔφη τε πρὸς αὐτούς, ²⁸ Ὑμεῖς ἐπίστασθε ὡς ἀθέμιτόν ἐστιν ἀνδρὶ Ἰουδαίῳ κολλᾶσθαι ἢ προσέρχεσθαι ἀλλοφύλῳ· κἀμοὶ ἔδειξεν ὁ θεὸς μηδένα κοινὸν ἢ ἀκάθαρτον λέγειν ἄνθρωπον· ²⁹ διὸ καὶ ἀναντιρρήτως ἦλθον μεταπεμφθείς. πυνθάνομαι οὖν, τίνι λόγῳ μετεπέμψασθέ με; ³⁰ καὶ ὁ Κορνήλιος ἔφη, Ἀπὸ τετάρτης ἡμέρας μέχρι ταύτης τῆς ὥρας ἤμην τὴν ἐνάτην προσευχόμενος ἐν τῷ οἴκῳ μου, καὶ ἰδοὺ ἀνὴρ ἔστη ἐνώπιόν μου ἐν ἐσθῆτι λαμπρᾷ, καί φησιν, ³¹ Κορνήλιε, εἰσηκούσθη σου ἡ προσευχὴ καὶ αἱ ἐλεημοσύναι σου ἐμνήσθησαν ἐνώπιον τοῦ θεοῦ. ³² πέμψον οὖν εἰς Ἰόππην καὶ μετακάλεσαι Σίμωνα ὃς ἐπικαλεῖται Πέτρος· οὗτος ξενίζεται ἐν οἰκίᾳ Σίμωνος βυρσέως παρὰ θάλασσαν. ³³ ἐξαυτῆς οὖν ἔπεμψα πρός σε, σύ τε καλῶς ἐποίησας παραγενόμενος. νῦν οὖν πάντες ἡμεῖς ἐνώπιον τοῦ θεοῦ πάρεσμεν ἀκοῦσαι πάντα τὰ προστεταγμένα σοι ὑπὸ τοῦ κυρίου.

³⁴ Ἀνοίξας δὲ Πέτρος τὸ στόμα εἶπεν, Ἐπ' ἀληθείας καταλαμβάνομαι ὅτι οὐκ ἔστιν προσωπολήμπτης ὁ θεός, ³⁵ ἀλλ' ἐν παντὶ ἔθνει ὁ φοβούμενος αὐτὸν καὶ ἐργαζόμενος δικαιοσύνην δεκτὸς αὐτῷ ἐστιν· ³⁶ τὸν λόγον ὃν ἀπέστειλεν τοῖς υἱοῖς Ἰσραὴλ εὐαγγελιζόμενος εἰρήνην διὰ Ἰησοῦ Χριστοῦ· οὗτός ἐστιν πάντων κύριος. ³⁷ ὑμεῖς

οἴδατε τὸ γενόμενον ῥῆμα καθ᾽ ὅλης τῆς Ἰουδαίας, ἀρξάμενος ἀπὸ τῆς Γαλιλαίας μετὰ τὸ βάπτισμα ὃ ἐκήρυξεν
Ἰωάννης, ³⁸ Ἰησοῦν τὸν ἀπὸ Ναζαρέθ, ὡς ἔχρισεν αὐτὸν
ὁ θεὸς πνεύματι ἁγίῳ καὶ δυνάμει, ὃς διῆλθεν εὐεργετῶν
καὶ ἰώμενος πάντας τοὺς καταδυναστευομένους ὑπὸ τοῦ
διαβόλου, ὅτι ὁ θεὸς ἦν μετ᾽ αὐτοῦ· ³⁹ καὶ ἡμεῖς μάρτυρες
πάντων ὧν ἐποίησεν ἔν τε τῇ χώρᾳ τῶν Ἰουδαίων καὶ ἐν
Ἱερουσαλήμ, ὃν καὶ ἀνεῖλαν κρεμάσαντες ἐπὶ ξύλου.
⁴⁰ τοῦτον ὁ θεὸς ἤγειρεν τῇ τρίτῃ ἡμέρᾳ καὶ ἔδωκεν αὐτὸν
ἐμφανῆ γενέσθαι, ⁴¹ οὐ παντὶ τῷ λαῷ, ἀλλὰ μάρτυσιν
τοῖς προκεχειροτονημένοις ὑπὸ τοῦ θεοῦ, ἡμῖν οἵτινες
συνεφάγομεν καὶ συνεπίομεν αὐτῷ μετὰ τὸ ἀναστῆναι
αὐτὸν ἐκ νεκρῶν· ⁴² καὶ παρήγγειλεν ἡμῖν κηρύξαι τῷ
λαῷ καὶ διαμαρτύρασθαι ὅτι αὐτός ἐστιν ὁ ὡρισμένος ὑπὸ
τοῦ θεοῦ κριτὴς ζώντων καὶ νεκρῶν. ⁴³ τούτῳ πάντες οἱ
προφῆται μαρτυροῦσιν, ἄφεσιν ἁμαρτιῶν λαβεῖν διὰ τοῦ
ὀνόματος αὐτοῦ πάντα τὸν πιστεύοντα εἰς αὐτόν.

⁴⁴ Ἔτι λαλοῦντος τοῦ Πέτρου τὰ ῥήματα ταῦτα ἐπέπεσεν τὸ πνεῦμα τὸ ἅγιον ἐπὶ πάντας τοὺς ἀκούοντας
τὸν λόγον. ⁴⁵ καὶ ἐξέστησαν οἱ ἐκ περιτομῆς πιστοὶ ὅσοι
συνῆλθαν τῷ Πέτρῳ, ὅτι καὶ ἐπὶ τὰ ἔθνη ἡ δωρεὰ τοῦ
ἁγίου πνεύματος ἐκκέχυται· ⁴⁶ ἤκουον γὰρ αὐτῶν λαλούντων γλώσσαις καὶ μεγαλυνόντων τὸν θεόν. τότε
ἀπεκρίθη Πέτρος, ⁴⁷ Μήτι τὸ ὕδωρ δύναται κωλῦσαί τις
τοῦ μὴ βαπτισθῆναι τούτους, οἵτινες τὸ πνεῦμα τὸ
ἅγιον ἔλαβον ὡς καὶ ἡμεῖς; ⁴⁸ προσέταξεν δὲ αὐτοὺς ἐν
τῷ ὀνόματι Ἰησοῦ Χριστοῦ βαπτισθῆναι. τότε ἠρώτη-
σαν αὐτὸν ἐπιμεῖναι ἡμέρας τινάς.

11 ¹ Ἤκουσαν δὲ οἱ ἀπόστολοι καὶ οἱ ἀδελφοὶ οἱ
ὄντες κατὰ τὴν Ἰουδαίαν ὅτι καὶ τὰ ἔθνη ἐδέξαντο τὸν
λόγον τοῦ θεοῦ. ² ὅτε δὲ ἀνέβη Πέτρος εἰς Ἱερουσαλήμ,

διεκρίνοντο πρὸς αὐτὸν οἱ ἐκ περιτομῆς, λέγοντες ³ὅτι
Εἰσῆλθες πρὸς ἄνδρας ἀκροβυστίαν ἔχοντας καὶ συνέφαγες αὐτοῖς. ⁴ἀρξάμενος δὲ Πέτρος ἐξετίθετο αὐτοῖς
καθεξῆς λέγων, ⁵Ἐγὼ ἤμην ἐν πόλει Ἰόππῃ προσευχόμενος, καὶ εἶδον ἐν ἐκστάσει ὅραμα, καταβαῖνον σκεῦός
τι ὡς ὀθόνην μεγάλην τέσσαρσιν ἀρχαῖς καθιεμένην ἐκ
τοῦ οὐρανοῦ, καὶ ἦλθεν ἄχρι ἐμοῦ· ⁶εἰς ἣν ἀτενίσας
κατενόουν, καὶ εἶδον τὰ τετράποδα τῆς γῆς καὶ τὰ θηρία
καὶ τὰ ἑρπετὰ καὶ τὰ πετεινὰ τοῦ οὐρανοῦ. ⁷ἤκουσα δὲ
καὶ φωνῆς λεγούσης μοι, Ἀναστὰς Πέτρε θῦσον καὶ φάγε.
⁸εἶπον δέ, Μηδαμῶς, κύριε· ὅτι κοινὸν ἢ ἀκάθαρτον
οὐδέποτε εἰσῆλθεν εἰς τὸ στόμα μου. ⁹ἀπεκρίθη δὲ
φωνὴ ἐκ δευτέρου ἐκ τοῦ οὐρανοῦ, Ἃ ὁ θεὸς ἐκαθάρισεν
σὺ μὴ κοίνου. ¹⁰τοῦτο δὲ ἐγένετο ἐπὶ τρίς, καὶ ἀνεσ-
πάσθη πάλιν ἅπαντα εἰς τὸν οὐρανόν. ¹¹καὶ ἰδοὺ ἐξαυτῆς τρεῖς ἄνδρες ἐπέστησαν ἐπὶ τὴν οἰκίαν ἐν ᾗ ἦμεν,
ἀπεσταλμένοι ἀπὸ Καισαρείας πρός με. ¹²εἶπεν δὲ τὸ
πνεῦμα μοι συνελθεῖν αὐτοῖς μηδὲν διακρίναντα. ἦλθον
δὲ σὺν ἐμοὶ καὶ οἱ ἓξ ἀδελφοὶ οὗτοι, ¹³καὶ εἰσήλθομεν εἰς
τὸν οἶκον τοῦ ἀνδρός. ἀπήγγειλεν δὲ ἡμῖν πῶς εἶδεν τὸν
ἄγγελον ἐν τῷ οἴκῳ αὐτοῦ σταθέντα καὶ εἰπόντα, Ἀπόστειλον εἰς Ἰόππην καὶ μετάπεμψαι Σίμωνα τὸν ἐπικαλούμενον Πέτρον, ¹⁴ὃς λαλήσει ῥήματα πρός σε, ἐν
οἷς σωθήσῃ σὺ καὶ πᾶς ὁ οἶκός σου. ¹⁵ἐν δὲ τῷ ἄρξασθαί με λαλεῖν ἐπέπεσεν τὸ πνεῦμα τὸ ἅγιον ἐπ᾽ αὐτοὺς
ὥσπερ καὶ ἐφ᾽ ἡμᾶς ἐν ἀρχῇ. ¹⁶ἐμνήσθην δὲ τοῦ ῥήματος
τοῦ κυρίου, ὡς ἔλεγεν, Ἰωάννης μὲν ἐβάπτισεν ὕδατι,
ὑμεῖς δὲ βαπτισθήσεσθε ἐν πνεύματι ἁγίῳ. ¹⁷εἰ οὖν
τὴν ἴσην δωρεὰν ἔδωκεν αὐτοῖς ὁ θεὸς ὡς καὶ ἡμῖν,
πιστεύσασιν ἐπὶ τὸν κύριον Ἰησοῦν Χριστόν, ἐγὼ τίς
ἤμην δυνατὸς κωλῦσαι τὸν θεόν; ¹⁸ἀκούσαντες δὲ ταῦτα

ἡσύχασαν, καὶ ἐδόξασαν τὸν θεὸν λέγοντες, Ἄρα καὶ τοῖς ἔθνεσιν ὁ θεὸς τὴν μετάνοιαν εἰς ζωὴν ἔδωκεν.

¹⁹ Οἱ μὲν οὖν διασπαρέντες ἀπὸ τῆς θλίψεως τῆς γενομένης ἐπὶ Στεφάνῳ διῆλθον ἕως Φοινίκης καὶ Κύπρου καὶ Ἀντιοχείας, μηδενὶ λαλοῦντες τὸν λόγον εἰ μὴ μόνον Ἰουδαίοις. ²⁰ ἦσαν δέ τινες ἐξ αὐτῶν ἄνδρες Κύπριοι καὶ Κυρηναῖοι, οἵτινες ἐλθόντες εἰς Ἀντιόχειαν ἐλάλουν καὶ πρὸς τοὺς Ἕλληνας, εὐαγγελιζόμενοι τὸν κύριον Ἰησοῦν. ²¹ καὶ ἦν χεὶρ κυρίου μετ’ αὐτῶν, πολύς τε ἀριθμὸς ὁ πιστεύσας ἐπέστρεψεν ἐπὶ τὸν κύριον. ²² ἠκούσθη δὲ ὁ λόγος εἰς τὰ ὦτα τῆς ἐκκλησίας τῆς οὔσης ἐν Ἱερουσαλὴμ περὶ αὐτῶν, καὶ ἐξαπέστειλαν Βαρνάβαν ἕως Ἀντιοχείας· ²³ ὃς παραγενόμενος καὶ ἰδὼν τὴν χάριν τὴν τοῦ θεοῦ ἐχάρη, καὶ παρεκάλει πάντας τῇ προθέσει τῆς καρδίας προσμένειν τῷ κυρίῳ, ²⁴ ὅτι ἦν ἀνὴρ ἀγαθὸς καὶ πλήρης πνεύματος ἁγίου καὶ πίστεως. καὶ προσετέθη ὄχλος ἱκανὸς τῷ κυρίῳ. ²⁵ ἐξῆλθεν δὲ εἰς Ταρσὸν ἀναζητῆσαι Σαῦλον, ²⁶ καὶ εὑρὼν ἤγαγεν εἰς Ἀντιόχειαν. ἐγένετο δὲ αὐτοῖς καὶ ἐνιαυτὸν ὅλον συναχθῆναι ἐν τῇ ἐκκλησίᾳ καὶ διδάξαι ὄχλον ἱκανόν, χρηματίσαι τε πρώτως ἐν Ἀντιοχείᾳ τοὺς μαθητὰς Χριστιανούς.

²⁷ Ἐν ταύταις δὲ ταῖς ἡμέραις κατῆλθον ἀπὸ Ἱεροσολύμων προφῆται εἰς Ἀντιόχειαν· ²⁸ ἀναστὰς δὲ εἷς ἐξ αὐτῶν ὀνόματι Ἄγαβος ἐσήμανεν διὰ τοῦ πνεύματος λιμὸν μεγάλην μέλλειν ἔσεσθαι ἐφ’ ὅλην τὴν οἰκουμένην, ἥτις ἐγένετο ἐπὶ Κλαυδίου. ²⁹ τῶν δὲ μαθητῶν καθὼς εὐπορεῖτό τις, ὥρισαν ἕκαστος αὐτῶν εἰς διακονίαν πέμψαι τοῖς κατοικοῦσιν ἐν τῇ Ἰουδαίᾳ ἀδελφοῖς· ³⁰ ὃ καὶ ἐποίησαν ἀποστείλαντες πρὸς τοὺς πρεσβυτέρους διὰ χειρὸς Βαρνάβα καὶ Σαύλου.

12 ¹ Κατ᾽ ἐκεῖνον δὲ τὸν καιρὸν ἐπέβαλεν Ἡρώδης ὁ βασιλεὺς τὰς χεῖρας κακῶσαί τινας τῶν ἀπὸ τῆς ἐκκλησίας. ² ἀνεῖλεν δὲ Ἰάκωβον τὸν ἀδελφὸν Ἰωάννου μαχαίρῃ. ³ ἰδὼν δὲ ὅτι ἀρεστόν ἐστιν τοῖς Ἰουδαίοις, προσέθετο συλλαβεῖν καὶ Πέτρον, ἦσαν δὲ ἡμέραι τῶν ἀζύμων, ⁴ ὃν καὶ πιάσας ἔθετο εἰς φυλακήν, παραδοὺς τέσσαρσιν τετραδίοις στρατιωτῶν φυλάσσειν αὐτόν, βουλόμενος μετὰ τὸ πάσχα ἀναγαγεῖν αὐτὸν τῷ λαῷ. ⁵ ὁ μὲν οὖν Πέτρος ἐτηρεῖτο ἐν τῇ φυλακῇ· προσευχὴ δὲ ἦν ἐκτενῶς γινομένη ὑπὸ τῆς ἐκκλησίας πρὸς τὸν θεὸν περὶ αὐτοῦ. ⁶ ὅτε δὲ ἤμελλεν προαγαγεῖν αὐτὸν ὁ Ἡρώδης, τῇ νυκτὶ ἐκείνῃ ἦν ὁ Πέτρος κοιμώμενος μεταξὺ δύο στρατιωτῶν, δεδεμένος ἁλύσεσιν δυσίν, φύλακές τε πρὸ τῆς θύρας ἐτήρουν τὴν φυλακήν. ⁷ καὶ ἰδοὺ ἄγγελος κυρίου ἐπέστη, καὶ φῶς ἔλαμψεν ἐν τῷ οἰκήματι· πατάξας δὲ τὴν πλευρὰν τοῦ Πέτρου ἤγειρεν αὐτὸν λέγων, Ἀνάστα ἐν τάχει. καὶ ἐξέπεσαν αὐτοῦ αἱ ἁλύσεις ἐκ τῶν χειρῶν. ⁸ εἶπέν τε ὁ ἄγγελος πρὸς αὐτόν, Ζῶσαι καὶ ὑπόδησαι τὰ σανδάλιά σου. ἐποίησεν δὲ οὕτως. καὶ λέγει αὐτῷ, Περιβαλοῦ τὸ ἱμάτιόν σου καὶ ἀκολούθει μοι. ⁹ καὶ ἐξελθὼν ἠκολούθει, καὶ οὐκ ᾔδει ὅτι ἀληθές ἐστιν τὸ γινόμενον διὰ τοῦ ἀγγέλου, ἐδόκει δὲ ὅραμα βλέπειν. ¹⁰ διελθόντες δὲ πρώτην φυλακὴν καὶ δευτέραν ἦλθαν ἐπὶ τὴν πύλην τὴν σιδηρᾶν τὴν φέρουσαν εἰς τὴν πόλιν, ἥτις αὐτομάτη ἠνοίγη αὐτοῖς, καὶ ἐξελθόντες προῆλθον ῥύμην μίαν, καὶ εὐθέως ἀπέστη ὁ ἄγγελος ἀπ᾽ αὐτοῦ. ¹¹ καὶ ὁ Πέτρος ἐν ἑαυτῷ γενόμενος εἶπεν, Νῦν οἶδα ἀληθῶς ὅτι ἐξαπέστειλεν κύριος τὸν ἄγγελον αὐτοῦ καὶ ἐξείλατό με ἐκ χειρὸς Ἡρώδου καὶ πάσης τῆς προσδοκίας τοῦ λαοῦ τῶν Ἰουδαίων. ¹² συνιδών τε ἦλθεν ἐπὶ τὴν οἰκίαν τῆς Μαρίας τῆς μητρὸς Ἰωάννου τοῦ ἐπικαλουμένου Μάρκου, οὗ ἦσαν ἱκανοὶ συνηθροισμένοι καὶ προσευχόμενοι.

¹³ Κρούσαντος δὲ αὐτοῦ τὴν θύραν τοῦ πυλῶνος προσῆλθεν παιδίσκη ὑπακοῦσαι, ὀνόματι Ῥόδη, ¹⁴ καὶ ἐπιγνοῦσα τὴν φωνὴν τοῦ Πέτρου ἀπὸ τῆς χαρᾶς οὐκ ἤνοιξεν τὸν πυλῶνα, εἰσδραμοῦσα δὲ ἀπήγγειλεν ἑστάναι τὸν Πέτρον πρὸ τοῦ πυλῶνος. ¹⁵ οἱ δὲ πρὸς αὐτὴν εἶπαν, Μαίνη. ἡ δὲ διϊσχυρίζετο οὕτως ἔχειν. οἱ δὲ ἔλεγον, Ὁ ἄγγελός ἐστιν αὐτοῦ. ¹⁶ ὁ δὲ Πέτρος ἐπέμενεν κρούων· ἀνοίξαντες δὲ εἶδαν αὐτὸν καὶ ἐξέστησαν. ¹⁷ κατασείσας δὲ αὐτοῖς τῇ χειρὶ σιγᾶν διηγήσατο αὐτοῖς πῶς ὁ κύριος αὐτὸν ἐξήγαγεν ἐκ τῆς φυλακῆς, εἶπέν τε, Ἀπαγγείλατε Ἰακώβῳ καὶ τοῖς ἀδελφοῖς ταῦτα. καὶ ἐξελθὼν ἐπορεύθη εἰς ἕτερον τόπον. ¹⁸ γενομένης δὲ ἡμέρας ἦν τάραχος οὐκ ὀλίγος ἐν τοῖς στρατιώταις, τί ἄρα ὁ Πέτρος ἐγένετο. ¹⁹ Ἡρώδης δὲ ἐπιζητήσας αὐτὸν καὶ μὴ εὑρών, ἀνακρίνας τοὺς φύλακας ἐκέλευσεν ἀπαχθῆναι, καὶ κατελθὼν ἀπὸ τῆς Ἰουδαίας εἰς Καισάρειαν διέτριβεν.

²⁰ Ἦν δὲ θυμομαχῶν Τυρίοις καὶ Σιδωνίοις· ὁμοθυμαδὸν δὲ παρῆσαν πρὸς αὐτόν, καὶ πείσαντες Βλάστον τὸν ἐπὶ τοῦ κοιτῶνος τοῦ βασιλέως ᾐτοῦντο εἰρήνην, διὰ τὸ τρέφεσθαι αὐτῶν τὴν χώραν ἀπὸ τῆς βασιλικῆς. ²¹ τακτῇ δὲ ἡμέρᾳ ὁ Ἡρώδης ἐνδυσάμενος ἐσθῆτα βασιλικὴν καὶ καθίσας ἐπὶ τοῦ βήματος ἐδημηγόρει πρὸς αὐτούς· ²² ὁ δὲ δῆμος ἐπεφώνει, Θεοῦ φωνὴ καὶ οὐκ ἀνθρώπου. ²³ παραχρῆμα δὲ ἐπάταξεν αὐτὸν ἄγγελος κυρίου ἀνθ᾽ ὧν οὐκ ἔδωκεν τὴν δόξαν τῷ θεῷ, καὶ γενόμενος σκωληκόβρωτος ἐξέψυξεν. ²⁴ ὁ δὲ λόγος τοῦ θεοῦ ηὔξανεν καὶ ἐπληθύνετο. ²⁵ Βαρνάβας δὲ καὶ Σαῦλος ὑπέστρεψαν ἐξ Ἱερουσαλήμ, πληρώσαντες τὴν διακο-

νίαν, συμπαραλαβόντες Ἰωάννην τὸν ἐπικληθέντα Μάρκον.

13 ¹⁹Ἦσαν δὲ ἐν Ἀντιοχείᾳ κατὰ τὴν οὖσαν ἐκκλησίαν προφῆται καὶ διδάσκαλοι ὅ τε Βαρνάβας καὶ Συμεὼν ὁ καλούμενος Νίγερ, καὶ Λούκιος ὁ Κυρηναῖος, Μαναήν τε Ἡρώδου τοῦ τετράρχου σύντροφος καὶ Σαῦλος. ²λειτουργούντων δὲ αὐτῶν τῷ κυρίῳ καὶ νηστευόντων εἶπεν τὸ πνεῦμα τὸ ἅγιον, Ἀφορίσατε δή μοι τὸν Βαρνάβαν καὶ Σαῦλον εἰς τὸ ἔργον ὃ προσκέκλημαι αὐτούς. ³τότε νηστεύσαντες καὶ προσευξάμενοι καὶ ἐπιθέντες τὰς χεῖρας αὐτοῖς ἀπέλυσαν. ⁴αὐτοὶ μὲν οὖν ἐκπεμφθέντες ὑπὸ τοῦ ἁγίου πνεύματος κατῆλθον εἰς Σελεύκειαν, ἐκεῖθέν τε ἀπέπλευσαν εἰς Κύπρον, ⁵καὶ γενόμενοι ἐν Σαλαμῖνι κατήγγελλον τὸν λόγον τοῦ θεοῦ ἐν ταῖς συναγωγαῖς τῶν Ἰουδαίων· εἶχον δὲ καὶ Ἰωάννην ὑπηρέτην. ⁶διελθόντες δὲ ὅλην τὴν νῆσον ἄχρι Πάφου εὗρον ἄνδρα τινὰ μάγον ψευδοπροφήτην Ἰουδαῖον, ᾧ ὄνομα Βαριησοῦς, ⁷ὃς ἦν σὺν τῷ ἀνθυπάτῳ Σεργίῳ Παύλῳ, ἀνδρὶ συνετῷ. οὗτος προσκαλεσάμενος Βαρνάβαν καὶ Σαῦλον ἐπεζήτησεν ἀκοῦσαι τὸν λόγον τοῦ θεοῦ· ⁸ἀνθίστατο δὲ αὐτοῖς Ἐλύμας ὁ μάγος, οὕτως γὰρ μεθερμηνεύεται τὸ ὄνομα αὐτοῦ, ζητῶν διαστρέψαι τὸν ἀνθύπατον ἀπὸ τῆς πίστεως. ⁹Σαῦλος δέ, ὁ καὶ Παῦλος, πλησθεὶς πνεύματος ἁγίου ἀτενίσας εἰς αὐτὸν ¹⁰εἶπεν, Ὦ πλήρης παντὸς δόλου καὶ πάσης ῥᾳδιουργίας, υἱὲ διαβόλου, ἐχθρὲ πάσης δικαιοσύνης, οὐ παύσῃ διαστρέφων τὰς ὁδοὺς κυρίου τὰς εὐθείας; ¹¹καὶ νῦν ἰδοὺ χεὶρ κυρίου ἐπὶ σέ, καὶ ἔσῃ τυφλὸς μὴ βλέπων τὸν ἥλιον ἄχρι καιροῦ. παραχρῆμα δὲ ἔπεσεν ἐπ᾽ αὐτὸν ἀχλὺς καὶ σκότος, καὶ περιάγων ἐζήτει χειραγωγούς. ¹²τότε ἰδὼν ὁ ἀνθύπατος τὸ γεγονὸς ἐπίστευσεν, ἐκπλησσόμενος ἐπὶ τῇ διδαχῇ τοῦ κυρίου.

[13] Ἀναχθέντες δὲ ἀπὸ τῆς Πάφου οἱ περὶ Παῦλον ἦλθον εἰς Πέργην τῆς Παμφυλίας. Ἰωάννης δὲ ἀποχωρήσας ἀπ᾽ αὐτῶν ὑπέστρεψεν εἰς Ἱεροσόλυμα. [14] αὐτοὶ δὲ διελθόντες ἀπὸ τῆς Πέργης παρεγένοντο εἰς Ἀντιόχειαν τὴν Πισιδίαν, καὶ ἐλθόντες εἰς τὴν συναγωγὴν τῇ ἡμέρᾳ τῶν σαββάτων ἐκάθισαν. [15] μετὰ δὲ τὴν ἀνάγνωσιν τοῦ νόμου καὶ τῶν προφητῶν ἀπέστειλαν οἱ ἀρχισυνάγωγοι πρὸς αὐτοὺς λέγοντες, Ἄνδρες ἀδελφοί, εἴ τις ἔστιν ἐν ὑμῖν λόγος παρακλήσεως πρὸς τὸν λαόν, λέγετε.

[16] Ἀναστὰς δὲ Παῦλος καὶ κατασείσας τῇ χειρὶ εἶπεν, Ἄνδρες Ἰσραηλῖται καὶ οἱ φοβούμενοι τὸν θεόν, ἀκούσατε. [17] ὁ θεὸς τοῦ λαοῦ τούτου Ἰσραὴλ ἐξελέξατο τοὺς πατέρας ἡμῶν, καὶ τὸν λαὸν ὕψωσεν ἐν τῇ παροικίᾳ ἐν γῇ Αἰγύπτῳ, καὶ μετὰ βραχίονος ὑψηλοῦ ἐξήγαγεν αὐτοὺς ἐξ αὐτῆς, [18] καὶ ὡς τεσσερακονταέτη χρόνον ἐτροφοφόρησεν αὐτοὺς ἐν τῇ ἐρήμῳ, [19] καὶ καθελὼν ἔθνη ἑπτὰ ἐν γῇ Χαναὰν κατεκληρονόμησεν τὴν γῆν αὐτῶν, [20] ὡς ἔτεσιν τετρακοσίοις καὶ πεντήκοντα. καὶ μετὰ ταῦτα ἔδωκεν κριτὰς ἕως Σαμουὴλ προφήτου. [21] κἀκεῖθεν ᾐτήσαντο βασιλέα, καὶ ἔδωκεν αὐτοῖς ὁ θεὸς τὸν Σαοὺλ υἱὸν Κείς, ἄνδρα ἐκ φυλῆς Βενιαμείν, ἔτη τεσσεράκοντα· [22] καὶ μεταστήσας αὐτὸν ἤγειρεν τὸν Δαυεὶδ αὐτοῖς εἰς βασιλέα, ᾧ καὶ εἶπεν μαρτυρήσας, Εὗρον Δαυεὶδ τὸν τοῦ Ἰεσσαί, ἄνδρα κατὰ τὴν καρδίαν μου, ὃς ποιήσει πάντα τὰ θελήματά μου. [23] τούτου ὁ θεὸς ἀπὸ τοῦ σπέρματος κατ᾽ ἐπαγγελίαν ἤγαγεν τῷ Ἰσραὴλ σωτῆρα Ἰησοῦν, [24] προκηρύξαντος Ἰωάννου πρὸ προσώπου τῆς εἰσόδου αὐτοῦ βάπτισμα μετανοίας παντὶ τῷ λαῷ Ἰσραήλ. [25] ὡς δὲ ἐπλήρου Ἰωάννης τὸν δρόμον, ἔλεγεν, Τί ἐμὲ ὑπονοεῖτε εἶναι, οὐκ εἰμὶ ἐγώ· ἀλλ᾽ ἰδοὺ ἔρχεται μετ᾽ ἐμὲ οὗ οὐκ εἰμὶ ἄξιος τὸ ὑπόδημα τῶν ποδῶν λῦσαι.

²⁶ ἄνδρες ἀδελφοί, υἱοὶ γένους Ἀβραὰμ καὶ οἱ ἐν ὑμῖν
φοβούμενοι τὸν θεόν, ὑμῖν ὁ λόγος τῆς σωτηρίας ταύτης
ἐξαπεστάλη. ²⁷ οἱ γὰρ κατοικοῦντες ἐν Ἰερουσαλὴμ καὶ
οἱ ἄρχοντες αὐτῶν τοῦτον ἀγνοήσαντες καὶ τὰς φωνὰς
τῶν προφητῶν τὰς κατὰ πᾶν σάββατον ἀναγινωσκομένας
κρίναντες ἐπλήρωσαν, ²⁸ καὶ μηδεμίαν αἰτίαν θανάτου
εὑρόντες ᾐτήσαντο Πιλᾶτον ἀναιρεθῆναι αὐτόν· ²⁹ ὡς δὲ
ἐτέλεσαν πάντα τὰ περὶ αὐτοῦ γεγραμμένα, καθελόντες
ἀπὸ τοῦ ξύλου ἔθηκαν εἰς μνημεῖον. ³⁰ ὁ δὲ θεὸς ἤγειρεν
αὐτὸν ἐκ νεκρῶν, ³¹ ὃς ὤφθη ἐπὶ ἡμέρας πλείους τοῖς
συναναβᾶσιν αὐτῷ ἀπὸ τῆς Γαλιλαίας εἰς Ἰερουσαλήμ,
οἵτινες νῦν εἰσὶν μάρτυρες αὐτοῦ πρὸς τὸν λαόν. ³² καὶ
ἡμεῖς ὑμᾶς εὐαγγελιζόμεθα τὴν πρὸς τοὺς πατέρας ἐπαγγελίαν γενομένην, ³³ ὅτι ταύτην ὁ θεὸς ἐκπεπλήρωκεν τοῖς
τέκνοις ἡμῶν ἀναστήσας Ἰησοῦν, ὡς καὶ ἐν τῷ πρώτῳ
ψαλμῷ γέγραπται, Υἱός μου εἶ σύ, ἐγὼ σήμερον γεγέν-
νηκά σε. ³⁴ ὅτι δὲ ἀνέστησεν αὐτὸν ἐκ νεκρῶν μηκέτι
μέλλοντα ὑποστρέφειν εἰς διαφθοράν, οὕτως εἴρηκεν
ὅτι Δώσω ὑμῖν τὰ ὅσια Δαυεὶδ τὰ πιστά. ³⁵ διότι καὶ
ἐν ἑτέρῳ λέγει, Οὐ δώσεις τὸν ὅσιόν σου ἰδεῖν διαφθοράν.
³⁶ Δαυεὶδ μὲν γὰρ ἰδίᾳ γενεᾷ ὑπηρετήσας τῇ τοῦ θεοῦ
βουλῇ ἐκοιμήθη καὶ προσετέθη πρὸς τοὺς πατέρας αὐτοῦ
καὶ εἶδεν διαφθοράν· ³⁷ ὃν δὲ ὁ θεὸς ἤγειρεν, οὐκ
εἶδεν διαφθοράν. ³⁸ γνωστὸν οὖν ἔστω ὑμῖν, ἄνδρες
ἀδελφοί, ὅτι διὰ τούτου ὑμῖν ἄφεσις ἁμαρτιῶν καταγ-
γέλλεται· ³⁹ ἀπὸ πάντων ὧν οὐκ ἠδυνήθητε ἐν νόμῳ
Μωϋσέως δικαιωθῆναι, ἐν τούτῳ πᾶς ὁ πιστεύων δικαι-
οῦται. ⁴⁰ βλέπετε οὖν μὴ ἐπέλθῃ τὸ εἰρημένον ἐν τοῖς
προφήταις, ⁴¹ Ἴδετε, οἱ καταφρονηταί, καὶ θαυμάσατε
καὶ ἀφανίσθητε, ὅτι ἔργον ἐργάζομαι ἐγὼ ἐν ταῖς ἡμέραις
ὑμῶν, ἔργον ὃ οὐ μὴ πιστεύσητε ἐάν τις ἐκδιηγῆται ὑμῖν.

⁴²'Εξιόντων δὲ αὐτῶν, παρεκάλουν εἰς τὸ μεταξὺ σάββατον λαληθῆναι αὐτοῖς τὰ ῥήματα ταῦτα. ⁴³λυθείσης δὲ τῆς συναγωγῆς ἠκολούθησαν πολλοὶ τῶν Ἰουδαίων καὶ τῶν σεβομένων προσηλύτων τῷ Παύλῳ καὶ τῷ Βαρνάβᾳ, οἵτινες προσλαλοῦντες αὐτοῖς ἔπειθον αὐτοὺς προσμένειν τῇ χάριτι τοῦ θεοῦ. ⁴⁴τῷ δὲ ἐρχομένῳ σαββάτῳ σχεδὸν πᾶσα ἡ πόλις συνήχθη ἀκοῦσαι τὸν λόγον τοῦ κυρίου. ⁴⁵ἰδόντες δὲ οἱ Ἰουδαῖοι τοὺς ὄχλους ἐπλήσθησαν ζήλου, καὶ ἀντέλεγον τοῖς ὑπὸ Παύλου λαλουμένοις ἀντιλέγοντες καὶ βλασφημοῦντες. ⁴⁶παρρησιασάμενοί τε ὁ Παῦλος καὶ ὁ Βαρνάβας εἶπαν, Ὑμῖν ἦν ἀναγκαῖον πρῶτον λαληθῆναι τὸν λόγον τοῦ θεοῦ· ἐπειδὴ ἀπωθεῖσθε αὐτὸν καὶ οὐκ ἀξίους κρίνετε ἑαυτοὺς τῆς αἰωνίου ζωῆς, ἰδοὺ στρεφόμεθα εἰς τὰ ἔθνη. ⁴⁷οὕτως γὰρ ἐντέταλται ἡμῖν ὁ κύριος, Τέθεικά σε εἰς φῶς ἐθνῶν τοῦ εἶναί σε εἰς σωτηρίαν ἕως ἐσχάτου τῆς γῆς. ⁴⁸ἀκούοντα δὲ τὰ ἔθνη ἔχαιρον καὶ ἐδόξαζον τὸν λόγον τοῦ κυρίου, καὶ ἐπίστευσαν ὅσοι ἦσαν τεταγμένοι εἰς ζωὴν αἰώνιον· ⁴⁹διεφέρετο δὲ ὁ λόγος τοῦ κυρίου δι' ὅλης τῆς χώρας. ⁵⁰οἱ δὲ Ἰουδαῖοι παρώτρυναν τὰς σεβομένας γυναῖκας τὰς εὐσχήμονας καὶ τοὺς πρώτους τῆς πόλεως, καὶ ἐπήγειραν διωγμὸν ἐπὶ τὸν Παῦλον καὶ Βαρνάβαν, καὶ ἐξέβαλον αὐτοὺς ἀπὸ τῶν ὁρίων αὐτῶν. ⁵¹οἱ δὲ ἐκτιναξάμενοι τὸν κονιορτὸν τῶν ποδῶν ἐπ' αὐτοὺς ἦλθον εἰς Ἰκόνιον· ⁵²οἱ δὲ μαθηταὶ ἐπληροῦντο χαρᾶς καὶ πνεύματος ἁγίου.

14 ¹Ἐγένετο δὲ ἐν Ἰκονίῳ κατὰ τὸ αὐτὸ εἰσελθεῖν αὐτοὺς εἰς τὴν συναγωγὴν τῶν Ἰουδαίων καὶ λαλῆσαι οὕτως ὥστε πιστεῦσαι Ἰουδαίων τε καὶ Ἑλλήνων πολὺ πλῆθος. ²οἱ δὲ ἀπειθήσαντες Ἰουδαῖοι ἐπήγειραν καὶ ἐκάκωσαν τὰς ψυχὰς τῶν ἐθνῶν κατὰ τῶν ἀδελφῶν.

³ ἱκανὸν μὲν οὖν χρόνον διέτριψαν παρρησιαζόμενοι ἐπὶ
τῷ κυρίῳ τῷ μαρτυροῦντι τῷ λόγῳ τῆς χάριτος αὐτοῦ,
διδόντι σημεῖα καὶ τέρατα γίνεσθαι διὰ τῶν χειρῶν
αὐτῶν. ⁴ ἐσχίσθη δὲ τὸ πλῆθος τῆς πόλεως, καὶ οἱ μὲν
ἦσαν σὺν τοῖς Ἰουδαίοις, οἱ δὲ σὺν τοῖς ἀποστόλοις.
⁵ ὡς δὲ ἐγένετο ὁρμὴ τῶν ἐθνῶν τε καὶ Ἰουδαίων σὺν τοῖς
ἄρχουσιν αὐτῶν ὑβρίσαι καὶ λιθοβολῆσαι αὐτούς, ⁶ συνιδόντες κατέφυγον εἰς τὰς πόλεις τῆς Λυκαονίας Λύστραν
καὶ Δέρβην καὶ τὴν περίχωρον· ⁷ κἀκεῖ εὐαγγελιζόμενοι
ἦσαν.

⁸ Καί τις ἀνὴρ ἐν Λύστροις ἀδύνατος τοῖς ποσὶν
ἐκάθητο, χωλὸς ἐκ κοιλίας μητρὸς αὐτοῦ, ὃς οὐδέποτε
περιεπάτησεν. ⁹ οὗτος ἤκουσεν τοῦ Παύλου λαλοῦντος,
ὃς ἀτενίσας αὐτῷ καὶ ἰδὼν ὅτι ἔχει πίστιν τοῦ σωθῆναι,
¹⁰ εἶπεν μεγάλῃ φωνῇ, Ἀνάστηθι ἐπὶ τοὺς πόδας σου
ὀρθός. καὶ ἥλατο, καὶ περιεπάτει. ¹¹ οἵ τε ὄχλοι ἰδόντες
ὃ ἐποίησεν Παῦλος ἐπῆραν τὴν φωνὴν αὐτῶν Λυκαονιστὶ
λέγοντες, Οἱ θεοὶ ὁμοιωθέντες ἀνθρώποις κατέβησαν
πρὸς ἡμᾶς, ¹² ἐκάλουν τε τὸν Βαρνάβαν Δία, τὸν δὲ
Παῦλον Ἑρμῆν, ἐπειδὴ αὐτὸς ἦν ὁ ἡγούμενος τοῦ λόγου.
¹³ ὅ τε ἱερεὺς τοῦ Διὸς τοῦ ὄντος πρὸ τῆς πόλεως, ταύρους
καὶ στέμματα ἐπὶ τοὺς πυλῶνας ἐνέγκας, σὺν τοῖς
ὄχλοις ἤθελεν θύειν. ¹⁴ ἀκούσαντες δὲ οἱ ἀπόστολοι
Βαρνάβας καὶ Παῦλος, διαρρήξαντες τὰ ἱμάτια αὐτῶν
ἐξεπήδησαν εἰς τὸν ὄχλον, ¹⁵ κράζοντες καὶ λέγοντες,
Ἄνδρες, τί ταῦτα ποιεῖτε; καὶ ἡμεῖς ὁμοιοπαθεῖς ἐσμὲν
ὑμῖν ἄνθρωποι, εὐαγγελιζόμενοι ὑμᾶς ἀπὸ τούτων τῶν
ματαίων ἐπιστρέφειν ἐπὶ θεὸν ζῶντα, ὃς ἐποίησεν τὸν
οὐρανὸν καὶ τὴν γῆν καὶ τὴν θάλασσαν καὶ πάντα τὰ
ἐν αὐτοῖς, ¹⁶ ὃς ἐν ταῖς παρῳχημέναις γενεαῖς εἴασεν
πάντα τὰ ἔθνη πορεύεσθαι ταῖς ὁδοῖς αὐτῶν· ¹⁷ καίτοι

οὐκ ἀμάρτυρον αὐτὸν ἀφῆκεν ἀγαθουργῶν, οὐρανόθεν
ὑμῖν ὑετοὺς διδοὺς καὶ καιροὺς καρποφόρους, ἐμπιπλῶν
τροφῆς καὶ εὐφροσύνης τὰς καρδίας ὑμῶν. ¹⁸ καὶ ταῦτα
λέγοντες μόλις κατέπαυσαν τοὺς ὄχλους τοῦ μὴ θύειν
αὐτοῖς.

¹⁹ Ἐπῆλθαν δὲ ἀπὸ Ἀντιοχείας καὶ Ἰκονίου Ἰουδαῖοι, καὶ πείσαντες τοὺς ὄχλους καὶ λιθάσαντες τὸν
Παῦλον ἔσυρον ἔξω τῆς πόλεως, νομίζοντες αὐτὸν τεθνηκέναι. ²⁰ κυκλωσάντων δὲ τῶν μαθητῶν αὐτὸν ἀναστὰς εἰσῆλθεν εἰς τὴν πόλιν. καὶ τῇ ἐπαύριον ἐξῆλθεν
σὺν τῷ Βαρνάβᾳ εἰς Δέρβην· ²¹ εὐαγγελιζόμενοί τε τὴν
πόλιν ἐκείνην καὶ μαθητεύσαντες ἱκανοὺς ὑπέστρεψαν
εἰς τὴν Λύστραν καὶ εἰς Ἰκόνιον καὶ εἰς Ἀντιόχειαν,
²² ἐπιστηρίζοντες τὰς ψυχὰς τῶν μαθητῶν, παρακαλοῦντες ἐμμένειν τῇ πίστει, καὶ ὅτι διὰ πολλῶν θλίψεων
δεῖ ἡμᾶς εἰσελθεῖν εἰς τὴν βασιλείαν τοῦ θεοῦ. ²³ χειροτονήσαντες δὲ αὐτοῖς κατ᾽ ἐκκλησίαν πρεσβυτέρους,
προσευξάμενοι μετὰ νηστειῶν παρέθεντο αὐτοὺς τῷ
κυρίῳ εἰς ὃν πεπιστεύκεισαν. ²⁴ καὶ διελθόντες τὴν
Πισιδίαν ἦλθον εἰς τὴν Παμφυλίαν, ²⁵ καὶ λαλήσαντες
ἐν Πέργῃ τὸν λόγον κατέβησαν εἰς Ἀττάλειαν, ²⁶ κἀκεῖθεν ἀπέπλευσαν εἰς Ἀντιόχειαν, ὅθεν ἦσαν παραδεδομένοι τῇ χάριτι τοῦ θεοῦ εἰς τὸ ἔργον ὃ ἐπλήρωσαν.
²⁷ παραγενόμενοι δὲ καὶ συναγαγόντες τὴν ἐκκλησίαν,
ἀνήγγελλον ὅσα ἐποίησεν ὁ θεὸς μετ᾽ αὐτῶν, καὶ ὅτι
ἤνοιξεν τοῖς ἔθνεσι θύραν πίστεως. ²⁸ διέτριβον δὲ
χρόνον οὐκ ὀλίγον σὺν τοῖς μαθηταῖς.

15 ¹ Καί τινες κατελθόντες ἀπὸ τῆς Ἰουδαίας ἐδίδασκον τοὺς ἀδελφοὺς ὅτι Ἐὰν μὴ περιτμηθῆτε τῷ ἔθει
τῷ Μωϋσέως, οὐ δύνασθε σωθῆναι. ² γενομένης δὲ στάσεως καὶ ζητήσεως οὐκ ὀλίγης τῷ Παύλῳ καὶ τῷ

Βαρνάβᾳ πρὸς αὐτούς, ἔταξαν ἀναβαίνειν Παῦλον καὶ
Βαρνάβαν καί τινας ἄλλους ἐξ αὐτῶν πρὸς τοὺς ἀποστόλους καὶ πρεσβυτέρους εἰς Ἰερουσαλὴμ περὶ τοῦ
ζητήματος τούτου. ³οἱ μὲν οὖν προπεμφθέντες ὑπὸ
τῆς ἐκκλησίας διήρχοντο τήν τε Φοινίκην καὶ Σαμάρειαν, ἐκδιηγούμενοι τὴν ἐπιστροφὴν τῶν ἐθνῶν, καὶ
ἐποίουν χαρὰν μεγάλην πᾶσιν τοῖς ἀδελφοῖς. ⁴παρα-
γενόμενοι δὲ εἰς Ἰερουσαλὴμ παρεδέχθησαν ὑπὸ τῆς
ἐκκλησίας καὶ τῶν ἀποστόλων καὶ τῶν πρεσβυτέρων,
ἀνήγγειλάν τε ὅσα ὁ θεὸς ἐποίησεν μετ᾽ αὐτῶν. ⁵ἐξανέ-
στησαν δέ τινες τῶν ἀπὸ τῆς αἱρέσεως τῶν Φαρισαίων
πεπιστευκότες, λέγοντες ὅτι Δεῖ περιτέμνειν αὐτοὺς
παραγγέλλειν τε τηρεῖν τὸν νόμον Μωϋσέως.
⁶Συνήχθησαν δὲ οἱ ἀπόστολοι καὶ οἱ πρεσβύτεροι
ἰδεῖν περὶ τοῦ λόγου τούτου. ⁷πολλῆς δὲ ζητήσεως
γενομένης ἀναστὰς Πέτρος εἶπεν πρὸς αὐτούς, Ἄνδρες
ἀδελφοί, ὑμεῖς ἐπίστασθε ὅτι ἀφ᾽ ἡμερῶν ἀρχαίων ἐν
ὑμῖν ἐξελέξατο ὁ θεὸς διὰ τοῦ στόματός μου ἀκοῦσαι
τὰ ἔθνη τὸν λόγον τοῦ εὐαγγελίου καὶ πιστεῦσαι. ⁸καὶ
ὁ καρδιογνώστης θεὸς ἐμαρτύρησεν αὐτοῖς δοὺς τὸ
πνεῦμα τὸ ἅγιον καθὼς καὶ ἡμῖν, ⁹καὶ οὐθὲν διέκρινεν
μεταξὺ ἡμῶν τε καὶ αὐτῶν, τῇ πίστει καθαρίσας τὰς
καρδίας αὐτῶν. ¹⁰νῦν οὖν τί πειράζετε τὸν θεόν, ἐπιθεῖναι ζυγὸν ἐπὶ τὸν τράχηλον τῶν μαθητῶν, ὃν οὔτε
οἱ πατέρες ἡμῶν οὔτε ἡμεῖς ἰσχύσαμεν βαστάσαι;
¹¹ἀλλὰ διὰ τῆς χάριτος τοῦ κυρίου Ἰησοῦ πιστεύομεν
σωθῆναι καθ᾽ ὃν τρόπον κἀκεῖνοι. ¹²ἐσίγησεν δὲ πᾶν
τὸ πλῆθος, καὶ ἤκουον Βαρνάβα καὶ Παύλου ἐξηγουμέ-
νων ὅσα ἐποίησεν ὁ θεὸς σημεῖα καὶ τέρατα ἐν τοῖς
ἔθνεσιν δι᾽ αὐτῶν.
¹³Μετὰ δὲ τὸ σιγῆσαι αὐτοὺς ἀπεκρίθη Ἰάκωβος

λέγων, Ἄνδρες ἀδελφοί, ἀκούσατέ μου. [14]Συμεὼν ἐξη-
γήσατο καθὼς πρῶτον ὁ θεὸς ἐπεσκέψατο λαβεῖν ἐξ
ἐθνῶν λαὸν τῷ ὀνόματι αὐτοῦ. [15]καὶ τούτῳ συμφωνοῦσιν οἱ λόγοι τῶν προφητῶν, καθὼς γέγραπται,
[16]Μετὰ ταῦτα ἀναστρέψω καὶ ἀνοικοδομήσω τὴν σκηνὴν
Δαυεὶδ τὴν πεπτωκυῖαν, καὶ τὰ κατεστραμμένα αὐτῆς
ἀνοικοδομήσω καὶ ἀνορθώσω αὐτήν, [17]ὅπως ἂν ἐκζητήσωσιν οἱ κατάλοιποι τῶν ·ἀνθρώπων τὸν κύριον, καὶ
πάντα τὰ ἔθνη ἐφ᾽ οὓς ἐπικέκληται τὸ ὄνομά μου ἐπ᾽
αὐτούς, λέγει κύριος ποιῶν ταῦτα [18]γνωστὰ ἀπ᾽ αἰῶνος.
[19]διὸ ἐγὼ κρίνω μὴ παρενοχλεῖν τοῖς ἀπὸ τῶν ἐθνῶν
ἐπιστρέφουσιν ἐπὶ τὸν θεόν, [20]ἀλλὰ ἐπιστεῖλαι αὐτοῖς
τοῦ ἀπέχεσθαι τῶν ἀλισγημάτων τῶν εἰδώλων καὶ τῆς
πορνείας καὶ τοῦ πνικτοῦ καὶ τοῦ αἵματος. [21]Μωϋσῆς
γὰρ ἐκ γενεῶν ἀρχαίων κατὰ πόλιν τοὺς κηρύσσοντας
αὐτὸν ἔχει ἐν ταῖς συναγωγαῖς κατὰ πᾶν σάββατον
ἀναγινωσκόμενος.

[22]Τότε ἔδοξε τοῖς ἀποστόλοις καὶ τοῖς πρεσβυτέροις
σὺν ὅλῃ τῇ ἐκκλησίᾳ, ἐκλεξαμένους ἄνδρας ἐξ αὐτῶν
πέμψαι εἰς Ἀντιόχειαν σὺν τῷ Παύλῳ καὶ Βαρνάβᾳ,
Ἰούδαν τὸν καλούμενον Βαρσαββᾶν καὶ Σίλαν, ἄνδρας
ἡγουμένους ἐν τοῖς ἀδελφοῖς, [23]γράψαντες διὰ χειρὸς
αὐτῶν, Οἱ ἀπόστολοι καὶ οἱ πρεσβύτεροι ἀδελφοὶ τοῖς
κατὰ τὴν Ἀντιόχειαν καὶ Συρίαν καὶ Κιλικίαν ἀδελφοῖς
τοῖς ἐξ ἐθνῶν χαίρειν. [24]ἐπειδὴ ἠκούσαμεν ὅτι τινὲς ἐξ
ἡμῶν ἐξελθόντες ἐτάραξαν ὑμᾶς λόγοις ἀνασκευάζοντες
τὰς ψυχὰς ὑμῶν, οἷς οὐ διεστειλάμεθα, [25]ἔδοξεν ἡμῖν
γενομένοις ὁμοθυμαδόν, ἐκλεξαμένους ἄνδρας πέμψαι
πρὸς ὑμᾶς σὺν τοῖς ἀγαπητοῖς ἡμῶν Βαρνάβᾳ καὶ
Παύλῳ, [26]ἀνθρώποις παραδεδωκόσι τὰς ψυχὰς αὐτῶν
ὑπὲρ τοῦ ὀνόματος τοῦ κυρίου ἡμῶν Ἰησοῦ Χριστοῦ.

²⁷ἀπεστάλκαμεν οὖν Ἰούδαν καὶ Σίλαν, καὶ αὐτοὺς διὰ λόγου ἀπαγγέλλοντας τὰ αὐτά. ²⁸ἔδοξεν γὰρ τῷ πνεύματι τῷ ἁγίῳ καὶ ἡμῖν, μηδὲν πλέον ἐπιτίθεσθαι ὑμῖν βάρος πλὴν τούτων τῶν ἐπάναγκες, ²⁹ἀπέχεσθαι εἰδωλοθύτων καὶ αἵματος καὶ πνικτῶν καὶ πορνείας, ἐξ ὧν διατηροῦντες ἑαυτοὺς εὖ πράξετε. ἔρρωσθε.

³⁰Οἱ μὲν οὖν ἀπολυθέντες κατῆλθον εἰς Ἀντιόχειαν, καὶ συναγαγόντες τὸ πλῆθος ἐπέδωκαν τὴν ἐπιστολήν. ³¹ἀναγνόντες δὲ ἐχάρησαν ἐπὶ τῇ παρακλήσει. ³²Ἰούδας τε καὶ Σίλας, καὶ αὐτοὶ προφῆται ὄντες, διὰ λόγου πολλοῦ παρεκάλεσαν τοὺς ἀδελφοὺς καὶ ἐπεστήριξαν· ³³ποιήσαντες δὲ χρόνον, ἀπελύθησαν μετ᾽ εἰρήνης ἀπὸ τῶν ἀδελφῶν πρὸς τοὺς ἀποστείλαντας αὐτούς. ³⁵Παῦλος δὲ καὶ Βαρνάβας διέτριβον ἐν Ἀντιοχείᾳ, διδάσκοντες καὶ εὐαγγελιζόμενοι μετὰ καὶ ἑτέρων πολλῶν τὸν λόγον τοῦ κυρίου.

³⁶Μετὰ δέ τινας ἡμέρας εἶπεν πρὸς Βαρνάβαν Παῦλος, Ἐπιστρέψαντες δὴ ἐπισκεψώμεθα τοὺς ἀδελφοὺς κατὰ πόλιν πᾶσαν ἐν αἷς κατηγγείλαμεν τὸν λόγον τοῦ κυρίου, πῶς ἔχουσιν. ³⁷Βαρνάβας δὲ ἐβούλετο συμπαραλαβεῖν καὶ τὸν Ἰωάννην τὸν καλούμενον Μάρκον· ³⁸Παῦλος δὲ ἠξίου, τὸν ἀποστάντα ἀπ᾽ αὐτῶν ἀπὸ Παμφυλίας καὶ μὴ συνελθόντα αὐτοῖς εἰς τὸ ἔργον, μὴ συμπαραλαμβάνειν τοῦτον. ³⁹ἐγένετο δὲ παροξυσμός, ὥστε ἀποχωρισθῆναι αὐτοὺς ἀπ᾽ ἀλλήλων, τόν τε Βαρνάβαν παραλαβόντα τὸν Μάρκον ἐκπλεῦσαι εἰς Κύπρον. ⁴⁰Παῦλος δὲ ἐπιλεξάμενος Σίλαν ἐξῆλθεν, παραδοθεὶς τῇ χάριτι τοῦ κυρίου ὑπὸ τῶν ἀδελφῶν· ⁴¹διήρχετο δὲ τὴν Συρίαν καὶ Κιλικίαν ἐπιστηρίζων τὰς ἐκκλησίας.

16 ¹Κατήντησεν δὲ εἰς Δέρβην καὶ εἰς Λύστραν. καὶ ἰδοὺ μαθητής τις ἦν ἐκεῖ ὀνόματι Τιμόθεος, υἱὸς γυναικὸς

Ἰουδαίας πιστῆς πατρὸς δὲ Ἕλληνος, ²ὃς ἐμαρτυρεῖτο ὑπὸ τῶν ἐν Λύστροις καὶ Ἰκονίῳ ἀδελφῶν. ³τοῦτον ἠθέλησεν ὁ Παῦλος σὺν αὐτῷ ἐξελθεῖν, καὶ λαβὼν περιέτεμεν αὐτὸν διὰ τοὺς Ἰουδαίους τοὺς ὄντας ἐν τοῖς τόποις ἐκείνοις· ᾔδεισαν γὰρ ἅπαντες τὸν πατέρα αὐτοῦ ὅτι Ἕλλην ὑπῆρχεν. ⁴ὡς δὲ διεπορεύοντο τὰς πόλεις, παρεδίδοσαν αὐτοῖς φυλάσσειν τὰ δόγματα τὰ κεκριμένα ὑπὸ τῶν ἀποστόλων καὶ πρεσβυτέρων τῶν ἐν Ἱεροσολύμοις. ⁵αἱ μὲν οὖν ἐκκλησίαι ἐστερεοῦντο τῇ πίστει καὶ ἐπερίσσευον τῷ ἀριθμῷ καθ᾽ ἡμέραν. ⁶διῆλθον δὲ τὴν Φρυγίαν καὶ Γαλατικὴν χώραν, κωλυθέντες ὑπὸ τοῦ ἁγίου πνεύματος λαλῆσαι τὸν λόγον ἐν τῇ Ἀσίᾳ· ⁷ἐλθόντες δὲ κατὰ τὴν Μυσίαν ἐπείραζον εἰς τὴν Βιθυνίαν πορευθῆναι, καὶ οὐκ εἴασεν αὐτοὺς τὸ πνεῦμα Ἰησοῦ· ⁸παρελθόντες δὲ τὴν Μυσίαν κατέβησαν εἰς Τρωάδα. ⁹καὶ ὅραμα διὰ νυκτὸς τῷ Παύλῳ ὤφθη, ἀνὴρ Μακεδών τις ἦν ἑστὼς καὶ παρακαλῶν αὐτὸν καὶ λέγων, Διαβὰς εἰς Μακεδονίαν βοήθησον ἡμῖν. ¹⁰ὡς δὲ τὸ ὅραμα εἶδεν, εὐθέως ἐζητήσαμεν ἐξελθεῖν εἰς Μακεδονίαν, συμβιβάζοντες ὅτι προσκέκληται ἡμᾶς ὁ θεὸς εὐαγγελίσασθαι αὐτούς. ¹¹ἀναχθέντες οὖν ἀπὸ Τρωάδος εὐθυδρομήσαμεν εἰς Σαμοθράκην, τῇ δὲ ἐπιούσῃ εἰς Νέαν πόλιν, ¹²κἀκεῖθεν εἰς Φιλίππους, ἥτις ἐστὶν πρώτη τῆς μερίδος Μακεδονίας πόλις, κολωνία. ἦμεν δὲ ἐν ταύτῃ τῇ πόλει διατρίβοντες ἡμέρας τινάς.

¹³Τῇ τε ἡμέρᾳ τῶν σαββάτων ἐξήλθομεν ἔξω τῆς πύλης παρὰ ποταμὸν οὗ ἐνομίζομεν προσευχὴν εἶναι, καὶ καθίσαντες ἐλαλοῦμεν ταῖς συνελθούσαις γυναιξίν. ¹⁴καί τις γυνὴ ὀνόματι Λυδία, πορφυρόπωλις πόλεως Θυατείρων, σεβομένη τὸν θεόν, ἤκουεν, ἧς ὁ κύριος διήνοιξεν τὴν καρδίαν προσέχειν τοῖς λαλουμένοις ὑπὸ

πορφυρόπωλης – ου (m.)
πορφωρόπωλις – ιδος (f.)

Παύλου. ¹⁵ ὡς δὲ ἐβαπτίσθη καὶ ὁ οἶκος αὐτῆς, παρε-
κάλεσεν λέγουσα, Εἰ κεκρίκατέ με πιστὴν τῷ κυρίῳ
εἶναι, εἰσελθόντες εἰς τὸν οἶκόν μου μένετε· καὶ παρεβιάσατο ἡμᾶς. ¹⁶ ἐγένετο δὲ πορευομένων ἡμῶν εἰς τὴν προσευχήν, παιδίσκην τινὰ ἔχουσαν πνεῦμα πύθωνα ὑπαντῆσαι
ἡμῖν, ἥτις ἐργασίαν πολλὴν παρεῖχεν τοῖς κυρίοις αὐτῆς
μαντευομένη. ¹⁷ αὕτη κατακολουθοῦσα τῷ Παύλῳ καὶ
ἡμῖν ἔκραζεν λέγουσα, Οὗτοι οἱ ἄνθρωποι δοῦλοι τοῦ θεοῦ
τοῦ ὑψίστου εἰσίν, οἵτινες καταγγέλλουσιν ὑμῖν ὁδὸν
σωτηρίας. ¹⁸ τοῦτο δὲ ἐποίει ἐπὶ πολλὰς ἡμέρας. διαπονηθεὶς δὲ Παῦλος καὶ ἐπιστρέψας τῷ πνεύματι εἶπεν,
Παραγγέλλω σοι ἐν ὀνόματι Ἰησοῦ Χριστοῦ ἐξελθεῖν
ἀπ' αὐτῆς· καὶ ἐξῆλθεν αὐτῇ τῇ ὥρᾳ. ¹⁹ ἰδόντες δὲ οἱ
κύριοι αὐτῆς ὅτι ἐξῆλθεν ἡ ἐλπὶς τῆς ἐργασίας αὐτῶν,
ἐπιλαβόμενοι τὸν Παῦλον καὶ τὸν Σίλαν εἵλκυσαν εἰς
τὴν ἀγορὰν ἐπὶ τοὺς ἄρχοντας, ²⁰ καὶ προσαγαγόντες αὐτοὺς τοῖς στρατηγοῖς εἶπαν, Οὗτοι οἱ ἄνθρωποι ἐκταράσσουσιν ἡμῶν τὴν πόλιν, Ἰουδαῖοι ὑπάρχοντες, ²¹ καὶ
καταγγέλλουσιν ἔθη ἃ οὐκ ἔξεστιν ἡμῖν παραδέχεσθαι
οὐδὲ ποιεῖν Ῥωμαίοις οὖσιν. ²² καὶ συνεπέστη ὁ ὄχλος
κατ' αὐτῶν, καὶ οἱ στρατηγοὶ περιρήξαντες αὐτῶν τὰ
ἱμάτια ἐκέλευον ῥαβδίζειν, ²³ πολλάς τε ἐπιθέντες αὐτοῖς
πληγὰς ἔβαλον εἰς φυλακήν, παραγγείλαντες τῷ δεσ-
μοφύλακι ἀσφαλῶς τηρεῖν αὐτούς· ²⁴ ὃς παραγγελίαν
τοιαύτην λαβὼν ἔβαλεν αὐτοὺς εἰς τὴν ἐσωτέραν φυλακὴν καὶ τοὺς πόδας ἠσφαλίσατο αὐτῶν εἰς τὸ ξύλον.
²⁵ κατὰ δὲ τὸ μεσονύκτιον Παῦλος καὶ Σίλας προσευχόμενοι ὕμνουν τὸν θεόν· ἐπηκροῶντο δὲ αὐτῶν οἱ δέσμιοι.
²⁶ ἄφνω δὲ σεισμὸς ἐγένετο μέγας, ὥστε σαλευθῆναι τὰ
θεμέλια τοῦ δεσμωτηρίου· ἠνεῴχθησαν δὲ παραχρῆμα
αἱ θύραι πᾶσαι, καὶ πάντων τὰ δεσμὰ ἀνέθη. ²⁷ ἔξυπνος

δὲ γενόμενος ὁ δεσμοφύλαξ καὶ ἰδὼν ἀνεῳγμένας τὰς
θύρας τῆς φυλακῆς, σπασάμενος μάχαιραν ἤμελλεν
ἑαυτὸν ἀναιρεῖν, νομίζων ἐκπεφευγέναι τοὺς δεσμίους.
²⁸ἐφώνησεν δὲ φωνῇ μεγάλῃ Παῦλος λέγων, Μηδὲν
πράξῃς σεαυτῷ κακόν· ἅπαντες γάρ ἐσμεν ἐνθάδε.
²⁹αἰτήσας δὲ φῶτα εἰσεπήδησεν, καὶ ἔντρομος γενόμενος
προσέπεσεν τῷ Παύλῳ καὶ τῷ Σίλᾳ, ³⁰καὶ προαγαγὼν
αὐτοὺς ἔξω ἔφη, Κύριοι, τί με δεῖ ποιεῖν ἵνα σωθῶ; ³¹οἱ
δὲ εἶπαν, Πίστευσον ἐπὶ τὸν κύριον Ἰησοῦν, καὶ σωθήσῃ
σὺ καὶ ὁ οἶκός σου. ³²καὶ ἐλάλησαν αὐτῷ τὸν λόγον
τοῦ κυρίου σὺν πᾶσιν τοῖς ἐν τῇ οἰκίᾳ αὐτοῦ. ³³καὶ
παραλαβὼν αὐτοὺς ἐν ἐκείνῃ τῇ ὥρᾳ τῆς νυκτὸς ἔλουσεν
ἀπὸ τῶν πληγῶν, καὶ ἐβαπτίσθη αὐτὸς καὶ οἱ αὐτοῦ
πάντες παραχρῆμα, ³⁴ἀναγαγών τε αὐτοὺς εἰς τὸν οἶκον
παρέθηκεν τράπεζαν, καὶ ἠγαλλιάσατο πανοικὶ πεπιστευκὼς τῷ θεῷ.

³⁵Ἡμέρας δὲ γενομένης ἀπέστειλαν οἱ στρατηγοὶ
τοὺς ῥαβδούχους λέγοντες, Ἀπόλυσον τοὺς ἀνθρώπους
ἐκείνους. ³⁶ἀπήγγειλεν δὲ ὁ δεσμοφύλαξ τοὺς λόγους
τούτους πρὸς τὸν Παῦλον ὅτι Ἀπέσταλκαν οἱ στρατηγοὶ
ἵνα ἀπολυθῆτε· νῦν οὖν ἐξελθόντες πορεύεσθε ἐν εἰρήνῃ.
³⁷ὁ δὲ Παῦλος ἔφη πρὸς αὐτούς, Δείραντες ἡμᾶς δημοσίᾳ
ἀκατακρίτους, ἀνθρώπους Ῥωμαίους ὑπάρχοντας, ἔβα-
λαν εἰς φυλακήν, καὶ νῦν λάθρα ἡμᾶς ἐκβάλλουσιν;
οὐ γάρ, ἀλλὰ ἐλθόντες αὐτοὶ ἡμᾶς ἐξαγαγέτωσαν.
³⁸ἀπήγγειλαν δὲ τοῖς στρατηγοῖς οἱ ῥαβδοῦχοι τὰ
ῥήματα ταῦτα. ἐφοβήθησαν δὲ ἀκούσαντες ὅτι Ῥωμαῖοί εἰσιν, ³⁹καὶ ἐλθόντες παρεκάλεσαν αὐτούς, καὶ
ἐξαγαγόντες ἠρώτων ἀπελθεῖν ἀπὸ τῆς πόλεως. ⁴⁰ἐξελ-
θόντες δὲ ἐκ τῆς φυλακῆς εἰσῆλθον πρὸς τὴν Λυδίαν,
καὶ ἰδόντες παρεκάλεσαν τοὺς ἀδελφούς, καὶ ἐξῆλθαν.

17 ¹ Διοδεύσαντες δὲ τὴν Ἀμφίπολιν καὶ τὴν Ἀπολλωνίαν ἦλθον εἰς Θεσσαλονίκην, ὅπου ἦν συναγωγὴ τῶν
Ἰουδαίων. ² κατὰ δὲ τὸ εἰωθὸς τῷ Παύλῳ εἰσῆλθεν
πρὸς αὐτούς, καὶ ἐπὶ σάββατα τρία διελέξατο αὐτοῖς
ἀπὸ τῶν γραφῶν, ³ διανοίγων καὶ παρατιθέμενος ὅτι τὸν
Χριστὸν ἔδει παθεῖν καὶ ἀναστῆναι ἐκ νεκρῶν, καὶ ὅτι
οὗτός ἐστιν Χριστὸς Ἰησοῦς, ὃν ἐγὼ καταγγέλλω ὑμῖν.
⁴ καί τινες ἐξ αὐτῶν ἐπείσθησαν καὶ <u>προσεκληρώθησαν</u>
τῷ Παύλῳ καὶ τῷ Σίλᾳ, τῶν τε σεβομένων Ἑλλήνων
πλῆθος πολύ, γυναικῶν τε τῶν πρώτων οὐκ ὀλίγαι.
⁵ ζηλώσαντες δὲ οἱ Ἰουδαῖοι καὶ προσλαβόμενοι τῶν
ἀγοραίων τινὰς ἄνδρας πονηροὺς καὶ ὀχλοποιήσαντες
ἐθορύβουν τὴν πόλιν, καὶ ἐπιστάντες τῇ οἰκίᾳ Ἰάσονος
ἐζήτουν αὐτοὺς προαγαγεῖν εἰς τὸν δῆμον· ⁶ μὴ εὑρόντες
δὲ αὐτοὺς ἔσυρον Ἰάσονα καί τινας ἀδελφοὺς ἐπὶ τοὺς
πολιτάρχας, βοῶντες ὅτι Οἱ τὴν οἰκουμένην ἀναστατώσαντες οὗτοι καὶ ἐνθάδε πάρεισιν, ⁷ οὓς ὑποδέδεκται Ἰά-
σων· καὶ οὗτοι πάντες ἀπέναντι τῶν δογμάτων Καίσαρος
πράσσουσιν, βασιλέα ἕτερον λέγοντες εἶναι Ἰησοῦν.
⁸ ἐτάραξαν δὲ τὸν ὄχλον καὶ τοὺς πολιτάρχας ἀκούοντας
ταῦτα, ⁹ καὶ λαβόντες τὸ ἱκανὸν παρὰ τοῦ Ἰάσονος καὶ
τῶν λοιπῶν ἀπέλυσαν αὐτούς.

¹⁰ Οἱ δὲ ἀδελφοὶ εὐθέως διὰ νυκτὸς ἐξέπεμψαν τόν
τε Παῦλον καὶ τὸν Σίλαν εἰς Βέροιαν, οἵτινες παραγενόμενοι εἰς τὴν συναγωγὴν τῶν Ἰουδαίων ἀπῄεσαν·
¹¹ οὗτοι δὲ ἦσαν εὐγενέστεροι τῶν ἐν Θεσσαλονίκῃ, οἵτινες
ἐδέξαντο τὸν λόγον μετὰ πάσης προθυμίας, καθ᾽ ἡμέραν
ἀνακρίνοντες τὰς γραφάς, εἰ ἔχοι ταῦτα οὕτως. ¹² πολλοὶ
μὲν οὖν ἐξ αὐτῶν ἐπίστευσαν, καὶ τῶν Ἑλληνίδων
γυναικῶν τῶν <u>εὐσχημόνων</u> καὶ ἀνδρῶν οὐκ ὀλίγοι· ¹³ ὡς
δὲ ἔγνωσαν οἱ ἀπὸ τῆς Θεσσαλονίκης Ἰουδαῖοι ὅτι καὶ

ἐν τῇ Βεροίᾳ κατηγγέλη ὑπὸ τοῦ Παύλου ὁ λόγος τοῦ
θεοῦ, ἦλθον κἀκεῖ σαλεύοντες καὶ ταράσσοντες τοὺς
ὄχλους. [14] εὐθέως δὲ τότε τὸν Παῦλον ἐξαπέστειλαν
οἱ ἀδελφοὶ πορεύεσθαι ἕως ἐπὶ τὴν θάλασσαν· ὑπέ-
μεινάν τε ὅ τε Σίλας καὶ ὁ Τιμόθεος ἐκεῖ. [15] οἱ δὲ
καθιστάνοντες τὸν Παῦλον ἤγαγον ἕως Ἀθηνῶν, καὶ
λαβόντες ἐντολὴν πρὸς τὸν Σίλαν καὶ τὸν Τιμόθεον, ἵνα
ὡς τάχιστα ἔλθωσιν πρὸς αὐτόν, ἐξῄεσαν.

[16] Ἐν δὲ ταῖς Ἀθήναις ἐκδεχομένου αὐτοὺς τοῦ
Παύλου, παρωξύνετο τὸ πνεῦμα αὐτοῦ ἐν αὐτῷ, θεωροῦντος κατείδωλον οὖσαν τὴν πόλιν. [17] διελέγετο μὲν
οὖν ἐν τῇ συναγωγῇ τοῖς Ἰουδαίοις καὶ τοῖς σεβομένοις
καὶ ἐν τῇ ἀγορᾷ κατὰ πᾶσαν ἡμέραν πρὸς τοὺς παρα-
τυγχάνοντας. [18] τινὲς δὲ καὶ τῶν Ἐπικουρείων καὶ
Στωϊκῶν φιλοσόφων συνέβαλλον αὐτῷ, καί τινες ἔλεγον,
Τί ἂν θέλοι ὁ σπερμολόγος οὗτος λέγειν; οἱ δέ, Ξένων
δαιμονίων δοκεῖ καταγγελεὺς εἶναι, ὅτι τὸν Ἰησοῦν καὶ
τὴν ἀνάστασιν εὐηγγελίζετο. [19] ἐπιλαβόμενοί τε αὐτοῦ
ἐπὶ τὸν Ἄρειον πάγον ἤγαγον, λέγοντες, Δυνάμεθα
γνῶναι τίς ἡ καινὴ αὕτη ἡ ὑπὸ σοῦ λαλουμένη διδαχή;
[20] ξενίζοντα γάρ τινα εἰσφέρεις εἰς τὰς ἀκοὰς ἡμῶν· βου-
λόμεθα οὖν γνῶναι τίνα θέλει ταῦτα εἶναι. [21] Ἀθηναῖοι
δὲ πάντες καὶ οἱ ἐπιδημοῦντες ξένοι εἰς οὐδὲν ἕτερον
ηὐκαίρουν ἢ λέγειν τι ἢ ἀκούειν καινότερον.

[22] Σταθεὶς δὲ Παῦλος ἐν μέσῳ τοῦ Ἀρείου πάγου
ἔφη, Ἄνδρες Ἀθηναῖοι, κατὰ πάντα ὡς δεισιδαιμονεστέρους ὑμᾶς θεωρῶ. [23] διερχόμενος γὰρ καὶ ἀναθεωρῶν
τὰ σεβάσματα ὑμῶν εὗρον καὶ βωμὸν ἐν ᾧ ἐπεγέ-
γραπτο, ἀγνώστῳ θεῷ. ὃ οὖν ἀγνοοῦντες εὐσεβεῖτε,
τοῦτο ἐγὼ καταγγέλλω ὑμῖν. [24] ὁ θεὸς ὁ ποιήσας τὸν
κόσμον καὶ πάντα τὰ ἐν αὐτῷ, οὗτος οὐρανοῦ καὶ γῆς

ὑπάρχων κύριος οὐκ ἐν χειροποιήτοις ναοῖς κατοικεῖ,
²⁵οὐδὲ ὑπὸ χειρῶν ἀνθρωπίνων θεραπεύεται προσδεό-
μενός τινος, αὐτὸς διδοὺς πᾶσιν ζωὴν καὶ πνοὴν καὶ τὰ
πάντα· ²⁶ἐποίησέν τε ἐξ ἑνὸς πᾶν ἔθνος ἀνθρώπων
κατοικεῖν ἐπὶ παντὸς προσώπου τῆς γῆς, ὁρίσας προστεταγμένους καιροὺς καὶ τὰς ὁροθεσίας τῆς κατοικίας
αὐτῶν, ²⁷ζητεῖν τὸν θεόν, εἰ ἄρα γε ψηλαφήσειαν αὐτὸν
καὶ εὕροιεν, καί γε οὐ μακρὰν ἀπὸ ἑνὸς ἑκάστου ἡμῶν
ὑπάρχοντα. ²⁸ἐν αὐτῷ γὰρ ζῶμεν καὶ κινούμεθα καὶ
ἐσμέν, ὡς καί τινες τῶν καθ᾽ ὑμᾶς ποιητῶν εἰρήκασιν,
Τοῦ γὰρ καὶ γένος ἐσμέν. ²⁹γένος οὖν ὑπάρχοντες τοῦ
θεοῦ οὐκ ὀφείλομεν νομίζειν, χρυσῷ ἢ ἀργύρῳ ἢ λίθῳ,
χαράγματι τέχνης καὶ ἐνθυμήσεως ἀνθρώπου, τὸ θεῖον
εἶναι ὅμοιον. ³⁰τοὺς μὲν οὖν χρόνους τῆς ἀγνοίας ὑπεριδὼν
ὁ θεὸς τὰ νῦν παραγγέλλει τοῖς ἀνθρώποις πάντας πανταχοῦ μετανοεῖν, ³¹καθότι ἔστησεν ἡμέραν ἐν ᾗ μέλλει
κρίνειν τὴν οἰκουμένην ἐν δικαιοσύνῃ, ἐν ἀνδρὶ ᾧ ὥρισεν,
πίστιν παρασχὼν πᾶσιν ἀναστήσας αὐτὸν ἐκ νεκρῶν.
³²Ἀκούσαντες δὲ ἀνάστασιν νεκρῶν, οἱ μὲν ἐχλεύαζον,
οἱ δὲ εἶπαν, Ἀκουσόμεθά σου περὶ τούτου καὶ πάλιν.
³³οὕτως ὁ Παῦλος ἐξῆλθεν ἐκ μέσου αὐτῶν. ³⁴τινὲς δὲ
ἄνδρες κολληθέντες αὐτῷ ἐπίστευσαν, ἐν οἷς καὶ Διονύσιος ὁ Ἀρεοπαγίτης καὶ γυνὴ ὀνόματι Δάμαρις, καὶ
ἕτεροι σὺν αὐτοῖς.

18 ¹Μετὰ ταῦτα χωρισθεὶς ἐκ τῶν Ἀθηνῶν ἦλθεν
εἰς Κόρινθον. ²καὶ εὑρών τινα Ἰουδαῖον ὀνόματι Ἀκύλαν, Ποντικὸν τῷ γένει, προσφάτως ἐληλυθότα ἀπὸ τῆς
Ἰταλίας, καὶ Πρίσκιλλαν γυναῖκα αὐτοῦ, διὰ τὸ διατεταχέναι Κλαύδιον χωρίζεσθαι πάντας τοὺς Ἰουδαίους
ἀπὸ τῆς Ῥώμης, προσῆλθεν αὐτοῖς, ³καὶ διὰ τὸ ὁμότεχνον εἶναι ἔμενεν παρ᾽ αὐτοῖς, καὶ ἠργάζετο· ἦσαν

γὰρ σκηνοποιοὶ τῇ τέχνῃ. ⁴διελέγετο δὲ ἐν τῇ συναγωγῇ κατὰ πᾶν σάββατον, ἔπειθέν τε Ἰουδαίους καὶ
Ἕλληνας. ⁵ὡς δὲ κατῆλθον ἀπὸ τῆς Μακεδονίας ὅ τε
Σίλας καὶ ὁ Τιμόθεος, συνείχετο τῷ λόγῳ ὁ Παῦλος, διαμαρτυρόμενος τοῖς Ἰουδαίοις εἶναι τὸν Χριστὸν Ἰησοῦν.
⁶ἀντιτασσομένων δὲ αὐτῶν καὶ βλασφημούντων ἐκτιναξάμενος τὰ ἱμάτια εἶπεν πρὸς αὐτούς, Τὸ αἷμα ὑμῶν
ἐπὶ τὴν κεφαλὴν ὑμῶν· καθαρὸς ἐγὼ ἀπὸ τοῦ νῦν εἰς
τὰ ἔθνη πορεύσομαι. ⁷καὶ μεταβὰς ἐκεῖθεν εἰσῆλθεν
εἰς οἰκίαν τινὸς ὀνόματι Ἰούστου σεβομένου τὸν θεόν,
οὗ ἡ οἰκία ἦν συνομοροῦσα τῇ συναγωγῇ. ⁸Κρίσπος δὲ
ὁ ἀρχισυνάγωγος ἐπίστευσεν τῷ κυρίῳ σὺν ὅλῳ τῷ
οἴκῳ αὐτοῦ, καὶ πολλοὶ τῶν Κορινθίων ἀκούοντες ἐπί-
στευον καὶ ἐβαπτίζοντο. ⁹εἶπεν δὲ ὁ κύριος ἐν νυκτὶ
δι' ὁράματος τῷ Παύλῳ, Μὴ φοβοῦ, ἀλλὰ λάλει καὶ μὴ
σιωπήσῃς, ¹⁰διότι ἐγώ εἰμι μετὰ σοῦ καὶ οὐδεὶς ἐπιθήσεταί
σοι τοῦ κακῶσαί σε, διότι λαός ἐστίν μοι πολὺς ἐν τῇ
πόλει ταύτῃ. ¹¹ἐκάθισεν δὲ ἐνιαυτὸν καὶ μῆνας ἓξ διδάσκων ἐν αὐτοῖς τὸν λόγον τοῦ θεοῦ.

¹²Γαλλίωνος δὲ ἀνθυπάτου ὄντος τῆς Ἀχαΐας κατεπέστησαν ὁμοθυμαδὸν οἱ Ἰουδαῖοι τῷ Παύλῳ καὶ ἤγαγον
αὐτὸν ἐπὶ τὸ βῆμα, ¹³λέγοντες ὅτι Παρὰ τὸν νόμον
ἀναπείθει οὗτος τοὺς ἀνθρώπους σέβεσθαι τὸν θεόν.
¹⁴μέλλοντος δὲ τοῦ Παύλου ἀνοίγειν τὸ στόμα εἶπεν
ὁ Γαλλίων πρὸς τοὺς Ἰουδαίους, Εἰ μὲν ἦν ἀδίκημά τι
ἢ ῥᾳδιούργημα πονηρόν, ὦ Ἰουδαῖοι, κατὰ λόγον ἂν
ἀνεσχόμην ὑμῶν· ¹⁵εἰ δὲ ζητήματά ἐστιν περὶ λόγου
καὶ ὀνομάτων καὶ νόμου τοῦ καθ' ὑμᾶς, ὄψεσθε αὐτοί·
κριτὴς ἐγὼ τούτων οὐ βούλομαι εἶναι. ¹⁶καὶ ἀπήλασεν αὐτοὺς ἀπὸ τοῦ βήματος. ¹⁷ἐπιλαβόμενοι δὲ
πάντες Σωσθένην τὸν ἀρχισυνάγωγον ἔτυπτον ἔμ-

πρόσθεν τοῦ βήματος· καὶ οὐδὲν τούτων τῷ Γαλλίωνι
ἔμελεν.

[18] Ὁ δὲ Παῦλος ἔτι προσμείνας ἡμέρας ἱκανάς, τοῖς
ἀδελφοῖς ἀποταξάμενος ἐξέπλει εἰς τὴν Συρίαν, καὶ
σὺν αὐτῷ Πρίσκιλλα καὶ Ἀκύλας, κειράμενος ἐν Κεγχρεαῖς τὴν κεφαλήν· εἶχεν γὰρ εὐχήν. [19] κατήντησαν
δὲ εἰς Ἔφεσον, κἀκείνους κατέλιπεν αὐτοῦ, αὐτὸς δὲ
εἰσελθὼν εἰς τὴν συναγωγὴν διελέξατο τοῖς Ἰουδαίοις.
[20] ἐρωτώντων δὲ αὐτῶν ἐπὶ πλείονα χρόνον μεῖναι οὐκ
ἐπένευσεν, [21] ἀλλὰ ἀποταξάμενος καὶ εἰπών, Πάλιν ἀνακάμψω πρὸς ὑμᾶς τοῦ θεοῦ θέλοντος, ἀνήχθη ἀπὸ τῆς
Ἐφέσου, [22] καὶ κατελθὼν εἰς Καισάρειαν, ἀναβὰς καὶ
ἀσπασάμενος τὴν ἐκκλησίαν κατέβη εἰς Ἀντιόχειαν,
[23] καὶ ποιήσας χρόνον τινὰ ἐξῆλθεν, διερχόμενος καθεξῆς
τὴν Γαλατικὴν χώραν καὶ Φρυγίαν, στηρίζων πάντας
τοὺς μαθητάς.

[24] Ἰουδαῖος δέ τις Ἀπολλὼς ὀνόματι, Ἀλεξανδρεὺς
τῷ γένει, ἀνὴρ λόγιος, κατήντησεν εἰς Ἔφεσον, δυνατὸς
ὢν ἐν ταῖς γραφαῖς. [25] οὗτος ἦν κατηχημένος τὴν ὁδὸν
τοῦ κυρίου, καὶ ζέων τῷ πνεύματι ἐλάλει καὶ ἐδίδασκεν
ἀκριβῶς τὰ περὶ τοῦ Ἰησοῦ, ἐπιστάμενος μόνον τὸ
βάπτισμα Ἰωάννου, [26] οὗτός τε ἤρξατο παρρησιάζεσθαι
ἐν τῇ συναγωγῇ. ἀκούσαντες δὲ αὐτοῦ Πρίσκιλλα καὶ
Ἀκύλας προσελάβοντο αὐτὸν καὶ ἀκριβέστερον αὐτῷ
ἐξέθεντο τὴν ὁδὸν τοῦ θεοῦ. [27] βουλομένου δὲ αὐτοῦ
διελθεῖν εἰς τὴν Ἀχαΐαν, προτρεψάμενοι οἱ ἀδελφοὶ
ἔγραψαν τοῖς μαθηταῖς ἀποδέξασθαι αὐτόν. ὃς παραγενόμενος συνεβάλετο πολὺ τοῖς πεπιστευκόσιν διὰ τῆς
χάριτος. [28] εὐτόνως γὰρ τοῖς Ἰουδαίοις διακατηλέγχετο
δημοσίᾳ ἐπιδεικνὺς διὰ τῶν γραφῶν εἶναι τὸν Χριστὸν
Ἰησοῦν.

διακατελεγχομαι to confute thoroughly

19 [1]Ἐγένετο δὲ ἐν τῷ τὸν Ἀπολλὼ εἶναι ἐν Κορίνθῳ Παῦλον διελθόντα τὰ ἀνωτερικὰ μέρη ἐλθεῖν εἰς
Ἔφεσον· καὶ εὑρεῖν τινὰς μαθητάς, [2]εἶπέν τε πρὸς
αὐτούς, Εἰ πνεῦμα ἅγιον ἐλάβετε πιστεύσαντες; οἱ
δὲ πρὸς αὐτόν, Ἀλλ᾽ οὐδὲ εἰ πνεῦμα ἅγιόν ἐστιν
ἠκούσαμεν. [3]εἶπέν τε, Εἰς τί οὖν ἐβαπτίσθητε; οἱ
δὲ εἶπαν, Εἰς τὸ Ἰωάννου βάπτισμα. [4]εἶπεν δὲ Παῦλος, Ἰωάννης ἐβάπτισεν βάπτισμα μετανοίας, τῷ λαῷ
λέγων εἰς τὸν ἐρχόμενον μετ᾽ αὐτὸν ἵνα πιστεύσωσιν,
τουτέστιν εἰς τὸν Ἰησοῦν. [5]ἀκούσαντες δὲ ἐβαπτίσθη-
σαν εἰς τὸ ὄνομα τοῦ κυρίου Ἰησοῦ, [6]καὶ ἐπιθέντος
αὐτοῖς τοῦ Παύλου χεῖρας ἦλθεν τὸ πνεῦμα τὸ ἅγιον
ἐπ᾽ αὐτούς, ἐλάλουν τε γλώσσαις καὶ ἐπροφήτευον.
[7]ἦσαν δὲ οἱ πάντες ἄνδρες ὡσεὶ δώδεκα.

[8]Εἰσελθὼν δὲ εἰς τὴν συναγωγὴν ἐπαρρησιάζετο ἐπὶ
μῆνας τρεῖς διαλεγόμενος καὶ πείθων τὰ περὶ τῆς βασιλείας τοῦ θεοῦ. [9]ὡς δέ τινες ἐσκληρύνοντο καὶ ἠπείθουν κακολογοῦντες τὴν ὁδὸν ἐνώπιον τοῦ πλήθους,
ἀποστὰς ἀπ᾽ αὐτῶν ἀφώρισεν τοὺς μαθητάς, καθ᾽ ἡμέραν διαλεγόμενος ἐν τῇ σχολῇ Τυράννου. [10]τοῦτο δὲ
ἐγένετο ἐπὶ ἔτη δύο, ὥστε πάντας τοὺς κατοικοῦντας
τὴν Ἀσίαν ἀκοῦσαι τὸν λόγον τοῦ κυρίου, Ἰουδαίους
τε καὶ Ἕλληνας. [11]δυνάμεις τε οὐ τὰς τυχούσας ὁ θεὸς
ἐποίει διὰ τῶν χειρῶν Παύλου, [12]ὥστε καὶ ἐπὶ τοὺς ἀσθε-
νοῦντας ἀποφέρεσθαι ἀπὸ τοῦ χρωτὸς αὐτοῦ σουδάρια
ἢ σιμικίνθια καὶ ἀπαλλάσσεσθαι ἀπ᾽ αὐτῶν τὰς νόσους
τά τε πνεύματα τὰ πονηρὰ ἐκπορεύεσθαι. [13]ἐπεχεί-
ρησαν δέ τινες καὶ τῶν περιερχομένων Ἰουδαίων ἐξορκιστῶν ὀνομάζειν ἐπὶ τοὺς ἔχοντας τὰ πνεύματα τὰ
πονηρὰ τὸ ὄνομα τοῦ κυρίου Ἰησοῦ, λέγοντες, Ὁρκίζω
ὑμᾶς τὸν Ἰησοῦν ὃν Παῦλος κηρύσσει. [14]ἦσαν δέ

[margin notes:]
upper inland
σκληρύνω
to harden
ἀφωρίζω
to separate
ἀσθενέω
to be sick
χρὼς ὁ
the skin
σουδά-
ριον
napkin
ἐπιχειρέω to take in hand
ἐξορκιστής

τινες Σκευᾶ Ἰουδαίου ἀρχιερέως ἑπτὰ υἱοὶ τοῦτο ποιοῦντες. ¹⁵ ἀποκριθὲν δὲ τὸ πνεῦμα τὸ πονηρὸν εἶπεν
αὐτοῖς, Τὸν Ἰησοῦν γινώσκω καὶ τὸν Παῦλον ἐπίσταμαι·
ὑμεῖς δὲ τίνες ἐστέ; ¹⁶ καὶ ἐφαλόμενος ὁ ἄνθρωπος ἐπ'
αὐτούς, ἐν ᾧ ἦν τὸ πνεῦμα τὸ πονηρόν, κατακυριεύσας
ἀμφοτέρων ἴσχυσεν κατ' αὐτῶν, ὥστε γυμνοὺς καὶ τε-
τραυματισμένους ἐκφυγεῖν ἐκ τοῦ οἴκου ἐκείνου. ¹⁷ τοῦτο
δὲ ἐγένετο γνωστὸν πᾶσιν Ἰουδαίοις τε καὶ Ἕλλησιν
τοῖς κατοικοῦσιν τὴν Ἔφεσον, καὶ ἐπέπεσεν φόβος ἐπὶ
πάντας αὐτούς, καὶ ἐμεγαλύνετο τὸ ὄνομα τοῦ κυρίου
Ἰησοῦ, ¹⁸ πολλοί τε τῶν πεπιστευκότων ἤρχοντο ἐξομολογούμενοι καὶ ἀναγγέλλοντες τὰς πράξεις αὐτῶν.
¹⁹ ἱκανοὶ δὲ τῶν τὰ περίεργα πραξάντων συνενέγκαντες
τὰς βίβλους κατέκαιον ἐνώπιον πάντων· καὶ συνεψή-
φισαν τὰς τιμὰς αὐτῶν καὶ εὗρον ἀργυρίου μυριάδας
πέντε. ²⁰ οὕτως κατὰ κράτος τοῦ κυρίου ὁ λόγος
ηὔξανεν καὶ ἴσχυεν.

²¹ Ὡς δὲ ἐπληρώθη ταῦτα, ἔθετο ὁ Παῦλος ἐν τῷ
πνεύματι διελθὼν τὴν Μακεδονίαν καὶ Ἀχαΐαν πορεύεσθαι εἰς Ἱεροσόλυμα, εἰπὼν ὅτι Μετὰ τὸ γενέσθαι με
ἐκεῖ δεῖ με καὶ Ῥώμην ἰδεῖν. ²² ἀποστείλας δὲ εἰς τὴν
Μακεδονίαν δύο τῶν διακονούντων αὐτῷ, Τιμόθεον καὶ
Ἔραστον, αὐτὸς ἐπέσχεν χρόνον εἰς τὴν Ἀσίαν.

²³ Ἐγένετο δὲ κατὰ τὸν καιρὸν ἐκεῖνον τάραχος οὐκ
ὀλίγος περὶ τῆς ὁδοῦ. ²⁴ Δημήτριος γάρ τις ὀνόματι,
ἀργυροκόπος, ποιῶν ναοὺς ἀργυροῦς Ἀρτέμιδος παρεί-
χετο τοῖς τεχνίταις οὐκ ὀλίγην ἐργασίαν, ²⁵ οὓς συναθροίσας καὶ τοὺς περὶ τὰ τοιαῦτα ἐργάτας εἶπεν, Ἄνδρες,
ἐπίστασθε ὅτι ἐκ ταύτης τῆς ἐργασίας ἡ εὐπορία ἡμῖν
ἐστιν, ²⁶ καὶ θεωρεῖτε καὶ ἀκούετε ὅτι οὐ μόνον Ἐφέσου
ἀλλὰ σχεδὸν πάσης τῆς Ἀσίας ὁ Παῦλος οὗτος πείσας

μετέστησεν ἱκανὸν ὄχλον, λέγων ὅτι οὐκ εἰσὶν θεοὶ οἱ
διὰ χειρῶν γινόμενοι. [27] οὐ μόνον δὲ τοῦτο κινδυνεύει
ἡμῖν τὸ μέρος εἰς ἀπελεγμὸν ἐλθεῖν, ἀλλὰ καὶ τὸ τῆς
μεγάλης θεᾶς ἱερὸν Ἀρτέμιδος εἰς οὐθὲν λογισθῆναι,
μέλλειν τε καὶ καθαιρεῖσθαι τῆς μεγαλειότητος αὐτῆς,
ἣν ὅλη ἡ Ἀσία καὶ ἡ οἰκουμένη σέβεται. [28] ἀκούσαντες
δὲ καὶ γενόμενοι πλήρεις θυμοῦ ἔκραζον λέγοντες,
Μεγάλη ἡ Ἄρτεμις Ἐφεσίων. [29] καὶ ἐπλήσθη ἡ πόλις
τῆς συγχύσεως, ὥρμησάν τε ὁμοθυμαδὸν εἰς τὸ θέατρον,
συναρπάσαντες Γάιον καὶ Ἀρίσταρχον Μακεδόνας,
συνεκδήμους Παύλου. [30] Παύλου δὲ βουλομένου εἰσελθεῖν εἰς τὸν δῆμον, οὐκ εἴων αὐτὸν οἱ μαθηταί· [31] τινὲς
δὲ καὶ τῶν Ἀσιαρχῶν, ὄντες αὐτῷ φίλοι, πέμψαντες
πρὸς αὐτὸν παρεκάλουν μὴ δοῦναι ἑαυτὸν εἰς τὸ θέατρον.
[32] ἄλλοι μὲν οὖν ἄλλο τι ἔκραζον· ἦν γὰρ ἡ ἐκκλησία
συγκεχυμένη, καὶ οἱ πλείους οὐκ ᾔδεισαν τίνος ἔνεκα
συνεληλύθεισαν. [33] ἐκ δὲ τοῦ ὄχλου συνεβίβασαν Ἀλέ-
ξανδρον, προβαλόντων αὐτὸν τῶν Ἰουδαίων· ὁ δὲ Ἀλέξανδρος κατασείσας τὴν χεῖρα ἤθελεν ἀπολογεῖσθαι τῷ
δήμῳ. [34] ἐπιγνόντες δὲ ὅτι Ἰουδαῖός ἐστιν, φωνὴ ἐγένετο μία ἐκ πάντων, ὡς ἐπὶ ὥρας δύο κραζόντων,
Μεγάλη ἡ Ἄρτεμις Ἐφεσίων. [35] καταστείλας δὲ ὁ
γραμματεὺς τὸν ὄχλον φησίν, Ἄνδρες Ἐφέσιοι, τίς
γάρ ἐστιν ἀνθρώπων ὃς οὐ γινώσκει τὴν Ἐφεσίων
πόλιν νεωκόρον οὖσαν τῆς μεγάλης Ἀρτέμιδος καὶ τοῦ
Διοπετοῦς; [36] ἀναντιρρήτων οὖν ὄντων τούτων δέον
ἐστὶν ὑμᾶς κατεσταλμένους ὑπάρχειν καὶ μηδὲν προπετὲς πράσσειν. [37] ἠγάγετε γὰρ τοὺς ἄνδρας τούτους
οὔτε ἱεροσύλους οὔτε βλασφημοῦντας τὴν θεὸν ἡμῶν.
[38] εἰ μὲν οὖν Δημήτριος καὶ οἱ σὺν αὐτῷ τεχνῖται
ἔχουσιν πρός τινα λόγον, ἀγοραῖοι ἄγονται καὶ ἀνθύ-

πατοί εἰσιν, ἐγκαλείτωσαν ἀλλήλοις. ³⁹ εἰ δέ τι περὶ
ἑτέρων ἐπιζητεῖτε, ἐν τῇ ἐννόμῳ ἐκκλησίᾳ ἐπιλυθήσεται.
⁴⁰ καὶ γὰρ κινδυνεύομεν ἐγκαλεῖσθαι στάσεως περὶ τῆς
σήμερον, μηδενὸς αἰτίου ὑπάρχοντος περὶ οὗ οὐ δυνησόμεθα ἀποδοῦναι λόγον περὶ τῆς συστροφῆς ταύτης.
⁴¹ καὶ ταῦτα εἰπὼν ἀπέλυσεν τὴν ἐκκλησίαν.

20 ¹ Μετὰ δὲ τὸ παύσασθαι τὸν θόρυβον μεταπεμψάμενος ὁ Παῦλος τοὺς μαθητὰς καὶ παρακαλέσας,
ἀσπασάμενος ἐξῆλθεν πορεύεσθαι εἰς Μακεδονίαν. ² διελθὼν δὲ τὰ μέρη ἐκεῖνα καὶ παρακαλέσας αὐτοὺς λόγῳ
πολλῷ ἦλθεν εἰς τὴν Ἑλλάδα, ³ ποιήσας τε μῆνας τρεῖς,
γενομένης ἐπιβουλῆς αὐτῷ ὑπὸ τῶν Ἰουδαίων μέλλοντι
ἀνάγεσθαι εἰς τὴν Συρίαν, ἐγένετο γνώμης τοῦ ὑποστρέφειν διὰ Μακεδονίας. ⁴ συνείπετο δὲ αὐτῷ ἄχρι
τῆς Ἀσίας Σώπατρος Πύρρου Βεροιαῖος, Θεσσαλονικέων δὲ Ἀρίσταρχος καὶ Σεκοῦνδος καὶ Γάιος Δερβαῖος καὶ Τιμόθεος, Ἀσιανοὶ δὲ Τυχικὸς καὶ Τρόφιμος·
⁵ οὗτοι δὲ προελθόντες ἔμενον ἡμᾶς ἐν Τρωάδι· ⁶ ἡμεῖς
δὲ ἐξεπλεύσαμεν μετὰ τὰς ἡμέρας τῶν ἀζύμων ἀπὸ
Φιλίππων, καὶ ἤλθομεν πρὸς αὐτοὺς εἰς τὴν Τρωάδα
ἄχρι ἡμερῶν πέντε, οὗ διετρίψαμεν ἡμέρας ἑπτά.

⁷ Ἐν δὲ τῇ μιᾷ τῶν σαββάτων συνηγμένων ἡμῶν
κλάσαι ἄρτον ὁ Παῦλος διελέγετο αὐτοῖς, μέλλων ἐξιέναι τῇ ἐπαύριον, παρέτεινέν τε τὸν λόγον μέχρι μεσο-
νυκτίου· ⁸ ἦσαν δὲ λαμπάδες ἱκαναὶ ἐν τῷ ὑπερῴῳ οὗ
ἦμεν συνηγμένοι. ⁹ καθεζόμενος δέ τις νεανίας ὀνόματι
Εὔτυχος ἐπὶ τῆς θυρίδος, καταφερόμενος ὕπνῳ βαθεῖ,
διαλεγομένου τοῦ Παύλου ἐπὶ πλεῖον, κατενεχθεὶς ἀπὸ
τοῦ ὕπνου ἔπεσεν ἀπὸ τοῦ τριστέγου κάτω καὶ ἤρθη
νεκρός. ¹⁰ καταβὰς δὲ ὁ Παῦλος ἐπέπεσεν αὐτῷ καὶ
συμπεριλαβὼν εἶπεν, Μὴ θορυβεῖσθε· ἡ γὰρ ψυχὴ

αἴρω   ἀρῶ   ἦρκα   ἦρα   ἤρθην   in. aor. ἀ

αὐτοῦ ἐν αὐτῷ ἐστίν. ¹¹ ἀναβὰς δὲ καὶ κλάσας τὸν
ἄρτον καὶ γευσάμενος, ἐφ᾽ ἱκανόν τε ὁμιλήσας ἄχρι
αὐγῆς, οὕτως ἐξῆλθεν. ¹² ἤγαγον δὲ τὸν παῖδα ζῶντα,
καὶ παρεκλήθησαν οὐ μετρίως.

¹³ Ἡμεῖς δὲ προελθόντες ἐπὶ τὸ πλοῖον ἀνήχθημεν
ἐπὶ τὴν Ἄσσον, ἐκεῖθεν μέλλοντες ἀναλαμβάνειν τὸν
Παῦλον· οὕτως γὰρ διατεταγμένος ἦν, μέλλων αὐτὸς
πεζεύειν. ¹⁴ ὡς δὲ συνέβαλλεν ἡμῖν εἰς τὴν Ἄσσον,
ἀναλαβόντες αὐτὸν ἤλθομεν εἰς Μιτυλήνην. ¹⁵ κἀκεῖθεν
ἀποπλεύσαντες τῇ ἐπιούσῃ κατηντήσαμεν ἄντικρυς
Χίου, τῇ δὲ ἑτέρᾳ παρεβάλομεν εἰς Σάμον, τῇ δὲ ἐχομένῃ ἤλθομεν εἰς Μίλητον. ¹⁶ κεκρίκει γὰρ ὁ Παῦλος
παραπλεῦσαι τὴν Ἔφεσον, ὅπως μὴ γένηται αὐτῷ χρονοτριβῆσαι ἐν τῇ Ἀσίᾳ· ἔσπευδεν γάρ, εἰ δυνατὸν
εἴη αὐτῷ, τὴν ἡμέραν τῆς Πεντηκοστῆς γενέσθαι εἰς
Ἱεροσόλυμα.

¹⁷ Ἀπὸ δὲ τῆς Μιλήτου πέμψας εἰς Ἔφεσον μετεκαλέσατο τοὺς πρεσβυτέρους τῆς ἐκκλησίας. ¹⁸ ὡς δὲ
παρεγένοντο πρὸς αὐτόν, εἶπεν αὐτοῖς, Ὑμεῖς ἐπίστασθε, ἀπὸ πρώτης ἡμέρας ἀφ᾽ ἧς ἐπέβην εἰς τὴν
Ἀσίαν, πῶς μεθ᾽ ὑμῶν τὸν πάντα χρόνον ἐγενόμην,
¹⁹ δουλεύων τῷ κυρίῳ μετὰ πάσης ταπεινοφροσύνης καὶ
δακρύων καὶ πειρασμῶν τῶν συμβάντων μοι ἐν ταῖς
ἐπιβουλαῖς τῶν Ἰουδαίων, ²⁰ ὡς οὐδὲν ὑπεστειλάμην
τῶν συμφερόντων τοῦ μὴ ἀναγγεῖλαι ὑμῖν καὶ διδάξαι
ὑμᾶς δημοσίᾳ καὶ κατ᾽ οἴκους, ²¹ διαμαρτυρόμενος Ἰουδαίοις τε καὶ Ἕλλησιν τὴν εἰς θεὸν μετάνοιαν καὶ
πίστιν εἰς τὸν κύριον ἡμῶν Ἰησοῦν Χριστόν. ²² καὶ
νῦν ἰδοὺ δεδεμένος ἐγὼ τῷ πνεύματι πορεύομαι εἰς
Ἱερουσαλήμ, τὰ ἐν αὐτῇ συναντήσοντά μοι μὴ εἰδώς,
²³ πλὴν ὅτι τὸ πνεῦμα τὸ ἅγιον κατὰ πόλιν διαμαρτύ-

ρεταί μοι λέγον ὅτι δεσμὰ καὶ θλίψεις με *μένουσιν.
²⁴ ἀλλ' οὐδενὸς λόγου ποιοῦμαι τὴν ψυχὴν τιμίαν ἐμαυτῷ ὡς τελειῶσαι τὸν δρόμον μου καὶ τὴν διακονίαν ἣν
ἔλαβον παρὰ τοῦ κυρίου Ἰησοῦ, διαμαρτύρασθαι τὸ
εὐαγγέλιον τῆς χάριτος τοῦ θεοῦ. ²⁵ καὶ νῦν ἰδοὺ ἐγὼ
οἶδα ὅτι οὐκέτι ὄψεσθε τὸ πρόσωπόν μου ὑμεῖς πάντες
ἐν οἷς διῆλθον κηρύσσων τὴν βασιλείαν. ²⁶ διὸ μαρτύρομαι ὑμῖν ἐν τῇ σήμερον ἡμέρᾳ ὅτι καθαρός εἰμι ἀπὸ
τοῦ αἵματος πάντων· ²⁷ οὐ γὰρ ὑπεστειλάμην τοῦ μὴ
ἀναγγεῖλαι πᾶσαν τὴν βουλὴν τοῦ θεοῦ ὑμῖν. ²⁸ προσέχετε ἑαυτοῖς καὶ παντὶ τῷ ποιμνίῳ, ἐν ᾧ ὑμᾶς τὸ
πνεῦμα τὸ ἅγιον ἔθετο ἐπισκόπους, ποιμαίνειν τὴν
ἐκκλησίαν τοῦ κυρίου, ἣν περιεποιήσατο διὰ τοῦ
αἵματος τοῦ ἰδίου. ²⁹ ἐγὼ οἶδα ὅτι εἰσελεύσονται
μετὰ τὴν ἄφιξίν μου λύκοι βαρεῖς εἰς ὑμᾶς, μὴ φειδό-
μενοι τοῦ ποιμνίου, ³⁰ καὶ ἐξ ὑμῶν αὐτῶν ἀναστήσονται
ἄνδρες λαλοῦντες διεστραμμένα τοῦ ἀποσπᾶν τοὺς μαθητὰς ὀπίσω ἑαυτῶν. ³¹ διὸ γρηγορεῖτε, μνημονεύοντες
ὅτι τριετίαν νύκτα καὶ ἡμέραν οὐκ ἐπαυσάμην μετὰ
δακρύων νουθετῶν ἕνα ἕκαστον. ³² καὶ τὰ νῦν παρατίθεμαι ὑμᾶς τῷ θεῷ καὶ τῷ λόγῳ τῆς χάριτος αὐτοῦ,
τῷ δυναμένῳ οἰκοδομῆσαι καὶ δοῦναι τὴν κληρονομίαν ἐν τοῖς ἡγιασμένοις πᾶσιν. ³³ ἀργυρίου ἢ χρυ-
σίου ἢ ἱματισμοῦ οὐδενὸς ἐπεθύμησα· ³⁴ αὐτοὶ γινώσκετε ὅτι ταῖς χρείαις μου καὶ τοῖς οὖσιν μετ' ἐμοῦ
ὑπηρέτησαν αἱ χεῖρες αὗται. ³⁵ πάντα ὑπέδειξα ὑμῖν,
ὅτι οὕτως κοπιῶντας δεῖ ἀντιλαμβάνεσθαι τῶν ἀσθενούντων, μνημονεύειν τε τῶν λόγων τοῦ κυρίου Ἰησοῦ,
ὅτι αὐτὸς εἶπεν, Μακάριόν ἐστιν μᾶλλον διδόναι
ἢ λαμβάνειν. ³⁶ καὶ ταῦτα εἰπών, θεὶς τὰ γόνατα
αὐτοῦ σὺν πᾶσιν αὐτοῖς προσηύξατο. ³⁷ ἱκανὸς δὲ

στρεφω στρεψω ἐστραμμαι ἐστραφην

κλαυθμὸς ἐγένετο πάντων, καὶ ἐπιπεσόντες ἐπὶ τὸν τράχηλον τοῦ Παύλου κατεφίλουν αὐτόν, ³⁸ ὀδυνώμενοι
μάλιστα ἐπὶ τῷ λόγῳ ᾧ εἰρήκει, ὅτι οὐκέτι μέλλουσιν τὸ
πρόσωπον αὐτοῦ θεωρεῖν. προέπεμπον δὲ αὐτὸν εἰς τὸ
πλοῖον.

21 ¹ Ὡς δὲ ἐγένετο ἀναχθῆναι ἡμᾶς ἀποσπασθέντας
ἀπ' αὐτῶν, εὐθυδρομήσαντες ἤλθομεν εἰς τὴν Κῶ, τῇ
δὲ ἑξῆς εἰς τὴν Ῥόδον, κἀκεῖθεν εἰς Πάταρα. ² καὶ
εὑρόντες πλοῖον διαπερῶν εἰς Φοινίκην, ἐπιβάντες ἀνήχθημεν. ³ ἀναφάναντες δὲ τὴν Κύπρον καὶ καταλιπόν-
τες αὐτὴν εὐώνυμον ἐπλέομεν εἰς Συρίαν, καὶ κατήλθομεν εἰς Τύρον· ἐκεῖσε γὰρ τὸ πλοῖον ἦν ἀποφορτιζόμενον
τὸν γόμον. ⁴ ἀνευρόντες δὲ τοὺς μαθητὰς ἐπεμείναμεν
αὐτοῦ ἡμέρας ἑπτά, οἵτινες τῷ Παύλῳ ἔλεγον διὰ τοῦ
πνεύματος μὴ ἐπιβαίνειν εἰς Ἱεροσόλυμα. ⁵ ὅτε δὲ ἐγένετο ἡμᾶς ἐξαρτίσαι τὰς ἡμέρας, ἐξελθόντες ἐπορεύο-
μεθα προπεμπόντων ἡμᾶς πάντων σὺν γυναιξὶ καὶ
τέκνοις ἕως ἔξω τῆς πόλεως, καὶ θέντες τὰ γόνατα ἐπὶ
τὸν αἰγιαλὸν προσευξάμενοι ⁶ ἀπησπασάμεθα ἀλλήλους καὶ ἐνέβημεν εἰς τὸ πλοῖον, ἐκεῖνοι δὲ ὑπέστρεψαν
εἰς τὰ ἴδια.

⁷ Ἡμεῖς δὲ τὸν πλοῦν διανύσαντες ἀπὸ Τύρου κατηντήσαμεν εἰς Πτολεμαΐδα, καὶ ἀσπασάμενοι τοὺς ἀδελφοὺς ἐμείναμεν ἡμέραν μίαν παρ' αὐτοῖς. ⁸ τῇ δὲ ἐπαύριον ἐξελθόντες ἤλθομεν εἰς Καισάρειαν, καὶ εἰσελθόντες
εἰς τὸν οἶκον Φιλίππου τοῦ εὐαγγελιστοῦ ὄντος ἐκ τῶν
ἑπτά, ἐμείναμεν παρ' αὐτῷ. ⁹ τούτῳ δὲ ἦσαν θυγατέρες
τέσσαρες παρθένοι προφητεύουσαι. ¹⁰ ἐπιμενόντων δὲ
ἡμέρας πλείους κατῆλθέν τις ἀπὸ τῆς Ἰουδαίας προφήτης ὀνόματι Ἄγαβος, ¹¹ καὶ ἐλθὼν πρὸς ἡμᾶς καὶ ἄρας
τὴν ζώνην τοῦ Παύλου, δήσας ἑαυτοῦ τοὺς πόδας καὶ

θνήσκω θανοῦμαι τέθνηκα ἔθανον

τὰς χεῖρας εἶπεν, Τάδε λέγει τὸ πνεῦμα τὸ ἅγιον,
Τὸν ἄνδρα οὗ ἐστιν ἡ ζώνη αὕτη οὕτως δήσουσιν ἐν
Ἰερουσαλὴμ οἱ Ἰουδαῖοι καὶ παραδώσουσιν εἰς χεί-
ρας ἐθνῶν. 12 ὡς δὲ ἠκούσαμεν ταῦτα, παρεκαλοῦμεν
ἡμεῖς τε καὶ οἱ ἐντόπιοι τοῦ μὴ ἀναβαίνειν αὐτὸν εἰς
Ἰερουσαλήμ. 13 τότε ἀπεκρίθη ὁ Παῦλος, Τί ποιεῖτε
κλαίοντες καὶ συνθρύπτοντές μου τὴν καρδίαν; ἐγὼ
γὰρ οὐ μόνον δεθῆναι ἀλλὰ καὶ ἀποθανεῖν εἰς Ἰερουσαλὴμ ἑτοίμως ἔχω ὑπὲρ τοῦ ὀνόματος τοῦ κυρίου
Ἰησοῦ. 14 μὴ πειθομένου δὲ αὐτοῦ ἡσυχάσαμεν εἰπόντες, Τοῦ κυρίου τὸ θέλημα γινέσθω.

15 Μετὰ δὲ τὰς ἡμέρας ταύτας ἐπισκευασάμενοι ἀνε-
βαίνομεν εἰς Ἰεροσόλυμα· 16 συνῆλθον δὲ καὶ τῶν μαθητῶν ἀπὸ Καισαρείας σὺν ἡμῖν, ἄγοντες παρ' ᾧ ξενισθῶμεν Μνάσωνί τινι Κυπρίῳ, ἀρχαίῳ μαθητῇ.

17 Γενομένων δὲ ἡμῶν εἰς Ἰεροσόλυμα, ἀσμένως ἀπεδέξαντο ἡμᾶς οἱ ἀδελφοί. 18 τῇ δὲ ἐπιούσῃ εἰσῄει ὁ
Παῦλος σὺν ἡμῖν πρὸς Ἰάκωβον, πάντες τε παρεγένοντο
οἱ πρεσβύτεροι. 19 καὶ ἀσπασάμενος αὐτοὺς ἐξηγεῖτο
καθ' ἓν ἕκαστον ὧν ἐποίησεν ὁ θεὸς ἐν τοῖς ἔθνεσιν διὰ
τῆς διακονίας αὐτοῦ. 20 οἱ δὲ ἀκούσαντες ἐδόξαζον τὸν
θεόν, εἶπάν τε αὐτῷ, Θεωρεῖς, ἀδελφέ, πόσαι μυριάδες
εἰσὶν ἐν τοῖς Ἰουδαίοις τῶν πεπιστευκότων, καὶ πάντες
ζηλωταὶ τοῦ νόμου ὑπάρχουσιν· 21 κατηχήθησαν δὲ
περὶ σοῦ ὅτι ἀποστασίαν διδάσκεις ἀπὸ Μωϋσέως τοὺς
κατὰ τὰ ἔθνη πάντας Ἰουδαίους, λέγων μὴ περιτέμνειν
αὐτοὺς τὰ τέκνα μηδὲ τοῖς ἔθεσιν περιπατεῖν. 22 τί οὖν
ἐστιν; πάντως δεῖ συνελθεῖν πλῆθος· ἀκούσονται γὰρ
ὅτι ἐλήλυθας. 23 τοῦτο οὖν ποίησον ὅ σοι λέγομεν. εἰσὶν ἡμῖν ἄνδρες τέσσαρες εὐχὴν ἔχοντες ἐφ' ἑαυτῶν·
24 τούτους παραλαβὼν ἁγνίσθητι σὺν αὐτοῖς, καὶ δαπά-

ἁγνίζω

νησον ἐπ' αὐτοῖς ἵνα ξυρήσονται τὴν κεφαλήν, καὶ γνώσονται πάντες ὅτι ὧν κατήχηνται περὶ σοῦ οὐδέν ἐστιν, ἀλλὰ στοιχεῖς καὶ αὐτὸς φυλάσσων τὸν νόμον. ²⁵ περὶ δὲ τῶν πεπιστευκότων ἐθνῶν ἡμεῖς ἐπεστείλαμεν κρίναντες φυλάσσεσθαι αὐτοὺς τό τε εἰδωλόθυτον καὶ αἷμα καὶ πνικτὸν καὶ πορνείαν. ²⁶ τότε ὁ Παῦλος παραλαβὼν τοὺς ἄνδρας τῇ ἐχομένῃ ἡμέρᾳ σὺν αὐτοῖς ἁγνισθεὶς εἰσῄει εἰς τὸ ἱερόν, διαγγέλλων τὴν ἐκπλήρωσιν τῶν ἡμερῶν τοῦ ἁγνισμοῦ, ἕως οὗ προσηνέχθη ὑπὲρ ἑνὸς ἑκάστου αὐτῶν ἡ προσφορά. ²⁷ ὡς δὲ ἔμελλον αἱ ἑπτὰ ἡμέραι συντελεῖσθαι, οἱ ἀπὸ τῆς Ἀσίας Ἰουδαῖοι θεασάμενοι αὐτὸν ἐν τῷ ἱερῷ συνέχεον πάντα τὸν ὄχλον, καὶ ἐπέβαλαν ἐπ' αὐτὸν τὰς χεῖρας, ²⁸ κράζοντες, Ἄνδρες Ἰσραηλῖται, βοηθεῖτε· οὗτός ἐστιν ὁ ἄνθρωπος ὁ κατὰ τοῦ λαοῦ καὶ τοῦ νόμου καὶ τοῦ τόπου τούτου πάντας πανταχῇ διδάσκων, ἔτι τε καὶ Ἕλληνας εἰσήγαγεν εἰς τὸ ἱερὸν καὶ κεκοίνωκεν τὸν ἅγιον τόπον τοῦτον. ²⁹ ἦσαν γὰρ προεωρακότες Τρόφιμον τὸν Ἐφέσιον ἐν τῇ πόλει σὺν αὐτῷ, ὃν ἐνόμιζον ὅτι εἰς τὸ ἱερὸν εἰσήγαγεν ὁ Παῦλος. ³⁰ ἐκινήθη τε ἡ πόλις ὅλη καὶ ἐγένετο συνδρομὴ τοῦ λαοῦ, καὶ ἐπιλαβόμενοι τοῦ Παύλου εἷλκον αὐτὸν ἔξω τοῦ ἱεροῦ, καὶ εὐθέως ἐκλείσθησαν αἱ θύραι. ³¹ ζητούντων τε αὐτὸν ἀποκτεῖναι ἀνέβη φάσις τῷ χιλιάρχῳ τῆς σπείρης ὅτι ὅλη συγχύννεται Ἰερουσαλήμ, ³² ὃς ἐξαυτῆς παραλαβὼν στρατιώτας καὶ ἑκατοντάρχας κατέδραμεν ἐπ' αὐτούς· οἱ δὲ ἰδόντες τὸν χιλίαρχον καὶ τοὺς στρατιώτας ἐπαύσαντο τύπτοντες τὸν Παῦλον. ³³ τότε ἐγγίσας ὁ χιλίαρχος ἐπελάβετο αὐτοῦ καὶ ἐκέλευσεν δεθῆναι ἁλύσεσι δυσί, καὶ ἐπυνθάνετο τίς εἴη καὶ τί ἐστι πεποιηκώς. ³⁴ ἄλλοι δὲ ἄλλο τι ἐπεφώνουν ἐν τῷ ὄχλῳ· μὴ δυναμένου δὲ αὐτοῦ γνῶναι τὸ ἀσφαλὲς διὰ

τὸν θόρυβον, ἐκέλευσεν ἄγεσθαι αὐτὸν εἰς τὴν παρεμβολήν. ³⁵ ὅτε δὲ ἐγένετο ἐπὶ τοὺς ἀναβαθμούς, συνέβη
βαστάζεσθαι αὐτὸν ὑπὸ τῶν στρατιωτῶν διὰ τὴν βίαν
τοῦ ὄχλου· ³⁶ ἠκολούθει γὰρ τὸ πλῆθος τοῦ λαοῦ κράζοντες, Αἶρε αὐτόν.

³⁷ Μέλλων τε εἰσάγεσθαι εἰς τὴν παρεμβολὴν ὁ Παῦλος λέγει τῷ χιλιάρχῳ, Εἰ ἔξεστίν μοι εἰπεῖν τι πρός
σε; ὁ δὲ ἔφη, Ἑλληνιστὶ γινώσκεις; ³⁸ οὐκ ἄρα σὺ
εἶ ὁ Αἰγύπτιος ὁ πρὸ τούτων τῶν ἡμερῶν ἀναστατώσας καὶ ἐξαγαγὼν εἰς τὴν ἔρημον τοὺς τετρακισχι-
λίους ἄνδρας τῶν σικαρίων; ³⁹ εἶπεν δὲ ὁ Παῦλος,
Ἐγὼ ἄνθρωπος μέν εἰμι Ἰουδαῖος, Ταρσεύς, τῆς Κιλικίας οὐκ ἀσήμου πόλεως πολίτης· δέομαι δέ σου, ἐπίτρεψόν μοι λαλῆσαι πρὸς τὸν λαόν. ⁴⁰ ἐπιτρέψαντος δὲ
αὐτοῦ ὁ Παῦλος ἑστὼς ἐπὶ τῶν ἀναβαθμῶν κατέσεισεν
τῇ χειρὶ τῷ λαῷ· πολλῆς δὲ σιγῆς γενομένης προσε-
φώνησεν τῇ Ἑβραΐδι διαλέκτῳ λέγων·

22 ¹ Ἄνδρες ἀδελφοὶ καὶ πατέρες, ἀκούσατέ μου
τῆς πρὸς ὑμᾶς νυνὶ ἀπολογίας. ² ἀκούσαντες δὲ ὅτι
τῇ Ἑβραΐδι διαλέκτῳ προσεφώνει αὐτοῖς, μᾶλλον
παρέσχον ἡσυχίαν. καί φησιν, ³ Ἐγώ εἰμι ἀνὴρ
Ἰουδαῖος, γεγεννημένος ἐν Ταρσῷ τῆς Κιλικίας, ἀνατεθραμμένος δὲ ἐν τῇ πόλει ταύτῃ, παρὰ τοὺς πόδας
Γαμαλιὴλ πεπαιδευμένος κατὰ ἀκρίβειαν τοῦ πατρῴου
νόμου, ζηλωτὴς ὑπάρχων τοῦ θεοῦ καθὼς πάντες ὑμεῖς
ἐστε σήμερον, ⁴ ὃς ταύτην τὴν ὁδὸν ἐδίωξα ἄχρι θανάτου, δεσμεύων καὶ παραδιδοὺς εἰς φυλακὰς ἄνδρας τε
καὶ γυναῖκας, ⁵ ὡς καὶ ὁ ἀρχιερεὺς μαρτυρεῖ μοι καὶ πᾶν
τὸ πρεσβυτέριον, παρ᾽ ὧν καὶ ἐπιστολὰς δεξάμενος
πρὸς τοὺς ἀδελφοὺς εἰς Δαμασκὸν ἐπορευόμην, ἄξων
καὶ τοὺς ἐκεῖσε ὄντας δεδεμένους εἰς Ἱερουσαλὴμ ἵνα

τιμωρηθῶσιν. [6] ἐγένετο δὲ μοι πορευομένῳ καὶ ἐγγί-
ζοντι τῇ Δαμασκῷ περὶ μεσημβρίαν ἐξαίφνης ἐκ τοῦ
οὐρανοῦ <u>περιαστράψαι</u> φῶς ἱκανὸν περὶ ἐμέ, [7] ἔπεσά τε
εἰς τὸ ἔδαφος καὶ ἤκουσα φωνῆς λεγούσης μοι, Σαοὺλ
Σαούλ, τί με διώκεις; [8] ἐγὼ δὲ ἀπεκρίθην, Τίς εἶ,
κύριε; εἶπέν τε πρὸς ἐμέ, Ἐγώ εἰμι Ἰησοῦς ὁ Ναζωραῖος, ὃν σὺ διώκεις. [9] οἱ δὲ σὺν ἐμοὶ ὄντες τὸ μὲν
φῶς ἐθεάσαντο, τὴν δὲ φωνὴν οὐκ ἤκουσαν τοῦ λαλοῦν-
τός μοι. [10] εἶπον δέ, Τί ποιήσω, κύριε; ὁ δὲ κύριος
εἶπεν πρός με, Ἀναστὰς πορεύου εἰς Δαμασκόν, κἀκεῖ
σοι λαληθήσεται περὶ πάντων ὧν τέτακταί σοι ποιῆσαι. [11] ὡς δὲ οὐκ <u>ἐνέβλεπον</u> ἀπὸ τῆς δόξης τοῦ φωτὸς
ἐκείνου, χειραγωγούμενος ὑπὸ τῶν συνόντων μοι ἦλθον
εἰς Δαμασκόν. [12] Ἀνανίας δέ τις, ἀνὴρ εὐλαβὴς κατὰ
τὸν νόμον, μαρτυρούμενος ὑπὸ πάντων τῶν κατοικούν-
των Ἰουδαίων, [13] ἐλθὼν πρὸς ἐμὲ καὶ ἐπιστὰς εἶπέν μοι,
Σαοὺλ ἀδελφέ, ἀνάβλεψον. κἀγὼ αὐτῇ τῇ ὥρᾳ ἀνέβλεψα εἰς αὐτόν. [14] ὁ δὲ εἶπεν, Ὁ θεὸς τῶν πατέρων
ἡμῶν προεχειρίσατό σε γνῶναι τὸ θέλημα αὐτοῦ καὶ
ἰδεῖν <u>τὸν δίκαιον</u> καὶ ἀκοῦσαι φωνὴν ἐκ τοῦ στόματος
αὐτοῦ, [15] ὅτι ἔσῃ μάρτυς αὐτῷ πρὸς πάντας ἀνθρώπους
ὧν ἑώρακας καὶ ἤκουσας. [16] καὶ νῦν τί μέλλεις; ἀναστὰς βάπτισαι καὶ ἀπόλουσαι τὰς ἁμαρτίας σου, ἐπικαλεσάμενος τὸ ὄνομα αὐτοῦ. [17] ἐγένετο δέ μοι ὑποστρέψαντι εἰς Ἰερουσαλὴμ καὶ προσευχομένου μου ἐν
τῷ ἱερῷ γενέσθαι με ἐν ἐκστάσει, [18] καὶ ἰδεῖν αὐτὸν
λέγοντά μοι, Σπεῦσον καὶ ἔξελθε ἐν τάχει ἐξ Ἱερουσαλήμ, διότι οὐ παραδέξονταί σου μαρτυρίαν περὶ ἐμοῦ.
[19] κἀγὼ εἶπον, Κύριε, αὐτοὶ ἐπίστανται ὅτι ἐγὼ ἤμην
φυλακίζων καὶ δέρων κατὰ τὰς συναγωγὰς τοὺς πιστεύοντας ἐπὶ σέ· [20] καὶ ὅτε <u>ἐξεχύννετο</u> τὸ αἷμα Στεφάνου

δέρω   1 aor.   ἔδειρα

τιμωρέω   to punish
περιαστρά   to shine
τω   round about
ἐμβλέπω   to see clearly
προχειρί-
ομαι   to appoint
ἐκχέω   to pour out
spill

τοῦ μάρτυρός σου, καὶ αὐτὸς ἤμην ἐφεστὼς καὶ συνευ
δοκῶν καὶ φυλάσσων τὰ ἱμάτια τῶν ἀναιρούντων αὐ
τόν. ²¹ καὶ εἶπεν πρός με, Πορεύου, ὅτι ἐγὼ εἰς ἔθνη
μακρὰν ἐξαποστελῶ σε.

²² Ἤκουον δὲ αὐτοῦ ἄχρι τούτου τοῦ λόγου, καὶ ἐπῆ
ραν τὴν φωνὴν αὐτῶν λέγοντες, Αἶρε ἀπὸ τῆς γῆς τὸν
τοιοῦτον· οὐ γὰρ καθῆκεν αὐτὸν ζῆν. ²³ κραυγαζόντων
δὲ αὐτῶν καὶ ῥιπτούντων τὰ ἱμάτια καὶ κονιορτὸν
βαλλόντων εἰς τὸν ἀέρα, ²⁴ ἐκέλευσεν ὁ χιλίαρχος εἰσά
γεσθαι αὐτὸν εἰς τὴν παρεμβολήν, εἴπας μάστιξιν ἀνε
τάζεσθαι αὐτόν, ἵνα ἐπιγνῷ δι' ἣν αἰτίαν οὕτως ἐπεφώ
νουν αὐτῷ. ²⁵ ὡς δὲ προέτειναν αὐτὸν τοῖς ἱμᾶσιν,
εἶπεν πρὸς τὸν ἑστῶτα ἑκατόνταρχον ὁ Παῦλος, Εἰ
ἄνθρωπον Ῥωμαῖον καὶ ἀκατάκριτον ἔξεστιν ὑμῖν
μαστίζειν; ²⁶ ἀκούσας δὲ ὁ ἑκατόνταρχος προσελθὼν
τῷ χιλιάρχῳ ἀπήγγειλεν λέγων, Τί μέλλεις ποιεῖν; ὁ
γὰρ ἄνθρωπος οὗτος Ῥωμαῖός ἐστιν. ²⁷ προσελθὼν
δὲ ὁ χιλίαρχος εἶπεν αὐτῷ, Λέγε μοι, σὺ Ῥωμαῖος
εἶ; ὁ δὲ ἔφη, Ναί. ²⁸ ἀπεκρίθη δὲ ὁ χιλίαρχος, Ἐγὼ
πολλοῦ κεφαλαίου τὴν πολιτείαν ταύτην ἐκτησάμην.
ὁ δὲ Παῦλος ἔφη, Ἐγὼ δὲ καὶ γεγέννημαι. ²⁹ εὐθέως
οὖν ἀπέστησαν ἀπ' αὐτοῦ οἱ μέλλοντες αὐτὸν ἀνετάζειν·
καὶ ὁ χιλίαρχος δὲ ἐφοβήθη, ἐπιγνοὺς ὅτι Ῥωμαῖός
ἐστιν καὶ ὅτι αὐτὸν ἦν δεδεκώς.

³⁰ Τῇ δὲ ἐπαύριον βουλόμενος γνῶναι τὸ ἀσφαλές,
τὸ τί κατηγορεῖται ὑπὸ τῶν Ἰουδαίων, ἔλυσεν αὐτὸν καὶ
ἐκέλευσεν συνελθεῖν τοὺς ἀρχιερεῖς καὶ πᾶν τὸ συνέ
δριον, καὶ καταγαγὼν τὸν Παῦλον ἔστησεν εἰς αὐτούς.

23 ¹ Ἀτενίσας δὲ τῷ συνεδρίῳ ὁ Παῦλος εἶπεν,
Ἄνδρες ἀδελφοί, ἐγὼ πάσῃ συνειδήσει ἀγαθῇ πεπο
λίτευμαι τῷ θεῷ ἄχρι ταύτης τῆς ἡμέρας. ² ὁ δὲ

ἀρχιερεὺς Ἀνανίας ἐπέταξεν τοῖς παρεστῶσιν αὐτῷ
τύπτειν αὐτοῦ τὸ στόμα. ³τότε ὁ Παῦλος πρὸς αὐτὸν εἶπεν, Τύπτειν σε μέλλει ὁ θεός, τοῖχε κεκονια-
μένε· καὶ σὺ κάθῃ κρίνων με κατὰ τὸν νόμον, καὶ παρανομῶν κελεύεις με τύπτεσθαι; ⁴οἱ δὲ παρεστῶτες
εἶπαν, Τὸν ἀρχιερέα τοῦ θεοῦ λοιδορεῖς; ⁵ἔφη τε ὁ
Παῦλος, Οὐκ ᾔδειν, ἀδελφοί, ὅτι ἐστὶν ἀρχιερεύς·
γέγραπται γὰρ ὅτι Ἄρχοντα τοῦ λαοῦ σου οὐκ ἐρεῖς
κακῶς. ⁶γνοὺς δὲ ὁ Παῦλος ὅτι τὸ ἓν μέρος ἐστὶ
Σαδδουκαίων τὸ δὲ ἕτερον Φαρισαίων, ἔκραζεν ἐν τῷ
συνεδρίῳ, Ἄνδρες ἀδελφοί, ἐγὼ Φαρισαῖός εἰμι, υἱὸς
Φαρισαίων· περὶ ἐλπίδος καὶ ἀναστάσεως νεκρῶν ἐγὼ
κρίνομαι. ⁷τοῦτο δὲ αὐτοῦ λαλήσαντος ἐγένετο στάσις τῶν Φαρισαίων καὶ Σαδδουκαίων, καὶ ἐσχίσθη τὸ
πλῆθος. ⁸Σαδδουκαῖοι μὲν γὰρ λέγουσιν μὴ εἶναι ἀνάστασιν μήτε ἄγγελον μήτε πνεῦμα, Φαρισαῖοι δὲ ὁμο-
λογοῦσιν τὰ ἀμφότερα. ⁹ἐγένετο δὲ κραυγὴ μεγάλη,
καὶ ἀναστάντες τινὲς τῶν γραμματέων τοῦ μέρους τῶν
Φαρισαίων διεμάχοντο λέγοντες, Οὐδὲν κακὸν εὑρί-
σκομεν ἐν τῷ ἀνθρώπῳ τούτῳ· εἰ δὲ πνεῦμα ἐλάλησεν
αὐτῷ ἢ ἄγγελος; ¹⁰πολλῆς δὲ γινομένης στάσεως
φοβηθεὶς ὁ χιλίαρχος μὴ διασπασθῇ ὁ Παῦλος ὑπ'
αὐτῶν, ἐκέλευσεν τὸ στράτευμα καταβὰν ἁρπάσαι αὐτὸν ἐκ μέσου αὐτῶν ἄγειν τε εἰς τὴν παρεμβολήν.

¹¹Τῇ δὲ ἐπιούσῃ νυκτὶ ἐπιστὰς αὐτῷ ὁ κύριος εἶπεν,
Θάρσει· ὡς γὰρ διεμαρτύρω τὰ περὶ ἐμοῦ εἰς Ἱερουσαλήμ, οὕτω σε δεῖ καὶ εἰς Ῥώμην μαρτυρῆσαι. ¹²γενο-
μένης δὲ ἡμέρας ποιήσαντες συστροφὴν οἱ Ἰουδαῖοι
ἀνεθεμάτισαν ἑαυτούς, λέγοντες μήτε φαγεῖν μήτε πιεῖν
ἕως οὗ ἀποκτείνωσιν τὸν Παῦλον. ¹³ἦσαν δὲ πλείους
τεσσεράκοντα οἱ ταύτην τὴν συνωμοσίαν ποιησάμενοι,

¹⁴ οἵτινες προσελθόντες τοῖς ἀρχιερεῦσιν καὶ τοῖς πρεσβυτέροις εἶπαν, Ἀναθέματι ἀνεθεματίσαμεν ἑαυτοὺς μηδενὸς γεύσασθαι ἕως οὗ ἀποκτείνωμεν τὸν Παῦλον. ¹⁵ νῦν οὖν ὑμεῖς ἐμφανίσατε τῷ χιλιάρχῳ σὺν τῷ συνεδρίῳ, ὅπως καταγάγῃ αὐτὸν εἰς ὑμᾶς ὡς μέλλοντας διαγινώσκειν ἀκριβέστερον τὰ περὶ αὐτοῦ· ἡμεῖς δὲ πρὸ τοῦ ἐγγίσαι αὐτὸν ἕτοιμοί ἐσμεν τοῦ ἀνελεῖν αὐτόν. ¹⁶ ἀκούσας δὲ ὁ υἱὸς τῆς ἀδελφῆς Παύλου τὴν ἐνέδραν, παραγενόμενος καὶ εἰσελθὼν εἰς τὴν παρεμβολὴν ἀπήγγειλεν τῷ Παύλῳ. ¹⁷ προσκαλεσάμενος δὲ ὁ Παῦλος ἕνα τῶν ἑκατοντάρχων ἔφη, Τὸν νεανίαν τοῦτον ἄπαγε πρὸς τὸν χιλίαρχον, ἔχει γάρ τι ἀπαγγεῖλαι αὐτῷ. ¹⁸ ὁ μὲν οὖν παραλαβὼν αὐτὸν ἤγαγεν πρὸς τὸν χιλίαρχον καί φησιν, Ὁ δέσμιος Παῦλος προσκαλεσάμενός με ἠρώτησεν τοῦτον τὸν νεανίσκον ἀγαγεῖν πρὸς σέ, ἔχοντά τι λαλῆσαί σοι. ¹⁹ ἐπιλαβόμενος δὲ τῆς χειρὸς αὐτοῦ ὁ χιλίαρχος καὶ ἀναχωρήσας κατ' ἰδίαν ἐπυνθάνετο, Τί ἐστιν ὃ ἔχεις ἀπαγγεῖλαί μοι; ²⁰ εἶπεν δέ ὅτι Οἱ Ἰουδαῖοι συνέθεντο τοῦ ἐρωτῆσαί σε ὅπως αὔριον τὸν Παῦλον καταγάγῃς εἰς τὸ συνέδριον ὡς μέλλων τι ἀκριβέστερον πυνθάνεσθαι περὶ αὐτοῦ. ²¹ σὺ οὖν μὴ πεισθῇς αὐτοῖς· ἐνεδρεύουσιν γὰρ αὐτὸν ἐξ αὐτῶν ἄνδρες πλείους τεσσεράκοντα, οἵτινες ἀνεθεμάτισαν ἑαυτοὺς μήτε φαγεῖν μήτε πιεῖν ἕως οὗ ἀνέλωσιν αὐτόν, καὶ νῦν εἰσὶν ἕτοιμοι προσδεχόμενοι τὴν ἀπὸ σοῦ ἐπαγγελίαν. ²² ὁ μὲν οὖν χιλίαρχος ἀπέλυσε τὸν νεανίσκον, παραγγείλας μηδενὶ ἐκλαλῆσαι ὅτι ταῦτα ἐνεφάνισας πρὸς ἐμέ. ²³ καὶ προσκαλεσάμενός τινας δύο τῶν ἑκατοντάρχων εἶπεν, Ἑτοιμάσατε στρατιώτας διακοσίους ὅπως πορευθῶσιν ἕως Καισαρείας, καὶ ἱππεῖς ἑβδομήκοντα καὶ δεξιολάβους

[marginal notes:]
ἐμβατ-ίζω, to notify
a lying-in-wait
ἐρωτάω
ἀναχωρέω, to withdraw
ἐθέμην, 2 aor. τίθημι

διακοσίους, ἀπὸ τρίτης ὥρας τῆς νυκτός, ²⁴ κτήνη τε
παραστῆσαι, ἵνα ἐπιβιβάσαντες τὸν Παῦλον διασώ-
σωσι πρὸς Φήλικα τὸν ἡγεμόνα, ²⁵ γράψας ἐπιστολὴν
ἔχουσαν τὸν τύπον τοῦτον·

²⁶ Κλαύδιος Λυσίας τῷ κρατίστῳ ἡγεμόνι Φήλικι
χαίρειν. ²⁷ τὸν ἄνδρα τοῦτον συλλημφθέντα ὑπὸ τῶν
Ἰουδαίων καὶ μέλλοντα ἀναιρεῖσθαι ὑπ' αὐτῶν ἐπιστὰς
σὺν τῷ στρατεύματι ἐξειλάμην, μαθὼν ὅτι Ῥωμαῖός
ἐστιν. ²⁸ βουλόμενός τε ἐπιγνῶναι τὴν αἰτίαν δι' ἣν
ἐνεκάλουν αὐτῷ, κατήγαγον αὐτὸν εἰς τὸ συνέδριον
αὐτῶν, ²⁹ ὃν εὗρον ἐγκαλούμενον περὶ ζητημάτων τοῦ
νόμου αὐτῶν, μηδὲν δὲ ἄξιον θανάτου ἢ δεσμῶν ἔχοντα
ἔγκλημα. ³⁰ μηνυθείσης δέ μοι ἐπιβουλῆς εἰς τὸν ἄνδρα
ἔσεσθαι ἐξ αὐτῶν, ἔπεμψα πρός σε, παραγγείλας καὶ
τοῖς κατηγόροις λέγειν αὐτοὺς ἐπὶ σοῦ.

³¹ Οἱ μὲν οὖν στρατιῶται κατὰ τὸ διατεταγμένον
αὐτοῖς ἀναλαβόντες τὸν Παῦλον ἤγαγον διὰ νυκτὸς εἰς
τὴν Ἀντιπατρίδα, ³² τῇ δὲ ἐπαύριον ἐάσαντες τοὺς
ἱππεῖς ἀπέρχεσθαι σὺν αὐτῷ, ὑπέστρεψαν εἰς τὴν
παρεμβολήν· ³³ οἵτινες εἰσελθόντες εἰς τὴν Καισάρειαν
καὶ ἀναδόντες τὴν ἐπιστολὴν τῷ ἡγεμόνι, παρέστησαν
καὶ τὸν Παῦλον αὐτῷ. ³⁴ ἀναγνοὺς δὲ καὶ ἐπερωτήσας
ἐκ ποίας ἐπαρχίας ἐστίν, καὶ πυθόμενος ὅτι ἀπὸ Κιλικίας, ³⁵ Διακούσομαί σου, ἔφη, ὅταν καὶ οἱ κατήγοροί
σου παραγένωνται, κελεύσας ἐν τῷ πραιτωρίῳ τοῦ
Ἡρῴδου φυλάσσεσθαι αὐτόν.

24 ¹ Μετὰ δὲ πέντε ἡμέρας κατέβη ὁ ἀρχιερεὺς
Ἀνανίας μετὰ πρεσβυτέρων τινῶν καὶ ῥήτορος Τερ-
τύλλου τινός, οἵτινες ἐνεφάνισαν τῷ ἡγεμόνι κατὰ τοῦ
Παύλου. ² κληθέντος δὲ αὐτοῦ ἤρξατο κατηγορεῖν ὁ
Τέρτυλλος λέγων, ³ Πολλῆς εἰρήνης τυγχάνοντες διὰ

σοῦ καὶ διορθωμάτων γινομένων τῷ ἔθνει τούτῳ διὰ
τῆς σῆς προνοίας, πάντῃ τε καὶ πανταχοῦ ἀποδεχόμεθα,
κράτιστε Φῆλιξ, μετὰ πάσης εὐχαριστίας. ⁴ ἵνα δὲ
μὴ ἐπὶ πλεῖόν σε ἐγκόπτω, παρακαλῶ ἀκοῦσαί σε
ἡμῶν συντόμως τῇ σῇ ἐπιεικείᾳ. ⁵ εὑρόντες γὰρ τὸν
ἄνδρα τοῦτον λοιμὸν καὶ κινοῦντα στάσεις πᾶσιν τοῖς
Ἰουδαίοις τοῖς κατὰ τὴν οἰκουμένην, πρωτοστάτην τε
τῆς τῶν Ναζωραίων αἱρέσεως, ⁶ ὃς καὶ τὸ ἱερὸν ἐπείρασεν βεβηλῶσαι, ὃν καὶ ἐκρατήσαμεν, ⁸ παρ᾽ οὗ δυνήσῃ αὐτὸς ἀνακρίνας περὶ πάντων τούτων ἐπιγνῶναι ὧν
ἡμεῖς κατηγοροῦμεν αὐτοῦ. ⁹ συνεπέθεντο δὲ καὶ οἱ
Ἰουδαῖοι φάσκοντες ταῦτα οὕτως ἔχειν.

¹⁰ Ἀπεκρίθη τε ὁ Παῦλος, νεύσαντος αὐτῷ τοῦ ἡγε-
μόνος λέγειν, Ἐκ πολλῶν ἐτῶν ὄντα σε κριτὴν τῷ
ἔθνει τούτῳ ἐπιστάμενος, εὐθύμως τὰ περὶ ἐμαυτοῦ ἀπολογοῦμαι, ¹¹ δυναμένου σου ἐπιγνῶναι ὅτι οὐ πλείους
εἰσίν μοι ἡμέραι δώδεκα ἀφ᾽ ἧς ἀνέβην προσκυνήσων εἰς
Ἱερουσαλήμ. ¹² καὶ οὔτε ἐν τῷ ἱερῷ εὗρόν με πρός τινα
διαλεγόμενον ἢ ἐπίστασιν ποιοῦντα ὄχλου, οὔτε ἐν ταῖς
συναγωγαῖς οὔτε κατὰ τὴν πόλιν. ¹³ οὐδὲ παραστῆσαι
δύνανταί σοι περὶ ὧν νυνὶ κατηγοροῦσίν μου. ¹⁴ ὁμο-
λογῶ δὲ τοῦτό σοι, ὅτι κατὰ τὴν ὁδὸν ἣν λέγουσιν
αἵρεσιν οὕτω λατρεύω τῷ πατρῴῳ θεῷ, πιστεύων πᾶσι
τοῖς κατὰ τὸν νόμον καὶ τοῖς ἐν τοῖς προφήταις γεγραμ-
μένοις, ¹⁵ ἐλπίδα ἔχων εἰς τὸν θεόν, ἣν καὶ αὐτοὶ οὗτοι
προσδέχονται, ἀνάστασιν μέλλειν ἔσεσθαι δικαίων τε
καὶ ἀδίκων. ¹⁶ ἐν τούτῳ καὶ αὐτὸς ἀσκῶ ἀπρόσκοπον
συνείδησιν ἔχειν πρὸς τὸν θεὸν καὶ τοὺς ἀνθρώπους
διαπαντός. ¹⁷ δι᾽ ἐτῶν δὲ πλειόνων ἐλεημοσύνας ποιήσων εἰς τὸ ἔθνος μου παρεγενόμην καὶ προσφοράς, ¹⁸ ἐν
αἷς εὗρόν με ἡγνισμένον ἐν τῷ ἱερῷ, οὐ μετὰ ὄχλου

οὐδὲ μετὰ θορύβου, τινὲς δὲ ἀπὸ τῆς Ἀσίας Ἰουδαῖοι,
[19] οὓς ἔδει ἐπὶ σοῦ παρεῖναι καὶ κατηγορεῖν, εἴ τι ἔχοιεν
πρὸς ἐμέ. [20] ἢ αὐτοὶ οὗτοι εἰπάτωσαν τί εὗρον ἀδίκημα
στάντος μου ἐπὶ τοῦ συνεδρίου, [21] ἢ περὶ μιᾶς ταύτης
φωνῆς ἧς ἐκέκραξα ἐν αὐτοῖς ἑστὼς ὅτι Περὶ ἀναστάσεως νεκρῶν ἐγὼ κρίνομαι σήμερον ἐφ' ὑμῶν.
[22] Ἀνεβάλετο δὲ αὐτοὺς ὁ Φῆλιξ, ἀκριβέστερον εἰδὼς
τὰ περὶ τῆς ὁδοῦ, εἴπας, Ὅταν Λυσίας ὁ χιλίαρχος
καταβῇ, διαγνώσομαι τὰ καθ' ὑμᾶς, [23] διαταξάμενος
τῷ ἑκατοντάρχῃ τηρεῖσθαι αὐτὸν ἔχειν τε ἄνεσιν καὶ
μηδένα κωλύειν τῶν ἰδίων αὐτοῦ ὑπηρετεῖν αὐτῷ.
[24] μετὰ δὲ ἡμέρας τινὰς παραγενόμενος ὁ Φῆλιξ σὺν
Δρουσίλλῃ τῇ ἰδίᾳ γυναικὶ οὔσῃ Ἰουδαίᾳ μετεπέμψατο τὸν Παῦλον, καὶ ἤκουσεν αὐτοῦ περὶ τῆς εἰς Χριστὸν Ἰησοῦν πίστεως. [25] διαλεγομένου δὲ αὐτοῦ περὶ
δικαιοσύνης καὶ ἐγκρατείας καὶ τοῦ κρίματος τοῦ μέλλοντος ἔμφοβος γενόμενος ὁ Φῆλιξ ἀπεκρίθη, Τὸ νῦν
ἔχον πορεύου, καιρὸν δὲ μεταλαβὼν μετακαλέσομαί
σε, [26] ἅμα καὶ ἐλπίζων ὅτι χρήματα δοθήσεται αὐτῷ
ὑπὸ τοῦ Παύλου· διὸ καὶ πυκνότερον αὐτὸν μεταπεμ-
πόμενος ὡμίλει αὐτῷ. [27] διετίας δὲ πληρωθείσης ἔλαβεν
διάδοχον ὁ Φῆλιξ Πόρκιον Φῆστον· θέλων τε χάριτα
καταθέσθαι τοῖς Ἰουδαίοις ὁ Φῆλιξ κατέλιπε τὸν Παῦλον δεδεμένον.

25 [1] Φῆστος οὖν ἐπιβὰς τῇ ἐπαρχίᾳ μετὰ τρεῖς
ἡμέρας ἀνέβη εἰς Ἱεροσόλυμα ἀπὸ Καισαρείας, [2] ἐνεφάνισάν τε αὐτῷ οἱ ἀρχιερεῖς καὶ οἱ πρῶτοι τῶν Ἰουδαίων κατὰ τοῦ Παύλου, καὶ παρεκάλουν αὐτὸν [3] αἰτούμενοι χάριν κατ' αὐτοῦ, ὅπως μεταπέμψηται αὐτὸν
εἰς Ἱερουσαλήμ, ἐνέδραν ποιοῦντες ἀνελεῖν αὐτὸν κατὰ
τὴν ὁδόν. [4] ὁ μὲν οὖν Φῆστος ἀπεκρίθη τηρεῖσθαι τὸν

Παῦλον εἰς Καισάρειαν, ἑαυτὸν δὲ μέλλειν ἐν τάχει ἐκπορεύεσθαι. [5] Οἱ οὖν ἐν ὑμῖν, φησίν, δυνατοὶ συγκαταβάντες, εἴ τι ἐστὶν ἐν τῷ ἀνδρὶ <u>ἄτοπον</u>, κατηγορείτωσαν αὐτοῦ. [6] διατρίψας δὲ ἐν αὐτοῖς ἡμέρας οὐ πλείους ὀκτὼ ἢ δέκα, καταβὰς εἰς Καισάρειαν, τῇ ἐπαύριον καθίσας ἐπὶ τοῦ βήματος ἐκέλευσεν τὸν Παῦλον ἀχθῆναι. [7] παραγενομένου δὲ αὐτοῦ περιέστησαν αὐτὸν οἱ ἀπὸ Ἱεροσολύμων καταβεβηκότες Ἰουδαῖοι, πολλὰ καὶ βαρέα αἰτιώματα καταφέροντες, ἃ οὐκ ἴσχυον ἀποδεῖξαι, [8] τοῦ Παύλου ἀπολογουμένου ὅτι Οὔτε εἰς τὸν νόμον τῶν Ἰουδαίων οὔτε εἰς τὸ ἱερὸν οὔτε εἰς Καίσαρά τι ἥμαρτον. [9] ὁ Φῆστος δὲ θέλων τοῖς Ἰουδαίοις χάριν καταθέσθαι, ἀποκριθεὶς τῷ Παύλῳ εἶπεν, Θέλεις εἰς Ἱεροσόλυμα ἀναβὰς ἐκεῖ περὶ τούτων κριθῆναι ἐπ' ἐμοῦ; [10] εἶπεν δὲ ὁ Παῦλος, Ἐπὶ τοῦ βήματος Καίσαρος ἑστώς εἰμι, οὗ με δεῖ κρίνεσθαι. Ἰουδαίους οὐδὲν ἠδίκηκα, ὡς καὶ σὺ κάλλιον ἐπιγινώσκεις. [11] εἰ μὲν οὖν ἀδικῶ καὶ ἄξιον θανάτου πέπραχά τι, οὐ <u>παραιτοῦμαι</u> τὸ ἀποθανεῖν· εἰ δὲ οὐδέν ἐστιν ὧν οὗτοι κατηγοροῦσίν μου, οὐδείς με δύναται αὐτοῖς <u>χαρίσασθαι</u>· Καίσαρα ἐπικαλοῦμαι. [12] τότε ὁ Φῆστος συλλαλήσας μετὰ τοῦ συμβουλίου ἀπεκρίθη, Καίσαρα ἐπικέκλησαι, ἐπὶ Καίσαρα πορεύσῃ.

[13] Ἡμερῶν δὲ διαγενομένων τινῶν Ἀγρίππας ὁ βασιλεὺς καὶ Βερνίκη κατήντησαν εἰς Καισάρειαν ἀσπασάμενοι τὸν Φῆστον. [14] ὡς δὲ πλείους ἡμέρας διέτριβον ἐκεῖ, ὁ Φῆστος τῷ βασιλεῖ ἀνέθετο τὰ κατὰ τὸν Παῦλον λέγων, Ἀνήρ τις ἐστὶν καταλελειμμένος ὑπὸ Φήλικος δέσμιος, [15] περὶ οὗ γενομένου μου εἰς Ἱεροσόλυμα ἐνεφάνισαν οἱ ἀρχιερεῖς καὶ οἱ πρεσβύτεροι τῶν Ἰουδαίων, αἰτούμενοι κατ' αὐτοῦ <u>καταδίκην</u>. [16] πρὸς

οὓς ἀπεκρίθην ὅτι οὐκ ἔστιν ἔθος Ῥωμαίοις χαρίζεσθαί
τινα ἄνθρωπον πρὶν ἢ ὁ κατηγορούμενος κατὰ πρόσωπον ἔχοι τοὺς κατηγόρους τόπον τε ἀπολογίας λάβοι
περὶ τοῦ ἐγκλήματος. ¹⁷ συνελθόντων οὖν αὐτῶν ἐνθάδε
ἀναβολὴν μηδεμίαν ποιησάμενος, τῇ ἑξῆς καθίσας ἐπὶ
τοῦ βήματος ἐκέλευσα ἀχθῆναι τὸν ἄνδρα· ¹⁸ περὶ οὗ
σταθέντες οἱ κατήγοροι οὐδεμίαν αἰτίαν ἔφερον ὧν ἐγὼ
ὑπενόουν πονηράν, ¹⁹ ζητήματα δέ τινα περὶ τῆς ἰδίας
δεισιδαιμονίας εἶχον πρὸς αὐτὸν καὶ περί τινος Ἰησοῦ
τεθνηκότος, ὃν ἔφασκεν ὁ Παῦλος ζῆν. ²⁰ ἀπορούμενος
δὲ ἐγὼ τὴν περὶ τούτων ζήτησιν ἔλεγον εἰ βούλοιτο
πορεύεσθαι εἰς Ἱεροσόλυμα κἀκεῖ κρίνεσθαι περὶ τούτων. ²¹ τοῦ δὲ Παύλου ἐπικαλεσαμένου τηρηθῆναι
αὐτὸν εἰς τὴν τοῦ Σεβαστοῦ διάγνωσιν, ἐκέλευσα τηρεῖσθαι αὐτὸν ἕως οὗ ἀναπέμψω αὐτὸν πρὸς Καίσαρα.
²² Ἀγρίππας δὲ πρὸς τὸν Φῆστον, Ἐβουλόμην καὶ αὐτὸς τοῦ ἀνθρώπου ἀκοῦσαι. Αὔριον, φησίν, ἀκούσῃ
αὐτοῦ.

²³ Τῇ οὖν ἐπαύριον ἐλθόντος τοῦ Ἀγρίππα καὶ τῆς
Βερνίκης μετὰ πολλῆς φαντασίας, καὶ εἰσελθόντων εἰς
τὸ ἀκροατήριον σύν τε χιλιάρχοις καὶ ἀνδράσιν τοῖς
κατ' ἐξοχὴν τῆς πόλεως, καὶ κελεύσαντος τοῦ Φῆστου
ἤχθη ὁ Παῦλος. ²⁴ καὶ φησιν ὁ Φῆστος, Ἀγρίππα
βασιλεῦ καὶ πάντες οἱ συμπαρόντες ἡμῖν ἄνδρες, θεωρεῖτε τοῦτον περὶ οὗ ἅπαν τὸ πλῆθος τῶν Ἰουδαίων
ἐνέτυχόν μοι ἔν τε Ἱεροσολύμοις καὶ ἐνθάδε, βοῶντες
μὴ δεῖν αὐτὸν ζῆν μηκέτι. ²⁵ ἐγὼ δὲ κατελαβόμην μηδὲν
ἄξιον αὐτὸν θανάτου πεπραχέναι, αὐτοῦ δὲ τούτου ἐπικαλεσαμένου τὸν Σεβαστὸν ἔκρινα πέμπειν. ²⁶ περὶ
οὗ ἀσφαλές τι γράψαι τῷ κυρίῳ οὐκ ἔχω· διὸ προήγαγον αὐτὸν ἐφ' ὑμῶν καὶ μάλιστα ἐπὶ σοῦ, βασιλεῦ

[marginal notes:]
ἀπορέ-
ομαι
to be in
doubt.

κίτιον

to
perceive

λείπω   λείψω   λέλειμμαι   ἐλίπον
ιαορ ἐλείφθην

Ἀγρίππα, ὅπως τῆς ἀνακρίσεως γενομένης σχῶ τί
γράψω· ²⁷ ἄλογον γάρ μοι δοκεῖ πέμποντα δέσμιον μὴ
καὶ τὰς κατ' αὐτοῦ αἰτίας σημᾶναι.

26 ¹Ἀγρίππας δὲ πρὸς τὸν Παῦλον ἔφη, Ἐπι-
τρέπεταί σοι περὶ σεαυτοῦ λέγειν. τότε ὁ Παῦλος
ἐκτείνας τὴν χεῖρα ἀπελογεῖτο, ²Περὶ πάντων ὧν ἐγκαλοῦμαι ὑπὸ Ἰουδαίων, βασιλεῦ Ἀγρίππα, ἥγημαι
ἐμαυτὸν μακάριον ἐπὶ σοῦ μέλλων σήμερον ἀπολογεῖσθαι, ³μάλιστα γνώστην ὄντα σε πάντων τῶν κατὰ
Ἰουδαίους ἐθῶν τε καὶ ζητημάτων· διὸ δέομαι μακροθύμως ἀκοῦσαί μου. ⁴τὴν μὲν οὖν βίωσίν μου τὴν ἐκ
νεότητος τὴν ἀπ' ἀρχῆς γενομένην ἐν τῷ ἔθνει μου ἔν
τε Ἱεροσολύμοις ἴσασι πάντες οἱ Ἰουδαῖοι, ⁵προγινώ-
σκοντές με ἄνωθεν, ἐὰν θέλωσι μαρτυρεῖν, ὅτι κατὰ τὴν
ἀκριβεστάτην αἵρεσιν τῆς ἡμετέρας θρησκείας ἔζησα
Φαρισαῖος. ⁶καὶ νῦν ἐπ' ἐλπίδι τῆς εἰς τοὺς πατέρας
ἡμῶν ἐπαγγελίας γενομένης ὑπὸ τοῦ θεοῦ ἕστηκα κρινόμενος, ⁷εἰς ἢν τὸ δωδεκάφυλον ἡμῶν ἐν ἐκτενείᾳ νύκτα
καὶ ἡμέραν λατρεῦον ἐλπίζει καταντῆσαι· περὶ ἧς
ἐλπίδος ἐγκαλοῦμαι ὑπὸ Ἰουδαίων, βασιλεῦ. ⁸τί ἄπιστον κρίνεται παρ' ὑμῖν εἰ ὁ θεὸς νεκροὺς ἐγείρει; ⁹ἐγὼ
μὲν οὖν ἔδοξα ἐμαυτῷ πρὸς τὸ ὄνομα Ἰησοῦ τοῦ Ναζωραίου δεῖν πολλὰ ἐναντία πρᾶξαι· ¹⁰ὃ καὶ ἐποίησα ἐν
Ἱεροσολύμοις, καὶ πολλούς τε τῶν ἁγίων ἐγὼ ἐν φυλακαῖς κατέκλεισα, τὴν παρὰ τῶν ἀρχιερέων ἐξουσίαν
λαβών, ἀναιρουμένων τε αὐτῶν κατήνεγκα ψῆφον, ¹¹καὶ
κατὰ πάσας τὰς συναγωγὰς πολλάκις τιμωρῶν αὐτοὺς
ἠνάγκαζον βλασφημεῖν, περισσῶς τε ἐμμαινόμενος αὐτοῖς ἐδίωκον ἕως καὶ εἰς τὰς ἔξω πόλεις. ¹²ἐν οἷς
πορευόμενος εἰς τὴν Δαμασκὸν μετ' ἐξουσίας καὶ ἐπιτροπῆς τῆς τῶν ἀρχιερέων, ¹³ἡμέρας μέσης κατὰ τὴν

ὁδὸν εἶδον, βασιλεῦ, οὐρανόθεν ὑπὲρ τὴν λαμπρότητα
τοῦ ἡλίου περιλάμψαν με φῶς καὶ τοὺς σὺν ἐμοὶ
πορευομένους· ¹⁴ πάντων καταπεσόντων ἡμῶν εἰς τὴν
γῆν ἤκουσα φωνὴν λέγουσαν πρός με τῇ Ἑβραΐδι
διαλέκτῳ, Σαοὺλ Σαούλ, τί με διώκεις; σκληρόν σοι
πρὸς κέντρα λακτίζειν. ¹⁵ ἐγὼ δὲ εἶπα, Τίς εἶ, κύριε;
Ὁ δὲ κύριος εἶπεν, Ἐγώ εἰμι Ἰησοῦς ὃν σὺ διώκεις.
¹⁶ ἀλλὰ ἀνάστηθι καὶ στῆθι ἐπὶ τοὺς πόδας σου· εἰς
τοῦτο γὰρ ὤφθην σοι, προχειρίσασθαί σε ὑπηρέτην καὶ
μάρτυρα ὧν τε εἶδες ὧν τε ὀφθήσομαί σοι, ¹⁷ ἐξαιρούμενός σε ἐκ τοῦ λαοῦ καὶ ἐκ τῶν ἐθνῶν, εἰς οὓς ἐγὼ
ἀποστέλλω σε, ¹⁸ ἀνοῖξαι ὀφθαλμοὺς αὐτῶν, τοῦ ἐπιστρέψαι ἀπὸ σκότους εἰς φῶς καὶ τῆς ἐξουσίας τοῦ
σατανᾶ ἐπὶ τὸν θεόν, τοῦ λαβεῖν αὐτοὺς ἄφεσιν ἁμαρτιῶν καὶ κλῆρον ἐν τοῖς ἡγιασμένοις πίστει τῇ εἰς ἐμέ.
¹⁹ ὅθεν, βασιλεῦ Ἀγρίππα, οὐκ ἐγενόμην ἀπειθὴς τῇ
οὐρανίῳ ὀπτασίᾳ, ²⁰ ἀλλὰ τοῖς ἐν Δαμασκῷ πρῶτόν τε
καὶ Ἱεροσολύμοις πᾶσάν τε τὴν χώραν τῆς Ἰουδαίας
καὶ τοῖς ἔθνεσιν ἀπήγγελλον μετανοεῖν καὶ ἐπιστρέφειν
ἐπὶ τὸν θεόν, ἄξια τῆς μετανοίας ἔργα πράσσοντας.
²¹ ἕνεκα τούτων με Ἰουδαῖοι συλλαβόμενοι ἐν τῷ ἱερῷ
ἐπειρῶντο διαχειρίσασθαι. ²² ἐπικουρίας οὖν τυχὼν
τῆς ἀπὸ τοῦ θεοῦ ἄχρι τῆς ἡμέρας ταύτης ἕστηκα μαρτυρόμενος μικρῷ τε καὶ μεγάλῳ, οὐδὲν ἐκτὸς λέγων ὧν
τε οἱ προφῆται ἐλάλησαν μελλόντων γίνεσθαι καὶ
Μωϋσῆς, ²³ εἰ παθητὸς ὁ Χριστός, εἰ πρῶτος ἐξ ἀναστάσεως νεκρῶν φῶς μέλλει καταγγέλλειν τῷ τε λαῷ καὶ
τοῖς ἔθνεσιν.

²⁴ Ταῦτα δὲ αὐτοῦ ἀπολογουμένου ὁ Φῆστος μεγάλῃ
τῇ φωνῇ φησίν, Μαίνῃ Παῦλε· τὰ πολλά σε γράμματα
εἰς μανίαν περιτρέπει. ²⁵ ὁ δὲ Παῦλος, Οὐ μαίνομαι,

φησίν, κράτιστε Φῆστε, ἀλλὰ ἀληθείας καὶ σωφροσύνης
ῥήματα ἀποφθέγγομαι. ²⁶ ἐπίσταται γὰρ περὶ τούτων
ὁ βασιλεύς, πρὸς ὃν καὶ παρρησιαζόμενος λαλῶ· λανθάνειν γὰρ αὐτόν τι τούτων οὐ πείθομαι οὐδέν· οὐ γάρ
ἐστιν ἐν γωνίᾳ πεπραγμένον τοῦτο. ²⁷ πιστεύεις, βασιλεῦ
Ἀγρίππα, τοῖς προφήταις; οἶδα ὅτι πιστεύεις. ²⁸ ὁ δὲ
Ἀγρίππας πρὸς τὸν Παῦλον, Ἐν ὀλίγῳ με πείθεις
Χριστιανὸν ποιῆσαι. ²⁹ ὁ δὲ Παῦλος, Εὐξαίμην ἂν τῷ
θεῷ καὶ ἐν ὀλίγῳ καὶ ἐν μεγάλῳ οὐ μόνον σε ἀλλὰ καὶ
πάντας τοὺς ἀκούοντάς μου σήμερον γενέσθαι τοιούτους
ὁποῖος κἀγώ εἰμι, παρεκτὸς τῶν δεσμῶν τούτων. ³⁰ ἀνέστη τε ὁ βασιλεὺς καὶ ὁ ἡγεμὼν ἥ τε Βερνίκη καὶ οἱ
συγκαθήμενοι αὐτοῖς, ³¹ καὶ ἀναχωρήσαντες ἐλάλουν
πρὸς ἀλλήλους λέγοντες ὅτι Οὐδὲν θανάτου ἢ δεσμῶν
ἄξιον πράσσει ὁ ἄνθρωπος οὗτος. ³² Ἀγρίππας δὲ τῷ
Φήστῳ ἔφη, Ἀπολελύσθαι ἐδύνατο ὁ ἄνθρωπος οὗτος εἰ
μὴ ἐπεκέκλητο Καίσαρα.

27 ¹ Ὡς δὲ ἐκρίθη τοῦ ἀποπλεῖν ἡμᾶς εἰς τὴν
Ἰταλίαν, παρεδίδουν τόν τε Παῦλον καί τινας ἑτέρους
δεσμώτας ἑκατοντάρχῃ ὀνόματι Ἰουλίῳ σπείρης Σεβαστῆς. ² ἐπιβάντες δὲ πλοίῳ Ἀδραμυττηνῷ μέλλοντι πλεῖν
εἰς τοὺς κατὰ τὴν Ἀσίαν τόπους, ἀνήχθημεν, ὄντος
σὺν ἡμῖν Ἀριστάρχου Μακεδόνος Θεσσαλονικέως· ³ τῇ
τε ἑτέρᾳ κατήχθημεν εἰς Σιδῶνα, φιλανθρώπως τε ὁ
Ἰούλιος τῷ Παύλῳ χρησάμενος ἐπέτρεψεν πρὸς τοὺς
φίλους πορευθέντι ἐπιμελείας τυχεῖν. ⁴ κἀκεῖθεν ἀναχθέντες ὑπεπλεύσαμεν τὴν Κύπρον διὰ τὸ τοὺς ἀνέμους
εἶναι ἐναντίους, ⁵ τό τε πέλαγος τὸ κατὰ τὴν Κιλικίαν
καὶ Παμφυλίαν διαπλεύσαντες κατήλθαμεν εἰς Μύρρα
τῆς Λυκίας. ⁶ κἀκεῖ εὑρὼν ὁ ἑκατοντάρχης πλοῖον
Ἀλεξανδρινὸν πλέον εἰς τὴν Ἰταλίαν ἐνεβίβασεν ἡμᾶς

Βραδυπλοέω

εἰς αὐτό. ⁷ ἐν ἱκαναῖς δὲ ἡμέραις βραδυπλοοῦντες καὶ
μόλις γενόμενοι κατὰ τὴν Κνίδον, μὴ προσεῶντος ἡμᾶς
τοῦ ἀνέμου, ὑπεπλεύσαμεν τὴν Κρήτην κατὰ Σαλμώνην,
⁸ μόλις τε παραλεγόμενοι αὐτὴν ἤλθομεν εἰς τόπον τινὰ
καλούμενον Καλοὺς λιμένας, ᾧ ἐγγὺς ἦν πόλις Λασαία.
⁹ ἱκανοῦ δὲ χρόνου διαγενομένου καὶ ὄντος ἤδη ἐπισφαλοῦς τοῦ πλοὸς διὰ τὸ καὶ τὴν _νηστείαν_ ἤδη
παρεληλυθέναι, παρῄνει ὁ Παῦλος ¹⁰ λέγων αὐτοῖς,
Ἄνδρες, θεωρῶ ὅτι μετὰ ὕβρεως καὶ πολλῆς ζημίας
οὐ μόνον τοῦ φορτίου καὶ τοῦ πλοίου ἀλλὰ καὶ τῶν
ψυχῶν ἡμῶν μέλλειν ἔσεσθαι τὸν πλοῦν. ¹¹ ὁ δὲ
ἑκατοντάρχης τῷ κυβερνήτῃ καὶ τῷ ναυκλήρῳ μᾶλλον
ἐπείθετο ἢ τοῖς ὑπὸ Παύλου λεγομένοις. ¹² _ἀνευθέτου_ δὲ
τοῦ λιμένος ὑπάρχοντος πρὸς παραχειμασίαν, οἱ πλείονες
ἔθεντο βουλὴν ἀναχθῆναι ἐκεῖθεν, εἴπως δύναιντο καταντήσαντες εἰς Φοίνικα παραχειμάσαι, λιμένα τῆς Κρήτης
βλέποντα κατὰ λίβα καὶ κατὰ χῶρον. ¹³ ὑποπνεύσαντος
δὲ νότου δόξαντες τῆς _προθέσεως_ κεκρατηκέναι, ἄραντες
ἆσσον παρελέγοντο τὴν Κρήτην. ¹⁴ μετ᾽ οὐ πολὺ δὲ
ἔβαλεν κατ᾽ αὐτῆς ἄνεμος τυφωνικὸς ὁ καλούμενος
εὐρακύλων· ¹⁵ συναρπασθέντος δὲ τοῦ πλοίου καὶ μὴ
δυναμένου _ἀντοφθαλμεῖν_ τῷ ἀνέμῳ ἐπιδόντες ἐφερόμεθα.
¹⁶ νησίον δέ τι ὑποδραμόντες καλούμενον Καῦδα ἰσχύσαμεν μόλις περικρατεῖς γενέσθαι τῆς σκάφης, ¹⁷ ἣν
ἄραντες βοηθείαις ἐχρῶντο, ὑποζωννύντες τὸ πλοῖον·
φοβούμενοί τε μὴ εἰς τὴν σύρτιν ἐκπέσωσιν, _χαλάσαντες_
τὸ σκεῦος, οὕτως ἐφέροντο. ¹⁸ _σφοδρῶς_ δὲ χειμαζομένων
ἡμῶν τῇ ἐξῆς ἐκβολὴν ἐποιοῦντο, ¹⁹ καὶ τῇ τρίτῃ αὐτόχειρες τὴν σκευὴν τοῦ πλοίου _ἔρριψαν·_ ²⁰ μήτε δὲ ἡλίου
μήτε ἄστρων _ἐπιφαινόντων_ ἐπὶ πλείονας ἡμέρας, χει-
μῶνός τε οὐκ ὀλίγου ἐπικειμένου, λοιπὸν _περιῃρεῖτο_

[margin notes:]
The day of Atonement: Sept. or Oct.

incommodious

purpose

ἀντο-φθαλμεω to face

χαλάω to slacken

χειμάζω to afflict with tempest

περιαιρεω

αὐτοχειρ with his own hand
ῥίπτω to cast

ἐπιφαινω to be visible

ἐλπὶς πᾶσα τοῦ σώζεσθαι ἡμᾶς. ²¹ πολλῆς τε ἀσιτίας
ὑπαρχούσης, τότε σταθεὶς ὁ Παῦλος ἐν μέσῳ αὐτῶν
εἶπεν, Ἔδει μέν, ὦ ἄνδρες, πειθαρχήσαντάς μοι μὴ
ἀνάγεσθαι ἀπὸ τῆς Κρήτης κερδῆσαί τε τὴν ὕβριν
ταύτην καὶ τὴν ζημίαν. ²² καὶ τὰ νῦν παραινῶ ὑμᾶς
εὐθυμεῖν· ἀποβολὴ γὰρ ψυχῆς οὐδεμία ἔσται ἐξ ὑμῶν
πλὴν τοῦ πλοίου. ²³ παρέστη γάρ μοι ταύτῃ τῇ νυκτὶ
τοῦ θεοῦ οὗ εἰμι ἐγώ, ᾧ καὶ λατρεύω, ἄγγελος ²⁴ λέγων,
Μὴ φοβοῦ, Παῦλε· Καίσαρί σε δεῖ παραστῆναι, καὶ
ἰδοὺ κεχάρισταί σοι ὁ θεὸς πάντας τοὺς πλέοντας μετὰ
σοῦ. ²⁵ διὸ εὐθυμεῖτε, ἄνδρες· πιστεύω γὰρ τῷ θεῷ ὅτι
οὕτως ἔσται καθ’ ὃν τρόπον λελάληταί μοι. ²⁶ εἰς νῆσον
δέ τινα δεῖ ἡμᾶς ἐκπεσεῖν. ²⁷ ὡς δὲ τεσσαρεσκαιδεκάτη
νὺξ ἐγένετο διαφερομένων ἡμῶν ἐν τῷ Ἀδρίᾳ, κατὰ
μέσον τῆς νυκτὸς ὑπενόουν οἱ ναῦται προσάγειν τινὰ
αὐτοῖς χώραν. ²⁸ καὶ βολίσαντες εὗρον ὀργυιὰς εἴκοσι,
βραχὺ δὲ διαστήσαντες καὶ πάλιν βολίσαντες εὗρον
ὀργυιὰς δεκαπέντε· ²⁹ φοβούμενοί τε μήπου κατὰ τραχεῖς
τόπους ἐκπέσωμεν, ἐκ πρύμνης ῥίψαντες ἀγκύρας τέσσαρας εὔχοντο ἡμέραν γενέσθαι. ³⁰ τῶν δὲ ναυτῶν
ζητούντων φυγεῖν ἐκ τοῦ πλοίου καὶ χαλασάντων τὴν
σκάφην εἰς τὴν θάλασσαν προφάσει ὡς ἐκ πρώρας
ἀγκύρας μελλόντων ἐκτείνειν, ³¹ εἶπεν ὁ Παῦλος τῷ ἑκατοντάρχῃ καὶ τοῖς στρατιώταις, Ἐὰν μὴ οὗτοι μείνωσιν
ἐν τῷ πλοίῳ, ὑμεῖς σωθῆναι οὐ δύνασθε. ³² τότε ἀπέκοψαν
οἱ στρατιῶται τὰ σχοινία τῆς σκάφης καὶ εἴασαν αὐτὴν
ἐκπεσεῖν. ³³ ἄχρι δὲ οὗ ἡμέρα ἤμελλεν γίνεσθαι, παρεκάλει ὁ Παῦλος ἅπαντας μεταλαβεῖν τροφῆς λέγων,
Τεσσαρεσκαιδεκάτην σήμερον ἡμέραν προσδοκῶντες
ἄσιτοι διατελεῖτε, μηθὲν προσλαβόμενοι. ³⁴ διὸ παρακαλῶ ὑμᾶς μεταλαβεῖν τροφῆς· τοῦτο γὰρ πρὸς τῆς

Marginal notes (left):
to be obedient
κερδαίνω to obtain a loss
to be driven to & fro
διΐστημι to proceed
πρύμνα the stern
προφασις a pretext
ἀποκόπτω to cut off
τροφη food
διατελέω to continue

Marginal notes (bottom):
κερδαίνω   κερδανῶ
κερδήσω
ιαον μ. κερδηθήσομ...

ὑμετέρας σωτηρίας ὑπάρχει· οὐδενὸς γὰρ ὑμῶν θρὶξ
ἀπὸ τῆς κεφαλῆς ἀπολεῖται. ³⁵ εἴπας δὲ ταῦτα καὶ
λαβὼν ἄρτον εὐχαρίστησεν τῷ θεῷ ἐνώπιον πάντων
καὶ κλάσας ἤρξατο ἐσθίειν. ³⁶ εὔθυμοι δὲ γενόμενοι
πάντες καὶ αὐτοὶ προσελάβοντο τροφῆς. ³⁷ ἤμεθα δὲ αἱ
πᾶσαι ψυχαὶ ἐν τῷ πλοίῳ διακόσιαι ἑβδομήκοντα ἕξ.
³⁸ κορεσθέντες δὲ τροφῆς ἐκούφιζον τὸ πλοῖον ἐκβαλλό-
μενοι τὸν σῖτον εἰς τὴν θάλασσαν. ³⁹ ὅτε δὲ ἡμέρα
ἐγένετο, τὴν γῆν οὐκ ἐπεγίνωσκον, κόλπον δέ τινα
κατενόουν ἔχοντα αἰγιαλόν, εἰς ὃν ἐβουλεύοντο εἰ δύναιντο
ἐξῶσαι τὸ πλοῖον. ⁴⁰ καὶ τὰς ἀγκύρας περιελόντες εἴων
εἰς τὴν θάλασσαν, ἅμα ἀνέντες τὰς ζευκτηρίας τῶν
πηδαλίων, καὶ ἐπάραντες τὸν ἀρτέμωνα τῇ πνεούσῃ
κατεῖχον εἰς τὸν αἰγιαλόν. ⁴¹ περιπεσόντες δὲ εἰς τόπον
διθάλασσον ἐπέκειλαν τὴν ναῦν, καὶ ἡ μὲν πρῷρα
ἐρείσασα ἔμεινεν ἀσάλευτος, ἡ δὲ πρύμνα ἐλύετο ὑπὸ
τῆς βίας. ⁴² τῶν δὲ στρατιωτῶν βουλὴ ἐγένετο ἵνα τοὺς
δεσμώτας ἀποκτείνωσιν, μή τις ἐκκολυμβήσας διαφύγῃ·
⁴³ ὁ δὲ ἑκατοντάρχης βουλόμενος διασῶσαι τὸν Παῦλον
ἐκώλυσεν αὐτοὺς τοῦ βουλήματος, ἐκέλευσέν τε τοὺς
δυναμένους κολυμβᾶν ἀπορρίψαντας πρώτους ἐπὶ τὴν
γῆν ἐξιέναι, ⁴⁴ καὶ τοὺς λοιποὺς οὓς μὲν ἐπὶ σανίσιν,
οὓς δὲ ἐπί τινων τῶν ἀπὸ τοῦ πλοίου. καὶ οὕτως ἐγένετο
πάντας διασωθῆναι ἐπὶ τὴν γῆν.

28 ¹ Καὶ διασωθέντες τότε ἐπέγνωμεν ὅτι Μελίτη ἡ
νῆσος καλεῖται. ² οἵ τε βάρβαροι παρεῖχαν οὐ τὴν τυχοῦσαν φιλανθρωπίαν ἡμῖν· ἅψαντες γὰρ πυρὰν προσελάβοντο πάντας ἡμᾶς διὰ τὸν ὑετὸν τὸν ἐφεστῶτα καὶ
διὰ τὸ ψύχος. ³ συστρέψαντος δὲ τοῦ Παύλου φρυγάνων τι πλῆθος καὶ ἐπιθέντος ἐπὶ τὴν πυράν, ἔχιδνα ἀπὸ
τῆς θέρμης ἐξελθοῦσα καθῆψεν τῆς χειρὸς αὐτοῦ. ⁴ ὡς

[marginal notes, right column]
ἀπολλυμι to destroy
κορέννυμι 'am h.
ἐκουφέσθην to satisfy
a boy
περιαιρέω to take away
ἀνίημι to loosen
ἐπικέλλω to run the ship aground
ἀσάλευτος unmovable
ἐκκολυμβάω to swim ashore
σανίς a plank
ἅπτω to light
ὑετὸν rain
ψῦχος cold
ἔχιδνα viper

[marginal notes, bottom]
συστρέφω to gather
φρυγανον to firewood
καθαπτω to fasten upon

δὲ εἶδον οἱ βάρβαροι κρεμάμενον τὸ θηρίον ἐκ τῆς χειρὸς αὐτοῦ, πρὸς ἀλλήλους ἔλεγον, Πάντως φονεύς ἐστιν ὁ ἄνθρωπος οὗτος, ὃν διασωθέντα ἐκ τῆς θαλάσσης ἡ δίκη ζῆν οὐκ εἴασεν. ⁵ ὁ μὲν οὖν ἀποτινάξας τὸ θηρίον εἰς τὸ πῦρ ἔπαθεν οὐδὲν κακόν. ⁶ οἱ δὲ προσεδόκων αὐτὸν μέλλειν πίμπρασθαι ἢ καταπίπτειν ἄφνω νεκρόν. ἐπὶ πολὺ δὲ αὐτῶν προσδοκώντων καὶ θεωρούντων μηδὲν ἄτοπον εἰς αὐτὸν γινόμενον, μεταβαλλόμενοι ἔλεγον αὐτὸν εἶναι θεόν. ⁷ ἐν δὲ τοῖς περὶ τὸν τόπον ἐκεῖνον ὑπῆρχεν χωρία τῷ πρώτῳ τῆς νήσου ὀνόματι Ποπλίῳ, ὃς ἀναδεξάμενος ἡμᾶς τρεῖς ἡμέρας φιλοφρόνως ἐξένισεν.

⁸ ἐγένετο δὲ τὸν πατέρα τοῦ Ποπλίου πυρετοῖς καὶ δυσεντερίῳ συνεχόμενον κατακεῖσθαι, πρὸς ὃν ὁ Παῦλος εἰσελθὼν καὶ προσευξάμενος, ἐπιθεὶς τὰς χεῖρας αὐτῷ, ἰάσατο αὐτόν. ⁹ τούτου δὲ γενομένου καὶ οἱ λοιποὶ οἱ ἐν τῇ νήσῳ ἔχοντες ἀσθενείας προσήρχοντο καὶ ἐθεραπεύοντο, ¹⁰ οἳ καὶ πολλαῖς τιμαῖς ἐτίμησαν ἡμᾶς καὶ ἀναγομένοις ἐπέθεντο τὰ πρὸς τὰς χρείας.

¹¹ Μετὰ δὲ τρεῖς μῆνας ἀνήχθημεν ἐν πλοίῳ παρακεχειμακότι ἐν τῇ νήσῳ, Ἀλεξανδρινῷ, παρασήμῳ Διοσκούροις. ¹² καὶ καταχθέντες εἰς Συρακούσας ἐπεμείναμεν ἡμέρας τρεῖς, ¹³ ὅθεν περιελθόντες κατηντήσαμεν εἰς Ῥήγιον. καὶ μετὰ μίαν ἡμέραν ἐπιγενομένου νότου δευτεραῖοι ἤλθομεν εἰς Ποτιόλους, ¹⁴ οὗ εὑρόντες ἀδελφοὺς παρεκλήθημεν παρ' αὐτοῖς ἐπιμεῖναι ἡμέρας ἑπτά· καὶ οὕτως εἰς τὴν Ῥώμην ἤλθαμεν. ¹⁵ κἀκεῖθεν οἱ ἀδελφοὶ ἀκούσαντες τὰ περὶ ἡμῶν ἦλθαν εἰς ἀπάντησιν ἡμῖν ἄχρι Ἀππίου φόρου καὶ Τριῶν ταβερνῶν, οὓς ἰδὼν ὁ Παῦλος εὐχαριστήσας τῷ θεῷ ἔλαβε θάρσος. ¹⁶ ὅτε δὲ εἰσήλθομεν εἰς Ῥώμην, ἐπετράπη τῷ Παύλῳ μένειν καθ' ἑαυτὸν σὺν τῷ φυλάσσοντι αὐτὸν στρατιώτῃ.

Marginal glosses:

κρεμάν-νυμι — to hang

πίμπρα.. — to swell

χωρίον τὸ — an estate

κατάκειμαι — to lie down

ἰάομαι — to cure

ἀσθένεια — sickness

παράσημος — marked

— on the second day

ἀπαντάω — to meet

¹⁷ Ἐγένετο δὲ μετὰ ἡμέρας τρεῖς συγκαλέσασθαι *to call together*
αὐτὸν τοὺς ὄντας τῶν Ἰουδαίων πρώτους· συνελθόντων
δὲ αὐτῶν ἔλεγεν πρὸς αὐτούς, Ἐγώ, ἄνδρες ἀδελφοί,
οὐδὲν ἐναντίον ποιήσας τῷ λαῷ ἢ τοῖς ἔθεσι τοῖς πα-
τρῴοις, δέσμιος ἐξ Ἱεροσολύμων παρεδόθην εἰς τὰς χεῖρας
τῶν Ῥωμαίων, ¹⁸ οἵτινες ἀνακρίναντές με ἐβούλοντο
ἀπολῦσαι διὰ τὸ μηδεμίαν αἰτίαν θανάτου ὑπάρχειν ἐν
ἐμοί· ¹⁹ ἀντιλεγόντων δὲ τῶν Ἰουδαίων ἠναγκάσθην ἐπι- *ἀντιλέγω to oppose*
καλέσασθαι Καίσαρα, οὐχ ὡς τοῦ ἔθνους μου ἔχων τι
κατηγορεῖν. ²⁰ διὰ ταύτην οὖν τὴν αἰτίαν παρεκάλεσα
ὑμᾶς ἰδεῖν καὶ προσλαλῆσαι· ἕνεκεν γὰρ τῆς ἐλπίδος
τοῦ Ἰσραὴλ τὴν ἅλυσιν ταύτην περίκειμαι. ²¹ οἱ δὲ *to be encompassed with*
πρὸς αὐτὸν εἶπαν, Ἡμεῖς οὔτε γράμματα περὶ σοῦ ἐδε-
ξάμεθα ἀπὸ τῆς Ἰουδαίας, οὔτε παραγενόμενός τις τῶν
ἀδελφῶν ἀπήγγειλεν ἢ ἐλάλησέν τι περὶ σοῦ πονηρόν.
²² ἀξιοῦμεν δὲ παρὰ σοῦ ἀκοῦσαι ἃ φρονεῖς· περὶ μὲν *to think it right*
γὰρ τῆς αἱρέσεως ταύτης γνωστὸν ἡμῖν ἐστιν ὅτι παν-
ταχοῦ ἀντιλέγεται. ²³ ταξάμενοι δὲ αὐτῷ ἡμέραν ἦλθον
πρὸς αὐτὸν εἰς τὴν ξενίαν πλείονες, οἷς ἐξετίθετο διαμαρτυρόμενος τὴν βασιλείαν τοῦ θεοῦ, πείθων τε αὐτοὺς περὶ τοῦ Ἰησοῦ ἀπό τε τοῦ νόμου Μωϋσέως καὶ
τῶν προφητῶν, ἀπὸ πρωῒ ἕως ἑσπέρας. ²⁴ καὶ οἱ μὲν *early*
ἐπείθοντο τοῖς λεγομένοις, οἱ δὲ ἠπίστουν. ²⁵ ἀσύμφωνοι
δὲ ὄντες πρὸς ἀλλήλους ἀπελύοντο εἰπόντος τοῦ Παύλου *to depart*
ῥῆμα ἓν ὅτι Καλῶς τὸ πνεῦμα τὸ ἅγιον ἐλάλησεν διὰ
Ἡσαΐου τοῦ προφήτου πρὸς τοὺς πατέρας ὑμῶν ²⁶ λέγων,
Πορεύθητι πρὸς τὸν λαὸν τοῦτον καὶ εἰπόν, Ἀκοῇ
ἀκούσετε καὶ οὐ μὴ συνῆτε, καὶ βλέποντες βλέψετε καὶ
οὐ μὴ ἴδητε· ²⁷ ἐπαχύνθη γὰρ ἡ καρδία τοῦ λαοῦ τούτου, *παχύνω*
καὶ τοῖς ὠσὶν βαρέως ἤκουσαν, καὶ τοὺς ὀφθαλμοὺς *to make thick, for*
αὐτῶν ἐκάμμυσαν· μήποτε ἴδωσιν τοῖς ὀφθαλμοῖς καὶ

καμμύω   to close

τοῖς ὠσὶν ἀκούσωσιν καὶ τῇ καρδίᾳ συνῶσιν καὶ ἐπιστρέψωσιν, καὶ ἰάσομαι αὐτούς. ²⁸ γνωστὸν οὖν ἔστω
ὑμῖν ὅτι τοῖς ἔθνεσιν ἀπεστάλη τοῦτο τὸ σωτήριον τοῦ
θεοῦ· αὐτοὶ καὶ ἀκούσονται.

³⁰ Ἐνέμεινεν δὲ διετίαν ὅλην ἐν ἰδίῳ μισθώματι, καὶ
ἀπεδέχετο πάντας τοὺς εἰσπορευομένους πρὸς αὐτόν,
³¹ κηρύσσων τὴν βασιλείαν τοῦ θεοῦ καὶ διδάσκων τὰ
περὶ τοῦ κυρίου Ἰησοῦ Χριστοῦ μετὰ πάσης παρρησίας
ἀκωλύτως.

στελλω   στελῶ   ἔσταλκα   ἐστάλην

ιαor. ἔστειλα

μισθωμα   a hired dwelling

NOTES.

*In the notices of various readings prefixed to each chapter it is not
intended to give more than the most important variants, and to indicate
the uncial authorities by which each is supported. Of versions the
Vulgate alone is specially noticed.*

CHAPTER I.

Readings varying from the *Text. recept.*

Title. πράξεις ἀποστόλων adopted on the authority of B, and as
describing the contents of the book better than any other. The book
is not *the* Acts of *the* Apostles, but merely *some* acts of *certain*
Apostles, which are related by the author, but intermixed with the
acts of others who were not Apostles, wherever such additions seem
needed to make the narrative clear. א gives πράξεις only, which
appears too brief, sufficient for the purposes of quotation, but not for
a complete title. א has the subscription πράξεις ἀποστόλων. The longer
forms bear marks of the reverent additions of a later date.

1. ὁ Ἰησοῦς with אAE. The omission in other MSS. is probably
due to the occurrence of o as the last letter of ἤρξατο.

3. τεσσεράκοντα is the spelling of אAB and other authorities.

6. ἠρώτων with אABC. The shorter form was most likely the
earlier. The same may be said too of βλέποντες in verse 11.

8. μου. The *Text. recept.* is the result of a conformity to the more
common construction.

10. ἐσθήσεσι λευκαῖς. This is the reading of אABC. The *Vulgate*
has 'in vestibus albis.' The *Text. recept.* has conformed to the
ordinary expression.

14. καὶ τῇ δεήσει omitted with אABCDE. The *Vulgate* has only
'oratione.' The insertion of the words is probably due to a marginal
note taken from Phil. iv. 6.

15. ἀδελφῶν with אABC. μαθητῶν seems to have been introduced
to avoid the occurrence of the same word in three consecutive verses.
The *Vulg.* has 'fratrum.'

16. ταύτην omitted with אABC and *Vulgate.*

17. ἐν for σὺν with all the most ancient authorities. The *Vulg.* has 'in.'

19. Ἀχελδαμάχ with אA. The form, though not easy to be accounted for, has also much support from the versions.

23. Βαρσαββᾶν with אABE. Μαθθίαν with BD, following the analogy of Μαθθαῖος in 13, which is there the form given by א also. But the authorities are inconsistent about the latter name.

25. τόπον for κλῆρον with ABCD. *Text. recept.* seems to have been a change made because τόπον occurs again in the verse. The *Vulg.* has 'locum,' א κλῆρον.

ἀφ' for ἐξ with אABCD.

Ch. I. 1—14. LINK CONNECTING THIS BOOK WITH ST LUKE'S GOSPEL. DETAILED ACCOUNT OF THE ASCENSION.

1. πρῶτον. The use of πρῶτος for the former of *two* things was not uncommon in later Greek. We have examples, Matth. xxi. 28; 1 Cor. xiv. 30; Heb. viii. 7; ix. 15; Rev. xxi. 1. We use *first* in the same way in English, and Cicero (*de Inventione*) in his second book (chap. iii.) calls the former book *primus liber.* The work here intended by it is the Gospel according to St Luke, also addressed to Theophilus.

τὸν μὲν πρῶτον λόγον. The clause which should have answered to this and been of the form τοῦτον δὲ τὸν δεύτερον κ.τ.λ. is omitted. The writer is carried on by the subject to speak of Christ's appearances and leaves the structure of his sentence incomplete.

λόγος is used in a similar way by Xenophon (*Anab.* ii. 1) in speaking of one 'book' of his history.

ἐποιησάμην, *I made.* The time is indefinite and we have no warrant in the text for that closer union of the two books, in point of date, which is made by the rendering of the A.V.

Θεόφιλε. Nothing is known of the person so called, except that from the adjective κράτιστος applied to him in Luke i. 3 he seems to have held some official position. Cf. Acts xxiii. 26; xxiv. 3; xxvi. 25. Some have however thought that had the title been an official one it would not have been omitted in this verse. The word is used without any official sense; cf. Josephus *Ant.* vi. 6, 8; where the Midianitish women speak to the Israelites as ὦ κράτιστοι νεανιῶν. But its employment elsewhere in the Acts favours the acceptance of it as a title. Josephus uses the word as a title in addressing Epaphroditus, to whom he dedicates the account of his life (*Vit. Joseph.* ad fidem). The suggestion, that θεόφιλος, = 'lover of God,' is a name adopted by the author to indicate any believer, is improbable. Such personification is unlike the rest of Scripture and is not supported by evidence.

ὦν. The relative, instead of standing as required by the governing verbs (ποιεῖν and διδάσκειν) in the accusative is attracted into the case of the preceding demonstrative. This grammatical peculiarity is very common. Cf. Acts iii. 21, 25, vii. 17; &c.

ἤρξατο. This is an emphatic word. The writer regards the Gospel as a record of work which Jesus *began*, and committed to others to be carried forward; and this later book is to be a history of the *beginning* of Christian congregations in various places, and after such a beginning has been made at Rome, then the metropolis of the civilized world, his proposed labour is brought to a close.

The Gospel was the record of Christ's work on earth, the Acts of His work from heaven. Hence the force of 'began' as applied to the former. His work was continued by the various 'beginnings' recorded in the Acts.

ποιεῖν τε καὶ διδάσκειν. So in St Luke (xxiv. 19) the disciples call Jesus 'a prophet mighty in *deed* and in *word*.' The acts and the life spake first and then the voice.

2. ἄχρι ἧς ἡμέρας. An instance of the incorporation of the antecedent into the relative clause, where it must take the case of the relative. Cf. Matth. vii. 2, ἐν ᾧ μέτρῳ μετρεῖτε=ἐν τῷ μέτρῳ, ἐν ᾧ μετρεῖτε.

διὰ πνεύματος ἁγίου. The preposition indicates the operation of that power of the Holy Spirit with which Jesus was filled after His baptism (Luke iv. 1). Chrysostom speaks of Christ's communication to the Twelve thus: πνευματικὰ πρὸς αὐτοὺς εἰπὼν ῥήματα οὐδὲν ἀνθρώπινον. Along with the charges which Jesus gave to His disciples there was bestowed on them too a gift of the Holy Ghost (John xx. 22), which at Pentecost was to be poured out in rich abundance, so that 'filled with the Holy Ghost' becomes a frequent phrase in the Acts to describe the divine endowment of the first evangelists. (Cf. Acts ii. 4, iv. 8, 31, vi. 3, 5, vii. 53, xi. 24, xiii. 9.)

3. μετὰ τὸ παθεῖν αὐτόν, *after He had suffered*. The death is included with the other forms of the passion.

ἐν πολλοῖς τεκμηρίοις. This use of ἐν for expressing the *means* by which anything is done, is from a translation of the Hebrew בְּ =in. Thus the LXX. have (Eccles. ix. 15) καὶ διασώσῃ αὐτὸς τὴν πόλιν ἐν τῇ σοφίᾳ αὐτοῦ.

A τεκμήριον is such an evidence as to remove all doubt. It is explained by Hesychius as σημεῖον ἀληθές. See also Aristot. *Rhet.* i. 2. So 3 Macc. iii. 24, καὶ τεκμηρίοις καλῶς πεπεισμένοι. The proofs which Christ gave of His true resurrection were His speaking, walking and eating with His disciples on several occasions after His resurrection, and giving to Thomas and the rest the clearest demonstration that He was with them in the same real body as before His death (Luke xxiv. 39, 43; John xx. 27; xxi. 13). As the verity of the Resurrection would be the basis of all the Apostolic teaching, it was necessary for the Twelve who were to be His witnesses to have every doubt removed.

δι' ἡμερῶν. The preposition intimates that the appearances of

Jesus to His disciples happened *from time to time* during the forty days, a force which is scarcely to be gathered from A.V. So Chrysostom who remarks οὐκ εἶπεν τεσσεράκοντα ἡμέρας ἀλλὰ δι' ἡμερῶν τεσσεράκοντα, ἐφίστατο γὰρ καὶ ἀφίπτατο πάλιν.

The period of forty days is only mentioned here, and it has been alleged as a discrepancy between St Luke's Gospel and the Acts that the former (Luke xxiv.) represents the Ascension as taking place on the same day as the Resurrection. It needs very little examination to disperse such an idea. The two disciples there mentioned (verse 13) were at Emmaus 'towards evening' on the day of the Resurrection. They came that night t⟩ Jerusalem and told what they had seen. But after this has been stated, the chapter is broken up at *v.* 36 (which a comparison with John (xx. 26—28) shews to be an account of what took place eight days after the Resurrection), and again at *vv.* 44 and 50, into three distinct sections, with no necessary marks of time to connect them. And in the midst of the whole we are told that Christ opened the minds of His disciples that they should understand the Scriptures. No reasonable person can suppose that all this was done in one day. Beside which the objectors prove too much, for according to their reasoning the Ascension must have taken place at night, after the two disciples had returned from Emmaus to Jerusalem.

ὀπτανόμενος. A rare word. It is used Tobit xii. 19 by the angel Raphael, πάσας τὰς ἡμέρας ὠπτανόμην ὑμῖν, and in the LXX. of 1 Kings viii. 8 about the staves on which the ark was carried, and which when it rested in the Most Holy place were not seen outside.

βασιλ. τοῦ θεοῦ. The more frequently used phrase is βασιλ. τῶν οὐρανῶν. Here the meaning is, the new society which was to be founded in Christ's name, and in which all members were to be His soldiers and servants and to bear His name. On the nature of the intercourse between Christ and His disciples during this period, see John xx. 21; Matth. xxviii. 20; Mark xvi. 15, 16; Luke xxiv. 45. They received their solemn commission, and were made to understand the Scriptures, and also were comforted by the promise of the Lord's constant presence to aid them in their great work.

4. συναλιζόμενος. This word is not found elsewhere in N. T., and in only one doubtful instance (Ps. cxl. 5) in the LXX., but is frequent in Herodotus, and several times found in Xenophon. Connected with ἀλής = close gathered together, its sense is 'being gathered in company,' and αὐτοῖς is to be supplied in thought. The *Vulgate* renders by 'convescens' = eating together, as if the word were derived from ἅλς, salt. This sense was put on the word by some of the Greek Fathers, Chrysostom expounding it by τραπέζης κοινωνῶν.

ἐπαγγ. τοῦ πατρός. That promise which God had made of old time through His prophet (Joel iii. 1—5) concerning the outpouring of His Spirit, which Jesus knew was shortly to be fulfilled. This promise is alluded to, Luke xxiv. 49, and is found in St John (xiv. 16, 26, xv. 26), 'The Comforter, which is the Holy Ghost, shall teach you all things'; 'He shall testify of Me.' This was to be their special preparation for their future work.

ἣν ἠκούσατέ μου. Here the language passes from the oblique to the direct form of narrative, as is not uncommon in Greek. Cf. Acts xxiii. 22 where a similar change occurs. See also Tobit viii. 21, καὶ εἶπεν αὐτῷ Ῥαγουήλ...λαβόντα τὸ ἥμισυ τῶν ὑπαρχόντων αὐτοῦ πορεύεσθαι μεθ' ὑγείας πρὸς τὸν πατέρα, καὶ τὰ λοιπὰ ὅταν ἀποθάνω καὶ ἡ γυνή μου.

μου. *Vulg.* 'per os meum.'

5. The variation in construction after βαπτίζειν, first the dative ὕδατι without a preposition and then with ἐν, is probably due to the difference of sense between baptism with water and with the Spirit. But βαπτίζειν ἐν ὕδατι is found (John i. 31) where there is no contrast between sacramental and spiritual baptism.

6. εἰ. This conjunction, at first used after some verb on which it was dependent, at last came to be employed in questions of an independent form. We may suppose that originally some such expression as 'Tell us' was understood before the 'if,' but in translating this sentence the *Vulgate* merely gives 'Domine, si restitues'...and the Latin *si* in Jerome's time had become a particle of direct interrogation. For other examples of εἰ thus used cf. Acts xix. 2, xxi. 37, xxii. 25.

βασιλείαν. Though they were being taught the nature of the kingdom of God, yet their minds were even still far from open, and ran on the thought of a temporal kingdom over Israel to be established by Jesus. The change from the spirit which dictated the question in this verse, to that in which St Peter (Acts ii. 38, 39) preached repentance and forgiveness to all whom the Lord should call, is one of the greatest evidences of the miracle of Pentecost. Such changes are only wrought from above.

7. οὐχ ὑμῶν ἐστίν, *it does not belong to you*, it is not your business. This sense of the genitive, implying *property* or *propriety*, is not uncommon in classical Greek. During the tutelage, as it may be called, of His disciples, Jesus constantly avoided giving a direct answer to the inquiries which they addressed to Him. He checked in this way their tendency to speculate on the future and drew their minds to their duty in the present. Cf. John xxi. 21, 22. Of this conduct Chrysostom writes : διδασκάλου γὰρ τοῦτό ἐστι, μὴ ἃ βούλεται ὁ μαθητὴς ἀλλ' ἃ συμφέρει μαθεῖν, διδάσκειν.

καιρούς. *Vulg.* 'momenta.' This word differs from χρόνος in being restricted to some well-defined point of time, while χρόνος embraces a more extended period. Cf. LXX. Neh. x. 34, where the wood for the altar is to be brought εἰς καιροὺς ἀπὸ χρόνων ἐνιαυτὸν κατ' ἐνιαυτόν, = at fixed points of time chosen out of larger periods, year by year. The A.V. has 'at times appointed year by year.' Cf. also for the idea of the words LXX. 2 Sam. xx. 5, καὶ ἐχρόνισεν ἀπὸ τοῦ καιροῦ οὗ ἐτάξατο αὐτῷ, 'he tarried longer than the set time which he had appointed him' (A.V.). The two nouns are found in conjunction LXX. Dan. ii. 21, vii. 12. Also in 1 Thess. v. 1.

ἐξουσίᾳ = *authority*, absolute disposal. 'Which the Father appointed by His own authority.' It is not the same word as that in the next verse, δύναμις, though the A.V. renders both by 'power.'

8. δύναμιν. The *Vulgate* renders 'virtutem,' and makes it govern the words in the genitive which immediately follow, 'Ye shall receive the influence of the Holy Spirit which shall come upon you.' It is better, with A.V., to render the genitive as genitive absolute, because of the participle included in the expression. The phrases δύναμις τοῦ πνεύματος and δ. πνεύματος ἁγίου do occur (Lk. iv. 14; Rom. xv. 13, 19), but not constructed as in this verse. The effect of this gift was to be something different from the profitless speculations to which they had just desired an answer, even 'a mouth and wisdom which their adversaries could neither gainsay nor resist' (Lk. xxi. 15).

Ἰερουσαλὴμ κ.τ.λ. The order here appointed for the preaching of the Gospel was exactly observed. At Jerusalem (Acts ii.—vii.), Judæa and Samaria (Acts viii. 1), and after the conversion of Saul, in all parts of Asia, Greece, and last of all at Rome.

ἕως ἐσχάτου τῆς γῆς. The precise expression occurs several times in the LXX. of Isaiah (xlviii. 20, xlix. 6, lxii. 11). See also Acts xiii. 47.

9. βλεπόντων αὐτῶν. The Ascension took place while the Eleven beheld, for they were to be witnesses of that event to the world as well as of the life, death, and resurrection. That the Eleven alone saw Christ go into heaven is told us, Mark xvi. 14. In the Gospel (Luke xxiv. 51), we are told that Christ was parted from them 'while He blessed them.'

10. πορευομένου αὐτοῦ, *as He went.* The 'up' of A.V. is not represented in the Gk.

καὶ ἰδού. The καί with the apodosis after expressions signifying *time* is very common in N.T. Greek and is to be classed with those where a similar untranslatable καί follows ἐγένετο δέ and like expressions. See *Winer-Moulton*, p. 756 n.

ἐν ἐσθήσεσι λευκαῖς. The plural rendering given by the *Vulgate* is strong evidence in favour of the reading of the older MSS., for the unusual Greek is not likely to have been put into the place of the more usual form. The two persons are called *men*, but were evidently angels. So one of the two angels which Mary saw in the sepulchre after the Resurrection is called (Mark xvi. 5), a young *man*, clothed in a long white garment. The Jews use the expression 'clad in white garments' in describing angelic or divine messengers. Cf. Luke xxiv. 4; Acts x. 30, xi. 13.

11. Γαλιλαῖοι. We know that most of the Twelve were called in Galilee, and it is very probable that they were all from the same district, as they would be called at the earliest portion of Christ's ministerial life, which was begun among His countrymen in the north. Below (v. 22) Peter speaks of the new disciple to fill the place of Judas, as one who must be fit to be a witness from the time when John was baptizing; so the Twelve must themselves have been companions of Jesus from that early period. Men of Galilee were easily known by their peculiar dialect. Thus when Peter is accused (Matth. xxvi. 73) of being a follower of Jesus, it is said to him, 'Surely thou art one of them, for thy speech bewrayeth thee,' a remark which shews plainly that Christ's immediate followers and friends were known as Galilæans.

οὕτως ἐλεύσεται. These words explain the statement which occurs in the abridged account of the Ascension given by St Luke in the Gospel (xxiv. 52), 'They returned to Jerusalem with great joy.' They had been supernaturally assured that He would return to them.

ὃν τρόπον. The manner in which an action is performed is often expressed both in classical and Hellenistic Greek by the simple accusative; cf. Jude 7, τὸν ὅμοιον τούτοις τρόπον ἐκπορνεύσασαι. When a relative and antecedent are to be used in this way, the antecedent is transferred not unfrequently, as here, into the relative clause. See Matth. xxiii. 37, ὃν τρόπον ὄρνις ἐπισυνάγει τὰ νοσσία. Also LXX. Ezek. xlii. 7; 2 Macc. xv. 40.

12. τοῦ καλουμένου, as well as the subsequent indication of the locality of mountain, shew us that he for whom the Acts was written was a stranger to these places.

'Ελαιῶνος. Here 'Ελαιών is given as the designation by which the mountain was known. Its name was = *Olivetum.*

ἐγγὺς 'Ιερουσαλήμ, *near unto Jerusalem.* The A.V. omits to translate the preposition. The mount of Olives is on the east of Jerusalem, between that city and Bethany.

σαββάτου ὁδόν. The journey which a Jew was allowed to take on the sabbath. This was put at two thousand yards or cubits (Heb. *ammoth*), and the Rabbis had arrived at the measure by a calculation based on their exposition of Exod. xvi. 29, 'Abide ye every man *in his place.*' Here the Hebrew word is *takhtav*, and this the Talmud (Erubin 51 a) explains to mean the four yards (which is the space allowed for downsitting and uprising), but in the same verse it says, 'Let no man go out of *his place,*' and here the word is *makom*, and this means two thousand yards. For *makom* is in another passage explained by *nisah* = flight, and *nisah* is explained by *gebul* = border, and *gebul* is explained elsewhere by *khuts* = extremity, and in one place *khuts* = two thousand yards. For it is written (Numb. xxxv. 5) 'And ye shall measure from the *extremity* of the city on the east side two thousand yards.'

So taking *khuts* as defined in the last passage, they made an equation *khuts = gebul = nisah = makom,* and made *makom* in Exod. xvi. 29 also equal to two thousand yards. The Scriptural passages on which the above reasoning is based are (1) Exod. xxi. 13 'I will appoint thee a *place* (*makom*) whither *he shall flee*' (*yanus*), and from the verb *yanus* the noun *nisah* is formed. (2) Numb. xxxv. 26 'But if the slayer shall at any time come without the border (*gebul*) of the city of his refuge whither he *is fled,*' a passage which connects *gebul* and *nisah.* (3) Numb. xxxv. 27 'If the avenger of blood shall find him *without* (*mikhuts*) the *border* of the city of his refuge,' where *gebul* is brought into connexion with *khuts.*

13. εἰσῆλθον, *they were come in*, i.e. entered into Jerusalem, coming from the open country where the Ascension had taken place.

εἰς τὸ ὑπερῷον, *into the upper room.* The occurrence of the article is probably because the room was the same which had been used before for the Last Supper (Mark xiv. 15; Luke xxii. 12). The noun is not the same here as in those passages, but it seems most probable that the disciples, strangers in Jerusalem, when they had shortly before found one such room which could be obtained, would hardly seek after another. The passover chamber moreover would be hallowed to them by what happened at the Last Supper. In the next clause καταμένοντες seems to imply that the Twelve had taken possession of the room while awaiting the fulfilment of the promise which Jesus had made to them.

The names of the Eleven are probably here recited again, though they had been given to Theophilus in the Gospel, that it might be on record, that though all of them at the arrest and trial forsook their Master, this was done by all but Judas only through fleshly weakness not through defection of heart. It may also be that their names are here given at the outset of the Acts, that it may be intimated thus, that though the separate works of each man will not be chronicled in these fragmentary 'Acts of Apostles,' yet all alike took their part in the labour which their Master had appointed for them.

Ἰάκωβος Ἀλφαίου...Ἰούδας Ἰακώβου. The A.V. renders these two identical constructions in different ways, making James *the son* of Alphæus, but Judas *the brother* of James. There is authority to be found for both renderings, though many more instances occur where the ellipse is the word *son*, than where it is *brother*. Judas is made to be the brother of James here, because in Jude 1 that Judas calls himself brother of James. But we cannot be sure that they were the same person, and in the list of the Twelve it is hardly conceivable that two different words were meant to be supplied with names which stand in close juxtaposition. It is better therefore to render Judas *the son* of James, for which insertion we have more abundant authority.

Σίμων ὁ Ζηλωτής. Ζηλωτής is a Greek rendering of the Hebrew word which is represented by Κανανίτης (Matth. x. 4; Mark iii. 18). That word signifies one who is very zealous for his opinions or his party, and was applied in our Lord's time to those Jews who were specially strict in their observance of the Mosaic ritual.

14. τῇ προσευχῇ. It would seem from the article here as if already some religious service had taken definite form among the disciples. This is almost implied too in the fact of their continuance therein with one accord, a description hardly consistent with mere individual supplication. The disciples had long before made the request 'Lord, teach us to pray' (Luke xi. 1), and during the three years of association with Jesus, the form given them as an example may very well have grown into the proportions suited for general worship.

σὺν γυναιξίν, best rendered '*with* certain *women.*' There is nothing

to define them, but from the first, women played a helpful part in
Christian offices.

τῇ μητρί. It is noteworthy how from first to last the Gospel history
shews our Lord acknowledging a human mother, and so causing her
to be cared for by His friends, but from the dawn of consciousness at
twelve years old never speaking but of a Father in heaven. The
blessed Virgin would naturally remain with St John, to whose care she
had been confided by Jesus at the Crucifixion (John xix. 27). This is
the last mention of the Virgin, and thus Scripture leaves her on her
knees. She is mentioned apart from the other women as having
a deeper interest in all that concerned Jesus than the rest could have.

ἀδελφοῖς. See Matth. xiii. 55; Mark vi. 3. The brethren of our
Lord are there named James, Joses (or Joseph), Simon and Judas.
Being mentioned here as persons distinct from the Eleven, we may
fairly conclude that James, the son of Alphæus, and James, the Lord's
brother, were different persons.

A change has come over these 'brethren' since the last mention of
them (John vii. 5). There we are told that they did not believe on
Jesus.

15—26. ELECTION OF AN APOSTLE TO FILL THE PLACE OF JUDAS ISCARIOT.

15. ἡμέραις. The days which intervened between the Ascension
and Pentecost.

Πέτρος. As in the Gospels, so here, Peter is always the moving
spirit and speaker among the Apostles, till he drops out of the history
and gives place to St Paul.

ἦν τε κ.τ.λ. This sentence is not well rendered in A.V. Better
'and there was a crowd of persons [*names*] gathered together, about a
hundred and twenty.' On this use of ὀνόματα=persons, cf. Rev. iii.
4, 'Thou hast a few *names* even in Sardis, which have not defiled
their garments.'

16. ἄνδρες ἀδελφοί. This form of beginning an address is common throughout the Acts (cf. i. 11, ii. 14, 22, 29, iii. 12, &c.), and an
objection has been raised against this uniformity. But we cannot but
suppose, that St Luke after collecting the speeches which were reported to him, cast them into a form fitted for insertion in his narrative.
This is only what a writer of history must do. Some introductory
words were necessary at the commencement of the speeches, and it is
probable that the uniformity found in these places is due to him and
not to those whose words he reports and supplies with the links needful to attach them to his narrative.

γραφή. A constant word for Old Testament Scripture (cf. John vii.
38, x. 35; Acts viii. 32, &c.), and often used in the plural in the same
sense (Matth. xxi. 42, xxii. 9, &c.).

ἣν προεῖπεν. The quotations made below are from Pss. lxix. 25 and
cix. 8, and these the minds of the disciples, being opened, comprehend

may be applied to the case of Judas, whose treachery more than fulfils
all the description of the Psalmist. The words which describe the
traitor-friend suit completely the conduct of Judas, but we are not on
that account to suppose that they had not a first fulfilment in the
life-history of him who wrote these Psalms, and the otherwise fierce
character of the imprecations they contain finds its best justification
when we learn how they are to be applied. While the Psalmist spake
of himself and of his own circumstances, the Holy Ghost was speaking
through him of what should happen to "the son of David."

17. ἐν ἡμῖν. This preposition is supported by the '*in nobis*' of the
Vulgate, and seems to give, more than is done by the σὺν of the *Text.
recept.* the sense that though Judas was counted *in* the Twelve, he
was not truly *of* them.

τὸν κλῆρον. The article is best rendered by the possessive pronoun
'*his* part.'

18. μὲν οὖν. These particles at the opening of the verse shew that
there is a break in the continuity of the narrative and that what follows, in verses 18 and 19, must be taken for a parenthesis. For
examples of such use of μὲν οὖν cf. Acts v. 41, xiii. 4, xvii. 30, xxiii.
22, xxvi. 9.

ἐκτήσατο, *acquired.* The word may be used not only of him who
gets something for himself, but of one who is the cause of its being
gotten by another. The field was bought by the chief priests (Matth.
xxvii. 5—8), but it was the return of the money by Judas, and the
difficulty of disposing of it in any other way, which brought about the
purchase of the field.

ἐκ μισθοῦ τῆς ἀδικίας. This expression is found only here and in
2 Pet. ii. 13, 15. It seems therefore to be a Petrine phrase. The
varied English of the A.V. in these places effectually obscures the
evidence of this. Though these verses are in the form of a parenthesis, St Luke most probably gathered the facts which they contain
from St Peter himself, or he would not thus have inserted them within
the compass of that Apostle's address.

πρηνὴς γενόμενος. Of course this occurred after he had hanged
himself, as is recorded by St Matthew (xxvii. 5). If the cord used by
Judas broke with his weight, it is easy to understand how all that is
related took place. The ground, to be suitable for an Eastern burial-
place must needs be rocky and cavernous. St Matthew intimates
that it was a clay-pit which had probably been long before dug out
for making pottery. When the body suspended over such a place fell
down on the hard bottom, a result would ensue like that described
2 Chron. xxv. 12, and which might well be described by the language in
the text.

ἐλάκησεν (from λάσκω). The word indicates that the occurrence was
attended by a loud sound. There is a passage in the apocryphal *Acta
Thomæ* § 33 which illustrates the language of this verse, and where
this rare verb occurs. ὁ δράκων φυσηθεὶς ἐλάκησε καὶ ἀπέθανε καὶ ἐξε-

χύθη ὁ ἰὸς αὐτοῦ καὶ ἡ χολή. The dragon burst asunder by reason of the poison which he had been compelled by the Apostle to suck back out of the body of a young man whom he had slain and whom the Apostle raised to life. The apocryphal story then goes on to tell how a chasm opened, so that the dragon was swallowed into the earth, while the Apostle, after commanding the hollow to be filled up, and houses to be built over it, adds, ἵνα οἴκησις γένηται τοῖς ξένοις, that it may be a dwelling-place for *the strangers.* Cf. Matt. xxvii. 7.

19. καὶ γνωστὸν ἐγένετο, *and it became known.* And hence the name of 'the Potter's Field' was by general consent changed to 'the Field of Blood.' The entire story, as St Luke tells it, must have been what in later days became widely known, for there is nothing of it in St Matthew's narrative, which only mentions the purchase to account for the change of name.

τῇ ἰδίᾳ διαλέκτῳ. i.e. in the Aramaic speech, which was the language of the dwellers in Jerusalem. The giving of this name must have taken place some time after the Day of Pentecost. So that St Luke is explaining parenthetically something in which evidence still remained, in the name, to bear witness to the terrible fate of Judas, and to the impression which it produced throughout all Jerusalem.

Ἀχελδαμάχ. This orthography, which has most authority, is not easy to explain. The Aramaic form would be חֲקַל דְּמָא, and for this we should expect an aspirate at the beginning of the word, and it is so represented in some authorities, as in *Vulg.*, which gives 'Haceldama.' When the word was made to commence with ἀ, the principle of compensation for the lost aspirate may have converted Hacel into Ἀχελ (cf. for the converse of this ἔχω, future ἕξω), and the final χ may be due to a desire to represent in some way the final נ of the Aramaic, which together with the preceding vowel-point might be deemed incompletely represented by α only.

20. γενηθήτω, *let it become* (or *be made*) *desolate.* The *Vulgate* gives 'fiat commoratio *eorum* deserta,' quoting exactly from Ps. lxix., where the pronoun is plural. But there is no authority for reading αὐτῶν instead of αὐτοῦ, and the singular is needed in this application of the verse to Judas. The further application of the prophecies to the Jewish nation, and their fulfilment in that case too, came at a later date, but were as terrible as the fulfilment upon Judas.

ἐπισκοπήν. An office involving oversight of others. In A. V. 'bishoprick,' and so in all previous versions except the Geneva, which has 'charge.' But 'office' which is the word used in Ps. cix. 8 is better.

It is this second prophecy which makes a new election necessary. Judas has perished, but the work must have another overseer and not be hindered by the sin of the traitor.

The former of these quotations stands in the LXX. (Ps. lxviii., Heb. lxix. 26) thus γενηθήτω ἡ ἔπαυλις αὐτῶν ἠρημωμένη, καὶ ἐν τοῖς σκηνώμασιν αὐτῶν μὴ ἔστω ὁ κατοικῶν. These variations are of interest as shewing the freedom with which the text was handled in quotation.

21.   ἐν παντὶ χρόνῳ. It seems then that Justus and Matthias had been companions of Jesus from a very early period, as no doubt were several others; for the Twelve were chosen out of a greater number, and the sending of the Seventy shews us that Jesus employed many more agents, and had many more who were ready to be employed, than the Twelve selected to be His closest companions.

εἰσῆλθεν καὶ ἐξῆλθεν. These verbs are used in connexion more than once in the LXX. (cf. Deut. xxxi. 2; Josh. xiv. 11; 1 Sam. xviii. 13), but in those passages (though the third sentence about David is not so manifestly like the other two) the reference is to some leadership in war or otherwise. Here the sentence seems to mean no more than 'passed His life' (cf. Acts ix. 28), unless the leadership of Jesus is to be understood in the preposition ἐφ' = over, which immediately follows. On the expression cf. Chrysostom's words: δείκνυσιν αὐτοὺς συνῳκηκότας αὐτῷ οὐχ ἁπλῶς ὡς μαθητὰς παρόντας.

22.   ἀρξάμενος. For it could not be long after His baptism that Jesus began to gather followers around Him, and some of these had been beforetime disciples of John, had perhaps been witnesses of the baptism of Jesus, and certainly had heard the frequent testimony borne to Him by the Baptist.

ἧς. This is perhaps not to be regarded as an attraction of the relative like that in verse 1, for the genitive of the time *when* is common in Greek, and this may be taken as an example of it. Cf. LXX. Levit. xxiii. 15, ἀπὸ τῆς ἡμέρας ἧς ἂν προσενέγκητε τὸ δράγμα. So too Deut. iv. 32; Baruch i. 19. The form ἀπὸ τῆς ἡμέρας ᾖ κ.τ.λ. occurs Numb. xv. 21; Josh. ix. 12, &c.

τῆς ἀναστάσεως. This, as the central point of the Christian faith, must be attested, and they would be the most cogent witnesses thereto who had known most of Jesus before His crucifixion. Cf. the language of Chrysostom on this as the chief subject of the Acts: καὶ γὰρ τοῦτο μάλιστά ἐστι τὸ βιβλίον, ἀπόδειξις ἀναστάσεως.

τούτων. Resuming the construction of the συνελθόντων at the beginning of the verse.

23.   ἔστησαν. They first exercised their own powers in selecting those who best fulfilled the condition laid down. Probably there were only few among the hundred and twenty, besides the Eleven and the selected two, who had been continuously in the company of Jesus.

Βαρσαββᾶν. A patronymic. The man's Jewish name was Joseph, and his father's Sabba. He had besides a Roman name, Justus. This was a common thing among the Jews to have one name among their own people, and another for use in their intercourse with non-Jews. Thus Saul becomes generally known as Paulus when he is to go forth on his missionary labours. Simon takes (from Christ, perhaps that by it he might become known to all the world) the name of Petrus, and Thomas is called Didymus.

If we may judge from his three appellations, and from his being set first in order, Joseph was the better known, and it may be of more repute among the brethren. But God's choice falls on Matthias.

24. προσευξάμενοι. They made a solemn supplication to God for His guidance. St Luke mentions the only point towards which the whole tenor of their petitions was directed, viz. for light to see God's choice. No doubt the prayers, like the speeches in the book, were of greater extent than is indicated in the sentence or two of abstract in which the author sums up for us their purport.

The participle προσευξάμενοι, though aorist, is used to express a simultaneous action with the verb, 'they prayed and (in their prayer) said.'

ἀνάδειξον. Having done their utmost to select fit persons, and having sought God's blessing on their endeavour, they now ask for some token by which they may be guided in the final choice. From the use of κύριε we may judge that the prayer was addressed to Christ, by whom at first the Twelve had been chosen. καρδιογνώστης is applied to God the Father (Acts xv. 8), but the Apostles (John ii. 25) had learnt that their Master 'knew what was in man.'

25. τόπον. Used in the sense of a position or office, Sirach xii. 12 μὴ ἀνατρέψας σε στῇ ἐπὶ τὸν τόπον σου. Cf. also 1 Cor. xiv. 16. The testimony of the Vulgate is in favour of τόπον, for κλῆρον could not be rendered by 'locum ministerii.'

διακονίας...καὶ ἀποστολῆς. The office is described by two words, the first of which is the more general, the second defining the character of the work which was to constitute the διακονία.

παρέβη, fell away. The periphrasis 'by transgression fell' of the A.V. gives the sense correctly, but does not shew that the whole expression is but a single verb in the original.

τὸν τόπον τὸν ἴδιον. He had been chosen for one place, but had made choice of another for himself. The writer does not define what this was, but what this phrase meant in a Jewish mouth is seen from the Baal Haturim on Numb. xxiv. 25, where the place to which Balaam went is explained as Gehenna, the place of torment. So too Midrash Koheleth Rabbah, vii. 1.

26. κλῆρους. The giving of lots was a provision in the Law (Lev. xvi. 8) by which one of the two goats offered on the great Day of Atonement was to be selected for the Lord. 'The goat upon which the Lord's lot fell' was offered for a sin offering. Most probably in this case each one of the Eleven wrote on a tablet the name of that one of the two men for whom in his heart he was prompted to vote, and he who had most votes was chosen to fill the vacant place among the Apostolic band.

St Chrysostom, on this passage, remarks that these events took place before Pentecost. After the Holy Ghost had been given they used no more casting of lots.

συγκατεψηφίσθη μετά, *he was numbered* (literally *together*) *with.* This is an example of redundancy of prepositions with which may be compared LXX. Ps. xlvi. 10, ἄρχοντες λαῶν συνήχθησαν μετὰ τοῦ θεοῦ Ἀβραάμ. See also Ezek. xxviii. 7.

CHAPTER II.

Readings varying from the *Text. recept.*

1. πάντες ὁμοῦ with אABC. The *Vulg.* has 'pariter.'

7. πρὸς ἀλλήλους omitted with אABC and *Vulg.*

12. τί θέλει with ABCD. *Vulg.* has 'quidnam vult.' א reads τί θέλοι without ἄν, which seems to confirm the correctness of the other uncials, θέλοι being only a slip of the scribe for θέλει.

17. ἐνυπνίοις with אABCD. There is the like variation between accusative and dative in the MSS. of the LXX.

22. Omit καὶ before αὐτοὶ with אABCDE and numerous cursives. The *Vulg.* inserts 'et.'

23. Omit λαβόντες with אABC and *Vulg.*

30. τὸ κατὰ σάρκα ἀναστήσειν τὸν Χριστόν omitted with אABCD. The *Vulg.* does not represent these words. The omitted words seem like a marginal exposition which in time made its way into the text.

31. ἡ ψυχὴ αὐτοῦ omitted with אABCD and *Vulg.* They appear to have been added to balance ἡ σάρξ in the following clause.

33. νῦν omitted with אABCD and *Vulg.*

36. αὐτὸν placed after κύριον with אABC. The *Vulg.* has 'dominum eum et Christum.'

38. ἔφη omitted with אAC, which however add, what the *Vulg.* appears to have read, φησίν after μετανοήσατε. There is much variation in the word as well as in its position in the different MSS. and versions.

Add ὑμῶν after ἁμαρτιῶν with אABC and *Vulg.*

41. ἀσμένως omitted with אABCD and *Vulg.*

42. Omit καὶ after κοινωνίᾳ with אABCD. The *Vulg.* has 'et communicatione fractionis panis,' which also supports the omission of καί.

47. Omit τῇ ἐκκλησίᾳ, and add from the commencement of the next chapter ἐπὶ τὸ αὐτό after ἡμέραν, so that chap. iii. will begin Πέτρος δέ. This reading is given by אABCG and is confirmed by the *Vulg.* and many other versions.

Ch. II. 1—13. The Holy Ghost given at Pentecost. Effect
first produced thereby on the Dwellers at Jerusalem.

1. ἐν τῷ συμπληροῦσθαι. This compound verb is not found in the
LXX. (nor in classical Greek in this sense), but the derived noun
occurs 2 Chron. xxxvi. 21 of the 'complete fulfilling' of a period of
time. The simple verb is used both of a period of time to be gone
through and of a point of time which has to be reached. See Numb.
vi. 5, and Jer. xxv. 12 compared with verse 34 of the same chapter.
The *Vulg.* gives 'cum complerentur dies Pentecostes,' as if the day
of the feast was regarded as the completion of the whole seven
weeks.

τὴν ἡμέραν τῆς Πεντηκοστῆς. Pentecost was the second of the
three great Jewish feasts, the Passover being the first, and the third
the Feast of Tabernacles. The name is derived from πεντηκοστός,
fiftieth; because it was kept on the fiftieth day after the Passover
Sabbath. In the Law it is called 'the feast of harvest, the firstfruits of thy labours' (Exod. xxiii. 16) and also, from being seven
weeks after the Passover, it is named 'the feast of *weeks*' (Exod.
xxxiv. 22; Deut. xvi. 9—10). The offering in this festival was the
two first loaves made from the first portion of the wheat-harvest
of the year, as a thank-offering.

The words of Chrysostom on the typical character of the Pentecostal feast are worthy of notice. τίς ἐστιν αὕτη ἡ Πεντηκοστή; ὅτε
τὸ δρέπανον ἐπιβάλλειν ἔδει τῷ ἀμήτῳ, ὅτε τοὺς καρποὺς συνάγειν ἐχρῆν.
εἶδες τὸν τύπον· βλέπε πάλιν τὴν ἀλήθειαν.

This day was probably chosen for the outpouring of the Spirit upon
the Apostles, that there might be a greater multitude present in
Jerusalem, and so the tidings of this gift might at once be spread
abroad. It is perhaps for this reason that the very word employed is
one which indicates that the day was *fully* come, and so all that were
intending to be present at the feast were there. We find in ix. 2
that there were Christians at Damascus before we read of any one of
the Apostolic band visiting that city. It may well be that among
those who saw the gifts now bestowed, and whose hearts were pierced
by Peter's sermon, there were some who went forth to this and other
cities, bearing the fame and teaching of the new society along with
them. In like manner, we cannot doubt that it was in order that
more might hear His words, that our Lord so frequently went to Jerusalem at the feasts (John iv. 45, v. 1, vii. 10, x. 22, &c.).

ὁμοῦ, *together.* This word and that which takes its place in the
Text. recept. i.e. ὁμοθυμαδόν occur frequently in this part of the Acts
and mark very strongly the unity which existed in the new society,
but which was so soon destined to be broken. For ὁμοθυμαδόν cf.
Acts i. 14, ii. 46, iv. 24, v. 12, &c. Beside this book the word is
only found in N. T. in Rom. xv. 6.

ἐπὶ τὸ αὐτό. Doubtless this was in the upper room in which the
disciples were wont to meet.

2. **ὥσπερ φερομένης πνοῆς βιαίας.** Literally 'as of a mighty wind borne along,' i.e. *as of the rushing of a mighty wind.* The verb here employed to express the rushing of the wind is used by St Peter (2 Ep. i. 17, 18) of 'the voice which came from heaven' at the Transfiguration, also (i. 21) of the gift of prophecy, and the motion of the prophets by the Holy Ghost.

3. **διαμεριζόμεναι γλῶσσαι ὡσεὶ πυρός,** *tongues like as of fire distributed among them.* Cf. Is. v. 24, where the Hebrew has 'tongue of fire' (see margin) while the A. V. gives only 'fire.' It is also to be noticed that the appearance is not called fire, but only compared to fire. The idea conveyed by the verb is that the flamelike tongues were distributing themselves throughout the assembly (the *Vulg.* has 'dispertitæ'), and the result is expressed by what follows; *and it sat upon each of them.* The intention of the writer is to describe something far more persistent than meteoric light or flashes of electricity. The sound which is heard fills the house, and the flame rests for some time on the heads of the disciples. (See ver. 33.)

4. This verse describes a great miracle, and its simplicity of statement marks it as the record of one who felt that no additional words could make the matter other than one which passed the human understanding.

ἤρξαντο λαλεῖν ἑτέραις γλώσσαις. These are spoken of as καιναὶ γλῶσσαι, new tongues (Mark xvi. 17). The meaning is, they spake in languages which before were unknown to them, and from the history it would appear that some of the company spake in one and some in another language, for the crowd of foreigners, when they come together, all find somebody among the speakers whom they are able to understand.

ἀποφθέγγεσθαι αὐτοῖς. The order is supported by the *Vulg.* 'dabat eloqui illis,' as well as by the oldest MSS.

5. **ἦσαν δὲ ἐν Ἱερουσαλήμ.** Probably, in addition to the visitors who had come to the feast, many religious Jews from foreign parts were permanent residents in Jerusalem, for it was to the Jew a thing much to be desired, that he might die and be buried near the Holy City. It is said (T. B. *Kethuboth,* 111 *a*), 'Every one that is buried in the land of Israel is in as good case as if he were buried under the altar,' and there are many other like expressions in the immediate context of this quotation. That among the crowd were some residents seems the more likely, because when they recognized the new tongues, some asked as though they were acquainted with the speakers, 'Are not these men Galilæans?'

εὐλαβεῖς, *devout.* The word is used of the aged Simeon (Luke ii. 25) and of the men who carried Stephen to his burial (Acts viii. 2). It is one of those Greek words which Christianity has taken hold of and dignified. In classical language its sense is merely = circumspect. The LXX. (according to some authorities) has it (Micah vii. 2) of the good, godly, merciful man; other MSS. read εὐσεβής there.

ἀπὸ παντὸς ἔθνους. This expression is hyperbolic. We say *from every part of the world*, when we only mean from a great many parts. Cf. also Deut. ii. 25, 'This day will I begin to put the fear of thee upon the nations that are under the whole heaven.' That the Jews were spread abroad very widely is seen from Josephus (*B. J.* II. 16, 4) where Herod Agrippa says 'There is not a nation in the world which does not contain some of us' (Jews). So Philo *In Flaccum*, § 7, says of them, τὰς πλείστας καὶ εὐδαιμονεστάτας τῶν ἐν Εὐρώπῃ καὶ Ἀσίᾳ κατά τε νήσους καὶ ἠπείρους ἐκνέμονται.

6. γενομένης δὲ τῆς φωνῆς ταύτης, *and when this sound was heard.* Φωνή though not the same word as ἦχος which is used for *sound* in verse 2, yet is never found in the sense of a *report* or *rumour*, as is given by the A.V. It is used for *crying aloud*, as in the mourning at Rama and Christ's cry on the cross (Matt. ii. 18), or in John the Baptist's preaching (Mark i. 3), and of voices from heaven frequently (Matt. xvii. 5; Mark i. 11; Luke iii. 22; Acts ix. 4, &c.), of the sound of the wind which is used as a figure for the gift of the Spirit in Christ's conversation with Nicodemus (John iii. 8), and constantly of the heavenly voices in the book of the Revelation (i. 10, v. 2, vi. 6, &c.). So in the LXX. we have φωνή with σάλπιγγος, βροντῆς, σεισμοῦ, and such like words, all indicating a loud noise.

The sound which was sent forth, though heard around in the city, was evidently such as could be traced to a central spot, for led by the sound, the multitude came together to the room in which the Apostles were assembled. It would need but a brief space for a crowd to gather, and all the new-comers found among the disciples, now divinely prepared to be Christ's heralds, some who were declaring what had come to pass, and the great things which God had wrought with them, in the different languages of the lands where the strangers had been born. This was clearly not a proclamation of the wonderful works of God in some one language, which the Spirit, acting upon the hearers, caused them to appreciate as if it were their own, for in that way the gift of the Holy Ghost ought to have been described as poured out, not on the speakers, but on the listeners.

ἤκουον. The verb is plural, in consequence of the plural idea contained in πλῆθος, though the verbs in immediate connexion with the noun are singular. For πλῆθος joined directly with a plural cf. Luke xxiii. 1 ἅπαν τὸ πλῆθος ἤγαγον αὐτόν. See also *Acta Apocryph. Philip.* 7 πολὺ πλῆθος ἐξ αὐτῶν ἀποφυγόντες ἀπὸ τοῦ ἐχθροῦ ἐπεστρέφοντο ἐπὶ τὸν Ἰησοῦν.

εἰς ἕκαστος is explanatory and distributive, and not to be regarded as a direct nominative to the verb. So too in verse 8, and also xi. 29.

7. οὐχ. This form, though the succeeding word has only the smooth breathing, is supported by the best MS. authority and adopted by Lachmann and Tischendorf. See also Acts xix. 23, where οὐχ ὀλίγος is read by Lach.; but not by Tisch. though it has the support of ℵAD. Similarly below in verse 26 of this chapter ἐφ᾽ ἐλπίδι is the reading favoured by Lachmann, Tischendorf and Tregelles, Tischendorf reading also ἐλπίδι.

8. τῇ ἰδίᾳ διαλέκτῳ. There is no description here of any jargon or incoherent speech. We are told of utterances tested by the ears of men who had spoken these languages from their youth. Cf. Chrysostom's words οὐ γὰρ ἁπλῶς ἐλάλουν, ἀλλά τινα θαυμαστὰ ἔλεγον. The only question on which from St Luke's description we are left in uncertainty is this: whether the disciples did or did not understand the new words which they were enabled to utter. The only other place in the New Testament which throws any light on this matter is St Paul's 1st Epistle to the Corinthians. For a consideration of the expressions which St Paul there employs concerning these marvellous gifts, see note after ver. 13.

9, 10. Under all the nationalities mentioned in these verses we are to understand the Jews, either by birth or conversion (as is indicated in the case of Rome), whose homes were in the countries named.

Πάρθοι. A people who occupied a wide extent of country south of the Caspian Sea, from which they were separated by Hyrcania. They stretched in the Apostolic times from India to the Tigris, and no doubt stand foremost in this list because of their great fame among the nations of the time.

Μῆδοι. Their country lay east of Assyria, north-west of Persia and south-west of the Caspian Sea.

Ἐλαμῖται. These dwelt in the district known to the Greeks and Romans as Susiana. It lay at the north of the Persian Gulf and was bounded on the west by the Tigris, touching Media on the North and Persia on the South and East. They were a Semitic people, perhaps taking their name from Elam, son of Shem (Gen. x. 22). 'Shushan in the province of Elam' is mentioned Dan. viii. 2.

Μεσοποταμίαν. The country between the Euphrates and the Tigris.

Ἰουδαίαν. These would comprise the Jews from the neighbouring towns.

Καππαδοκίαν...Παμφυλίαν. These were all countries within Asia Minor, Pontus lying in the N.E. and forming, on the north, part of the shore of the Euxine. Cappadocia was south of Pontus, Phrygia was westward of Cappadocia, separated from it by Lycaonia, while Pamphylia stretched on the south coast of Asia Minor between Lycia on the W. and Cilicia on the E. By Asia in this verse, and everywhere else in the Acts is meant the Roman province known as Proconsular Asia. It comprised all the western coast of Asia Minor and may be roughly considered as embracing the countries known as Mysia, Lydia and Caria. Its capital was Ephesus, and in this district were the seven churches of the Apocalypse.

Αἴγυπτον. The cities of the north of Egypt, and especially Alexandria, were the abodes of great numbers of Jews.

Λιβύη was the name anciently applied to the African continent. The 'parts of it about Cyrene' means the district called Cyrenaica. This lay E. of the Syrtis Major and contained five chief cities of which

Cyrene was the best known. We find Simon a Cyrenian living in Jerusalem at the time of the Crucifixion (Matt. xxvii. 32). Josephus has a passage (*Antiq.* xiv. 7, 2) which testifies to the wide dispersion of the Jews at this time, and also mentions specially Egypt and the parts of Libya about Cyrene as full of them. It runs thus:

'Strabo in another place bears witness to this [the wealth and influence of the Jews]; saying that when Sulla crossed over into Greece to war against Mithridates, he also sent Lucullus to put down *in Cyrene* the revolution raised there by *our nation, of whom the whole world is full*. His words are: There were four classes in the city of the Cyrenians, that of citizens, that of husbandmen, that of resident aliens, and *the fourth of the Jews. Now this last class has already spread into every city, and it is not easy to find a place in the world which has not admitted this tribe and which is not swayed by them.* And with regard to Egypt and Cyrene as being under the same governors, and many portions of other countries, it has come to pass that they imitate them [the Jews], and also give special support to companies of the Jews, and flourish from their adoption of the ancestral laws of the Jews. For instance, in Egypt there is a special district set apart for the Jews, and beside this *a large part of the city of Alexandria is apportioned to this race.* And a special magistrate is appointed for them, who governs their nation and administers judgment, and takes charge of their contracts and agreements as if he were the governor of an independent state.' Philo *in Flaccum*, § 8, confirms what is said here about Alexandria, telling that two districts, out of the five into which that city was divided, were known as Ἰουδαϊκαί, while Jews also lived in parts of the other three.

οἱ ἐπιδημοῦντες Ῥωμαῖοι. Render, *sojourners from Rome, both Jews &c.* We know from the allusions to them in Latin writers that Jews were numerous in Rome (Hor. *Sat.* 1. 5; Juv. x. 14, &c.). It is most probable that converts from among these Romans founded the Church which we learn from Acts xxviii. 14, 15 was flourishing there when St Paul first came to that city.

προσήλυτοι. This word, signifying *one who has come over*, is mainly employed of converts from heathenism to the religion of the Jews. It is of very frequent occurrence in the LXX. of the last four books of Moses.

11. Κρῆτες. Natives of the well-known island which lies south of the Cyclades in the Mediterranean, and is now called *Candia*. Christianity may perhaps have been spread in Crete also from the converts of Pentecost. Titus was made bishop of Crete.

Ἄραβες. Inhabitants of the great peninsula which stretches between the Red Sea and the Persian Gulf.

τὰ μεγαλεῖα. Literally, *the great works* of God. *Vulg.* 'magnalia.' The word is rendered 'wonderful works' (as A.V.) in Ecclus. xxxvi. 8. In the same way it is said (xiii. 46) of the first Gentile converts on whom the Holy Ghost came, 'They heard them speak with tongues

and *magnify God.*' And of those to whom the Spirit was given at
Ephesus (xix. 6), 'They spake with tongues and *prophesied.*'

12. διηποροῦντο, *were perplexed.* They were in no doubt about
the facts. Their eyes and ears were trusty witnesses. But they were
at a loss how to account for what they heard and saw.

13. ἕτεροι δὲ κ.τ.λ., *but others mocking said: They are full of
new wine.* γλεῦκος, not a common word, is found in LXX. of Job
xxxii. 19

In the above description of the events of the day of Pentecost, the
meaning which St Luke intends to convey is very plain in every respect,
except that we cannot with certainty gather from it whether the disciples, as well as speaking new languages, also understood what they
uttered. It would seem most reasonable to conclude that the Holy
Spirit with the one power also bestowed the other, and this may have
been so in the case of the disciples at Pentecost, even though it was
not so at other times and under other circumstances. The only
Scripture which bears upon the question is St Paul's 1st Epistle to
the Corinthians (xii. 10—xiv. 30). There among the gifts of the
Spirit the Apostle enumerates "*divers kinds of tongues*" (xii. 10, 30)
and as what might be a separate gift not included in the first, "*the
interpretation of tongues*" (xii. 10). He mentions in the next chapter
the *tongues of angels* as well as of men (xiii. 1), but not in such an
enumeration as to connect the words with our inquiry. It should be
borne in mind that all which the Apostle says in the Epistle is addressed to the Corinthians, not as missionary labourers but as members
of a settled Christian Church, and he is instructing them what the
best gifts are after which they should seek. Now their labours and
utterances were to be among their own people and mostly among
those already professing Christianity. St Paul repeatedly dwells on
'the Church' as the scene of their labours, which expression without
necessarily always implying an edifice (which however here seems to
be its meaning, see xiv. 23, 24) indicates a Christian community. The
Apostle tells them that gifts of tongues are not for these. Tongues
are for a sign not to them that believe but to the unbelieving. To
speak with tongues was therefore not the best gift to be desired for
the Church at Corinth. Yet we can fancy that some members longed
for such a power, and it is to such as these that the Apostle's remarks
are directed. In such a congregation as theirs, he tells them, 'he
that speaketh in a tongue, speaketh not unto men, but unto God'
(xiv. 2), meaning to teach them that if a man had this gift he would
yet profit his neighbours nothing, for they would not be men of a
foreign speech like the crowd at Pentecost, or like those in foreign
lands which the Christian missionaries must visit. Next he adds
'he that speaketh in a tongue edifieth himself' (xiv. 4), for he feels
the power and tells of the great works of God. The Apostle could
wish 'they all spake with tongues,' if, that is, there were an advantage to the Church therein, but under their circumstances he
rather wishes for them the gift of prophecy, or power of exposition
of the Scriptures and preaching. We next come to those sentences

which bear directly upon our inquiry (xiv. 13), 'Let him that speaketh in a tongue pray that he may interpret.' There were then in the Corinthian Church examples of that division of these closely connected gifts which in the recital of spiritual gifts the Apostle seems to imply; some spake with tongues who could not interpret, and others could interpret who did not speak with tongues. And the next words confirm this view, 'If I pray in a tongue my spirit prayeth' (and in this way I edify myself), 'but my understanding is unfruitful.' Therefore the Apostle desires that form of power for himself which in a congregation shall exercise both spirit and understanding. He himself had this gift in great fulness, but in the Church it is not that which he would desire to use, lest the unlearned should not be able to say 'Amen' to his giving of thanks. For in the ordinary church-assembly if the gift of tongues were exercised, it would seem madness to those Corinthian unbelievers who came in, and heard a speaker uttering a foreign language to a congregation who were all Greeks, and their minister a Greek likewise. St Paul therefore ordains that if any man speak in a tongue in the Church, he must have an interpreter, or else must keep silence. From which ordinance also it appears that there were those who, though endowed with the gift of speaking with tongues, were yet not able to interpret to the congregation the words which they were empowered to speak.

In these passages we have all the references to this gift of the Holy Ghost which seem to help us to appreciate in some degree what its character was. Whatever may have been the case at Pentecost, certainly in the Corinthian Church the power of speaking seems not always to have had with it the power of interpretation, though in some cases it had, and all were to pray for the one to be given with the other. Yet in this whole account it is to be borne in mind that we have no indication that such gifts were frequent in Corinth, but only that the members of the Church longed to possess them. From this wish the Apostle dissuades them, because their duty was to minister to believers rather than to unbelievers, whereas on those occasions where the gift was most markedly bestowed, as related by the author of the Acts, viz. at the house of Cornelius, and in the heathen and multilingual maritime city of Ephesus, as well as at the outpouring on Pentecost, there was the probability of having an audience on whom such a display of God's gifts would be likely to produce the same kind of effect as that produced in Jerusalem on the first manifestation.

14—21. SKETCH OF ST PETER'S SERMON. REFUTATION OF THE MOCKERS.

14. Πέτρος σὺν τοῖς ἕνδεκα. The Twelve naturally take the leading place among the disciples, and Peter, who is usually the spokesman in the Gospels, begins the general address now, directing it principally to those who were dwellers in Jerusalem and the neighbouring country, for it was more likely to be these who gave vent to the mocking speeches than the foreigners who would better recognize the astounding nature of what had come to pass.

ἀπεφθέγξατο, *spake forth* unto them. The word is the same that is used to describe the gift which they had just received. 'They spake as the Spirit gave them *utterance*,' lit. 'to speak forth' (ii. 4). St Paul employs it when Festus had said he was mad. 'I *speak forth* the words of truth and soberness' (xxvi. 25).

ἐνωτίσασθε. The word signifies 'to take anything into the ears.' It is only found here in N.T. but is very common in the LXX., especially in the Psalms. Cf. also Gen. iv. 23 (Lamech's address); Job xxxii. 10, xxxiv. 16, xxxvii. 13.

15. μεθύουσιν. Wine was drunk by the Jews with flesh only, and, founding the custom on Exodus xvi. 8, they ate bread in the morning, and flesh in the evening, and so took no wine till late in the day. So Eccles. x. 16, 17, by the 'princes who eat *in the morning*' are meant those who eat to the full of all sorts of food and so take wine, and their opposites are next described as those who eat in due season for strength and not for *drunkenness*.

The paraphrase of this passage given in the Targum is worth notice in illustration of the text of the Acts. It reads, 'Woe to thee, O land of Israel, when there shall reign over thee Jeroboam the wicked, and shall exterminate from the midst of thee the offering of the morning sacrifice, and when thy lords shall eat bread before any man has offered the perpetual offering of the morning. Blessed art thou, land of Israel, at the time when Hezekiah the son of Ahaz (who is of the genealogy of the house of David) shall reign, who will be a mighty hero in the law, and fulfil all the duties of the commandments, and then thy princes shall only eat bread after the perpetual offering has been offered (i.e. their eating shall be) at the fourth hour, from the labour of their hands in the strength of the law, and not in faintness and blindness of the eyes.'

ὥρα τρίτη. Only one quarter of the day was over. The Jews divided the day and night each into twelve parts, calling them hours, though their length varied according as the daylight was less or more. When day and night were equal, the third hour would be nine o'clock in the morning.

16. διὰ τοῦ προφήτου, *through the prophet*. διὰ is the preposition generally used in such phrases, and denotes that the prophet was the instrument by whose intervention God spake. Joel himself (i. 1) calls his prophecy 'the word of the Lord that came unto Joel.' The quotation is from Joel ii. 28—32. The order of sentences differs here from the Hebrew (which is represented by the A.V. of Joel), but agrees with the LXX. very nearly, only for ἐν ταῖς ἐσχ. ἡμέραις the LXX. has μετὰ ταῦτα, and omits σημεῖα in verse 19.

17. ἐν ταῖς ἐσχάταις ἡμέραις. In the language of the Old Testament prophets these words signify the coming of the Messiah (cf. Is. ii. 2; Micah iv. 1).

18. καί γε may be rendered, *Yea and*, or *And truly*. Cf. Acts xvii. 27 where καί γε is the correct reading. The *Vulg.* gives 'et quidem.'

προφητεύσουσιν. Fulfilled also in the case of Agabus (xi. 28), and of the Ephesian converts (xix. 6), and of the daughters of Philip the Evangelist (xxi. 9).

19. τέρατα. Even when the Kingdom of Christ shall have come, mighty troubles will still prevail. Christ Himself gave the same lesson (Matth. xxiv. 21—30).

20. ἐπιφανῆ, *notable.* The Hebrew word in Joel means *terrible.* But the Hebrew verbs *to fear* and *to see* are often confounded in the LXX. version, with which the quotation in the text agrees. The prophecy of Joel had a partial fulfilment in the destruction of Jerusalem by Nebuchadnezzar, but it also looked onward to its later destruction by the Romans.

21. σωθήσεται. Eusebius (*H. E.* III. 5. 3) tells how the Christians were warned to leave Jerusalem before its destruction, and went into a city of Perea called Pella.

22—36. RECITAL OF GOD'S TESTIMONY BY THE RESURRECTION TO THE MESSIAHSHIP OF JESUS.

22. ἄνδρες Ἰσραηλῖται. As the prophecies which St Peter is about to put forward were given before the nation was rent into two parts, he calls them by a name which points to their union and common descent from Jacob.

Ἰησοῦν τὸν Ναζωραῖον. This accusative, taken up by the following τοῦτον, continues in suspense till the close of the next verse.

ἄνδρα. St Peter begins with the humanity of Jesus, as a point on which they would all agree.

ἀποδεδειγμένον. Publicly demonstrated, or *set forth.* Cf. the words of Nicodemus (John iii. 2) 'No man can do these miracles that thou doest except God be with him.' The sense of the participle is given by the gloss of D, which reads δεδοκιμασμένον.

εἰς ὑμᾶς. Render, *unto you.* The testimony was not given *among* them only (as A.V.), but *unto* them. Cf. John xii. 37 'Though He had done so many miracles before them yet they believed not on Him.'

δυνάμεσι κ.τ.λ. These distinct names are given to Christ's marvellous works according to the light in which they are viewed. The first name, δυνάμεις, lit. **powers,** is applied to them because they proclaimed the might of Him who wrought them; they are named τέρατα, **wonders,** because they called forth that feeling when they were wrought; and σημεῖα, **signs,** because they point out their author as divine.

οἷς. Attracted into the case of the antecedent, as in i. 1, though here that case is dative. See note there.

ὁ θεός. St Peter does not advance at once to the declaration that Christ is God, but speaks of Jesus as God's agent, in the mighty works which their own eyes had seen.

23. ἔκδοτον. Given up unto you as God had decreed He should be, for the sake of man's redemption.

διὰ χειρὸς ἀνόμων, *by the hand of wicked* (lit. lawless) *men.* διὰ χειρός is a literal translation of a Hebrew expression = by means of. Cf. Lev. viii. 36 'Things which the Lord commanded *by the hand* of Moses.' See also 2 Kings xiv. 25, though in both those passages the LXX. has ἐν χειρί. But διὰ χειρός in the same sense is found 2 Kings xiv. 27; 1 Chron. xi. 3, xxix. 5, &c.

24. τὰς ὠδῖνας τοῦ θανάτου. The expression occurs in LXX. Ps. xvii. 5, &c.

25. Δαυεὶδ κ.τ.λ. The passage which St Peter quotes is from Ps. xvi. 8—11, and he argues that it could not be of himself that the Psalmist there spake, for they had evidence that the words could not be truly said of him. But having regard to God's promise David spake of Him who was to be born from his line, as identified with himself. St Peter's quotation is from the LXX.

εἰς αὐτόν, *in reference to him.* The preposition indicates the direction of the thoughts of him who spoke. Cf. *Winer-Moulton*, p. 495.

προορώμην. The πρό is used here as a strengthening of the following ἐνώπιόν μου, and in the same sense. The *foresaw* of A.V. is equal to no more than *saw.* The Hebrew text would be rendered, *I set.*

26. ἡ γλῶσσά μου. The Hebrew = my glory. For this exposition of *glory,* cf. Ps. cviii. 1, where the A.V. has, according to the Hebrew, 'I will give praise even *with my glory,*' while the Prayer-Book Version renders 'with the best member that I have.' If however we are to be guided by the Hebrew parallelism 'the glory' is *the soul* or *life.* Cf. Ps. vii. 5, 'Let him tread my life upon the earth, and lay my glory (A.V. honour) in the dust.' On the use of a similar expression by the Arabs for any member of the body of special honour, see Gesenius s. v. כבוד‎.

κατασκηνώσει. Lit. *shall tabernacle.*

27. εἰς ᾅδην, *in Hades,* i.e. in the unseen world. So too in verse 31 where we have the more usual expression εἰς ᾅδου (understanding δόμον), but in the Psalm from which quotation is made, the best text of the LXX. gives the accusative there too.

δώσεις, *Thou wilt suffer* [lit. give].

τὸν ὅσιόν σου, *Thy Holy One.* The Hebrew word in the Psalm conveys the idea of *beloved,* as well as *godly* or *pious.*

28. πληρώσεις κ.τ.λ. This is an example of how the LXX. sometimes paraphrases. The Hebrew text literally translated is, 'in thy presence is fulness of joy.'

29. ἐξὸν εἰπεῖν. Here ἔστι is the verb to be supplied. Render 'It is allowed me = I *may* freely *say* unto you concerning the patriarch David that *he both died and was buried.*' Here St Peter begins his argument with a statement which none of them will gainsay. St Paul

makes use of the selfsame argument (xiii. 36) 'David after he had served his own generation...fell on sleep and was laid unto his fathers.'

τὸ μνῆμα. The existence of the sepulchre is evidence that David did not rise again. The sepulchre of the House of David was a famous object in the Holy City. Among the marvels of Jerusalem mentioned in the *Aboth de-Rabbi Nathan* (c. 35), we are told, 'There are no graves made in Jerusalem except the tombs of the House of David and of Huldah the Prophetess, which have been there from the days of the first prophets.'

On the burial of David in Zion, cp. 1 Kings ii. 10 with 2 Sam. v. 7.

30. ὅρκῳ ὤμοσεν. See Ps. cxxxii. 11 'Of the fruit of thy body will I set upon thy throne.'

ἐκ καρποῦ κ.τ.λ. Render, *of the fruit of his loins one should sit* [*or,* he would set *one*] *on his throne;* for καθίζειν is used both transitively and intransitively.

31. περὶ τῆς ἀναστάσεως τοῦ Χριστοῦ, *of the resurrection of the Christ,* i.e. the Messiah, Jehovah's Anointed.

ὅτι οὔτε ἐγκατελείφθη, *that neither was He left in Hades nor did His flesh,* &c. The ἡ ψυχὴ αὐτοῦ of the *Text. recept.* has been introduced to make this application accord more exactly with the words of the prophecy quoted in verse 27. At first perhaps the addition was innocently placed as a note on the margin, but the next copyist incorporated it.

32. ἀνέστησεν, *raised up* (from the dead). The word takes up the ἀνάστασις of the previous verse. The English cannot mark by similarity of word the forcible character of the Greek, which would be given in sense somewhat thus: 'David spake of a *resurrection,* which manifestly was not his own, but here is now come to pass the *resurrection* of Jesus, of which we all are witnesses.' The πάντες is probably to be confined to Peter and the Eleven, with whom he is more closely connected in this speech (see ver. 14) than with the rest.

33. ὑψωθείς, *exalted* (into heaven), for the Apostles are witnesses not only of the Resurrection but of the Ascension also.

τήν τε ἐπαγγελίαν πν. τ. ἁγ. Called in i. 4 ἡ ἐπαγγελία τοῦ πατρός. The promise was made by the Father, and the Holy Ghost was the gift promised. Christ's words were, 'I will pray the Father, and He shall give you another Comforter' (John xiv. 16). What was at first an ἐπαγγελία has now attained its fulfilment, so that λαβών implies the complete fruition of all that was promised.

ἐξέχεεν, *He hath poured forth.* Thus fulfilling the promise in the prophecy quoted verse 17: ἐκχεῶ ἀπὸ τοῦ πνεύματός μου.

βλέπετε καὶ ἀκούετε. It would seem from this that the appearance, like as of fire, which rested upon each of them, remained visible for some time, thus making it evident how different this was from any meteoric flashes into which some have endeavoured to explain away the miracle which St Luke describes.

34. οὐ...ἀνέβη, *he ascended not.* He went down to the grave, and 'slept with his fathers.'

λέγει δέ. The passage is from Ps. cx. 1. David saith, speaking as a prophet, and concerning the same person, whom though He is to be born of the fruit of his loins, he is yet taught by the Spirit to call his Lord. The words of this Psalm were admitted by the Jews themselves in their discourse with Jesus (Matt. xxii. 44, 45) to be spoken of the Christ.

κύριος τῷ κυρίῳ μου. The sense is, *the Lord* [Jehovah] *said unto* [Him whom I must even now call] *my Lord,* since I foresee how great He shall be.

κάθου ἐκ δεξιῶν μου. A common Oriental expression for sharing power and sovereignty. Cf. the request of the mother of James and John when she desired places of influence for her sons in the future kingdom, which she supposed would be an earthly one (Matth. xx. 21).

35. ὑποπόδιον. To put the foot on the neck of a prostrate enemy was in the Eastern world a token of complete conquest. (Cf. Josh. x. 24.)

36. γινωσκέτω. This appeal could only be made to Israel, for they alone knew of the promises and prophecies in which the Christ had been foretold.

ὅτι καὶ κ.τ.λ. Render, *that God hath made Him both Lord and Christ, even this Jesus whom ye crucified.* Thus closes the argument. Its steps are: Jesus, who has been crucified, has been by God raised from the grave, by God exalted to heaven, and set at His right hand, and thus proved to be the Lord and the Anointed One.

37—40. Effect of St Peter's Sermon.

37. κατενύγησαν τὴν καρδίαν. The verb, without the following noun, is found LXX. Gen. xxxiv. 7 (*were grieved* A.V.) and κατανενυγμένον τῇ καρδίᾳ, Ps. cviii. 16 of one 'broken in heart.' The sense here is, they were stung with remorse at the enormity of the wickedness which had been committed in the crucifixion, and at the blindness with which the whole nation had closed their eyes to the teaching of the prophecies which had spoken of the Messiah.

πρὸς τὸν Πέτρον κ.τ.λ. For these men, who had so clearly set before them the error of the whole people, were the most likely to know what could be done to atone for it.

ἄνδρες ἀδελφοί. See i. 16 note.

38. μετανοήσατε. This was in accordance with the directions of Jesus before His Ascension (Luke xxiv. 47) 'that repentance and remission of sins should be preached in His name.' On the omission of both ἔφη and φησίν in this verse, cf. Acts xxv. 22, xxvi. 28, where the best MSS. are without any verb=he said. It should be noticed that the *Vulg.* has 'Pœnitentiam (inquit) agite.'

βαπτισθήτω. The verb is here singular from the close connexion with the distributive ἕκαστος, but the plural with which the verse commenced is resumed immediately in λήμψεσθε.

The exhortation to baptism is in accord with Christ's injunction (Matth. xxviii. 19), and though there the baptism is directed 'to be in the name of the Father and of the Son and of the Holy Ghost,' and here it is only said 'in the name of Jesus Christ,' we are not to suppose any change made from the first ordinance, but only that as the Church was to be called Christ's, so in mentioning the Sacrament for the admission of its members His name was specially made prominent. It was belief in Christ as the Son of God which constituted the ground of admission to the privileges of His Church. This made the whole of St Peter's Creed (Matt. xvi. 16) when Christ pronounced him blessed.

δωρεὰν τ. ἁγ. πν. This is expressly stated to have been bestowed on some of the first converts (see viii. 17, x. 44, &c.), and the prompt repentance of these earliest hearers of the truth would not be without its reward.

39. ἐπαγγελία must be taken to embrace the same gifts which it included in i. 4 and ii. 33.

καὶ τοῖς τέκνοις. As under the old covenant the promises were made (Gal. iii. 16) 'to Abraham and his seed,' so is it to be under the new dispensation.

τοῖς εἰς μακράν. Peter knew from the first, we see, that the Gentiles were to be admitted to the same privileges as Israel. But Christ's commission said they were to preach *first* in Jerusalem and in Judæa. Peter needed the vision of the great sheet let down from heaven to tell him *when* God's time was come for the extension of the work; and though in his dream the natural prejudice of his race was asserted, yet when he awoke he went 'without gainsaying as soon as he was sent for' (x. 29), as he says to Cornelius. For Christ's words had been 'Go, teach *all nations.*'

The expression οἱ εἰς μακράν means those persons, whom to reach you have to go out *into* the distance.

προσκαλέσηται. Render, *shall call unto Him.* Thus the force of the preposition will be given, which disappears in A.V.

40. ἑτέροις τε λόγοις πλείοσιν. This is a very important statement. We learn from it that there is no attempt made by the writer of the Acts to produce more than the substance and character of what was here said. And we may be sure that he uses the same rule always. We need not therefore be startled if we find an address followed by mighty results, even though St Luke's abstract of it may only extend over a few verses.

διεμαρτύρατο, *he charged*, as 1 Tim. v. 21; 2 Tim. ii. 14, iv. 1. Peter's address was not of the nature of testimony but a direction what the penitents were to do.

σκολιᾶς. Literally *crooked.* The expression 'crooked generation' is found in A.V. (Deut. xxxii. 5) where the Greek of the LXX. is the

same as here and in Phil. ii. 15.   γενεὰ σκολιά is also the text in
Ps. lxxvii. (lxxviii.) 8.

41—47.   THE FIRST CONVERTS AND THEIR BEHAVIOUR.

41.   προσετέθησαν. Render, *there were added on that day about
three thousand souls*, i.e. to the hundred and twenty who composed the
community when the day began.   In *v.* 47 it is said '*the Lord* added.'

42.   προσκαρτεροῦντες. This means that they allowed nothing to
interfere with the further teaching which the Apostles no doubt gave
to the newly baptized.   The converts would naturally seek to hear all
the particulars of the life of Him whom they had accepted as Lord and
Christ, and such narratives would form the greatest part of the teaching of the Apostles at the first.

The phrase ἡ διδαχὴ τῶν ἀποστόλων has acquired a new interest
since the recent discovery and publication of a MS. with that title.
But the subjects treated of in this new discovery, a work manifestly of
the first or beginning of the second century, are not such as could be
spoken of immediately after the Pentecostal outpouring of the Spirit.
They relate to the Church when she has taken a firm hold on the
world.

κοινωνίᾳ, that communion, or holding all things common, of which
a more full description is given in the following verses, and which
would bind them most closely into one society.

Chrysostom calls this 'an angelic republic': τοῦτο πολιτεία ἀγγελικὴ
μηδὲν αὐτῶν λέγειν ἴδιον εἶναι. ἐντεῦθεν ἡ ῥίζα τῶν κακῶν ἐξεκόπη, καὶ
δι᾽ ὧν ἔπραττον ἔδειξαν ὅτι ἤκουσαν.

The omission of the conjunction after κοινωνίᾳ makes a division
between the educational and social duties on one hand, and the
strictly devotional on the other.

τῇ κλάσει τοῦ ἄρτου. The earliest title of the Holy Communion
and that by which it is mostly spoken of in Scripture.   (See Acts
xx. 7 ; 1 Cor. x. 16, &c.)   In consequence of the omission here and
elsewhere of any mention of the wine, an argument has been drawn
for communion in one kind.   But it is clear from the way in which
St Paul speaks of the bread and the cup in the same breath, as it were,
that such a putting asunder of the two parts of the Sacrament which
Christ united is unwarranted by the practice of the Church of the
Apostles.

It is worth notice that in the 'Teaching of the XII Apostles' to
which allusion has just been made, the directions concerning the cup
stand first.   See chap. 9 περὶ δὲ τῆς εὐχαριστίας, οὕτως εὐχαριστή-
σατε. πρῶτον περὶ ποτηρίου· κ.τ.λ.

ταῖς προσευχαῖς. There is the article here too.   Render, *the
prayers.*   See note on i. 14.

43.   πάσῃ ψυχῇ. Even the mockers were afraid to continue their
jeers in the face of such preaching and such lives.

τέρατα καὶ σημεῖα. See note on verse 22.   The purposes now
chiefly aimed at by the miracles were to arrest attention and bear

evidence to the new teaching. So they are not here spoken of as δυνάμεις.

44. ἦσαν ἐπὶ τὸ αὐτὸ κ.τ.λ. With the words of the angels still in their ears (i. 11) 'This same Jesus shall so come in like manner as ye have seen Him go into heaven,' the disciples were no doubt full of the thought that the return of Jesus was not far distant. Such an opinion spreading among the new disciples would make them ready to resign their worldly goods, and to devote all things to the use of their brethren. For so the spreading of a knowledge of Christ could be made the chief work of the whole body of believers.

45. κτήματα...ὑπάρξεις. The *Vulg.* distinguishes the words by rendering 'possessiones et substantias.' The former of the Greek words seems to imply those means which were at the time actively employed in the acquisition of more wealth; this would include farming and trade stock, &c., while ὕπαρξις refers rather to realized property (cf. however iv. 34). Soon, it seemed, there would be no need for either, and the produce of their sale was the most convenient form in which the bounty could be used for those who needed it.

καθότι ἄν τις χρείαν εἶχεν, *according as any man had need.* We gather from this that the first converts kept their homes and things needful for themselves, but held the rest as a trust for the Church to be bestowed whenever need was seen. This is an earlier stage than that in which the money was brought and put at the disposal of the Apostles.

The verb εἶχεν is in the indicative notwithstanding the preceding καθότι ἄν, because the writer's intention is to describe a fact, viz. that there were persons in need.

46. καθ' ἡμέραν τε κ.τ.λ., *and day by day attending continually with one accord,* &c.

At the Temple they were likely to meet with the greatest number of devout listeners; and we shall find that the first Christians did not cease to be religious Jews, but held to all the observances of their ancient faith, its feasts, its ritual, and its hours of prayer, as far as they could do so consistently with their allegiance to Jesus. We find (xxi. 20—24) the elders of the Church in Jerusalem urgent on St Paul that he should shew his zeal for the Law by taking upon him the vow of a Nazirite, and should so quiet the scruples of Jews, and of such Christian brethren who were more zealous for the Law than St Paul himself, and the Apostle saw no reason why he should not comply with their request.

κλῶντές τε κατ' οἶκον ἄρτον. Render, *breaking bread at home;* though the A.V., if rightly understood, gives the sense very well. What is meant is, that the specially Christian institution of the breaking of bread was not a part of the service in the Temple, but was observed at their own homes, the congregations meeting now at one house, now at another. The *Vulg.* has 'circa domos.' The connexion of the Lord's Supper with the Passover meal at its institution made the Christian Sacrament essentially a service which could be celebrated, as on the first occasion it was, in the dining-room of a dwelling-house.

τροφῆς, i.e. their ordinary meals.

ἀγαλλιάσει, *with gladness.* Because those who were able to contribute to the support of the poorer members of the Church were delighted to do so, and thus all over-anxious care for the morrow was removed from the whole community.

ἀφελότητι καρδίας. *Vulg.* 'simplicitate cordis.' Having but one end in view, that the faith of Christ should be as widely spread abroad as possible.

47. χάριν, *favour.* As it was said of Christ, 'The common people heard Him gladly' (Mark xii. 37), so it seems to have been with the Apostles. The first attack made on them is (iv. 1) by the priests, the Captain of the Temple, and the Sadducees.

τοὺς σωζομένους. For this use of the present participle in relation to a work or condition begun, but only as yet in progress and not complete, cf. LXX. Judges xiii. 8 (Manoah's question to the angel), τί ποιήσωμεν τῷ παιδίῳ τικτομένῳ; The child spoken of is not born, but will be, for God has promised it. So here the men were put into the way of salvation, but not yet saved, though made through hope to be heirs of salvation. The rendering of the text is, *and the Lord added day by day together such as were in the way of salvation.*

CHAPTER III.

Readings varying from the *Text. recept.*

1. Πέτρος δέ. In accordance with the change made in the last verse of chap. II.

7. ἤγειρεν αὐτόν with אABCG. The *Vulg.* has the pronoun twice expressed.

11. αὐτοῦ instead of τοῦ ἰαθέντος χωλοῦ with אABCDE. *Vulg.* 'cum teneret autem Petrum.'

13. Omit αὐτὸν after ἠρνήσασθε with אABC and many cursives. *Vulg.* 'et negastis ante faciem Pilati.'

18. αὐτοῦ after Χριστὸν with אABCDE. *Vulg.* 'Christum suum.'

20. προκεχειρισμένον is the reading of אABCDEP. The *Vulg.* favours the *Text. recept.* in giving 'qui prædicatus est.' But that sense is out of harmony with verse 25 where the people are called υἱοὶ τῆς διαθήκης. See notes.

21. τῶν ἁγίων for πάντων ἁγίων with אABCD. *Vulg.* 'per os sanctorum, &c.'

ἀπ᾽ αἰῶνος before αὐτοῦ with אABC. The *Vulg.* has 'suorum a sæculo prophetarum,' which does not leave ἀπ᾽ αἰῶνος to the end of the verse.

22. Omit γὰρ πρὸς τοὺς πατέρας with אABC. *Vulg.* 'Moses quidem dixit.'

26. Omit Ἰησοῦν with אBCDE and *Vulg.*

Cʜ. III. 1—10. Healing of the Lame Man at the Beautiful
Gate of the Temple.

1. ἀνέβαινον, *were going up.* The verb is in the imperfect
tense and to render it exactly adds much to the vividness of the
narrative. On the close attachment always seen between Peter and
John, Chrysostom observes, πανταχοῦ φαίνονται οὗτοι πολλὴν ἔχοντες
πρὸς ἀλλήλους ὁμόνοιαν. τούτῳ νεύει ὁ Πέτρος. ὁμοῦ εἰς τὸν τάφον ἔρχον-
ται οὗτοι. περὶ αὐτοῦ φησὶν τῷ Χριστῷ, οὗτος δὲ τί ;
The Temple stood above the city on Mt Moriah.

τὸ ἱερόν. While earnestly labouring for the spread of Christ's teaching, they did not cast off their regard for that schoolmaster which
had been appointed to bring men to Christ.

ἐπί. The preposition indicates the period of time *towards* which
their movement tended, and may be well rendered *for the hour,*
&c. They were on their way, and would get there at the time
appointed for prayer. This is not the most common use of ἐπί with
the accusative of time. It more frequently denotes that space of
time *over* which any action is extended. Cf. Acts xiii. 31 ἐπὶ ἡμέρας
πλείους=during many days. See *Winer-Moulton,* pp. 508, 509.

We read in Scripture of three specified hours of prayer in accordance with which the Psalmist speaks of his own custom (Ps. lv. 17),
'Evening, and morning, and at noon will I pray.' And in like
manner Daniel prayed 'three times a day' (Dan. vi. 10). Cf. also
'The Teaching of the twelve Apostles,' chap. 8, τρὶς τῆς ἡμέρας οὕτω
προσεύχεσθε. The hour of morning prayer was the third hour, and
Peter went up to the housetop to pray (Acts x. 9) about the sixth
hour, which was noon, and the evening prayer was this to which
Peter and John were going up.

ἐνάτην. This orthography has the support of much authority.
See Tischendorf's *Prolegomena,* p. 49, ed. 7.

At the Equinox the ninth hour would be three o'clock in the after-
noon, but when the daylight was longer it would be later, so that if
there were 18 hours' day and 6 hours of darkness, each hour of the
day would be an hour and a half long, and the hours of the night
only half an hour each. At such time the ninth hour would be at
half-past four. See ii. 15 note.

2. ἐκ. Just as when this preposition is used with words *directly*
indicative of time, the idea here contained in it is of a starting-point
since which a certain state has been continuous. Cf. Acts xxiv. 10,
ἐκ πολλῶν ἐτῶν ὄντα κριτήν. Render, *a certain man who was lame,*
otherwise ὑπάρχων is not represented.

ἐβαστάζετο...ἐτίθουν. The imperfect tenses imply that this was
done regularly every day, and the position in which he had been daily

set for the greater part of his forty years' life (see iv. 22) made it certain that he would be widely and well known. In the same fashion Bartimaeus sat by the wayside to beg (Mark x. 46).

πρὸς τὴν θύραν...ὡραίαν. The gateways of the Temple gave admission to the inner court from the court of the Gentiles and the court of the women. There were three on the north and the same number on the south, but the Beautiful Gate meant in this verse was probably the gate on the east which led from the court of the women. The other gates, Josephus says (*B. J.* v. 5, 3), were overlaid with gold and silver, but this one was 'made of Corinthian bronze, and much surpassed in worth those enriched with silver and gold.'

τοῦ αἰτεῖν, *to ask.* This form of construction of the infinitive with *τοῦ* to indicate *purpose* is abundantly common in N.T. and LXX. Cf. Gen. iv. 15, *καὶ ἔθετο κύριος ὁ θεὸς σημεῖον τῷ Κάϊν τοῦ μὴ ἀνελεῖν αὐτὸν πάντα τὸν εὑρίσκοντα αὐτόν.*

ἐλεημοσύνην. Not a classical word, but very common in the LXX., first, for the feeling of mercy which dictates the giving of alms, and then, for the gift itself, as here. For the latter sense see Tobit xii. 8, *ἀγαθὸν προσευχὴ μετὰ νηστείας καὶ ἐλεημοσύνης......καλὸν ποιῆσαι ἐλεημοσύνην ἢ θησαυρίσαι χρυσίον.* Also Ecclus. iii. 14, 30, xxxv. 2.

From this word comes the English *alms,* formerly spelt *almesse,* or *awmous,* and in German it has become *almosen.*

3. λαβεῖν. This infinitive is redundant. A similar pleonasm is found Mark i. 17.

4. ἀτενίσας δέ. So of St Paul in a similar case (xiv. 9). And doubtless too here Peter 'perceived that the man had faith to be healed.' For his first act after his cure—'he entered into the temple'—bespeaks a devout frame of mind, and we may judge that though his infirmity had kept him at the gate for forty years, he had felt earnestly a longing to enter.

5. ἐπεῖχεν, *gave heed.* The verb requires *τὸν νοῦν,* or something similar, to be supplied with it. The sense is 'turned (his attention).' Cf. Ecclus. xxxiv. 2, *ὁ ἐπέχων ἐνυπνίοις,* 'he that pays attention to dreams'; and verse 18 of the same chapter, *τίνι ἐπέχει;* 'To what does he pay attention?'

6. οὐχ ὑπάρχει μοι. The Apostles, we may see from this, made no claim for themselves upon the contributions of the richer converts. There seems to be a difference intended in the kind of possession, *ὑπάρχω* being used of the worldly belongings, *ἔχω* of the spiritual gifts, as being the best, and the most surely held.

Render the second clause, 'What I have that give I thee.' We are nowhere told how much time had passed since the day of Pentecost, but it is probable that this was not the first miracle which Peter wrought (see ii. 43). For he speaks as not without experience of what works God will enable him to do. His language is that of firm assurance, 'what I have,' though in a moment he adds 'in the name of Jesus Christ.'

Ναζωραίου. According to St John's account, the name Nazareth was included in the title on Christ's cross (John xix. 19), and we can see that the place was despised in the eyes of the Jews (John i. 46) from Nathanael's question to Philip. This despised origin, as well as the shameful death, of Jesus, was a stumblingblock to the Jews.

ἔγειρε καὶ περιπάτει. There is some variation in the MSS. here, some having only the last verb. As it stands, the text is exactly the same as the words which Christ used (Luke v. 23) at the cure of the paralytic. Hence objectors have alleged that St Luke in the Acts has based his history here on those recorded words of Jesus. But what is more natural than that St Peter at such a time when speaking and acting in Christ's name should employ Christ's very words?

7. αἱ βάσεις αὐτοῦ καὶ τὰ σφυρά. These words are found nowhere else in the N.T. They are of a technical character, and their use, together with the other features of exact description of the cripple's case, indicate that we have before us the language of the physician (Col. iv. 14). And it is hardly possible to dwell too strongly on indications of this kind, which indirectly mark in the history something which is likewise noted in the Epistles. Those who would assign the second century as the date of the composition of the Acts, must assume for their supposed writer the keenest appreciation of every slight allusion in the letters of St Paul, and at the same time an ability to let his knowledge peep out only in hints like that which we find in this verse. Such persons, while rejecting all that is miraculous in the story as we have it, ask us to believe in such a writer as would himself be almost a miracle, for his powers of observation and the skill with which he has employed them.

βάσις in the LXX. is generally used of some basement or foundation on which a thing may rest, but it occurs with the meaning of this verse in Wisdom xiii. 18, where, in speaking of an idolater, it is said he makes petitions περὶ ὁδοιπορίας [ἱκετεύει] τὸ μηδὲ βάσει χρῆσθαι δυνάμενον, 'for a good journey unto that which cannot set a foot forward.'

8. ἐξαλλόμενος, *leaping up.* Thus manifesting his faith by his instant obedience, though his limbs must have shrivelled with forty years' want of use.

περιεπάτει. Every word seems to express the man's joy. *He kept walking* is the sense of this imperfect.

εἰσῆλθεν, *he went in.* As we see afterwards, he did not want to leave his benefactors. Beside this, it was the best use he could make of his new powers, to go to the Temple with the other worshippers. Of this conduct Chrysostom says, διὰ τοῦ μετὰ τὸ ἄλλεσθαι αἰνεῖν τὸν θεόν, οὐκ ἐκείνους θαυμάζων ἀλλὰ τὸν θεὸν τὸν δι' ἐκείνων ἐνεργήσαντα· οὕτως εὐχάριστος ἦν ὁ ἀνήρ.

ἀλλόμενος. He cannot put his strength sufficiently to exercise by the calm pace of those who have been walking all their lives. His exultant 'leaping' was a part of his 'praising God.'

We can hardly fail to see, if we compare the narrative of this miracle with that of the similar one wrought at Lystra by St Paul (xiv.), to which we have already referred, that St Luke has used faithfully the materials with which he was furnished by 'eye-witnesses,' and has given the accounts as he received them without any colouring of his own. In this chapter we have a description such as a painter would desire; the scene is brought vividly before us, and all the characters are in lively action. It is just such an account as we find in St Mark's Gospel of the cure of the demoniac child (Mark ix. 14—27), and both are quite in accord with all that we know of St Peter's mode of speaking, and from St Peter it is most probable that the narrative in this chapter (like the substance of the Second Gospel) is derived. On the contrary, the story of the cure wrought at Lystra by St Paul is told in the fewest possible words and with no touch of the graphic power of which this description is so full. The difference bespeaks the faithfulness of the writer of the Acts, and shews us that he has left the narratives as they came to his hand, without any attempt to stamp on them an individuality of his own.

9. πᾶς ὁ λαός, *all the people.* There was no lack of testimony to the reality of the cure. Many of the witnesses must have known the cripple for years. The Jewish authorities (iv. 16) admit the unimpeachable character of the evidence.

10. ἐπεγίνωσκον. This verb is rendered *they took knowledge* in iv. 13, and that is the better sense here. It can hardly be intended to say that the whole of the people present knew the man. For the construction which brings from the predicate-sentence its subject and makes it the object in the antecedent clause, cf. below, ix. 20, ἐκήρυσσεν τὸν Ἰησοῦν ὅτι οὗτός ἐστιν ὁ υἱὸς τοῦ θεοῦ.

πρός with an accusative of the aim or purpose. Cf. xxvii. 12, πρὸς παραχειμασίαν, 'for the purpose of wintering in.'

11—26. St Peter's Discourse to the Crowd.

11. Σολομῶντος. As the name of Solomon was so intimately connected with the Jewish temple, it is natural enough that one of its porches (or cloisters) should be called after him. There is no account of any such porch in Solomon's own temple, but Josephus tells us (*Ant.* xx. 9. 7) that there was an eastern porch in Herod's temple called by this name. The mention of this feature in the building is a sign that the writer, from whom St Luke drew, was one acquainted with the localities about which he speaks, and that the account was written before the fall of Jerusalem, or he would not have said '*is called,*' or if he had done so would have been convicted of inconsistency of language by those to whom his work was first presented.

ἔκθαμβοι is in the plural, because the notion of λαός is a plural one.

12. ἰδὼν δέ. Seeing, viz. their astonishment, as we may gather from his opening words, τί θαυμάζετε.

ἀπεκρίνατο, *gave answer,* i.e. to their looks, for there had been no words. This word, like the Hebr. יַעַן, is frequently used for the first utterance of a speaker, unevoked by any question. Cf. (LXX. and Hebrew) Deut. xxi. 7, xxvi. 5, xxvii. 14. So too Acts v. 8, where

Peter is said to have *answered* Sapphira, though she had said nothing, as far as we are told, and where the Apostle's words are a *question.*

ἐπὶ τούτῳ, 'at this *man*,' as is evidenced by the pronoun being αὐτόν at the end of the verse.

ἰδίᾳ δυνάμει. As he had said to the crippled man, so now he makes it clear to the crowd, that the name of Jesus is the power to which the cure is due.

εὐσεβείᾳ. That extreme devotion to God was sometimes conceived to obtain miraculous power for its reward may be gathered from such narratives as the raising of the widow's son by Elijah (1 Kings xvii. 24). The mother seeing her son restored to her says, 'Now by this I know that thou art a man of God.' Cf. also Nicodemus' statement, John iii. 2.

πεποιηκόσιν τοῦ περιπατεῖν αὐτόν, *having made him to walk.* This genitive of the infinitive is such a harsh construction after a verb with which a direct infinitive would be expected, that it is worth while to give a few illustrations of it, mainly from the LXX. 1 Chron. xvii. 6 οἷς ἐνετειλάμην τοῦ ποιμαίνειν τὸν λαόν μου, compared with 1 Kings xvii. 4 καὶ τοῖς κόραξιν ἐντελοῦμαι διατρέφειν σε ἐκεῖ. So too Is. v. 6 ταῖς νεφέλαις ἐντελοῦμαι τοῦ μὴ βρέξαι εἰς αὐτὸν ὑετόν. The construction is also found Gen. xxxvii. 18 ἐπονηρεύοντο τοῦ ἀποκτεῖναι αὐτόν, Exod. ii. 18 διὰ τί ἐταχύνατε τοῦ παραγενέσθαι σήμερον; 'How is it that ye are come so soon to-day?' (A.V.) Cf. also *Acta Andr. Apocryph.* 14 ἄλλοι οὖν καὶ ἄλλοι ἐπετήδευον τοῦ λῦσαι αὐτόν, and *Acta Petri et Pauli,* 5, ᾐτήσαντο Καίσαρα τοῦ ἀποστεῖλαι ἐν πάσαις ταῖς ἐπαρχίαις αὐτοῦ.

13. ὁ θεὸς Ἀβραὰμ κ.τ.λ. The crowd of listening Jews must have been sorely troubled to be told that they had been guilty of such rebellion against the God of their fathers.

παῖδα αὐτοῦ, *His servant.* The use of this word would carry the minds of the hearers back, as St Peter no doubt intended, to Isaiah xlii. 1, 'Behold my *servant* whom I uphold,' a passage which St Matthew (xii. 18) applies to Jesus.

ἠρνήσασθε. When to Pilate's question (John xix. 15), 'Shall I crucify your king?' they had answered, 'We have no king but Caesar.'

κατὰ πρόσωπον. This is a rendering of a Hebrew form לִפְנֵי, and is common in the LXX. Cf. 1 Sam. xiv. 13, xvi. 8; 1 Kings i. 23.

κρίναντος. Render, *when he had given sentence to release Him.* For Pilate had pronounced Jesus innocent (John xix. 4).

14. τὸν ἅγιον. Whom even the demoniac (Mark i. 24) had confessed to be '*the Holy One* of God.'

φονέα, i.e. Barabbas, who had committed murder (Mark xv. 7; Luke xxiii. 19). Ἄνδρα seems here joined with φονέα, as ἄνθρωπος so often is with nouns that signify some occupation which is discreditable (γόης, συκοφάντης), to increase the odiousness of the term. So we have ἀνὴρ γεωργός for a tributary servant, LXX. Gen. xlix. 15, a sort of *adscriptus glebæ.*

THE ACTS H

15. ἀρχηγὸν τῆς ζωῆς, *the prince of life.* The same word applied to
Jesus (Heb. xii. 2) is rendered '*author* and finisher of our faith,' and in
the same epistle (ii. 10) 'the *captain* of their salvation.' It is probably
in the latter sense that St Peter, whose thoughts are on the resurrection, uses the word here, thinking of Christ as the firstfruits of them
that slept (1 Cor. xv. 20), but the other sense, that 'in Him was life'
(John i. 4), is also embraced in the word.

ἤγειρεν, *raised,* i.e. once for all.

οὗ. This pronoun takes up the preceding ὅν, and refers to Jesus,
'*whose witnesses we are.*' Not merely of the Resurrection did the
Apostles bear witness, but of all Christ's teaching and deeds. Cf. i. 22,
where Matthias was chosen to be such a witness.

16. καὶ ἐπὶ τῇ πίστει κ.τ.λ., *and on the ground of faith in His
name, His name hath made strong this man whom ye see and know.*
This use of *name*=power, and even as an absolute equivalent for God,
is very Jewish; cf. iv. 12. The usage grew out of such passages as
Ps. cvi. 8, 'He saved them for *His name's* sake.' In the literature of
the Jews great power was attributed to the name of God even when
only inscribed, e.g. as it was said in tradition to have been on the
rod of Moses. By this power he is reported to have wrought the
miracles in Egypt and in the wilderness. But St Peter's language
here explains that it is no such power of which he is now speaking,
for the name of Jesus does not work the miracle *per se*, but only
because of the faith of the believer.

For ἐπί=*on account of,* cf. Luke v. 5, ἐπὶ τῷ ῥήματί σου χαλάσω τὸ
δίκτυον=on account of thy bidding. See *Winer-Moulton,* p. 491, who
explains it as='induced by.'

ἡ πίστις ἡ δι' αὐτοῦ. Cf. the same Apostle's words (1 Pet. i. 21),
τοὺς δι' αὐτοῦ πιστούς, 'you who through Him are believers.' Christ
is 'the *author* and *finisher* of our faith.'

ὁλοκληρίαν, *complete soundness.* The word occurs in the LXX. Is.
i. 6, οὐκ ἔστιν ἐν αὐτῷ ὁλοκληρία. Also in later Greek writers, as Plutarch.

17. κατὰ ἄγνοιαν, *through ignorance.* Ignorance has many degrees
and may arise from many causes. The Jewish multitude were ignorant from want of teaching, their rulers from mental perverseness in
looking only on one part of the prophecies concerning the Messiah.
Yet of both of these it may be said that through ignorance (i.e. want of
knowledge, however caused) they crucified Jesus. Compare the words
of Chrysostom, ἀλλ' ὅμως δίδωσιν αὐτοῖς ἐξουσίαν ἀρνήσασθαι καὶ μετα-
γνῶναι ἐπὶ τοῖς γεγεννημένοις· μᾶλλον δὲ καὶ ἀπολογίαν ὑπὲρ αὐτῶν συντί-
θησιν εὐπρόσωπον, καὶ λέγει· ὅτι μὲν οὖν ἀθῷον ἀνῃρεῖτε, ᾔδειτε· ὅτι δὲ
τὸν ἀρχηγὸν τῆς ζωῆς, ἴσως ἠγνοεῖτε. καὶ ἐντεῦθεν οὐκ αὐτοὺς μόνους
ἀφίησιν ἐγκλημάτων, ἀλλὰ καὶ τοὺς τῶν κακῶν ἀρχιτέκτονας.

18. τὸν Χριστὸν αὐτοῦ. Render, *by the mouth of all the prophets
that His Christ should suffer.* The purpose of the whole of the Scripture is to set forth the redemption of men through the *suffering* of
Christ. So that from the first mention of the bruising of the heel of

the seed of the woman (Gen. iii. 15), there had been a constant chain of testimony that the Christ should suffer. The ignorance of the Jews was manifested in this, that they would only see what spake of the sovereignty of the Messiah, and so rejected Him who came to give His life as a ransom for men.

οὕτως. Emphatic. By turning your evil deed to a purpose of salvation. So Chrysostom, ὅρα πόσῃ τοῦ θεοῦ ἡ σοφία, ὅτ' ἂν ταῖς ἑτέρων πονηρίαις εἰς τὸ δέον ᾖ κατακεχρημένη.

19. μετανοήσατε, *repent;* seeing how great your offence is, but yet that sin done in ignorance may be pardoned.

ἐπιστρέψατε. Literally, *turn again,* i.e. from the evil of your ways. So (xi. 21) 'a great number believed and *turned* unto the Lord.' The phrase 'be converted' of the A.V. has received much augmentation of meaning since 1611.

ἐξαλειφθῆναι. A very common word in the LXX. for the blotting-out of offences. The idea is, they are written down, but may be erased. Cf. Jerem. xviii. 23, τὰς ἁμαρτίας αὐτῶν μὴ ἐξαλείψῃς. So Pss. l. (li.) 1, 11, cviii. (cix.) 14; 2 Macc. xii. 42.

ὅπως ἄν. These particles cannot be translated '*when* the times... shall come,' but '*that* the times...may come.' They indicate a purpose, the accomplishment of which still lies in doubt. So the Apostle's argument is, Repent, that your sins may be blotted out, *that in this way* (i.e. by your penitence) the times of refreshing-may come. ὅπως ἄν is rendered in this sense (Acts xv. 17), 'That the residue of men might [better *may*] seek after the Lord.' See also Luke ii. 35.

καιροὶ ἀναψύξεως. Literally, 'appointed times of refreshing.' These God hath appointed and keeps in His own power, but the penitence of men can hasten them. They are called 'times of refreshing,' i.e. peace and blessedness, for the Apostle describes them afterwards as the coming of the Christ. But by the prophecies which he quotes he shews that the refreshing is for those only who repent (vers. 23) and hear the prophet whom God sends. The anticipation of a speedy return of Christ from heaven was common among the first believers. St Peter here does not directly state this opinion, but we can see how current it was from St Paul's Second Epistle to the Thessalonians, where he finds it necessary to warn the Christians of that Church against the disquiet which the immediate expectation of the second Advent was causing among them.

ἀνάψυξις is used in LXX. Exod. viii. 15 of the relief which Pharaoh felt when the plague of frogs was removed.

20. καὶ ἀποστείλῃ. The construction is continued from ὅπως ἄν in the previous verse. Render, *and that He may send.*

προκεχειρισμένον, *the Christ which was appointed for you,* **even Jesus**. This reading and sense agree with the proof which St Peter presently cites (ver. 25), 'Ye are the children of the covenant which God made with our fathers.' The Christ, the Messiah had been appointed and promised unto the Jewish nation, and now the promise of the covenant is fulfilled in Jesus.

21. δέξασθαι. And Peter and the rest could bear witness that He was gone into heaven, His work on earth being finished.

ἀποκαταστάσεως πάντων, *restoration of all things*, i.e. at Christ's second coming. But this phrase, 'the restoration of all things,' is used in two senses in N.T. For it is said (Matt. xvii. 11 ; Mark ix. 12) that Elias must 'first come and restore all things.' There the beginning of Christ's Kingdom is meant. As Christ's death was for all men's redemption, the restoration of all things may be said to have begun then. In the present verse the words have reference to the time when the course of that restoration shall be completed.

ὧν ἐλάλησεν. For the attraction of the relative, see note on **i. 1.** Render, *of which* [times] *God hath spoken.*

22. Μωϋσῆς μέν, *Moses indeed said.* Here the Apostle cites the prophecies to which he has been alluding. First from Deut. xviii. 15 (though not quoting the LXX. quite exactly) he points out that the prophet who had been promised was to be of their brethren, as Moses had been. This was a comparison which the Jews themselves were fond of making, and they often identified the prophet of whom Moses spake with the Messiah. Thus the *Midrash Rabbah* on Eccl. i. 9 says, 'Rabbi Berakhiah in the name of Rabbi Yizkhak [Isaac] says : "As was the former redeemer so shall the latter redeemer be." While of the former redeemer it is said (Exod. iv. 20), "And Moses took his wife and his sons and set them upon an ass," so of the latter: for it says (Zech. ix. 9), "He is lowly and riding upon an ass." And while the former redeemer brought down manna, as it says (Exod. xvi. 4), "Behold I will rain bread from heaven for you," so the latter redeemer will bring down manna. For it says (Ps. lxxii. 16), "There shall be abundance of corn in the earth." And as the former redeemer caused the well to spring up (see Num. xxi. 17), so the latter redeemer shall also cause the waters to spring up. For it says (Joel iii. 18), "A fountain shall come forth of the house of the Lord, and shall water the valley of Shittim."'

ὡς ἐμέ, *like unto me.* This is a rendering of the Hebrew כ, and is very common in the LXX. Cf. Jud. viii. 18 καὶ εἶπαν Ὡς σὺ ὡς αὐτοί, εἰς ὁμοίωμα υἱοῦ βασιλέως.

ἀκούσεσθε, i.e. those who have 'ears to hear' when the prophet comes and speaks. The next verse shews that all the nation were not included in the 'ye.'

24. καὶ πάντες δὲ οἱ προφῆται. To other prophecies St Peter only makes a general reference. We learn (*Midrash Shemuel*, c. 24) that Samuel was called by the Jews the Rabban, the chief and teacher, of the prophets and there are several reasons why he is put in this foremost place. (1) We never read of a school of the prophets before his time. (2) His mother Hannah is the first person in Holy Writ who speaks of the Messiah (1 Sam. ii. 10), 'God's anointed.' (3)

Jewish tradition says that the man of God who came to Eli (1 Sam. ii. 27) was Elkanah. The Targum on 1 Sam. x. 12, 'But who is their *father?*' explains *father* by *Rabbi*, and refers the word to Samuel, so that the question in that verse would imply, 'Why do you wonder at Saul among the prophets? Who is it that instructs the prophets? Is it not Samuel? And has not Saul been with him just now and been anointed by him?' All this could be said without the speaker having any knowledge that Saul was to be king. For the use of *father* as=*teacher* or *Rabbi* cf. Elisha's cry to Elijah (2 Kings ii. 12), 'My father, my father.'

ὅσοι ἐλάλησαν καὶ κατήγγειλαν. Render, *as many as spake they also told of these days*. The προ which is prefixed to the latter verb in the *Text. recept.* seems to have been introduced with the notion that the words of a prophet must of necessity be predictive. Whereas the prophet was one who spake *for* God, gave a message in His name, but was not necessarily a foreteller of the future.

25. υἱοὶ τῶν προφητῶν. Render, *sons of the prophets*, i.e. of the same race as they, and hence what they spake is meant for you. For you is the prophet raised up whom Moses foretold.

καὶ τῆς διαθήκης, and [sons] *of the covenant*, i.e. heirs to its promises and obligations. So (2 Kings xiv. 14) *hostages* are called literally *sons of the pledgings* or compacts. LXX. οἱ υἱοὶ τῶν συμμίξεων. So the two anointed ones are called LXX. Zech. iv. 14 υἱοὶ τῆς πιότητος.

λέγων. The quotation is from Gen. xxii. 18, but the LXX. instead of πᾶσαι αἱ πατριαὶ has πάντα τὰ ἔθνη.

26. ὑμῖν πρῶτον. That the house of Israel might first receive the blessing, and be God's instruments in spreading it abroad.

ἀναστήσας. The word is used here not of the resurrection of Jesus, but recalling the promise of Moses, cited in *v.* 22 that a prophet should be *raised up* (ἀναστήσει κύριος) and sent unto the people.

τὸν παῖδα αὐτοῦ, *His servant*. See note on verse 13.

εὐλογοῦντα, *to bless you* (literally, *blessing you*), i.e. by the appointed times of refreshing alluded to in verse 19. The way and means to this blessing is to be by the repentance and turning again to which the Apostle has been exhorting them. And to effect this they must turn away from their iniquities, but for doing this he assures them they will find present help in Christ.

Such a construction as this of a present participle after an aorist tense has sometimes been explained as though it were equal to a future. It is better to regard the action expressed by the participle as having begun from the point of time indicated by the verb. So here, the blessing was ready for the faithful as soon as ever Christ was sent. Cf. *Winer-Moulton*, p. 429.

ἐν τῷ ἀποστρέφειν, *in turning away* every one of you from his iniquities. This word is very common in the LXX. in this sense.

See Ezek. xviii. 27, ἐν τῷ ἀποστρέψαι ἄνομον ἀπὸ τῆς ἀνομίας αὐτοῦ. Also Ezek. iii. 19, xxxiii. 14 and Jonah iii. 10, ἀπέστρεψαν ἀπὸ τῶν ὁδῶν αὐτῶν τῶν πονηρῶν.

CHAPTER IV.

Readings varying from the *Text. recept.*

6. Ἄννας κ.τ.λ. All the names in this verse are in the nominative with אAB. The *Vulg.* has also nominatives but the construction of the previous verse in the Latin brings the words there also into the same case.

8. τοῦ Ἰσραὴλ omitted with אAB. The *Vulg.* also omits, but reads 'Principes populi et seniores, audite.'

11. οἰκοδόμων instead of οἰκοδομούντων with אABD. The *Vulg.* has a participle.

17. ἀπειλῇ omitted with אABD. Unrepresented in the *Vulg.*

18. αὐτοῖς omitted with אABDE. The *Vulg.* gives the pronoun only once, 'vocantes eos.'

19. εἶπον πρὸς αὐτούς with אABDE, and the *Vulg.* agrees with this.

24. ὁ Θεὸς after σὺ omitted with אAB. *Vulg.* has 'tu es qui fecisti.'

25. ὁ τοῦ πατρὸς ἡμῶν διὰ πνεύματος ἁγίου στόματος Δαυεὶδ παιδός σου. This is the reading of אABE. The *Vulg.* in some degree confirms it, having 'qui Spiritu sancto per os patris nostri David, pueri tui.' But the reading is full of difficulty and there is probably some error. The *Vulg.* would seem to have had τοῦ πατρὸς ἡμῶν after στόματος, and, it may be, another διὰ preceding that word. Dr Hort suggests that τοῦ πατρὸς may be a corruption for τοῖς πατράσιν, and that στόματος &c. may be taken in apposition with what precedes, the mouth of David being represented as the mouth of the Holy Ghost.

27. After ἀληθείας add ἐν τῇ πόλει ταύτῃ with אABDE. *Vulg.* 'in civitate ista.'

32. ἡ omitted before καρδία and ψυχή with אABD.

33. δυνάμει μεγάλῃ (the order of the *Vulg.*) with אABD and several cursives.

34. ἦν for ὑπῆρχεν with אABF.

36. Ἰωσὴφ with אABDE and *Vulg.*, also several cursives and some other versions.

Ch. IV. 1—12. First Arrest of the Apostles. Their Hearing
AND DEFENCE.

1. λαλούντων δέ. Some little time must have elapsed since Pentecost, for now the movements of the Apostles have become a matter of
concern to the Jewish authorities. See their complaint (v. 28). There
is no note of time at the beginning of chap. iii. It need not have been
a long period, for news soon spread in the city, as we learn from the
events related in the previous chapter.

ἐπέστησαν, *came upon them*, i.e. to arrest them. The same word
is used (xxiii. 27) of the action of the chief captain. See note there.

οἱ ἱερεῖς. Those whose duty it was at the time to take charge of the
Temple services, and who probably had taken offence at the multitudes
assembled in the Temple court. The division of the priests was into
twenty-four courses, each of which was to serve in the Temple for
a week, see 1 Chron. xxiv. 1—19; 2 Chron. xxiii. 8. It was during
such service in the order of his course, that the promise of the birth of
John the Baptist was made to Zacharias the priest (Luke i. 5—8).
Some versions render *high-priests*, but these were only gathered to the
council on the following day.

ὁ στρατηγὸς τοῦ ἱεροῦ. There is mentioned in the O. T. an officer
whose title is 'the ruler of the house of God,' ὁ ἡγούμενος οἴκου κυρίου
(or τοῦ θεοῦ), (1 Chron. ix. 11; 2 Chron. xxxi. 13; Neh. xi. 11). He
was not a military officer, but had charge of the guard of priests and
Levites who watched the Temple at night. There are two titles given
to such an officer in the later writings of the Jews. (1) the *memunneh*
(T. Babl. *Tamid* I.), a kind of prefect of the Temple guard; and (2) a
higher officer called 'the captain of the mountain of the [Lord's]
house.' (T. Babl. *Middoth* II.) Rabbenu Shimshon describes this
second officer as 'the Commander who was set over every watch of
those that watched in the less sacred portion of the Temple.' He was
apparently a civil as well as a religious official, for we find (v. 26) that
he goes with 'the officers' to make the second arrest of the Apostles.

οἱ Σαδδουκαῖοι. This was the name of one of the most influential
sects among the Jews in our Lord's time. Their name has been
variously explained. The Jewish authorities state that the name,
which they write *Tsedukim*, is derived from *Tsadok* (Zadok) the proper
name, and that thus they are 'the followers of Zadok.' The Zadok
from whom they derive the title is said to have been a disciple of
Antigonus of Socho. This Antigonus is the second in order of the
Jewish Fathers whose sayings are recorded in the *Pirke Aboth*, and
the commentators thereon mention two of his pupils, Baithos and
Zadok, to the latter of whom and to his followers they attribute the
teaching that 'there was nothing for them in the world to come.' But
it is perhaps more probable, from their constant connexion with the
priests, that the name of the Sadducees was derived from the more
famous Zadok who became high priest in the reign of king Solomon
(1 Kings ii. 35). We read of the distinction of his descendants as
'the sons of Zadok,' and 'the priests the Levites of the seed of

Zadok,' even as late as the description of Ezekiel's temple (Ezek. xl. 46, xliv. 15). The probability of this priestly descent of the sect of the Sadducees is strengthened by the way in which they are mentioned Acts v. 17, 'Then rose up *the high priest and all they that were with him* (*which is the sect of the Sadducees*).' The derivation which makes their name the plural of the Hebrew adjective *Tsaddik*, =righteous, has not much authority to support it.

The teaching of the Sadducees is partly described (Acts xxiii. 8). They 'say that there is no resurrection, neither angel nor spirit.' In addition to this they attached no authority to the Oral Law, while the Pharisees maintained that the greater portion thereof had been transmitted to them from Moses. The Sadducees also taught the doctrine of the freedom of the will of men. The statement that they rejected all the Old Testament Scriptures except the Pentateuch has no confirmation in Josephus, and has arisen from a confusion of the Sadducees with the Samaritans. Josephus (*Antiq.* xviii. 1. 4) says 'their doctrine is accepted only by a few, but yet by those of the greatest dignity,' a statement fully borne out by the influential position in which we find them when the history of the Acts opens. They play no very prominent part in the Gospel history, because the teaching of Christ while on earth was directed more specially against the formalism and outward show of religion that prevailed among the Pharisees. It is when the doctrine of the resurrection begins to be preached that the hostility of the Sadducees makes itself most apparent.

2. διαπονούμενοι. The word is found in LXX. (Eccles. x. 9) of the pain and risk which a man incurs in removing stones. Here the pain is mental, they were *sorely grieved*. It is used (xvi. 18) of St Paul's feeling when the 'damsel possessed with a spirit of divination' cried after him at Philippi.

Chrysostom's words on this sentence are: διεπονοῦντο οὐ μόνον ὅτι ἐδίδασκον, ἀλλ' ὅτι οὐκ αὐτὸν μόνον ἔλεγον ἐγηγέρθαι, ἀλλὰ καὶ ἡμᾶς δι' ἐκεῖνον ἀνίστασθαι. οὕτως ἰσχυρὰ ἐγένετο ἡ ἀνάστασις ὡς καὶ ἑτέροις αὐτὸν αἴτιον γενέσθαι ἀναστάσεως.

διδάσκειν. The scribes and priests would have made teaching a monopoly of their own, and would be the more vexed because these new teachers were ἄνθρωποι ἀγράμματοι. See verse 13.

καταγγέλλειν ἐν τῷ Ἰ. κ.τ.λ. Render, *and published in Jesus the resurrection from the dead.* This would rouse the feelings of the Sadducees. The resurrection is said to be *in* Jesus, because His resurrection was a pledge that all should rise. '*In* Christ all shall be made alive' (1 Cor. xv. 22). The language of the Apostles in the Acts does not dwell on this as a consequence of the resurrection of Jesus, for the Apostles set forth at first what was historical rather than doctrinal teaching. Their language was a proclamation, not an argument.

τὴν ἀνάστασιν τὴν ἐκ νεκρῶν, *the resurrection from the dead.* Here this expression seems to mean exactly the same as ἀνάστασις νεκρῶν in xxiv. 21, viz. the general resurrection. The latter expression is the more common, being found nine or ten times (in Acts xxiv. 15 modern editors omit νεκρῶν), and means most frequently the general resurrection, though it is applied to Christ's resurrection in Acts xxvi. 23; Rom. i. 4; while in 1 Cor. xv. 21 it signifies the general resurrection implied in the particular raising up of Jesus.

ἡ ἀνάστασις τῶν νεκρῶν is found twice (Matt. xxii. 31; 1 Cor. xv. 42) of the general resurrection; and the form in this verse (ἡ ἀνάστασις ἡ ἐκ νεκρῶν) is found again in Luke xx. 35, there, as here, signifying the resurrection of all men. Like this is ἡ ἐξανάστασις ἡ ἐκ νεκρῶν of Phil. iii. 11. And we have once (1 Pet. i. 3) ἀνάστασις Ἰησοῦ Χριστοῦ ἐκ νεκρῶν.

When the verb (ἐγείρω, ἀνίστημι, &c.) is used, the preposition which most usually follows it is ἐκ; commonly ἐκ νεκρῶν, now and then ἐκ τῶν νεκρῶν. In St Matthew we have, three times, ἀπὸ τῶν νεκρῶν (xiv. 2, xxvii. 64, xxviii. 7).

It appears that the preposition most commonly employed after the verb was also put after the derived noun (as 1 Pet. i. 3); and once or twice the preposition was used, as here, in the adjectival form (ἡ ἐκ νεκρῶν) appended to the noun.

Those sentences where the verb is used refer nearly always to Christ's coming up from among the dead, or to some particular rising, like that of Lazarus or John the Baptist; but once in Mark xii. 25 there is a wider sense. Where the noun is found the phrase is nearly always of the general resurrection, though the examples given above shew that it is sometimes restricted to our Lord's rising again.

3. τήρησιν, *ward*, safe keeping, i.e. in a prison-house. And it is worth noticing on the use of it, that the Jews only employed imprisonment for this precautionary purpose. It was not a mode of punishment with them, and where we find mention of it so used in the Scripture records, the authorities who inflicted it were not Jewish.

ἑσπέρα ἤδη, *already eventide*. The Apostles had gone up to the Temple about the ninth hour, so sundown would soon come on, and the Jews were not allowed to give judgment in the night, while their day ceased at the twelfth hour. The Rabbis founded the prohibition on Jer. xxi. 12, 'O house of David, thus saith the Lord, Execute judgment *in the morning*.' In Mishna *Sanhedrin* IV. 1 it is said: 'Judgments about money may be commenced in the day and concluded in the night, but judgments about life must be begun in the day and concluded in the day.' And even the rule about the declaration of the new moon, which was looked on as a judicial proceeding, is similarly regulated (Mishna *Rosh ha-Shanah* III. 1), and it may not be declared unless the examination of the witnesses and all other preliminaries enjoined before its proclamation be completed before dark.

4. πολλοὶ δέ, *but many* &c.; i.e. they were not deterred by the arrest of the Apostles.

ἐπίστευσαν, *believed*, i.e. on Him (Jesus) whom Peter had set before them as the Prophet of whom Moses had spoken.

ἐγενήθη, *came to*, *amounted to*. Thus the Christian brotherhood had gained nearly two thousand adherents since the day of Pentecost (cf. ii. 41).

5. ἐπὶ τὴν αὔριον, *on the morrow*, when the investigation was permitted to be held.

τοὺς ἄρχοντας καὶ τοὺς πρεσβυτέρους. Here we may see that the party of the Sadducees was at this time the party of power and influence.

καὶ τοὺς γραμματεῖς. Not only did the Scribes copy, but they also expounded the Law. And the teaching of the followers of Jesus would probably differ as much as did His own from the lessons of the Scribes. Cf. Matth. vii. 29.

ἐν Ἱερουσαλήμ. This is the preposition in the best MSS. Some of the authorities may have resided away from the city, and had to be summoned. Hence συναχθῆναι, to be gathered together.

6. καὶ Ἄννας ὁ ἀρχιερεύς, *and Annas the high-priest was there.* The verb in this sentence is understood. Annas (called Ananus in Josephus) son of one Seth was made high-priest (A.D. 7) by the Roman governor Quirinus [Cyrenius], and so continued till A.D. 14 (Joseph. *Antiq.* XVIII. 2. 1). We do not find that he was ever again appointed to the office, though St Luke here calls him high-priest. But the way in which he is mentioned at the time of the trial of Christ, who was brought, as we read, before Annas first (John xviii. 13), and sent by him afterwards bound unto Caiaphas, shews that, though not actual high-priest, yet in the eyes of the people of Jerusalem his position was one which justified them in bringing Jesus to him as soon as he was seized. It is difficult to explain from the words of the New Test. the relation of these two men in their office. Caiaphas is expressly called high-priest by St John, yet we are not told why Christ was not at once brought to him. It may be that one was acting high-priest, while the other was *nasi* or president of the Sanhedrin. Moreover it is not improbable that Annas, having been high-priest before, and only deposed from the office by the Roman governor Gratus, would, both during the short high-priesthood of his son Eleazar (A.D. 16), and the longer high-priesthood of Caiaphas, his son-in-law (A.D. 25—37), exercise much influence by reason of his age and experience, and might from his former tenure of the office even be spoken of as high-priest. It is clear that he was at the head of one of the most influential Jewish families, for before his death, five of his sons had been high-priests (Joseph. *Antiq.* xx. 9. 1). We can see from Luke iii. 2, where both Annas and Caiaphas are said to be high-priests, that there was some laxity in the common use of the title. So far only does the New Testament carry us, but when we come to examine the Old Testament, and the records of later Jewish literature, there seems every reason to conclude that the expressions which seem somewhat hard to reconcile are exactly those which would naturally be employed. We find that Moses, who is himself counted (Ps. xcix. 6) high-priest on the same level with Aaron, anointed not Aaron only, but his sons at the same time (Exod. xl. 12—15) to be high-priests. Also (Numb. xxxi. 6) Phinehas the son of Eleazar is sent to the war against the Midianites with 'the holy

instruments' (i.e. the Urim and Thummim), which shews that he was high-priest at the same time as Eleazar his father. Again in later times (2 Kings xxv. 18) we have mention made of 'Seraiah the chief priest and Zephaniah the second priest,' which the Targum explains as 'high-priest and Sagan' or deputy high-priest. The Talmud makes it very clear that there was a special arrangement for providing on some occasions such a deputy for the high-priest. Thus (Mishna *Joma* I. 1) it says, 'Seven days before the day of atonement they remove the high-priest from his house to the chamber of the assessors, and they provide another priest in his place lest any disqualification should befall him.' On this passage Rashi's note is '*to be high-priest instead of him*': and a little later on in the same treatise (T. B. *Joma* 39 a) it is said concerning the services of the Day of Atonement: 'Rabbi Khanina the Sagan of the priests (and so one qualified to speak on the duties of the office) said: "Why does the Sagan stand on the right hand of the high-priest (when the lots are being cast for the goats)?" The answer is, "So that if any disqualification should befall him, the Sagan may go in (to the Holy of Holies) and perform the service in his stead."' Cp. also *Midrash Rabbah* on Leviticus (par. 20 *ad fin.*). 'If there was any defilement on Aaron, Eleazar served (as high-priest), and if there was any defilement on Eleazar, Ithamar served.' (On the slight matters which caused such ceremonial defilement, see note on x. 28.) And in the same chapter we find 'Had not Elisheba (Exod. vi. 23, the wife of Aaron) joy in this world who saw five crowns (i.e. subjects for rejoicing) in one day; her brother-in-law (Moses) a king (Deut. xxxiii. 5); her brother (Naashon) *nasi*, i.e. president of the Sanhedrin; her husband high-priest; her two sons, Sagans of the high-priest; and Phinehas her grandson anointed for the war?' These notices make it clear that from the earliest times down to a period posterior to the date of the Acts, there were occasions, and these not unfrequent, when two men were called high-priests at the same time.

That one who had been high-priest should still retain the title may be seen from the principle laid down in several places in the Talmud, (see Mishna *Shekalim* VI. 6, *ed. princ. Jerus.*), viz. that 'you may elevate in a sacred office or service, but you cannot bring down': as with us 'once a Bishop, always a Bishop.' The illustration given is that you might lay the shewbread on a marble table first, and after-wards on a golden one, but the contrary order of proceeding was for-bidden. (For another illustration, see note on vi. 3.) Therefore Annas, having been high-priest could, according to Jewish usage, never be called by any lower title.

The relationship between Annas and Caiaphas and the seniority of the former is enough to explain the conduct of the crowd in bringing Jesus to him first: while the omission of the word high-priest (Acts iv. 6) with the name of Caiaphas is no more a proof that he was not also known to be high-priest, as well as Annas, than the words of St Mark's Gospel (xvi. 7), 'Go your way, tell His disciples and Peter' can be made evidence that Peter was not one of the disciples. For a similar phrase see chap. v. 29 and the note there.

καὶ **Καϊάφας**, *and Caiaphas*. He was called Joseph Caiaphas (Joseph. *Ant.* XVIII. 22), and was son-in-law of Annas.

καὶ **Ἰωάννης**, *and John*. This is the same name as Johanan, and Lightfoot concludes that this person was the famous Johanan ben Zaccai, who by his influence with Vespasian procured permission for many of the Jews to settle in Jamnia (Jafneh) after the destruction of their city, and himself became head of the synagogue there.

καὶ **Ἀλέξανδρος**, *and Alexander*, of whom we have no other notice than this. The adoption of a Greek name, and his being by that best known, is a sign that foreign influence was at this time strong among the Jews.

ἀρχιερατικοῦ. The adjective is of rare occurrence. It occurs of the chief priest's dress τὸ ἔνδυμα τὸ ἀρχιερατικόν in the *Acta Philippi in Hellade* §§ 9 and 23; also Joseph. *Ant.* XI. 8. 2. Here 'the kindred of the high priest' would most likely all of them belong to the sect of the Sadducees.

7. ἐν τῷ μέσῳ, *in the midst*. The council or Sanhedrin was assembled in the *Beth-din* or Judgment-hall.

ἐν ποίᾳ δυνάμει, *by what power*. The noun here is the same which is used often for 'a mighty work,' and so has the force of 'miraculous power.'

ἢ ἐν ποίῳ ὀνόματι. Literally 'in what name.' But ὄνομα is constantly used in the sense of *authority*. In this second member of the sentence, the literal translation is the most forcible. Cf. Peter's very words in iii. 6.

8. πνεύματος ἁγίου. The Spirit of God which had come upon him had changed Peter 'into another man.' Cf. 1 Sam. x. 6.

ἄρχοντες τοῦ λαοῦ. This was the highest tribunal which the Jews possessed.

καὶ πρεσβύτεροι. The council was composed of the *chief priests*, i.e. the heads of each of the twenty-four classes into which the priests were divided, the *scribes*, men who were skilled in all the Jewish law, and the *elders*, grave and learned men chosen to complete the number, which is stated to have been in all seventy-one.

9. εἰ. This conjunction followed as here by the verb in the indicative = if, as is really the case; and so in sense is equivalent to ἐπεί, since, but may still be rendered 'if.'

ἀνακρινόμεθα κ.τ.λ. Render, *we are examined concerning a good deed done to an impotent man*. Both the nouns are without the article. This of itself however is not conclusive, as may be seen below in verse 11, εἰς κεφαλὴν γωνίας. Not unfrequently after a preposition the article is omitted even where a definite sense is required. But in this verse the definiteness begins in the οὗτος which follows immediately.

εὐεργεσία very often means *well-doing, kindness of spirit*, generally, but it is used of a concrete act, as here, in 2 Macc. ix. 26, ἀξιῶ μεμνημένους τῶν εὐεργεσιῶν, 'I claim that ye should remember my good actions.'

ἐν τίνι οὗτος σέσωσται, *by what means this man is made whole.*
The demonstrative pronoun should be expressed in the translation (it
is not so in A.V.) for it is emphatically inserted in the Greek. The
man was there for all to see (cf. verse 14) and probably St Peter
pointed him out as he spake.

σέσωσται. The verb σώζω primarily refers to the body, and means
the keeping of that safe and sound, and out of peril of death. Then
it is used for healing, bringing the body into a sound state out of an
unsound one. But as disease and death are the consequences of sin,
the scriptural use of the word was elevated, and it meant in the end
the salvation of the soul.

10. ἐν τῷ ὀνόματι, *in the name,* as before in verse 7.

ὑμεῖς ἐσταυρώσατε, *ye crucified.* For though the Roman soldiers
were the actual agents in the crucifixion, it was the Jewish people
and their rulers who set the Roman power in motion and urged it to
the last extremity. The pronoun is therefore emphatically inserted.

ἐν τούτῳ. Refer back to the previous ἐν, and so render, *in this
name.*

11. οὗτος, *this,* viz. Jesus.

ὑφ᾽ ὑμῶν τῶν οἰκοδόμων. Render, *of you the builders.* The article
has its proper force. The council are fitly called the builders, for on
them depended the whole religious and civil government of the people.
St Peter, with his mind now enlightened to apply the Scriptures, uses
the words of the Psalmist (cxviii. 22) as spoken prophetically of
Christ. Christ had already (Matt. xxi. 42) applied these words to
Himself and to the way in which He was being rejected of the Jews, in
the close of one of His parables which the Pharisees felt had been
spoken against them.

The rendering of the Psalm by the Apostle does not altogether
accord with the words of the LXX.

εἰς κεφαλὴν γωνίας, *the head of the corner.* Christ, now exalted
into heaven, is no longer the despised, but is become the most important, stone in the new building of the Christian society, cf. Eph.
ii. 20—22. St Peter uses this quotation in his Epistle (1 Pet. ii. 7),
and joins with it a passage (Isa. xxviii. 16) where the like figure is
employed prophetically of the Messiah, 'the foundation stone laid in
Zion.'

For the expression cf. LXX. Jerem. xxviii. 26, λίθος εἰς γωνίαν and
Job xxxviii. 6 ὁ βαλὼν λίθον γωνιαῖον.

12. καί...ἡ σωτηρία. Render, *and salvation is not in any other,* i.e.
salvation in all the fulness of its conception. St Peter thus intimates
that the cure of the lame man is only a sign of the power of salvation
for the soul which was in Jesus. The people were to draw from the
effect produced by 'Arise and walk,' the conclusion that the same
power could as surely give the greater blessing, 'thy sins be forgiven
thee' (Matt. ix. 5). Cf. on σώζω, verse 9, and the use of σωθῆναι
immediately.

τὸ δεδομένον ἐν ἀνθρώποις, i.e. communicated to men by God, as a means of salvation.

δεῖ implies the necessity of seeking our salvation in this name, if we are ever to find it.

13—22. THE APOSTLES ARE DISMISSED UNPUNISHED.

13. θεωροῦντες. This is not the common verb for *seeing*, but implies that they beheld with some astonishment.

παρρησίαν, a freedom and readiness of speech not to be expected in unlearned men. This it was which made them wonder.

τοῦ Πέτρου...καὶ Ἰωάννου. It appears then, though St Luke has not recorded a word of his, that St John had also shewn boldness of speech on this occasion. Another evidence that St Luke has not aimed to report complete speeches of those about whom he writes.

ἰδιῶται. Render, *common men*. The word signifies *plebeian*, as opposed to men of noble birth.

ἐπεγίνωσκόν τε αὐτούς. These words have been interpreted as though they meant that the members of the Sanhedrin now for the first time discovered the relation in which the two Apostles stood to Jesus. Those who press such a rendering must overlook the force of the very same verb as used in iii. 10, 'They *knew* that it was he which sat for alms.' The men of whom this is said had known the cripple for years, but now observed in addition that he was a cripple no longer, though still the same man whom they had so long seen begging. Just so with the Jewish authorities; they could hardly fail to have known the connexion of the preachers with Jesus after the sermon on the Day of Pentecost and the events which followed it, and now they *further* (ἐπὶ) notice that as the Master's words had been powerful, so there was like power in the language of those who had been with Him. We are told (John xviii. 15) of one disciple, taken always to be St John himself, that he was known to the high-priest before the Crucifixion.

14. τόν τε ἄνθρωπον. It has been asked on this verse: Why did the sight of the healed man so utterly confound the judges that they had not a word to say? We may see from what happened afterwards that there were men in the council not without the thought that God was really working through the Apostles. Gamaliel says (v. 39) 'If this work be of God'; and if this feeling operated in him, the recognised head of the Jewish court, it is not unlikely that others were also silent with the consideration that 'haply they might be fighting against God.'

Chrysostom says the miracle spake as forcibly as did the Apostles: οὐχ ἧττον δὲ τῆς τούτων φωνῆς ἠφίει φωνὴν τὸ θαῦμα καὶ τὸ σημεῖον. ὃ δὴ καὶ μάλιστα ἐνέφραξεν αὐτῶν τὰ στόματα.

15. ἔξω τοῦ συνεδρίου, i.e. to retire from the council-chamber while the members of the council considered in conference what course should be taken. συνέβαλλον is the word used (xvii. 18) of the conference of the Stoic and Epicurean philosophers with St Paul at Athens.

16. γνωστόν, *well-known, patent to all.* For the word, which is less common in the singular than in the plural, cf. Ecclus. xxi. 7 γνωστὸς μακρόθεν ὁ δυνατὸς ἐν γλώσσῃ.

πᾶσιν...φανερόν, *manifest to all them that dwell in Jerusalem.* Because all the inhabitants knew the beggar at the Temple-gate, and that he had been lame all his life. There could only be two grounds on which, in reference to the cure of the cripple, the Apostles could be worthy of punishment: (1) If it were a case of imposture, but this nobody in the council or anywhere else insinuated, or (2) if the miracle had been wrought by some unlawful agency (Deut. xiii.). The question of the Sanhedrin points in this direction, 'By what power have ye done this?' But Peter from the first (iii. 13) had ascribed the miracle to the 'God of Abraham, Isaac and Jacob,' and again testifies that it is God through Jesus Christ that hath made the man whole. So that there was no charge possible on the second ground.

17. διανεμηθῇ, *be spread abroad,* i.e. the fame of the miracle and the consequent belief in the divinity of Jesus.

ἐπὶ τῷ ὀνόματι. The notion in the preposition here is that of *resting upon.* The Apostles were no more to make the name of Jesus the basis and groundwork of their addresses, nor to refer to it as the source of their power.

18. καλέσαντες, *having called them,* i.e. back again into the council-chamber.

παρήγγειλαν, *they commanded.* The verb is frequently used of our Lord's strict injunctions that His miracles should not be published abroad (Mark vi. 8; Luke v. 14, &c.).

τὸ καθόλου, *at all.* This not very common adverb is found in verse 26 of the Song of the Three Children, καὶ οὐχ ἥψατο αὐτῶν τὸ καθόλου τὸ πῦρ.

19. ὁ δὲ Πέτρος καὶ Ἰωάννης. Both alike express their determination to publish the news of Christ's life and resurrection. The reason why both names are here mentioned may be that each was separately appealed to for a promise to desist. For an instance of like firmness in a good cause cf. 2 Macc. vii. 30.

κρίνατε, *judge ye,* i.e. come to whatever decision you please. Our minds are made up, and 'we are not careful to answer you in this matter.'

20. εἴδαμεν καὶ ἠκούσαμεν, *we saw and heard.* For the witness is to be concerning the whole life of Jesus.

21. προσαπειλησάμενοι, *having further threatened.* The first threats must have been made as soon as the Apostles were called back into the council-hall, as was suggested in verse 17. They did not see their way to do more than threaten, because the people were sure that the lame man had been healed and that there was no charge against the Apostles for which they deserved punishment. They could not say that the miracle was untrue, for there was the man standing by, and proving its reality; and they could not inflict a punishment 'for a good deed,' nor could they find any ground for an accusation in the declaration that the man had been healed in the name of Jesus.

On the contrast between the courage of the Apostles and the terror of the Sanhedrin Chrysostom says: τοιοῦτον ἡ φιλοσοφία. ἐκεῖνοι ἐν ἀπορίᾳ, οὗτοι ἐν εὐφροσύνῃ· ἐκεῖνοι πολλῆς γέμοντες αἰσχύνης, οὗτοι μετὰ παρρησίας πάντα πράττοντες· ἐκεῖνοι ἐν τῷ δεδοικέναι, οὗτοι ἐν τῷ θαρρεῖν. τίνες γὰρ ἦσαν, εἰπέ μοι, οἱ φοβούμενοι; οἱ λέγοντες ἵνα μὴ ἐπὶ πλέον διανεμηθῇ εἰς τὸν λαὸν ἢ οἱ λέγοντες οὐ δυνάμεθα ἃ εἴδαμεν καὶ ἠκούσαμεν μὴ λαλεῖν; καὶ ἐν ἡδονῇ καὶ ἐν παρρησίᾳ καὶ ἐν εὐφροσύνῃ μείζονι πάντων οὗτοι· ἐκεῖνοι ἐν ἀθυμίᾳ ἐν αἰσχύνῃ ἐν φόβῳ. τὸν γὰρ λαὸν ἐδεδοίκεσαν. ἃ ἐβούλοντο ἐφθέγξαντο οὗτοι, ἐκεῖνοι ἃ ἐβούλοντο οὐκ ἐποίησαν. τίνες ἦσαν ἐν δεσμοῖς καὶ ἐν κινδύνοις;

τὸ πῶς κολάσωνται, i.e. on what pretext, or in what way they might punish them, without enraging the multitude. For the form of the sentence cf. 1 Thess. iv. 1 παρελάβετε παρ' ἡμῶν τὸ πῶς δεῖ ὑμᾶς περιπατεῖν.

22. ἐτῶν... τεσσεράκοντα, *above forty years old.* To one who looked on the circumstances, as St Luke, with a physician's eye (Col. iv. 14), this feature would be most noticeable. For limbs unused shrink and wither, and become disproportionate to the other parts of the frame.

ἐφ' ὃν γεγόνει τὸ σημεῖον κ.τ.λ. Literally, 'on whom this sign of healing was wrought.' The A.V. rendering σημεῖον by *miracle* has given somewhat of its sense by using the verb *shewed.*

23—31. THE APOSTLES RELEASED. THEIR PRAYER AND ITS ANSWER.

23. πρὸς τοὺς ἰδίους, *to their own company,* who were perhaps still abiding in the upper room which they had occupied before Pentecost. Because St Peter on a later occasion (xii. 12) made his way, after his delivery from prison, to the house of Mary the mother of John Mark where many were gathered together praying, some have thought that this was the house where the Apostles had dwelt from the first. Such men at such a time would have neither means (see iii. 6) nor inclination to change from house to house, and Christ's injunction (Luke x. 7) 'Go not from house to house' was given with a purpose which the Apostles would be likely to bear in mind and act upon.

24. οἱ δὲ ἀκούσαντες, *and they, having heard it,* viz. the report of the threats.

ἦραν φωνήν, *lifted up their voice.* The compound verb ἐπαίρειν is the more common in classical Greek in this phrase. Both forms are found in the LXX. For αἴρειν φωνὴν cf. Judges xxi. 2; 1 Sam. xi. 4, and ἐπαίρειν occurs Judges ix. 7; Ruth i. 9, 14. The words of the prayer which follows have so direct a reference to the circumstances which had just occurred that we cannot interpret otherwise than that to the prayer, uttered by the lips of one, all the rest, with one mind, pronounced fervent Amens. 'The author (says Zeller) takes no forbidden liberty when he collects the concordant expressions of individuals into one common expression.'

δέσποτα, LORD, lit. *Master*. The word is not often used of God (as Luke ii. 29) or Christ, but it is worth notice that St Peter (2 Pet. ii. 1) and St Jude (4) apply it to Jesus.

σὺ ὁ ποιήσας, *Thou that hast made*. The ὁ θεός of the *Text. Recept.* is an expository note, meant to explain δέσποτα.

25. ὁ τοῦ πατρὸς…παιδός σου. Render, *who by the Holy Ghost* [through] *the mouth of our father David thy servant.* See textual note. If *through* be omitted in this rendering then the latter clause becomes an apposition in explanation of the words 'by the Holy Ghost.'

The Apostle now proceeds to apply the words of the second Psalm, which has been admitted by the Jews themselves to be Messianic, to the circumstances under which Christ was put to death.

The words of the LXX. are here quoted exactly.

ἔθνη, *the nations*, or *the Gentiles* as it is rendered in verse 27.

The Psalm in its first application probably referred to some revolt against the king of Israel. We have such a revolt mentioned in David's reign (2 Sam. viii.), where the Syrians, Moabites, Ammonites and other nations were conquered by David, after being in vain rebellion.

27. ἐπ' ἀληθείας, *of a truth*. This expression is both classical and is also found often in the LXX. as Dan. ii. 8, 47; Job ix. 2, xix. 4, xxxvi. 4; Is. xxxvii. 18, for the Hebrew אָמְנָם = verily.

The Apostle proceeds to apply the language of the Psalmist to the events which preceded the Crucifixion. Thus the words ἐν τῇ πόλει ταύτῃ find a natural place here, as given by the best authorities.

παῖδα, *servant*, as in iii. 13.

ἔχρισας, *Thou hast anointed*, i.e. by the descent of the Holy Ghost upon Him at His baptism.

Ἡρώδης. The representative of the rulers of the Jews. This particular Herod was Antipas the son of Herod the Great by his Samaritan wife Malthace. He was tetrarch of Galilee and Perea (Luke iii. 19), and because our Lord belonged to Galilee, Pilate took occasion to send Jesus to be examined by him, as Herod was in Jerusalem to keep the feast of the Passover.

καὶ Πόντιος Πιλάτος, who was the Roman Governor; and so in his person were represented many nations at this time under the sway of Rome. His officials and soldiers would be drawn from all lands, and the mockery to which Jesus was exposed at their hands might well be described as the rage of the Gentiles.

Pontius Pilate was the sixth Roman procurator of Judæa; he was appointed A.D. 25—6 in the twelfth year of Tiberius, and continued to hold the office till A.D. 36, when he was sent to Rome by Vitellius under an accusation brought against him by the Samaritans. Of his after life and his death there are many legends, but no history.

28. ποιῆσαι, *to accomplish.* God made the passions, which the enemies of Jesus indulged, to be the instruments for working out His will. So men, when they suppose they are choosing their own way, have the ends thereof shapen by God, 'rough hew them how they will.' Their misdeeds are made to execute the will of God, yet they are not on that account exempt from blame.

ἡ χείρ σου. The verb (προώρισεν, =preordained) which follows is due to the intervening noun βουλή=counsel. Such a zeugma is not uncommon. And in χείρ is conveyed the idea of *grandeur* and *majesty*, so that the need for a different verb is scarcely felt. For an instance of zeugma, cf. *Acta Pauli et Theclæ* 43, ᾤκησεν ἐν σπηλαίῳ ἐσθίουσα βοτάνας καὶ ὕδωρ.

29. ἔπιδε, *look upon.* The verb is employed in heathen writings very often of the *oversight* and *notice* of the gods, and is common in the LXX. for God's providential care. Cf. Job xxii. 12; Ps. cxii. 6; Ezek. viii. 12, and 2 Macc. vii. 6 ὁ κύριος ὁ θεὸς ἐφορᾷ.

δούλοις. The Apostles use this word of themselves, they are Christ's *bond-servants.* For Jesus the word is παῖς. Cf. verse 30. St Paul constantly calls himself δοῦλος Ἰησοῦ Χριστοῦ or the like. Cf. Rom. i. 1; Phil. i. 1; Titus i. 1, &c.

παρρησίας, *boldness,* freedom of speech, as above, verse 13. Christ had promised that this should be given to them (Luke xxi. 15), and they are able to feel (cf. below, verse 31) that His promise is fulfilled.

30. ἐν τῷ τὴν χεῖρά σου ἐκτείνειν σε. Literally, 'while Thou stretchest forth Thine hand.' Thus the mighty works were to be a sign and testimony to the words which the Apostles spake, to demonstrate that they were God's words, and that none could do the works which they did except God were with him. (John iii. 2.)

παιδός σου, *Thy servant* (as in verse 27).

31. ἐσαλεύθη ὁ τόπος. That they might feel at once that the God of all nature, to whom they had appealed (ver. 24), was among them. In their immediate need an immediate answer is vouchsafed, and a token with it that their prayer was heard. Cp. xvi. 26 of the shaking of the prison at Philippi after the prayers of Paul and Silas.

ἐλάλουν. The imperfect tense indicates that they went on preaching, speaking the word which God gave unto them, without regard to the threats of the council.

32—37. UNANIMITY AND LOVE AMONG THE FIRST CHRISTIANS.

32. καρδία καὶ ψυχὴ μία, *one heart and soul.* This was a Hebrew form of expressing complete accord. So (1 Chron. xii. 38) καὶ ὁ κατάλοιπος Ἰσραὴλ ψυχὴ μία τοῦ βασιλεῦσαι τὸν Δαυίδ. Also cf. such expressions as (1 Sam. xiv. 7; 2 Kings x. 15) ὡς ἡ καρδία σοῦ καρδία μοῦ. In some MSS. there is an addition to this verse, καὶ οὐκ ἦν διάκρισις (some have χωρισμός) ἐν αὐτοῖς οὐδεμία. This is followed by several versions and quoted by the Fathers. It has not found its way into the Received Text, but is just such a marginal explanation as a scribe would be sure sooner or later to incorporate.

καὶ οὐδὲ εἷς κ.τ.λ., *and not one of them said.* This is much stronger than the rendering of the A.V. Each felt that he held his possessions only as a trust, and if occasion called for it, they were to be given up. Such love towards one another, Christ had foretold, should be a mark of His disciples (John xiii. 35). All those who have sketched a perfect society, as Plato in his *Republic,* and Sir Thos. More in his *Utopia,* have placed among their regulations this kind of community of goods which was established by the first Christians. In theory it is the perfection of a commonwealth, but there is need of perfection in the citizens before it can be realized. There can be no question that an expectation of Christ's immediate return from heaven, acting along with the unity of thoughts and feeling, made these men willing to part with their possessions and goods, there being, as we shall see from the case of Ananias, no constraint upon them to do so.

33. ἀπεδίδουν τὸ μαρτύριον, *they gave their witness.* The article should have its force. See above on verse 12. The verb is also much stronger than the usual verb 'to give.' It is used for 'paying a debt' (Matth. xviii. 29; Luke vii. 42) and for 'rendering an account' (Matth. xii. 36; Heb. xiii. 17): so that there is implied in it the sense of *obligation* under which the Apostles so constantly declare themselves placed (cf. above, verse 20).

χάρις τε μεγάλη, *and great grace* (or *favour*). Like their Master, while experiencing the favour of God, they were also finding favour with men. Cf. Acts v. 13.

34. οὐδὲ γὰρ ἐνδεής τις ἦν. The A.V. omits to translate γὰρ, but it is essential to the sense. *For neither was there,* &c. This was one reason for their favour among men. All could see and admire the spirit of self-sacrifice which was exhibited by what they were doing. See ii. 44, 45 and the notes there.

τὰς τιμὰς τῶν πιπρασκομένων. The language here expressly avoids saying that these men sold all they had. They sold some things, and the sum realized by what was sold was offered to the common store. We never hear that a similar fund was raised in any place except Jerusalem.

35. παρὰ τοὺς πόδας. To lay a thing at, or under, any one's feet was a significant act. Here it denoted that entire control was given to the Apostles over the bestowal of these sums. For the figure, cp. Ps. viii. 6, and Cicero *pro Flacco* (xxvii. § 68) '*ante pedes prætoris*' in foro expensum est auri pondo centum paullo minus.'

διεδίδετο δὲ κ.τ.λ. Render, *and distribution was made unto each according as any had need.* There were no doubt many who were not

I 2

in need, and they of course lived on their own. The distribution was intended only for the needy, as widows, &c., and for those who could not otherwise support themselves while they took part, as many did, in the active propagation of the new faith. It may be, too, that some were deprived of the means of support because they had become Christians. Cf. the threat of the authorities, John ix. 22.

36. Ἰωσήφ. The oldest MSS. give this as the form of the word. Barnabas, who was so called, was afterwards the companion of St Paul in his first missionary journey (Acts xiii. 2), and is often mentioned by St Luke. He was invited by St Paul to join him on his second journey, but as they disagreed about taking John Mark with them, they did not labour again, as far as we know, in the same field, and the writer leaves Barnabas (xv. 39) with the mention that 'he took Mark and sailed to Cyprus.'

μεθερμηνευόμενον. The interpretation is added for the sake of Theophilus, who may have had no knowledge of Hebrew (see on i. 19).

υἱὸς παρακλήσεως. Probably, *son of exhortation*, rather than, *of consolation*. The Hebrew noun *nebuah* is from the same root as the common word for *prophet*. The title may have been given to Barnabas from his ability as a preacher (xi. 23), though in this he seems (Acts xiv. 12) to have been less prominent than St Paul, as most men must have been. In describing the work of Barnabas in xi. 23 the verb used (παρεκάλει), 'he exhorted,' is that from which the noun in this verse is derived, and is akin to the word παράκλητος, which is so often translated 'Comforter' when applied to the Holy Ghost, but rendered 'advocate' in 1 John ii. 1 when used of the intercession of Jesus.

Λευΐτης, *a Levite.* In the Holy Land, the Levites had no portion assigned unto them, but were scattered through all the tribes; the same regulation may not, however, have applied to the Levites in other countries; and we are not informed where the field was situated which Barnabas sold. He may also have been a married man, and have held lands from his marriage.

Κύπριος. The island of Cyprus, still called by the same name, is in the Eastern part of the Mediterranean Sea. We find Jews settled there in the Maccabean times (1 Macc. xv. 23). It was one of the places to which Paul and Barnabas went in their missionary journey, and it had been previously visited by some of the Christian teachers who were driven from Jerusalem by the persecution which succeeded the death of Stephen (Acts xi. 19).

37. ἀγροῦ, *a field.* Joseph is perhaps chosen as an example of the primitive liberality of the Christian community, because there was something remarkable in the kind of gift, or the nature of the sacrifice which he made. And the character of the man, who was to play a part in the history of the Acts, is also set before us by his first recorded action.

Chrysostom says: μέλλει διηγεῖσθαι τὸ κατὰ Ἀνανίαν λοιπὸν καὶ

Σάπφειραν, καὶ θέλων δεῖξαι τὸν ἄνδρα χείριστα ἡμαρτηκότα, πρῶτον μέμνηται τοῦ κατωρθωκότος.

τὸ χρῆμα, *the money*, the price realized. The word is seldom found in the singular in this sense. Perhaps it is so used here to indicate the compactness, the entirety of what was brought. It was the sum without deduction, in contrast to the proceeding which follows in the next chapter.

CHAPTER V.

Readings varying from the *Text. recept.*

2. αὐτοῦ omitted with אABD.

5. ταῦτα omitted with אABD.   So also *Vulg.* and other versions.

8. πρὸς αὐτήν for αὐτῇ with אABD.

9. εἶπε omitted with אBD.   *Vulg.* has 'Petrus autem ad eam.'

10. πρὸς for παρὰ with אABD.

12. τέρατα πολλὰ ἐν τῷ λαῷ with אABDE.   *Vulg.* has 'prodigia multa in plebe.'

15. καὶ εἰς for κατὰ with אABD.   *Vulg.* has 'ita ut in plateas.'
     κλιναρίων for κλινῶν with אABD.
     κραβάττων as in אABD.   *Vulg.* has 'grabatis.'

16. εἰς omitted with אAB.   The *Vulg.* has no preposition.

18. αὐτῶν omitted with אABD.   The *Vulg.* has no pronoun.

19. τῆς before νυκτὸς omitted with אABD.

22. οἱ δὲ παραγενόμενοι ὑπηρέται with אAB.   The *Vulg.* has 'cum autem venissent ministri.'

23. μὲν omitted with אABD.
     ἔξω omitted with אABDEP.   It is not represented in *Vulg.*
     ἐπὶ for πρὸ with אABD.   *Vulg.* has 'ante.'

24. ἱερεὺς καὶ ὁ omitted as in אABD.   *Vulg.* has only 'magistratus templi.'

25. λέγων omitted with אABDEP.   It is not represented in *Vulg.*

28. οὐ omitted with אAB, also unrepresented in *Vulg.*

32. αὐτοῦ omitted with אAD.   *Vulg.* 'et nos sumus testes horum verborum.'

34. ἀνθρώπους for ἀποστόλους with אAB.   *Vulg.* 'homines.'

36. ᾧ προσεκλίθη ἀνδρῶν ἀριθμὸς ὡς τετρακοσίων with אABC.

37. ἱκανὸν omitted with אAB.   *Vulg.* has only 'populum.'

38.   ἄφετε for ἐάσατε with אABC.

39.   δυνήσεσθε with אBCDE.   *Vulg.* 'poteritis.'
      αὐτούς for αὐτό with אABCDE.   *Vulg.* 'illud.'

40.   αὐτούς omitted with אABC.   *Vulg.* 'eos.'

41.   κατηξιώθησαν ὑπὲρ τοῦ ὀνόματος ἀτιμασθῆναι with אABC.
Vulg. 'digni habiti sunt pro nomine Jesu contumeliam pati.'

42.   τὸν Χριστὸν Ἰησοῦν with אAB.   *Vulg.* 'Christum Jesum.'

CH. V. 1—11. ACCOUNT OF ANANIAS AND SAPPHIRA.

The narrative with which this chapter commences is one which
none but a veracious narrator would have inserted where it stands.
The last chapter concludes with a description of the unity of heart
and soul which prevailed among the brethren, and expressly notices
that all were filled with the Holy Ghost.   But as among the twelve
Apostles there was a Judas, so into the infant Church there had intruded two at least whose professions were not sincere, and who were
unworthy of the gifts of grace which, with the rest, they had received.

We cannot but be surprised that persons like Ananias and Sapphira should have thought it *worth while* to act as they did.   Why
join the Christian community at all?   Or why not leave it when they
found what was required of them?   But there is in some characters an
innate and incorrigible duplicity.   It is clear that there must have
been a strong conviction of the truth of Christianity.

The offence of Ananias and Sapphira shewed contempt for God,
vanity and ambition in the offenders, and utter disregard of the corruption which they were bringing into the society.   Such sin, committed
in despite of the light which they possessed, called for a special mark
of divine indignation, and to those who, likewise filled with the Spirit,
knew all that had been done and why it was done, there is no shock
produced by the terrible doom of the sinners.   Nor is any language
employed in the narration but the simplest and plainest.   A late
compiled story would have enlarged and spoken apologetically on the
reasons for such a judgment, and would not have presented us with
a bare recital of facts without comment.

1.   Ἀνανίας.   The name was common.   See Acts ix. 10—17, and
xxiii. 2, xxiv. 1.   It is the same as *Hananiah*, Jer. xxviii. 1; Dan. i.
6, 7, &c., where it is the Hebrew name of Shadrach, which is spelt
Ananias in the *Benedicite*, and that form of the name is found Tobit
v. 12.   It signifies 'one to whom Jehovah has been gracious.'

Σαπφείρη.   The name is probably derived from σάπφειρος, *sapphire*,
the precious stone so called.   Similar derivations may be found in
Beryllus (βήρυλλος), and the more common name *Margaret* (μαργα-
ρίτης), though the latter may have gone through more than one stage
in its passage from a common noun to a proper name.

κτῆμα. In verse 3 it is called χωρίον, a piece of land, but the word may be applied to any kind of property. It is used (Matth. xix. 22) of the young man who had 'great possessions.' The LXX. use it (Hos. ii. 15) of vineyards.

2. ἐνοσφίσατο, *kept back, withheld*, bringing only a part and pretending it was the whole. The portion withheld can hardly have been large, or the disproportion between what was offered and the value of the property sold and represented as sacrificed to the common cause would have been too apparent. νοσφίζομαι is rendered (Tit. ii. 10) *to purloin*, and is used 2 Macc. iv. 32 of the golden vessels which Menelaus *stole*. It has the stronger sense constantly in classical Greek.

συνειδυίης, *being privy to it.* This is mentioned to shew that the offence was an aggravated one, and had not been committed without deliberation and set purpose. She was a willing accomplice in the intended fraud.

παρὰ τοὺς πόδας...ἔθηκεν. Thus professing equal devotion with all the others who were making sacrifices for the cause of the faith. We are not told what Ananias and his wife hoped to gain by their act, whether in reputation among the people (ii. 47), or, by giving what was supposed to be their whole estate (which may be implied in the vague word *possession*), to procure for themselves in perpetuity a maintenance from the common funds. The former ambition was most probably what led to their offence. They thought more of the display made at the Apostles' feet than of the offence before God's eyes. And we know from St Peter's Epistle (2 Pet. ii. 3) that it was soon foretold that men would arise in the Christian community who 'through covetousness would with feigned words make merchandise of' the society, and at a later date (Jude 11) these men are described as those who run 'greedily after the error of Balaam for reward.' We may therefore be convinced that in the example of Ananias we have a typical instance of the kind of offence into which at this time the Christian community was in danger of being tempted.

3. διατί. Stronger probably than the simple τί. 'On what account? to what temptation have you listened?' It may be an indication that it would have been possible to resist the evil influence, had Ananias desired to do so.

ἐπλήρωσεν, *filled.* The idea seems to be that of complete occupation. The heart is so charged and possessed with one purpose, that there is no room left for any other influence. Cf. LXX. Eccles. viii. 11, ἐπληροφορήθη καρδία υἱῶν τοῦ ἀνθρώπου ἐν αὐτοῖς τοῦ ποιῆσαι τὸ πονηρόν.

σατανᾶς. The word, which is Hebrew, signifies 'an adversary,' and is especially applied to the prince of evil spirits, as the great adversary of all good. It is used in LXX. of 1 Kings xi. 14, 23, 25 in its primary sense of an 'adversary' raised up against king Solomon, but in the sense of 'Satan' Ecclus. xxi. 27.

τὸ πνεῦμα τὸ ἅγιον, *the Holy Ghost*, for it was the power of the Holy Ghost that was manifested in the Apostles. It is much to be noticed how from the first the Apostles disclaim any power in themselves. It is Christ who works the miracles, the God of Abraham who gives the power of healing, and the Holy Ghost who is grieved by sins like that of Ananias. There is no trace of any seeking after consideration for themselves and their deeds among the records of these Acts of Apostles, and no sign could be more indicative of the earliest age of the Christian Church.

4. οὐχὶ μένον σοὶ ἔμενεν. To bring out the force of the repeated verb render, *whiles it remained, did it not remain thine own?* that is, there was no compulsion on Ananias to sell it, the only thing expected from him being that, if he were moved to sell, he should honestly set forth what he had done. There seems to have been no necessity to give at all to the common fund unless a man felt that he could well afford to do so, nor to give all that he either had, or had realized by any sale, provided only he made honest declaration of what his gift really was. This is implied in the words which follow, which declare that the sum produced by any sale was at the seller's disposal until he made it over to the common fund.

ἔθου ἐν τῇ καρδίᾳ. The precise phrase occurs in LXX. of Dan. i. 8, and is rendered 'Daniel purposed in his heart'; cf. also Haggai ii. 19. The force of the expression is 'to lay anything (as a plan or a precept) deep in the heart,' and it implies long and stedfast deliberation on the part of this offender. The offence of Ananias was not a case of yielding to a sudden temptation, but the plan had been accepted into the heart, and fostered there till there seemed to be a way of carrying it out. Satan had filled his heart, and he had made no effort to cast out the intruder.

οὐκ ἐψεύσω ἀνθρώποις, *thou hast not lied unto men.* That is, the grave portion of the offence is not the lie to men, but the lie to God. In verse 3 the Apostle said that the deception had been practised towards the Holy Ghost, and so is expressed the Divinity of the third Person of the Trinity.

5. ἀκούων. The present tense seems to indicate the immediate result of the Apostle's words, spoken in the power of the Spirit with which he was filled. Here is no description of a death from apoplexy or mental excitement under the rebuke of the Apostle, but a direct intervention of the divine power.

Terrible as this divine judgment was, we cannot wonder that it should be inflicted, for it was so done to check that kind of offence which brought in all the troubles of the early Church, and which though they be not so punished now, when Christ's Church has attained more firm hold on the world, yet would, if not terribly visited in these earlier days, have overthrown the whole work of the Apostles. Of a like character is the apparent severity of the penalty inflicted on Aaron's sons, Nadab and Abihu, at the commencement of the Jewish priesthood (Lev. x. 2); and the way in which Aaron and his family are forbidden to mourn for those whom God so punished may teach us what interpretation to put upon the judgment inflicted on Ananias and Sapphira. For they were of the members of the infant Church; they had presumed to come nigh unto God and in a wrong spirit. On them, we may conclude, some gifts had been bestowed, and in this they differed from Simon Magus (viii. 20) and Elymas (xiii. 11), with whom they are sometimes compared. So that the words which God spake of Nadab and Abihu may be used of these offenders, 'I will be sanctified in them that come nigh Me.' We see what evils the spirit of greed and hypocrisy wrought in the Corinthian Church, even to the profanation of the Lord's Supper (1 Cor. xi. 17—21). Every good institution would have been thus perverted and, as is said of some in later times (Jude 4), they would have 'turned the grace of God into lasciviousness.' The very community of goods which here was instituted for a time, was in this way perverted and turned into an argument for a community of all things, which resulted in the vices for which the Nicolaitans are so severely censured (Rev. ii. 6, 15). The death of Ananias and his wife is the finger of God interposed to save His Church from danger, just as He interposed to build it up by stretching forth His hand to heal, and that through the name of His Servant Jesus mighty works might be wrought by the first preachers.

ἐξέψυξεν, *gave up the ghost.* ἐκψύχω is not classical, but is found in LXX. (of some MSS.) in Judges iv. 21 and in Ezek. xxi. 7. It is only used in the N.T. concerning the death of this husband and wife, and of the end of Herod Agrippa (Acts xii. 23), but is found *Acta Andr. et Matth. Apocr.* 19 used of men suddenly falling down dead.

φόβος μέγας. A great fear, which would deter those who were not sincere from making a profession of Christianity. This result would help the stability of the young community, which would have been sorely hindered by hypocritical members.

6. οἱ νεώτεροι, *the younger men.* Some have thought that already an organized body had been formed whose business it was to take charge of funerals. But it seems unlikely that, at a time when assistance had not been provided to relieve the Apostles from 'serving tables' and distributing the funds to those who needed (vi. 1—4), there should already have been an organization for this less pressing necessity. The use of another word, νεανίσκοι, for these same persons in verse 10 seems to shew that οἱ νεώτεροι was not an official designation, but that those who are meant are those most able physically to perform such an office as is here described. On the way in which the Jews regarded attention to funeral rites see note on viii. 2.

συνέστειλαν, *wound him up,* i.e. in the robe which he was at the moment wearing. The middle voice is used in classical Greek in the sense of 'gathering one's robe about one.'

ἔθαψαν. We know from what took place after the Crucifixion that graves were made ready beforehand; and in the caves where the dead were deposited, as we can see from the account of the raising of Lazarus, there (John xi. 43) needed little preparation, for they were closed by the simple means of a stone placed at the cave's mouth. It would not therefore need much time to complete the whole work of

burial.   In hot climates burial must needs follow quickly after
death.   Cf. the brief time which Jehu allowed to pass after Jezebel's
death (2 Kings ix. 34) before he gave orders for her burial.

7. ὡρῶν τριῶν διάστημα, *the space of three hours.*   This was
time enough for the bestowal of the dead body, but yet so short that
news of the death of her husband had not reached Sapphira.   It may
have been that their home was in the country at a distance from
Jerusalem, and that the husband alone came in to offer the money by
reason of the distance.

διάστημα is found of a distance in space in LXX. of Gen. xxxii. 16;
Ezek. xli. 8, xlv. 2; 2 Macc. xiv. 44, but not of an interval of time.
διάστημα τετραετές occurs Polyb. ix. 1. 1; and ἡμιωρίου διάστημα, the
space of half an hour, *Apocryph. Act. Andreæ* 14.

καὶ ἡ γυνή.   The construction is broken here.   We should have
expected an accusative and infinitive in dependence on ἐγένετο.   But
such interruptions are not uncommon after a clause beginning with ἐγένετο.   Cf. Luke viii. 1, 22, ix. 28, &c.   The construction is due to
the Hebrew form יְהִי followed by וְ.

μὴ εἰδυῖα.   μὴ here cannot be held to differ from οὐ.   There is a
direct statement of a fact, present, and nothing which can convert the
words in any sense into a mere thought or conception.

8. ἀπεκρίθη, *answered.*   This verb is not unfrequently used both in
LXX. and N.T. where no question has preceded, and often where no
remark has gone before (see Deut. xxvi. 5, xxvii. 14; Dan. ii. 14, 26;
Matth. xi. 25; Luke iii. 16).   The peculiarity here is that St Peter's
words are not an answer but a *question.*
The word is similarly used before a question *Act. Andr. et Matth.
Apocr.* 26.

τοσούτου, *for so much.*   St Peter mentioned the sum which Ananias
had brought in, or perhaps it was still lying on the ground where he
had first put it down.

9. τί ὅτι.   This form, which occurs also in verse 4, is to be explained by the ellipsis of ἐστί.   'Why *is it* that...'

πειράσαι, *to tempt.*   They would make trial whether the Spirit of
the Lord would make their deception known.   Nothing could render
more manifest their want of faith, their unfitness to be members of
the society, than such an attempt.

οἱ πόδες.   The footsteps of the young men as they returned were
probably now audible without.

καὶ ἐξοίσουσίν σε, *and they shall carry thee out,* i.e. to burial likewise.   St Peter, as before, was prompted by the Holy Ghost in what
he said, and was enabled to predict the punishment of Sapphira for
her persistent dissembling.   We are not told that he knew beforehand
what would befal Ananias, but as the Spirit shewed him what was to
come on the wife we may perhaps conclude that he knew what the fate
of the husband would be also.

10. πρὸς τοὺς πόδας αὐτοῦ, *at his feet.* Close to the place where the money, for which they had sinned, had been laid, and where perhaps it was still lying. For we cannot think that St Peter would be willing to mix an offering given in such a hypocritical spirit with the more pure offerings of the other brethren. It may be that as he spake, in verse 8, he pointed to the money still lying there unaccepted, 'Did ye sell the land *for so much ?*'

εἰσελθόντες. The young men came to join the congregation again, for the worship appears not to have ceased during the time between the death of Ananias and the arrival of Sapphira. And this may be the explanation of the wife's ignorance of her husband's fate. None had gone forth but the younger men to bury the dead body.

πρὸς τὸν ἄνδρα αὐτῆς, *beside her husband.*

11. καὶ ἐγένετο κ.τ.λ., *and great fear came upon the whole Church, and upon all that heard these things.*

To produce such a fear as should deter others from a like offence was God's intention in this miracle of punishment. And St Luke seems to have pointed to the reason by making here for the first time any mention of 'the Church' (see note on ii. 47). The true ἐκκλησία must be free from such hypocritical professors, or its work could not advance. The lesson was to be stamped into the hearts of all who were fit to be of ' the Church,' though at the same time it would strike deep into the minds of all others who learnt how the Spirit of God had punished the lying lips of those who sought the praise of men rather than that of God.

12—16. MIRACULOUS POWERS OF THE APOSTLES. CONTINUED GROWTH OF THE CHURCH.

12. διὰ δὲ τῶν χειρῶν, *and by the hands.* This may be only a Hebrew mode of expressing *by,* and need not necessarily be pressed to imply *imposition of hands.* Cf. (Josh. xiv. 2) 'By lot was their inheritance, as the Lord commanded by the hand (ἐν χειρὶ) of Moses.' But as in the description of our Lord's miracles we very often read 'He laid *His hands* upon a few sick folk' (Mark vi. 5, &c.), and as it is said of the Apostles (Mark xvi. 18) 'they shall lay *their hands* on the sick and they shall recover,' it seems better to understand the words here of such acts of imposition of hands, though we presently find (ver. 15) that the multitudes believed that a cure could be wrought without such an act.

ἐγίνετο. The imperfect tense, probably to indicate that such occurrences were numerous at the first.

ἅπαντες. The reference in this sentence must be to such assemblies as were held by the Apostles for conference and instruction when they went up at the usual times of prayer. Thus ἅπαντες will signify the whole company assembled on some such occasions, and not embrace every person who had joined the new teaching.

ἐν τῇ στοᾷ Σολομῶντος, *in Solomon's porch.* Probably this became a recognized meeting-place of those who wished to tell and to hear more of the new teaching.

13. τῶν δὲ λοιπῶν, *but of the rest*, &c., i.e. of those not yet interested in the movement. The sense is that the assemblies of Christians made the porch of Solomon their special rendezvous when they went up to the Temple, seeing that it was there that the first addresses in the Temple-precincts had been given by St Peter. And while they were so assembled none of the other people who had not yet joined the new community ventured to attach themselves intrusively to the Christian body. The verb κολλᾶσθαι is used of Philip (viii. 29) when he is commanded 'Go near and *join thyself* to this chariot,' where the action meant by it is one that was to press some notice of Philip upon the eunuch. From such intrusion all who were not Christians held back, and left the worshippers in Solomon's porch alone.

ἀλλ' ἐμεγάλυνεν κ.τ.λ., *howbeit the people magnified them.* The fear inspired by what had happened, though it deterred those who might have tried to join the community from other than sincere motives, did not produce an unfavourable feeling among the people, but quite the contrary.

For the English 'magnify' in the sense of *praise* cf. the opening of the *Magnificat*, 'My soul doth magnify the Lord.'

14. προσετίθεντο, *were added.* And the tense implies the continuous growth of the Church. The addition of this verse makes clear what has just been said about the sense of κολλᾶσθαι, that it implied insincere intrusion into the Christian assemblies. For the number of the faithful went on increasing.

15. ὥστε καὶ εἰς τὰς πλατείας, *so that even into the streets.* These words are a description of one way in which the new believers gave evidence of their faith. To bring a sick person on a couch to the presence of Jesus was accepted by Him (Mark ii. 5) as a sign of true faith, and for the sake of the faith shewn by those who brought him the paralytic was made whole. So here, though we are not told of any cures, we may conclude that to the like faith God would give a like blessing.

ἐπὶ κλιναρίων, *on beds.* In the east the warm climate made it possible to bring the sick into the open air, as we read more than once in the Gospels.

ἵνα ἐρχομένου Πέτρου κ.τ.λ., *that, as Peter came by, at least his shadow might fall on some one of them.* Peter is alone mentioned here because he was the most prominent figure, but we are not to conclude that no mighty works were done by the rest. These men who gave such an exhibition of faith have been described (ver. 14) as *believers in the Lord.* There can therefore be no question as to what they regarded as the power which was to heal their sick. They did not believe on Peter, though they magnified him as the Lord's instrument; they did not ascribe healing power to Peter's shadow, though it might please God to make that a sacrament of healing, as to Israel in old times

He had made the brazen serpent. They had seen health bestowed through the Apostle by the name of Christ, and to demonstrate their faith in that name, they bring their afflicted friends into the way of salvation.

κἄν. The explanation of the καί here is that in the first clause there is some word or two suppressed. The full idea is 'that as Peter came by *they might be in the way and so* his shadow,' &c.

16. τὸ πλῆθος κ.τ.λ., *the multitude of the cities round about.* The word πόλις is not unfrequently used of places which are comparatively small. So of Nazareth (Matth. ii. 23), Nain (Luke vii. 11) and Arimathea (Luke xxiii. 51). With τῶν πέριξ πόλεων cf. *Acta Andr. et Matth. Apocr.* 26, οὓς ὁ μακάριος ἐξέβαλεν ἐκ τῶν πέριξ χωρῶν.

The preposition being omitted before Ἱερουσαλήμ, it becomes the accusative under the government of συνήρχετο, a verb with the sense of motion *to* a place.

ὀχλουμένους, *troubled, vexed.* The word is found also Luke vi. 18, and nowhere else in N.T. As it occurs often in the works of Greek medical writers, it points to Luke as having been a physician. Cf. for its use concerning evil spirits, Tobit vi. 7, ἐάν τινα ὀχλῇ δαιμόνιον ἢ πνεῦμα πονηρόν, ταῦτα δεῖ καπνίσαι ἐνώπιον ἀνθρώπου ἢ γυναικὸς καὶ μηκέτι ὀχληθῇ.

ὑπὸ πνευμάτων ἀκαθάρτων, *by unclean spirits.* It was recognized that the power of the Apostles extended not only to physical, but also to spiritual maladies. Indeed the whole history being of a supernatural character, the cures wrought on ordinary maladies were of the nature of signs and wonders, and spake of a power which was not human. The power here displayed is that which in Christ's own life was confessed to be that of the Son of God (Luke iv. 40, 41).

Unclean spirits are those which are called *wicked* (πονηρά) in other parts of the New Testament (Matth. xii. 45, &c.); and the former epithet is probably applied to them because an unclean life had made the afflicted man the subject of this possession, or because in his state of frenzy he wandered into places where he would incur ceremonial defilement, as the demoniac who had his dwelling among the tombs (Mark v. 3); the latter adjective indicates the evil effects so often patent in the condition of the afflicted person, as loss of speech, hearing and other senses, the belief of the Jews being that spirits afflicted with such maladies were the cause of the like affliction in human beings.

ἅπαντες, *all of them.* For it was only a complete faith which had prompted the bringing them unto the Apostles, and to such faith *all things* had been promised by Christ (Mark ix. 23).

17—32. ARREST OF THE TWELVE. THEIR MIRACULOUS DELIVERANCE AND THEIR DEFENCE BEFORE THE SANHEDRIN.

17. ἀναστὰς δέ. The 'rising up' is due to the indignation caused by the spread of the Christian teaching. The word ἀναστάς has this sense of movement in opposition. See below, of the insurrections of

Theudas and Judas (*vv.* 36, 37) and in vi. 9 of the disputants with Stephen.

The rendering should be, *but the high-priest rose up*. While the multitudes thronged to be healed, the effect on the authorities was to rouse them to opposition.

πάντες οἱ σὺν αὐτῷ. A phrase more comprehensive than that used in iv. 6, 'as many as were of the kindred of the high-priest.' The opposition has had time to gather its forces, and now represents not only the family of Annas, but the heads of the party of the Sadducees.

αἵρεσις, *the sect*. It is the word from which our English *heresy* comes. But St Paul uses it of his own mode of worship (though there shewing that the Jews attached an ill meaning to it), in his defence (Acts xxiv. 14) before Felix, 'after the way which they call *a sect.*' But he employs it without any sense of blame (xxvi. 5) about the Pharisees, and it is used of them also xv. 5. With a bad sense it is applied to the Nazarenes (xxiv. 5), and similarly xxviii. 22.

It is used disparagingly in *Apocr. Act. Phil. in Hellad.* 10, Ἰησοῦς ...ὃς ἐδίδαξεν τὴν αἵρεσιν ταύτην. The words are in the mouth of the Jewish high-priest.

τῶν Σαδδουκαίων. From verse 21 it will be seen that the statement of Josephus concerning the influence of this sect is fully borne out (*Ant.* XIII. 11. 6), that they had the rich on their side. We have no certain evidence in Scripture that Annas was a Sadducee, but Josephus (*Ant.* xx. 9. 1) tells us that his son Ananus [or Annas] was of this sect.

ζῆλον, *jealousy*. This is rather the sense of the word than 'indignation' as A.V. Of course the one was bred of the other. But what is here described is an outbreak of party feeling in a body who were jealous of the spread of this teaching about a resurrection.

18. ἐπὶ τοὺς ἀποστόλους. The whole twelve are now arrested. The new teachers must be put down. It is clear from this, though St Luke has only mentioned the speeches of Peter, with some slight notice that John also was a speaker, that all the Apostles were busy, and could have been quoted as preachers and teachers had it been any part of the compiler's purpose to write a history of all the Apostles.

ἐν τηρήσει δημοσίᾳ, *in public ward*. See note on iv. 3. This was meant to be a temporary imprisonment, till next day when the council could be gathered.

19. ἄγγελος δὲ κ.τ.λ., *but an angel of the Lord by night*, &c. As if for a protest against the actions of those who taught that 'there was neither angel nor spirit.' There is no possibility of explaining St Luke's words into anything but a miraculous deliverance. He gives no word that can be twisted into any other meaning. It was not an earthquake, it was not a friendly human being who interposed to procure the release of the Apostles. The writer readily acknowledges in this very chapter the effect of such intervention on the part of Gamaliel, but he is here speaking of supernatural aid. If it be remarked that the Apostles make no mention of their miraculous

deliverance when they are called upon for their defence, it may be
answered that they in no case dwell on the miracles either wrought by
or for them, except where they have been wrought under the eyes of
men and are to be used as signs of the divine power which was
working in and for the Church. To enter on a description of a
miracle which had been wrought in the lonely night, as this deliverance had been, and to ground their claims to be heard upon circumstances of which the eyes of those to whom they speak could not bear
testimony, is foreign to the whole character of the Apostolic ministry.

διὰ νυκτός.   *διά* cannot have here the sense *throughout* which is
most usual when it is constructed with a genitive. Here the expression means no more than *at night*, for the release took place at one
point of time only. It is found in this sense in xvi. 9.

20. πορεύεσθε καὶ σταθέντες κ.τ.λ., *go ye and stand and speak.* There
was to be no attempt made to conceal their escape. They were to go
back to the same place where their most frequent teachings had been
given before, and were to continue the same teaching. They are not
directed to appeal to the multitude for sympathy, nor to try and
excite any feeling against those who had arrested them.

τὰ ῥήματα τῆς ζωῆς ταύτης.   This has been explained as if it meant
no more than 'these words of life' (see *Winer-Moulton*, pp. 297, 298).
But this weakens the sense immensely. The Apostles were to preach
this new life through the resurrection. It was Christ's own message
(John xi. 25) 'I am the Resurrection and the Life.' It was the words
of *this life* which the Sadducees could not away with. But spite of
all opposition the same teaching about the life to come is to be persisted in.

21. ὑπὸ τὸν ὄρθρον, *at break of day.* The words indicate a time
as soon as possible after day dawn. They lost no time in obeying the
command. How early it was possible for them to come to the Temple
we find from the directions in the Talmud concerning the morning
sacrifice. It is said (Mishna *Joma* III. 1) 'The Memunneh (see note
on iv. 1) said to them: Go ye out (on to the Temple wall or roof) and
see whether the time for killing the sacrifice has arrived. If it had
arrived, the outlooker said, "It has flashed forth" (i.e. day has dawned).
Matthia ben Shemuel said [that the form of question was], "Has the
whole face of the east become lit up as far as to Hebron? And the
man answered, Yes." So that the first sacrifice took place at the very
peep of day.' A like explanation is found Mishna *Tamid* III. 2.

παραγενόμενος, *having come*, i.e. into the council-chamber, to
consider what steps to take about their prisoners.

συνεκάλεσαν τὸ συνέδριον, *they called together the council;* i.e.
the Sanhedrin proper. This was evidently deemed to be a matter of
the gravest character, for, as we see from Gamaliel's presence, it was
not the Sadducees alone who were summoned to the council.

τὴν γερουσίαν.   The word occurs many times in LXX. of the Pentateuch, and in the Apocryphal books, and is variously rendered
elders, council, or *senate* (see 1 Macc. xii. 6 ; 2 Macc. i. 10, iv. 44,

xi. 27). The name indicates that they were older men, who probably were invited as assessors to join the council by reason of their age and consequent weight of character. We can find from the Jewish literature that such assessors were often appointed. In the extract Mishna *Joma* I. 1, quoted on iv. 6, the word for 'assessors' is *parhedrin*, i.e. the Greek πάρεδροι, and the adoption of such a word into the Jewish vocabulary shews that the institution which it describes was of so permanent a nature as to justify the adoption of a foreign expression to describe it.

22. οἱ δὲ παραγενόμενοι ὑπηρέται, *but the officers that came.* The word may refer to some military body, or it may have been only some of the Levitical guard who were sent. The same word is used (Luke iv. 20) for the 'minister' of the synagogue.

23. τοὺς φύλακας, *the guards*, who were of course unconscious that their prisoners were gone.

ἐπὶ τῶν θυρῶν. This, the oldest reading, is not the usual mode of expressing *by, at, beside.* ἐπὶ with the genitive usually means *upon* or *over*, which can hardly be meant here. We find however ἐπὶ τῶν θυρῶν = at the doors, 1 Macc. i. 55, and the singular ἐπὶ τῆς θύρας, in a like sense, LXX. Numb. xi. 10, xii. 5, xxvii. 2.

24. ἤκουσαν τοὺς λόγους τούτους, *heard these words*, i.e. the report of the officers who had been to the prison. ὁ στρατηγὸς τοῦ ἱεροῦ. On this officer see on iv. 1, and on ἀρχιερεῖς iv. 23.

διηπόρουν, *they doubted of them*, i.e. they were at a loss about what was said, and did not know what step to take next. It is worthy of notice that when the Apostles are brought before them in the end, the magistrates avoid all questions about how they had been released. They clearly wished to have no more testimony to the supernatural powers which had been so often manifested in connexion with Jesus and His followers. Caiaphas and his party could not be ignorant how Jesus Himself had risen out of His grave to the great terror of the Jewish guard set over it. Holding the opinions which they did, we can quite understand their perplexity and their silence on the subject, at all events before the disciples and the multitude.

25. παραγενόμενος δέ τις, *and there came one*, &c. The Apostles made no attempt at concealment, and the judgment-hall was at no great distance from the place in which they were teaching.

εἰσὶν ἐν τῷ ἱερῷ κ.τ.λ. Render, *are in the Temple, standing and teaching*, &c. The words look back to the command of the angel in ver. 20, and shew that Peter and his fellows were obedient thereto. This *standing* implies the prominent and undaunted position which the Apostles had taken up. They were not like prisoners who had escaped, and so were seeking a place to hide themselves; but like men whose work had been interfered with, and who, as soon as they were able, had come back to it again.

26. οὐ μετὰ βίας, *without violence.* Nor can we suppose that the Apostles were at all likely to offer resistance, for their examination before the council would afford them an opportunity of proclaiming the message of the Gospel.

On this verse Chrysostom says ὦ τῆς ἀνοίας· ἐφοβοῦντό, φησι, τὸν ὄχλον. τί γὰρ αὐτοὺς ὁ ὄχλος ὠφέλει; δέον τὸν θεὸν φοβηθῆναι τὸν καθάπερ πτηνοὺς ἀεὶ τῶν χειρῶν αὐτοὺς ἐξαρπάζοντα τῶν ἐκείνων, οἱ δὲ μᾶλλον τὸν ὄχλον φοβοῦνται.

μὴ λιθασθῶσιν. After a past tense, as ἐφοβοῦντο, the verb would be expected to be in the optative not in the subjunctive mood. The subjunctive is explained as implying more certainty of a result. Here = 'lest they should be stoned,' as surely they would have been. We have already had evidence of the favour with which the disciples were looked upon by the people, and we can see from the account of the death of Stephen that a sudden outbreak of popular rage might result in the death of him against whom this feeling was displayed. And that the Jewish people were ready enough thus to take the law into their own hands, we can see from the Gospel history (John x. 31—33), and the parables of Jesus speak of such proceedings as though they were of no very rare occurrence (Matth. xxi. 35).

28. παραγγελίᾳ κ.τ.λ., *we strictly charged you.* The charge had been given (iv. 18) only to Peter and John, but the magistrates assume that it has been conveyed by them to their companions.

For this manner of expressing *intensity,* by the dative case of a cognate noun joined to the verb, cf. Luke xxii. 15 ἐπιθυμίᾳ ἐπεθύμησα = 'I have earnestly desired.' Other examples are in John iii. 29; Acts xxiii. 14.

ἐπὶ τῷ ὀνόματι τούτῳ, i.e. resting all your teaching upon this name. They go at once to that which is the great offence in their eyes. The name of Jesus of Nazareth, whom they knew to have been crucified, but who was proclaimed to be alive again, and whose followers manifested such mighty works, was the object against which their power was directed.

πεπληρώκατε τὴν Ἱερουσαλήμ, *ye have filled Jerusalem.* The best of evidence, coming from the mouths of adversaries, that the Apostles had actively fulfilled the first part of Christ's directions (i. 8).

καὶ βούλεσθε κ.τ.λ., *and ye wish to bring this man's blood upon us.* It is a marvellous spectacle to see judges take the place of culprits, and deprecate accusation where they would naturally be dealing out penalties. But the invocation of the people before Christ's crucifixion, 'His blood be upon us and upon our children' (Matth. xxvii. 25), was felt by the council to be likely to be brought to fulfilment.

29. καὶ οἱ ἀπόστολοι, *and the Apostles.* It is quite like the style of the New Testament to say 'Peter and the Apostles' (cf. Mark xvi. 7). It is not implied hereby that Peter was excluded from the number of the Apostles, but, as he probably was the chief speaker, his name is singled out for prominence in the narrative (see note on iv. 6). Here again we have evidence that St Luke has made no attempt to do more than produce for us the substance of such speeches as he notices.

πειθαρχεῖν δεῖ. Render, *we must obey*. The argument is that of Peter and John (iv. 19) on a former occasion, though here there is more stress laid on the impossibility of doing otherwise.

30. **ὁ θεὸς τῶν πατέρων ἡμῶν.** The Apostles point out, just as Peter did (iii. 13), that there is no severance of themselves from the worship of the Covenant God of Israel. On the contrary they were teaching that His promise through Moses had now been fulfilled, since in Jesus the promised prophet had appeared. Cf. Deut. xviii. 15, and St Peter's speech, Acts iii. 22.

ὃν ὑμεῖς κ.τ.λ. Render, *whom ye hanged on a tree and slew.* This sentence describes the Roman, and not the Jewish mode of execution. By the Jewish law only those who were already dead were to be hanged (Deut. xxi. 22; Josh. x. 26).

In the word **διεχειρίσασθε** the Apostles point out that the guilt of the Crucifixion was as truly upon the Jews as if they had slain Jesus with their own hands. The phrase κρεμάσαντες ἐπὶ ξύλου is used again (x. 39) by St Peter, and by nobody else in the N.T. He also has ξύλον = tree, for σταυρός, a cross, in 1 Pet. ii. 24, 'He bare our sins in His own body on the *tree.*'

31. **ἀρχηγὸν καὶ σωτῆρα,** *a prince and a Saviour.* If Christ seeks to rule it is that He may save those who take His yoke upon them.

τῇ δεξιᾷ, *by His right hand,* as in ii. 33. The right hand is the symbol of might. Cf. 'His right hand, and His holy arm, hath gotten Him the victory' (Ps. xcviii. 1).

δοῦναι μετάνοιαν, *for to give repentance,* thus offering the way of salvation to all those who were ready to accept it. These words to a Jew would have great significance, for they had a saying (T. B. *Sanhedrin* 113 a) that salvation was one of the things which God kept in His own power. If Christ then was to bestow this gift on Israel He must be owned by them as God.

32. **καὶ ἡμεῖς ἐσμὲν μάρτυρες τῶν ῥ. τ.,** *and we are witnesses of these things,* i.e. of the Crucifixion, Resurrection and Ascension.

καὶ τὸ πνεῦμα τὸ ἅγιον, *and so is the Holy Ghost.* Christ had said, while alive, concerning the Holy Ghost, 'He shall testify of Me' (John xv. 26). And this He now did in the minds of the Apostles by 'bringing all things to their remembrance,' and by enlightening them to see how Christ's life had fulfilled the prophecies, and also in the mighty powers which through the outpouring of the Spirit they now possessed.

τοῖς πειθαρχοῦσιν, *to them that obey Him.* Thus the disciples declare that the obedience to God, which at the outset (ver. 29) they had proclaimed as their bounden duty, was also the reason why the Holy Ghost had been bestowed upon them. They leave it to be gathered that what God has done He will do again, and bestow like gifts of grace on others who are willing to obey Him.

33—42. Effect of the Apostles' Defence. Counsel of Gamaliel. Release and subsequent Conduct of the Twelve.

33. διεπρίοντο. The active voice of this verb is used (LXX. 1 Chron. xx. 3) in its literal sense of 'to saw asunder,' the passive generally in the figurative sense of the rending of the heart. In Acts vii. 54, where the word occurs again, ταῖς καρδίαις is added, and it is necessary to supply those words here to complete the sense. The effect described is not the compunction which leads to repentance, but the irritation that results in more furious anger.

ἐβουλεύοντο, *they took counsel.* Some good MSS. read ἐβούλοντο, *they wished.* The Vulgate has *cogitabant.*

34. ἀναστὰς δέ τις, *but there stood up one,* &c. See note on verse 25. Gamaliel rose to oppose the plan or wish.

Φαρισαῖος. It may very well be believed that some small sympathy towards the Christian teachers would be roused in the breast of a Pharisee, because they maintained, as he did, the doctrine of a resurrection, but there is nothing in the speech of this Pharisee beyond a policy of inactivity, bred perhaps of despair.

Γαμαλιήλ. This Gamaliel, called here νομοδιδάσκαλος, is no doubt the same person who is mentioned (Acts xxii. 3) as the teacher of St Paul. He is known in Jewish writings as Gamaliel ha-Zaken (i.e. the old), and was the grandson of Hillel. He was alive during the time when Herod was beautifying the Temple. For in *Tosephta Shabbath* xiv. we read, 'Rabbi Jose said, It happened that Rabbi Khalaphta went to Rabban Gamaliel (the younger, and grandson of the Gamaliel in our text) to Tiberias, and found him sitting at the table of Rabbi Jochanan ben-Nozâph, and in his (Gamaliel's) hand was the book of Job in Targum (i.e. in the Chaldee paraphrase), and he (Gamaliel) was reading in it. Rabbi Khalaphta said to him, I remember concerning Rabban Gamaliel the elder, the father of thy father, that he was sitting on a step in the Temple mount, and they brought before him the book of Job, in Targum, and he said to the builder, "Sink it (bury it) under this course of the wall."' This could only have been when the walls were in building.

Gamaliel is said to have died 18 years before the Temple was destroyed.

In T. B. *Abodah Zarah* 11 a, in allusion to the custom of burning beds, clothes, and other things, at the funerals of great men (see Jer. xxxiv. 5), it is said, 'When Rabban Gamaliel the elder died, Onkelos the proselyte burned in his honour the worth of 70 minæ of Tyrian money.'

So great was Gamaliel's fame that we read (Mishna *Sotah* ix. 15) when he died 'the glory of the Torah ceased, and purity and sanctity died out also.' We can therefore understand that he was 'had in reputation among all the people.'

βραχύ τι, *a little space,* i.e. for a short time. He could then say more unrestrainedly what he wished to say to his colleagues.

τοὺς ἀνθρώπους, *the men.* In Gamaliel's mouth they would not be styled *apostles.*

35. προσέχετε ἑαυτοῖς. The phrase implies the need of thought. *Attendite vobis* (Vulg.). It is not a warning against some danger that might result. 'Think well over what ye mean to do.'

ἐπί. The preposition seems to go better with προσέχετε than with πράσσειν. 'Think well *upon* these men,' rather than, 'what ye mean to do *with* these men.'

36. Θευδᾶς, *Theudas.* Gamaliel proceeds to give illustrations that mere pretenders will come to nought. But about the mention of Theudas much discussion has been raised, because it is declared that the statements of Gamaliel contradict the facts recorded by Josephus, and therefore cannot be received as historic. In this way discredit would be thrown on all the rest of his speech.

It is true that Josephus mentions a Theudas (*Ant.* xx. 5. 1) who rose up and professed himself a prophet, in the time when Fadus was procurator of Judæa, about A.D. 45 or 46, and persuaded a great part of the people to take their goods and follow him to the river Jordan, through which he promised he would afford them a miraculous passage. This man, who, with many of his followers, was destroyed, could clearly not be the leader of the revolt which took place before that raised by Judas of Galilee in the time of the taxing which took place some few years after our Lord was born. But when we turn to the history which Josephus gives of the events which preceded this rebellion of Judas we find him saying (*Ant.* xvii. 10. 4), 'At this time [i.e. in the days when Varus was president of Syria] there were *ten thousand* other disorders in Judæa, which were like tumults.' Of these innumerable disturbances he gives account of no more than four, but presently in the same chapter says: 'Judæa was full of robberies, and whenever the several companies of the rebels could light upon any one to head them, he was created a king immediately.' Then in a brief space after (*Ant.* xviii. 1. 1) Josephus proceeds to mention Judas of Galilee, though he calls him sometimes (*Ant.* xviii. 1. 6, xx. 5. 2; *B. J.* ii. 8. 1, and 17. 8) a Galilean and sometimes a Gaulonite (xviii. 1. 1), and his rebellion in the days of the taxing. Now amid so many outbreaks, spoken of but not described, there is no violence in supposing that one may have been led by a Theudas, a name not very uncommon, and thus the order of events as stated by Gamaliel would be perfectly correct. The *great multitude* of the followers of the later Theudas indicates a far larger number than the *four hundred* of whom Gamaliel speaks. Moreover while Gamaliel's Theudas was killed and his followers dispersed, Josephus says that many of the adherents of his Theudas were slain, and many taken prisoners. There seems, therefore, more reason to identify this Theudas of whom mention is made by Gamaliel with some of the *ten thousand* rebels whom Josephus speaks of before the time of the census, than to suppose that Gamaliel, who is correct in his account of Judas, has mentioned in the other case a rebel who did not rise till long after the time of which he is speaking.

That such false leaders were numerous and had caused a terror in the minds of the more thoughtful among the Jews we can see from the Jewish literature which has come down to us. Thus (T. B. *Sanhedrin* 97 b) Rabbi Shemuel bar Nachmani on the authority of Rabbi Jonathan, expounding Habakkuk ii. 3, says, 'It means, may his spirit be blown away (perish) whosoever over-anxiously calculates about the ends. For people have said [in consequence of such calculations] when the end [so calculated] came, and he [Messiah] did not come, that He would never come at all. Yet wait anxiously for Him, for it says, if He tarry wait anxiously for Him.' We have here the despairing echo of Gamaliel's words, 'Let them alone.'

λέγων εἶναί τινα, *saying that he was somebody.* Of course each one of these leaders professed himself to be the Messiah, for that was what the people in their distress were ever looking for.

προσεκλίθη. This reading is better supported than προσεκολλήθη. It is not easy to decide which the *Vulgate* represents by *consensit.* There is some little degree more of *attachment* implied in προσεκλίθη. Cf. its use 2 Macc. xiv. 24 ψυχικῶς τῷ ἀνδρὶ προσεκέκλιτο, 'he loved the man from his heart.'

The passive voice is here used in the sense of the middle, 'joined themselves.'

37. Ἰούδας ὁ Γαλιλαῖος. With this account agrees the history of Josephus (*Ant.* XVIII. 1. 1), except, as has been already noticed, he calls Judas Γαυλανίτης, but as when speaking of the same man again (XX. 5. 2) he calls him Γαλιλαῖος, and in the same sentence alludes to the history before narrated, 'as we have shewn in a foregoing book,' we can have no hesitation in accepting Gamaliel's story as the correct one, while at the same time we may learn from this example what value we ought to place on the accuracy of Josephus when we have to weigh his statements against those of the New Testament.

τῆς ἀπογραφῆς, *of the taxing.* Not the same which is mentioned Luke ii. 2. That was rather an *enrolment* or census-taking preliminary to taxation. The revolt of Judas, about seven years later, was caused by the actual imposition of a tax. Josephus says of it (XVIII. 1. 1): 'Cyrenius came into Judæa to take an account of their substance,' and afterwards: 'Judas said that this taxation was no better than an introduction to slavery, and exhorted the nation to assert their liberty.'

ἀπέστησεν λαὸν ὀπίσω αὐτοῦ, *drew away people* (i.e. some of the people) *after him.*

ἀπώλετο, *he perished.* Josephus gives no notice of the fate of Judas and his party, though he mentions the revolt several times and says (*B. J.* II. 8. 1) that this 'Judas was a teacher of a peculiar sect of his own.'

38. ἐὰν ᾖ. This construction, = '*if it should be* (and we do not yet know whether it may be) *of men*' is followed by εἰ with the indicative ἐστί in the next verse. The latter form is often used to mean '*if it is* (as indeed it is)'; but we can hardly suppose this to be Gamaliel's meaning, yet he may have employed this form to indicate that he felt there was more to be said in favour of the Apostles, backed as they were by such mighty signs, than could be alleged for previous movements.

καταλυθήσεται, *it will be overthrown.*

39. οὐ δυνήσεσθε καταλῦσαι αὐτούς, *ye will not be able to overthrow them.*

μήποτε, *lest haply.* The construction looks back to verse 35, προσέχετε ἑαυτοῖς.

40. προσκαλεσάμενοι κ.τ.λ., *having called the Apostles,* i.e. to return again into the judgment-hall.

δείραντες, *having beaten them,* as being the guilty parties. (See Deut. xxv. 1—3.)

41. κατηξιώθησαν ὑπὲρ τοῦ ὀνόματος ἀτιμασθῆναι. The Apostles count as glory what the world would count as shame. Cf. Gal. vi. 14, 'God forbid that I should *glory* save in the *cross* of our Lord Jesus Christ.' This figure of speech (called oxymoron, and consisting in the effective contrast of words opposite in meaning) is common in the New Testament. Cp. 2 Cor. vi. 8—10.

ὑπὲρ τ. ὀ. Render, *for the Name.* That name of which St Peter had said (iv. 12), 'There is none other name under heaven, given among men, whereby we must be saved.'

42. ἐν τῷ ἱερῷ καὶ κατ' οἶκον. Render, *in the Temple and at home,* as in ii. 46. These are the two fields of labour; in the Temple, where they had apparently come to be expected by the converts, and after that public teaching there were other meetings in private houses, whither those might come who could not go to the Temple.

τὸν Χριστὸν Ἰησοῦν, *Jesus the Christ,* the Messiah, God's Anointed. This is *the Name* of the previous verse.

CHAPTER VI.

Readings varying from the *Text. recept.*

3. ἁγίου omitted after πνεύματος with ℵBCD. *Vulg.* 'sancto.'

8. χάριτος instead of πίστεως with ℵABD. *Vulg.* 'gratia.'

13. λαλῶν ῥήματα omitting βλάσφημα with ℵABCD. *Vulg.* 'loqui verba' only.

τούτου omitted with ℵDEHP. *Vulg.* 'locum sanctum' only.

Ch. VI. 1—7. Murmuring about the Distribution of the
common Fund. Measures for allaying it.

By the confession of the high-priest himself (Acts v. 28) Jerusalem
was now filled with the teaching of the Christians, and thus the first
step was accomplished in the course which Christ had ordained (i. 8)
for the publication of the Gospel. Now, therefore, the historian of
the Church's progress turns to deal with other events and different
persons, because he has to tell of a persecution which caused Christian
missionaries to go forth for the next stage of the work, the spread of
the faith through Judæa and Samaria (viii. 1). The means which
God employed for this end are not such as an inventor in the second
century would have been likely to hit upon, nor such as any writer
who merely desired to magnify the Apostles would have adopted.
A system for the more effectual relief of the widows among the congregation is devised, and an outburst of popular rage, causing the
death of one of the dispensers of the relief-funds, disperses the greater
part of the Church of Jerusalem. A person who was free to choose
(as an inventor would have been) would scarcely have selected one of
the seven deacons for the first Christian martyr, and have left the
Apostles out of sight, while giving the history of Stephen. The
choice of such a writer would have surely fallen upon one of the Twelve
to be the first to die for the faith.

1. ἐν δὲ ταῖς ἡμέραις ταύταις, *now in these days.* The words
refer back to verse 14 of the previous chapter, where we read 'believers
were added to the Lord, multitudes (πλήθη) both of men and women.'

πληθυνόντων κ.τ.λ. Render, *when the number of the disciples was
multiplying.* The participle is in the present tense, and its meaning
should be fully expressed. It was at the time when this sudden increase was in progress that the difficulty arose which led to the murmuring. The numbers of the society increased so rapidly that the
superintendence of the relief of the needy claimed the full devotion of
the Apostles, and proved in the end more than they could discharge.

ἐγένετο γογγυσμός, *there arose a murmuring.* The noun is not
classical, but is found in the LXX. of Exodus (xvi. 7, 8, 9, 12) and
Numbers (xvii. 5, 10), as well as in Wisdom (i. 10, 11) and in Ecclus.
xlvi. 7, κοπάσαι γογγυσμὸν πονηρίας, 'to appease the murmuring of
wickedness.' By the readiness with which the Apostles took measures
to remedy what was complained of, we may infer that there had been
shewn sufficient cause for complaint. This may easily have come to
pass without any fault on the part of the Twelve, simply from the
sudden growth of the number of Christians. Chrysostom's remark is
οὐ γάρ ἐστιν ἀκρίβειαν ἐν πλήθει εἶναι.

τῶν Ἑλληνιστῶν. Properly applied to Greek-speaking Jews. These
were either (1) Jews who had been born in countries where Greek was
the vernacular, and so did not speak Hebrew, nor join in the Hebrew
services of the Jews of the Holy Land, but had synagogues of their
own in Jerusalem; or else (2) they were proselytes. In either case
they had embraced Christianity as Jews for as yet the Gospel had

been preached to Jews only. That provision was made for a Greek service for the foreign Jews we may see from T. Jerus. *Sotah*, VII. 1 (Gemara), 'Rabbi Levi, the son of Hithah, went to Cæsarea, and heard the voice of the people saying the *Shema* (the name given to the Hebrew confession "Hear, O Israel, the Lord thy God, Jehovah is one," from its first word) in Hellenistic. He desired to prevent them. Rabbi Jose heard of it and was angry, and said, Thus I say, that whosoever does not know how to read it correctly in Hebrew shall not read it at all [in that language], but does his duty [by reading it] in any language which he knows how to speak.'

πρὸς τοὺς Ἑβραίους, *against the Hebrews.* These were the Jews by birth, whose home was in the Holy Land, and who spoke that Aramaic dialect which the N. T. calls Hebrew.

ὅτι...αἱ χῆραι αὐτῶν, *because their widows were* (overlooked, or) *neglected,* &c. Such widows, speaking a foreign language and being desolate, would be the persons most likely to be overlooked amid the increasing number of applicants for help.

ἐν τῇ διακονίᾳ κ.τ.λ. This noun is rendered in xi. 29 by *relief,* and, from the class of persons on whose behalf the complaint was made, it is clear that it bears the same sense here. The word διάκονος (deacon) has therefore been used as the name of these officers, whose appointment was at first made that they might have care of and distribute the funds contributed by the rich members for the relief of the needy. The appellation is nowhere directly given to the seven. They are still the seven in xxi. 8. The deacons of the Pastoral Epistles are a later provision. We can nevertheless see from St Stephen's work that the labours of the seven were not confined to relief-duties alone, for he is a mighty preacher and endued with gifts of the Holy Ghost in the same way as the Apostles. It is deserving of notice that, before we find any special arrangements made for what we now understand by 'divine service,' the regulation of the relief of those in need had become so engrossing a part of the duty of the Twelve as to have thrust aside in some degree the prayers and ministration of the word, which were especially their charge. In these early days they appear to have acted according to St James' teaching (i. 27), 'Pure religion (θρησκεία) and undefiled before God and the Father is this, to visit the fatherless and widows in their affliction, and to keep himself unspotted from the world.'

2. οἱ δώδεκα, *the Twelve.* They had found that there was cause for the complaint, and at once set about providing a remedy.

τὸ πλῆθος τῶν μαθητῶν. We are not from this to suppose that an attempt was made to gather every one who in Jerusalem called himself a Christian, but that a large and special meeting was convened, before which the Apostles laid their plan. The funds had been given by various persons, and were for the common relief; it was therefore fit that a change in the distributors should be considered in common.

οὐκ ἀρεστόν ἐστιν. Render, *it is not pleasing* (or *fit*). 'Non est æquum,' *Vulg.* The duties were not properly distributed. Those were now engrossed in business duties who alone could be the true exponents of Christ's life and teaching.

καταλείψαντας κ.τ.λ., *that we should forsake the Word of God.* The verb is a strong one, and implies that the whole time of the Twelve was being consumed by these cares for the temporal wants of the brethren.

διακονεῖν τραπέζαις, *to serve tables*, means to preside at the bench or counter where the money was distributed. Cf. the *τρά-πεζαι* of the money-changers (Matth. xxi. 12), who are themselves called *τραπεζῖται* (Matth. xxv. 27).

διακονεῖν is to discharge the *διακονία* mentioned in verse 1.

3. ἐπισκέψασθε οὖν κ.τ.λ., *but look ye out from among you.* If the selection were committed to the whole body there could hardly fail to be an end put to the oversight and so to the murmuring.

ἀδελφοί, *brethren.* One of the earliest names employed in addressing the members of the Church, and particularly suitable to this occasion.

μαρτυρουμένους. Literally, *attested, well reported of*, as in 1 Tim. v. 10. The same word is rendered *of good report* afterwards in x. 22.

ἑπτά. The number *seven* was probably fixed on because that was the number of persons chosen to manage public business in Jewish towns. See Mishna *Megillah* III. 1, 'The men of the city who dispose of city market-places may buy with the price thereof a synagogue, or if they sell a synagogue, they may buy an ark (to keep the Law in), or if they sell an ark, they may buy wrappers (the ornamental and costly covers in which the Law was rolled) for the Law, and if they sell these wrappers they may buy books (i.e. the Prophets and the Hagiographa), and if they sell books they may buy a copy of the Torah, but if they have sold a Torah they may not buy books,' and so on in the contrary order.

On this ordinance it is said, T. B. *Megillah* 26 a, 'Raba says, This is only applicable when *the seven good men of the city* sell anything in the presence of the men of the city.'

πλήρεις πνεύματος καὶ σοφίας, *full of the Spirit and of wisdom.* They were to be approved both by God and man. Men could judge of their wisdom, and God had in these days shed forth the Spirit on many.

καταστήσομεν, *we will appoint.* Some authorities read *καταστή-σωμεν*, and that appears to be represented by *constituamus* of the *Vulgate*. While leaving to the assembled brethren the selection of the men, the Apostles keep some control still with themselves. They certainly would judge best concerning the spiritual fitness of the chosen seven.

τῇ προσευχῇ καὶ τῇ διακονίᾳ τοῦ λόγου, *to prayer and to the ministry of the word*, which explains what is meant by 'to forsake the word of God' in verse 2. Here again we have the word *διακονία* to describe the Apostle's duty of preaching and teaching. Each office was, if

duly performed, a part of the service which was laid upon the whole
Church. Cp. Milton, Sonnet xiv., 'They also serve who only stand
and wait.'

4. προσκαρτερήσομεν, *we will give ourselves continually.* The
word is of frequent use to describe the earnest, stedfast character of
the early disciples. Thus i. 14 of their continuance in prayer; ii. 42
of continuing stedfastly in the Apostles' doctrine. Cf. also ii. 46 and
Rom. xii. 12.

5. καὶ ἤρεσεν κ.τ.λ., *and the saying pleased the whole multitude.*
The construction ἤρεσεν ἐνώπιον is not classical but is common in the
LXX. Cf. Deut. i. 23; 2 Sam. iii. 36; 1 Kings iii. 10. In 1 Macc.
viii. 21 we have the very expression καὶ ἤρεσεν ὁ λόγος ἐνώπιον αὐτῶν. There was clearly no thought of neglecting any, and when
the oversight was known and a remedy proposed all were rejoiced
thereat.

καὶ ἐξελέξαντο κ.τ.λ., *and they chose out Stephen,* &c. If we may
judge of the men's nationality from the names they bear, every one
of the seven was of the Grecians. The names are all Greek, and
such a choice marks the desire of all the Church to put an end to
every cause of complaint, and as it were to say, We know that as we
should not wilfully overlook a Greek who was in need, so no Greek
Christian would of purpose neglect a Hebrew widow, and to shew
our trust we choose Greeks to have the whole oversight of this duty.
Of the men who were chosen, except Stephen, we hear in future
only of Philip (viii. 5) as a preacher in Samaria, and he is supposed
to be, and probably is, the same person as 'Philip the evangelist' mentioned xxi. 8.

There is a tradition that Nicolas was the originator of that error of
the Nicolaitans against which St John speaks in such condemnatory
terms in the Apocalypse (Rev. ii. 6, 15). Irenæus and Tertullian both
make this statement, and if there was a Judas among the Apostles,
one of the seven *may* have been an apostate. But even in the early
ages of the Church there was much uncertainty about this matter,
and there is no very trustworthy evidence for connecting this Nicolas
with the licentious body whom St John condemns.

Νικόλαον προσήλυτον 'Αντιοχέα. Some have thought that, from
this description of Nicolas, he was the only proselyte among the
seven, but the distinction of such a special addition may have been
given to him because he came from Antioch, while the other six were
of Jerusalem.

6. ἐνώπιον τῶν ἀποστόλων, *before the Apostles.* That they might
confirm, as they had proposed to do, the selection made by the congregation.

ἐπέθηκαν αὐτοῖς τὰς χεῖρας. The laying on of hands thus became
the solemn mode of dedication to the ministry of Christ's Church.

7. ηὔξανεν, *increased,* i.e. the word of God was more widely published now that the Apostles were freed from secular cares, and left

to give themselves unto the ministry of the word. (Cf. for the expression xii. 24, xix. 20.)

πολύς τε ὄχλος τῶν ἱερέων, *a great company of the priests.* To these men the sacrifice would be greater than to the ordinary Israelite, for they would experience the fullest weight of the hatred against the Christians, and would lose their status and support, as well as their friends. This is no doubt the reason why such special mention is made of them.

ὑπήκουον τῇ πίστει, *became obedient to the faith.* As faith in Christ was the first demand made on those who desired to enter the new communion, it is easy to understand how the Christian religion gained from the first the name of 'the Faith.' Cf. xiii. 8, xiv. 22, xvi. 5, xxiv. 24.

8—15. OF STEPHEN'S PREACHING, ARREST AND ACCUSATION.

8. πλήρης χάριτος, *full of grace.* The *Text. recept.* has arisen from a desire to make this verse conform to verse 5.

δυνάμεως, *power,* i.e. of working miracles, with which he at least among the seven seems to have been endued equally with the Apostles.

On this Chrysostom remarks ὅρα, πῶς καὶ ἐν τοῖς ἑπτὰ ἦν τις πρόκριτος καὶ τὰ πρωτεῖα εἶχεν. εἰ γὰρ καὶ ἡ χειροτονία κοινή, ἀλλ᾽ ὅμως οὗτος ἐπεσπάσατο χάριν πλείονα.

9. ἀνέστησαν δέ, *but there arose.* There is a danger that *then* in the A. V. may be taken as a mark of time = τότε (as in verse 11).

τινες τῶν...καὶ τῶν. As an explanation of occurrence of τῶν twice and no more, it has been suggested that only two synagogues are meant, and that one was that of the Libertini, Cyrenians and Alexandrians, the other that of the Jews from Cilicia and Asia. But the necessity for the repetition of the τῶν arises because while the first three names represent cities, Rome, Cyrene, and Alexandria, the others Cilicia and Asia are names of districts, and as ἀπὸ must therefore be put before Κιλικίας the article is needed before the preposition to make a complete construction, τῶν ἀπὸ Κιλικίας standing as if = Κιλίκων.

Render : *some of them that were of the synagogue called the synagogue of the Libertines and of the Cyrenians and of the Alexandrians.* For the number of synagogues in Jerusalem was very great. The Λιβέρτινοι were most likely the children of some Jews who had been carried captive to Rome by Pompey (B.C. 63), and had been made freedmen (*libertini*) by their captors, and after their return to Jerusalem had formed one congregation and used one synagogue specially. There is an interesting illustration of this severance of congregations among the Jews from a like cause in the description of the modern Jewish communities in Malabar and Cochin. It is in a MS. in the Cambridge University Library (Oo. 1. 47) which was written in 1781. 'At this time are found in their dwelling-places about forty white householders, and in all the other places are black Jews found, and their forefathers *were the slaves* of the white Jews, and now the black

Jews, as found in all the places, are about five hundred householders, and they have ten synagogues, while the white Jews have only one. And the white Jews dwell all together and their ritual is distinct from that of the black Jews, and they will not count them [the black Jews] among the ten [necessary for forming a congregation] except a few families of them; but if any of the white Jews go to their [the black Jews'] synagogues, they will admit him as one of the ten.'

On the Jews in Cyrene see note on ii. 10.

There were Jews resident in Alexandria in Christ's time and had been long before, as we learn from the history of the Septuagint version, and in the Talmud we are told they were very numerous. Thus, T. B. *Succah* 51 b, it is said, 'Rabbi Jehudah said: He that has not seen the amphitheatre at Alexandria (apparently used for the Jewish worship) in Egypt has not seen the glory of Israel. They say it was like a great Basilica with gallery above gallery. Sometimes there were in it double the number of those who went out from Egypt, and there were in it seventy-one seats of gold corresponding to the seventy-one members of the great Sanhedrin, each one of them worth not less than twenty-one myriads of talents of gold, and there was a platform of wood in the midst thereof, and the minister of the synagogue stood upon it with flags in his hand, and when the time [in the service] came that they should answer Amen, then he waved with the flag and all the people answered Amen.' In spite of the exaggeration of the numbers in this story we may be certain from it that there was a very large Jewish population in Alexandria, and that they were likely to have a separate synagogue in Jerusalem. For another portion of this story see note on xviii. 3. See also Joseph. *Ant.* xiv. 7, § 2 and xiv. 10, § 1.

τῶν ἀπὸ Κιλικίας. Cilicia was at the S.E. corner of Asia Minor. One of its principal towns was Tarsus, the birthplace of St Paul, and there were no doubt many other Jews there, descendants of those Jews whom Antiochus the Great introduced into Asia Minor (Joseph. *Ant.* xii. 3. 4), two thousand families of whom he placed there as well-disposed guardians of the country. St Paul himself may have been one of these.

'Ασίας. See note on ii. 9.

συνζητοῦντες, *disputing*. The word is used of the captious questionings of the Pharisees (Mark viii. 11) and of the scribes (Mark ix. 14) with Jesus and His disciples.

10. ἀντιστῆναι, *to resist*. The very word used in Christ's promise (Luke xxi. 15), οὐ δυνήσονται...ἀντιστῆναι ἅπαντες ἀντικείμενοι ὑμῖν.

11. ὑπέβαλον, *they suborned*. Suborn=to provide, but nearly always used in a bad sense. *Subornation* of perjury is the legal phrase for procuring a person who will take a false oath.

λέγοντας, *which said*. The charge here laid against Stephen is afterwards (verse 14) defined. Blasphemous words against Moses and against God was the construction which these witnesses put upon language which had probably been uttered by Stephen in the same way as Christ had said (John iv. 21), ' The time cometh when ye shall

neither in this mountain, nor yet at Jerusalem, worship the Father.'
The reflection of Chrysostom is: ὦ ἀναίσχυντοι· πράγματα ποιεῖτε
βλάσφημα εἰς τὸν θεόν, καὶ οὐ φροντίζετε. καὶ Μωσέως φροντίζειν προσ-
ποιεῖσθε; διὰ τοῦτο πρόσκειται Μωσῆς ἐπειδὴ τὰ τοῦ θεοῦ οὐ σφόδρα
αὐτοῖς ἔμελεν, καὶ ἄνω καὶ κάτω Μωσέως μέμνηνται.

12. συνεκίνησάν τε τὸν λαόν, *and they stirred up the people*, who
would be easily roused, if they were told that the glory of the Temple
was spoken against.   It was an object of much admiration, as we can
see from many parts of the Gospels.   Cf. Matth. xxiv. 1.

τοὺς πρεσβυτέρους καὶ τοὺς γραμματεῖς.   Neither elders nor scribes
would need much rousing, their anger was kindled already. Cf. iv. 5.

ἐπιστάντες συνήρπασαν, *they came upon him and caught him*.   The
words indicate a good deal of violence, and this action is a fit prelude
to the still greater outburst when Stephen's defence was concluded
(vii. 57).

13. μάρτυρας ψευδεῖς, *false witnesses*.   Their falseness consists in
the perverted turn which they gave to the words of Stephen.   Though
we have no speech of his hitherto recorded, we can see from the character of his defence in the next chapter that he must have been heard
to declare that the worship of God was no longer to be restricted as it
had been to the Temple at Jerusalem.   And just as in the accusation
of Christ (Matth. xxvi. 61) the witnesses (called, as here, false, and for
a like reason) perverted a saying of Jesus, 'Destroy this temple and in
three days I will raise it up,' which St John (ii. 21) explains, into 'I
am able to destroy the temple of God and to build it in three days,' so
the words of Stephen, which spake of a worship now 'to be bound to
no fixed spot, and fettered by no inflexible externality' (Zeller), were
twisted into an utterance against the Temple and the Law, called in ver.
11 blasphemy against Moses and against God; and by the use of these
two phrases as equivalent the one to the other, they shew us how God
and Moses meant for them no more than their Temple and its ritual.

οὐ παύεται λαλῶν ῥήματα, *ceaseth not to speak words*.

14. ἀκηκόαμεν γάρ, *for we have heard*.   No doubt there was some
handle afforded for their statement by St Stephen's language, just as
in the case of Jesus Himself.   We may gather what the character of
that language must have been from vii. 48, 'the Most High dwelleth not in temples made with hands.' And to Jewish people at this
time to sever worship from Jerusalem was the same thing as to
destroy the Temple.   The attempt which has been made to shew that
the charge against Stephen is merely a reproduction of that made
against Jesus is seen to be futile when we observe that in Stephen's
case the witnesses know nothing of 'the raising up again of the
temple,' and that Stephen himself, by not contradicting but explaining their accusation in his defence, points out that their statement had
a widely different origin from that which gave cause to the accusation
of Jesus.

15. ἀτενίσαντες, *looking stedfastly*, which was what they would naturally do when he was about to make his defence.

ὡσεὶ πρόσωπον ἀγγέλου, *as it had been the face of an angel.* Either because of the dignity which Stephen's natural look displayed —he was calm and undisturbed, confident in his good cause and supported by the Spirit—or as his gaze soon afterwards (vii. 56) beheld the open heavens and the glory of Christ enthroned on high, it may be that this verse speaks of what was supernatural, and that the face of Stephen was already illumined with the radiancy of the new Jerusalem. Chrysostom on this heavenly illumination says οὕτως ἔστι καὶ ἐν ἐλάττονι ὄντας βαθμῷ λάμπειν.

We have the same expression used about St Paul in *Acta Pauli et Theclæ* 2, ἀγγέλου πρόσωπον εἶχεν, and in the preceding line it is also said of him that he was χάριτος πλήρης, as Stephen is described in verse 8 of this chapter.

For a similar phrase see note on vii. 20.

CHAPTER VII.

Readings varying from the *Text. recept.*

1. ἄρα before ταῦτα omitted with ℵABC. The *Vulg.* has nothing to express it.

5. δοῦναι αὐτῷ with BCDHP. *Vulg.* 'dare illi.'

7. ὁ θεὸς εἶπεν with ℵABC.

11. τὴν Αἴγυπτον with ℵABC. *Vulg.* 'in universam Ægyptum.'

12. σιτία εἰς Αἴγυπτον with ℵABCE.

13. Omit τοῦ before Ἰωσήφ with BC. In ℵAE we have τὸ γένος αὐτοῦ. *Vulg.* 'genus ejus.'

14. Ἰακὼβ τὸν πατέρα with ℵABCDE. *Vulg.* 'Jacob patrem suum.'

Omit the second αὐτοῦ with ℵABCHP.

15. καὶ κατέβη with ℵACEP.

16. ᾧ for ὅ with ℵABCDE.

ἐν for τοῦ before Συχέμ, with ℵBC.

17. ὡμολόγησεν for ὤμοσεν with ℵABC. *Vulg.* 'confessus erat.'

18. ἐπ' Αἴγυπτον added after ἕτερος with ℵABC. *Vulg.* 'in Ægypto.'

19. Omit ἡμῶν after πατέρας with ℵBD.

τὰ βρέφη ἔκθετα with ℵABC.

20. Omit αὐτοῦ with ℵABCHP.

21 ἐκτεθέντος δὲ αὐτοῦ with ℵABCD. *Vulg.* 'exposito autem illo.'

22. ἐν πάσῃ σοφίᾳ with אACE.

  ἐν before ἔργοις omitted with אABCDH. *Vulg.* has 'in.'

25. Omit αὐτοῦ after ἀδελφοὺς with אBC. *Vulg.* 'fratres' only.

  σωτηρίαν αὐτοῖς with אABCD. *Vulg.* 'salutem illis.'

27. ἐφ' ἡμῶν with אABCHP.

30. Omit κυρίου with אABC. *Vulg.* has 'angelus' only.

31. Omit πρὸς αὐτόν with אAB. *Vulg.* has 'vox Domini, dicens.'

32. Omit ὁ θεὸς before Ἰσαὰκ and Ἰακώβ with אABC. The *Vulg.* has 'Deus' in each place.

33. ἐφ' ᾧ with אABCD.

34. ἀποστελῶ with אABCDE. *Vulg.* 'mittam.'

35. ἀπέσταλκεν σὺν χειρὶ with אABDE. *Vulg.* 'misit cum manu.'

36. ἐν γῇ Αἰγύπτῳ with אAEHP. *Vulg.* 'in terra Ægypti.'

37. ἀναστήσει ὁ θεὸς ἐκ with אABD. *Vulg.* 'suscitabit Deus de.'

  αὐτοῦ ἀκούσεσθε omitted with אABHP. *Vulg.* has 'ipsum audietis.'

39. ἐν before ταῖς καρδίαις with אABC.

40. ἐγένετο for γέγονεν with אABC.

43. Omit ὑμῶν before Ῥεφάν with BD. *Vulg.* has 'vestri.'

44. Omit ἐν before τοῖς πατράσιν with אABCDHP.

46. οἴκῳ for θεῷ with אBDH. *Vulg.* has 'Deo.'

48. ναοῖς omitted with אABCDE. *Vulg.* has 'in manufactis' only.

51. καρδίαις for τῇ καρδίᾳ with אACD. *Vulg.* 'cordibus.'

52. ἐγένεσθε for γεγένησθε with אABCDE.

56. διηνοιγμένους with אABC.

CH. VII. 1—53. STEPHEN'S DEFENCE.

1. εἶπεν δὲ κ.τ.λ., *and the high-priest said:* thus calling on Stephen for his defence.

εἰ ταῦτα. On εἰ with the indicative as a simple particle of interrogation see note on i. 6. The usage is largely confined to St Luke.

2. ἄνδρες ἀδελφοὶ καὶ πατέρες. Render, *Brethren and fathers.* For an account of the argument in Stephen's speech and its connexion with the whole design of the writer of the Acts, see *Introduction,* p. xv.

ὁ θεὸς τῆς δόξης. The expression occurs in LXX. of Ps. xxviii. 3, but is not common. It is probably used here because Stephen is about to speak of the several stages of God's manifestation. The equivalent of these words is applied (John i. 14) to the supreme manifestation in the incarnate Son. 'We beheld His glory, the glory as of the only-begotten of the Father.'

τῷ πατρὶ ἡμῶν, *to our father.* There is another reading ὑμῶν, due probably to the correction of some one who remembered that Stephen was a Greek. But even if he were merely a proselyte he might use this expression, for Abraham is regarded as the father of proselytes. On Genesis xii. 5, 'the souls which they had gotten [Heb. *made*] in Haran,' the Targum of Onkelos explains, 'the souls which they (Abraham and his family) had brought to serve the Law,' i.e. made proselytes: and on the same text *Berashith Rabbah*, p. 39, has: 'Rabbi Eliezer, the son of Zimra, said: If all the men in the world were to combine to create even a single gnat, they could not infuse into it a soul; and thou sayest, 'The souls which they *made*.' But these are the proselytes whom they brought in. Yet, if so, why does it say they *made* them? This is to teach these that when anybody brings near the stranger, and makes him a proselyte, it is as good as if he had created him.'

Μεσοποταμίᾳ. The ancestral home of Abraham is called 'Ur of the Chaldees' (Gen. xi. 31), and it is said (Josh. xxiv. 2, 3) to have been 'on the other side of the flood,' i.e. beyond the Euphrates. It is not possible to determine the site of Ur, but the most probable opinion seems to be that which places it at Edessa, now called *Orfah*, and said to have been called *Orrha* in early times. If this were the place, the journey thence to Charran (O.T. Haran), i.e. *Carrhæ*, would not have been so very formidable for the father of the patriarch to undertake, and at Charran Terah remained till he died (Gen. xi. 32). Abraham, when without his father, could remove with greater ease to the distant Canaan.

πρὶν ἢ κατοικῆσαι, *before he dwelt.* The verb implies a settled residence, though not necessarily a permanent abode. It is used (Matth. ii. 23) of Joseph and Mary *dwelling* at Nazareth, and (Matth. iv. 13) of the less fixed *dwelling* of Jesus at Capernaum.

3. καὶ εἶπεν πρὸς αὐτόν, *and said unto him.* It does not appear from the narrative in Genesis whether there had been some divine communication which caused the first removal from Ur to Haran. We are only told (xi. 31) that Terah took his family and removed, but as it is there added 'to go into the land of Canaan,' and as in the following chapter, where God's order to remove is expressly given (xii. 1), it is also said that 'they went forth to go into the land of Canaan,' we may reasonably conclude that the first removal had been enjoined by God, and that it was only on account of Terah's age that the country for which they set forth was not reached at once. In Gen. xv. 7 God says 'I am the Lord that brought thee out of Ur of the Chaldees,' language which implies a command given for the first removal. Cp. Neh. ix. 7. Gen. xii. 1 should be rendered 'Now the Lord *said* unto Abram,' not 'had said,' as A.V.

ἔξελθε ἐκ τῆς γῆς σου, *Get thee out of thy land.*   Let γῆ be translated alike in both clauses of the verse.   In Gen. xii. 1 the words καὶ
ἐκ τοῦ οἴκου τοῦ πατρός σου are added after συγγενείας σου.   Although
the emigrants halted at Haran, their destination was known to be
Canaan before they started from Ur.   (See Gen. xi. 31.)

4.   Χαλδαίων, *of the Chaldæans.*   The Chaldæans were the people
of that country which had Babylon for its capital.   The extent of the
country signified by 'the land of the Chaldæans' must have varied at
different periods.

μετὰ τὸ ἀποθανεῖν τὸν π. α., *after his father was dead.*   According
to the order of the narrative in Genesis, this seems to be so; but when
the ages of Terah and Abraham are noticed, it appears that Abraham
left Haran before his father's death.   For Terah was 70 years old when
Abraham was born (Gen. xi. 26), and Abraham was 75 years old when
he departed out of Haran (Gen. xii. 4), so that of Terah's 205 years
there were yet (205 – 145) = 60 years unexpired when his son went
away.   On this chronological difficulty Jewish literature has the explanation (*Midrash Rabbah* on Genesis, cap. 39) that God absolved
Abraham from the care of his father, and yet lest Abraham's departure
from Terah should lead others to claim the same relaxation of a commandment for themselves, Terah's death is noticed in Holy Writ
before Abraham's departure, and it is also added, to explain the
mention of *death*, that 'the wicked (and among them Terah is
reckoned, see Josh. xxiv. 2) are called dead while they are alive.'

μετῴκισεν αὐτόν, *he caused him to migrate.*   The 'removed him'
of the A.V. is somewhat vague.

εἰς ἥν, *in which.*   The use of εἰς in this way after κατοικέω and
similar verbs is due to the implied idea 'ye have come into and dwell.'
Cf. Matth. ii. 23, iv. 13, where the construction is made easy by a previous ἐλθών, which in the present verse must be mentally supplied.

5.   καὶ οὐκ ἔδωκεν αὐτῷ κ.τ.λ., *and he gave him no inheritance in
it.*   The first settlement of Abraham in Canaan is said (Gen. xii. 6) to
have been at the place of Sichem [Shechem] at the plain [rather, *oak*]
of Moreh.   He next dwelt on the east of Bethel, and in both these
places he probably purchased land, for he built an altar at each; and
on returning from Egypt (xiii. 3) he came 'to the place where his tent
had been at the beginning, between Bethel and Hai,' which he hardly
could have done unless the land had been his own, for he 'was very
rich in cattle.'

οὐδὲ βῆμα ποδός, *not so much as to set his foot on.*   The expression
is in LXX. Deut. ii. 5.   The land which God gave to Abraham's seed
would be held on a very different tenure from that on which Abraham
held that which he bought or hired.

καὶ ἐπηγγείλατο.   The promise 'unto thy seed will I give this land'
was first made (Gen. xii. 7) when Abraham was at the place of
Shechem, and in its greater fulness when he returned from Egypt
(xiii. 15, 16).

THE ACTS   L οὐκ ὄντος αὐτῷ τέκνου, *when he had no child.* We cannot learn from Holy Writ how long a time after the promise Abraham lived before Isaac was born, but we can see that it was a long period, for when he went down to Egypt Sarah was a fair woman in the prime of her beauty (Gen. xii. 14), and she was 'waxed old' (xviii. 12) before her son was born.

6. ἐλάλησεν δέ. The words are in substance taken from Gen. xv. 13, 14, though here turned into an indirect narration.

ἔτη τετρακόσια, *four hundred years.* This number agrees with that stated in Genesis; but in Exod. xii. 40, and also by St Paul (Gal. iii. 17), the time is said to have been *four hundred and thirty* years. The period is reckoned so as to include part of the lives of the patriarchs in Canaan, and the variation may be accounted for if one number dates back to the first call, and the second only to the departure from Haran; or the one may be reckoned from the time of the covenant of circumcision, and the other from the promise of the land. Or it may be that one is merely a round number and the other an attempt at greater exactness. We can come to no certain conclusion in the matter, but we can see that both numbers were current among the Jews, for Josephus (*Ant.* II. 15. 2) makes the time 430 years, and elsewhere (*Ant.* II. 9. 1, and *Bell. Jud.* v. 9. 4) 400 years.

7. ᾧ ἐὰν δουλεύσουσιν, *to whom they shall be in bondage.* This construction of the future indicative after ἐὰν is not uncommon in the LXX. Cf. Deut. v. 27, λαλήσεις πάντα ὅσα ἂν λαλήσει κύριος ὁ θεός. So too Judges x. 18, xi. 24, &c. In all these instances a future indicative stands also in the antecedent clause.

On God's suffering Israel to be in bondage Chrysostom has ὁρᾷς; ὁ ἐπαγγειλάμενος, ὁ δοὺς τὴν γῆν, πρότερον τὰ κακὰ συγχωρεῖ· οὕτω καὶ νῦν, εἰ καὶ βασιλείαν ἐπηγγείλατο, ἀλλ' ἀφίησιν ἐγγυμνάζεσθαι τοῖς πειρασμοῖς.

ἐξελεύσονται, *they shall come forth.* The first prophecy of this exodus (Gen. xv. 14) adds μετὰ ἀποσκευῆς πολλῆς, 'with great substance.'

καὶ λατρεύσουσίν μοι κ.τ.λ., *and shall serve me in this place.* These words are not in the promise given to Abraham, but are taken from Exod. iii. 12, where the original promise is repeated and sent to the Israelites through Moses. The place meant in that verse is Sinai, called there Horeb, the mountain of God. Stephen in his speech combines the two that he may describe the promise in its fulness, and he mentions the worship of God in that place, because the one great object of his address is to demonstrate that what is laid to his charge concerning the highest worship of God being no longer restricted to the Temple and Jerusalem, is nothing more than what they were taught by a study of their own history.

8. διαθήκην περιτομῆς, *the covenant of circumcision.* This was given the year before Isaac was born (Gen. xvii. 21).

9. ζηλώσαντες, *moved with envy.*   The same word is used (xvii. 5) of the hostile feelings of the Jews at Thessalonica against Paul and Silas. In the history (Gen. xxxvii. 4), it is said in the LXX. οἱ ἀδελφοὶ ἐμίσησαν αὐτόν, but below in verse 11, ἐζήλωσαν αὐτόν.

ἀπέδοντο, *they sold.*   The same word in LXX. Gen. xxxvii. 28.

καὶ ἦν ὁ θεὸς μετ᾿ αὐτοῦ, *and God was with him.*   The statement (with κύριος for ὁ θεὸς) is thrice repeated Gen. xxxix. 2, 21, 23, and is used by Stephen to give point to his argument that God's presence is not circumscribed, and so His worship should not be tied to a special place.

10. For the history, see Genesis xxxix.—xli.

ἡγούμενον.   This same word is employed about Joseph in Ecclus. xlix. 15 οὐδὲ ὡς Ἰωσὴφ ἡγούμενος ἀδελφῶν, στήριγμα λαοῦ.

11. ἐφ᾿ ὅλην τὴν Αἴγυπτον, *over all Egypt.*

χορτάσματα, *sustenance.*   The word is generally used of food for cattle rather than men.   See LXX. Gen. xxiv. 25, 32, &c. But we may suppose that, though in the history the sufferings of the people are most noticed, the famine also affected the supplies of cattle-food, and the one word is used to embrace all.

12. ὄντα σιτία εἰς Αἴγυπτον, *that there was corn in Egypt.*   The force of the preposition implies 'to be had by going down *into* Egypt.' See above on verse 4.

σιτία is found in the LXX. Prov. xxx. 22 ἐὰν ἄφρων πλησθῇ σιτίων, 'if a fool be filled with meat.'   But it is not a common word, which will account for σῖτα taking its place in later MSS.

πρῶτον, *first,* i.e. before he himself went away from Canaan into Egypt.

13. ἀνεγνωρίσθη, *was made known.*   The verb used in the LXX. (Gen. xlv. 1) of this event.

φανερὸν ἐγένετο, *became known.*   The LXX. has ἀκουστὸν ἐγένετο, 'it was heard of,' but this is in reference to the *report* of the coming of Joseph's brethren.

14. ἐν ψυχαῖς ἑβδομήκοντα πέντε, *threescore and fifteen souls.* The form of expression is a copy of LXX. (Deut. x. 22) ἐν ἑβδομή-κοντα ψυχαῖς κατέβησαν οἱ πατέρες σου, and the ἐν is simply a transla-tion of the Hebrew בְּ, the idea being 'they went down [consisting] *in* so many souls.'

The number, threescore and fifteen, is taken from the LXX. In the Hebrew (Gen. xlvi. 8—27) the number is but seventy, including Jacob himself. The five additional names given in the LXX. are Machir the son and Galaad the grandson of Manasseh, and the two sons of Ephraim, Taam and Soutalaam, with Soutalaam's son, Edom. So in Exodus i. 5 the Hebrew has 70, and the LXX. 75.   There were many traditions current on this subject, and the Rabbis notice too that 69 persons (they exclude Jacob) are reckoned for 70 in the ac-count given Gen. xlvi. In the *Midrash Shemuel,* c. 32, there are

various suggestions thrown out. First it is said the one wanting was
Jochebed, who became wife of Amram and mother of Moses, for it is
mentioned (Numb. xxvi. 59) that she was a daughter of Levi born in
Egypt, and the tradition is that she was born 'between the walls,' i.e.
just as the people were entering Egypt, and so she is to be counted in
the number. Another tradition is attached to Gen. xlvi. 23, 'The sons
of Dan, Hushim.' As the last word is a plural form, and *sons* are
spoken of in the verse, therefore it is thought that there were two
Hushim, an elder and a younger. Also (T. B. *Baba Bathra* 123 a *ad
fin.*) there is mentioned the tradition that there was a twin with
Dinah. We may thus see that there were traditions current which
probably were well known to the translators of the LXX., and gave
rise to their number. They however are not consistent, for in Deuteronomy (x. 22) they give 70 as the number which went down into
Egypt. Stephen, as was to be expected from the other quotations in
this book, and also because he was a Grecian Jew, follows the LXX.

15. καὶ κατέβη Ἰακώβ, *and Jacob went down.* Now the whole race
whom God had chosen to himself was in Egypt, away from the land
of promise, and remained there for a long period, yet God was with
them in their exile, and His worship was preserved for the whole time.
This seems the point which Stephen desires to emphasize by so frequent a repetition of the words 'into Egypt.'

καὶ ἐτελεύτησεν αὐτὸς κ. ο. π. ἡ., *and he died, himself, and our
fathers.* Of the transportation of the bodies of the patriarchs to
Canaan we have no record in Holy Writ. Josephus (*Ant.* II. 8. 2)
says 'the posterity and sons of these men, after some time, carried
their bodies and buried them at Hebron.' In the discussion of
Exodus xiii. 19 *Carry up my bones away hence with you*, it is said
(*Mechilta*, ed. Weiss, 1865, Vienna, 8vo. p. 30) that the bodies of the
patriarchs were carried out of Egypt with the returning Israelites, and
it is argued that this is implied in the expression *with you*, which Moses
quotes as uttered by Joseph, who must have known that his brethren
to whom he was speaking would all be dead before the exodus.
Therefore *with you* could only be used if their bodies were to be trans-
ported as well as his own.

16. εἰς Συχέμ, *to Sychem,* i.e. the O. Test. 'Shechem.'

ἐν Συχέμ, *in Sychem.* The place and the son of Emmor had the
same name, the place from the man or *vice versâ*. And hence came
the substitution of τοῦ for ἐν.

The statement in this verse about Abraham's purchase of land from
Emmor appears incapable of being reconciled with the record of the
Old Testament. There we find (Gen. xlix. 30) that Abraham bought
the field and cave of Machpelah, which is before Mamre (i.e. Hebron),
from Ephron the Hittite. This is there spoken of as the general
burial-place of the family; there were buried Abraham and Sarah,
Isaac and Rebekah, and Jacob's wife Leah. And of Jacob we read
(Gen. xxxiii. 19) 'he bought a parcel of a field where he had spread
his tent, at the hand of the children of Hamor, Shechem's father.'

We are not told that this was for a burial-place, and it is rather to be judged that it was not so, because it is added 'he erected there an altar.' Moreover it is in Machpelah that Jacob desires to be buried (Gen. xlvii. 30, xlix. 30) and is buried (l. 13). We have seen (note on verse 5) that 'the place of Shechem' was one of the resting-places of Abraham when he came first into Canaan, and that probably he bought a possession there, for he built an altar. The bones of Joseph were laid in Shechem (Josh. xxiv. 32). There were two burial-places connected with the patriarchal families. In the report of Stephen's speech we find that Abraham is said to have bought what Jacob really purchased, but there may also have been land purchased by Abraham 'in the place of Shechem.' We have only to suppose that in his speech Stephen, speaking of the burial of the whole family, mentioned, in accordance with the tradition of Josephus, the burial-place of the fathers in Hebron, which Abraham bought, and noticed the laying of Joseph's bones at Shechem which Jacob bought, and that into the report of what he said a confusion has been introduced by the insertion of Abraham's name for Jacob's in the abbreviated narrative. We have pointed out in several places that the speeches recorded can be no more than abstracts of what was said, and the degree of inaccuracy here apparent might readily be imported in the formation of such an abstract, and yet the original speech have correctly reported all the traditions.

Stephen dwells on 'Shechem' in the same way as before he had dwelt on 'Egypt,' to mark that in the ancient days other places were held in reverence by the chosen people, and that of old God had been worshipped in Shechem, though at the time when he was speaking it was the home of their enemies the Samaritans.

17. καθὼς δὲ ἤγγιζεν κ.τ.λ., *but as the time of the promise drew nigh*, i.e. the time for its fulfilment. The fathers 'all died in faith, not having received the promises, but having seen them afar off,' Heb. xi. 13.

ἧς, *which*. For the attraction, see note on i. 1.

ὡμολόγησεν ὁ θεός, *God had vouchsafed*. The same word is used (Matth. xiv. 7) of the promise made by Herod to the daughter of Herodias. Cf. also LXX. Jerem. li. 25, ποιοῦσαι ποιήσομεν τὰς ὁμολογίας ἡμῶν ἃς ὡμολογήκαμεν, 'we will surely perform our vows that we have vowed.' And in verse 26 immediately following we have the same various reading as in our text, ὤμοσα and ὡμολόγηκα, the latter being the text in Trommius, the former the variation; in Holmes and Parsons this arrangement is reversed, while Tischendorf only gives ὤμοσα.

ηὔξησεν ὁ λαός, *the people grew*. Another point in Stephen's argument. God's blessing went with them into Egypt (Exod. i. 7, 12). The number of those who came out of Egypt was (Exod. xii. 37) 'six hundred thousand on foot that were men, besides children.'

18. βασιλεὺς ἕτερος ἐπ' Αἴγυπτον, *another king over Egypt.*

19. κατασοφισάμενος τὸ γένος ἡμῶν, *dealt subtilly with our race and,* &c. The expression is from the LXX. (Exod. i. 10), κατασοφισώ-μεθα αὐτούς are the words of the new king.

ἐκάκωσεν τοὺς πατέρας, *he evil entreated our fathers.* In the account of the taskmasters, the LXX. says they were appointed ἵνα κακώσωσιν αὐτοὺς ἐν τοῖς ἔργοις. Beside the hard tasks put upon the people according to the record in Exodus, Josephus adds (*Ant.* II. 9. 1) that the Egyptians 'made them to cut a great many channels for the river, and set them to build pyramids; forced them to learn all sorts of mechanical arts and to accustom themselves to hard labour.'

τοῦ ποιεῖν τὰ βρέφη ἔκθετα αὐτῶν, *in causing their young children to be cast out.* The words are rather a description of what the Egyptian king did in his tyranny (Exod. i. 22), than (as A. V.) of what the Israelites were driven to by their despair.

With the genitival infinitive in this clause, expressive of that wherein the κάκωσις consisted, cf. 1 Kings xvi. 33, καὶ προσέθηκεν Ἀχαὰβ τοῦ ποιῆσαι παροργίσματα τοῦ παροργίσαι τὸν κύριον θεὸν τοῦ Ἰσραήλ.

εἰς τὸ μὴ ζωογονεῖσθαι, *to the end that they might not live.* The verb is used, in the active voice, three times (Exod. i. 17, 18, 22) of the conduct of the midwives in saving the children alive. Cf. also the remarkable use of the word in Luke xvii. 33.

20. ἀστεῖος τῷ θεῷ, *exceeding fair.* Literally, 'fair unto (i.e. in the sight of) God.' This is a Hebrew mode of expressing a high degree of any quality. Thus (Jonah iii. 3) 'Nineveh was an exceeding great city' is 'a city great unto God.' Similar instances are found Gen. x. 9, xxiii. 6, xxx. 8, &c. Cf. also 1 Cor. ix. 2; 2 Cor. x. 4. In the *Pirke de-Rabbi Eliezer,* c. 48, we have 'The parents of Moses saw his face as (that of) an angel of God.'

21. ἀνείλατο, *took him up.* The word of the LXX. (Exod. ii. 5). Jewish tradition says that the king had no son, and so Moses was designed by the king's daughter to succeed to the kingdom. See Josephus (*Ant.* II. 9. 7), where she speaks of him as 'a *child of a divine form* and generous mind.'

22. ἐπαιδεύθη Μωϋσῆς, *Moses was instructed.* As was to be expected if he were designed for the kingdom. The wisdom on which the Jewish traditions most dwell is the power of magic, and such knowledge as Pharaoh's wise men are represented as having in the book of Exodus.

ἦν δὲ...αὐτοῦ, *and was mighty in his words and deeds.* Josephus (*Ant.* II. 10. 2) tells that Moses was a great captain among the Egyptians and led that people to victory against the Ethiopians.

23. ὡς δὲ ἐπληροῦτο...χρόνος. Render, *but when he was well-nigh forty years old.* The verb intimates that the forty years were just being completed. For the fixing of this time we have no authority in the Old Testament. We learn thence that Moses was eighty years old when he was sent to speak before Pharaoh for the deliverance of the Israelites (Exod. vii. 7), and that he was a hundred and twenty years old when he died (Deut. xxxiv. 7). In *Midrash Tanchuma* on Exodus ii. 6, we are told ' Moses was in the palace of Pharaoh twenty years, but some say *forty* years, and forty years in Midian, and forty years in the wilderness.' Stephen's words agree with this tradition, which no doubt was known in his day to every Jew.

ἀνέβη ἐπὶ τὴν καρδίαν. The phrase is not classical, but is found in the LXX. frequently, as 2 Kings xii. 4; Is. lxv. 16; Jer. iii. 16 and Ezek. xxxviii. 10, ἐν τῇ ἡμέρᾳ ἐκείνῃ ἀναβήσεται ῥήματα ἐπὶ τὴν καρδίαν σου, ' in that day shall things come into thy heart.'

ἐπισκέψασθαι, *to visit*. The same verb is used in Luke vii. 16, ' God hath visited His people,' and means to look upon generally with kindness (cf. ἐπισκέπτεσθαι, James i. 27), and this is the old sense of the English *visit*. See Shaksp. *Rich. II.* I. 3. 275:

> 'All places that the eye of heaven *visits*.'

24. καταπονουμένῳ, *oppressed*. The word is used 2 Macc. viii. 2 of the suffering Jews in the time of Judas Maccabæus, though some MSS. there give καταπατούμενον = *downtrodden*.

πατάξας, *having smitten*, i.e. to death, as is seen by the context. See Exod. ii. 12, where the same word is used.

25. ἐνόμιζεν δὲ συνιέναι...σωτηρίαν αὐτοῖς. Render, *and he supposed that his brethren understood that God by his hand was giving them deliverance.* There is no condition in the sentence. The traditions, in the atmosphere of which Stephen moved, represent the death of the Egyptian as no mere ordinary killing by superior strength, but as brought about by mysterious divine power, which Moses feeling within himself expected his kindred to recognize.

26. αὐτοῖς μαχομένοις, *unto them as they strove*, viz. to ' two men of the Hebrews' (see Exod. ii. 13). The quotation which follows makes plain what was otherwise not yet clear, that the persons contending in this second case were Israelites. Similarly in verse 24 there had been no mention of an ' Egyptian' or anything to make clear who the doer of the wrong was. But the minds of the hearers supplied all these details without difficulty.

συνήλλασσεν. The tense implies a continuous endeavour, though without result.

28. ὃν τρόπον ἀνεῖλες, *as thou killedst*. The Israelite knew of the slain Egyptian, whose body Moses had hidden in the sand, but as things stood between Egyptians and Israelites he would hardly think of laying a charge against a fellow Israelite, though he was ready at once to use his knowledge to alarm Moses, when any interference with himself was attempted.

29. ἐν τῷ λόγῳ τούτῳ. The preposition marks the occasion. *Upon this speech.* Josephus (*Ant.* II. 11. 1) makes no mention of this reason for the flight of Moses, but says that the Egyptians were jealous of him, and told the king ' that he would raise a sedition, and bring innovations' into the land. And in consequence of the plots against him bred of these suspicions Moses fled away secretly.

καὶ ἐγένετο πάροικος, *and became a sojourner.* *Madian* is the Greek form for the Hebrew *Midian*, which form would, for clearness' sake, be better here. By 'the land of Midian,' which is only found in Scripture history, is probably meant the peninsula on which Mount Sinai stands (see Exod. iii. 1).

υἱοὺς δύο. These sons were Gershom and Eliezer; their mother was Zipporah the daughter of Jethro (Exod. xviii. 2—4).

30. ἐτῶν τεσσεράκοντα, *forty years*, thus making, with the forty years mentioned in verse 23, eighty years, the age at which Moses went unto Pharaoh (Exod. vii. 7).

ὤφθη ... ἄγγελος, *an angel appeared to him.* It is better to write *Sinai* than to conform to the Greek spelling Σινᾶ. See previous verse.

31—34. These verses give in substance the history as recorded in Exod. iii. 2—10.

34. ἰδὼν εἶδον, *I have seen, I have seen.* Literally, 'having seen I have seen.' This construction is employed in the LXX. continually to represent the Hebrew infinitive absolute, which was used to give emphasis to the finite verb. The English of A.V. in Exod. iii. 7 (where the LXX. has the same Greek as here) is well given, 'I have surely seen.'

ἀποστελῶ. The tense is the same in Exod. iii. 10.

35. Stephen now addresses himself to another point and shews how in old time the people had rejected Moses, though he had the witness of God that his commission was divine. He wishes to teach his hearers that they are now acting in like manner towards Jesus.

τοῦτον ὁ θεὸς...ἀπέσταλκεν σὺν χειρί, *him God sent with the hand.* Here Stephen appeals to history. God, he says, sent back the rejected Moses to be a ruler and deliverer, and he leaves them to draw the conclusion that what God had done in the case of Moses, he would also do in the case of the prophet whom Moses had foretold as one who was to be like himself. Cp. Gal. iv. 23; 1 Tim. ii. 14; Heb. vii. 6.

σὺν χειρί implies *with the power.* Cf. Acts xi. 21, 'the hand of the Lord was with them.'

ἀγγέλου. That this angel was Jehovah Himself, is seen from Exod, iii. 4, 'when the *Lord* saw that he turned aside to see, *God* called unto him.' So that the whole phrase = 'with the power of God.'

36. οὗτος ἐξήγαγεν, *this man led them out,* having God's power with him.

σημεῖα ἐν γῇ Αἰγύπτῳ, *signs in the land of Egypt.* There is much authority for the reading ἐν τῇ Αἰγύπτῳ.

ἐν ἐρυθρᾷ θαλάσσῃ, *in the Red Sea.* The Jewish traditions make the plagues sent on the Egyptians at the Red Sea more than those which had been sent to them in Egypt. Thus in the *Mechilta* (ed. Weiss, p. 41) the Egyptians are said to have received *ten* plagues in Egypt, but *fifty* at the Red Sea, because the magicians speak of the afflictions in Egypt (Exod. viii. 19) as 'the *finger* of God,' while at the Red Sea it is said (Exod. xiv. 31), 'and Israel saw that great work [Heb. *hand*] which the Lord did upon the Egyptians.'

37. προφήτην. The prophecy is in Deut. xviii. 15, and has been already quoted by St Peter (iii. 22) as referring ultimately to the Messiah. Its quotation to those who had rejected Jesus is the key-note of what is more openly expressed in ver. 51, 'as your fathers did, so do ye.'

38. ἐν τῇ ἐκκλησίᾳ, *in the congregation,* i.e. with the congregation of Israel assembled at Mt. Sinai.

μετὰ τοῦ ἀγγέλου, *with the angel.* As in 35, the angel is God Himself; just so in ver. 31 the voice which spake is called 'a voice of the Lord.'

Σινᾶ, *Sinai.*

καὶ τῶν πατέρων ἡμῶν, *and with our fathers.* Jewish tradition says that the whole world was present at Sinai. Thus *Midrash Rabbah* on Exodus, cap. 28 *ad fin.*: 'Whatever the prophets were to utter in prophecy in every generation they received from Mount Sinai'; and presently after, commenting on the words of Moses (Deut. xxix. 15), *him that is not here with us this day,* it is said, 'these are the souls which were yet to be created,' i.e. to be sent into the world; and to explain (Deut. v. 22) *and he added no more* (on which they found the teaching that all revelation was completely given at Sinai), they say, 'the one voice was divided into seven voices, and these were divided into the seventy tongues,' which Jewish tradition held to be the number of the languages of the world.

ὃς ἐδέξατο λόγια ζῶντα, *who* [i.e. Moses] *received living oracles.* Moses is thus shewn to have been a mediator (see Gal. iii. 19), and thus to have prefigured the mediator of a better covenant (Heb. viii. 6) and of the New Testament (Heb. ix. 15), even Jesus (Heb. xii. 24).

The oracles are called *living,* just as 'the word of God' is called *living* [A.V. *quick*] (Heb. iv. 12), because it is a discerner of the thoughts and intents of the heart. On this effect cf. St Paul's language concerning the Law (Rom. vii. 9), 'when the commandment came, sin revived, and I died.' But there is at the same time the other sense in the word, which appears when (John vi. 51) Christ calls Himself 'the *living* bread which came down from heaven.' For the Law pointed onward to Christ, who should lead His people 'unto *living* fountains of waters' (Rev. vii. 17). For the thought, cf. 1 Pet. i. 23, 'the word of God which *liveth* and abideth for ever.'

39. ᾧ οὐκ ἠθέλησαν ὑπήκοοι γενέσθαι κ.τ.λ., *to whom our fathers would not be obedient.* For they said (Numb. xiv. 4) 'Let us make a captain, and let us return into Egypt.' This was after the return of

the spies, when the people became discontented with the leadership of Moses and Aaron.

καὶ ἐστράφησαν ἐν ταῖς καρδίαις αὐτῶν, *and in their hearts turned back into Egypt*, as is told Exod. xvi. 3; Numb. xi. 4, 5, in which passages the desires of the people are all represented as turned to the good things which they had enjoyed in the land of their slavery.

40. θεοὺς οἳ προπορεύσονται, *gods which shall go before us.* The verse is almost exactly in the words of the LXX. of Exod. xxxii. 1.

41. καὶ εὐφραίνοντο, *and they rejoiced.* It was not the voice of them that shout for the mastery, nor of them that cry for being overcome, but *the noise of them that sing* which Moses (Exod. xxxii. 18) heard when he came down from the mount.

42. ἔστρεψεν δὲ ὁ θεός, *but God turned*, i.e. changed His treatment of the people. Cf. Is. lxiii. 10, 'but they rebelled and vexed His Holy Spirit, therefore He was turned (ἐστράφη) to be their enemy.' The word is not often found in this sense.

λατρεύειν τῇ στρατιᾷ τοῦ οὐρανοῦ, *to serve the host of heaven.* God had previously warned them against this kind of idolatry (Deut. iv. 19), but we learn from the records of their historians (2 Kings xvii. 16) and their prophets (Jer. xix. 13; Zeph. i. 5) that the warning was given in vain.

ἡ στρατιὰ τοῦ οὐρανοῦ is a Hebrew notion, and the expression is often found in the LXX. Jer. vii. 18, viii. 2; 2 Chron. xxxiii. 3; Zeph. i. 5.

ἐν βίβλῳ τῶν προφητῶν. The Hebrews divided their Scriptures into three sections, the Law, the Prophets, and the Hagiographa (called the Psalms, Luke xxiv. 44), and each of these parts is looked upon as a special and separate book. The Law comprised the five books of Moses. The earlier prophets were the books of Joshua, Judges, Samuel, and Kings: the later prophets were Isaiah, Jeremiah, Ezekiel and the twelve which we now call Minor Prophets. The Hagiographa consisted of the following books in the order here given: Psalms (and the expression of Luke xxiv. 44 will be understood because the Psalms stand first in this section), Proverbs, Job, the Song of Songs, Ruth, Lamentations, Ecclesiastes, Esther (these five last mentioned were called the five rolls, being written on separate rolls for use at special festival services), Daniel, Ezra, Nehemiah, and Chronicles.

μὴ σφάγια κ.τ.λ. Render, *did ye offer unto me slain beasts and sacrifices forty years in the wilderness, O house of Israel?* The whole passage to the end of ver. 43 is a quotation from Amos (v. 25—27). The question in this verse is to be answered in the negative, for in their hearts, though they were sacrificing to Jehovah, they had turned back into Egypt, and such service God counts as no service at all.

43. καὶ ἀνελάβετε. Render, *and ye took up.* The conjunction is the ordinary copulative, and the thought is continuous, 'your hearts were after your idols, and ye took up their images,' more truly than my ark. In the Hebrew the word for 'took up' is that regularly employed for the 'bearing' the ark of the covenant. So the prophet reproaches them with paying to Moloch honour which they had been taught to render to Jehovah.

τὴν σκηνήν, *the tabernacle.* The Hebrew word which the LXX. have rendered σκηνή is not the usual form for that word. It seems probable that it is intended for a proper name, *Siccuth.*

καὶ τὸ ἄστρον...αὐτοῖς, *the star of your god Rephan, the figures which ye made to worship them.* This clause differs widely from the Hebrew, which gives, 'and Chiun your images, the star of your god which ye made to yourselves.' The LXX. seem to have read the words in a different order. *Rephan,* which is by them substituted for *Chiun,* is said to be the Egyptian name for Saturn (see Spencer *de Leg. Heb.* p. 667), and may have been used by them as an equivalent for the other name which is found nowhere else but in Amos. The whole idea of the passage seems to be that the stars were being worshipped, and so it is an illustration suited for Stephen's argument. προσκυνεῖν αὐτοῖς is an addition not in the LXX.

ἐπέκεινα Βαβυλῶνος, *beyond Babylon.* The Hebrew of Amos and the LXX. say beyond *Damascus.* But as Babylon was the place most connected in the mind of the Jew with captivity, the alteration in the quotation may be due either to the prominence of such connexion in Stephen's mind, or in the thoughts of the reporter of the speech, who thus inadvertently wrote Babylon. At this point Stephen closes the digression which began at the 37th verse, and which is meant to point out that the Jews are doing towards Jesus just what their fathers did to Moses and against God. He now resumes the argument that God's worship was not meant to be always fixed to one place.

44. ἡ σκηνὴ τοῦ μαρτυρίου, *the tabernacle of the testimony.* This name is found first in Exod. xxxviii. 21 (xxxvii. 19, LXX.). The ark is also called ἡ κιβωτὸς τοῦ μαρτυρίου, as in Exod. xxv. 21, &c. The name was no doubt given because all the contents of the ark, which was the most sacred part of the tabernacle fittings, were testimonies to God's rule or to His power exerted for His people. Aaron's rod, the pot of manna, and the tables of the Law were all stored up therein. And this ark, above which God made His presence seen, was in the wilderness and moving from place to place.

ἦν τοῖς πατράσιν ἡμῶν, *our fathers had,* &c. Concerning a historic religion, like that of the Jews, this was, or ought to have been, a weighty argument.

καθὼς διετάξατο ὁ λαλῶν, *even as He had appointed who spake,* &c. For the command see Exod. xxv. 9, 40, xxvi. 30, xxvii. 8.

45. ἣν καὶ εἰσήγαγον διαδεξάμενοι κ.τ.λ., *which also our fathers having received it after,* &c. All the generation that came out of Egypt was dead at the entry into Canaan except Caleb and Joshua.

μετὰ Ἰησοῦ, *with Joshua.* See above on verses 29 and 30.

ἐν τῇ κατασχέσει κ.τ.λ., *when they took possession* [lit. in their taking possession] *of the nations whom God thrust out before the face of our fathers, unto the days of David.* Till this time the tabernacle existed, and, as the history tells us, was not always in one place in the land of Canaan, and at the time when the first proposal for a permanent temple is made by David (2 Sam. vii. 2) and approved by Nathan, God forbids the building of it by David. All which goes to strengthen Stephen's argument that the worship should not be fettered to one place.

46. εὑρεῖν σκήνωμα τῷ οἴκῳ 'Ιακώβ, *to find a tabernacle for the house of Jacob.* This is the reading preferred by most critics. Tischendorf says '*τῷ οἴκῳ* minime sensu caret, sed facile apparet cur *τῷ θεῷ* a tot testibus cum omnibus interpretibus substitutum sit.'

The text must mean ' to find a fit place in which the house of Jacob might worship.' But the reference is so clearly to Ps. cxxxii. 5, ' until I find out a place for the Lord, an habitation for the mighty God of Jacob,' that it seems impossible to accept the evidence of אBDH when ACEP and all the versions are on the other side.

Moreover St Stephen's argument has nothing to do with the place of worship of the house of Israel, but with the fact that God's tabernacle, where His presence dwelt, was frequently changed, and that David was anxious to change it again, having no feeling that God's presence was tied to one place. On this Chrysostom says ὁρᾷς, ὅτι ἐκεῖ τόπος ἅγιός ἐστιν, ἔνθα ἂν ᾖ θεός.

48. οὐχ…ἐν χειροποιήτοις κατοικεῖ, *dwelleth not in places made with hands.* Stephen allows that in the days of Solomon there seemed to be a more permanent abode appointed for God's worship, but instantly points out that God through His prophet (Isaiah lxvi. 1, 2) had taught that He was not controlled by or confined to any place.

49. ὁ οὐρανὸς κ.τ.λ. The quotation is nearly verbatim from the LXX.

51. σκληροτράχηλοι, *Ye stiffnecked.* A charge often brought against the Jews in the Old Testament, cf. Exod. xxxii. 9, xxxiii. 3, &c., so that it is a very suitable expression when Stephen is declaring that the people of his time were 'as their fathers.'

ἀπερίτμητοι, *uncircumcised.* As the rite of circumcision was the sign of submission to the Jewish religion in its fullest requirements, so the word *uncircumcised* became a synonym for obstinate resistance to what God had revealed, and the phrase in the text consequently signifies ' ye who shut your heart and ears against the truth.'

ἀπερίτμητα τὰ ὦτα occurs Jer. vi. 10 and ἀπερίτμητοι καρδίας Jer. ix. 26. Cf. also Levit. xxvi. 41; Ezek. xliv. 7, 9.

It seems very likely that at this part of his discourse Stephen saw that the language he had been using was distasteful to his audience. Observing this effect he proceeds with language which implied how far they were from being God's people, though they called themselves Israelites. They were in his eyes as those whom they named 'sinners of the Gentiles.' (Gal. ii. 15.)

ἀεί, *always.* From the days of Moses to whom your fathers

would not be obedient, down to the days of Jesus whom ye have crucified.

52. τίνα κ.τ.λ., *which of the prophets did not your fathers persecute?* Cf. the history 2 Chron. xxxvi. 16, 'they mocked the messengers of God and despised His words and misused His prophets.'
And Christ (Matth. xxiii. 37) brought the same charge against Jerusalem, 'thou that killest the prophets.'

τοῦ δικαίου, *of the righteous One.* Jesus is so named by St John
(1 John ii. 1), and the name also occurs with the same application
Acts iii. 14, xxii. 14, where the same rendering should be given that
the passages may be brought into due connexion.

ἐγένεσθε, *ye are become.* Thus proving yourselves true children of
those who misused the prophets of old time.

53. οἵτινες κ.τ.λ., *ye who received the Law,* from Sinai.

εἰς διαταγὰς ἀγγέλων. Literally, 'unto ordinances of angels,' which
signifies '*at the ministration* of angels' or 'as it was ordained by angels.'
St Paul (Gal. iii. 19) has the same expression concerning the Law, that
it was 'ministered by angels.' The LXX. have in Deut. xxxiii. 2,
speaking of the giving of the Law, ἐκ δεξιῶν αὐτοῦ ἄγγελοι μετ᾽ αὐτοῦ, and Josephus (*Ant.* xv. 5. 3) represents the same tradition,
'We have learned from God the most excellent of our doctrines and
the most holy part of our Law *by angels*.' So *Pesikta Rabbathi*, par.
xxi., 'There came down with the Holy One to Sinai twenty-two
thousand ministering angels, like the camp of the Levites.'

καὶ οὐκ ἐφυλάξατε, *and ye kept it not.* Stephen here points back
along the whole history of the Jews, and shews how the Law, which
was intended to lead men to Christ, had not been guarded in its best
sense, the spirit having been sacrificed to the letter, and so the result
had been that they rejected and slew Him of whom the whole Law was
speaking. The Law, given by angels, was the glory of Israel, the perverse use of it had proved their shame and destruction.

54—60. EFFECT OF THE SPEECH. DEATH OF STEPHEN.

54. ἀκούοντες δὲ ταῦτα διεπρίοντο κ.τ.λ., *now when they heard
these things they were cut to the heart.* On the verb, which is only
found here and in v. 33, see note there. It expresses the sort of cutting
that would be made by a saw, its effect is always one of irritation,
and at last it came to be synonymous with gnashing the teeth for rage,
with which expression it is here combined.

καὶ ἔβρυχον τοὺς ὀδόντας ἐπ᾽ αὐτόν, *and gnashed their teeth at him.*

55. δόξαν θεοῦ, *the glory of God.* Some visible sign of God's
presence, such as the Shechinah had been to the Jews of old. See
Exod. xvi. 10, xxiv. 17, in the latter of which passages it is described
as like devouring fire. It is defined by the Jews as some concentra-
tion of God's omnipresence.

καὶ Ἰησοῦν ἑστῶτα, *and Jesus standing.* Stephen was permitted
to behold Jesus triumphing in the flesh in which He had been crucified.

The position of *standing* rather than that of *sitting* as described elsewhere (Matth. xxvi. 64, &c.) may have been to indicate the readiness
of Jesus to strengthen and help His martyr.

56. τὸν υἱὸν τοῦ ἀνθρώπου, *the Son of Man.* This title, which in
the Gospels is only used by Christ when speaking of Himself, is here
first employed by another, and can fitly be so employed now, for the
prophecy which Christ uttered of Himself (Matth. xxvi. 64), 'hereafter
ye shall see *the Son of Man* sitting on the right hand of power,' is
now fulfilled, and its fulfilment is to be preached to the world.

57. κράξαντες δέ, *but they cried out...and,* &c.

συνέσχον τὰ ὦτα, *stopped their ears,* thus shewing that they
merited the description given in ver. 51. The verb signifies to com-
press, to hold tight together, and is often used in the LXX. of the
shutting of heaven that there should be no rain. Cf. Deut. xi. 17;
1 Kings viii. 35, &c. On the action thus described cf. T. B. *Kethuboth* 5 b, 'Wherefore is the whole ear hard but the flap soft? That
if any hear an unbecoming word he may *press up* the flap and shut
his ear.'

καὶ ὥρμησαν ὁμοθυμαδόν, *and rushed with one accord.* As though
he had been one convicted of idolatry, in which case (Deut. xiii. 9, 10)
'the hand of *all the people*' was to be upon the offender.

58. ἔξω τῆς πόλεως, *out of the city.* In accordance with the Law
(Lev. xxiv. 14) the person to be stoned must be carried without the
camp, and to the people of Jerusalem the walls of the city were as
the limits of the camp. Though there was much popular excitement
exhibited in this proceeding, we are not to think that it was looked
upon by those who were actors in it as other than the carrying out of
the law.

There was a place set apart for such punishment. The person to
be stoned was placed on an elevation twice the height of a man,
from whence with his hands bound he was thrown down, and then
a stone as much as two men could carry was rolled down upon him
by the witnesses, after which all the people present cast stones
upon him.

καὶ οἱ μάρτυρες, *and the witnesses,* who must take a prominent
part in the infliction of the penalty.

τὰ ἱμάτια αὐτῶν, *their clothes,* i.e. their loose outer garments, that
they might be more ready for the task which they had to discharge.
The law which ordained that the first stone should be thrown by the
witnesses (Deut. xvii. 7) was meant to restrain hasty accusation.
Men would only bring an accusation for grave reasons when they
knew that their own hands must be first upon the condemned person.

νεανίου, *of a young man.* Saul was already of such an age that the
authorities could entrust him (ix. 2) with the duty of going to Damascus
to arrest the Christians in that city. The Greek word is applied to
persons up to the age of forty. In the Epistle to Philemon (9) St Paul
speaks of himself as *aged.* That Epistle was probably written about

A.D. 63, and the death of Stephen took place about A.D. 35, therefore Saul may well have been then between 30 and 40 years of age.

καλουμένου Σαύλου, *called Saul.* The name is the same as that of the first King of Israel, and signifies 'one asked for' (i.e. in prayer). This Saul was also of the tribe of Benjamin, and had come from his home at Tarsus in Cilicia to attend on the lessons of the great teacher Gamaliel (Phil. iii. 5, 6; Acts xxii. 3).

59. ἐπικαλούμενον, *calling upon* the Lord. The noun must be supplied from the Κύριε which immediately follows.

The verb ἐπικαλέομαι is used afterwards of St Paul's appeal to Cæsar, Acts xxv. 11, xxvi. 32, xxviii. 19.

δέξαι τὸ πνεῦμά μου, *receive my spirit,* i.e. at its departure from my body, which he perceived was close at hand.

60. θεὶς δὲ τὰ γόνατα, *and kneeling down:* to pray, probably before the stoning commenced. This shews that the proceeding of the people was somewhat deliberate, and not a mere act of mob violence.

τιθέναι τὰ γόνατα is common in N.T., but is not classical, nor found in the LXX., where κάμπτειν is the usual verb. On Stephen's kneeling Chrysostom remarks ὅθεν θεῖος αὐτοῦ καὶ ὁ θάνατος γέγονεν.

μὴ στήσῃς αὐτοῖς, *lay not to their charge.* More literally, 'set it not down against them.' The verb is the same as in LXX. Zech. xi. 12, καὶ ἔστησαν τὸν μισθόν μου τριάκοντα ἀργυροῦς, 'and they weighed (or *set*) as my price thirty silverlings,' from which sense the text may be explained = 'charge it not upon them.'

It is to be observed that both the prayers of Stephen are addressed to Jesus as God. The tone of both cannot but bring to the memory the words of Jesus addressed to the Father in His agony, 'Into thy hands I commend My spirit' (Luke xxiii. 46) and 'Father, forgive them, for they know not what they do' (Luke xxiii. 34). As Christ had died, so did His servant learn to die.

ἐκοιμήθη, *he fell asleep.* The verb is common in the LXX. in the phrase ἐκοιμήθη μετὰ τῶν πατέρων αὐτοῦ, of the kings when they die. It is also used (Matth. xxvii. 52) of 'the saints which slept' and arose after the Crucifixion. How far its use in the Old Test. Scriptures implies a belief in an awakening is not easy to decide, for the word is used of death in the classical writers. Cf. Soph. *Electra* 509.

VIII. 1. συνευδοκῶν, *consenting,* i.e. approving of all that was done. The verb is found 1 Macc. i. 57, εἴ τις συνευδόκει τῷ νόμῳ, of assenting or approving of a law; and 2 Macc. xi. 35, καὶ ἡμεῖς συνευδοκοῦμεν, 'therewith we also are well pleased.' The word implies entire approbation. So Luke xi. 48, συνευδοκεῖτε, 'ye allow (i.e. praise and approve of) the deeds of your fathers.' St Paul also says of himself (Acts xxii. 20), 'when the blood of Thy martyr Stephen was shed I also was standing by and consenting (συνευδοκῶν) unto his death.'

CHAPTER VIII.

Readings differing from the *Text. recept.*

2. ἐποίησαν with ℵABCD.

7. πολλοί for πολλῶν with ℵABCE.

8. ἐγένετο δὲ πολλὴ χαρά with ℵABC. *Vulg.* has 'magnum gaudium.'

10. ἡ καλουμένη μεγάλη, with ℵABCDE. *Vulg.* has 'quæ vocatur magna.'

22. κυρίου for θεοῦ with ℵABCDE. *Vulg.* has 'Deum.'

27. The second ὅς omitted with ℵACD. It is unrepresented in the *Vulg.*

30. Ἠσαΐαν τὸν προφήτην with ℵABC. *Vulg.* has 'Isaïam prophetam.'

37. The whole of this verse is omitted with ℵABCHLP. The *Vulgate* represents it. But see note.

Ch. VIII. 1—4. Persecution after the Death of Stephen.

1. ἐγένετο δὲ ἐν ἐκείνῃ τῇ ἡμέρᾳ, *and there arose on that day*, &c. The persecution was in immediate succession to the death of Stephen. Having once proceeded to such a length, the rage of the people turned upon the whole Christian body.

ἐπὶ τὴν ἐκκλησίαν, *against the Church*, i.e. the congregation or community of Christians which had been formed in the city since the day of Pentecost.

πάντες δὲ διεσπάρησαν, *and they were all scattered abroad.* Thus the rage of their enemies brought about the dispersion which Christ had foretold (Acts i. 8). On this Chrysostom remarks οὐκ ἄρα μάτην ἔλεγον ὅτι οἰκονομίας ὁ διωγμὸς ἦν, εἰ μὴ γὰρ γέγονεν οὐκ ἂν οἱ μαθηταὶ διεσπάρησαν.

By the word πάντες we need not understand every member of the Christian body, but only those who had been most active, and so were in special danger from the persecution. We find (ver. 3) that there were many left, both men and women, in the city, whom Saul seized upon as 'disciples of the Lord' and carried to prison. Perhaps Ananias who visited Paul at Damascus (ix. 19, 25) may have been among those now scattered abroad, but see ix. 2 note.

τῆς Ἰουδαίας καὶ Σαμαρείας, *of Judæa and Samaria.* According to the order of extension indicated by Jesus. The teaching of the Apostles must have been with great power to break through the long-standing prejudices of their Jewish converts against the Samaritans. On these prejudices it is enough to refer to John iv.

πλὴν τῶν ἀποστόλων, *except the Apostles.* Jerusalem would of necessity be looked upon as the headquarters of the Christian band. Thither all the wanderers would refer for guidance and help. The Twelve therefore must remain at their post, in spite of all the persecution.

2. συνεκόμισαν, *they carried to burial.* The verb is found in classical Greek for 'to help in burying,' cf. Soph. *Ajax*, 1048 τόνδε τὸν νεκρόν…μὴ συγκομίζειν; also Thuc. VI. 71 συγκομίσαντες δὲ τοὺς ἑαυτῶν νεκρούς, 'having carried forth their own dead,' where the corpses however were to be burned not buried.

The Jews paid great attention to funeral rites. Cp. *Midrash Rabbah* on Gen. xlvii. 29 (par. 96), 'Deal kindly and truly with me,' literally, 'Do with me kindness and truth.' "Is there then a kindness of falsehood, that he says, kindness and truth? How is this? There is a common proverb which says, 'Is the son of thy friend dead?' Put on the load (i.e. bear the burden with him). Is thy friend himself dead? Put off the load (his survivors will not requite you for your sympathy). Therefore he says to him, 'If thou wilt do me a kindness after my death, that is a kindness of truth.' And in all Ashkenazic prayer-books it is said: 'These are the works of which a man reaps the interest in this world, and the capital endures in the world to come: the honouring of father and mother, the doing of acts of mercy,…*the bearing forth the dead,* the reconciliation of a man to his neighbour, but the study of the Torah is above them all.'" Cp. Mishna *Peah* I. 1.

εὐλαβεῖς, *devout.* See note on ii. 5.

καὶ ἐποίησαν κοπετὸν μέγαν, *and made great lamentation.* κοπετός is not a classical word but is frequent in the LXX., most generally with the cognate verb, as κόπτεσθαι κοπετόν Gen. l. 10; Zech. xii. 10; 1 Macc. ii. 70, &c. But ποιῆσαι κοπετόν occurs Jer. vi. 26; Micah i. 8. The word signifies the beating on the breast which is one of the outward expressions of great sorrow. The Hebrew word for mourning (Gen. xxiii. 2; 2 Sam. iii. 31 &c.) has the same sense. It must have needed no little courage at such a time to perform the funeral rites for one who had fallen as Stephen had, by the fury of the whole people.

3. ἐλυμαίνετο, *he made havock of.* His own words (xxii. 4) are 'I persecuted this way unto the death, binding and delivering into prisons both men and women.' For the verb cf. LXX. Ps. lxxix. 13 ἐλυμήνατο αὐτὴν σῦς ἐκ δρυμοῦ, of the rage and ravages of a wild beast.

κατὰ τοὺς οἴκους εἰσπορευόμενος, *entering into every house.* Having authority from the high-priests probably (as ix. 14), and making search everywhere that none should escape.

γυναῖκας. He had no mercy on sex. See also ix. 2.

εἰς φυλακήν, *to prison.* To be kept till there should be an opportunity of bringing them to judgment, which was a slow process because of the numerous arrests. No persecutor equals in zeal the religious persecutor.

4. διῆλθον, *went about*. This was the effect on the whole body. The history turns at once to a single instance of the dispersion, and describes its results.

5—13.   PHILIP'S PREACHING IN SAMARIA AND ITS EFFECT.

5. Φίλιππος δέ, *But Philip*. He is the second named in the list of the seven deacons (vi. 5). He is only mentioned in this chapter and xxi. 8, where he is called Philip the Evangelist.

εἰς τὴν πόλιν, *into the city*, i.e. the capital city of the district of Samaria. It was at this time called *Sebaste*=Augusta, in honour of Augustus Cæsar (Joseph. *Ant.* xv. 8, 5).

ἐκήρυσσεν, *he proclaimed*. This word, connected with κῆρυξ, points out the preachers as the heralds of a king, while εὐαγγελίζεσθαι, in the previous verse, speaks rather of the glad tidings which was the characteristic of their message.

αὐτοῖς, i.e. Σαμαρείταις, to the people of Samaria, understood in the previous Σαμαρείας. Cf. xx. 2, where αὐτούς refers to the *people* of Macedonia, though the country only is named in the verse before.

τὸν Χριστόν, *the Christ*, the Messiah, the king whose message Philip proclaimed.

6. προσεῖχον δὲ οἱ ὄχλοι, *and the multitudes gave heed*. We know from John iv. 25, 29, 42, that some among the Samaritans were looking for the advent of the Messiah. The field had been already in some degree prepared for Philip's labours: hence the abundant fruit.

τὸν νοῦν must be mentally supplied with προσεῖχον as below in verses 10 and 11, and in xvi. 14, and, with a slightly different sense, in xx. 28.

ἐν τῷ ἀκούειν κ.τ.λ., *when they heard and saw the signs which he wrought*. Lit. 'in the hearing.' They heard what had been done in other places and saw what was done each under his own observation. The miracles are described by that characteristic which they were specially intended to have in this instance. They were to be *signs* that the message which Philip was bringing was from God. The signs here enumerated are such as could leave no doubt in the minds of those who witnessed the cures.

7. πολλοὶ γὰρ κ.τ.λ., *for many of those which had unclean spirits that cried with a loud voice came forth*. This reading is confirmed by the *Vulg.* 'multi enim eorum qui habebant spiritus immundos clamantes voce magna exibant.' But accepting the reading we see that the writer has passed in thought from the persons to the spirits by which they were possessed, and has made the verb refer to the latter. Of the many attempts to correct the oldest texts Tischendorf says 'locus retractando corruptus est.'

On unclean spirits see v. 16, note.

9. Σίμων. From the verb μαγεύω used in describing the arts of Simon, he is usually spoken of as Simon *Magus*, i.e. the sorcerer or magician. According to Justin Martyr (*Apol.* 1. 26) he was born at Gitton, a village of Samaria. The history which is given of him after the events mentioned in this chapter describes him as persistently hostile to St Peter and as following that Apostle to Rome to oppose his teaching. But much that is related is of very doubtful authority. He is said to have been deified at Rome, but it seems probable that Justin mistook a tablet, with an inscription 'Semoni Sanco deo fidio' which was erected in honour of the Sabine Hercules, for a record of divine honours paid to this Simon Magus. The tablet was discovered at Rome in the sixteenth century.

ἐν τῇ πόλει, *in the city.* He had made Samaria a sort of head-quarters. The sorcery which Simon and men like him used was probably no more than a greater knowledge of some of the facts of chemistry. By this they at first attracted attention and then traded on the credulity of those who came to consult them. From the time of their sojourn in Egypt the Jews had known of such impostors, and in their traditional literature some of the 'wisdom' of Moses partakes of this character.

ἐξιστάνων τὸ ἔθνος, *amazing the nation.* For not only the people of the city, but of the whole district had run after him.

εἶναί τινα ἑαυτὸν μέγαν, *that he was some great one* (cf. v. 36). The expectation of the Messiah was strong among the Samaritans, and the general expectation that some great person was to arise among the Jews, while it dictated the form in which impostors would proclaim themselves, also aided them in procuring credence for what they said.

10. ἀπὸ μικροῦ ἕως μεγάλου, *from the least to the greatest*, i.e. one and all. The expression is common in the LXX. Thus God smites the people of Gath (1 Sam. v. 9) ἀπὸ μικροῦ ἕως μεγάλου, 'both small and great' (A.V.). So 1 Sam. xxx. 19; 2 Chron. xxxiv. 30, &c.

ἡ δύναμις τ. θ. ἡ καλουμένη μεγάλη, *the power of God that is called great.* We can see from the language of the N.T. that 'power' was a word current to express *angelic or heavenly influences* (Rom. viii. 38; 1 Pet. iii. 22); and without assuming such a partition of the celestial host as is seen in the later Alexandrine writings we can understand the thought of these Samaritans that in Simon they had an incarnation of divine power, which deserved the title of *great* preeminently.

11. ἱκανῷ χρόνῳ, *for a long time.* For the dative similarly used of a space of time, see xiii. 20. Simon's birthplace was in Samaria, and it is most probable that he had lived there a great part of his life. Tradition (*Clement. Hom.* II. 22) makes him to have been educated in Alexandria, but he is also said to have been a pupil of Dositheus, a Gnostic teacher in Samaria, so that he had probably been but a short time away from his native country.

ταῖς μαγείαις, *with sorceries.* μαγεῖαι are mentioned in the 'Teaching of the Twelve Apostles' (§ 5) among those works which belong to the 'way of death'; and οὐ μαγεύσεις is one of the prohibitions (§ 2) contained in the second commandment of the 'Teaching.'

12. εὐαγγελιζομένῳ περὶ τῆς βασιλείας κ.τ.λ., *preaching concerning the kingdom of God.* Christ had prepared the Apostles for this work during the forty days after the resurrection (i. 3) by the things which He spake unto them about the kingdom which was to be begun.

καὶ τοῦ ὀνόματος Ἰησοῦ Χριστοῦ, *and concerning the Name of Jesus Christ*, i.e. its true meaning and the evidence that to Jesus the name Christ was truly applied.

13. ὁ δὲ Σίμων...ἐπίστευσεν, *and Simon himself believed also.* We can see from the history which follows that the belief here described was of a very imperfect nature. It perhaps amounted to no more than the conviction that in Philip was some power greater than his own. We have an example of a like imperfect belief described in like words in St John's Gospel (viii. 31), 'then said Jesus to those Jews which *believed* on Him,' and all that follows in the chapter shews that the belief which they professed was not enough to prevent them from plotting for Christ's death.

καὶ βαπτισθείς, *and when he was baptized.* Chrysostom (*Hom. XVIII. in Act.*) asks why it came to pass that such a man was admitted to baptism, and answers the question ὥσπερ καὶ τὸν Ἰούδαν ὁ Χριστὸς ἐξελέξατο. But St Luke's language here (ἐξίστατο) implies that Simon was possessed with the same feeling towards Philip which the people of Samaria had towards himself.

θεωρῶν τε κ.τ.λ., *beholding the signs and great miracles wrought.* There is apparently a distinction intended by St Luke between the belief of the Samaritans and that of Simon. When they believed (verse 12) it was the preaching and the glad tidings to which they most gave heed, but the verb used in this verse (θεωρῶν) seems to paint Simon as one who gazed with wonder only on a sight which was beyond him to explain.

14—25. PETER AND JOHN SENT DOWN TO SAMARIA. CONDUCT OF SIMON MAGUS.

14. οἱ ἐν Ἱεροσολύμοις ἀπόστολοι, *the Apostles which were at Jerusalem*, the whole Twelve still abiding there, as noted in verse 1, and evidently all taking their part in the administration of the affairs of the Church, though it does not fall within St Luke's purpose to notice what each did or said.

ὅτι δέδεκται κ.τ.λ., *that Samaria had received the word of God.* There was a communication kept up between the fugitives from Jerusalem and the Twelve even from the first. Samaria here means the district, for although Philip's preaching was in one city, the newly-baptized would spread abroad in every part, and carry the teaching forth as the woman of Samaria did her 'new learning' (John iv. 28). They had received the word of God as their countrymen before, so as to 'know that this is indeed the Christ, the Saviour of the world.'

ἀπέστειλαν, *they sent.* We gather from this passage that there was no special preeminence assigned to any among the Twelve in these earliest days. Peter and John were sent forth on their mission by the decision of the whole body. These two were probably chosen for such a work, as they had taken the most active part and in concert (iii. 1) in establishing the Church in Jerusalem.

15. καταβάντες, *when they were come down.* Used often of leaving Jerusalem, the centre of all religious life, to go into other parts. So the contrary verb ἀναβαίνειν is employed (Luke ii. 42) to describe the journey to the Holy City.

ὅπως λάβωσι, *that they might receive.* The subjunctive mood comes after ὅπως even when preceded by a past tense, as here, when the result intended is regarded as something which will surely come to pass. Cf. Acts xxv. 26, προήγαγον αὐτὸν ἐφ' ὑμῶν...ὅπως σχῶ τί γράψω.

πνεῦμα ἅγιον, *the Holy Ghost,* or rather (as the word has no article) 'a gift of the Holy Ghost.' It is clear from the whole history that special gifts of the Holy Ghost, bestowed at this period on the Christian converts in various places, were not given except through the Apostles. The case of Ananias, sent by God's special command to Saul, differs from all others. Peter could promise it (ii. 38) to those who should repent and be baptized, but the Samaritan converts whom Philip had made received no share of such powers till the arrival of Peter and John. But the Apostles make it manifest by their prayer that the gift was not theirs either to impart or withhold, but was 'of God,' as Peter calls it (ver. 20).

16. ὑπῆρχον. This verb seems to be used with somewhat of its original force = 'to make a beginning.' These men had taken one step, and had been baptized and thus admitted into the community.

εἰς τὸ ὄνομα, *into the name* The preposition, which is the same that is used by Christ (Matth. xxviii. 19) at the institution of the Sacrament, implies the tie by which the new converts are in baptism bound to Christ as His followers, servants, worshippers.

17. τότε ἐπετίθεσαν κ.τ.λ., *then they laid their hands on them,* that there might be some outward sign of this imparted grace. So Ananias (ix. 17) laid his hands on Saul, and he received the Holy Ghost. But on Cornelius and his companions (x. 44) the same gift was bestowed while Peter spake unto them.

18. ἰδὼν δέ, *and when Simon saw,* &c. Simon's conduct now makes it clear how limited his faith had been. As he offered to buy the power, so we may be sure he meant to sell it. His faith had only sprung from his amazement.

προσήνεγκεν κ.τ.λ., *he offered them money.* From Simon's name all trafficking in sacred things has since been called 'simony.'

19. δότε κἀμοὶ τὴν ἐξουσίαν ταύτην, *give me also this power.* The character of the man is shewn by what he asks for. He does not desire the Holy Ghost for himself as a spiritual gift to seal his baptism, but that he may be able to bestow what he looks upon as a higher power than his own magic. On this verse Chrysostom remarks οὐκ ἂν οὕτως εἶπεν εἰ μὴ αἰσθητόν τι ἐγίνετο. The gift of the Holy Ghost had been made apparent by the new powers conferred on those who received it. Their works and words Simon had seen and heard, and hence his application to the Apostles.

20. τὸ ἀργύριον...ἀπώλειαν, *thy silver perish with thee.* εἰς ἀπώλειαν is a frequent expression in the LXX. Thus for the king's threat 'ye shall be cut to pieces' (A.V.) we find Dan. ii. 5, iii. 29 ἔσεσθε εἰς ἀπώλειαν. The expression also occurs Is. xiv. 23; Esther vii. 4; Ezek. xxviii. 7, &c. It is clear from what follows that the terrible invocation of doom upon this offender is to be qualified by the condition supplied from ver. 22, where repentance and prayer are pointed out as means whereby even so great a sinner may find forgiveness. And St Peter may have thus joined Simon in the same destruction as his money, because he foresaw that there was little or no hope that such a man could be brought to repentance unless the consequence of his sin were set before him in all its terror.

ὅτι τὴν δωρεὰν κ.τ.λ., *because thou thoughtest to acquire the gift of God for money.* Simon had given no heed to the prayer which the Apostles had offered to God that this gift of the Spirit might be sent down. He did not regard it as 'the gift of God' but only thought, if he could but once buy it, it would be his own at all times and for ever.

21. μερὶς οὐδὲ κλῆρος. These two words are constantly found together in the LXX. of Deuteronomy where the Levites are spoken of, who had no inheritance or possession in the land of Canaan. Thus Deut. xii. 12 ὁ Λευίτης, ὅτι οὐκ ἔστιν αὐτῷ μερὶς οὐδὲ κλῆρος μεθ᾽ ὑμῶν. So xiv. 27, 29, xviii. 1.

ἐν τῷ λόγῳ τούτῳ, *in this matter.* Or, more literally, 'in this word'; and if that rendering be taken, the reference will be to the λόγον θεοῦ mentioned in verse 14.

ἡ γὰρ καρδία σου οὐκ ἔστιν εὐθεῖα, *for thy heart is not right,* &c. This expression or its equivalent (εὐθὺς τῇ καρδίᾳ) is very common in the LXX. of the Psalms, as Pss. vii. 10, x. 2, xxxi. 11, &c. The passage which most nearly accords with this verse is Ps. lxxvii. 37, ἡ δὲ καρδία αὐτῶν οὐκ εὐθεῖα μετ᾽ αὐτοῦ.

22. μετανόησον οὖν ἀπὸ τ. κ., *repent therefore,* &c. On this condition not only could the stern wish of Peter be averted, but the anger of God also. We see therefore that the words of the Apostle in ver. 20 must have been coupled in his mind with such condition, but the further language of this verse seems to imply that to Peter's mind there was not much hope of such repentance. The phrase μετανοεῖν ἀπό is found in LXX. (Jer. viii. 6) ἄνθρωπος ὁ μετανοῶν ἀπὸ τῆς κακίας αὐτοῦ.

δεήθητι τοῦ κυρίου, *and pray the Lord.* This is what one would look for in the sentence, rather than 'pray God' (*Text. recept.*), for the offence was directly against Christ. Simon, with corrupt motives, was seeking to be enrolled among those who were called by Christ's name.

εἰ ἄρα, *if perhaps.* The Apostle sees how full the mind of Simon has been of the scheme which he has conceived, and the knowledge of this seems expressed in the εἰ ἄρα with which this clause begins. He will not declare that there is not hope even for such an offender, but the covetousness, which is idolatry, makes repentance almost impossible. See Chrysostom's words, διὰ τοῦτο καὶ εἶπεν, εἰ ἄρα ἀφεθήσεταί σοι, ὅτι ᾔδει ἀδιόρθωτον ὄντα.

ἡ ἐπίνοια, *the thought*. ἐπίνοια is found only here in N.T., but is not uncommon in the LXX. It implies a deliberate, well matured plan. Cf. Wisdom xiv. 12, ἀρχὴ γὰρ πορνείας ἐπίνοια εἰδώλων. Also see 2 Macc. xii. 45.

23. εἰς γὰρ χολὴν πικρίας. The preposition εἰς=*into* is not easy to explain here. Some have thought that εἰς, like ἐν, is used as representing בְּ. By others the construction has been compared with that of the Hebrew preposition לְ = *for*, after the verb 'to be' in passages such as Ezek. xxxvii. 22 'I will make them one nation,' literally '*unto* one nation.' But instances of this construction are not common enough in the O.T. for an imitation of it in the N.T. to be probable. It seems better therefore not to take 'gall of bitterness' and 'bond of iniquity' as thus in apposition with the subject of the sentence, but rather to regard the preposition as used with the sense of motion towards a place or state and subsequent rest there. So it is found in Luke xi. 7, 'my children are with me *in* (εἰς) bed,' where the meaning is, 'they have come into, and are remaining in, bed.' So that the sense here would be 'thou hast advanced towards, and art involved in, the gall of bitterness,' &c. The expression χολὴ πικρίας is a modification of words which are found more than once in the LXX. Cf. Deut. xxix. 18 ῥίζα ἄνω φύουσα ἐν χολῇ καὶ πικρίᾳ. Similarly Deut. xxxii. 32 σταφυλὴ χολῆς, βότρυς πικρίας. See also Lament. iii. 15.

σύνδεσμον ἀδικίας, *the bond of iniquity*. The expression is found in the LXX. (Is. lviii. 6). The whole sentence thus implies that Simon had gone from one evil to another till he had reached and was remaining in a stage which deserved the reprobation spoken against idolatry in the O.T., and that he had allowed evil to make him its prisoner.

24. ὅπως μηδὲν ἐπέλθῃ κ.τ.λ., *that none of these things which ye have spoken come upon me*. Simon shews from the character of his petition that he is not moved by a true spirit of repentance. He utters no word of sorrow for the evil of his thought, but only petitions that he may suffer no punishment. Yet we can see that he had not taken the expression of St Peter in ver. 20 as a curse invoked upon him by the Apostle, but only as a declaration of the anger of God and of the certainty of a penalty upon the wilful continuance in such sin. His entreaty may be compared with that oft-repeated petition of Pharaoh to Moses (Exod. viii. 8, 28, ix. 28, x. 17), 'Intreat the Lord for me,' extorted by fear and followed by no change of conduct.

25. οἱ μὲν οὖν...λαλήσαντες...εἰς Ἱεροσόλυμα...εὐηγγελίζοντο, *they therefore, when they had testified and spoken the word of the Lord, returned towards Jerusalem, and preached the Gospel to many villages*

of the Samaritans. Peter and John had not been sent forth to make an extended missionary journey, but only to confirm the work of the Evangelists who had first preached and baptized in Samaria, by laying their hands upon the converts. This done they returned to their place in Jerusalem, but by the way preached in such villages of Samaria as lay in their road.

On this return Chrysostom remarks διατὶ πάλιν ἁπίασιν ἐκεῖ ἔνθα ἡ τυραννὶς ἦν, ἔνθα ἡ ἀρχὴ τῶν κακῶν, ἔνθα οἱ μάλιστα φωνῶντες; καθάπερ ἐν τοῖς πολέμοις οἱ στρατηγοὶ ποιοῦσι καὶ τὸ πονοῦν τοῦ πολέμου μέρος καταλαμβάνουσι τὸ αὐτὸ καὶ οὗτοι ἐργάζονται.

26—40. PHILIP BAPTIZES AN ETHIOPIAN EUNUCH.

26. ἄγγελος δέ, *and an angel.* God does not let His agents languish for want of occupation. Peter and John are sent to complete the work of Philip in Samaria, but Philip meanwhile is divinely directed to another scene of labour.

ἐλάλησεν πρὸς Φίλιππον, *spake unto Philip.* Most probably in a vision, as to Cornelius (x. 3) and to Peter (xi. 5).

κατὰ μεσημβρίαν, *toward the south.* Gaza was the southernmost of the five great cities which the Philistines had formerly occupied, and was on the route which a traveller from Jerusalem to Egypt would follow. In 96 B.C. the city of Gaza had been destroyed and its inhabitants massacred by Alexander Jannæus (Joseph. *Ant.* XIII. 13. 3), but it had been rebuilt by Gabinius (*Ant.* XIV. 5. 3), though it is said that the restored city was nearer the sea than the ancient one. It continued to be a city of importance (see *Ant.* XV. 7. 3 and XVII. 11. 4), and it cannot therefore be to the city that the word 'desert', which follows, must be referred. From Samaria Philip would come directly south, and leaving Jerusalem on the east strike the road at some distance from that city.

ἀπὸ Ἱερουσαλὴμ εἰς Γάζαν, *from Jerusalem unto Gaza.* There was more than one road from Jerusalem to Gaza; the more northern route went first to Ascalon and then by the coast to Gaza, another road was by Hebron and through the more desert country which lay to the west of it, and this is most likely the road intended in the narrative.

αὕτη ἐστὶν ἔρημος, *this is desert.* With αὕτη it is best to supply ἡ ὁδός. If the words had been inserted as an explanation by the writer in reference to Gaza, they would scarcely have been so curt, whereas if we regard them as a portion of the speech of the angel they contain all that was needed for Philip's instruction. That road toward Gaza which passed through the desert explains exactly the place to which he was to go.

27. ἀνὴρ Αἰθίοψ. The deletion of the second ὅς in this verse leaves the nominative with a verb to which it may be joined, which was not the case in the *Text. recept.*

Ethiopia, like Cush in the O.T., is a general name given to the country which is now called Nubia and Abyssinia. Its northern portion was the great kingdom of Meroë, which we know was ruled over by queens for a long period (Plin. *H. N.* VI. 29), and it is from this kingdom, most probably, that the eunuch had come. Jews were abundant in Egypt, and this man had become a proselyte to their religion.

Κανδάκης, *of Candace.* We are told by Pliny (l. c.) that this was the name of a series of queens of Meroë, just as Pharaoh at an early period, and Ptolemy subsequently, were general names for the kings of Egypt, and Cæsar for the Roman emperors.

ἐπὶ πάσης τῆς γάζης αὐτῆς, *over all her treasure.* γάζα is a word of Persian origin, and is found in nearly the same form in the Hebrew text of Ezra v. 17, vi. 1, vii. 20, and Esther iv. 7, into which books it has come directly from the Persian.

ἐληλύθει προσκυνήσων, *had come to worship,* which proselytes did, as well as Jews. This we learn from the enumeration of those who were present at the feast of Pentecost (ii. 10), among whom proselytes are expressly named. So (John xii. 20) we find Greeks coming up to the feasts at Jerusalem.

28. ἦν τε ὑποστρέφων, *and was returning,* i.e. at the termination of the feast.

ἀνεγίνωσκεν τὸν προφήτην Ἠσαΐαν, *read Isaiah the prophet.* He was evidently reading aloud (see ver. 30), and this was common among orientals, and was specially the practice of the Jews, who accompanied the reading with a good deal of bodily motion and considered this helpful to study. Thus T. B. *Erubin* 53 b *ad fin.* 'Beruriah found a student who was reading, but not aloud; she pushed him and said to him, Is it not written "Only when it is well ordered then it is kept"? If it is put in order by all thy two hundred and forty-eight limbs [thy study] will abide, but if not it will not abide. We have heard of a pupil of Rabbi Eliezer who studied but not aloud, and after three years he had forgotten his learning.' And a little afterwards we read, 'Shemuel said to Rab Jehudah, Clever fellow! Open thy mouth when thou readest the Bible, and open thy mouth when thou studiest the Mishna, in order that the reading may abide, and that thy life may be prolonged. For it says (Prov. iv. 22), For life are they to them that find them' (or as the Rabbis preferred to read it, 'to them that utter them forth').

29. εἶπεν δὲ τὸ πνεῦμα τῷ Φιλίππῳ, *and the Spirit said unto Philip,* i.e. by some inward prompting.

πρόσελθε καὶ κολλήθητι κ.τ.λ., *go near and join thyself to this chariot.* No doubt this royal treasurer had a numerous retinue, and a single traveller on a desert road would be doing what was natural in attaching himself to a train of people who were journeying in the same direction. Philip would therefore be able to approach and hear what was read without being deemed an intruder.

30. προσδραμὼν δέ, *and having run up,* i.e. to overtake and get near the chariot.

ἆρά γε γινώσκεις, *dost thou understand?* i.e. how the words are to be applied, and to whom they relate.

31. ἐάν. For an example of ἐάν with future indicative cf. Luke xi. 12, ἐὰν αἰτήσει ᾠόν.

ὁδηγήσει με, *shall guide me.* The eunuch living far away from the received expounders of the Scriptures, feels that in a dark passage like that which he was reading he has need of trained instruction. He uses therefore the word which is employed for the guidance given by teacher to pupil. Our Lord uses it (Matth. xv. 14; Luke vi. 39) reproachfully of the blind guidance which the scribes and Pharisees in His day were giving to the people who came to them for instruction. He uses the same word for the guidance of the Holy Spirit (John xvi. 13). The word is common in LXX. version of the Psalms. Cf. also Eccles. ii. 3 and Wisdom ix. 11, ὁδηγήσει με...σωφρόνως καὶ φυλάξει με ἐν τῇ δόξῃ αὐτῆς, where divine wisdom is the guide spoken of. It was a marked feature in the teaching of the Jews that explanations of Scripture were passed on from generation to generation, and that only was highly valued by them which a man had received from his teachers. Such a system (unhappily not without its parallels in the history of the Christian Church) accounts for the permanence of all their traditions.

παρεκάλεσέν τε, *and he besought.* The verb implies a very earnest request, and betokens the great desire which the eunuch had for more enlightenment.

32. ἡ δὲ περιοχή, *now the place,* &c. The word περιοχή is of rare occurrence in this sense, but Cicero uses it in *Epist. ad Attic.* XIII. 25. It means the section of a book, rather than a particular place. Compare the use of the verb in 1 Pet. ii. 6, περιέχει ἐν τῇ γραφῇ, 'it is contained in the Scripture.' The eunuch was studying the whole description of the sufferer whom the prophet is describing.

αὕτη, *this.* The verses quoted here are Isaiah liii. 7, 8, and are given word for word from the LXX., which it is most probable that the eunuch was reading, as, being made in Egypt, that version was most likely to be circulated among those Jews with whom this man would be brought into communication. Philip also belonging to the Grecians (vi. 5) would be most familiar with the Greek translation. It will be seen that the translation differs in some points from the original, but yet it is sufficiently close in sense to express the intention of the prophet or rather the 'mind of the Spirit' in the prophecy, and on this translation therefore Philip founds his teaching.

33. ἐν τῇ ταπεινώσει, *in His humiliation.* The Hebrew text signifies 'through oppression and through judgment (i.e. punishment) he was taken away.'

τὴν γενεὰν κ.τ.λ., *who shall declare His generation?* i.e. who shall describe His contemporaries, men who under a form of judicial punishment oppressed the sufferer, and put Him to death?

ὅτι αἴρεται ἀπὸ τῆς γῆς ἡ ζωὴ αὐτοῦ, *for His life is taken from the earth.* The Hebrew has 'for He was cut off out of the land of the living.' It will be seen from a comparison of the Hebrew and the LXX. that the latter is in some parts rather a paraphrase than a translation.

Some of the Jews interpreted this passage of a suffering prophet, but most generally it was applied to the suffering nation. Although the notion of a suffering Messiah fell very much into the background, yet it is to be found in some Rabbinical interpretations of Isaiah. In the Targum of Jonathan the Messianic and the national application of the words run side by side. On the whole subject, see Perowne, *Psalms* (5th edition), Appendix.

34. περὶ ἑαυτοῦ, *concerning himself.* As Isaiah lxi. 'The Spirit of the Lord God is upon me, &c.,' was held by the Jews to refer to Isaiah, so the eunuch enquires whether the words he has been reading may have the same reference.

35. καὶ ἀρξάμενος ἀπὸ τῆς γραφῆς ταύτης κ.τ.λ., *and he began at this Scripture, and preached unto him Jesus.* It can hardly be doubted that during his sojourn in Jerusalem the eunuch had heard the history of the new teachers who had created such an excitement in the city. Thus he would have had some story told him of the founder of the new community, but his informants would have been Jews, and he would only have heard from them a version of what had been done of such a sort as to make him account Jesus one of the many deceivers who abounded in those times.

36. ὡς δὲ ἐπορεύοντο κατὰ τὴν ὁδόν, *and as they went on the way.* We must suppose that Philip travelled for some time with the eunuch, for not only has he explained that in Jesus was fulfilled all that the prophets had spoken concerning the sufferings of the Messiah, but has taught him that believers in Jesus are to be admitted into the Christian Church by baptism, of which sacrament he desires to be a partaker at once.

On the full teaching which the eunuch had received from Philip, Chrysostom says, ὅρα πῶς τὰ δόγματα ἀπηρτισμένα εἶχε, καὶ γὰρ ὁ προφήτης πάντα περιεῖχε, τὴν σάρκωσιν, τὸ πάθος, τὴν ἀνάστασιν, τὴν ἀνάληψιν, τὴν κρίσιν τὴν μέλλουσαν. ἃ δὴ καὶ πολλὴν τὴν ἐπιθυμίαν αὐτῷ μάλιστα ἐνεποίησαν. αἰσχύνθητε ὅσοι ἀφώτιστοι τυγχάνετε.

37. εἶπεν δὲ ὁ Φίλιππος, Εἰ πιστεύεις ἐξ ὅλης τῆς καρδίας ἔξεστιν. Ἀποκριθεὶς δὲ εἶπεν, Πιστεύω τὸν υἱὸν τοῦ θεοῦ εἶναι τὸν Ἰησοῦν Χριστόν. These words stand in the *Text. recept.* as verse 37, but are omitted in the oldest MSS. They probably found their way into the text, of those MSS. in which they stand, from the margin. Such a margin would be readily formulated by those who thought perhaps that the question in verse 36 required a definite answer, and who, when the Church had become more extended, and formal professions of faith were the rule before baptism, felt that there was a want of completeness in the narrative unless some such confession were supposed to have been made. Thus the margin became a kind of exposition, and in the end found acceptance in the text.

Though found in some MSS. of the Vulgate it is absent from the best, and was not in that which Beda used.

38. ἐκέλευσεν στῆναι τὸ ἅρμα, *he commanded the chariot to stand still,* i.e. he bade the chariot-driver halt.   Of course the whole retinue would be witnesses of what took place, and they may perhaps be regarded as the nucleus of a congregation to be established in Ethiopia. Tradition tells us that the eunuch laboured to evangelize his countrymen, and none were more likely to be influenced by his teaching than those who were present at his baptism and were, with him, witnesses of the way in which Philip was taken from them.

κατέβησαν κ.τ.λ., *they went down both into the water,* as was the custom among the Jews.   Thus John baptized his followers in the Jordan.   It is worth notice that in the 'Teaching of the Twelve Apostles' recently discovered provision is made for baptism by affusion (chap. vii.), ἔκχεον εἰς τὴν κεφαλὴν τρὶς ὕδωρ εἰς ὄνομα πατρὸς καὶ υἱοῦ καὶ ἁγίου πνεύματος.

39. πνεῦμα κυρίου κ.τ.λ., *the Spirit of the Lord caught away Philip.*   Just as Obadiah expected that Elijah would be carried away while he himself went on his errand to Ahab (1 Kings xviii. 12). Compare the language of Ezekiel (iii. 12, 14, viii. 3, &c.), 'So the spirit lifted me up (ἀνέλαβε) and took me away.'

Chrysostom says of this removal of Philip : συμφερόντως οὖν ἥρπασεν αὐτὸν τὸ πνεῦμα, ἐπεὶ ἠξίωσεν ἂν καὶ συνεπανελθεῖν αὐτῷ ὁ εὐνοῦχος, ὃν καὶ ἐλύπησεν ἂν ἐκεῖνος, ἀνανεύσας καὶ ἀρνησάμενος οὐδέπω καιροῦ ὄντος.

καὶ οὐκ εἶδεν αὐτὸν οὐκέτι ὁ εὐνοῦχος, *and the eunuch saw him no more.*   This marvellous removal of Philip would confirm the eunuch and his companions in their faith.   They would recognize that he who had been sent unto them was a man of God.

ἐπορεύετο γὰρ τὴν ὁδὸν αὐτοῦ χαίρων, *for he went on his way rejoicing.*   The words explain why Philip was no more seen of the eunuch. He was not like the sons of the prophets at Jericho, who went to seek Elijah when they heard of his being carried away.   The eunuch was filled with joy at the new light which God had sent to him, and felt no anxiety for the safety of Philip, being sure that he was cared for by the same hand which had sent him forth.

40. Φίλιππος δὲ εὑρέθη, *but Philip was found,* i.e. he appeared again and continued the work of his ministry.   Εὑρέθη is the exact translation of a Hebrew verb which in the A.V. is often rendered 'to be present.'   Cf. Esther i. 5 'that were present,' and in the margin 'Hebrew, *found.*'

εἰς Ἄζωτον, *at Azotus.*   The preposition εἰς, =*into,* in such a connexion may be explained as implying 'he had come *into* the city and was staying there.'   The LXX. text of the passage from Esther alluded to in the last note is a good illustration of this sentence, ἐποίησεν ὁ βασιλεὺς πότον τοῖς ἔθνεσιν τοῖς εὑρεθεῖσιν εἰς τὴν πόλιν.   See above on verse 23 and *Winer-Moulton*, p. 516.

Azotus is the ancient Ashdod (1 Sam. v. 1—7), one of the five chief cities of the Philistines when the Israelites settled in Canaan.

εἰς Καισάρειαν, *to Cæsarea.*   This was Cæsarea Sebaste, so called in honour of Augustus (Greek, Σεβαστός) Cæsar (Joseph. *Ant.* xvi.

5. 1). It was the chief city of Palestine under the Roman rule, and lay at the extreme north of the plain of Sharon. It is mentioned in the Acts as the place at which Cornelius was stationed (x. 1), and it seems that Philip subsequently made his home there (xxi. 8).

CHAPTER IX.

Readings varying from the *Text. recept.*

3. ἐκ for ἀπὸ with אABCL. *Vulg.* 'de.'

5. ὁ δέ instead of ὁ δὲ κύριος εἶπεν with ABC. *Vulg.* 'et ille' only.

5, 6. σκληρόν σοι πρὸς κέντρα λακτίζειν. τρέμων τε καὶ θαμβῶν εἶπεν, Κύριε, τί με θέλεις ποιῆσαι; καὶ ὁ κύριος πρὸς αὐτόν omitted with אABCEHLP. The *Vulg.* represents it.

8. οὐδὲν for οὐδένα with אAB. *Vulg.* 'nihil.'

12. ἐν ὁράματι omitted with אA. The *Vulg.* also does not represent it.

18. ὡς for ὡσεὶ with אAB.

παραχρῆμα omitted with אABCHP. Not represented in *Vulg.*

19. ὁ Σαῦλος omitted with אABCE. Not in *Vulg.*

20. For Χριστόν read Ἰησοῦν with אABCE. *Vulg.* 'Jesum.'

26. ὁ Σαῦλος omitted with אABC. Not in *Vulg.*

29. Ἰησοῦ omitted with אABE. Not in *Vulg.*

31. ἡ μὲν οὖν ἐκκλησία with אABC. *Vulg.* 'ecclesia quidem.'

38. Μὴ ὀκνήσῃς with אABCE. *Vulg.* 'Ne pigriteris.'

ἡμῶν for αὐτῶν with אABCE. *Vulg.* 'nos.'

42. ἐπίστευσαν πολλοὶ with אABCE. *Vulg.* 'crediderunt multi.'

Ch. IX. 1—9. Saul's Mission to Damascus and his Conversion.

1. ὁ δὲ Σαῦλος, *but Saul.* The δέ takes up the previous δέ in viii. 1, where Saul was last alluded to. On this resumptive use of δέ cf. *Winer-Moulton*, p. 553.

ἐμπνέων ἀπειλῆς, *breathing threatening.* This was the atmosphere in which he was constantly living during his search for the Christians. The rendering 'breathing out' (A.V.) gives a wrong sense. Cf. LXX. Josh. x. 40 πᾶν ἐμπνέον ζωῆς ἐξωλόθρευσεν, 'he utterly destroyed everything which drew the breath of life.'

εἰς τοὺς μαθητάς, *against the disciples.* We are not told of any other death, but Stephen's, in which Saul was an active participator, but we can gather from his own words (Acts xxvi. 10) 'when they were put to death, I gave my voice [vote] against them' that the protomartyr was not the only one who was killed in the time of this persecution. It has been suggested that the zeal which Saul shewed at the time of Stephen's death led to his election into the Sanhedrin, and so he took a judicial part in the later stages of the persecution, and, it may be from a desire to justify the choice of those who had placed him in authority, he sought to be appointed over the enquiry after the Christians in Damascus. We gather from xxvi. 10 that before this inquisitorial journey he had been armed with the authority of the chief priests in his search after the Christians in Jerusalem.

τῷ ἀρχιερεῖ, *to the high-priest.* He would be the person through whom the power, which the great Sanhedrin claimed to exercise in religious matters, over Jews in foreign cities, would be put in motion.

2. ἐπιστολάς, *letters.* These are the papers which constituted his 'authority and commission' (xxvi. 12). From that passage we learn that the issuing of these papers was the act of the whole body, for Paul there says they were 'from the chief priests.'

Δαμασκόν, *Damascus.* Of the history of this most ancient (Gen. xiv. 15) city in the world, see the *Dictionary of the Bible.* It had from the earliest period been mixed up with the history of the Jews, and great numbers of Jews were living there at this time, as we can see from the subsequent notices of their conduct in this chapter. We are told by Josephus (*B. J.* II. 20. 2) that ten thousand Jews were slaughtered in a massacre in Damascus in Nero's time, and that the wives of the Damascenes were almost all of them attached to the Jewish religion.

πρὸς τὰς συναγωγάς, *to the synagogues,* viz. those which existed in Damascus. As at Jerusalem, so in Damascus, the synagogues were numerous, and occupied by different classes and nationalities. Greek-Jews were sure to be found in so large a city.

τινας...τῆς ὁδοῦ ὄντας, *any that were of the Way.* For εἰμί with this genitive of a class or particular character, cf. 1 Thess. v. 5 οὐκ ἐσμὲν νυκτὸς οὐδὲ σκότους, and just afterwards (verse 8) ἡμεῖς δὲ ἡμέρας ὄντες.

The name 'the Way' soon became a distinctive appellation of the Christian religion. The fuller expression 'the way of truth' is found 2 Pet. ii. 2; and the brief term is common in the Acts. See xix. 9, 23, xxii. 4, xxiv. 14, 22.

ἄνδρας τε καὶ γυναῖκας, *whether they be men or women.* We can mark the fury with which Saul raged against the Christians from this mention of the 'women' as included among those whom he committed and desired to commit to prison. Cp. viii. 3 and xxii. 4. The women played a more conspicuous part among early Christians than they were allowed to do among the Jews. See note on i. 14.

εἰς Ἱερουσαλήμ, *unto Jerusalem,* as to the head-quarters of Jewish authority, where the whole power of the great Sanhedrin might be employed to crush out the new teaching.

3. ἐν δὲ τῷ πορεύεσθαι, *and as he journeyed.* There were two roads by which Saul could make his journey, one the caravan road which led from Egypt to Damascus, and kept near the coast line of the Holy Land till it struck eastward to cross the Jordan at the north of the Lake of Tiberias. To join this road Saul must have at first turned

westward to the sea. The other way led through Neapolis and crossed the Jordan south of the Sea of Tiberias, and passing through Gadara went north-eastward to Damascus. We have no means whereby to decide by which road Saul and his companions took their way. The caravan road was a distance of 136 miles, and occupied six days for the journey.

ἐγένετο αὐτὸν ἐγγίζειν, *it came to pass that he drew nigh.* This accusative and infinitive after ἐγένετο is frequent in St Luke's writings, but it also occurs in other parts of N. T.; cf. Mark ii. 23, καὶ ἐγένετο παραπορεύεσθαι αὐτὸν διὰ τῶν σπορίμων. Cf. *Winer-Moulton,* p. 406.

The party must have reached the near neighbourhood of the city, for his companions (ver. 8) 'led him by the hand and brought him into Damascus' after the vision.

φῶς ἐκ τοῦ οὐρανοῦ, *a light from heaven.* In xxii. 6 we are told that the time of the day was 'about noon' when the vision was seen, and in xxvi. 13 Paul says that 'at mid-day' the light was 'above the brightness of the sun.' The mid-day glare of an Eastern sun is of itself exceedingly bright, and the hour was chosen, we cannot doubt, in order that 'the glory' of this heaven-sent light should not be confounded with any natural phenomenon. It was in the midst of this glory that Christ was seen by Saul (1 Cor. xv. 8), so that he can enumerate himself among those who had beheld the Lord after His resurrection.

4. καὶ πεσὼν ἐπὶ τὴν γῆν ἤκουσεν, *and he fell to the earth and heard.* The fall was in consequence of the dazzling intensity of the brightness. From xxvi. 14 we find that not only Saul but his companions were struck down by the light, though there was more in the vision which he beheld than was made evident to them, and by reason of the greater glory which was manifested to him his natural sight was blinded.

φωνήν. By using the accusative case here and the genitive in verse 7, St Luke seems to point out that there was a difference between the hearing which Saul experienced and that of his companions. St Paul in xxii. 9 marks the distinction in his own narrative of what occurred. Speaking of his companions, he says τὴν φωνὴν οὐκ ἤκουσαν, though here in verse 7 we have ἀκούοντες μὲν τῆς φωνῆς said of them.

Taking all the instances together the correct conclusion seems to be that when ἀκούειν signifies *direct* hearing, it may have after it a genitive case and participle, but not an accusative and participle. Thus the construction of λέγουσαν in this verse must be taken as an apposition to φωνήν, *a voice that said,* &c. So also must be explained the construction in xxvi. 14.

Saul during the vision heard articulate sounds, a voice which spake to him, but his companions were only conscious of a sound from which they comprehended nothing.

Of a similar supernatural communication to Hyrcanus the high

priest we have (Joseph. *Ant.* XIII. 10. 3) φασὶ γὰρ ὅτι…αὐτὸς ἐν τῷ
ναῷ θυμιῶν μόνος ὢν ὁ ἀρχιερεὺς ἀκούσειε φωνῆς ὡς οἱ παῖδες αὐτοῦ νενι-
κήκασιν ἀρτίως τὸν Ἀντίοχον. In this case the sound was that of
intelligible words.

Σαοὺλ Σαούλ, τί με διώκεις; *Saul, Saul, why persecutest thou Me?*
It is very noteworthy that in all the three accounts of the vision the
Greek text of Saul's name is a transliteration of the Hebrew, shewing
that we have here a very close adherence to the words of Jesus. The
Lord spake in the language of His people, and both the evangelist
and the apostle have preserved for us this remarkable feature of the
heavenly address. The only other place where the Hebrew form of
Saul's name is retained is in the speech of Ananias when (ix. 17) he
comes to see the convert in his blindness. As he also had received
a communication from Jesus in connexion with Saul's conversion, we
can understand how the same form of the name would have been
given to him. Moreover he was himself, to judge from his name, a
Hebrew, and therefore that form would be most natural on his lips.
Except in these cases St Luke always employs the Greek form of the
word.

Christ speaks of Himself as persecuted by Saul, because 'in all the
affliction of His people He is afflicted' (Is. lxiii. 9), and 'whoso toucheth
them toucheth the apple of His eye' (Zech. ii. 8).

5. εἶπεν δέ, Τίς εἶ, κύριε, *and he said, Who art thou, Lord?* Saul
is sensible of the divine nature of the vision, and shews this by his
address. The appearance of Christ, though in a glorified body, must
have been like that which He wore in His humanity, and since Saul
does not recognize Jesus we may almost certainly conclude that
he had not known Him in His ministerial life.

ὁ δέ, *and he* said. The verb is needed for the sense in English,
but the Greek could dispense with it, as is done below in verse 11.
See also xix. 2.

ἐγώ εἰμι Ἰησοῦς, ὃν σὺ διώκεις, *I am Jesus whom thou persecutest.*
The emphatic contrast of the pronouns is to be noticed, though it
cannot be represented in a translation. In xxii. 8 St Paul gives the
fuller form of the sentence, *I am Jesus of Nazareth.* The Lord speaking from heaven, and employing this His human name, at once and
for ever puts an end to Saul's rage and persecution. Him whom
he must own as Lord is the same who was Jesus of Nazareth. Thus
he sees, what his master Gamaliel had before suggested (v. 39),
that to persecute 'the Way' is 'to fight against God.'

5, 6. The words here omitted by the best MSS. have found their
way into the text in this place from the desire of some early students
of the Acts to make a complete narrative of Saul's conversion by
combining with what is here said the additional particulars given in
xxvi. 14 and xxii. 10. To do this some slight adaptations of the
words became necessary, and hence the form in the *Text. recept.* The
excluded words are more in place in the personal narratives of
St Paul than here, where the account is that of the historian.

6. ἀλλὰ ἀνάστηθι, *but arise.* Saul had continued prostrate during the vision, just where he had been struck down at first.

εἰς τὴν πόλιν, *into the city.* Here is another proof that the party of travellers had arrived very nearly at Damascus. Tradition here, as in many other instances, has fixed on a spot as the scene of this divine vision. It is placed outside the eastern gate, and about a mile from the city. Such a situation answers very well, but its fitness is the only ground for attaching any weight to the tradition.

ὅ τι σε δεῖ ποιεῖν, *what thou must do.* It is very uncommon in N.T. Greek to find ὅ τι in an indirect question, the usual form being τί. Cf. Matth. xx. 22, οὐκ οἴδατε τί αἰτεῖσθε, and numerous other instances. See also *Winer-Moulton*, p. 210.

It will be noticed that, in xxvi. 16—18, St Paul gives an abstract of the labours for which Christ had designed him, and the words in that passage appear as a portion of the divine communication made before Saul entered Damascus. In that narrative however no mention is made of Ananias or his visit, but the Apostle has given instead a brief notice of the message which Ananias brought to him, and therein is contained a declaration of those things which Jesus in the vision only spake of as 'what thou must do.'

7. οἱ δὲ ἄνδρες κ.τ.λ., *and the men which journeyed with him stood speechless.* Cf. Dan. x. 7, 'I Daniel alone saw the vision, for the men that were with me saw not the vision, but a great quaking fell upon them.'

Saul was not only furnished with authority, but also with men who were to carry out his intentions and bring the prisoners to Jerusalem. Painters have represented the travellers as riding on horseback, but there is no warrant for this in any form of the narrative.

εἱστήκεισαν means here 'remained fixed,' 'did not move.' For they were not on their feet, but had been stricken down as well as Saul (xxvi. 14).

ἐνεός is found in LXX. Is. lvi. 10 κύνες ἐνεοί, and in Epist. Jerem. 41 ἐνεὸν μὴ δυνάμενον λαλῆσαι.

ἀκούοντες μὲν τῆς φωνῆς, *hearing the voice.* On the case and its probable significance see above on verse 4.

μηδένα δὲ θεωροῦντες, *but beholding no man.* θεωρέω is used by Stephen (vii. 56), 'I behold the heavens opened.' So here of the glorious vision of Jesus which Saul beheld but not his companions. In their astonishment, and guided by the sound, Saul's companions lifted up their faces to the sky, but as with the words so with the appearance of Jesus; it was unseen by all but one, but to him was manifest enough to form a ground of his confidence in his Apostolic mission: 'Have I not seen Jesus Christ our Lord?' (1 Cor. ix. 1).

8. ἀνεῳγμένων δὲ...οὐδὲν ἔβλεπεν, *but when his eyes were opened he saw nothing.* The vision had struck him blind. He opened his eyes, but their power had been taken away. Thus his physical condition becomes a fit representation of the mental blindness which he

THE ACTS

N

afterwards (xxvi. 9) deplores: 'I verily thought with myself that I ought to do many things contrary to the name of Jesus of Nazareth.'

χειραγωγοῦντες δέ, *but they led him by the hand and*, &c. His companions had seen nothing of the blinding glory, and so saw all things as before.

9. ἡμέρας τρεῖς, *three days*. During this time we cannot but think the illumination of his mind was being enlarged by the Spirit. He had been convinced by the vision that Jesus was risen from the dead and ascended into heaven. But more than this was needed for the preparation of this mighty missionary. He himself (Gal. i. 16) speaks of God revealing His Son not only *to* but *in* him, and that his conferences were not with flesh and blood, and we are told below (ver. 12) that the coming of Ananias had been made known unto him by vision. To this solemn time of darkness may also perhaps be referred some of those 'visions and revelations of the Lord' which the Apostle speaks of to the Corinthians (2 Cor. xii. 1—4). While his bodily powers were for a time in suspense, he may fitly describe himself as not knowing whether what he saw was revealed to him 'in the body or out of the body,' and it was the spiritual vision only which saw the third heaven and paradise, and the spirit heard those 'unspeakable words which it is not lawful for a man to utter.' The Apostle no doubt received other divine revelations while he was in retirement in Arabia.

μὴ βλέπων. It is impossible to discern any difference here between μή and what the sense could have been with οὐ, and the absence of any such difference is made more apparent by the οὐ which follows twice over in the next clause. On the use of μὴ in such sentences, cf. *Winer-Moulton*, p. 610.

καὶ οὐκ ἔφαγεν, *and he did not eat*. The mental anguish for a time overpowered the natural craving for food. The newly-called Apostle was contemplating in all its enormity his sin in persecuting the Church of Christ, and though there were times of comfort and refreshing before Ananias came, yet the great thought which filled Saul's mind would be sorrow for his late mad and misdirected zeal, and so the three days of blindness formed a period of deep penitence.

10—22. SAUL'S SIGHT RESTORED. HE PREACHES IN DAMASCUS.

10. ἦν δέ τις μαθητὴς...'Ανανίας. *Now there was a certain disciple at Damascus, named Ananias*. Of this disciple we have no further mention in Holy Writ except in chap. xxii. 12, where St Paul describes him as 'a devout man according to the Law, having a good report of all the Jews which dwelt' at Damascus. Whether he had become a Christian during the life of Jesus, or was among the Jewish converts on the Day of Pentecost or at some subsequent time, and had been forced to flee from Jerusalem by the persecution which followed on the death of Stephen, we are not told, but we can gather, from the words which he employs in expressing his reluctance to visit Saul, that he had much and trustworthy communication still with the Holy

City, for he knows both of the havock which the persecutor has caused, and of the purpose of his mission to Damascus. On the name Ananias see v. 1, note.

On the sending of Ananias Chrysostom asks τί δήποτε οὐδένα τῶν κορυφαίων ἀποστόλων οὔτε ἐκάλεσεν οὔτε ἀπέστειλε πρὸς τὴν τοῦ Παύλου κατέχησιν; and answers the question thus: ὅτι οὐκ ἐχρῆν δι᾿ ἀνθρώπων ἐνάγεσθαι ἀλλὰ δι᾿ αὐτοῦ τοῦ χριστοῦ· ἐπεὶ καὶ οὗτος ἐδίδαξεν μὲν αὐτὸν οὐδέν, ἐβάπτισε δὲ μόνον.

ἐν ὁράματι, *in a vision.* As Saul had been prepared for the visit by a vision, so Ananias is by a vision instructed to go to him. Dean Howson's remarks (*Life and Epistles of St Paul*, I. 101) on this preparation and its similarity to the preparation of Peter and Cornelius deserve to be dwelt on. 'The simultaneous preparation of the hearts of Ananias and Saul, and the simultaneous preparation of those of Peter and Cornelius—the questioning and hesitation of Peter and the questioning and hesitation of Ananias—the one doubting whether he might make friendship with the Gentiles, the other doubting whether he might approach the enemy of the Church—the unhesitating obedience of each when the Divine will was made clearly known—the state of mind in which both the Pharisee and the Centurion were found—each waiting to see what the Lord would say unto them—this close analogy will not be forgotten by those who reverently read the two consecutive chapters, in which the baptism of Saul and the baptism of Cornelius are narrated in the Acts of the Apostles.' When so much criticism has been expended to shew that the Acts is a work of fiction written at a late period to minimize certain differences supposed to exist between the teaching of St Paul and that of St Peter, it is well to know that others have seen, in these undoubted analogies, proofs of the working of a God who is ever the same, and who would have all men to be saved through Jesus Christ.

11. ἐπὶ τὴν ῥύμην τὴν καλουμένην εὐθεῖαν, *into the street which is called Straight.* ἐπὶ with the accusative signifies 'upon,' and here the sense given by it is that of motion first *to* the street, and then *along* it.

ῥύμη is only a word of late classical authors. In N.T. it is used in contradiction to πλατεία, which is a wide, open space. So ῥύμη=lane. It is found in like contrast in LXX. of Is. xv. 3; also it occurs in Tobit xiii. 18; Ecclus. ix. 7 μὴ περιβλέπου ἐν ῥύμαις πόλεως, where the context suggests a reference to the less public and open places of the city.

A long, straight street still runs through Damascus, and is probably (so persistent is every feature of Oriental life) the same in which Ananias found Saul in the house of Judas.

12. ἀναβλέψῃ, *he may receive his sight.* Here we have ὅπως with the conjunctive after a past tense. But as the event alluded to is yet in the future, it is easy to explain the construction.

13. ἤκουσα ἀπὸ πολλῶν, *I have heard from many.* These words seem to indicate a longer residence of Ananias in Damascus than he could have made if he had only left Jerusalem after the death of

Stephen; and so do the words (xxii. 12) which speak of his good report among all the Jews that dwelt at Damascus. And what a tale they tell us of Saul's zeal against the Church.

τοῖς ἁγίοις σου, *to Thy saints.* The Christian converts were probably called 'saints,' i.e. 'holy persons,' at a very early period after the death of Christ because of the marvellous outpourings of the Holy Spirit upon the first converts, cf. 1 Pet. i. 15. The word is of frequent occurrence in the greetings of St Paul's Epistles.

14. τοὺς ἐπικαλουμένους τὸ ὄνομά σου, *those that call on thy name.* 'To call on Christ's name' is equivalent to being a believer in Him. The expression is found in 1 Cor. i. 2 in apposition to ἅγιοι, and thus we see what in Pauline language is meant by 'saints' when used of the whole body of the Christian Church.

15. σκεῦος ἐκλογῆς, *a chosen vessel.* Literally, 'a vessel of election.' This is a Hebrew form of expression. Cf. LXX. Jerem. xxii. 28, where it is said of king Coniah that he is ὡς σκεῦος οὗ οὐκ ἔστι χρεία. So in Hosea viii. 8 Israel is called σκεῦος ἄχρηστον.

This qualitative genitive (where one noun serves to another in the place of an adjective) is a common construction in Hebrew because that language is poor in adjectives.

τοῦ βαστάσαι τὸ ὄνομά μου, *to bear My name.* This shall be the load which I will lay upon this My chosen servant.

This use of the infinitive with the article in the genitive to express *purpose* or *design* is very common both in the LXX. and in the N. T. Greek. In the former it is the constant form for rendering the infinitive with ל. Cf. Gen. i. 14 and almost every chapter in the Bible. In the N. T. the frequency of this usage is probably due to a familiarity with the LXX., though the classical writers use such a genitival infinitive occasionally. Cf. *Winer-Moulton*, pp. 410, 411.

ἐνώπιον ἐθνῶν, *before the Gentiles.* This was doubtless a revelation to Ananias, who as a devout Jew would not yet have contemplated the inclusion of the whole world in the Church of Christ. The Gentiles are placed first in the enumeration, because among them specially was Saul's field of labour to be. For the wide spirit in which the Apostle embraced his commission, see Rom. i. 13, 14, &c.

καὶ βασιλέων, *and kings.* As before Agrippa (xxvi. 1, 32) and at Rome in consequence of the appeal unto Cæsar.

16. ὑπὲρ τοῦ ὀνόματός μου παθεῖν, *to suffer for My name.* It was no light burden which the new convert was to bear. Cf. his own words (xx. 23), 'the Holy Ghost witnesseth in every city, saying that bonds and afflictions abide me.' The truth of this is borne out by that long list of the Apostle's sufferings which he enumerates in his letter to the Corinthians (2 Cor. xi. 23—28), and the less detailed list in the same Epistle (vi. 4, 5).

17. Σαούλ. See above on verse 4.

ὁ κύριος...Ἰησοῦς. Ananias is guided to combine the name 'Lord,' which Saul had used when he beheld the vision of glory, with 'Jesus' which Christ had Himself uttered in answer to Saul's question, 'Who art thou?' Thus his mission would bring at once its warrant to the mind of Saul. He was now confirmed from without of the verity of all he had seen in the way, and would recognize in Ananias the teacher who was to explain to him what he should do.

πλησθῇς πνεύματος ἁγίου, *be filled with the Holy Ghost.* On this occasion the hands laid on him to whom the gift was imparted were not those of an Apostle, except in so far as Ananias was Christ's ἀπόστολος in this special case.

18. ὡς λεπίδες, *as it had been scales.* The word λεπίς is used by Hippocrates as a technical term for a disease of the eye, and λεπίζω is found (Tobit iii. 17, xi. 13) used to describe the peeling-process by which such a disease was cured. καὶ ἐλεπίσθη ἀπὸ τῶν κάνθων τῶν ὀφθαλμῶν αὐτοῦ τὰ λευκώματα, 'and the whiteness *pilled away* from the corners of his eyes' (A.V.). λευκώματα is rendered in the margin (Tob. ii. 10) 'white films'; they were clearly something like the 'scales' which caused Saul's blindness, and a process for the cure thereof is called (iii. 17) λεπίσαι τὰ λευκώματα, 'to *scale* away the whiteness of Tobit's eyes.' St Paul (xxii. 11) ascribes his blindness to the glory of the heavenly light, and it may have been some secretion, caused by the intensity of that vision, which formed over them, and at his cure fell away. Some have thought that his constant employment of an amanuensis, and the mention of the large characters in which he wrote in his Epistle to the Galatians (vi. 11) 'ye see in what large letters I have written to you,' are indications that the Apostle suffered permanently in his eyesight from the heavenly vision.

On the recovery of St Paul's sight, Chrysostom remarks καὶ ἵνα μὴ νομίσῃ φαντασίαν τις εἶναι τὴν πήρωσιν, διὰ τοῦτο αἱ λεπίδες.

καὶ ἀνέβλεψεν, *and he recovered his sight.* Render thus also in the previous verse.

καὶ ἀναστὰς ἐβαπτίσθη, *and he arose and was baptized.* In the fuller account (xxii. 16) we learn that the exhortation to be baptized was part of the message with which Ananias was charged, and so he was divinely commissioned to receive Saul thus into the Christian Church.

19. καὶ λαβὼν τροφήν, *and when he had taken meat.* Needed after his three days' fast, but (says Calvin) 'he refreshed not his body with meat until his soul had received strength.'

ἐγένετο δὲ...ἡμέρας τινάς, *and he was certain days with the disciples which were at Damascus.* ἡμέρας τινάς is found again x. 48, xv. 36, xvi. 12, xxiv. 24 and xxv. 13, and in all cases the time indicated by them must have been brief. It was for this amount of time that Peter tarried with Cornelius; the words are applied to a short period spent by Paul and Barnabas at Antioch, to the time of St Paul's stay at Philippi, to the short time during which Paul was detained at Cæsarea before his hearing by Felix, and to a like period between the arrival of Festus and the visit which Agrippa made to salute him as the new governor. In most of these instances the time intended must have been very brief, and it is important to notice this here, because in verse 23 we shall find another expression, ἡμέραι ἱκαναί, which is translated 'many days' and seems designed by the writer to indicate a somewhat longer period. It is clear, from the way in which 'disciples' are here mentioned, that there was a numerous body of Christians in Damascus at this early period. Saul dwelt with them now not as an enemy but as a brother, by which name Ananias had been directed to greet him.

20. ἐκήρυσσεν τὸν Ἰησοῦν κ.τ.λ., *he proclaimed Jesus that He is the Son of God.* This is undoubtedly the correct reading. The preaching which was to be to the Jews a stumbling-block was that Jesus of Nazareth was the Christ, their long-expected Messiah.

Saul went, as was Christ's custom also, into the synagogues as the most likely places where to find an audience who would listen to his proclamation. His letters to the synagogues (ver. 2) were not delivered, but he came as the herald of one of higher authority than the chief priests. For St Paul's constant practice of teaching in the Jewish synagogues see xiii. 5, xiv. 1, xvii. 1, 10, xviii. 4, 19, xix. 8.

Chrysostom's note on this practice from the first is ὅρα, εὐθέως διδάσκαλος ἦν ἐν ταῖς συναγωγαῖς· οὐκ ᾐσχύνετο τὴν μεταβολήν, οὐκ ἐδεδοίκει ἐν οἷς λαμπρὸς ἦν ταῦτα καταλύων· οὐχ ἁπλῶς ἦν διδάσκαλος ἀλλὰ ἐν ταῖς συναγωγαῖς.

The construction is not entirely simple, for a portion of the predicative clause has been attracted into the antecedent part of the sentence. The simpler order would have been ἐκήρυσσεν ὅτι Ἰησοῦς ἐστιν κ.τ.λ. But κηρύσσειν Ἰησοῦν (or Χριστόν) had a distinct sense on the lips of the early Christians (cf. Acts viii. 5; 1 Cor. i. 23, &c.), which will account for the order of the words here.

21. ἐξίσταντο δὲ πάντες, *but all were amazed.* Saul's fame as a persecutor of Christians was apparently well known to the Jews of Damascus, and the authorities of the synagogues may have been instructed beforehand to welcome him as a zealous agent. If so their amazement is easy to understand. It is clear from what follows in this verse that they knew of his mission and the intention thereof, though Saul did not bring them his 'commission and authority.' We should gather also from the strong expression ὁ πορθήσας 'he that destroyed,' used to describe Saul's career in Jerusalem, that the slaughter of the Christians there had not been limited to the stoning of Stephen.

ἐληλύθει, ἵνα...ἀγάγῃ, *came hither that he might bring.* The subjunctive after the past tense seems however to indicate that in the mind of the speaker the intention is still thought to be persistent. 'He came that he may (as he is resolved to do) bring,' &c.

22. Σαῦλος δὲ μᾶλλον ἐνεδυναμοῦτο, *but Saul increased the more in strength,* i.e. became more and more energetic in his labours, and the Holy Ghost gave him more power. His fitness for the labour on which he was entering was very great. He possessed all the Jewish learning of a zealous pupil of Gamaliel, and now that he had seen

Jesus in the glory of the Godhead, he could use his stores of learning for the support of the new teaching in such wise as to commend it to those Jews who were looking for the consolation of Israel. But these would naturally be the smallest portion of his hearers. The rest of the Jews were confounded. They heard their Scripture applied by a trained mind, and shewn to be applicable to the life of Jesus. They could not at this time make an attack on Saul, for they were paralysed by what they heard, and it was only when some time had elapsed that they resolved to continue in their rejection of Jesus, and then, at a later time, their persecution of Saul began.

συμβιβάζων, *proving.* This word is used again xvi. 10 and translated there in A.V. 'assuredly gathering.' The idea conveyed by it is that of putting things side by side, and so making a comparison and forming a conclusion. Thus Saul, well equipped with a knowledge of the ancient Scriptures, set before his hearers a description of the Messiah as He is there portrayed, and relating the life history of Jesus, shewed them that in Him the Scriptures of the prophets had been fulfilled.

The word is used often in the LXX. of teaching and instructing. Thus Exod. xviii. 16 καὶ συμβιβάζω αὐτοὺς τὰ προστάγματα θεοῦ, where the sentence relates to judging between one and another. Cf. also Deut. iv. 9.

23—25. A Plot against Saul's Life. His Flight from Damascus.

23. ἡμέραι ἱκαναί, *many days.* As the visit to Jerusalem mentioned in ver. 26 seems to follow closely upon the events narrated in ver. 25, and as that visit was not made till after the retirement into Arabia of which St Paul speaks (Gal. i. 17, 18) thus: 'Neither went I up to Jerusalem to them that were Apostles before me, but I went into Arabia and returned again unto Damascus. Then after three years I went up to Jerusalem to see Peter,' we must place the visit to Arabia between the events recorded in ver. 22 and the fresh narration which commences in this verse. St Luke has marked, as it seems, the two periods as distinct by calling one time of residence 'certain days,' and the other 'many days.' The following seems to have been the order of events. Saul preached for 'certain days' in Damascus immediately after his conversion. He then made his journey into Arabia, either for preaching or for retirement and spiritual communion, after which he made a second visit to Damascus, on which latter occasion his enemies sought to take his life. This latter visit is here spoken of as lasting 'many days.' The words thus translated are used in several places of the Acts; as in this chapter, ver. 43, of the stay made by Peter at Joppa after the raising of Dorcas; also xviii. 18, of the time, 'a good while,' which St Paul spent in Corinth after he had been brought before Gallio; and in xxvii. 7 of the 'many days' of slow sailing during the Apostle's voyage to Rome. It is clear from these examples that the period covered by the words is very indefinite, but if we reckon the 'three years' (Gal. i. 18) from Saul's conversion, then the first and last times of residence in Damascus would be included in that period, and we need not then extend either the stay in Arabia or the duration of this later visit to Damascus over a great while, especially if we remember that, to a Jew, one whole year with the end of the preceding and the beginning of the succeeding one was counted for three years.

συνεβουλεύσαντο, *they took counsel.* The deliberation and previous preparation implied in this expression are such as would take place, not among the people who were 'confounded' by Saul's first preaching, but when they had become enraged against him after his second visit, when his words would be even more full of power than before, by reason of the time spent in Arabia, in spiritual communion to prepare himself for the labours which God had set before him.

24. ἐγνώσθη δὲ τῷ Σαύλῳ ἡ ἐπιβουλὴ αὐτῶν, *but their plot was known to Saul.* Perhaps the information was given by some of the Christian disciples, who would be well disposed to him from what they had heard from Ananias. These certainly manifested their zeal towards him in aiding him to make his escape from Damascus.

παρετηροῦντο δὲ καὶ τὰς πύλας, *and they watched the gates also.* The gates were the places to which one fleeing from death would naturally make his way. St Paul says (2 Cor. xi. 32), of the circumstances under which this plot was made against his life, that 'in Damascus the governor (ὁ ἐθνάρχης) of king Aretas kept the city of the Damascenes with a garrison, desirous to apprehend me.' Hence it appears that it was no mere attack made by the Jews resident in Damascus, but they had gained the support of the authorities for the time being. We do not know enough of the history of Syria and Arabia at this period to be able to explain with certainty how an ethnarch of Aretas, who was king of Arabia Petræa, came to be holding Damascus. But we do know (Joseph. *Ant.* XVIII. 3. 1—4) that Aretas had been at war with Herod Antipas, tetrarch of Galilee, who in consequence of his attachment to his brother Philip's wife, had forsaken his own wife, who was the daughter of Aretas. Herod had appealed to Rome, and had been promised the help of the Roman power, but the death of Tiberius (A.D. 37) checked the march of Vitellius, the Roman governor of Syria, into Arabia, and he thereupon returned to Antioch. It may have been that Aretas, encouraged by this withdrawal, had advanced, and in the general confusion had taken possession of Damascus. He had, in a former stage of the war, destroyed the army of Herod; and some of the Jews, who hated Herod, spake of this destruction of his troops as a divine judgment for his murder of John the Baptist. We can understand then that the Jews in Damascus might under such circumstances favour Aretas, and in return for their support be aided by his ethnarch in an attempt on the life of Saul.

Or the occupation of Damascus by Aretas may have been (as Dean Howson suggests) in consequence of the change of policy which took place so widely at the death of Tiberius; and Caligula, in contradiction of what his predecessor had been designing, to crush Aretas, may have put the Arabian king in command of the city of Damascus for a time.

25. λαβόντες δὲ οἱ μαθηταὶ αὐτοῦ κ.τ.λ., *but his disciples took him by night and*, &c. This well-supported reading favours the explanation of ἡμέραι ἱκαναί given in verse 23. On his second visit to Damascus, more than ever filled with the Spirit, he stayed long enough to gather about him a band of followers who accepted him as their leader in spiritual things.

διὰ τοῦ τείχους, *through the wall*, i.e. by some opening in the wall, on which probably stood, as is often the case in Eastern cities, some of the dwelling-houses. In 2 Cor. xi. 33 St Paul says, 'and through a window in a basket was I let down by the wall and escaped.' Such apertures can be found in the walls of houses in all defenced cities, and it was by such a way that Rahab let the spies escape from Jericho (Josh. ii. 15), and Michal aided David's escape (1 Sam. xix. 12). The basket here mentioned (σπυρίς) is of the same kind as that spoken of (Matth. xv. 37) at the feeding of the Four Thousand in the mountain district west of the Sea of Galilee. It appears to have been large and soft, fit for carrying a great quantity of miscellaneous articles from the plain into the hills, while the baskets (κόφινοι) spoken of at the feeding of the Five Thousand (Matth. xiv. 20) were such as the multitude, which in that case had followed Jesus on foot out of the cities, would be likely to carry in their hands. In a basket of the former kind Saul might easily be wrapped and then lowered over the city wall.

26—31. SAUL VISITS JERUSALEM. HE IS SENT AWAY TO TARSUS. THE CHURCHES HAVE REST.

26. παραγενόμενος δὲ εἰς Ἱερουσαλήμ, *and when he was come to Jerusalem.* Saul had never visited Jerusalem since the day when he set out on his inquisitorial journey to Damascus, and as he had been a long time in Arabia since then, his name may very well have fallen out of the memory of many in the Holy City, or knowing little of what had happened to him in the meantime they might esteem him still only as their determined enemy.

ἐπείραζεν κολλᾶσθαι τ. μ., *he assayed to join himself to the disciples.* If as a Jew he had gone to Alexandria or any other city where Jews were numerous, his first thought would have been to search out his co-religionists; so he acts now. He seeks to join the Christian community. But his own language (Gal. i. 16) shews us that he had made no attempt to spread the news of his changed feelings among the Christian congregations. 'I conferred not with flesh and blood,' he says, 'but I went into Arabia, and returned to Damascus.' An absence of three years, mainly in a region whence little news could come of his conversion and labours, and the memory of what evil he had done in days gone by, was enough to justify some hesitation about receiving him, on the part of the disciples.

καὶ πάντες ἐφοβοῦντο αὐτόν, *and they were all afraid of him.* The rendering of καὶ by *but* (A.V.) is unjustifiable. There is not any adversative sense. Saul tried to become a member of the Church, and they were not willing to receive him.

In Gal. i. 18 St Paul says his wish was to see Peter, and this we can very well understand, for though Saul had received his commission directly from Jesus, there were many things in the history of the life of Christ which could be best learned from the lips of him who had been with Jesus from the commencement of His ministry. But at first Saul came to the Christians at Jerusalem as an ordinary believer.

μὴ πιστεύοντες κ.τ.λ., *not believing that he was a disciple.* From this we can see how little was known in Jerusalem of the history of Saul since his conversion, and we can understand those words of his own (Gal. i. 22), 'I was unknown by face unto the churches of Judæa which were in Christ.' God had been training him for his work among the Gentiles, and although he was brought to Jerusalem that all might know that the Gospel was one, and that Saul was sent forth even as the Twelve, yet no attempt is made by St Luke at this point, where, according to some theories, it might have been most expected, to set forth the unanimity of Paul and Peter. It is left for St Paul himself to tell us of his desire to see Peter, and the historian only says they all were afraid of him.

27. Βαρνάβας δὲ κ.τ.λ., *but Barnabas took him and brought him to the Apostles,* i.e. to such of the Apostles as happened to be then in Jerusalem. During a short space of fifteen days it is easy to understand that all but Peter and James might be absent from Jerusalem. St Paul tells us he only saw these two during his visit (Gal. i. 19), and all that he says is perfectly consistent with St Luke's narrative. Barnabas, who introduced Saul to the Apostles, has already been mentioned as a Levite of Cyprus (iv. 36), and from the proximity of Cyprus to Cilicia, and the distinction of the schools of Tarsus, a conjecture has been hazarded that Barnabas may have been known to Saul before they came to Jerusalem. This would explain how it came to pass that while the other disciples were afraid of him, Barnabas listened to his statement and repeated it to the rest of the Church.

ἐπιλαβόμενος αὐτόν. This verb, which signifies to take hold of a person by the hand for the purpose of leading, is generally constructed with the genitive of the limb (as τῆς χειρός) or of the person (αὐτοῦ). When as here the accusative follows it, the construction appears due to the other verb (ἤγαγεν), so that the whole idea 'took and led' must be taken as requiring this case.

πῶς ἐν τῇ ὁδῷ κ.τ.λ., *how he had seen the Lord in the way.* It is worthy of notice in how many forms the statement of the appearance of Jesus to Saul is repeated. This was indeed the turning-point of the Apostle's life, Jesus of Nazareth seen as the glorified Son of God.

ἐπαρρησιάσατο, *he had spoken boldly* (as in verse 29). Whether the knowledge of Barnabas on this subject was derived from Saul himself or from other sources we are not told, but in the political turmoil of the times (see ver. 24, note) we may easily suppose that the teachings of a preacher who appeared for a brief space, and then retired from Damascus, and who had only lately reappeared, would not be widely known among the Church at Jerusalem.

28. καὶ ἦν μετ' αὐτῶν, *and he was with them*, i.e. for the fifteen days during which his visit lasted he was received into the fellowship of the Church.

On εἰσπορευόμενος καὶ ἐκπορευόμενος see note on i. 21.

29. Tischendorf marks the beginning of this verse at ἐλάλει, and not, as other editors, at παρρησιαζόμενος.

ἐλάλει τε καὶ συνεζήτει πρὸς τοὺς Ἑλληνιστάς, *and he spake and disputed against the Grecians*. These Ἑλληνισταί were the Greek Jews at whose instigation Stephen had been put to death. Now Saul, who had consented unto that martyrdom, is exposed to the like persecution. The very same word (συζητεῖν, to dispute) is here used which was employed to describe the controversies with the proto-martyr (vi. 9), and it is found nowhere else in this book. But it is worth notice that the attack is now reversed. The Grecians disputed with Stephen, now Saul disputes with them. Chrysostom comments thus on Saul's preaching to the Greeks: ἐκεῖνοι γὰρ οἱ ἄλλοι οὐδὲ ἰδεῖν αὐτὸν ἠθέλησαν οἱ βαθεῖς Ἑβραῖοι.

οἱ δὲ ἐπεχείρουν ἀνελεῖν αὐτόν, *but they sought to slay him*. The same expression is used above (verse 23) of the attempts of Saul's enemies in Damascus.

30. ἐπιγνόντες δὲ οἱ ἀδελφοί, *and when the brethren were aware of it*. The disciples in Jerusalem, just as those in Damascus, got information about the plot which was being laid against Saul.

κατήγαγον αὐτὸν εἰς Καισάρειαν, *they brought him down to Cæsarea*, i.e. to the seaport so called, not to Cæsarea Philippi, for the latter place was only touched by the road which led from Tyre to Damascus. The former was a place from which Tarsus could be reached either by sea or by the road which ran northward along the coast of Syria.

εἰς Ταρσόν, *to Tarsus*, where he was born, and which perhaps, next to Jerusalem, would appear to be the best centre from which his work could be carried on. For an account of Tarsus and its fame as a seat of heathen learning, see *Dict. of the Bible.*

31. ἡ μὲν οὖν ἐκκλησία...εἰρήνην, *so the Church throughout all Judæa and Galilee and Samaria had peace*. The sense is that the whole Christian body enjoyed a time of quiet, not as A.V. (with *Text. recept.*), the various congregations. The cause of this peace for the Christians was that the attention of their persecutors, the Jews, was turned from them to resist the attempt made by Caligula (Joseph. *Ant.* XVIII. 8. 2) to have his statue erected in the Temple at Jeru-salem. This profanation was averted partly by the determined opposi-tion of the Jews, and partly by the intercession of king Agrippa with the mad emperor.

κατά with the genitive of place, as here, implies the spreading of the act or condition spoken of *over* and *throughout* the place mentioned. Cf. Luke iv. 14 *φήμη ἐξῆλθεν καθ᾽ ὅλης τῆς περιχώρου*, 'the fame went forth over all the surrounding district.'

Examples of this sense are not very common, but it occurs in verse 42 below and in Acts x. 37.

32—35. PETER HEALS A PARALYTIC AT LYDDA.

32. διὰ πάντων, *through all quarters.* The history now turns from Saul to Peter, to shew us that when the former had been prepared for his special work, the latter was taught by revelation that the time had arrived for the next and complete extension of. the Church among all nations. Peter had been labouring, as no doubt all the rest of the Twelve also (for we have seen that only two were at Jerusalem when Saul came thither), in building up the Churches in Judæa and Samaria, and the narrative of two miracles which follow in the history makes intelligible to us the position of Peter when Cornelius is warned to send for him.

On the connexion of this portion of the history with the preceding Chrysostom says *μέλλει περὶ Πέτρου λέγειν, καὶ ὅτι πρὸς τοὺς ἁγίους κάτεισιν. ἵν᾽ οὖν μὴ φόβου τοῦτο νομίσῃ τις, πρότερον ὡς εἶχον αἱ ἐκκλησίαι διηγεῖται, δεικνὺς ὅτι διωγμὸς ὅτε ἦν, ἐν Ἱεροσολύμοις ἦν, ὅτε δὲ πανταχοῦ ἐν ἀσφαλείᾳ τὰ τῆς ἐκκλησίας, τότε λοιπὸν καὶ τὰ Ἱεροσόλυμα ἀφίησιν· οὕτως ἦν θερμὸς ὁμοῦ καὶ σφοδρός. οὐ γὰρ ἐπειδὴ εἰρήνη ἦν ἐνόμιζε μηδὲν δεῖσθαι τῆς αὑτοῦ παρουσίας.*

τοὺς ἁγίους. See note on verse 13.

Λύδδα, *Lydda.* The Hebrew *Lod,* 1 Chron. viii. 12. It was afterwards called *Diospolis.* It was near to Joppa, and a day's journey from Jerusalem. Josephus (*Ant.* xx. 6. 2) calls it 'a village not less than a city in largeness.'

33. ἐξ ἐτῶν ὀκτὼ κατακείμενον κ.τ.λ., *which had kept his bed eight years.* There could therefore be no doubt cast upon the miraculous nature of his cure.

34. ἰᾶταί σε Ἰησοῦς Χριστός, *Jesus Christ maketh thee whole.* As in the cure of the cripple at the Temple gate (iii. 6), the Apostle makes known that he is but the messenger, and that the healer is Christ. We are not told that Æneas was a disciple, but it may be inferred that he was among 'the saints,' and that thus Peter was brought unto him.

καὶ στρῶσον. The noun *τὴν κλίνην,* or some equivalent, must be understood after this verb.

35. καὶ εἶδαν αὐτὸν πάντες, *and they all saw him.* No doubt his case of eight-years-long paralysis was well known to the dwellers in the village and neighbourhood, and to see such a one about in their midst again would be a cause for general remark and enquiry into the manner of his restoration. 'When the Scripture saith *all* it doth not comprehend every one, how many soever it noteth, but it putteth

all for the more part, or for many, or for the common sort of men'
(Calvin on this verse).

τὸν Σάρωνα, *Saron.* The O.T. *Sharon.* It is doubtful whether
by this name is intended some village in the neighbourhood of Lydda
or the whole district known as the 'plain of Sharon,' and extending
along the coast from Joppa to Cæsarea. No place of this name has
been noticed in the neighbourhood, and as in the original the word
has the article, 'the Sharon,' it is better to refer it to the district.

οἵτινες ἐπέστρεψαν ἐπὶ τὸν κύριον, *and they turned unto the Lord.*
ὅστις in this and similar sentences is almost like the Latin *quippe qui*,
when it can be rendered 'and in fact.' So here the force of this
strengthened relative is somewhat of this kind, 'they saw him, and as
a fact in consequence of their seeing, they turned.'

36—43. DORCAS RAISED TO LIFE. PETER'S STAY AT JOPPA.

36. ἐν Ἰόππῃ, *in Joppa.* The seaport town on the coast of
Palestine almost directly west from Jerusalem. For its history, see
Dict. of the Bible.

μαθήτρια, *a* (female) *disciple.* The word is only found here in N.T.
and is rare in other Greek authors. It is probably used to shew that
under the Gospel there is no distinction between male and female
(Gal. iii. 28), all alike are disciples.

Ταβιθά, *Tabitha.* This is the Aramaic form of a Hebrew word
(found 2 Sam. i. 19) which signifies a *gazelle*, which is also the meaning of the Greek Δορκάς.

πλήρης ἀγαθῶν ἔργων, *full of good works.* A favourite form of
expression with St Luke. Cp. 'Stephen full of faith and power'
(vi. 8); Elymas, 'full of all subtilty' (xiii. 10); and the Ephesians
'full of wrath' (xix. 28). The sense is 'given up to' or 'devoted to.'

37. ἀσθενήσασαν αὐτὴν ἀποθανεῖν, *that she fell sick and died.*
The proceedings which followed on her death are evidence of its
reality. The probable reason for deferring the burial was the knowledge that Peter was close at hand, and the hope of the disciples that
the power of Jesus might be exercised through him for the restoration
to life of so eminent a disciple as Dorcas.

λούσαντες δέ, *and when they had washed her.* No doubt it was the
women who prepared the body for burial, but the historian, speaking
generally, writes not λούσασαι but the masculine.

38. παρακαλοῦντες, Μὴ ὀκνήσῃς διελθεῖν ἕως ἡμῶν, *entreating him,
Delay not to come on to us.* Thus διελθεῖν has its full force, which is
lost in A.V. It is as though their supplication were, 'We have heard
of the mighty works which Jesus has wrought by thy hands; extend
thy journey to us, for we are in great need.'

39. ἀναστὰς δὲ Πέτρος, *and Peter arose.* We may be sure that
the Apostle knew, by the Spirit, that it would please God to do something for the help of the distress at Joppa when he set out with the
messengers.

καὶ παρέστησαν αὐτῷ πᾶσαι αἱ χῆραι κλαίουσαι, *and all the widows stood by him weeping.* These were the women who, with the dead Dorcas, had been busy in the good works to which they were all devoted. The petition of such a company was sure to have power with the Apostle, and their action shews how they place the good deeds of her whom they had lost far above their own. The χῆραι became a recognized class of women earnest in good works and separate from the world. See the directions concerning them which St Paul gives to Timothy, 1 Tim. v. 3—5, 9, 11, 16.

40. ἐκβαλὼν δὲ...ὁ Πέτρος, *but Peter put them all forth.* Cf. Christ's action (Matth. ix. 25) at the raising of Jaïrus' daughter, on which occasion Peter had been present.

καὶ θεὶς τὰ γόνατα προσηύξατο, *and kneeled down and prayed.* For the first part of the phrase, cf. vii. 60. St Peter's request no doubt here was that the consolation to be given to these mourners might be the restoration of the dead woman to life.

καὶ ἐπιστρέψας πρὸς τὸ σῶμα, *and turning him to the body.* When he felt within him that his prayer would be answered.

Ταβιθὰ ἀνάστηθι, *Tabitha, arise.* If St Peter spake in the Aramaic dialect, as is most probable, his utterance *Tabitha cumi* must have been nearly the same as that of our Lord (Mark v. 41), *Talitha cumi,* at the raising of the daughter of Jaïrus. But when we find both these utterances interpreted in the places where they occur, it is astonishing that some should suggest that the *Tabitha* of this verse is an adaptation of the *Talitha* of the Gospel.

41. φωνήσας δὲ τοὺς ἁγίους καὶ τὰς χήρας, *and when he had called the saints and widows.* These words make it evident that the petition sent to Peter had been the supplication of the whole Christian Church of Joppa, 'Come on unto us and help us.'

42. καθ᾽ ὅλης τῆς Ἰόππης. See above, verse 31, note.

καὶ ἐπίστευσαν πολλοὶ ἐπὶ τὸν κύριον, *and many believed on the Lord.* There seems to be intended by these words a fuller acceptance of the faith of Jesus than when it is said 'they turned to the Lord' (see above, ver. 35). The belief here wrought by the resurrection of Dorcas is like that mentioned (John xi. 45) of those who were won to the faith by the raising of Lazarus.

43. ἡμέρας ἱκανάς. On the indefinite nature of the length of time indicated here, see verse 23, note.

παρά τινι Σίμωνι βυρσεῖ, *with one Simon a tanner.* The trade of a tanner was held as abominable by the Jews. A wife, it is said, could claim a divorce from a husband who became a tanner. See Mishna *Khethuboth* VII. 10 where is recorded the following story: 'It happened at Sidon that a tanner died, and left a brother who was also a tanner. The sages held that his (childless) widow had a right to plead, Thy brother I could bear but I cannot bear thee, and so in this case the woman might refuse to marry her husband's brother.'

It is a sign that in the mind of St Peter some usages and prejudices of the Jews were already becoming of small account, when he makes his abode at the house of Simon a tanner. Such a step prepares us for the history of the next chapter, where he is instructed to go and preach to and baptize the Gentile Cornelius.

CHAPTER X.

Readings varying from the *Text. recept.*

1. ἦν omitted with אABCEL. *Vulg.* has 'erat.'

5. Σίμωνά τινα with ABC. *Vulg.* 'Simonem quemdam.'

6. οὗτος λαλήσει σοι τί σε δεῖ ποιεῖν omitted with אABCELP. The *Vulg.* represents these words.

7. For τῷ Κορνηλίῳ read αὐτῷ with אABCE. *Vulg.* 'qui loque-batur illi.'

Omit αὐτοῦ after οἰκετῶν, with אABCE.

10. ἐγένετο for ἐπέπεσεν with אABC. *Vulg.* 'cecidit.'

11. Omit ἐπ' αὐτὸν after καταβαῖνον with אABCE. The words are not represented in the *Vulg.*

δεδεμένον καὶ omitted with אABCE. They are not represented in the *Vulg.*

12. καὶ τὰ θηρία omitted with אABC. Unrepresented in *Vulg.*

16. εὐθὺς for πάλιν with אABCE. *Vulg.* 'statim.'

17. καὶ before ἰδοὺ omitted with אAB. Unrepresented in *Vulg.*

21. τοὺς ἀπεσταλμένους ἀπὸ τοῦ Κορνηλίου πρὸς αὐτόν omitted with אABDELP, and unrepresented in *Vulg.*

23. ἀναστὰς for ὁ Πέτρος with אABD. *Vulg.* 'surgens.'

30. νηστεύων καὶ omitted with אABC. Unrepresented in *Vulg.*

ὥραν omitted with אABCD.

32. ὃς παραγενόμενος λαλήσει σοι omitted with אAB. Not represented in *Vulg.*

33. τοῦ κυρίου for τοῦ θεοῦ with אABCE. *Vulg.* 'Domino.'

39. ἐσμεν omitted with אABCDE.

48. Ἰησοῦ Χριστοῦ for τοῦ κυρίου with אABE. *Vulg.* has 'Domini Jesu Christi.'

———•———

CH. X. 1—8. CORNELIUS IS DIVINELY WARNED TO SEND FOR PETER.

1. St Luke now brings to our notice the circumstances which attended the first preaching of the Gospel to the Gentiles. The Apostles, though informed by Christ's commission that they were to 'teach all nations,' yet tarried the Lord's leisure, and waited till the Spirit, who

was their constant guide, shewed them a door opened for such extension of their labours. The first Gentile converts seem to have been
living in some sort of communion with the Jews of Cæsarea, for Cornelius, the representative figure among them, was 'of good report
among all that nation,' but yet from the complaints of the brethren
at Jerusalem, when they heard what Peter had done, we can see that
Cornelius was one of the 'sinners of the Gentiles.' 'Thou wentest in
to men uncircumcised and didst eat with them' expresses the shock
which the strict observers of the Law experienced in this new development of the Church; and even Peter himself, though chosen to inau-
gurate the preaching to the Gentiles, was not always proof against the
scruples and remonstrances of his brethren of the Circumcision (Gal.
ii. 12).

ἀνὴρ δέ τις. The substantive verb is omitted by the best authorities. The rendering would therefore be, *Now a certain man...which
gave much alms...saw in a vision.*

Cæsarea is the same place which is mentioned viii. 40, and was
usually the residence of the Roman Procurator (see xxiii. 23—26, xxv.
1—4). The soldiers over whom Cornelius was centurion were the
necessary troops to support the state and authority of the Roman
representative, who at this time was Herod Agrippa, whom Claudius
had made king over Judæa and Samaria.

ὀνόματι Κορνήλιος, *by name Cornelius.* The name shews he was a
Roman, and perhaps he may have been of the famous Cornelian Gens.
But there were also many plebeians of this name, for Sulla (Appian
B. C. I. 100) bestowed the Roman franchise on 10,000 slaves and called
them after his own name, 'Cornelii.'

ἑκατοντάρχης, *a centurion.* We find also the Latin word κεντυρίων in
N.T. (Mark xv. 39, 44, 45). The centurion's was not a distinguished
office. He was commander of the sixth part of a cohort, i.e. of half a
maniple. The name must have been given to such officer when his
command was over a *hundred* men. The Roman legion in these times
was divided into ten cohorts, and each cohort into three maniples, so
that the nominal strength of the legion would be 6000 men.

ἐκ σπείρης, *of the band,* i.e. the cohort. See Polyb. XI. 23. 1 τοῦτο
δὲ καλεῖται σύνταγμα τῶν πεζῶν παρὰ Ῥωμαίοις κοόρτις. Such a troop
was stationed in Jerusalem at the time of the Crucifixion (Matth.
xxvii. 27). σπεῖρα is found in the LXX. used of Jewish troops (Judith
xiv. 11; 2 Macc. viii. 23, xii. 20, 22).

τῆς καλουμένης Ἰταλικῆς, *called the Italian band.* The name at
first would be given to it from the country in which it was raised, but
no doubt it would afterwards be recruited from other parts, and yet
still retain its original title. Tacitus (*Hist.* I. 59 &c.) mentions an
Italian legion. A centurion of a similar band, which was styled
'Augustan,' is mentioned (xxvii. 1) below.

2. εὐσεβής, *a devout man,* i.e. he was a worshipper of the true
God, but had not joined himself to the Jews in the observance of the
Law. The language of St Peter in verse 28 shews us that he was not

a proselyte. It is noteworthy that wherever in the N.T. we find mention made of Roman centurions they appear to have been good men, Matth. viii. 5; Luke vii. 2, xxiii. 47.

σὺν παντὶ τῷ οἴκῳ αὐτοῦ, *with all his house.* The earnestness of his devotion to God is evidenced by the character of his household. (Cf. Abraham's character, Gen. xviii. 19.) If his family be here meant, he had instructed them in the worship of God, and had provided that those who attended on him should also be of the same character. The soldier, whom he sends to Peter, is called εὐσεβής likewise. Chrysostom says here ἀκούσωμεν ὅσοι τῶν οἰκείων ἀμελοῦμεν.

τῷ λαῷ, *to the people.* This must mean the Jewish people among whom he was stationed. So of the centurion mentioned Luke vii. 5 it is said by the Jews 'He loveth our nation and hath built us a synagogue.'

δεόμενος τοῦ θεοῦ διαπαντός, *praying to God always.* This devotional habit of the centurion is manifested through the whole narrative. See especially verse 30.

3. εἶδεν ἐν ὁράματι φανερῶς, *he saw in a vision openly,* i.e. he was not in a trance, as we read afterwards concerning Peter, but was employed in prayer when the angel appeared. See below ver. 30.

ὡσεὶ περὶ ὥραν ἐνάτην, *about the ninth hour.* The ὡσεὶ makes the point of time less definite. Cornelius was observing the Jewish hour of prayer, and at some time during his devotions the vision was seen by him.

ἄγγελον τοῦ θεοῦ, *an angel of God,* called in verse 30 ἀνὴρ ἐν ἐσθῆτι λαμπρᾷ.

4. ὁ δὲ ἀτενίσας, *and when he had fastened his eyes on him.* The dazzling brightness of the vision would first rivet the centurion's gaze, and the terror would come afterwards when he realized that he was in the presence of an angel. Cf. Manoah's alarm from a similar cause. Judges xiii. 21, 22.

ἔμφοβος. When found in classical Greek, which is rare, this word has the sense of 'terrible.' It occurs twice in the LXX. with the meaning 'afraid' as here. Cf. Ecclus. xix. 24 and 1 Macc. xiii. 2, εἶδεν τὸν λαὸν ὅτι ἐστὶν ἔντρομος καὶ ἔμφοβος.

τί ἐστιν, κύριε; *what is it, Lord?* His words express his readiness to do whatever he may be bidden.

αἱ προσευχαί σου καὶ αἱ ἐλεημοσύναι σου ἀνέβησαν, *thy prayers and thine alms have gone up.* ἀναβαίνω is used Ezek. viii. 11 of the rising up of the cloud of incense, and this is the figure here. Cf. Rev. viii. 3, 4, also Rev. v. 8, 'vials full of odours which are the prayers of saints.' See too Ps. cxli. 2.

εἰς μνημόσυνον ἔμπροσθεν τοῦ θεοῦ, *for a memorial before God.* They have been such that God remembers them and is now about to answer them. The portion of the meal-offering which the priest was commanded to burn upon the altar to be an offering of a sweet savour unto the Lord (Lev. ii. 2) was called a *μνημόσυνον*, and the allusion is to offerings of this kind. Cf. the words of the angel (Tobit xii. 12), 'I did bring the *remembrance* (*μνημόσυνον*) of your prayers before the Holy One.'

6. The words omitted from the text in this verse (see notes on readings) are an adaptation of xi. 14, where St Peter is giving an account of his visit to Cornelius, and are another example of the desire naturally prevalent to make the narrative complete in the early chapters by adding on the margin any particulars which can be gathered from the subsequent narrative. Put at first as marginal illustrations and expansions, they found in early times their way into the text through the agency of copyists.

7. ὡς δὲ ἀπῆλθεν κ.τ.λ., *and when he was departed.* The reality (see *φανερῶς* in verse 3) of the angelic presence is strongly marked by this language, which speaks of his going away just as if he had been any human visitor.

τῶν προσκαρτερούντων αὐτῷ, *of those that attended on him.* So of the judges in the History of Susanna (verse 7), οὗτοι προσεκαρτέρουν ἐν τῇ οἰκίᾳ Ἰωακείμ, 'These kept much at Joachim's house,' where '*keep*' is in the sense still common in the Universities and elsewhere, of '*live*,' '*abide*,' '*dwell*.' So here the soldier was attached to the personal service of Cornelius. Compare that other centurion's retinue (Luke vii. 8) where the master says to one 'Go,' and his order is at once obeyed.

8. ἐξηγησάμενος ἅπαντα αὐτοῖς, *when he had declared all things unto them.* The confidence which Cornelius placed in those who attended on him is shewn by this open communication with them at once on the subject of his vision. They had known all his former hopes and prayers, and so were fit persons to be made sharers in what seemed to be the answer.

9—16. PETER IS PREPARED BY A VISION FOR THE COMING OF CORNELIUS' MESSENGERS.

9. ἀνέβη Πέτρος ἐπὶ τὸ δῶμα, *went up upon the housetop.* With the flat roofs of houses, to which access could be obtained from outside without passing through the rooms of the building, the housetop formed a convenient place for retirement. It was the place chosen by Samuel (1 Sam. ix. 25, 26) for his conference with Saul before he anointed him king. Cp. also 2 Sam. xi. 2.

προσεύξασθαι, *to pray.* We find that the housetop was used as a place for religious observances (Jer. xix. 13, xxxii. 29; Zeph. i. 5). These are instances of worship paid to false gods; and we find a similar example of altars on the top of the roofs of a part of the Jewish temple (2 Kings xxiii. 12) LXX., τὰ θυσιαστήρια τὰ ἐπὶ τοῦ δώματος τοῦ ὑπερῴου Ἄχαζ, but in Nehemiah (viii. 16) at the celebration of the Feast of Tabernacles we read καὶ ἐποίησαν ἑαυτοῖς σκηνὰς ἀνὴρ ἐπὶ τοῦ δώματος αὐτοῦ. So that these places were not used only for purposes of idolatrous worship, though in the O.T. they are noticed most frequently in that connexion.

περὶ ὥραν ἕκτην, *about the sixth hour*, i.e. midday, and the second of the Jewish stated hours of prayer. We see from verses 23 and 24 that the journey from Joppa to Caesarea occupied more than one day, so that the vision of Cornelius took place on the day before the trance of St Peter, and the messengers had time almost to accomplish their journey before the Apostle, by his vision, was prepared to receive them. The distance between the two places was 30 Roman miles.

10. πρόσπεινος, *very hungry*. The word is found nowhere else.

ἤθελεν γεύσασθαι, *he would have eaten*. γεύομαι is not commonly used for taking a meal, but (LXX. Gen. xxv. 30) the hungry Esau says γεῦσόν με ἀπὸ τοῦ ἑψήματος τοῦ πυροῦ.

παρασκευαζόντων δὲ αὐτῶν, *but while they made ready*. The persons to whom reference is made in αὐτῶν have been in no way indicated, but the mind readily supplies the οἰκέται to whom the wish for food would be communicated.

ἐγένετο ἐπ᾽ αὐτὸν ἔκστασις, *he fell into a trance*. The word ἔκστασις is used by the LXX. (Gen. ii. 21) of the deep sleep sent upon Adam, and also (Gen. xv. 12) of that which came upon Abraham, when it was revealed unto him that his seed should be captives in a strange land, before they entered on the possession of Canaan. In like manner here, the vision was disclosed mentally to St Peter, all things being presented to him as in a dream.

Chrysostom says, τί ἐστιν ἔκστασις; πνευματική, φησί, θεωρία γέγονεν αὐτῷ. τοῦ σώματος, ὡς ἂν εἴπῃ τις, ἐξέστη ἡ ψυχή.

11. καὶ θεωρεῖ τὸν οὐρανὸν ἀνεῳγμένον, *and he beholdeth heaven opened*. For θεωρέω of the vision of things heavenly, cf. vii. 56, ix. 7. The opened heaven made it clear to Peter that the teaching of the vision was sent from God.

σκεῦός τι ὡς ὀθόνην μεγάλην, τέσσαρσιν ἀρχαῖς καθιέμενον ἐπὶ τῆς γῆς, *a certain vessel as it had been a great sheet let down by four corners upon the earth*. The word ἀρχαί is used (LXX. Exod. xxviii. 23, xxxix. 15) of the extremities of the high-priest's breastplate to which rings were to be attached for fastening it upon the ephod. What St Peter saw was an extended sheet, the four corners of which were held up as it were by cords let down from the four extremities of the opened sky. The significance of the outstretched sheet, as a figure of the wide world, and the four corners as the directions into which the Gospel was now to be borne forth into all the world has often been dwelt upon.

12. ἐν ᾧ ὑπῆρχεν, *in which were*, i.e. as it seemed in the vision.

πάντα τὰ τετράποδα κ.τ.λ., *all manner of fourfooted beasts and creeping things of the earth and fowls of the air*. The vision represented the entire animal creation. There were present living creatures typical of each kind, not a multitude of the same sort of birds and beasts.

13. ἀναστὰς Πέτρε θῦσον καὶ φάγε, *rise, Peter, kill and eat.* He was hungry before he fell into the trance. In the vision there is presented the means of satisfying his hunger. But with this there comes an instruction to disregard the Mosaic distinction about clean and unclean meats. His waking mind is able to interpret this, and he sees that now all nations alike are to be included among God's people.

On ἀναστάς Chrysostom remarks ἴσως ἐπὶ γόνατα κείμενος εἶδε τὴν ὀπτασίαν. And then he continues ὅτι δὲ καὶ θεῖον ἦν τὸ γινόμενον δῆλον ἔκ τε τοῦ ἄνωθεν ἰδεῖν καταβαῖνον, ἔκ τε τοῦ ἐν ἐκστάσει γενέσθαι. τὸ δὲ καὶ φωνὴν ἐκεῖθεν ἐνεχθῆναι, καὶ τὸ τρὶς τοῦτο γενέσθαι, καὶ τὸν οὐρανὸν ἀνεῳχθῆναι, καὶ τὸ ἐκεῖθεν ἥκειν, καὶ τὸ ἐκεῖ ἀναρπασθῆναι πάλιν μέγα δεῖγμα τοῦ θεῖον εἶναι τὸ πρᾶγμα.

14. μηδαμῶς, κύριε, *not so* (by no means), *Lord.* Cf. Ezek. iv. 14, where the prophet being shewn that the children of Israel shall eat defiled bread among the Gentiles, exclaims in words very like St Peter's, 'There never came abominable flesh into my mouth.' For the care with which the devout Jew observed the ceremonial distinction between clean and unclean, see Dan. i. 8—12; 2 Macc. vi. 18.

οὐδέποτε...πᾶν. From the usage of the Hebrew, the N.T. writers frequently use οὐ (μή)...πᾶς where the classical authors would use οὐδείς and μηδείς. Cf. Matth. xxiv. 22, οὐκ ἂν ἐσώθη πᾶσα σάρξ. So Rom. iii. 20; Ephes. iv. 29, &c. In the LXX. cf. Exod. xx. 10 (of the Sabbath-day), οὐ ποιήσεις ἐν αὐτῇ πᾶν ἔργον. Also, with another case than the nominative or accusative, 2 Chron. xxxii. 15, οὐ μὴ δύνηται ὁ θεὸς παντὸς ἔθνους καὶ βασιλείας τοῦ σῶσαι τὸν λαὸν αὐτοῦ.

κοινὸν καὶ ἀκάθαρτον, *common and unclean.* The use of κοινός in the sense of 'impure' according to the Mosaic code is, as were all the ordinances about which this language was employed, peculiar to the Jews. But it is easy to trace the steps by which the word came to be used thus. All persons who were not Jews were viewed as the 'common' rabble, shut out from God's covenant (cf. κοινοὶ ἄνθρωποι, Joseph. *Ant. J.* xII. 2, 14), then whatever practices of these outcasts differed from those of the chosen people were called 'common' things, and as these 'common' things were those forbidden by the Law, all such prohibited things or actions became known as 'common.' Cf. Mark vii. 2, where '*defiled* hands' is the rendering of χεῖρες ἄνιπτοι. κοινός is not used by the LXX. as the rendering of any passage where unclean beasts are spoken of, but appears first in this sense in that version, 1 Macc. i. 50, 65 τοῦ μὴ φαγεῖν κοινά.

15. καὶ φωνὴ πάλιν κ.τ.λ., *and a voice came again the second time.* As there is no verb in the sentence, ἐγένετο, as in 13, must be supplied. ἐκ δευτέρου defines precisely what was not definite with πάλιν only.

ἃ ὁ θεὸς ἐκαθάρισεν σὺ μὴ κοίνου, *what God hath cleansed that make not thou common.* The heaven-sent voice revokes what had been enjoined from heaven at the giving of the Law. The power which made the restriction can remove it. That it would be removed

Christ had intimated (Matth. xv. 11), 'Not that which goeth into the mouth defileth a man.' The old dispensation is now to give place to the new, and Peter is taught by the vision that men are not to make such distinctions and separations for themselves. 'For meat destroy not the work of God' (Rom. xiv. 20). That the Christian religion was meant to abrogate these ceremonial regulations may be gathered also from Christ's language (Mark vii. 18, 19) about that which goeth into a man not defiling him, which He is expressly stated to have spoken, καθαρίζων πάντα τὰ βρώματα, 'making (or declaring) all meats pure.'

16. τοῦτο δὲ ἐγένετο ἐπὶ τρίς, *and this was done three times.* The threefold repetition of the vision was meant to leave no doubt in the Apostle's mind about its nature, and the reception of the whole into heaven again was designed to point out that it was a lesson which God had as directly sent as of old He sent the Law on Sinai. Cf. the repetition of Pharaoh's dream (Gen. xli. 32) and Joseph's explanation thereof. Peter would also remember when he came out of his trance the thrice-repeated charge given to him by Jesus (John xxi. 15—17), 'Feed My sheep.'

ἐπὶ τρίς is not classical and is seldom found. It occurs in xi. 10 in the repetition of this history.

17—24. ARRIVAL OF THE MESSENGERS FROM CORNELIUS. PETER GOES WITH THEM TO CÆSAREA.

17. ὡς δὲ ἐν ἑαυτῷ διηπόρει, *now while he was much perplexed in himself.* διαπορέω implies ' to be thoroughly at a loss, and not to know which way to turn.' It is used (Luke ix. 7) of Herod's perplexity about Christ, when men said that John the Baptist was risen from the dead. Peter, aroused from his trance, was to apply what he had seen and heard, but he knew not how to begin the work.

ἀπὸ τοῦ Κορνηλίου, *from Cornelius.* There is no great certainty in this verse whether the preposition is ἀπό or ὑπό. It could not in this case make much difference to the sense, but with passive verbs the more common preposition is ὑπό when the action done is with the knowledge of the agent. ἀπό might in some cases (though not here) mean coming *from* without the direct consciousness of him from whom the persons came.

ἐπέστησαν ἐπὶ τὸν πυλῶνα, *stood at the porch.* The position of the house had been described to Cornelius (ver. 6), and when his messengers found the details true, it must have given them confidence that their errand was to be a successful one.

18. καὶ φωνήσαντες κ.τ.λ., *and called, &c.,* i.e. they attracted by a call the attention of the persons in the house, and brought some one out. These messengers, like Cornelius himself, were most probably Gentiles, but Gentiles of such a sort as to respect Jewish scruples, and so might not feel justified in entering a Jewish house without giving notice of their presence.

19. τοῦ δὲ Πέτρου διενθυμουμένου περὶ τοῦ ὁράματος, *now while Peter pondered over the vision.* He was turning over his difficulty in his mind, and asking what God would have him learn by this lesson about the abolition of differences in meats. And while he was thus pondering the explanation came.

εἶπεν τὸ πνεῦμα αὐτῷ, *the Spirit said to him.* Thus the arrival of the messengers was, by an inward admonition of the Spirit, connected with the vision which he had just seen.

τρεῖς, i.e. the two servants and the soldier whom Cornelius had sent (see verse 7).

20. κατάβηθι, *get thee down.* Peter was still on the housetop.

μηδὲν διακρινόμενος, *doubting nothing.* The same words are rendered Jas. i. 6 'nothing wavering' (A.V.). There is a difference in the best MSS. between the reading here and in xi. 12, where instead of the middle voice we have the active, μηδὲν διακρίναντα. This latter signifies 'making no distinction,' i.e. between Jew and Gentile. We must bear in mind that this phrase was used by the Apostle when events had taught him precisely what the vision and the spiritual exhortation meant. The Spirit's teaching is given little by little as Christ had told His disciples that it should be, 'He shall *guide* you (lit., lead you on the way) unto all truth' (John xvi. 13). The vision had given no hint of a journey to be taken; now Peter is informed of it, and so too when the end of the journey is reached the 'nothing wavering' is shewn to mean 'putting no distinction between Jews and other men,' and thus the vision was made intelligible little by little and the perplexity removed.

22. μαρτυρούμενός τε ὑπὸ ὅλου τοῦ ἔθνους, *of good report among all the nation,* i.e. for the alms-deeds which he did, and on account of his reverence for the true God. They say not only among the people of Cæsarea was the piety of Cornelius known, but among all the Jews.

ἐχρηματίσθη, *was divinely warned.* This word and the noun derived from it are constantly used of messages from above. Thus we find the verb where we are told of Joseph's warnings (Matth. ii. 12, 22), of Simeon's divine revelation (Luke ii. 26), and of the admonitions sent to Moses (Heb. viii. 5), and to Noah (Heb. xi. 7). For the noun, see 2 Macc. ii. 4, χρηματισμοῦ γενηθέντος αὐτῷ, 'being warned of God,' (A.V.).

ἀκοῦσαι ῥήματα παρὰ σοῦ, *to hear words of thee,* i.e. to receive commandments from thee and learn what God would have him to do (cp. xi. 14). By the Jews the Ten Commandments are constantly called "the ten *words*," and Moses in recapitulating them (Deut. v. 5) speaks of them as τὰ ῥήματα κυρίου.

23. εἰσκαλεσάμενος οὖν αὐτοὺς ἐξένισεν, *then he called them in and lodged them.* This was the first step towards laying aside the scruples to which the Jews were so much attached.

τῇ δὲ ἐπαύριον ἀναστὰς ἐξῆλθεν σὺν αὐτοῖς, *and on the morrow he arose and went forth with them.* They would start in the early part of the day to get through as much of their way as they could on the first day.

καί τινες τῶν ἀδελφῶν κ.τ.λ., *and certain of the brethren from Joppa accompanied him.* In xi. 12 we are told that there were *six* of them, and in verse 45 of this chapter they are called οἱ ἐκ περιτομῆς πιστοί. So these men were Jewish Christians, and Peter took them for his companions that he might, if need were, afterwards appeal to them for testimony of what had been done, and to explain why he had acted as he did. No doubt they were informed by him of the message which the servants of Cornelius had brought, and the good repute of this devout man would weigh with them and make them ready to go.

24. τῇ δὲ ἐπαύριον κ.τ.λ., *and the morrow after they entered into Cæsarea.* Their road lay the way along the coast, and as Apollonia was situate about halfway between Joppa and Cæsarea, it is most likely that they passed the night there.

ὁ δὲ Κορνήλιος ἦν προσδοκῶν αὐτούς, *and Cornelius was waiting for them.* His attitude of preparation shews how convinced the man was of the reality of his vision, and that God was about to give him an answer to his prayers.

τοὺς συγγενεῖς αὐτοῦ καὶ τοὺς ἀναγκαίους φίλους, *his kinsmen and near friends.* The whole narrative shews that Cornelius must have been a long while stationed at Cæsarea, for his good deeds to have become known to the whole nation. An officer in such a permanent post would be very likely to have his kindred round about him. We can hardly doubt also that they were people of like mind with Cornelius in their faith and worship, and so had naturally been told of the answer which he was expecting, and invited to be present when Peter arrived.

25—33. ARRIVAL OF PETER. CORNELIUS EXPLAINS WHY HE HAS SENT FOR HIM.

25. ὡς δὲ ἐγένετο τοῦ εἰσελθεῖν τὸν Πέτρον, *and as Peter was come in.* This is a solitary case in the N.T. of the substantival infinitive in such a construction, and it is very difficult to see an explanation of it. That it could so stand is clear from a parallel sentence in *Acta Barnab. Apocryp.* 7 ὡς δὲ ἐγένετο τοῦ τελέσαι αὐτοὺς διδάσκοντας. It seems as if the genitive of the infinitive in both these instances were regarded as a genitive absolute would be. So that the sense = 'when Peter went in' 'when they had finished teaching.' What occurred in Cæsarea was prior to St Peter's entry into the house. We read of that in verse 27.

προσεκύνησεν, *worshipped,* i.e. paid him the religious reverence which the supernatural direction of the angel concerning Peter would be likely to prompt. This act of obeisance in the Roman officer marks most strongly his sense that Peter was God's messenger. Such acts were not usual among Roman soldiers.

26. ὁ δὲ Πέτρος ἤγειρεν αὐτόν, *but Peter raised him up.* Cf. with the way in which Peter declines such reverence the language of the angel to St John (Rev. xix. 10) refusing similar worship. 'See thou do it not. I am thy fellow-servant.'

27. καὶ συνομιλῶν αὐτῷ εἰσῆλθεν, *and as he talked with him he went in.* So the previous part of the interview had been without. The action of Cornelius in thus coming forth to meet Peter is in the spirit of that other centurion in the Gospel, who said (Luke vii. 6) 'I am not worthy that thou shouldest enter under my roof.' συνομιλέω (which is a very rare word) indicates the communication made during an interview of some length. The subsequent remarks of St Peter shew us that he had been told many things by Cornelius, which are not specially mentioned, but comprehended under this word 'talked.'

καὶ εὑρίσκει συνεληλυθότας πολλούς, *and finds many that were come together.* Cornelius had won many attached friends by his high character, and now of all that God shall communicate to him he wishes them to be sharers with himself.

28. ὑμεῖς ἐπίστασθε, *ye know.* The pronoun is perhaps meant to be emphatic. Ye, who, though ye be not Jews, have lived in friendship with Jewish people and so know their customs.

ὡς ἀθέμιτόν ἐστιν κ.τ.λ., *how that it is an unlawful thing*, &c. It is said expressly by Maimonides, *Hilechoth Rozeah, &c.* XII. 7 'It is forbidden to a Jew to be alone with heathens, because they are suspected of (lightly) shedding blood, nor must he associate with them on the road.' And in the *Midrash Rabbah* on Leviticus, cap. 20 (*ad fin.*), there is an interesting example of the sort of ceremonial defilement which association with the heathen might bring about, 'It happened that Shimeon the son of Kimkhith (who was high-priest) went out to speak with the king of the Arabians, and there came a fleck of spittle from the king's mouth upon the priest's garment and so he was unclean; and his brother Judah went in and served instead of him in the high-priest's office. That day their mother saw two of her sons high-priests.' The Apostle speaks of the prohibition as a thing well known to those who heard him, and the action of the messengers of Cornelius in standing outside the house of Simon and calling out some one to question in the open air shews that they were aware of the dislike of the Jews to associate with Gentiles. We have evidence that this dislike was well known wherever the Jews resided from the words of Juvenal (XIV. 103), 'Non monstrare vias eadem nisi sacra colenti.' So Tacitus (*Hist.* v. 5) 'separati epulis, discreti cubilibus.'

κολλᾶσθαι, *to keep company.* Literally 'to join himself.' The word is used in the command to Philip (viii. 29) 'Go near and *join thyself* to this chariot;' and signifies intimate intercourse. The ordinary dealings of life must constantly have forced Jews to be in the company of Gentiles, but it was to be avoided if possible.

ἀλλοφύλῳ, *to one of another nation.* In the historical books of the Old Test. (Samuel, Kings, &c.), ἀλλόφυλοι is the constant rendering of the name of the Philistines. This helps us to see what the force of the word would be in a Jew's mouth when speaking to one of the uncircumcised.

κἀμοὶ ἔδειξεν ὁ θεὸς κ.τ.λ., *but God hath shewed me that I should not call any man common or unclean.* The Spirit's command, 'Go with them doubting nothing, for I have sent them,' has taught Peter how he is to interpret the figure shewn to him in his vision.

29. ἀναντιρρήτως, *without gainsaying,* i.e. I have followed the guidance of the Spirit, though I did not see fully what God would have me do.

30. ἀπὸ τετάρτης ἡμέρας, *four days ago.* The notion of the phrase is 'from the fourth day,' i.e. which will be the fourth if we reckon backwards.

μέχρι ταύτης τῆς ὥρας ἤμην τὴν ἐνάτην προσευχόμενος, *until this hour I was observing the ninth hour of prayer.* These words shew us that the time of Peter's arrival at Cæsarea was after the ninth hour of the day. The prayer-service to which Cornelius refers had begun and been continued for a time before the appearance of the angel.

ἀνήρ...ἐν ἐσθῆτι λαμπρᾷ, *a man...in bright clothing.* See i. 10 note and above on verse 3 of this chapter.

33. ἀκοῦσαι πάντα τὰ προστεταγμένα σοι ὑπὸ τοῦ κυρίου, *to hear all things that are commanded thee of the Lord.* Cornelius infers that as he had been instructed to send for Peter, so Peter had God's command for his conduct and speech. By 'hear' the centurion meant also 'to obey.' To one so directed from heaven the words of the Apostle would be divine orders. We learn also (xi. 14) that the message which Peter would bring had been described to him as one 'whereby he and all his house might be saved.' To hear then was to do.

34—43. SPEECH OF PETER TO CORNELIUS AND HIS FRIENDS.

34. ἐπ' ἀληθείας καταλαμβάνομαι κ.τ.λ., *of a truth I perceive that God is no respecter of persons.* The verb καταλ. implies the grasping of something with the mind which has hitherto not been comprehended, and indicates some degree of strangeness in what is accepted. St Peter is constrained to say, I am now fully convinced, from what I have heard of God's angel appearing to Cornelius, and from the connexion of that vision with my own, that God is making Himself known to all the workers of righteousness (ἐν παντὶ ἔθνει), whether they be Jews or Gentiles.

προσωπολήμπτης. This word is found nowhere else. A kindred verb occurs James ii. 9, and a noun in Rom. ii. 11; Col. iii. 25; James ii. 1. But πρόσωπον λαμβάνειν is not an unfrequent expression in the LXX.; see Lev. xix. 15; Job xiii. 8, xlii. 8; Ecclus. xxxv. 13, and a good instance is Malachi ii. 9 οὐκ ἐφυλάξασθε τὰς ὁδούς μου ἀλλὰ ἐλαμβάνετε πρόσωπα ἐν νόμῳ, 'Ye have not kept my ways, but have been partial in the law' (A.V.).

35. δεκτὸς αὐτῷ ἐστίν, *is accepted with Him,* i.e. is acceptable unto

Him. God has no longer a chosen people, but calleth all men to repent, and will accept all penitents.

36. τὸν λόγον ὃν ἀπέστειλεν κ.τ.λ. The construction in this verse and in the following is very involved. τὸν λόγον seems, in the intention of the speaker, to have been used first with reference to the language in the previous verse, and to have meant the message there recited, that whoever feareth God and worketh righteousness is accepted with Him. And the sentence begins thus: *This message which God sent to the children of Israel when He published the good news of peace through Jesus Christ* (*He is Lord of all*). Here the speaker should have introduced a verb like the οἴδατε which presently follows, but instead of doing so, he resumes the τὸν λόγον, by another expression τὸ ῥῆμα, and leaves the first sentence in suspense, continuing thus: *That saying ye yourselves know which was published throughout all Judæa.* Then he returns in thought to the word εὐαγγελιζόμενος, and makes his speech refer to the same subject, viz. to God who published the good news of peace, *beginning* (the publication by Jesus Christ) *from Galilee after the baptism which John preached.* In the next sentence the message and the saying of the previous clause find concrete expression, and are taken up with the name of Him in *whom* they centred: *Jesus of Nazareth, how God anointed Him with the Holy Ghost and with power.*

37. ὑμεῖς οἴδατε τὸ γενόμενον ῥῆμα. The ῥῆμα is the teaching about Jesus which went forth when John the Baptist began to preach, and seems to be more restricted in sense than the λόγος which refers to the whole message of salvation through Christ. About the Baptist and his preaching, Peter either assumes Cornelius and his friends to have heard, as so many must have done during Christ's ministerial life, or he speaks from what he had gathered in his previous conversation with Cornelius. Hence he says, 'Ye know of the history of Jesus.'

καθ' ὅλης τῆς... See on ix. 31.

38. Ἰησοῦν τὸν ἀπὸ Ναζαρέθ, *Jesus of Nazareth.* In Him was the whole accomplishment of the ῥῆμα and the λόγος. This was the entire scope of what had been preached even from the first: Jesus who had lived as a man in Nazareth, had yet been God's Anointed Son, the promised Messiah, and shewn to be so by the mighty works which He did.

τοὺς καταδυναστευομένους κ.τ.λ., *those that were oppressed of the devil.* The verb, not much used in classical Greek, is very common, especially in the active voice, in the LXX. The cure of those oppressed by the devil is perhaps mentioned as shewing that the power of Jesus was to be not only over physical but over moral evil likewise, and this alone is mentioned because in the healing of the greater, the power to cure the less evil is implied.

ὅτι ὁ θεὸς ἦν μετ' αὐτοῦ, *for God was with Him.* Of which presence the mighty works were the σημεῖα. Cf. Nicodemus' confession (John iii. 2), 'No man can do these signs that Thou doest except God be with him.'

39. καὶ ἡμεῖς μάρτυρες, *and we are witnesses.* Because they had seen His mighty works through His whole ministerial life (Luke xxiv. 48).

ὧν ἐποίησεν. For this attraction see note on i. 1.

ὃν καὶ ἀνεῖλαν κ.τ.λ., *whom also they slew, hanging Him on a tree.* He does not mention here, before a Gentile audience, who the offenders were; though to the Jews themselves (ii. 23) he dwells on the sin, that he may thereby move his hearers on whom the guilt lay. For the expression κρεμάσαντες ἐπὶ ξύλου, see chap. v. 30, note.

40. καὶ ἔδωκεν αὐτὸν ἐμφανῆ γενέσθαι, *and gave Him to be made manifest.* The literal translation implies more than the A.V. Christ was not *openly shewed*, but by many proofs it was made clear to those who saw Him that it was the same body which had been wounded on the cross that was alive again, though the resurrection had bestowed on it a character and a glory which had not been observed before.

41. οὐ παντὶ τῷ λαῷ, *not to all the people.* For they, having rejected Moses and the prophets, who foretold Christ's coming, and the nature of His kingdom, were not likely, as Jesus Himself had said of some others of like character, to be converted by the rising of any one from the dead.

μάρτυσιν τοῖς προκεχειροτονημένοις ὑπὸ τοῦ θεοῦ, *to witnesses chosen before by God.* The article joined with the participle, while the noun has none, gives special prominence to the fact of the previous choice of the Apostles by God, = 'even those who were,' &c. Christ Himself (John xvii. 6) calls them 'those whom Thou hast given Me.'

ἡμῖν, *to us.* Cf. 1 Cor. xv. 6—8.

οἵτινες συνεφάγομεν κ.τ.λ. The relative is emphatic. *Who* (to make our testimony undeniable) *did eat and drink with Him after He rose from the dead.* See Luke xxiv. 42, 43. And in the narrative John xxi. 12—15 it is to be inferred, especially from the last verse, that Jesus Himself partook of the food which He gave to the rest.

42. καὶ παρήγγειλεν ἡμῖν κηρύξαι τῷ λαῷ, *and He commanded us to proclaim to the people.* This was among the commandments alluded to Acts i. 2. Compare the charge given by Christ, Matth. xxviii. 19, where the wide commission 'Go ye, teach *all nations*,' is one that anticipated the preaching of the Gospel not only to Cornelius, but to all other Gentiles.

ὅτι αὐτός ἐστιν ὁ ὡρισμένος κ.τ.λ., *that it is He which was ordained of God to be the Judge of quick and dead.* Of this the Apostles could testify for they had heard it from Christ's own lips. Cf. His words to the Jews (John v. 22, 27), 'For the Father judgeth no man, but hath committed all judgment unto the Son,' 'and hath given Him authority to execute judgment also, because he is the Son of man.'

43. τούτῳ πάντες οἱ προφῆται μαρτυροῦσιν, *to Him give all the prophets witness.* Cornelius and his friends could be referred to the prophets, for though not Jews, they were students and followers of Jehovah's law. The prophetic words to which allusion is specially made are such as Jer. xxxi. 34 'They shall all know Me, from the least of them unto the greatest of them.' Also Joel ii. 32 ' Whosoever shall call on the name of the Lord shall be delivered.' So that under the Law the redemption of the Gentiles was seen afar off.

πάντα τὸν πιστεύοντα, *every one that believeth*. So that not circumcision but faith was now the key to the Kingdom of Heaven.

44—48. THE HOLY GHOST IS SENT UPON CORNELIUS AND HIS FRIENDS, AND THEY ARE SUBSEQUENTLY BAPTIZED.

44. ἐπὶ πάντας τοὺς ἀκούοντας, *on all them which heard*. On the nature of this hearing, which made the men fit to receive so great a gift, see above on verse 33.

45. οἱ ἐκ περιτομῆς, *they of the circumcision*, i.e. those six Jewish Christians mentioned in xi. 12 as companions of St Peter from Joppa.

46. ἤκουον γὰρ αὐτῶν κ.τ.λ., *for they heard them speak with tongues and magnify God*. As to those first called in the Jewish Church, so here to the first called of the Gentiles, God pours forth His gifts of grace. This was the Gentile Pentecost. (See ii. 11.)

47. μήτι τὸ ὕδωρ δύναται κωλῦσαί τις τοῦ μὴ βαπτισθῆναι τούτους; *can any man forbid water, that these should not be baptized?* Here is another instance of the genitival infinitive so common in N.T. Greek. But here, as κωλύειν may have a genitive of the thing from which any one is hindered, the construction offers less difficulty. The μὴ before βαπτισθῆναι is an instance of the Greek fondness for doubling negative ideas. Cf. Eur. *Phoeniss.* 1268 κωλύειν τινὰ μὴ θανεῖν, where the negative only renders emphatic the sense of the verb.

Though the gift of the Spirit has been made so apparent, yet St Peter does not omit the outward sign which Christ had ordained (Matth. xxviii. 19) for the admission of members into His Church.

ὡς καὶ ἡμεῖς, *as well as we*. And in precisely the same kind of manifestation.

48. προσέταξεν δὲ κ.τ.λ., *and he commanded them to be baptized*. Peter seems to have refrained from baptizing converts, and we know that St Paul did so, and the latter indicates a reason which may have influenced all the Twelve to appoint others to baptize, lest factions should arise, and men sever the Christian unity by calling themselves by the name of some one of the Apostles. Cp. 1 Cor. i. 13—16.

ἐν τῷ ὀνόματι Ἰησοῦ Χριστοῦ, *in the name of Jesus Christ*. The name of Jesus Christ is perhaps specially mentioned with a thought of the danger just alluded to. The converts were to be Christians. But see also ii. 38 note.

ἐπιμεῖναι ἡμέρας τινάς, *to tarry certain days*. It is probable that Peter consented to stay and to become the guest of Cornelius and his friends (see xi. 1—3); and thus shewed that he was prepared to act according to the teaching of the vision. We know that afterwards (Gal. ii. 11—13) he wavered in his determination, and was rebuked by

St Paul for so doing; but even the account of that rebuke shews us that Peter had laid aside his Jewish prejudices in a great degree, and had only acted in the way which was blamed, through the influence of some still strict Jews who had come from Jerusalem to Antioch. St Luke is not to be supposed to be ignorant of that wavering action of St Peter because he does not mention it. For a similar Christian reticence, in a like case, see xiii. 13 and note there.

CHAPTER XI.

Readings varying from the *Text. recept.*

3. ὅτι εἰσῆλθες. This order is in agreement with אABD, and is supported by the *Vulg.* 'quare introisti.'

8. ὅτι κοινόν. The omission of πᾶν agrees with אABDE and has the support of *Vulg.*

9. μοι omitted after ἀπεκρίθη δὲ with אAB. *Vulg.* 'Respondit autem vox.'

12. μηδὲν διακρίναντα with אAB. *Vulg.* 'Nihil hæsitans.'

13. αὐτῷ omitted after εἰπόντα with אAB. The *Vulg.* adds 'sibi.'
ἄνδρας omitted with אABD. Unrepresented in *Vulg.*

20. Ἕλληνας for Ἑλληνιστάς with אAD. *Vulg.* 'Græcos.'

22. οὔσης added after ἐκκλησίας τῆς with אBE.
διελθεῖν omitted with אAB. *Vulg.* 'Barnabam usque ad Antiochiam.'

25. ὁ Βαρνάβας omitted with אAB. *Vulg.* represents it.

26. καὶ εὑρὼν ἤγαγεν εἰς, with אAB. The first αὐτὸν is also omitted in E. *Vulg.* has 'quem cum invenisset, perduxit Antiochiam,' which supports the omission of the second αὐτόν.

28. μεγάλην after λιμόν with אABD, and so ἥτις to agree with it instead of ὅστις.

Καίσαρος omitted with אABD. Unrepresented in *Vulg.*

––––––––––––––

Ch. XI. 1—18. THE JUDÆO-CHRISTIANS BLAME PETER. HE MAKES HIS DEFENCE AT JERUSALEM.

1. ἤκουσαν δέ, *now they heard.* The report of what had happened at Cæsarea reached Jerusalem before Peter's return. Hence it seems that he accepted the hospitality of the new converts.

ὅτι καὶ τὰ ἔθνη ἐδέξαντο τὸν λόγον τοῦ θεοῦ, *that the Gentiles also had received the word of God.*

Where animate objects *and especially persons* are spoken of it is common in both classical and N.T. Greek for nouns in the neuter plural to be joined with a plural verb. Cf. Matth. xxvii. 52 πολλὰ σώματα τῶν κεκοιμημένων ἁγίων ἠγέρθησαν. For an instance of this usage about things inanimate see below verse 13, note. At the news of the acceptance of the word of God by the Gentiles, had there been no additional information about Peter's eating with Cornelius, the disciples would have rejoiced, and would have welcomed this further spread of the word, as they did (viii. 14) the conversion of the Samaritans, but to some, who were not only Christians, but strict observers of Jewish ritual, it was a cause of offence that Peter had consented to become the guest of a Gentile.

2. διεκρίνοντο πρὸς αὐτόν, *they contended with him.* The verb is the same which is used (x. 20), with a negative, μηδὲν διακρινόμενος, *nothing doubting,* and presently in this chapter (xi. 12) μηδὲν διακρίναντα *making no difference.* The contention of these opponents of Peter's conduct was that the difference between Jew and Gentile should still be maintained, and that any close fellowship (such as was involved in living at the same board) with those who accepted Christianity otherwise than through the gate of submission to the Mosaic Law should be avoided. As the Jews felt it their duty (x. 28) to behave towards Cornelius and such as he before they became Christians, so would the Judaizing feeling have prompted the Jewish Christians to deal with him still. And when we think on the prejudice which, by generations of ceremonial observance, had grown up among the Jews, we cannot wonder greatly at what they did. A whole nation is not brought to a change of feeling in a day.

οἱ ἐκ περιτομῆς, *they that were of the circumcision.* This must have been the whole Church, at the time when the event occurred, for there were no Christians as yet except Jews and proselytes. But St Luke's narrative was compiled at a time when 'they that were of the circumcision' had become a distinct party, and when their influence had begun to work division in the Christian societies. He therefore employs a name which when he wrote was full of significance, although it had its origin only in the circumstances to which he here applies it. Those who had been born Jews and knew of Jesus as conforming to the Law, and who had not heard of Peter's vision nor seen the gift of the Holy Ghost to Cornelius and his friends, as those who had been with Peter had done, were to be pardoned, if their scruples caused them to question the conduct of the Apostle at this time; yet when they heard his story they were satisfied (see ver. 18), but many Jewish Christians elsewhere continued to make this subject a cause of contention. See xv. 1.

3. πρὸς ἄνδρας ἀκροβυστίαν ἔχοντας, *to men uncircumcised.* The expression here employed testifies to the strength of feeling against what Peter had done. The men with whom he had mixed are not called Gentiles only, but the uncircumcised, the word of greatest reproach on the lips of a Jew.

καὶ συνέφαγες αὐτοῖς, *and didst eat with them.* Among whom there would be no ceremonial observance about either the character of the food or the way of its preparation.

4. ἀρξάμενος δὲ Πέτρος ἐξετίθετο αὐτοῖς καθεξῆς, *but Peter began and rehearsed the matter in order to them.*

5. καθιεμένην. The participle is here in agreement with ὀθόνην. In the parallel passage in the previous chapter, it was made to agree with σκεῦος. The one construction is as correct as the other.

6. κατενόουν, *I beheld.* So LXX. (Exod. xxxiii. 8) καὶ κατενοοῦσαν ἀπιόντος Μωυσῆ, of the people watching Moses as he went up the mountain. Cf. also Ps. xc. (xci.) 8, xciii. 9.

11. καὶ ἰδού...ἐν ᾗ ἦμεν, *and behold immediately there stood three men before the house in which we were.* The Apostle is speaking to the congregation at Jerusalem, who would know of any companions who might have gone with him to Lydda and Joppa. Therefore he includes them in his words. It is most in harmony with what was done in other cases that he should not have gone forth unaccompanied.

12. μηδὲν διακρίναντα, *making no difference.* On this change of the verb from the middle to the active voice, and for a reason why Peter, after having been at Cæsarea and having heard the statement of Cornelius and seen the gift of the Spirit, adopted this form in his address at Jerusalem, see x. 20 note.

ἦλθον δὲ σὺν ἐμοὶ καὶ οἱ ἓξ ἀδελφοὶ οὗτοι, *and these six brethren accompanied me.* Those who had been his companions to Cæsarea were brought on by Peter to Jerusalem, that their testimony might support his statement, and that they might declare to the rest of Judæo-Christians what they had witnessed. It may be that these men, or some of them, had been his companions in his journey described (ix. 32) as made 'throughout all quarters.'

13. ἀπήγγειλεν δὲ ἡμῖν πῶς εἶδεν τὸν ἄγγελον, *and he related to us how he had seen the angel.* Before St Peter made this defence, and long before St Luke put it down in the Acts, the story of Cornelius and his vision would be well known, and so the definite article would be used in speaking of it, i.e. '*the* angel' of whom all men had heard.

In N.T. Greek the general usage is to put the forms used for direct interrogation (as πῶς, πότε) where the classical writers would usually write the corresponding relative forms, ὅπως, ὁπότε. So Matth. vi. 28 καταμάθετε τὰ κρίνα τοῦ ἀγροῦ πῶς αὐξάνουσιν.

ἀπόστειλον εἰς Ἰόππην, *send to Joppa.* The insertion of ἄνδρας here is one of the numerous instances where in the repetition of a narrative an attempt has been made to bring the different passages into exact verbal agreement. There have been times when devout men thought much of this verbal accord. It is therefore worth notice that the writers of the N.T. disregarded it utterly. The words in such a solemn inscription as that above the Cross differ in all the four Gospels, and St Peter, when in the Second Epistle (i. 17) he speaks of the heavenly voice heard at the Transfiguration, varies verbally from each of the accounts of the Evangelists.

15. ἐν δὲ τῷ ἄρξασθαί με λαλεῖν, *and as I began to speak.* A somewhat more precise statement than that of the previous chapter, which was (x. 44) ἔτι λαλοῦντος τοῦ Πέτρου. It would appear from these words of Peter that he had hardly begun his address before the gift of the Spirit descended.

ἐν ἀρχῇ, *at the beginning*, i.e. at the feast of Pentecost.

16. τοῦ ῥήματος τοῦ κυρίου, *the word of the Lord;* recorded above i. 5. The ὡς ἔλεγεν which follows is inserted to introduce the exact words of Christ.

17. πιστεύσασιν, *who believed.* The participle refers alike to the preceding αὐτοῖς and ἡμῖν, and thus the two cases are made parallel exactly as in the narrative of verse 15. For just as in the case of Peter and the Apostles, their faith was existing before the gift of the Spirit, so in Cornelius and in his companions there existed a degree of faith, or there could have been no sincere prayer offered by them.

ἐγὼ τίς ἤμην δυνατὸς κωλῦσαι τὸν θεόν; *who was I that I could withstand God?* There are in reality two questions here merged into one. Who was I? Was I able to withstand...? So also Luke xix. 15 τίς τί διεπραγματεύσατο = who had traded, and what he had made thereby.

18. ἡσύχασαν, *they held their peace.* But though those who listened to St Peter's narrative were satisfied that God had now called Gentiles as well as Jews to be of His Kingdom, there were others who, some perhaps with a real but misguided zeal for the Law, some, as St Paul says (Gal. vi. 13), from vain-glory, maintained the necessity for the observance of the older covenant, and hence arose dissensions in the Church from a very early time.

19—26. FURTHER SPREAD OF THE GOSPEL AS FAR AS ANTIOCH.

19. ἐπὶ Στεφάνῳ, *about Stephen.* See above viii. 1.

ἕως Φοινίκης, *as far as Phœnicia.* A still wider circuit for the Gospel messengers. Phœnicia contained the important seaports of Tyre and Sidon. For its history see *Dict. of the Bible.*

Κύπρου. *Cyprus.* See iv. 36.

'Αντιοχείας. *Antioch.* The capital city of Syria, about 16 miles from the sea-coast, on the river Orontes. It was the residence of the Roman pro-consul of Syria. St Paul made this his starting point in all his three missionary journeys. For its history see *Dictionary of the Bible.*

εἰ μὴ μόνον 'Ιουδαίοις, *but unto the Jews only.* For they had not been warned, as Peter was, that the time was come to carry out Christ's prophetic command (Acts i. 8) to its fullest extent.

20. ἦσαν δέ τινες...Κύπριοι καὶ Κυρηναῖοι, *but some of them were men of Cyprus and Cyrene.* In whose minds, from their more cosmopolitan education, there was less scruple about mixing with Gentiles than existed among the Jews of Palestine, the home of the nation, and by consequence the stronghold of their prejudices.

ἐλάλουν πρὸς τοὺς Ἕλληνας, *spake unto the Greeks.* The N.T. uses Ἑλληνισταί to mean those Jews who had been born in some foreign land and spoke the Greek language, or else for proselytes; but Ἕλληνες, when the heathen population is spoken of. Now it is clear that it would have been no matter of remark had these men preached to Ἑλληνισταί, Greek-Jews, for of them there was a large number in the Church of Jerusalem, as we see from the events related in chap. vi. 1, and most probably these Grecian and Cyprian teachers were themselves Greek-Jews; but what calls for special mention by St Luke is that they, moved perhaps by some spiritual impulse, addressed their preaching in Antioch to the Gentiles as well as to the Jews. The time was ripe for such a work, and God who had prompted Peter by a vision, moved these men by His Spirit.

21. καὶ ἦν χεὶρ κυρίου μετ' αὐτῶν, *and the hand of the Lord was with them.* The expression is a common one in the O.T. to express the direct interposition of God in the affairs of the world. Cf. 1 Sam. v. 3, καὶ ἐβαρύνθη χεὶρ κυρίου ἐπὶ τοὺς Ἀζωτίους. So too 1 Sam. vii. 13: and of His interposition for good, see Is. xli. 20. Cf. also Exod. viii. 19, xiv. 31.

πολύς τε ἀριθμὸς ὁ πιστεύσας ἐπέστρεψεν κ.τ.λ., *and a great multitude that believed turned unto the Lord.* These probably, like Cornelius had been prepared, by their knowledge of Jehovah through Judaism, to accept the teaching of the Christian missionaries.

22. ἠκούσθη δὲ ὁ λόγος κ.τ.λ., *and the report concerning them, &c.* i.e. concerning these Gentile converts. These events took place, and were known to the Church in Jerusalem, before they heard of the visit of Peter to Cornelius. But what had happened at Antioch caused the Church no disturbance, because we read of no such breaking through the restrictions of the ceremonial Law as was made in Cæsarea when Peter took up his abode with Cornelius. The Jewish preachers mingled no further with the Gentiles to whom they preached at Antioch than the intercourse of everyday life forced them to do constantly.

καὶ ἐξαπέστειλαν Βαρνάβαν, *and they sent forth Barnabas.* He was sent forth, as Peter and John before had been sent into Samaria (viii. 14), to confirm and give the sanction and direction of the mother Church to the work which had begun at a new centre. Barnabas being a native of Cyprus would most likely be well known to the Cyprians who were preaching at Antioch, and so he was a most fit person to be selected for this errand.

23. καὶ ἰδὼν τὴν χάριν τὴν τοῦ θεοῦ, *and having seen the grace of God,* i.e. as it was exhibited in the faith, and consequent turning to Christ, of these Gentiles.

ἐχάρη, *was glad.* Seeing nothing in the new movement which could call for disapproval, while the addition of new members to the Church was a source of joy.

καὶ παρεκάλει, *and exhorted.* He is called υἱὸς παρακλήσεως in iv. 36.

τῇ προθέσει τῆς καρδίας, *with purpose of heart.* Lit. 'in the purpose of their heart.' Their determination was at present formed, and they had turned to the Lord; the purport of Barnabas' exhortation was

that continuing in the same determination they should hold fast their
faith, and allow nothing to shake their attachment to Christ. The
heathen converts to Christianity had much to endure for Christ's sake,
and to the weak there were many temptations to relapse.

24. πλήρης πνεύματος ἁγίου καὶ πίστεως, *full of the Holy Ghost
and faith.* The same description is given of Stephen (vi. 5), and a
man of like character with that most eminent among the Greek-Jews
would exert much influence in Antioch, where Greeks and Greek-Jews
were the chief part of the population. It was in consequence of the
persecution after Stephen's death that these preachers had come to
Antioch, and some of them were probably of those Grecians who had
been forward in the work for which Stephen was martyred.

καὶ προσετέθη ὄχλος ἱκανός, *and much people was added.* No
doubt the joyful approval of Barnabas, representing the Mother-
Church of Jerusalem, would help forward the zeal of the preachers at
Antioch.

25. ἀναζητῆσαι Σαῦλον, *for to seek Saul.* That he, to whom the
Lord had appeared, and who had been marked as a 'chosen vessel'
(ix. 15) to bear the name of Christ before the Gentiles, might come
with him to share in this new work of preaching to the Gentiles at
Antioch.

26. ἐνιαυτὸν ὅλον, *a whole year.* This long period, spent with
success in the first field where the preaching to the Gentiles had
begun, will account for the constant return of the Apostle of the
Gentiles to Antioch after each of his three missionary journeys. He
had preached at Damascus and at Jerusalem, but it was always with
his life in his hand. At Antioch he first found a quiet Church with a
wide scope for all his earnestness.

χρηματίσαι τε πρώτως κ.τ.λ., *and the disciples were called Christians
first in Antioch.* It is most probable that this name was given them
by the heathen in ridicule. The disciples of Jesus never give it to
themselves, and as the use of it would imply that those who bore it
were the followers of the Messiah, the Christ, it is certain it would
not be given to them by the Jews. The reason for a new distinctive
term is apparent. When these new Gentile converts were joined to
the Church of Antioch, none of the former distinctive appellations
would embrace the whole body. They were no longer all Nazarenes
or Galilæans or Greek-Jews, and as to the people of Antioch they
probably seemed a strange medley, they would not be unlikely to
apply to them such a hybrid form as 'Christian,' a Greek word with
a Latin termination. The name is probably used in mockery by
Agrippa (Acts xxvi. 28) 'With but little persuasion thou wouldest
fain make me a Christian,' but in the only other and later instance
of the use of the name in the N.T. (1 Pet. iv. 16) we can see that
what had been at first a taunt had soon come to be a name in
which to glory, 'If any man suffer as a Christian, let him not be
ashamed.'

χρηματίζω, having, as a first meaning, 'to do some business,' came afterwards, because persons of certain callings are named from what they do, to have the sense of ' to be named ' as here.

27—30. AGABUS AT ANTIOCH FORETELLS A FAMINE, AND IN CON-
SEQUENCE THE CHURCH AT ANTIOCH SENDS RELIEF TO JERU-
SALEM.

27. ἐν ταύταις δὲ ταῖς ἡμέραις, *and in those days*, i.e. during the year when Barnabas and Saul were labouring in Antioch, and the Church increasing there rapidly in consequence.

προφῆται, *prophets.* That there should be prophets in the Church was but the fulfilment of the prophecy of Joel which Peter had quoted in his Pentecostal sermon (ii. 17). We cannot gather from the N. T. records any clear description of what office is to be understood by the word 'prophet.' The men to whom it is applied are sometimes occupied in preaching and explaining the word of God, and sometimes have the power of foretelling future events, as Agabus did here. See Acts xiii. 1, xv. 32, xix. 6, xxi. 9, 10; Rom. xii. 6; 1 Cor. xii. 10, 28, 29, xiii. 2, 8, xiv. 6, 29—37; Eph. ii. 20.

28. εἷς ἐξ αὐτῶν ὀνόματι Ἄγαβος, *one of them, named Agabus.* He is mentioned again in xxi. 10, where, after the fashion of some of the prophets of the O. T., he by a significant action, as well as by his words, foretells the imprisonment of St Paul at Jerusalem.

διὰ τοῦ πνεύματος. So too xxi. 11 the words of Agabus are prefaced by τάδε λέγει τὸ πνεῦμα τὸ ἅγιον.

λιμὸν μεγάλην, *great dearth.* This noun is usually masculine, but the grammarians notice that, as St Luke makes it here, it is sometimes feminine. The Megarean in Aristoph. *Acharn.* 743 uses it as feminine.

This famine is mentioned by Josephus (*Ant.* xx. 2. 5) who tells how Helena, queen of Adiabene, being at Jerusalem, succoured the people by procuring for them corn from Alexandria and a cargo of figs from Cyprus. The date of this severe famine was A.D. 45.

ἐφ' ὅλην τὴν οἰκουμένην, *throughout all the world.* ἡ οἰκουμένη is the phrase used for the whole Roman empire, as in Luke ii. 1, but here perhaps it has a wider signification. Though one region might be specially afflicted by the failure of its crops, all the rest of the Roman empire would be sure to suffer in some degree at the same time, and especially when famines were, as at this time, of frequent recurrence.

ἐπὶ Κλαυδίου, *in the days of Claudius.* The reign of Claudius (A.D. 41—54) was remarkable for the famines with which various parts of the empire were afflicted. The first, second, fourth, ninth and eleventh years of this emperor's reign are recorded as years of famine in some district or other. See Suetonius, *Claudius*, 28; Tacitus, *Ann.* XII. 43; Josephus, *Ant.* xx. 2. 5; Dio Cassius, IX. p. 949; Euseb. *H. E.* II. 8.

29. τῶν δὲ μαθητῶν καθὼς εὐπορεῖτό τις, *and the disciples each man according to his ability*, i.e. the disciples of the Church at Antioch.

εἰς διακονίαν, *for relief*. Lit. 'for ministry': a phrase which recalls the ἡ διακονία ἡ καθημερινή of vi. 1. The relief from Antioch was to be distributed in that way, for no doubt the Christian Church in Judæa would be much impoverished. At first the poorer converts had been sustained by the common fund, but persecution had driven away great numbers of the Christians, and those would be most likely to depart who possessed means to support themselves in other places. Thus the Mother-Church would be deprived of those members who were best able to give relief in such a severe time of distress.

30. πρὸς τοὺς πρεσβυτέρους, *to the elders*. This is the first time we come upon the πρεσβύτεροι in the Christian history. In xx. 17 they are again mentioned, and shortly afterwards (verse 28) in the same narrative they are named ἐπίσκοποι = overseers, bishops. No doubt at first the office of elder or presbyter comprised, beside the work of teaching, the general oversight of one, or it may be more Churches. Cf. Phil. i. 1 where the two orders of the ministry are described as 'bishops (= presbyters) and deacons.' As the Church increased in numbers these duties were separated, and the general superintendence and control assigned to one who was called overseer or bishop.

διὰ χειρὸς Βαρνάβα καὶ Σαύλου, *by the hand of Barnabas and Saul*. The character and labours of these two had marked them out as the most fit men to be bearers of this help, and it was from Jerusalem that Barnabas had been sent at first to Antioch.

CHAPTER XII.

Readings varying from the *Text. recept.*

9. αὐτῷ omitted with אABD. *Vulg.* represents it.

13. αὐτοῦ for τοῦ Πέτρου with אABDLP. *Vulg.* 'eo.'

20. ὁ Ἡρώδης omitted with אABD. Unrepresented in *Vulg*.

25. καὶ omitted after συμπαραλαβόντες with אAB. Unrepresented in *Vulg*.

Ch. XII. 1—12. Herod's Persecution of the Church. Peter's Miraculous Deliverance from Prison.

1. κατ' ἐκεῖνον δὲ τὸν καιρόν, *now about that time*. The events narrated in this chapter must have occurred very shortly before Herod's death. The date will therefore be about A.D. 43.

Ἡρώδης ὁ βασιλεύς. This was Herod Agrippa I. He was the son of Aristobulus, and grandson of Herod the Great. See Table of the Herods in Archdeacon Farrar's St Luke (*Cambridge Gk. Test. for Schools*), Introduction, p. li.

ἐπέβαλεν...τὰς χεῖρας κακῶσαι, *stretched forth his hands to injure.*
Agrippa according to Josephus (XIX. 7. 3) was anxious to be esteemed
a devout Jew: 'He loved to live continually at Jerusalem, and was
exactly careful in the observance of the laws of his country. He
therefore kept himself entirely pure, nor did any day pass over his head
without its appointed sacrifice.' Such a man might easily be roused,
by the Jews whom he was so anxious to please, to the perpetration
of cruelties upon the Christians.

On the seizure of St James, Chrysostom says, Τοῦτό ἐστιν ὁ ἔλεγεν
ὁ Χριστός. τὸ μὲν ποτήριον ὁ μέλλω πίνειν πίεσθε, καὶ τὸ βάπτισμα ὁ
ἐγὼ βαπτίζομαι βαπτισθήσεσθε.

2. Ἰάκωβον τὸν ἀδελφὸν Ἰωάννου, *James, the brother of John.* This
was one of the two sons of Zebedee, who had been among the three
specially favoured disciples of Jesus. It is therefore likely that he
would take a leading part in the labours of the Church. Thus Agrippa's attention would be drawn to him as a proper person to be first
struck down. All the accusations which had been laid against
Stephen, that the Christian leader spake against the Temple and the
Law, would be used with effect to such a zealous observer of Mosaic
ritual as Herod Agrippa was.

μαχαίρῃ, *with the sword.* This was the third in order of the modes
of execution appointed among the Jews. These modes were (1) stoning,
(2) burning, (3) the sword, and (4) strangulation. In connexion with
the execution of James the words of the Mishna are interesting: 'The
ordinance for putting to death by the sword is as follows: the man's
head is cut off with the sword as is wont to be done *by royal command.*'
See Surenhusius on *Sanhedrin*, p. 248, where there is a discussion
about the position of the prisoner, whether he should stand erect or
have his head on a block.

3. ἰδὼν δὲ ὅτι ἀρεστόν ἐστιν τοῖς Ἰουδαίοις, *and because he saw it
pleased the Jews,* which with him was so great an object. Josephus,
in contrasting Agrippa with the Herod who ruled before him, says the
latter was 'more friendly to the Greeks than to the Jews,' but in this
respect Agrippa 'was not at all like him.'

προσέθετο συλλαβεῖν καὶ Πέτρον, *he proceeded further to take Peter
also.* Literally, 'he added to take &c.' This is the literal rendering cf
a common Hebrew form. Cf. LXX. Gen. iv. 2, καὶ προσέθετο τεκεῖν
τὸν ἀδελφὸν αὐτοῦ, 'and she *bare again* his brother,' and Gen. xxxvii.
8, καὶ προσέθεντο ἔτι μισεῖν αὐτὸν ἕνεκεν τῶν ἐνυπνίων αὐτοῦ, 'and they
hated him yet the more for his dreams.' Peter was the other most conspicuous figure among the Twelve, for John, as in his Gospel he keeps
himself from view under the designation 'that other disciple' (John
xx. 2, 3, xxi. 20, 23), so in the work of the early Church is but little
noticed after the first persecution at Jerusalem.

ἦσαν δὲ ἡμέραι τῶν ἀζύμων, *and those were the days of unleavened
bread.* The phrase refers to the whole Passover feast, as may be seen
from Luke xxii. 1 ἡ ἑορτὴ τῶν ἀζύμων ἡ λεγομένη πάσχα.

4. ἔθετο εἰς φυλακήν, *he put him in prison*, to be kept a prisoner till the termination of the feast, when he might be brought to trial.

παραδοὺς τέσσαρσιν τετραδίοις κ.τ.λ., *having delivered him to four quaternions of soldiers to guard him.* A quaternion was a set of four men, which was the number at one time occupied in the work of the guard, two soldiers being chained to the prisoner, and two keeping guard outside. These latter are called (ver. 10) 'the first and second ward.' There were four such sets appointed to have charge of Peter, one company for each of the four watches by day and by night.

A similar arrangement for keeping guard, though not over a prisoner, is mentioned Philo *in Flaccum* 13, where an officer is sent to arrest Flaccus, and it is said στρατιώτην δέ τινα τῶν ἐν τοῖς τετραδίοις φυλακῶν καθ' ὁδὸν εὑρὼν κελεύει δεικνύναι τὴν οἰκίαν στρατάρχου.

βουλόμενος μετὰ τὸ πάσχα, *intending after the Passover.* The A.V. renders πάσχα by 'Easter,' meaning thereby to shew that the whole feast, and not the day of the sacrifice only, is spoken of. That this meaning, and not the single day of the Paschal feast is intended by the Greek, seems clear from the elaborate preparation made, as for a longer imprisonment than was the rule among the Jews. Peter was arrested at the commencement of the Passover feast (14th of Nisan), and the king's intention was to proceed to sentence and punish him when the feast was at an end on the 21st of Nisan.

ἀναγαγεῖν αὐτὸν τῷ λαῷ, *to bring him forth to the people.* That they might see his zeal for Judaism by the sentence which he should pass upon Peter. The same verb is used (Luke xxii. 66) of bringing Jesus before the council, ἀνήγαγον αὐτὸν εἰς τὸ συνέδριον.

5. ἐτηρεῖτο ἐν τῇ φυλακῇ, *was kept* [guarded] *in the prison.* Another indication of the intended longer duration of the imprisonment, and that he was not arrested on the day of the Paschal sacrifice with the purpose of being brought forth on the morning of the 15th of Nisan, as some have maintained.

προσευχὴ δὲ ἦν ἐκτενῶς γινομένη κ.τ.λ., *but prayer was earnestly made by the Church unto God for him.* The adverb ἐκτενῶς is thus used in LXX. of earnest crying unto God. Joel i. 14; Jonah iii. 8. So Judith iv. 12 καὶ ἐβόησαν πρὸς τὸν θεὸν Ἰσραὴλ ὁμοθυμαδὸν ἐκτενῶς τοῦ μὴ δοῦναι εἰς διαρπαγὴν τὰ νήπια αὐτῶν. The prayers of the Church were offered by assemblies of Christians meeting in various private houses (see verse 12), for the persecution would now render public Christian services dangerous, as we know was often the case in the early days of Christianity.

6. ὅτε δὲ ἤμελλεν προαγαγεῖν αὐτὸν ὁ Ἡρώδης, *and when Herod was about to bring him forth.* This is an additional note of the lapse of some space between the arrest and the intended punishment of the Apostle.

φύλακές τε πρὸ τῆς θύρας, *and guards before the door*, i.e. those two soldiers of the quaternion who were not chained to the prisoner. See above on verse 4.

7. καὶ ἰδοὺ ἄγγελος κυρίου ἐπέστη, *and behold an angel of the Lord came upon him.* The phrase is word for word the same as in Luke ii. 9, and the words which follow there καὶ δόξα κυρίου περιέλαμψεν αὐτοὺς have much resemblance to the further description here.

καὶ...ἐν τῷ οἰκήματι, *and a light shined in the cell.* οἴκημα, though applicable to any dwelling-place, is used in classical Greek for such places as a tavern, a cage for birds, a store-room, and for a prison (as here) in Thuc. IV. 47, παραλαβόντες δὲ αὐτοὺς οἱ Κερκυραῖοι ἐς οἴκημα μέγα καθεῖρξαν. The light in the cell was due to the presence of the angel who came in the glory of the Lord.

ἤγειρεν αὐτόν, *he roused him up.* The verb indicates that the angel woke Peter from his sleep, not that he helped him to arise, as might be supposed from the A. V.

8. ζῶσαι, *gird thyself.* To gird up the loose Oriental robe was a necessity before undertaking any expeditious movement. So to Gehazi, (LXX.) 2 Kings iv. 29, Elisha says Ζῶσαι τὴν ὀσφύν σου, and uses the same phrase (2 Kings ix. 1) to that one of the sons of the prophets whom he is about to send to Ramoth-Gilead.

περιβαλοῦ τὸ ἱμάτιόν σου, *cast thy garment about thee.* The ἱμάτιον was the outer garment as distinguished from the under one, which is χιτών. The ἱμάτια were stripped off by those who stoned Stephen (Acts vii. 58), and in the LXX. the constant phrase for rending the loose robe as a sign of horror is διέρρηξαν τὰ ἱμάτια αὐτῶν, while the dress made for Adam and Eve is described as χιτῶνες δερμάτινοι (Gen. iii. 21), and it was the χιτών which Ahab (1 Kings xxi. 27) rent, that he might put sackcloth upon his flesh. Cf. also 'Teaching of the Twelve Apostles,' chap. i. ἐὰν ἄρῃ τις τὸ ἱμάτιόν σου, δὸς αὐτῷ καὶ τὸν χιτῶνα.

10. διελθόντες δὲ πρώτην φυλακὴν καὶ δευτέραν, *and when they were past the first and second ward,* i.e. the warders, who were stationed one nearer to the inner door of the prison and another at some further distance away.

ἦλθαν ἐπὶ τὴν πύλην κ.τ.λ., *they came unto the iron gate that leadeth into the city.* This description, with the words which immediately follow about the street into which they came, make it probable that the prison in which Peter was kept was in the midst of the city.

αὐτομάτη, *of its own accord,* i.e. without any human agency. Cf. the description of the fire which appeared to the Egyptians when they were oppressing the holy nation (Wisdom xvii. 6), διεφαίνετο δ' αὐτοῖς μόνον αὐτομάτη πυρὰ φόβου πλήρης.

ἀπέστη ὁ ἄγγελος ἀπ' αὐτοῦ, *the angel departed from him,* giving no more aid now that the Apostle could make his way without supernatural assistance. Cf. Chrysostom's words, τὰ μέν τοι ἔνδον γενόμενα θαυμασιώτερα ἦν, τοῦτο δὲ λοιπὸν ἀνθρωπινώτερον. ὅτε οὐδὲν κώλυμα ἦν τότε ἀπέστη ὁ ἄγγελος.

11. καὶ ὁ Πέτρος ἐν ἑαυτῷ γενόμενος, *and when Peter was come to himself.* This and the other subjective features of the narrative shew that the account must have been derived from St Peter himself.

No one else could describe the astonishment and the after realization that all was truly enacted and no vision.

In Luke xv. 17 the phrase is εἰς ἑαυτὸν γενόμενος where it is a moral and spiritual, not a physical, awakening and resipiscence that is spoken of.

καὶ πάσης τῆς προσδοκίας τοῦ λαοῦ τῶν Ἰουδαίων, *and from all the expectation of the people of the Jews.* Their gratification had been great at the death of James, and now they hoped to see another of the Apostles condemned and executed.

12. συνιδών τε, *and when he comprehended the matter,* i.e. had taken in all the circumstances and decided what was best to be done. The same word is used (xiv. 6) of the disciples getting news of an intended attack, and making up their minds to flee before it took place.

Μαρίας τῆς μητρὸς Ἰωάννου κ.τ.λ., *Mary the mother of John, whose surname was Mark.* This Mary was the sister to Barnabas as we learn in Col. iv. 10, where Mark is called sister's son to Barnabas. This relationship accounts for the way in which the uncle clung to his nephew, even when St Paul declined to have Mark as a companion on their second proposed missionary journey. We do not read of the father of Mark anywhere, so it is probable that Mary was a widow, and, like her brother, was possessed of means which enabled her to put a house, or a part thereof, at the service of the Church, as a meeting-place for prayer.

συνηθροισμένοι καὶ προσευχόμενοι, *gathered together and praying.* Probably Mary's house was a regular place for Christian assemblies. At one time they would meet for one purpose, at another for another, but just when Peter was delivered their object in meeting had been to make supplication for his deliverance.

13—19. SURPRISE OF THE BRETHREN AND ANGER OF HEROD.

13. τὴν θύραν τοῦ πυλῶνος, *the door of the gate.* θύρα is the wicket which was opened for any one's admission, while πυλών is the porch into which admission was obtained through the θύρα. ἡ θύρα τοῦ πυλῶνος occurs in the LXX. Ezek. xl. 11; also in Judges xviii. 16, 17, in which latter place the expression applies to the gate of a city, which had also its wicket.

ὑπακοῦσαι, *to hearken.* Perhaps we have here a trace of the danger which at this time surrounded the disciples from this zeal for Judaism on the part of Herod. Saul had entered into every house and carried off men and women to prison (viii. 3), and there was a prospect of a like persecution. So Rhoda was not minded to open till she knew who was seeking for admission.

14. καὶ ἐπιγνοῦσα τὴν φωνὴν τοῦ Πέτρου, *and when she knew Peter's voice.* We know that there was something easily recognized in it, and he was known by his speech on a former occasion (Matth. xxvi. 73).

ἀπὸ τῆς χαρᾶς οὐκ ἤνοιξεν τὸν πυλῶνα, *she opened not the gate for gladness*. Cf. with this action the description of the disciples, Luke xxiv. 41; when they recognized Jesus 'they believed not for joy.'

On this Chrysostom remarks: καλῶς καὶ τοῦτο γέγονε· ἵνα μὴ καὶ ἐκεῖνοι ἐκπλαγῶσιν εὐθέως ἰδόντες καὶ ἀπιστήσωσιν, ἀλλ᾽ ἐγγυμνασθῇ ἡ διάνοια, καὶ ὅπερ ἔθος ἡμῖν ποιεῖν, εὑρεθῇ πράττουσα καὶ αὐτή.

15. ἡ δὲ διϊσχυρίζετο, *but she confidently affirmed*. In the time of the A.V. *constantly* had the meaning of *confidently*, which it has now lost. διϊσχυρίζομαι is in N.T. only here and in St Luke xxii. 59. It occurs in *Acta Petri et Pauli Apocryph*. §§ 34 and 39, οἱ δὲ τῷ Σίμωνι κολληθέντες τὸν Πέτρον διϊσχυρίζοντο μάγον. The word is often found in classical Greek.

ὁ ἄγγελός ἐστιν αὐτοῦ, *it is his angel*. The author of the Epistle to the Hebrews expresses (i. 14) in part the opinion of the Jews concerning angels when he asks, 'Are they not all ministering spirits sent forth to do service to them who shall be heirs of salvation?' The Jewish belief was that each man had a guardian angel assigned to him. Cf. *Midrash Rabbah* on Eccles. iv. 4, where it is said that 'six hundred thousand of the angels of the presence came down on Sinai at the giving of the Law, and each one bore a crown to crown Israel, one for each Israelite.' Cf. also our Lord's language (Matt. xviii. 10).

17. πῶς, *how*. See on ix. 27 note.

ὁ κύριος αὐτὸν ἐξήγαγεν ἐκ τῆς φυλακῆς, *the Lord had brought him out of the prison*. Cf. his exclamation in verse 11.

ἀπαγγείλατε, *carry word*. The A.V. has endeavoured to give the full sense by 'Go, shew,' but this seems as though it represented two verbs instead of one.

Ἰακώβῳ, *unto James*. This is no doubt the James who is afterwards (xv. 13) described as presiding over the council at Jerusalem concerning circumcision, and giving his sentence on that question. Thus he seems to have been at the head of the Church at Jerusalem, and to him it was natural for Peter to send the first news of his deliverance.

This James must have been either the son of Alphæus or else the James who is called one of the Lord's brethren, but it is not easy to decide whether the persons called by these names were one and the same. It seems however safest not to identify the Apostle, James the son of Alphæus, with the Lord's brother, for these brethren of Jesus did not believe in Him till a very late period of His ministerial life, long after the Twelve were chosen. But the James in St Luke's narrative here is probably the Lord's brother, because St Paul gives to the James who was one of the pillars of the Church at Jerusalem (Gal. ii. 9) when St Paul visited that city, the express title of 'the Lord's brother' (Gal. i. 19). This James, bishop of Jerusalem, was, as we learn from a tradition preserved by Eusebius (*H. E.* II. 23), cast down from the pinnacle of the Temple, whither the Jews had brought him, in the expectation that he would disown Christ. When, on the contrary, he still held to his belief, he was thrown down, and not being killed by the fall, was slain by a blow from the club of a fuller.

καὶ τοῖς ἀδελφοῖς, *and to the brethren,* i.e. to the rest of the Christian congregation. Though it was in the middle of the night when his deliverance took place, Peter sends to the various centres where, as in the house of Mary, prayer was also being offered to God for his deliverance.

ἐπορεύθη εἰς ἕτερον τόπον, *he went into another place.* The peril of death was so imminent if he had been seized that he takes refuge by hiding where he cannot be found. The times are altered since the day when, after his former deliverance, he could dare to go and speak in the day-dawn to the people in the Temple. Then the populace were a protection to the Church and saved them from violence of the authorities, now the Jewish people are in expectation of a second execution.

18. τάραχος οὐκ ὀλίγος ἐν τοῖς στρατιώταις, *no small stir among the soldiers.* For the guards who had been chained to the prisoner would discover as soon as they awoke that he had escaped from between them, and they would know that their life would probably answer for the life of Peter.

19. μὴ εὑρών. It is difficult to imagine any more literal statement than these words, and there can be no distinction in such a sentence between μὴ and οὐ.

ἐκέλευσεν ἀπαχθῆναι, *commanded that they should be put to death.* This is the A.V., and gives the sense better than the literal rendering 'commanded that they should be led forth.' This 'leading forth' was the prelude to execution. The verb ἀπάγειν is frequent in the accounts of the trial and Crucifixion of Jesus in the Gospels.

κατελθών...εἰς Καισάρειαν διέτριβεν. The preposition goes with κατελθών; *he came down to Cæsarea and abode there.* By Caligula there had been conferred on Herod Agrippa the tetrarchies of Herod Philip and Lysanias mentioned Luke iii. 1. He afterwards received the tetrarchy of Antipas, and was honoured with the title of king. He therefore, and not a Roman governor, was in power at Cæsarea at this date, for Josephus tells us (*Ant.* xx. 8. 2) that he had received from Claudius, Judæa and Samaria in addition to the districts over which he had ruled under Caligula.

20—25. Death of Herod Agrippa I. Growth of the Church.

20. ἦν δὲ θυμομαχῶν, *now he was highly displeased.* The word is of very rare occurrence, being found once in Polybius and once in Diodorus Siculus, and nowhere else. It implies a very deep seated feeling of anger.

Τυρίοις καὶ Σιδωνίοις, *with them of Tyre and Sidon.* These cities were still seats of maritime industry, and perhaps Herod's regard for the people of Berytus (*Beyrout*), another Phoenician seaport a little north of Sidon, may have been connected as cause or effect with his anger at the people of the two older cities. Josephus (xix. 7. 5) gives an account of splendid buildings which this king provided for Berytus. It is clear that the way in which the royal anger had made itself felt was one which interfered with the commercial prosperity of Tyre and Sidon.

ὁμοθυμαδὸν δὲ παρῆσαν πρὸς αὐτόν, *but they came with one accord to him,* i.e. they joined in a common embassy and sent persons from both towns to make representations and to use their influence to appease Herod's anger.

Βλάστον τὸν ἐπὶ τοῦ κοιτῶνος τοῦ βασιλέως, *Blastus the king's chamberlain.* The name Blastus is Roman, and the man had probably taken office under this eastern king because he was high in the favour of the Roman emperor.

ᾐτοῦντο εἰρήνην, *they asked for peace.* We are not to understand from these words that Agrippa was making *war* on Tyre and Sidon, but only that he was on unfriendly terms with them and was impeding their trade.

διὰ τὸ τρέφεσθαι αὐτῶν τὴν χώραν ἀπὸ τῆς βασιλικῆς, *because their country was nourished by the king's country.* The extent of Herod's rule was very great, and if he encouraged another port, and made regulations by which traffic was diverted from the towns of Tyre and Sidon, it was in his power to take away from them at least one-half of the commerce which was their support.

21. τακτῇ δὲ ἡμέρᾳ, *and upon a set day.* The day was one appointed (as Josephus tells us) for holding a festival on which to make vows for the safety of the Roman emperor.

ὁ Ἡρώδης ἐνδυσάμενος ἐσθῆτα βασιλικήν, *Herod having arrayed himself in royal apparel.* See the extract from Josephus given below.

23. παραχρῆμα δὲ ἐπάταξεν αὐτὸν ἄγγελος κυρίου κ.τ.λ., *and immediately an angel of the Lord smote him...and he was eaten of worms.* Cf. the fate of Antiochus Epiphanes (2 Macc. ix. 9), and Herod the Great's death (Josephus, *Ant.* XVII. 6. 5). The passage in which Josephus describes these events is so important in its bearing on the N. Test. narrative that it deserves to be read in its entirety. He writes (*Ant.* XIX. 8. 2), "Now when Agrippa had reigned three years over all Judæa he came to the city Cæsarea, which was formerly called Strato's Tower, and there he exhibited shows in honour of Cæsar, upon his being informed that there was *a certain festival celebrated to make vows for his safety.* At which festival a great multitude was gotten together of the principal persons and such as were of dignity throughout his province. *On the second day of which shows he put on a garment made wholly of silver* and of a con- texture truly wonderful, and came into the theatre early in the morn- ing, at which time the silver of his garment being illuminated by the fresh reflection of the sun's rays upon it, shone out after a surprising manner, and was so resplendent as to spread a dread and shuddering over those that looked intently upon it, and presently his flatterers cried out, one from one place and another from another (though not for his good), that he was a god. And they added, '*Be thou merciful to us,* for although we have hitherto reverenced thee only as a man yet

shall *we henceforth own thee as superior to mortal nature.*' Upon this the King *did neither rebuke them nor reject their impious flattery.* But as he presently afterwards looked up he saw an owl sitting upon a certain rope over his head, and immediately understood that this bird was the messenger of ill tidings, as it had once been the messenger of good tidings to him, and fell into the deepest sorrow. A violent pain also arose in his belly, having begun with great severity. He therefore looked upon his friends and said, 'I whom you call a god, *am commanded presently to depart this life,* while Providence thus reproves the lying words you just now said to me; and I who was called by you immortal, *am immediately to be hurried away by death.* But I am bound to accept what *Providence allots as it pleases God,* for we have by no means lived ill, but in a splendid and happy manner.' *When he had said this his pain became violent.* Accordingly he was carried into the palace, and the rumour went abroad everywhere that *he would certainly die in a little time......* And when he had been quite worn out by the pain in his bowels for five days he departed this life."

We can see from this extract that among the throng who flattered Herod, there were some who were suing for *mercy* to be shewn to them; that the day was a *set day,* that Herod was *clad in royal robes,* that the flattery consisted in *calling him a god,* that *he did not rebuke* them; that he was *stricken immediately* so that he had to be carried to his palace, that he acknowledged that the *stroke came from God as a rebuke for accepting such flattery,* and everybody expected him to *die at once.*

With reference to the latter portion in which Josephus speaks of a violent pain increasing in vehemence very rapidly, and the N. Test. says he was eaten of worms, it is noticeable that, in the account of the death of Antiochus, already alluded to, we have these two features of the same disease mentioned and that they are described separately. First, 2 Macc. ix. 5, 'The Lord Almighty, the God of Israel, smote him with an incurable and invisible plague, for as soon as he had spoken these words a pain of the bowels that was remediless came upon him and sore torments of the inner parts.' Then after a verse or two describing the pride of Antiochus we read, 'So that the worms rose up out of the body of this wicked man.'

Josephus (by whom Herod, as one who favoured Jews, was regarded as of no bad character, and was moreover looked upon with an eye of admiration as having been raised to the highest pitch of power through Roman influence, to which Josephus himself was very ready to pay court) has merely described the form in which the malady made itself apparent at first, and has left out the more loathsome details from the death story of one who in his eyes was a great king : while Holy Writ has given the fuller account, because the object of the writer of the Acts was to emphasize in all its enormity the sin for which Josephus tells us that Herod himself felt that he was stricken. The points of accord in the two accounts are so many, and the difference so slight and so easy to be accounted for, that this extract from Josephus must always be regarded as a most weighty testimony to the historic accuracy and faithfulness of St Luke's narrative. For other instances of death by this loathsome malady, see Herodotus ɪᴠ. 205; Eusebius ᴠɪɪɪ. 16; Tertullian *ad Scapul.* ɪɪɪ. A similar account is given of the death of Philip II. of Spain.

24. ὁ δὲ λόγος τοῦ θεοῦ ηὔξανεν καὶ ἐπληθύνετο, *but the word of God grew and multiplied.* Cf. vi. 7 and xix. 20. 'The seed is the word,' said Christ, and so the Christian historian tells us that the word was as seed,—when it was cast forth diligently it waxed and brought forth fruit.

25. ὑπέστρεψαν ἐξ Ἰερουσαλήμ, *returned from Jerusalem,* i.e. to their labours among the Gentile converts in Antioch.

πληρώσαντες τὴν διακονίαν, *when they had fulfilled their ministration.* ἡ διακονία here means the giving into the care of the Church the contributions of the disciples in Antioch for the support of their brethren in Judæa during the famine which Agabus had foretold (xi. 28).

Ἰωάννην, *John.* See above on verse 12.

CHAPTER XIII.

Readings varying from the *Text. recept.*

1. τινες omitted with אABD. Unrepresented in *Vulg.*

4. αὐτοὶ for οὗτοι with אAB. *Vulg.* 'ipsi.'

6. ὅλην added before τὴν νῆσον with אABCDE. *Vulg.* 'universam insulam.'

9. καὶ before ἀτενίσας omitted with אABCL. Not represented in *Vulg.*

15. εἴ τις ἔστιν ἐν υμῖν λόγος with אABC. *Vulg.* 'si quis est in vobis sermo.'

18. ἐτροφοφόρησεν for ἐτροποφόρησεν with ACE. *Vulg.* 'mores eorum sustinuit.'

19. αὐτοῖς omitted after κατεκληρονόμησεν with אBD. *Vulg.* has 'eis.'

20. ὡς ἔτεσιν τετρακοσίοις καὶ πεντήκοντα. καὶ μετὰ ταῦτα with אABC. Supported by *Vulg.*

25. τί ἐμὲ for τίνα με with אAB. *Vulg.* 'Quem me.'

33. τοῖς τέκνοις ἡμῶν with אABCD. *Vulg.* 'filiis nostris.'

ἐν τῷ πρώτῳ ψαλμῷ with D. *Vulg.* 'in Psalmo secundo.' But see notes.

40. ἐφ' ὑμᾶς omitted with אBD. *Vulg.* 'vobis.'

42. ἐξιόντων δὲ αὐτῶν for ἐξιόντων δὲ ἐκ τῆς συναγωγῆς τῶν Ἰουδαίων with ℵABCDEI. *Vulg.* 'exeuntibus autem illis.'

τὰ ἔθνη omitted with ℵACDI. Unrepresented in *Vulg.*

44. κυρίου for θεοῦ with ℵAB. *Vulg.* 'Dei.'

50. καὶ before τὰς εὐσχήμονας omitted with ℵABCD. *Vulg.* 'et.'

51. αὐτῶν omitted with ℵABC. Unrepresented in *Vulg.*

Ch. XIII. 1—12. Beginning of Saul's First Missionary Journey. He visits Cyprus.

1. ἦσαν δὲ ἐν Ἀντιοχείᾳ κατὰ τὴν οὖσαν ἐκκλησίαν, *now there were at Antioch in the Church which was there.*

We now come to the history of those three great journeys which the Apostle of the Gentiles undertook in his special work. It is fitting that the point of departure should be Antioch, the city in which Gentiles had first in large numbers been joined to the Church, and where as yet there had risen no difficulty about the way in which they were received.

προφῆται καὶ διδάσκαλοι, *prophets and teachers.* Cf. ii. 17. The words of Joel were now to receive a wider fulfilment.

We see from the 'Teaching of the Twelve Apostles,' chap. xiii. that these two classes of instructors became recognized in the Church. πᾶς δὲ προφήτης ἀληθινός, θέλων καθῆσαι πρὸς ὑμᾶς, ἄξιός ἐστι τῆς τροφῆς αὐτοῦ, ὡς αὕτως διδάσκαλος ἀληθινός ἐστιν ἄξιος καὶ αὐτός, ὥσπερ ὁ ἐργάτης, τῆς τροφῆς αὐτοῦ.

Συμεὼν ὁ καλούμενος Νίγερ, *Simeon that was called Niger.* The first name points out the man as of Jewish origin, and the second is a Latin adjective = *black*, which may have been assumed, or given to him, as a name from his dark complexion. Jews were, and are still, in the habit of having another name beside their national one, for use when they mixed among foreign nations.

Λούκιος ὁ Κυρηναῖος, *Lucius of Cyrene.* This name is Latin, though his birthplace or home may indicate that he was one of the Jews who abounded in Cyrene and other parts of northern Africa. Perhaps he is the person mentioned Rom. xvi. 21.

Μαναήν, *Manaen*, i.e. Menahem. The name is Jewish, and is found in Josephus (*Ant.* xv. 10. 5) as the name of an Essene who foretold that Herod the Great would become king. It may well be that the name became, when the prophecy had received its fulfilment, a favourite one among those who were attached to or favoured the rulers of the Herodian family.

Ἡρώδου τοῦ τετράρχου σύντροφος, *the foster-brother of Herod the tetrarch.* The *Vulg.* gives 'collectanus.' Herod the tetrarch (Antipas) had a brother Archelaus by the same mother. Manaen would hardly be said to have 'been brought up with' (as A.V.) one brother and not with the other.

The various connections and nationalities of the men who are here named are worthy to be noticed when we reflect on the work which was to have its beginning from Antioch. One a Cypriote, another a Cyrenian, another a Jew, but from his double name accustomed to mix among non-Jews, one a connection of the Idumean house of Herod, and Saul, the heaven-appointed Apostle of the Gentiles,—the list may be deemed in some sort typical of 'all the world,' into which the Gospel was now to go forth.

2. λειτουργούντων δὲ αὐτῶν τῷ κυρίῳ, *and as they ministered to the Lord.* The verb λειτουργέω is the one usually employed by the LXX. for the ministerial services in the Temple, as it is also Heb. x. 11, but the parallelism with the next verse, where the service here mentioned is described as 'fasting and *prayer*,' shews us that we are not to attach the former strict signification to it. Such has been the mind of the Church also, for from this verb comes our word 'Liturgy.' The old order is giving place to the new, and the terminology is receiving a new sense.

καὶ νηστευόντων, *and fasted,* i.e. as a solemn act of devotion in the prospect of the work which was before them.

εἶπεν τὸ πνεῦμα τ. ἅ., *the Holy Ghost said,* speaking to and through the prophets who were there.

ἀφορίσατε δή μοι κ.τ.λ., *separate me Barnabas and Saul.* Saul had from the first been a 'vessel of election,' and so specially severed for this work, and we can see why Barnabas, who had been the first to introduce Saul to the Church at Jerusalem, and whose education may have been very like his own, (for there was much inter-communication between Cyprus and Tarsus,) was appointed to be the sharer of Saul's labours.

The verb ἀφορίζω is used in the LXX. (Numb. viii. 11) of the *separation* of the Levites for God's service, and (Exod. xiii. 12) of living things specially devoted to the Lord.

εἰς τὸ ἔργον κ.τ.λ., *for the work whereunto I have called them.* As the one portion of this admonition was from the Holy Ghost, we may perhaps be warranted in concluding that the whole course of this first great missionary journey was pointed out also by the Spirit. There is no notice of a deliberation in the Church about the best way for the Apostles to set forth.

ὃ προσκέκλημαι. It is usual in Greek not to repeat with the relative the preposition which stands before the antecedent. Cf. Luke xii. 46, ἥξει ὁ κύριος τοῦ δούλου ἐκείνου ἐν ἡμέρᾳ ᾗ οὐ προσδοκᾷ. The middle force of προσκέκλημαι though not possible to be represented in a translation should not be lost sight of. The Holy Ghost says 'I have called them *for myself.*'

3. τότε νηστεύσαντες. This verse indicates that there was a solemn dedication service at the end of the ministration and fasting with which the devotions of the Church had commenced.

4. ἐκπεμφθέντες ὑπὸ τοῦ ἁγίου πνεύματος, *sent forth by the Holy Ghost.* This repetition marks the solemn character which St Luke and also his informant attached to this new form which the Christian work was taking.

εἰς Σελεύκειαν, *unto Seleucia*, which was the seaport of Antioch at the mouth of the river Orontes.

ἀπέπλευσαν εἰς Κύπρον, *they sailed to Cyprus.* Probably, if not specially directed, the missionary Apostles were induced to take this route because Cyprus was the birthplace of one of them, and there were in the island already many Jews resident, and also some Cypriote Christians (xi. 20), who perhaps had been in Jerusalem at the feast of Pentecost among the various nationalities then assembled, and who had, when driven away by persecution, turned their steps homeward and preached Jesus to their fellow countrymen (xi. 19).

5. γενόμενοι ἐν Σαλαμῖνι, *when they were at Salamis.* Salamis was the nearest port of Cyprus for voyagers from Seleucia. It is at the eastern end of the island in the bay which is now called Famagousta.

ἐν ταῖς συναγωγαῖς τῶν Ἰουδαίων, *in the synagogues of the Jews*, who were in sufficient numbers in Salamis to need several synagogues.

εἶχον δὲ καὶ Ἰωάννην ὑπηρέτην, *and they had also John as their minister.* This is John Mark, the nephew of Barnabas (see on xii. 12). His office may have been to baptize, from which service the Apostles seem to have refrained where it was possible (see above on x. 48). But there is perhaps also implied in the word ὑπηρέτης some degree of the same service which in old times Elisha rendered to Elijah (2 Kings iii. 11). The same Greek word is used for the minister in a synagogue (Luke iv. 20).

6. διελθόντες δὲ ὅλην τὴν νῆσον ἄχρι Πάφου, *and when they had gone through the whole island unto Paphos.* Probably teaching at other places in the same way as they had done in Salamis. Paphos was the capital of Cyprus, and therefore the residence of the Roman governor. It was the more modern city, not the old city of Paphos, to which Paul and Barnabas came. See *Dictionary of the Bible.*

εὗρον ἄνδρα τινὰ μάγον ψευδοπροφήτην Ἰουδαῖον, *they found a certain man, a magician, a false prophet, a Jew.* That there were living among the Jews persons well known as pretenders to magic powers we can see from a story told T. B. *Berakhoth* 59 a, of a certain Rab Katina who, in his walk, as he was passing the door of one who was known as a professor of witchcraft and magic arts, felt a slight shock of an earthquake. He thereupon called out and asked 'Does this wizard diviner know what that shock is?' Upon this the man cried with a sanctimonious promptness worthy of his profession, 'In the hour when the Holy One, blessed be He, remembers His children who dwell in sorrow among the nations of the world, He lets fall two tears into the great sea, and that is the cause of the tremor of the earth.' Chaldæan astrologers and impostors are mentioned by Juvenal (vi. 562, xiv. 248) and Horace (*Sat.* i. 2. 1) and by many other Latin writers, and these were probably Babylonian Jews. So also Lucian, *Necromantia*, where a wonderful story is told of a magician named Mithrobarzanes. Also Lucian, *Philopseudes*, where one of the wonder-workers is called 'A Syrian from Palestine.'

Βαρίησοῦς, *Bar-Jesus*. This was his Jewish name. The Arabic name or title, *Elymas* = wise, was a self-assumed designation; and for that reason he is called 'Magus' = the magician, a name originally applied to the Persian priests, who were deemed the *wise* men of the realm both in policy and religion, though their title in after times was degraded to baser arts and persons.

7. ὃς ἦν σὺν τῷ ἀνθυπάτῳ Σεργίῳ Παύλῳ, *which was with the pro-consul Sergius Paulus*. Under Augustus the Roman provinces were divided into two classes, one class of which (needing the presence of troops for their government, and the possession of which gave the emperor the control of the army) was called imperatorial, while the others were called senatorial provinces. The former were governed by an officer named *propraetor*, the latter by a *proconsul*. We know from Dio Cassius (LIII. 12) that Cyprus was originally an imperatorial province, and therefore under a propraetor. This also Strabo confirms (XIV. 685), but says that Augustus made it over to the people along with Cyprus and part of Galatia, and took instead of these Dalmatia for one of his provinces, so that the government was at St Paul's visit held by a *proconsul* for the Roman senate, as is here recorded; and this is another instance of the historic faithfulness of St Luke's record.

Of Sergius Paulus we know nothing, but the opportunities now afforded, by the English occupation of Cyprus, for the investigation of the antiquities of the island, may lead to some discovery of his name and office in coin or description.

ἀνδρὶ συνετῷ, *a prudent man*. The presence of such a man as Elymas among his staff shews that the proconsul was a man of inquiring mind, and the same characteristic is displayed by his desire to hear Barnabas and Saul.

8. ζητῶν διαστρέψαι τὸν ἀνθύπατον ἀπὸ τῆς πίστεως, *seeking to turn aside the proconsul from the faith*. Sergius had not yet accepted the doctrine of the Apostles, though we may presume that both he and Elymas had heard much about their teaching since their landing at Salamis. Report going before had roused the proconsul's curiosity and the magician's fear, and the wish of the latter was to divert the attention of Sergius, that he might not send for the new teachers.

On this Chrysostom has: ὅρα τοῦτον, ὅτε μὲν τοῖς ἄλλοις ἐκήρυττον οὐ σφόδρα ἀγανακτοῦντα, ἐπειδὴ δὲ τῷ ἀνθυπάτῳ προσίεσαν τότε. τὸ δὲ θαυμαστὸν τοῦ ἀνθυπάτου, ὅτι καὶ προκατειλημμένος τῇ μαγείᾳ ἐκείνου ἤθελεν ἀκοῦσαι τῶν ἀποστόλων.

9. Σαῦλος δέ, ὁ καὶ Παῦλος, *but Saul, who also is called Paul*. In spite of Elymas, the proconsul had been determined in his purpose, and Saul had come before him. At this point we first meet the name by which the great Apostle is best known throughout the Christian

THE ACTS

Church, and many reasons have been given why he assumed this name, and why at this time. Some have thought that the name was adopted from the proconsul's, his first convert of distinction, but this is utterly alien to all we know of the character of St Paul, with his sole glory in the cross of Christ. Far more likely is he to have been attracted to it, if it were not his before, by the meaning of the Latin word (*paullus* = little, see Ter. *And.* 1. 5. 31; *Adelph.* 5. 4. 22), and its fitness to be the name of him who called himself the *least* of the Apostles. But perhaps he did only what other Jews were in the habit of doing when they went into foreign lands, and chose him a name of some significance (for the Jews were fond of names with a meaning) among those with whom he was about to mix. Dean Howson (*Life and Letters of St Paul*, 1. p. 164) compares Joses — Jason; Hillel — Iulus, and probably the similarity of sound did often guide the choice of such a name, and it may have been so with the Apostle's selection. St Luke, recognizing that the history of St Paul is now to be his chief theme and that the work for which that Apostle was separated was now begun, names him henceforth only by the name which became most current in the Churches.

The article ὁ before καὶ belongs to the understood καλούμενος, and is not to be considered a substitute for the relative.

πλησθεὶς πνεύματος ἁγίου, *filled with the Holy Ghost.* So we learn that the punishment inflicted on Elymas was dictated to the Apostle by the Spirit, and that he knew, from the inward prompting thereof, what would be the result to the offender.

ἀτενίσας εἰς αὐτὸν εἶπεν, *fastened his eyes on him and said.* For Elymas was standing by, ready to catch at anything which he could turn to the discredit of the Apostles. This is meant by St Paul's rebuke of him, as διαστρέφων τὰς ὁδοὺς κυρίου τὰς εὐθείας.

10. ἐχθρὲ πάσης δικαιοσύνης, *enemy of all righteousness.* We may judge from this expression that St Paul recognised an earnest zeal for truth in the inquiries of the proconsul, and that his wrath against Elymas was not only because of what he did at the time, but for the tendency of all his teachings. He had led astray for a long time one who was desirous to understand the ways of the Lord. That there were such anxious inquirers among the Greeks and Romans we can see from the case of Cornelius and his friends. These were sure to seek to Jews for guidance, and in Elymas and such as he they found false guides.

11. χεὶρ κυρίου, *the hand of the Lord*, i.e. of that Jehovah whose ways Elymas had perverted, for it could only have been after the Jewish faith that Sergius Paulus had made his inquiries of Elymas, who instead of teaching him to know the Lord, seduced him by his own pretensions.

For the expression cf. LXX. Exod. ix. 3, ἰδοὺ χεὶρ κυρίου ἐπέσται ἐν τοῖς κτήνεσί σου, and 1 Sam. xii. 15, καὶ ἔσται χεὶρ κυρίου ἐφ' ὑμᾶς.

τυφλὸς μὴ βλέπων, *blind, not seeing.* As the infliction is still in the future, and so only a conception in the mind of St Paul, however firmly settled, it is reasonable to use the subjective negative μὴ. Cf.

for an exactly similar expression Luke i. 20, σιωπῶν καὶ μὴ δυνάμενος λαλῆσαι.

ἄχρι καιροῦ, *for a season.* The punishment inflicted on Elymas is lighter than that of Ananias and Sapphira, because in their case the hypocrisy of their conduct would have brought ruin to the Church, if it had not been severely punished, and their sin was against greater light and gifts of grace than had been bestowed on the magician of Cyprus.

ἀχλὺς καὶ σκότος, *a mist and a darkness.* There is a gradation in the words which implies that the withdrawal of his sight was somewhat gradual. At first the eyes began to cloud over, and as the film increased upon them he became quite blind.

καὶ περιάγων ἐζήτει χειραγωγούς, *and he went about seeking some to lead him by the hand.*

περιάγειν = to lead about, is also used in N.T. in the intransitive sense, 'to go about,' cf. Mark vi. 6, καὶ περιῆγεν τὰς κώμας κύκλῳ διδάσκων.

χειραγωγός is rare, and only here in N.T. The verb is found in the LXX. (some texts) Judges xvi. 26.

As Elymas perceives the darkness closing in upon him he turns in the direction where he had last noticed some friend, and endeavours to get a guide. For such a man would wish to shew as little as possible how exactly the Apostle's words had come to pass.

12. τότε ἰδὼν ὁ ἀνθύπατος κ.τ.λ., *then the deputy, when he saw what was done, believed.* He was convinced by the miracle and by the words with which it was accompanied that the Apostles were teachers of that way of the Lord after which he had been seeking in vain from Elymas. We are not told that Sergius was baptized, but we have other instances of the like omission of notice (see verse 48), yet as baptism was the appointed door into Christ's Church, such omission of the mention thereof should not be thought to warrant us in believing that the sacrament was neglected on any occasion.

13—15. THE APOSTLES VISIT PAMPHYLIA AND PISIDIA. JOHN MARK RETURNS TO JERUSALEM.

13. ἀναχθέντες δὲ ἀπὸ τῆς Πάφου, *now having sailed from Paphos.* Their course would be N.W. to reach the south coast of Asia Minor.

On the prompt departure from Paphos, Chrysostom says: ὅρα καὶ αὐτοὺς οὐκ ἐγχρονίζοντας αὐτόθι ἅτε τοῦ ἀνθυπάτου λοιπὸν πιστεύσαντος οὐδὲ μαλακισθέντας τῇ κολακείᾳ καὶ τῇ τιμῇ, ἀλλ' εὐθέως τοῦ ἔργου ἐχομένους καὶ τὴν ἀντίπεραν χώραν ὁρμῶντας.

οἱ περὶ Παῦλον, *Paul and his company.* Literally 'those around Paul.' Henceforth the Apostle of the Gentiles is made the central figure of nearly every scene in the Acts.

ἦλθον εἰς Πέργην τῆς Παμφυλίας, *they came to Perga in Pamphylia.* Pamphylia was about the middle part of the southern seaboard of Asia Minor, and Perga was its capital. We are not told of any missionary labours in Perga at this time, either because there was no opening for their commencement, or it may be that the Apostles were troubled at the departure of Mark. They did preach in Perga on their return visit (xiv. 25).

Ἰωάννης δὲ κ.τ.λ., *and John departing from them returned to Jerusalem.* There is no reason given for his departure either here or elsewhere, but the cause assigned had clearly not been one which satisfied St Paul (xv. 38). John Mark, most probably the same person as the writer of the second Gospel, afterwards was an earnest labourer for Christ, and St Paul (Col. iv. 10) speaks of him with affection. If St Luke knew the cause of his present withdrawal, the remembrance of his subsequent zeal sealed his lips on the subject. Cf. x. 48 note.

14. αὐτοὶ δὲ διελθόντες ἀπὸ τῆς Πέργης, *but they having passed through from Perga.* διέρχομαι is a very correct expression and should be precisely rendered. The direction in which they went obliged them to cross a whole district. See below.

εἰς Ἀντιόχειαν τὴν Πισιδίαν, *to Antioch in Pisidia.* Pisidia lay inland to the N. of Pamphylia, and Antioch was at its extreme northern point.

Dean Howson (*Life and Epistles of St Paul,* i. 175) suggests that it was perhaps in this journey that St Paul and his companion were exposed to those 'perils of robbers' of which he speaks 2 Cor. xi. 26. Pisidia was a mountainous district rising gradually towards the north, and the quotations given by Dr Howson from Xenophon and Strabo shew that there was a great deal of brigand-like life even in these times, from which Paul and his company may have been in danger.

εἰς τὴν συναγωγήν, *into the synagogue.* Though he is the Apostle of the Gentiles, it is always to the synagogue that St Paul first makes his way. The Law of Moses ought to be a better schoolmaster to bring men to Christ than the law of nature.

15. μετὰ δὲ τὴν ἀνάγνωσιν τοῦ νόμου καὶ τῶν προφητῶν, *and after the reading of the Law and the Prophets.* Which was a prominent portion of the synagogue-service. For the better understanding of what was here done, and also at the time when our Lord 'stood up for to read' in the synagogue at Nazareth (Luke iv. 15) it seems worth while to give in detail an account of the manner in which the Scriptures are read in the Jewish synagogues. For this see the Excursus at the end of this chapter.

ἀπέστειλαν οἱ ἀρχισυνάγωγοι πρὸς αὐτούς, *the rulers of the synagogue sent unto them.* These were the persons who had the control of the arrangements for calling up readers and preachers.

εἴ τις ἔστιν ἐν ὑμῖν λόγος παρακλήσεως, *if ye have any word of exhortation.* The sense of λόγος παρακλήσεως is well seen from Heb. xiii. 22, where the writer calls his whole epistle by that name. λόγοι παρακλήσεως are spoken of 1 Macc. x. 24, where the A.V. renders 'words of encouragement,' while a similar expression, ἡ ἐν τοῖς ἀγαθοῖς λόγοις παράκλησις (2 Macc. xv. 11), is rendered 'comfortable and good words.'

16—41. PAUL'S SPEECH AT ANTIOCH.

16. κατασείσας τῇ χειρί, *beckoning with his hand.* Cf. xii. 17, where it is explained that the gesture was for the purpose of procuring silence.

ἄνδρες Ἰσραηλῖται καὶ οἱ φοβούμενοι τὸν θεόν, *men of Israel and ye that fear God.* The audience consisted of born Jews and proselytes as well as perhaps some Gentiles. (See verses 42 and 43.) When the audience and the subject and the end aimed at were so entirely in accord on all three occasions we cannot be surprised that the address of St Paul at Antioch partakes largely of the character, and also of the language, of those of St Peter at Pentecost and St Stephen in his defence. St Paul had heard the last of these, and the vision on the way to Damascus had taught him to speak with boldness on the truth of the Resurrection.

17. ὁ θεὸς...τοὺς πατέρας ἡμῶν, *the God of this people of Israel chose our fathers.* He commends his words to their hearing by dwelling on the historic facts of their national life as God's chosen people. In that history the LXX. continually represents God's choice of Israel by this word ἐξελέξατο. Cf. Deut. vii. 7, xiv. 2; Ps. xxxiii. 12, lxxvii. 70, &c.

ἐν τῇ παροικίᾳ, *when they dwelt as strangers.* The expression occurs Wisdom xix. 10, ἐμέμνηντο γὰρ ἔτι τῶν ἐν τῇ παροικίᾳ αὐτῶν, where the allusion is to the sojourn in Egypt. In the LXX. of Ezra it is also found (viii. 35), οἱ υἱοὶ τῆς παροικίας, of those who were in Babylon.

18. ἐτροφοφόρησεν αὐτούς, *He bare them as a nursing father.* This is the expression in Deut. i. 31, where the LXX. have rendered, καὶ ἐν τῇ ἐρήμῳ ταύτῃ...ὡς τροφοφορήσει σε κύριος ὁ θεός σου ὡς εἴ τις τροφοφορήσαι ἄνθρωπος τὸν υἱὸν αὐτοῦ. The allusion of St Paul is so clearly to this passage that there can be no hesitation about the choice of reading. ἐτροποφόρησεν is well supported by MS. authority, and is represented in the A.V., and in the text of the Revised Version, 'he suffered their manners.' But for this reading, true as it is to the facts, there is no such close parallel to be found in the books of Moses, while the other is equally true to fact, much more beautiful, and borne out by the words of the LXX., with which we can have no doubt that St Paul was very familiar.

19. ἔθνη ἑπτά, *seven nations.* They are enumerated (Deut. vii. 1) before the people went over Jordan, viz. the Hittites, the Girgashites, the Amorites, the Canaanites, the Perizzites, the Hivites, and the Jebusites.

κατεκληρονόμησεν τὴν γῆν αὐτῶν ὡς ἔτεσιν κ.τ.λ., *he gave their land for an heritage about the space of four hundred and fifty years.* According to the received chronology there was about this length of time between the call of Abraham and the death of Joshua. So that the land is regarded as a κληρονομία from that early time. But it is dangerous to found any conclusions on chronology based, as the O.T. chronology must be, on such insufficient data.

καὶ μετὰ ταῦτα ἔδωκεν κριτὰς ἕως Σαμουὴλ προφήτου, *and after these things He gave them judges until Samuel the prophet.* On Samuel as *the prophet* above all others cf. iii. 24, note.

21. κἀκεῖθεν, *and after that.* The word indicates *from that point* in their history where Samuel appears they began to clamour for a king, and thus the local becomes a temporal meaning in the adverb.

τὸν Σαοὺλ υἱὸν Κείς, ἄνδρα ἐκ φυλῆς Βενιαμείν, *Saul the son of Kish, a man of the tribe of Benjamin.* And to the speaker himself some part of this description applied, for he also was of the tribe of Benjamin.

The forty years' duration of Saul's reign is only to be gathered indirectly from Holy Writ, but Josephus (*Ant.* VI. 14. 9) expressly states that time as the length of his reign, and as Ishbosheth, Saul's son, whom Abner set on the throne after his father's death was forty years old when he began to reign (2 Sam. ii. 10), we may conclude that the length assigned in the text is correct.

22. εὗρον Δαυεὶδ κ.τ.λ., *I have found David, &c.* This sentence is a combination and adaptation from two separate verses out of the O. Test. (1) 'I have found David my servant,' Ps. lxxxix. 20; (2) 'The Lord hath sought Him a man after His own heart, and the Lord hath commanded him to be captain over His people,' 1 Sam. xiii. 14.

23. τούτου ὁ θεὸς...κατ' ἐπαγγελίαν ἤγαγεν...Ἰησοῦν, *from this man's seed hath God according to promise brought unto Israel a Saviour Jesus.* The promise alluded to here is preserved for us in Ps. cxxxii. 11 'Of the fruit of thy body will I set upon thy seat,' and in many other similar declarations in the prophets. Cf. Zech. iii. 8, 9.

24. πρὸ προσώπου is only the rendering of the Hebrew לִפְנֵי = *at the face of,* and means no more than πρό, and the A.V. has rightly rendered it only by *before.*

βάπτισμα μετανοίας, *the baptism of repentance,* i.e. baptism which was to be an outward sign of an inner change of life and mind. Cf. Mark i. 4.

25. τί ἐμὲ ὑπονοεῖτε εἶναι, *what think ye that I am?* For John's words see Matth. iii. 11; Mark i. 7; Luke iii. 16; John i. 20, 27.

26. οἱ ἐν ὑμῖν φοβούμενοι τὸν θεόν. Cf. above on verse 16.

ὑμῖν ὁ λόγος...ἐξαπεστάλη, *to you was the word of this salvation sent forth.* Some of the oldest authorities read ἡμῖν here, and for the Apostle to say 'to us' is quite in accord with the language of verse 17, 'God chose *our* fathers.' Through the whole address he avoids, as far as may be, wounding any Jewish prejudice, and so classes himself with his hearers where the subject allows him to do so.

In λόγος σωτηρίας the reference is to the σωτήρ mentioned in verse 23, so that the meaning is 'the message of the work of Jesus as Saviour.'

There appears to be a reference in the aorist ἐξαπεστάλη to the first announcement of the message of salvation.

27. τοῦτον ἀγνοήσαντες, *because they knew Him not.* Cf. the very similar language of St Peter at the Temple (iii. 17), 'I wot that through ignorance ye did it, as did also your rulers,' and see note there.

28. καὶ μηδεμίαν αἰτίαν θανάτου εὑρόντες, *and though they found no cause of death in Him.* These words are part of the declaration of Pilate (Luke xxiii. 22).

29. πάντα τὰ περὶ αὐτοῦ γεγραμμένα, *all the things which have been written of Him.* Various prophecies received their fulfilment in Christ's sufferings, some in the betrayal, others in harsh treatment, and agony which preceded His death, the greatest of them all.

30. ὁ δὲ θεὸς ἤγειρεν αὐτὸν ἐκ νεκρῶν, *but God raised Him from the dead.* This was the proof that God had now fulfilled the promise made unto Abraham and to David, that of their seed should one come, in whom all the nations of the earth should be blessed, even as St Paul says below, by being justified from all things, from which they could not be justified by the law of Moses. And elsewhere (Rom. i. 4) the Apostle says that Jesus 'was declared to be the Son of God with power, according to the spirit of holiness, *by the resurrection from the dead.*'

31. ἀπὸ τῆς Γαλιλαίας, *from Galilee.* The Apostles, and the main body of Christ's followers, were drawn from Galilee, in so much that, before the Crucifixion, Galilæans was a name by which they were known (Mark xiv. 70).

οἵτινες νῦν εἰσὶν μάρτυρες αὐτοῦ, *who now are His witnesses.* St Paul has not mentioned the Ascension of Jesus, but when he says that *now* men are His witnesses, it is implied that Christ was no longer on earth for men to see Him. The Apostle also thus marks out what was the especial work of those who had companied with Jesus during His life.

32. καὶ ἡμεῖς ὑμᾶς εὐαγγελιζόμεθα, *and we declare unto you glad tidings.* While the companions of Jesus are to be His witnesses, we are His Evangelists, the bringers of the good news of His salvation.

τὴν...ἐπαγγελίαν..., *of the promise which was made unto the fathers.* Thus ἐπαγγελίαν becomes the direct object of the verb εὐαγγελιζόμεθα.

33. ὅτι ταύτην ὁ θεὸς ἐκπεπλήρωκεν. Render, *how that God hath completely fulfilled this.* The 'glad tidings' are about the promise, and the precise message which is the cause for gladness is contained in the announcement that the promise has been fulfilled, and the strengthened form of the verb (ἐκπεπλήρωκεν) marks the completeness of this fulfilment.

τοῖς τέκνοις ἡμῶν, *unto our children.* This well-supported reading certainly merits Tischendorf's remark, 'insolenter illud quidem dictum est.' We should naturally expect what the *Text. recept.* has given, 'to

us their children.' But when the complete force of the preceding
verb is taken into account, the sentence may be explained. The
promise was made to Abraham, and generation after generation was
born and passed away, having received the promises only by faith.
Even the generation contemporary with Jesus was not born to the
complete fulfilment, but now after Christ's resurrection Christians
may say 'for our children' the promises are utterly fulfilled.

ἀναστήσας Ἰησοῦν, *in that He hath raised up Jesus again,* i.e. from
the dead. This is necessary to the Apostle's argument, which is on
the resurrection of Jesus as a proof that He was the Messiah. The
quotation which follows need not refer alone to the birth of Jesus into
this world. He was also the *first-begotten* from the dead, the firstfruits of them that slept.

ἐν τῷ πρώτῳ ψαλμῷ, *in the first Psalm.* What we now call the
first and second Psalms were originally joined into one, which will
account for what is now Ps. ii. 7 being named as in the text. Justin
Martyr (*Apol.* I. 40) treats the whole from μακάριος ἀνήρ ('Blessed is
the man' &c.) to μακάριοι πάντες οἱ πεποιθότες ἐπ' αὐτόν (the close of the
present second Psalm) as all one composition and on one subject. So
Tertullian (*Adv. Marc.* IV. 22) writes 'in primo psalmo, "filius meus
es tu, hodie genui te."'

34. οὕτως εἴρηκεν, *He* [i.e. God] *hath spoken on this wise.* The
quotation is from Is. lv. 3.

δώσω ὑμῖν τὰ ὅσια Δαευὶδ τὰ πιστά, *I will give you the sure
(faithful) mercies of David.* τὰ ὅσια is often used by the LXX. to represent the Hebrew word for 'mercies' as here. St Paul speaking to the
people of Antioch no doubt used the Greek version, though he would
carry the Hebrew thought along with him. But having τὰ ὅσια as the
explanation of the 'everlasting covenant' of which Isaiah is speaking,
St Paul at once connects τὰ ὅσια with the τὸν ὅσιον of Ps. xvi. 10,
where it is said God will not give *His Holy One* to see corruption.

35. διότι καὶ ἐν ἑτέρῳ λέγει, *because He saith also in another place.*
These words of Ps. xvi., which David was inspired to utter, cannot
refer to David himself, and this St Paul now proceeds to shew. Cf.
on the whole passage ii. 29—31 notes.

36. Δαυεὶδ μὲν γὰρ...ἐκοιμήθη, *for David, after he had served his
own generation by the counsel of God, fell on sleep.* There are several
other constructions possible in this verse. Thus βουλῇ might be taken
as dependent on ὑπηρετήσας, 'after that in his own generation he had
served the counsel of God, fell asleep.' Or βουλῇ might be taken after
ἐκοιμήθη, 'he fell asleep by the counsel of God.' But the A.V. seems
preferable. For it must be borne in mind that the contrast which
most aids the Apostle's argument is that, while David's services could
benefit only those among whom he lived, and could not be extended
to other generations, Christ by His Resurrection, never more to die
and see corruption, is a Saviour for all generations, and remission of
sins through Him can be promised to every one that believeth.

38.   ἄφεσις ἁμαρτιῶν, *forgiveness of sins.*   Just as Jesus in His life-time on earth declared that His miracles were only signs that 'the Son of man hath power on earth to forgive sins,' so the Apostles preach concerning the Resurrection.   Cf. x. 43, the conclusion of St Peter's speech in the house of Cornelius.

39.   ἀπὸ πάντων ὧν, *from all things from which.*   On the non-repetition of a preposition before the relative when it precedes the antecedent, see note above on verse 2.

40.   μὴ ἐπέλθῃ, *lest there come about,* viz. a moral and spiritual overthrow as great as the destruction which the Chaldæans and Nebuchadnezzar wrought upon the land and people at the time of the Babylonish captivity, to which the prophecy (Hab. i. 5) quoted in the next verse refers.

41.   ἴδετε, οἱ καταφρονηταί, *behold, ye despisers.*   This the render-ing of the LXX. and of some other versions.   The Hebrew text gives, as A.V., 'Behold, ye among the heathen.'   The LXX. either had, or thought they had, a different text.

ἔργον δ οὐ μὴ πιστεύσητε, *a work which ye shall in no wise believe.* It is the result of long-continued evil-doing that those who live in it grow incredulous and proof against all warnings.   Their hearts are allowed to wax gross and their ears to become dull of hearing.

42—52.   FURTHER PREACHING BOTH TO JEWS AND GENTILES.   JEALOUSY OF THE JEWS, AND EXPULSION OF THE APOSTLES FROM ANTIOCH.

42.   ἐξιόντων δὲ αὐτῶν, παρεκάλουν, *and as they were going out, they besought.*   The congregation had been in the synagogue where we may presume that only Jews and proselytes were assembled.   We do not read of Gentiles among the throng of listeners until the next sabbath. The τὰ ἔθνη of the *Text. recept.* makes the verse unintelligible.

εἰς τὸ μεταξὺ σάββατον.   In 44 we have the expression τῷ δὲ ἐρχο-μένῳ σαββάτῳ, and some thinking a difference of meaning intended would render here 'during the intervening week.'   This does not seem needed, but as is pointed out in the Excursus on ver. 15 the Jewish congregations had a portion of the Law read in the synagogues not only on the Sabbath, but on the Monday and on the Thursday mornings, that they might not be for three days without hearing the Scripture.   The peculiar expression in this verse *may* apply to the meetings in the synagogue on those days, when the people desired to hear once more the message which St Paul had just preached to them.

τὰ ῥήματα ταῦτα.   Render, *these tidings,* to mark that the word is not λόγος.   Cf. x. 37.

43.   τῶν σεβομένων προσηλύτων, *of devout proselytes.*   This name may have been used to distinguish those proselytes who conformed entirely to Judaism from the proselytes of the gate.

ἔπειθον αὐτοὺς προσμένειν τῇ χάριτι τοῦ θεοῦ, *persuaded them to continue in the grace of God*, as Barnabas in like circumstances had urged on the converts at Antioch in Syria (xi. 23). Here, though we have no mention of actual converts, the Apostles must have had regard to the 'purpose of their hearts' when they spake to these inquirers as though they were already 'in the grace of God.'

44. σχεδὸν πᾶσα ἡ πόλις, *almost the whole city*. Shewing that the Apostles must have been labouring diligently, both among Jews and heathen during the intervening days.

45. ἐπλήσθησαν ζήλου, *they were filled with jealousy*. That spirit of exclusion, which was so engrafted in the Jewish race, asserted itself as soon as they saw the Gentiles gathered to hear the Apostles. The teaching of men who would admit all mankind to the same privileges was abhorrent to them. For themselves and for proselytes they could accept a message as God-sent, and tolerate some modifications in their teaching and practice, but they could not endure that the Gentiles should be made equal with God's ancient people.

ἀντιλέγοντες καὶ βλασφημοῦντες, *contradicting and blaspheming*. Cf. the singular conduct of the Jews at Corinth under like circumstances (xviii. 6). There is considerable authority for omitting ἀντιλέγοντες καί here. It may be that they fell out because of the previous ἀντέλεγον in the verse. The sense seems better conveyed by their retention. They contradicted and, in doing so, became blasphemers.

46. ὑμῖν ἦν ἀναγκαῖον κ.τ.λ., *it was necessary that the word of God should first have been spoken to you*. That, as Christ came first unto His own, so His messengers should declare their glad tidings first unto Jews, but if they received not the word, then it was to be proclaimed to all who would receive it.

καὶ οὐκ ἀξίους κρίνετε ἑαυτούς, *and adjudge yourselves unworthy*, i.e. you pronounce a sentence upon yourselves by your actions. Cf. Matth. xxii. 8, 'They that were bidden' to the marriage-supper were found in this fashion to be unworthy. He who sent to call them had deemed them worthy, but they made it clear they were not so by their refusal to come.

47. οὕτως γὰρ ἐντέταλται ἡμῖν ὁ κύριος, *for thus hath the Lord commanded us*. The Lord's command which the Apostle quotes is from Isaiah xlix. 6, and it shews that from the prophetic times the reception of the Gentiles was made manifest in the counsels of God. Whatever application be made of the words of the Prophet (i.e. to whomsoever the 'thee' be referred) it is clear that, with the Jews, the Gentiles also are to be recipients of the promised blessings.

48. καὶ ἐπίστευσαν ὅσοι ἦσαν τεταγμένοι εἰς ζωὴν αἰώνιον, *and as many as were ordained unto eternal life believed*. In the controversies on predestination and election this sentence has constantly been brought forward. But it is manifestly unfair to take a sentence out of its context, and interpret it as if it stood alone. In ver. 46 we are told that the Jews had adjudged themselves unworthy of eternal life, and all that is meant by the words in this verse is the opposite of that expression. The Jews were acting so as to proclaim themselves unworthy; the Gentiles were making manifest their desire to be deemed worthy. The two sections were like opposing troops, ranged (τεταγμένοι=marshalled) by themselves, and to some degree, though not unalterably, looked upon as so arranged by God on different sides. Thus the Gentiles were ordering themselves, and were ordered unto eternal life. The text says no word to warrant us in thinking that none could henceforth change sides. Nor is the rendering 'ordained' necessarily an evidence of the Calvinistic bias of our translators. The same rendering is found in other English versions and the Rhemish, strange to say, is even stronger, having 'pre-ordinate.'

50. τὰς σεβομένας γυναῖκας τὰς εὐσχήμονας, *the devout women of honourable estate.* We read that in Damascus, and we may suppose that it was likely to be the case in other large towns and cities in which Jews abounded, the wives of the men in high position among the heathen were much inclined to the Jewish religion (Josephus, *B. J.* II. 20. 2). These would be easily moved by the Jews to take action against the Apostles.

τοὺς πρώτους τῆς πόλεως, *the chief men of the city,* i.e. the heathen magistrates. As the Jews in Jerusalem had appealed to Pilate and the Roman power to carry out their wishes at the Crucifixion, so the Jews in Antioch excite the heathen authorities against Paul and Barnabas.

ἀπὸ τῶν ὁρίων, *from their borders.* The old English word 'coasts' (A.V.) did not mean only land bordering on the sea as now, but any borderland.

51. οἱ δὲ ἐκτιναξάμενοι τὸν κονιορτὸν κ.τ.λ., *but they having shaken off the dust of their feet against them.* This significant action, like that of the 'shaking of the raiment' (xviii. 6), implied that those against whom it was done were henceforth left to go their own way. Cf. Matt. x. 14.

Ἰκόνιον, *Iconium.* A city in Pisidia to the east of Antioch. It is still a large town, and preserves a trace of its old name, being now called Konieh. See *Dict. of the Bible.*

52. οἱ δὲ μαθηταὶ ἐπληροῦντο χαρᾶς, *and the disciples were filled with joy.* Rejoicing in accordance with the Lord's exhortation (Matt. v. 12) when men reviled and persecuted them, which was the very treatment which they had received in Antioch.

καὶ πνεύματος ἁγίου, *and with the Holy Ghost.* This inward presence of the Comforter was the spring from which came the fulness of joy. On this Chrysostom says, πάθος γὰρ διδασκάλου ταρρησίαν οὐκ ἐγκόπτει ἀλλὰ προθυμότερον ποιεῖ τὸν μαθητήν.

ON THE JEWISH MANNER OF READING THE SCRIPTURES.

The Jewish division of the Scriptures is (1) the Law, i.e. the Five Books of Moses. (2) The Prophets, under which title the Jews include Joshua, Judges, 1 and 2 Samuel, 1 and 2 Kings, as well as Isaiah, Jeremiah, Ezekiel, and the twelve Minor Prophets. (3) The Hagiographa, containing Psalms, Proverbs, Job, the Song of Solomon[1], Ruth, Lamentations, Ecclesiastes, Esther, Daniel, Ezra, Nehemiah, and the two Books of Chronicles. The command which enjoins the reading of the Pentateuch is found Deut. xxxi. 10, 'At the end of every seven years in the solemnity of the year of release in the Feast of Tabernacles, when all Israel is come to appear before the Lord thy God in the place which He shall choose, thou shalt read this Law before all Israel in their hearing. Gather the people together, men and women and children and thy stranger that is within thy gates that they may hear.'

This appointment, which prescribes the reading of the *whole* Pentateuch on the Feast of Tabernacles, was probably soon found to be impracticable, and it is not unlikely that from a very early time the people arranged to read through the Pentateuch in seven years by taking a small portion on every Sabbath, beginning with the Sabbath after the Feast of Tabernacles in one year of release, and ending with the Feast of Tabernacles in the next year of release. Thus would they in some sort be fulfilling the commandment. That such an early subdivision of the Pentateuch into small portions took place seems likely from what we know of the later arrangements for the reading of the Law. The existence of such a plan for reading would account for *some* of the divisions which exist (otherwise unexplained) in various copies of the Jewish Law.

For (1) we learn (T. B. *Megillah*, 29 b) that the Jews of Palestine broke up the Pentateuch into sections for each Sabbath in such a manner as to spread the reading thereof over three years (and a half?). They arranged no doubt that the concluding portions of their second reading should be on the Feast of Tabernacles in the year of release; and they began again on the following Sabbath. In this way they read through the whole Law twice in the seven years, and by concluding it on the Feast of Tabernacles in the year of release observed the commandment[2], and hereby may be accounted for some other of the unused subdivisions of the copies of the Jewish Law.

---

[1] The five small books, the Song of Solomon, Ruth, Lamentations, Ecclesiastes and Esther, are for synagogue-use written each on a separate roll, and so are named the five Megilloth (*rolls*) and are read respectively, The Song of Solomon at the Feast of Passover, Ruth at Pentecost, Lamentations on the 9th of Ab (the anniversary of the destruction of the Temple), Ecclesiastes on the Feast of Tabernacles and Esther at Purim.

[2] This arrangement is still observed partially in the Jewish "Temple" at Hamburg, founded in 1818, and there was a little while ago (see *Jewish Chronicle*, Feb. 7, 1879) a movement on foot for introducing a similar arrangement in the West London Synagogue of British Jews.

2. The Babylonian Jews in the 4th century after Christ, and probably much earlier, and all Jews down to this day have the Pentateuch so divided that it is read through *once* every year, such reading
beginning on the Sabbath after the Feast of Tabernacles, and concluding on the so-called last day of that Feast in the next year, the day
really being the day of 'rejoicing in the Law' (*simkhath Torah*). Thus
they bring their reading to an end in each year, and so of course in
the release-year, on the day appointed, and observe the command in
this manner.

This comparatively modern, though almost universally prevailing
arrangement, accounts for the present larger divisions of the Law for
reading, and these divisions have each of them its proper name. For
the whole Pentateuch has 54 weekly portions, one for each Sabbath.
No year however contains 54 Sabbaths, and beside this, some festivals
(or rather, holy convocations) may fall on the Sabbath, and when
that happens the Scripture appointed for the festival is read, and not
the appointed weekly portion in its sequence. In order that the
whole Law may still be read through on the Sabbaths, it is provided
that occasionally two weekly sections are combined and read on one
Sabbath[1].

These weekly sections of the Pentateuch (*Parshioth*) are each divided
into seven portions, and seven readers are called up from the congregation. These are to be (1) an Aaronite (and if such be in the congregation he may not be passed over), (2) a Levite, (3) five ordinary Israelites.
These must all be males and at least 13 years and one day old. Prac-
tically, in Europe at least, though these are still called up in the congregations, they do not themselves read, but a reader is appointed to read
for them. There are congregations in which as a mark of honour
more than seven are called up, but this is discountenanced by some
Rabbis as likely to lead to abuses.

When the reading of the Law in this manner is concluded the
seventh section or part thereof is repeated, and any person may be
asked to do this. Such reader is called *Maphtir*, i.e. the Haphtarist
(the person whose reading terminates the reading of the Law). With
this is connected the subsequent reading of the selected portions of
the Prophets.

In olden times the Haphtarist was also the person invited to be the
preacher, and this must have been the position occupied by St Paul at
Antioch, and by Jesus in the synagogue at Nazareth.

The sections of the Prophets selected for Sabbath reading and called
Haphtaroth have always some bearing upon the appointed portion of
the Law for that Sabbath, e.g. with the first section of Genesis (Gen.
i. 1—vi. 8), which contains the account of the Creation, there is appointed as the prophetical reading the passage (Isaiah xlii. 5—21),
which begins 'Thus saith God the Lord, He that created the heavens,'
&c. With the next section of the Law which contains the history of
Noah (Gen. vi. 8—xi. 32), the prophetical reading is Isaiah liv. 1—10,

---

[1] Of course there will be less need for this arrangement in an intercalated
year, which will have four sabbaths extra.

in which passage is found 'This is as the waters of Noah unto me.'
The next section of the Law (Gen. xii. 1—xvii. 27) contains the history of Abraham, and the reading from the Prophets begins with
Isaiah xl. 27—xli. 16, and in the passage there occurs 'Who raised up
the righteous man from the East, called him to his foot,' &c., and a
like arrangement is observed throughout the year.

On the Sabbath afternoons the Jews in their synagogues read, to
three people, the first seventh of the portion of the Law which is set
apart for the following Sabbath, and they do the same on Monday
morning and on Thursday morning. So that during the week this
part is read four times over.

No prophetic portions are read with this, but (T. B. *Shabbath*,
116 b) in the old times, as early as the commencement of the 3rd
century, we find that on the Sabbath afternoons portions of the Hagiographa were read along with this smaller section of the Law, and we
cannot doubt that the same principle would be observed in their
selection, and that passages similar in character to the selections from
the Pentateuch would be chosen in these cases also, though we have
no indication what they were.[1]

Festivals and Fasts had their own portions of the Pentateuch appointed, and therewith corresponding portions of the Prophets.

On quasi-festival Sabbaths the ordinary portions of the Law were
read, but besides this occasionally other additional portions of the Law
were chosen for the Haphtarist to read with reference to the festival,
and instead of the usual prophetical section appointed for these days,
such passages from the Prophets were chosen as bore on the nature
of the quasi-festival.

These quasi-festivals are
  (1) Should the Sabbath be (*a*) the day before the New Moon, or (*b*)
      the day coincident with the New Moon.
      Partaking of the character of a quasi-festival there is also the so-
      called 'great Sabbath,'[2] which is the Sabbath that precedes the
      Passover. On this day the portion of the Law to be read is
      neither varied nor increased, but as in (1) the appointed Haph-
      tarah is changed for one of a suitable character. The same sort
      of change of the Haphtarah, but not of the portion of the Law
      to be read, takes place for the Sabbath between New Year and
      the Day of Atonement (1—10 of the month Tishri).
  (2) The Maccabæan festival of the Dedication, which as it lasted
      for 8 days might include two Sabbaths.
  (3) Four semi-festivals which are in one string.
      a. The Sabbath preceding the New Moon of Adar, or coinci-
            dent with that New Moon. This is called *Shekalim* (= the
            shekels), and the special portion of the Law then additionally
            read is Exod. xxx. 11—16.

---

[1] Thus would be accounted for many still unexplained divisions in the
Hagiographa.
[2] It may be mentioned that the name 'great Sabbath' is by the Italian Jews
applied also to the Sabbath preceding Pentecost.

    b.   The Sabbath before Purim (the Haman-festival) called *Zacor* = remember, for which the special additional portion of the Law is Deut. xxv. 17—19.

    c.   The Red Heifer Sabbath. This is a moveable feast, but must fall between (*b*) and (*d*). It is a preparation of Purification for Passover, and its special additional portion of the Law is Num. xix.

    d.   *Ha-Khodesh* = the month. The Sabbath preceding or coincident with the New Moon of Nisan, for which the special portion of the Law is Exod. xii. 1—20.

(4) To the above six must be added two Sabbaths if they fall in the middle holidays of the Feasts of Passover and Tabernacles, for such Sabbaths are even of a higher dignity than the other quasi-festivals.

(5) The three Sabbaths before the commemoration of the destruction of the city and Temple by Titus, and its previous destruction by Nebuchadnezzar[1]. On these Sabbaths the portion of the Pentateuch appointed for the day is retained, but prophetic portions are selected which suit the circumstances. These are known as the three Sabbaths [commemorative] of Punishment and Troubles.

(6) Besides these there are seven Sabbaths called 'Sabbaths of Consolation,' for which, in the same way, special prophetic passages are read, which must all be chosen from the latter part of Isaiah (chap. xl. and after), and in one of them probably occurred the passage (Isaiah lxi. 1), read by Jesus in the synagogue at Nazareth[2]. For although at present the Haphtarah from that chapter is marked to begin at verse 10, there are indications in some MSS.[3] that the selected portion formerly commenced at an earlier point, and this for coherence could hardly be elsewhere than at verse 1. It seems probable that in post-Christian times the verses read by our Lord have designedly been cut off from the special prophetic passage. For although any charge against the Jews of altering the *words* of Scripture on account of Christianity must be dismissed as utterly unfounded, it is on the other hand beyond question that they abolished the most ancient and hallowed custom of *reading the ten words* during the morning prayers daily, 'because of the murmuring of the heretics' (*minin*), and by this word (*minin*) the Jews meant the earliest Judæo-Christians (T. B. *Berakhoth* 12 a) who, after Christ's example in the Sermon on the Mount, laid great stress on the Ten Commandments of the Moral Law to the depreciation of ceremonial regulations.

---

[1] Both these events are commemorated on the same day (9th of Ab).

[2] That there is no anachronism in supposing that these 'Sabbaths of Consolation' were observed in our Lord's time may be inferred from the strict way in which the Jewish traditions always identify, in everything but time, the destruction of the two temples by Nebuchadnezzar and by Titus, and the observances in connexion therewith. And we take it as a further proof of the antiquity of this observance that though there are slight variations in the ordinary Haphtaroth, in the various Jewish rituals, those for the 'Sabbaths of Consolation' are the same in all.

[3] See a South-Arabian (*Yemen*) Codex, Brit. Museum MSS. *Oriental* 1470.

CHAPTER XIV.

Readings varying from the *Text. recept.*

3. καί before διδόντι omitted with ABDEP. Not represented in *Vulg.*

8. ὑπάρχων omitted with אABCDE. Unrepresented in *Vulg.*

13. αὐτῶν after πόλεως omitted with אABCDE. Not represented in *Vulg.*

14. ἐξεπήδησαν for εἰσεπήδησαν with אABCDE. *Vulg.* 'exsilierunt.'

17. ἀγαθουργῶν for ἀγαθοποιῶν with אABC.

23. κατ᾽ ἐκκλησίαν πρεσβυτέρους with אABCD. *Vulg.* 'per singulas ecclesias presbyteros.'

28. ἐκεῖ omitted with אABCD. Not represented in *Vulg.*

Ch. xiv. 1—7. Preaching at Iconium. The Apostles forced to flee.

1. κατὰ τὸ αὐτὸ εἰσελθεῖν αὐτοὺς εἰς τὴν συναγωγήν, *that they went both together into the synagogue.* These words probably refer not to one special visit, but to repeated occasions in which Paul and Barnabas appeared as fellow-labourers before the Jewish congregation in Iconium.

For an example of κατὰ τὸ αὐτό in this sense, cf. LXX. 1 Sam. xi. 11, καὶ οὐχ ὑπελείφθησαν ἐν αὐτοῖς δύο κατὰ τὸ αὐτό.

καὶ λαλῆσαι οὕτως, *and so spake,* i.e. on various occasions, on some of which not Jews only but Gentiles were hearers of the word.

Ἑλλήνων, *of the Greeks.* St Luke elsewhere uses Ἕλληνες to mean *Gentiles* and Ἑλληνισταί to mean *Greek-Jews.* But it has been thought that in this verse Ἕλληνες can only mean Greek-Jews, and that the word is here used differently from the other places where it is found in the Acts. Such supposition does not seem necessary. Clearly the visit of the Apostles to Iconium lasted a considerable time, and it is not to be supposed that while there they refrained from speaking the word of their message in any place but in the solitary synagogue. They went, as their wont was, to the synagogue first, that place was the scene of their joint labours on many occasions, and there many of the Jews were won to the faith. But the Apostles spake elsewhere the same glad tidings which they published to the Circumcision, and by this labour many Gentiles also were converted. This seems a simpler explanation than to make St Luke say Ἕλληνες here, when he means Ἑλληνισταί. The verse condenses the account of the Apostolic labours, marks that their commencement was at the synagogue, that Jews became believers, and then without further specification of a place of preaching adds 'and of the Gentiles,' to complete the description of the whole result.

2. **οἱ δὲ ἀπειθήσαντες Ἰουδαῖοι.** Render, *but the Jews that were disobedient.* The same verb is found John iii. 36, where the rendering should be 'he that *obeyeth not* the Son shall not see life.' The word is stronger than 'unbelieving,' it expresses unbelief breaking forth into rebellion, and so exactly describes the character of these Jews who were persecuting Paul and Barnabas. It is noteworthy throughout the Acts that persecution seems nearly in every case to have originated with the Jews.

Cf. for the verb Baruch i. 19, ἕως τῆς ἡμέρας ταύτης ἤμεθα ἀπειθοῦντες πρὸς κύριον θεὸν ἡμῶν, καὶ ἐσχεδιάζομεν πρὸς τὸ μὴ ἀκούειν τῆς φωνῆς αὐτοῦ.

ἐκάκωσαν τὰς ψυχάς, *made their minds evil affected.* The verb is not frequently found in this sense. The precise phrase κακῶσαι τὰς ψυχάς (ψυχήν) is found twice in LXX. (Numb. xxix. 7, xxx. 14), but there it is of affliction put on a person's own soul by a fast or a vow. It is also used (Acts xii. 1) to describe the harm done to the Church by Herod Agrippa. Here it implies not only an ill disposition aroused towards the brethren, but also that injury was done to the minds in which such feeling was stirred up.

3. **ἱκανὸν μὲν οὖν χρόνον διέτριψαν,** *long time therefore abode they.* There are two results described in this and the following verse as the consequences of the Jewish opposition. First, a long stay was necessary that, by the words of the Apostles and by the mighty deeds following wherewith God confirmed them, the faith of the new converts might be fully established before the Apostles departed. Secondly, there came about a division among the people; the Christians and non-Christians became distinctly marked parties.

παρρησιαζόμενοι ἐπὶ τῷ κυρίῳ, *speaking boldly in the Lord.* The preposition implies dependence and rest upon something. The παρρησία of the Apostles came from the Lord, and was sustained by Him. He made them bold by His works of power in support of their message.

τῷ λόγῳ τῆς χάριτος αὐτοῦ, *the word of His grace.* So named because the word of the truth of the Gospel is a message of grace and favour.

4. **οἱ μὲν ἦσαν σὺν τοῖς Ἰουδαίοις,** *part held with the Jews.* For a similar division see the history of the preaching at Thessalonica, xvii. 4, 5. That His word should cause such division had been foretold by Jesus (Luke xii. 51).

5. **ὡς δὲ ἐγένετο ὁρμή,** *but when there was an onset made.* The noun does not necessarily imply that any direct attack had been made, which, from what follows, we can see was not the case. It rather refers to the excitement, urging, and instigation which the Jews were applying to their heathen companions, and which was likely to end in violence. Chrysostom says οὐ γὰρ ἐδιώκοντο, ἀλλ' ἐπολεμοῦντο μόνον.

σὺν τοῖς ἄρχουσιν, *with their rulers.* The religious animosity calling in the civil power, as on other occasions, to work its wishes.

καὶ λιθοβολῆσαι αὐτούς, *and to stone them.* We can see from this that the prompting to violence came from the Jews. Stoning was their punishment for blasphemy, and such they would represent the teaching of the Apostles to be. We need not suppose that any regular legal stoning like that of Stephen was intended, or that to accomplish that object the rulers here mentioned were such Jewish authorities as could be gathered together in Iconium, and that they are indicated by a vague term because they had no very settled position. The previous verb 'to use them despitefully' rather points to the opposite conclusion, and marks the intended proceeding as a piece of mob-outrage, for which the countenance of any authority was gladly welcomed.

In connexion with St Paul's residence at Iconium, there exists a story of the conversion of a maiden named Thecla, of which the apocryphal *Acts of Paul and Thecla* represents the form into which the legend had grown in the fourth century. Thecla, who was espoused to Thamyris, is said to have been deeply affected by the preaching of the Apostle, which she accidentally heard, and when St Paul was put in prison on the accusation of being a magician, she bribed the gaoler and visited the prisoner, and was fully instructed by him in the Christian faith. The Apostle was punished and sent away from Iconium. Thecla was condemned to die for her refusal to marry Thamyris, but was miraculously saved, and after many troubles joined St Paul in his missionary travels, and ultimately made her home in the neighbourhood of Seleucia, where she led the life of a nun till her death, which took place when she was ninety years old.

This story may at first have had some basis of truth to rest on, but it has been so distorted with inconsistent details, that it is impossible now to judge what the foundation of it may have been.

6. συνιδόντες, *they being ware of it.* The Apostles were not without friends among the people, and of the party which sided with them there would be some who could get information about any attack which was being planned against them. It is to be noticed that throughout the history there is no attempt to exaggerate the sufferings of the Christian teachers. Here was a narrow escape from stoning, and as such it is recorded with no more expansion than is absolutely unavoidable.

κατέφυγον...καὶ τὴν περίχωρον, *fled unto the cities of Lycaonia, Lystra and Derbe, and unto the region round about.* From the violence of a mob excited by the Jews they fled into a wilder region where were few or no Jews, and the cities are enumerated in the order in which they were visited, while some to which they went are unnamed but included in the general term 'the region round about.' The flight of the Apostles is exactly in accord with Christ's injunction (Matt. x. 23).

8—18. CURE OF A CRIPPLE AT LYSTRA. THE HEATHEN PEOPLE
REGARD THE APOSTLES AS GODS.

8. ἐν Λύστροις, *at Lystra.* This place lay almost south from Iconium, if the site generally assigned to it, at the foot of the *Kara-dagh*, be the correct one. See *Dict. of the Bible.* It is most probable that this was the home of Timothy. We cannot conclude this absolutely from xvi. 1, because both Derbe and Lystra are there mentioned, but in xx. 4 we have an enumeration in which are the words 'Gaius of Derbe and Timotheus,' where the form of the expression makes it almost certain that the latter was not of Derbe. Further, when St Paul recalls to Timothy his sufferings undergone at this period (2 Tim. iii. 10, 11), he says 'Thou hast fully known......the persecutions and afflictions which came unto me at Antioch, at Iconium, at Lystra,' words which seem to connect Timothy with the last-named place, and when taken in connexion with the other passages to be conclusive that Timothy did not live at Derbe.

That Timothy was made a convert to Christianity at this first visit of St Paul is plain from xvi. 1, where on the Apostle's second visit he is called 'a disciple.' It is also clear from the same passage (xvi. 3) that there could have been but few Jews at Lystra at this time, or else the son of a religious Jewess would hardly have remained uncircumcised till he had reached man's estate. Some, however, have thought that this may have come to pass through the influence of the Greek father of Timothy.

ἀδύνατος τοῖς ποσὶν ἐκάθητο, *there sat a certain man impotent in his feet.* Perhaps this cripple, like that other in Jerusalem (iii. 2), was brought by his friends to some much frequented place that he might ask alms of them that passed by. There is no mention of a synagogue in Lystra, and it is very improbable that there was one. The Apostles therefore would seek out some place of public resort where they might proclaim their message, and such a position would also be most adapted for the purposes of a begging cripple.

It is worth while to notice once again in what precise and peculiar terms Luke, the physician, describes the nature of this and other maladies which claim mention in the history.

9. οὗτος ἤκουσεν κ.τ.λ., *this man heard Paul speaking.* The aorist leaves it quite indefinite whether the man heard on this one occasion only, or had listened to frequent teachings, and so become filled with faith in what was taught.

ὃς ἀτενίσας αὐτῷ, *who fastening his eyes upon him.* This verb is common with St Luke, and seems to indicate that the person using it was an eye-witness of what he relates. It occurs several times of St Paul, as in xiii. 9, where he fixes his gaze on Elymas, and xxiii. 1, where he attentively beholds the council. From the context of the latter passage, in which we learn that the Apostle did not recognize the high-priest, some have thought that this straining earnest gaze, so frequently ascribed to St Paul, was due to some weakness of sight remaining ever since his blindness at the time of his conversion.

καὶ ἰδὼν ὅτι ἔχει πίστιν τοῦ σωθῆναι, *and seeing that he had faith to be healed.* The man's heart shone out in his face, and the Spirit within the Apostle recognized that here was a fit object to be made, by his cure, a sign unto the men of Lystra. Cf. Mark x. 23.

The genitival infinitive τοῦ σωθῆναι may here be regarded as a noun regularly governed by πίστιν.

10. εἶπεν μεγάλῃ φωνῇ, *said with a loud voice,* i.e. raising his tone above that in which his ordinary address was given. Chrysostom says, διατὶ μεγάλῃ φωνῇ; ὥστε τοὺς ὄχλους πιστεῦσαι, having their attention called to the cure which followed at once upon the words.

ἀνάστηθι ἐπὶ τοὺς πόδας σου ὀρθός, *stand upright on thy feet.* It has been noticed in chap. iii. how different is the narration of this miracle from that wrought by St Peter at the Beautiful Gate of the Temple. The two cures were of exactly the same character, and had the historian been giving his own words only and aiming at producing a harmony in his picture between the words and works of St Paul and St Peter, no finer opportunity could have been found than by making the narratives in these two places as much as possible alike. A careful perusal leaves the impression that the latter may have been written from personal observation (see below on verse 22) or from the information of St Paul, but that the former was drawn from an entirely different authority, and that the historian has faithfully preserved the distinct character of the two sources from which he derived his information.

καὶ ἥλατο καὶ περιεπάτει, *and he leaped and walked.* The difference in tense is to be remarked in these verbs. ἥλατο is aorist as expressing one act, the upward spring, which shewed once for all that the cure was wrought; περιεπάτει is imperfect, and indicates that the act of walking was continued, that he henceforth was able to exercise his new power.

11. Λυκαονιστί, *in the speech of Lycaonia.* Which would come more naturally to their lips than any other. The people were bilingual, and St Paul had been speaking to them in Greek. This fact may give us some additional light on the question of what the gift of tongues was which was bestowed upon the Apostles. Clearly, from what we see here, it was not such a power as enabled them at once to understand and converse in the various dialects of all the people into whose countries they might be brought in their missionary labours. For it is manifest that neither Paul nor Barnabas understood the cry of these Lycaonians. If they had, we cannot suppose that they would have allowed a moment to elapse before they corrected the false impression which the words conveyed, and at which, when they came to know its purport, they expressed such horror. They, however, left the place where the multitude of listeners had been assembled, and departed to their own lodgings without any knowledge of what the mistaken people were about to do.

On this compare the words of Chrysostom, Ἀλλ᾽ οὐκ ἦν τοῦτο (the intention to offer sacrifice) οὐδέπω δῆλον. τῇ γὰρ οἰκείᾳ φωνῇ ἐφθέγγοντο λέγοντες ὅτι οἱ θεοὶ ὁμοιωθέντες ἀνθρώποις κατέβησαν πρὸς ἡμᾶς. διὰ τοῦτο οὐδὲν αὐτοῖς ἔλεγον. ἐπειδὴ δὲ εἶδον τὰ στέμματα τότε ἐξελθόντες διέρρηξαν τὰ ἱμάτια.

οἱ θεοὶ ὁμοιωθέντες κ.τ.λ., *the gods are come down to us.* Nothing was more familiar to the heathen mind than the thought of the gods assuming human shape and going about among mankind, and it has often been noticed that the scene of the legend of Baucis and Philemon

related by Ovid (*Metam.* VIII. 611 seqq.), and in which Jupiter and
Mercury are said to have wandered on earth and to have been received
as guests by Baucis and Philemon, is laid in Phrygia, which province
was close to Lycaonia.

12. ἐκάλουν τε τὸν Βαρνάβαν Δία, τὸν δὲ Παῦλον Ἑρμῆν, *and
they called Barnabas, Jupiter* [Zeus]; *and Paul, Mercurius* [Hermes].
Of course this was not known until afterwards. We can understand
how the heathen people concluded that if any deity came to visit them
with a beneficent purpose it would be that god Jupiter whose temple
was before their city, and to whom therefore their chief worship was
paid; and Mercury was counted as the principal attendant on Jupiter,
and moreover as the god of eloquence. It was obvious, therefore, to
assign that name to the chief speaker, and the name of Jupiter to that
one of the two Apostles who had the more commanding presence.
That St Paul was not such a figure we know from his own words,
and tradition describes him as ἀνὴρ μικρὸς τῷ μεγέθει, ψιλὸς τῇ κε-
φαλῇ, ἀγκύλος ταῖς κνήμαις, *Acta Pauli et Theclæ*, 2. Of the aspect
of Barnabas, Chrysostom writes, ἐμοὶ δοκεῖ καὶ ἀπὸ τῆς ὄψεως ἀξιοπρεπὴς
εἶναι ὁ Βαρνάβας.

ἐπειδὴ αὐτὸς ἦν ὁ ἡγούμενος τοῦ λόγου, *because he was the chief
speaker.* This character is always assigned to Hermes by the heathen
writers. Cf. Macrobius, *Sat.* I. 8, 'Scimus Mercurium vocis et ser-
monis potentem,' and Iamblichus, *de Mysteriis* ad init., says of him θεὸς
ὁ τῶν λόγων ἡγεμών.

13. ὅ τε ἱερεὺς τοῦ Διὸς τοῦ ὄντος πρὸ τῆς πόλεως, *the priest of
Jupiter, which was before their city,* i.e. 'whose temple was before their
city.' Zeus was their tutelar divinity, and it was to his priest that
the people ran with their cry, and brought him, with all the prepara-
tions for a sacrifice, to the gate of the house where the Apostles were
lodged.

ταύρους καὶ στέμματα, *oxen and garlands.* The latter were sometimes
put on the heads of the victims, and sometimes used by the worshippers
for their own decorations at religious rites. Probably in this case they
were meant to make gay some temporary altar.

ἐπὶ τοὺς πυλῶνας, *unto the gates.* Even though we have the plural
here it seems impossible to regard the word as used of the gates of the
city, because of the action of the Apostles (ἐξεπήδησαν) who sprang
forth upon the intending worshippers. The word must refer to the
entrance of the house where the Apostles lodged. They were within
the house, and as it was meet to offer the victims to the supposed gods
in their presence rather than on the altar at Jupiter's temple, it was
to the house of their host that the procession came.

14. ἀκούσαντες δέ, *but when they heard.* As they did first from
the clamour and excitement of the would-be worshippers.

ἐξεπήδησαν, *they sprang out.* They were horror-stricken at what
was contemplated, and with garments rent to shew, by signs (for there
would be many among the crowd who could understand little of what
they said) as well as by words, their repudiation of such worship,

they sprang forth from the house, through the vestibule, and into the midst of the crowd, that they might put an end to the delusion of the people. Cf. Matth. xxvi. 65.

15. εὐαγγελιζόμενοι, *preaching unto you.* Literally, 'bringing you good tidings' as the message must be which makes known to men a living God in the place of a dumb idol.

ἀπὸ τούτων τῶν ματαίων ἐπιστρέφειν, *that ye should turn from these vain things.* τὰ μάταια is a frequent expression in the LXX. for 'false gods'; cf. 2 Kings xvii. 15, καὶ ἐπορεύθησαν ὀπίσω τῶν ματαίων. Also Jer. ii. 5; Levit. xvii. 7, &c.

16. ὃς ἐν ταῖς παρῳχημέναις γενεαῖς κ.τ.λ., *who in bygone genera-tions suffered all the heathen to walk in their own ways.* On this cf. Acts xvii. 30; Rom. i. ii.

πορεύεσθαι ταῖς ὁδοῖς. This phrase in the LXX. almost always has the preposition ἐν, but it is found without a preposition (according to some MSS.) in 2 Chron. xi. 17.

God had chosen Israel only for His own people before the coming of Christ, and had given to the rest of the world no revelation of Himself except what they could read in the pages of the book of nature. But that, St Paul says, spake clearly of a careful Creator and Preserver of the world.

17. οὐκ ἀμάρτυρον αὐτὸν ἀφῆκεν, *He left not Himself without witness.* This is the same argument which the Apostle employs (xvii. 27) to the more philosophic multitude whom he addressed on Mars' Hill. God's natural teaching is meant to speak alike to all men. Cf. also the similar reasoning in Rom. i. 19, 20.

ὑμῖν ὑετοὺς διδούς, *giving you rain.* The reading ἡμῖν of the *Text. recept.* seems unnatural. For the Apostle could not include himself amongst those to whom God's appeal had been made through the gifts of nature only.

A few rather unusual words and forms which occur in this verse have suggested to some that we have here a fragment of a Greek poem on the bounties of nature, which the Apostle quotes, as he sometimes does quote the Greek poets, to illustrate his speech from the language familiar to his hearers. Attempts have therefore been made to arrange the words into some dithyrambic metre. But it is hardly probable that St Paul would quote Greek poetry to the people in Lycaonia, to whom Greek was not sufficiently familiar for them to appreciate its literature to the extent which this supposition presumes, and certainly the other quotations which he makes from Greek authors (Acts xvii. 28; 1 Cor. xv. 33; Tit. i. 12) are used to much more cultured audiences.

τὰς καρδίας ὑμῶν, *your hearts,* to correspond with the first part of the verse. With the Greeks καρδία was the seat of the appetites, so that there could be no harshness in such an expression as 'to fill the heart with food.'

18. τοῦ μὴ θύειν αὐτοῖς, *that they had not done sacrifice unto them.* Here the genitival infinitive is in strict government by the verb κατέπαυσαν, which like other verbs of detention and hindering can be properly constructed with a genitive.

19—28. CHANGE OF FEELING IN THE MULTITUDE. PAUL IS STONED. THE APOSTLES VISIT DERBE, AND THEN RETURN, BY THE ROUTE BY WHICH THEY CAME, TO ANTIOCH IN SYRIA.

19. ἀπὸ ᾽Αντιοχείας καὶ ᾽Ικονίου ᾽Ιουδαῖοι, *certain Jews from Antioch and Iconium.* Their anger, like that of 'the circumcision' in Jerusalem, was roused against the Apostles, whom they knew to be born Jews, but whom they saw casting away the legal restraints to which they themselves clung. They therefore followed them to other places and represented them no doubt as renegade Jews, and probably taught the heathen people, that what they had seen done was done by evil powers and not by beneficent ones. Some such argument they must have used. The mighty work of the cured cripple bore witness to the *reality* of the Apostle's power. It was only left, therefore, to ascribe it to evil agency, as the Jews aforetime said of Christ, 'He casteth out devils through Beelzebub.'

πείσαντες τοὺς ὄχλους, *having persuaded the multitudes.* Dean Howson (*Life and Epistles of St Paul,* I. 208) quotes from the Scholiast on Homer (*Il.* IV. 89—92) the following, ἄπιστοι γὰρ Λυκάονες, ὡς καὶ ᾽Αριστοτέλης μαρτυρεῖ, a passage which is confirmed by the fickle conduct of the people on this occasion. For a similar sudden change of temper in the populace, cf. the conduct of the multitude at Jerusalem just before the Crucifixion, and the sudden alteration of opinion in the people of Melita (Acts xxviii. 6).

καὶ λιθάσαντες τὸν Παῦλον, *and having stoned Paul.* Their jealous rage carried them to such a length that they became themselves the active agents in taking vengeance on the 'chief speaker' of the two missionaries. This must be the stoning to which Paul alludes (2 Cor. xi. 25), 'Once was I stoned.' And Paley (*Horæ Paulinæ,* p. 69) calls attention to the close agreement between the history of St Luke and the letter of St Paul. At Iconium St Paul had just escaped stoning; at Lystra he was stoned. The two circumstances are mentioned by the historian, only the actual suffering by the Apostle himself. Nothing but truth to guide them, says Paley, could have brought the two writers so close 'to the very brink of contradiction without their falling into it.'

ἔσυρον ἔξω τῆς πόλεως, *they drew him out of the city.* The stoning had not been in a place set apart for such executions, for there were few Jews in Lystra, but had been done publicly in the midst of the city, perhaps in the place of common resort where St Paul had been wont to preach.

νομίζοντες αὐτὸν τεθνηκέναι, *thinking that he was dead.* As they had apparently every reason to do, when the body could be dragged along the road.

20. κυκλωσάντων δὲ τῶν μαθητῶν αὐτόν, *but as the disciples stood round about him.* Among this ring of disciples we may well believe that the young Timothy was included. Braving all danger that might attend on their act, the believers at Lystra gathered about what they, as well as his assailants, deemed the corpse of their teacher, and their sorrowing thoughts were perhaps concerned how they might procure for it reverent burial.

ἀναστὰς εἰσῆλθεν εἰς τὴν πόλιν, *he rose up and came into the city.* The word ἀναστάς conveys the impression that this was a resurrection from the dead, and that the restoration of the Apostle, and his immediate exhibition of vigour, and boldness to enter again into the city, was the effect of a miracle. That one stoned and left for dead by a savage mob should revive and go about as if nothing had befallen him must have been a still more striking evidence of the mighty power of God present with these teachers than what the people had seen before in the restoration of the cripple.

On the zeal of the Apostle and his readiness to return to the scene of his danger, Chrysostom remarks οὐδαμοῦ δὲ λέγει ὅτι ὑπέστρεψαν χαίροντες ὅτι σημεῖα ἐποίησαν, ἀλλ' ὅτι κατηξιώθησαν ὑπὲρ τοῦ ὀνόματος αὐτοῦ ἀτιμασθῆναι.

καὶ τῇ ἐπαύριον ἐξῆλθεν, *and the next day he departed.* Having been sheltered for the night in the house of some disciple, perhaps in that of Eunice and Lois, the mother and grandmother of Timothy, of whose faith the Apostle speaks (2 Tim. i. 5) as though he had been witness of its fruits in their lives.

σὺν τῷ Βαρνάβᾳ εἰς Δερβήν, *with Barnabas to Derbe.* Barnabas, it seems, had not been an object of jealousy to the Jews. His power, though great as the 'son of exhortation or consolation,' was not so demonstrative as that of his fellow Apostle. Derbe, the town to which the Apostles next went, was to the east of Lystra. We have no mention of any other places in Lycaonia than these two as visited by Paul and Barnabas, but from ver. 6 we gather that their preaching was extended to other parts of the surrounding country.

21. μαθητεύσαντες ἱκανούς, *and having made many disciples.* According to Christ's words (Matth. xxviii. 19), μαθητεύσατε πάντα τὰ ἔθνη. Of course teaching was a part of the process, but μαθητεύειν implies a stage beyond that. Perhaps 'Gaius of Derbe,' whom St Luke mentions as one of Paul's companions in a subsequent journey (xx. 4), may have been one of these. This is the more probable because he is there mentioned in the same clause with Timothy, who undoubtedly was converted by St Paul during this visit to Lycaonia.

ὑπέστρεψαν, *they returned.* Thus going back over the ground which they had travelled before, that they might provide for the spread of that seed of the word which they had imperilled themselves so greatly to sow.

22. ἐπιστηρίζοντες τὰς ψυχὰς τῶν μαθητῶν, *confirming the souls of the disciples.* The strengthening indicated by ἐπιστηρίζειν is of that kind which St Peter was charged to afford to his fellow disciples. 'When

thou art converted *strengthen* (στήρισον) thy brethren,' i.e. by warnings and exhortations drawn from thy own trials and thy deliverance from them. We see that this was the purport of St Paul's charge to the Churches.

τῇ πίστει, *in the faith.* This expression seems to point to the existence of a definite creed. ἡ πίστις is certainly so used in later books of the N. T. Cf. Col. i. 23; 1 Pet. v. 9, &c.

καὶ ὅτι διὰ πολλῶν θλίψεων δεῖ ἡμᾶς κ.τ.λ., *and that we must through many tribulations enter into the kingdom of God.* From the use of the pronoun 'we' in this sentence some have thought that, although unmentioned, the writer of the Acts was present with Paul and Barnabas in this first missionary journey as well as in the others. St Luke only indicates his presence at Troas and elsewhere in the same manner (xvi. 10—12, &c.), though in those passages the mention is more conclusive than in the verse before us.

23. χειροτονήσαντες, *having ordained.* The word is found elsewhere in N. T. only in 2 Cor. viii. 19. It is used of the like ordination in the 'Teaching of the Twelve Apostles,' 15, χειροτονήσατε οὖν ἑαυτοῖς ἐπισκόπους καὶ διακόνους ἀξίους τοῦ κυρίου. So Philo *de præm. et pœn.* 9, ὑπὸ θεοῦ χειροτονηθείς. So too Josephus, *Ant.* VI. 4. 2.

κατ᾽ ἐκκλησίαν πρεσβυτέρους, *elders in every Church,* i.e. men who should have the oversight, and take care for the growth of these infant Churches when the Apostles were gone. It appears, then, that the Church in these places must have gone on without any regular ministry. On the appointment of Elders cf. xi. 30.

προσευξάμενοι μετὰ νηστειῶν, *having prayed with fasting.* They used the same solemn service, at the dedication of these men to their duties, which had been used when they were themselves sent forth from Antioch for their present labour (xiii. 3).

On this conduct Chrysostom says: εἶδες θερμότητα Παύλου; προσευ-ξάμενοι, φησί, μετὰ νηστειῶν παρέθεντο αὐτοὺς τῷ κυρίῳ. ὅρα· μετὰ νηστειῶν αἱ χειροτονίαι. πάλιν νηστεία τὸ καθάρσιον τῶν ἡμετέρων ψυχῶν.

παρέθεντο κ.τ.λ., *they commended them to the Lord.* Cf. St Paul's parting commendation (καὶ τανῦν παρατίθεμαι ὑμᾶς) of the elders of Ephesus (xx. 32) who had come to meet him at Miletus. The Lord was able here also to build these men up, and to give them an inheritance among those which are sanctified.

25. καὶ λαλήσαντες ἐν Πέργῃ τὸν λόγον, *and when they had spoken the word in Perga.* Which, for some unstated reason, they appear not to have done as they passed through it before. See xiii. 13, 14, note.

εἰς Ἀττάλειαν, *to Attalia.* A seaport of Pamphylia, at the mouth of the river Catarrhactes. For its history see *Dictionary of the Bible.* The Apostles had sailed, as they came from Paphos, directly to Perga, which they reached by coming some way up the river Cestrus. Now they go by land from Perga to the seacoast at Attalia, where there was more likelihood of finding a vessel in which they could sail into Syria.

26. ὅθεν ἦσαν παραδεδομένοι τῇ χάριτι τοῦ θεοῦ, *from whence they had been commended to the grace of God.* It is necessary to recur to the more usual meaning of παραδίδοσθαι before we reach the whole sense of these words. It is most commonly used of giving up to enemies, and of exposing to danger; and that there were dangers and foes in abundance before them those who sent out Barnabas and Paul knew, but while sending them into danger, they had faith in the grace of God for them.

27. καὶ συναγαγόντες τὴν ἐκκλησίαν, *and having gathered the Church together,* i.e. the Christian congregation at Antioch who had been moved by the Spirit (xiii. 2) to send them forth. It was fitting therefore that to them should be made a declaration of the results of the Apostolic mission.

ὅσα ἐποίησεν ὁ θεὸς μετ' αὐτῶν, *all that God had done with them.* The expression occurs again in xv. 4. The preposition implies that they felt through the whole work that their motto was *Immanuel=* God with us, cooperating and conspiring with every effort. Chrysostom on this verse says, οὐκ εἶπον ὅσα αὐτοὶ ἐποίησαν, ἀλλ' ὅσα ὁ θεὸς μετ' αὐτῶν.

ἤνοιξεν τοῖς ἔθνεσι θύραν πίστεως, *had opened the door of faith unto the Gentiles,* i.e. had made faith the ground of admission to His kingdom. It was now no longer through circumcision that men should enter in and be known as God's people. The Gospel privileges were offered to every one that believed. The phrase ἀνοίγειν θύραν in this sense first occurs here: cf. 1 Cor. xvi. 9; 2 Cor. ii. 12; Col. iv. 3; Rev. iii. 8.

28. διέτριβον δὲ χρόνον...μαθηταῖς, *and they abode no little time with the disciples.* St Paul was naturally more attached to Antioch than to Jerusalem, for here was the centre where Gentiles had first formed a Church, and where consequently he found most sympathy with his special labours.

The termination of St Paul's first missionary journey seems a fitting place to notice the general character of the Apostle's labours as they are set forth for us by the historian. A space of three or four years at least must be assigned for the duration of this first mission, and as the district traversed was comparatively small, a considerable time must have been spent at each place which was chosen for a centre of labour. This is very clear from St Luke's narrative. He tells us (xiii. 49) how 'the word of God was published throughout all the region.' He speaks also (xiii. 52, xiv. 22) of 'the disciples' as though converts had been made in no small numbers. Again at Iconium he mentions (xiv. 1) that 'a great multitude both of Jews and Greeks believed,' and (xiv. 3) that 'long time' was spent there in striving to overcome the opposition of the 'unbelieving Jews,' and at last the whole city seems to have been divided through the influence of the missionaries into two great and warmly opposing factions. Such results were not produced by a couple of unknown Jewish preachers except after long-extended labour. At Lystra they abode long enough to attract crowds to their discourses and to form a congregation of earnest disciples, who did not allow the work to die out. Another proof of the abundant fruit of their labours is the necessity for ordaining elders in the various centres and providing for orderly Church government. It took too no short time, we may feel sure, to secure converts of such a character as to be fit for the presidential offices in every Church. And the subsequent language of St Paul (xv. 36) where he speaks of revisiting their brethren in every city where they 'had before preached the word of the Lord,' shews that he believed a good foundation had been laid in the various places where they had ministered. We judge from this that the plan of the mission was that Barnabas and Paul made a stay in some centre of population, and there continued their preaching till converts enough and of such a character had been gained to continue the work when the Apostles departed, and some of them so far instructed as to be fit to become teachers to the rest.

It is however when we read of the Christian congregations that the narrative of St Luke becomes most replete with interest. The vision by which St Paul was called (Acts xxii. 21) declared him expressly chosen to be the Apostle of the Gentiles. In his letter to the Galatians he confirms (Gal. ii. 7) what St Luke tells us on this point in the history. Yet the history exhibits him to us as quite acting up to the feelings which he himself has expressed (Rom. x. 1), where he declares that his heart's desire for Israel is that they may be saved, and it shews us how his whole life was in accord with the language of that same Epistle (Rom. xi. 1) when he completely identifies himself with the children of Israel. Throughout all this missionary tour the Apostle in no instance neglects to publish the glad tidings of salvation first to his own people. The Jews reject him in one place, yet he still goes to their brethren first at the next station to which he comes. In Cyprus both he and Barnabas went first to the synagogue in Salamis. It is true that they preached mightily unto the Gentiles, but the Jews had heard their message first. At Antioch it was in the synagogue that their mission was commenced. They took their places there as ordinary Jewish worshippers, and were asked by the rulers to address the congregation as being brethren and of the same faith. The address which St Paul made on that occasion, the summary of which St Luke has preserved for us, echoes in more than one place the language of the Epistle to the Romans. While in the latter St Paul says (iii. 28) 'we conclude that a man is justified by faith without the deeds of the Law,' the historian relates (Acts xiii. 39) that he said to the Antiochene congregation in similar terms, 'By Him all that believed are justified from all things from which ye could not be justified by the law of Moses.' In the same way we find in the Epistle St Paul explains to the Romans (x. 19) that God's purpose had been to rouse His ancient people to jealousy by them that are no people, so at Antioch the history tells us how he said, 'It was necessary that the word of God should be first spoken to you, but seeing ye adjudge yourselves unworthy of everlasting life, lo, we turn to the

Gentiles.' This is quite in harmony too with Rom. i. 16. There the Gospel is proclaimed to be 'the power of God unto salvation to every one that believeth,' but the order in which it is offered is 'to the Jew first, and afterward to the Gentiles.'

To notice the unanimity of the language of St Paul's chief Epistle with that of such abstracts of his speeches as are furnished by St Luke has much interest and is of much importance. For there are those who maintain that the St Paul of the Acts is a very different person in character and teaching from the St Paul of the Epistles. To establish such an opinion, those passages in the letters have been singled out and unduly dwelt on, wherein the Apostle speaks severely of the opposition which he met with from the Jews. A theory has been started that in the early Church there were two opposing parties, one named from Peter, the other from Paul, and that the Acts of the Apostles is a work of a late date written with the view of bringing about harmony between them. It cannot therefore be too prominently set forward, that in the narrative of St Luke there is a great deal for which we find an exact counterpart in St Paul's Epistles. And if the comparison of the history with the letters be extended as far as the materials at our command permit, at every step it will become more and more apparent, that the agreement between the Apostle and the historian exists, because the latter is faithful to what he saw and heard, and his record therefore cannot but harmonize with the spirit and words of him who was the chief actor in the history.

CHAPTER XV.

Readings varying from the *Text. recept.*

7. ἐν ὑμῖν ἐξελέξατο ὁ θεὸς with ℵABC. *Vulg.* has 'Deus in nobis elegit.'

8. αὐτοῖς after δοὺς omitted with ℵAB. *Vulg.* only represents the pronoun once, though having 'dans illis.'

11. Χριστοῦ omitted with ℵABEHLP. *Vulg.* has 'Domini Jesu Christi.'

14. ἐπὶ omitted before τῷ ὀνόματι with ℵABCDE. Not represented in *Vulg.*

17, 18. κύριος ποιῶν ταῦτα γνωστὰ ἀπ' αἰῶνος. διὸ...with ℵBC. The *Vulg.* gives 'Dominus faciens hæc. Notum a sæculo est Domino opus suum. Propter quod...' But on the verses see notes.

23. τάδε after αὐτῶν omitted with ℵAB. *Vulg.* has only 'per manus eorum.'

καὶ οἱ before ἀδελφοὶ omitted with ℵABCD. *Vulg.* has 'et seniores fratres.'

24. λέγοντες περιτέμνεσθαι καὶ τηρεῖν τὸν νόμον omitted with ℵABD. Not represented in *Vulg.*

33. ἀποστείλαντας αὐτούς for ἀποστόλους with אABCD. *Vulg.* 'ad eos qui miserant illos.'

34. ἔδοξεν δὲ τῷ Σίλᾳ ἐπιμεῖναι αὐτοῦ omitted with אABEHLP. *Vulg.* has 'Visum est autem Silæ ibi remanere,' and continues with words not represented in *Text. recept.*, and only partly in D, viz. 'Judas autem solus abiit Jerusalem.'

36. εἶπεν πρὸς Βαρνάβαν Παῦλος with אABC. So *Vulg.* 'dixit ad Barnabam Paulus.'

ἡμῶν after ἀδελφοὺς omitted with אABCDE. Not represented in *Vulg.*

37. ἐβούλετο for ἐβουλεύσατο with אABCE. *Vulg.* 'volebat.'

καὶ before τὸν Ἰωάννην with אB, but the καὶ without the succeeding article appears also in CE. *Vulg.* has 'et Joannem.'

39. δὲ for οὖν after ἐγένετο with אABD. *Vulg.* 'autem.'

40. κυρίου for θεοῦ with אABD. *Vulg.* 'Dei.'

Ch. XV. 1—5. At Antioch some maintain that Gentile Converts must be circumcised. A Mission to Jerusalem about the question. Reception of those who were sent.

The history now approaches that subject of controversy which was certain to arise as soon as Christianity spread beyond the limits of the people of Israel. The first converts to the new faith were made among the Jews, but few of them were likely to cast aside those prejudices of religion in which they had long been educated. As soon as Gentiles who had not first become proselytes to Judaism joined the Christian Church, Jewish exclusiveness received a violent shock, and there was no small danger lest the new community should be rent asunder almost at its beginning. 'The covenant,' by which expression the devout Jew specially meant 'circumcision,' was constituted a cry by Judaizing agitators, and the opposition, first brought into prominence at Antioch, proved a continuous source of trial through the whole ministry of St Paul, and has left its traces on most of the writings both of the N. T. and of early Christian literature.

1. καὶ τινες κατελθόντες ἀπὸ τῆς Ἰουδαίας, *and certain which came down from Judæa*, i.e. to Antioch. The words of the new comers would derive authority from the place whence they had come, and would be received as the latest ordinance of the heads of the Church at Jerusalem. Thus the mission of inquiry to Jerusalem was rendered necessary.

ἐδίδασκον τοὺς ἀδελφούς, *taught the brethren*. These were a mixed body, composed of Jews, proselytes and Gentiles (see xi. 19, 20, and the notes there). Thus it was precisely the place where such a question would arise. Gentile converts who had not passed into Christianity by the gate of Judaism would be sure to be regarded as wanting something by the people in whose mouths 'uncircumcised' had been from old times the bitterest term of reproach. (Cf. 1 Sam. xvii. 26 and Acts xi. 3.) The tense of the verb used implies that these men were persistent in their teaching, they kept constantly to this theme.

τῷ ἔθει τῷ Μωϋσέως, *after the custom of Moses.* The word is found before (Acts vi. 14) 'the customs which Moses delivered' and signifies those rites and usages which had their foundation in the Law (cf. Luke i. 9, ii. 42; Acts xxi. 21) and so were more than a 'manner' or 'fashion.' Cf. also John vii. 22, for circumcision as the ordinance given to the people by Moses.

ἔθος is not common in the LXX. and appears to be only once used (2 Macc. xi. 25) for the observances of the Jewish religion.

The dative case is put here to express the rule or order by which a thing is done, but a much more frequent mode of expressing this is, as in xvii. 2, by κατά with the accusative. But cf. 2 Macc. vi. 1 τοῖς τοῦ θεοῦ νόμοις πολιτεύεσθαι.

οὐ δύνασθε σωθῆναι, *ye cannot be saved.* Such a statement was likely to cause debate and questioning among those who had just learnt (xiv. 27) that 'God had opened the door of faith' (independent of the observance of the ceremonial Law) 'unto the Gentiles.'

2. γενομένης δὲ στάσεως καὶ ζητήσεως, *and when there arose a debate and questioning.* στάσις does not necessarily imply angry dissension, but only a division. The members of the Church took opposite sides in the matter. Of course Paul and Barnabas would be with those who maintained that circumcision was no longer necessary.

ἔταξαν, *they appointed,* i.e. the brethren of the Church at Antioch did so. The verb, as well as the whole context, shews that the mission was sent, in an orderly fashion, by the whole Christian community, to which the question was one of most vital importance, probably affecting a large part of their members.

καὶ τινας ἄλλους ἐξ αὐτῶν, *and certain other of them,* who would represent the position of the men who had come from Judæa.

πρὸς τοὺς ἀποστόλους καὶ πρεσβυτέρους, *unto the Apostles and elders.* Peter, John and James we find were now at Jerusalem, and they seem, from other notices in the N.T. (Gal. i. 18, 19, and ii. 9), to have been the Apostles who continued to live in the holy city. These with the elders appear now as the governing body of the infant Church. And Jerusalem was for the Jew, until its destruction, the place of chief authority (cf. Is. ii. 3). The overthrow of the holy city did as much as anything to help on the knowledge of the universality of the Christian religion. Those who had been bred in Judaism could not (as devout Jews to this day do not) cast away the thought that Jerusalem is 'the place where men ought to worship.'

3. προπεμφθέντες, *being brought on their way.* It was not an uncommon mark of affection or respect that a part of the Church at any place should attend its chief teachers for a short way on their journeys. (Cf. *infra* xx. 38, xxi. 16.) And for the antiquity of the custom among the Jews, see Gen. xviii. 16, where when the heavenly visitors were departing from Abraham it is said (LXX.), συνεπορεύετο μετ' αὐτῶν συμπροπέμπων αὐτούς.

Among the companions of Paul and Barnabas on this journey must have been Titus, for we read of him, and of the question raised about his circumcision, in St Paul's own notice of this visit (Gal. ii. 3).

διήρχοντο τήν τε Φοινίκην καὶ Σαμάρειαν, *they passed through both Phœnicia and Samaria.* The road would take them along the coast through Berytus, Tyre and Sidon, which at this time were places of great importance, and most likely to have bodies of Christians among their inhabitants.

ἐκδιηγούμενοι τὴν ἐπιστροφὴν τῶν ἐθνῶν, *declaring the conversion of the Gentiles.* This would naturally be St Paul's great theme. Among those who were going up to Jerusalem with him would be members of the Judaizing party, but their presence was no check on the Apostle's zeal that all men should hear of the bringing in of Gentiles to the faith of Christ. The verb ἐκδιηγεῖσθαι implies that he gave his story with all details, and we may be sure that he dwelt on the way in which the Spirit of God had set a seal upon the work, though the converts of whom he spake were all uncircumcised.

πᾶσιν τοῖς ἀδελφοῖς, *unto all the brethren,* i.e. in the Churches through which they passed, in which places the brethren must have been in great part Jews, though there might be proselytes also among them. We see therefore that it was only some of the Jews who demanded from the Gentiles complete conformity to the Law. At Jerusalem (ver. 5) the Judaizing party is described as 'certain of the sect of the Pharisees which believed,' and the Gospel history represents the Pharisees on all occasions as determined supporters of the ceremonial law. Probably their party was most numerous at Jerusalem, where all the ritual observances could be most completely carried out. In the more remote congregations the joy over the Gentile conversions would be more unalloyed.

4. παρεδέχθησαν ὑπὸ τῆς ἐκκλησίας, *they were received by the Church.* The ἐκκλησία is perhaps named first because there would on such a visit be an assembly of the whole Christian body to hear the story of the missionary labours of Paul and Barnabas before the question about which they had specially been sent from Antioch came to be discussed. The account of the spreading of the faith was for all, while the question of circumcision would be discussed only by the heads of the Church, and those who could speak with authority. This preliminary meeting must have lasted for a considerable time, even if only a mere abstract of the labours, sufferings and success of Paul and Barnabas were given to those who met them. Such a recital was the best introduction that could be conceived for the question which was afterwards to be discussed and legislated on.

μετ' αὐτῶν, *with them.* On this preposition cf. xiv. 27. That the Apostles had a true notion of themselves as only instruments, though Christ deigned to be a fellow-worker (Mark xvi. 20) with them, is seen below in verse 12 where the preposition used is διά (by).

5. ἐξανέστησαν δέ τινες τῶν...Φαρισαίων, *but there rose up certain of the sect of the Pharisees.* The margin of the A.V. takes this sentence as part of the narration of Paul and Barnabas, 'there rose up, said they, certain, &c.' But it is much more natural to consider it to be St Luke's account of what happened at Jerusalem. The teachers at Antioch had not been described as Pharisees, though they probably were so. Yet in no other passage of the N.T. are the Pharisees mentioned away from Jerusalem. As soon as the Apostolic narrative was heard by the Church, certain of that party *stood forth from* the Church body and lodged their protest against what had been done. The Pharisaic teaching concerning the necessity of circumcision was based on such passages as Is. lvi. 6, where the covenant mentioned was held to be that of circumcision. They also supported their position by such passages as Is. lii. 1, where the uncircumcised are excluded from the Holy City.

πεπιστευκότες, *which believed,* i.e. had accepted Christ as the promised Messiah. But we can see from the position of these men that there was no thought at first by so doing of making a complete break with Judaism.

λέγοντες ὅτι Δεῖ, *saying, It is needful,* &c. The words are a direct utterance, and St Luke sets before us the very words spoken before the Church assembly.

The visit of St Paul to Jerusalem which St Luke here describes is now generally admitted to be the same of which St Paul speaks in Gal. ii. 1—9. The chronology offers no obstacle to this conclusion, while the purpose of the visit and the companionship of Barnabas and the persons who were at the head of the Church in Jerusalem are all accordant in the two notices. In the Epistle St Paul tells us that he took Titus with him, and nothing is more likely than that while he had the company of some members of the Judaizing party, he would also take a companion with him from among those converts on whose behalf he was making the journey. He says too that it was 'by revelation' that he went up, while the narrative of the Acts represents him as sent by the Church of Antioch. But here need be no contradiction. An inward monition may have furnished the true reason why the Apostle consented to make an appeal to the central authorities in Jerusalem. St Luke would not necessarily be aware of this; it was important in St Paul's argument to the Galatians that he should mention it. (For a fuller comparison of the two notices, see Bp Lightfoot's *Ep. to Galatians*, note, pp. 122—127.)

6—12. THE COUNCIL AT JERUSALEM; THE DEBATE AND THE SPEECH OF
         PETER. NARRATION OF THE WORK OF BARNABAS AND PAUL.

6. συνήχθησαν δὲ οἱ ἀπόστολοι καὶ οἱ πρεσβύτεροι, *and the Apostles and elders were gathered together.* These words refer to a formal summoning to discuss the difficult question which had been brought forward. That there was a space between the first welcome of the Apostles by the Church and the assembly of the synod suits St Paul's words (Gal. ii. 2) that he explained his position 'privately to them which were of reputation.' This private conference was a necessary preparation for the more public discussion, which alone is noticed by the history.

ἰδεῖν περί, *to consider about.* The use of ἰδεῖν in this sense and construction is rare. But compare our own familiar idiom 'to see about anything.'

7. πολλῆς δὲ ζητήσεως κ.τ.λ., *and when there had been much questioning.* For the Pharisaic element would find its warmest supporters at Jerusalem. And it is to that party that the disputing must be ascribed, for it is plain, from the summing-up of St James at the close of the discussion, that the other Apostles were of the same mind with Paul and Barnabas, and as is said in the Epistle to the Galatians (ii. 9), 'they gave unto them the right hands of fellowship.'

ἀναστὰς Πέτρος εἶπεν, *Peter rose up and said.* It is to be noted that Paul and Barnabas leave arguments and reasons to be put forward by those who had laboured most among Jewish converts, and content themselves with a recital of what God had wrought through them in their journey among the Gentiles.

ἀφ᾽ ἡμερῶν ἀρχαίων. Literally 'from early days.' The A.V. '*a good while ago*' is very idiomatic, and sufficiently close in sense. St Peter is alluding to the conversion of Cornelius (chap. x.), which probably took place some ten years before the meeting of this synod. That was at an early period of the Apostolic ministry, and the great and numerous events which had intervened made the time seem long ago.

ἐν ὑμῖν ἐξελέξατο ὁ θεός, *God made choice among you.* This, the reading of the oldest authorities, shews Peter as putting himself and his fellow Apostles on the same level with the whole Christian body which he is addressing. God might have chosen whom He would to receive the instruction of the sheet let down from heaven.

διὰ τοῦ στόματός μου, *by my mouth.* That he may not seem to be claiming a distinction for himself as the one chosen of God for this work, St Peter is careful to call himself no more than the mouthpiece of God.

8. ὁ καρδιογνώστης, *which knoweth the hearts.* καρδιογνώστης is only here and in Acts i. 24, and on both occasions it is St Peter who uses it. Such a witness could admit of no appeal. God himself had put the uncircumcised on the same level with the circumcised by giving to them the same gifts of the Spirit.

9. καὶ οὐθὲν διέκρινεν, *and put no difference,* i.e. made no distinction. The Apostle looks on God's testimony to the Gentiles in two lights. What was given to the new converts was the same which had been given at the first outpouring of the Spirit. And God made no mark of distinction to sever Jews from Gentiles. Faith had purified the hearts of Cornelius and his house, and the outward observances of the Law of Moses were of no account when the heart was clean before

Him who alone could judge of the purity thereof. In these words of his St Peter clearly agrees to all that St Paul had taught about the admission of the Gentiles.

τῇ πίστει καθαρίσας τὰς καρδίας αὐτῶν, *having purified their hearts by faith.* When he uses καθαρίσας St Peter is clearly thinking of the vision and the voice ἃ ὁ θεὸς ἐκαθάρισεν σὺ μὴ κοίνου.

10. νῦν οὖν, *now therefore,* i.e. after you have had so much evidence of God's acceptance of the Gentiles, both in the early days and in the journeys of St Paul and Barnabas.

τί πειράζετε τὸν θεόν; *why tempt ye God?* Men are said 'to tempt God' when they distrust His guidance, and in consequence disobey His revealed will (cf. Ps. xcv. 9). So the Jews *tempted* God in the wilderness (Heb. iii. 9) when they saw His mighty works and yet murmured at His leaders; so they are said to have *tempted* Christ (1 Cor. x. 9) when they were punished by the fiery serpents; and Ananias and Sapphira are said to 'have agreed to *tempt* the Spirit of the Lord,' by acting as though they thought they could deceive God in their offering. From these instances the force of the question in the text will be seen. Those who should act as the Pharisaic party would recommend, would be distrusting God's knowledge of the hearts of men, and refusing to be guided by what His Spirit had made known in the conversion of Cornelius.

ἐπιθεῖναι κ.τ.λ., *to put a yoke.* The infinitive is sometimes used as here to express the way or manner in which anything is done, and is in force something like a gerund, 'by placing a yoke.' Cf. 1 Pet. iv. 3, 'The time past of our life sufficeth us (κατειργάσθαι) for having wrought the will of the heathen.'

ζυγόν, *a yoke.* So St Paul (Gal. v. 1) calls the ceremonial law ζυγὸν δουλείας. Christ uses the word ζυγός as a designation for His own precepts, knowing that a yoke was needed for the guidance of men, but He calls it ζυγὸς χρηστός, 'an easy and profitable yoke,' Matth. xi. 30.

ἰσχύσαμεν βαστάσαι, *are able to bear.* How this was felt is shewn by the Rabbinic injunction to 'make a hedge about the Law,' i.e. so to fence in its precepts by additional regulations of their own, that there should be no chance of infringing the commandment. These additions, commandments of men, as our Lord styles them, had made the ceremonial observances into a killing load. 'The yoke of the commandments' was a Rabbinic expression (T. B. *Berachoth* II. 2) and referred to the penalties for disobedience, the duty of laying up the commands in the heart, of binding them upon the hands, and as frontlets between the eyes, of teaching them to children, and speaking of them at all times, and writing them upon the doorposts and the gates. So that 'the yoke' was a heavy one for the teacher as well as for the learner.

11. ἀλλά, *but.* There is much implied in this one word. The Apostle means 'But all this has been changed by God's new revela-

tion of Himself, and we should cease this tempting of Him, for we believe (if we are truly in Christ) that salvation is for all men.'

διὰ τῆς χάριτος τοῦ κυρίου Ἰησοῦ, *through the grace of the Lord Jesus.* A new and living way has been opened, and it is not in any conformity to the Jewish Law that we now look for salvation.

καθ' ὃν τρόπον κἀκεῖνοι, *even as they*, i.e. even as they believe. Thus the argument is: If our belief and hope are the same, and no other, than theirs, why should these new converts be urged to adopt observances which form to us no ground for our hope of salvation?

After this point in the N.T. history St Peter's name appears no more, and when we call to mind the opposition which, at the close of the first, and in the second, century was represented as existing between the teaching of Paul and Peter, we cannot think that it was without meaning that this last appearance of the Apostle of the circumcision in the Scripture story sets him before us in full accord with the Apostle of the Gentiles. The collision between Paul and Peter at a later period in Antioch (Gal. ii.) came about because the latter had forgotten for a time his own statement that 'God is no respecter of persons.' But like the παροξυσμός between Paul and Barnabas there was no rupture in the Church in consequence of the rebuke which St Paul administered to his fellow-apostle.

12. ἐσίγησεν δὲ πᾶν τὸ πλῆθος, *then all the multitude kept silence.* We see here, though the Apostles and Elders are alone mentioned (verse 6) as being gathered together, that the assembly was a very large one. The cause of their silence was the voice of authority with which he could speak through whom God had first opened the door of faith to the Gentiles. For while he told what God had done, he related how he, like themselves, had much prejudice to overcome before his mission to Cornelius.

καὶ ἤκουον, *and gave audience.* The verb is plural to correspond with the plural sense of πλῆθος, and the use of the imperfect tense is to indicate the continuous attention to the whole narrative of that, the first missionary journey for the spread of the faith.

ὅσα...σημεῖα καὶ τέρατα, *what signs and wonders.* The two nouns are the same which occur in the prayer of the disciples (iv. 30) 'that *signs and wonders* may be done through the name of Thy holy servant Jesus.' The prayer had been abundantly answered in the experience of Paul and Barnabas.

δι' αὐτῶν, *by them*, i.e. through them as instruments. See above on verse 4.

13—21. JAMES SUMS UP THE DISCUSSION, AND PRONOUNCES THE DECISION OF THE CHURCH ON THIS CONTROVERSY.

13. αὐτούς, i.e. Paul and Barnabas.

Ἰάκωβος, *James*, i.e. the brother of our Lord who was so called, and who was at the head of the Church in Jerusalem. See above on xii. 17.

ἀκούσατέ μου, *hearken unto me.* The president's summary takes no note of the 'much questioning' (v. 7) but points out that a divine revelation had been made to Peter, and that it was accordant with the words of Old Testament prophecy. On these warrants he based his decision.

14. Συμεών, *Symeon.* This more Jewish form of the name of the Apostle Peter is found also at the commencement of St Peter's second Epistle. The Jews after they came to have much intercourse with Gentiles had frequently two forms of name, one of which was employed on religious and solemn occasions, the other in intercourse with non-Jews and in the ordinary transactions of life. Thus in the Apocrypha (1 Macc. v. 17, &c.) the name of the Maccabean prince is written *Simon*, though on his coins it stands *Symeon* (see Gesenius, s.v.).

καθὼς πρῶτον ὁ θεὸς ἐπεσκέψατο, *how God did first visit,* i.e. the way in which the first Gentile convert was made. It was some time after the mission of the Holy Ghost on the Apostles that Cornelius was converted. 'At the first' of the A.V. gives a wrong idea.

λαὸν τῷ ὀνόματι αὐτοῦ, *a people for His name.* Thus the 'chosen people' were no longer to be Jews only, and so those ceremonial ordinances which had hitherto marked out Jews from Gentiles were seen to be no longer necessary.

The force of this dative is best perceived when we remember that God's 'name' is often used for 'Himself.' There is no harshness in the case, when the expression is regarded as the equivalent 'to take for Himself.'

15. καὶ τούτῳ συμφωνοῦσιν, *and to this agree,* i.e. with this action on God's part the statements of His prophets are in harmony. They had foretold that it should be so. Only one prophet is here quoted, viz. Amos (ix. 11, 12), but the audience would recall other like passages, as St Paul does Rom. xv. 9—12, quoting from the books of Moses, David and Isaiah.

16. μετὰ ταῦτα, *after these things.* It will be seen on reference to the words of Amos that the quotation here given is not made from the Hebrew, which is correctly represented by the A.V. in the book of Amos. Whether St James himself spoke at the synod in Greek, or St Luke has represented in Greek what the speaker himself uttered in Aramaic, we cannot know. But the words in the text correspond very nearly with the LXX. which here (either because they read the Hebrew consonants differently or because they merely gave the sense without attempting an exact rendering) varies from the Hebrew text. Yet St Luke does not give exactly the words of the LXX. He may have quoted from memory or have modified them somewhat to adapt them to the form of his sentence. The words of the LXX. run thus, ἐν τῇ ἡμέρᾳ ἐκείνῃ ἀναστήσω τὴν σκηνὴν Δαυὶδ τὴν πεπτωκυῖαν, καὶ ἀνοικοδομήσω τὰ πεπτωκότα αὐτῆς, καὶ τὰ κατεσκαμμένα αὐτῆς ἀναστήσω, καὶ ἀνοικοδομήσω αὐτὴν καθὼς αἱ ἡμέραι τοῦ αἰῶνος, ὅπως ἐκζητήσωσιν οἱ

κατάλοιποι τῶν ἀνθρώπων καὶ πάντα τὰ ἔθνη ἐφ' οὓς ἐπικέκληται τὸ
ὄνομά μου ἐπ' αὐτούς, λέγει κύριος ὁ ποιῶν πάντα ταῦτα.

ἀναστρέψω καὶ ἀνοικοδομήσω, *I will return and will build.* This is
not the form of the expression either in the Hebrew text or in the
LXX., but it is a common Hebrew formula to signify 'I will do a
thing again.' Cf. Eccles. iv. 1 καὶ ἐπέστρεψα ἐγὼ καὶ εἶδον, 'I
returned and considered'=I considered once again. Similarly Eccles.
iv. 7, ix. 11. The occurrence of this formula favours the opinion that
St James, in this specially Jewish synod, spoke in Aramaic of which
St Luke has given us a literal translation.

τὴν σκηνὴν Δανείδ, *the tabernacle of David.* The Hebrew word
used in Amos signifies one of those booths used by the people at the
Feast of Tabernacles, when they lived in frail dwellings in order to
be reminded that God was their protector. This word may be applied
to the estate of the Jews when the Deliverer should come, to indicate
that they should be brought very low, but yet should find in Him a
Saviour.

17. ὅπως ἂν ἐκζητήσωσιν...τὸν κύριον, *they might seek after the
Lord.* The Hebrew of Amos (see A.V.) differs widely here; and in
the LXX. τὸν κύριον is not expressed. But the Spirit enabled St James
to give the full interpretation of the prophetic words. The original
paints the restored tabernacle, and of course the people of David
restored along with it, as possessors of the remnant of Edom and all
the heathen. The nations shall be joined unto the Lord's people.
The LXX., as an exposition, speaks of 'the residue of men seeking
unto the restored tabernacle.' St James makes both clear by shewing
that 'to seek after the Lord' is to be the true up-building both of the
house of David and of all mankind besides.

The Hebrew word for 'man' is *Adam*, which differs very slightly
from the word *Edom*. So that the variation between 'remnant of
Edom' in the Hebrew and 'residue of men' in the LXX. may be due
only to the various reading of that noun.

ὅπως with ἂν implies an end aimed at, but the attainment of it is
still dependent on circumstances. Cf. *Winer-Moulton*, p. 389.

ἐφ' οὓς ἐπικέκληται τὸ ὄνομά μου ἐπ' αὐτούς, *upon whom My name is
called.* An Aramaic mode of saying 'who are called by My name.'
The expression is so translated James ii. 7 (A.V.). Cf. for the
Greek Jerem. xli. 15 (LXX.) ἐν τῷ οἴκῳ οὗ ἐπεκλήθη τὸ ὄνομά μου ἐπ'
αὐτῷ.

18. ποιῶν ταῦτα γνωστὰ ἀπ' αἰῶνος. This is the reading supported
by most authority, and the sense must be either (1) 'the Lord who
maketh these things known from the beginning of the world,' or (2)
'the Lord, who doeth these things that were known from the beginning of the world.' The first of these renderings is the more difficult
to understand, and it must be taken as somewhat hyperbolic. God
made known by His prophets the calling of the Gentiles in very early
days, and this early revelation may be all that is intended by the
stronger phrase. But the second sense seems to suit better with the

context. This reception of the Gentiles seems to the Jew a new and
startling thing, but God has revealed it by His prophets, and He who
is doing it is but carrying out what He had known and designed from
the beginning of the world.

19. διὸ ἐγὼ κρίνω, *wherefore I decide.* The pronoun is emphatically
expressed, and indicates that the speaker is one who may decide with
authority.

μὴ παρενοχλεῖν κ.τ.λ., *that we trouble not them,* &c. The verb is
only found here in N.T., but is somewhat frequent in the LXX. Thus
of the fire around the Three Children (Song of Three Child. 26) it is
said οὐκ ἐλύπησεν οὐδὲ παρηνώχλησεν αὐτούς. 'It neither hurt nor
troubled them.' Cf. also 1 Macc. x. 35, 63, where the word is used as
here in a public proclamation. The notion is of putting an obstacle
in any one's way. St James's idea is 'We will not by needless impe-
diments hinder the new converts from joining us.'

τοῖς ἀπὸ τῶν ἐθνῶν ἐπιστρέφουσιν ἐπὶ τὸν θεόν, *them which from the
Gentiles are turning to God.* The same phrase is used elsewhere in the
Acts (cf. ix. 35, xiv. 15, xxvi. 20) and its full significance is explained
when in xi. 21 it is said of the converts at Antioch πολὺς ἀριθμὸς
πιστεύσας ἐπέστρεψεν ἐπὶ τὸν κύριον. It was belief in Christ as the Son
of God which constituted this true turning.

20. ἀλλὰ ἐπιστεῖλαι αὐτοῖς, *but that we write unto them.* ἐπιστέλλω
is used primarily of a charge sent by a messenger, but also, as in Heb.
xiii. 22, is often used of what is sent by letter (and hence comes the
English word *epistle*), and there can be little doubt that this is the
sense in the present case, for though messengers were sent, they
carried with them the decision of the synod of Jerusalem in a formal
manner committed to writing (*v.* 23).

τοῦ ἀπέχεσθαι τῶν ἀλισγημάτων τῶν εἰδώλων, *that they abstain from
pollutions of idols.* This is explained in *v.* 29 by 'meats offered (i.e.
sacrificed) to idols.' Of the necessity for such an injunction in the
early Church, where congregations were to be now composed of both
Jews and Gentiles, we can judge from St Paul's argument to the
Corinthians (1 Cor. viii. 1—10, x. 19), and we can also see how he
would have the Gentile converts deal tenderly with the scruples of
their Jewish fellow-worshippers, however needless they themselves
might deem such scruples.

Here the genitival infinitive is used where in ordinary Greek a
simple infinitive would have been written. Cf. above, vii. 19 note.

The noun ἀλίσγημα is only found in N.T. and the verb ἀλισγέω in
LXX. Dan. i. 8; Mal. i. 7, 12, and in a passage somewhat illustrative
of this verse, Ecclus. xl. 29 ἀλισγήσει τὴν ψυχὴν αὐτοῦ ἐν ἐδέσμασιν
ἀλλοτρίοις, though the food there spoken of has not been offered to
idols.

As the ordinance of the synod is for the settling of Jewish minds,
we may understand the sort of offence which they were likely to feel.
It was of the same nature as the feeling of Daniel when he refused to
eat of the food supplied by King Nebuchadnezzar. Meat was often

sold in the markets from beasts that had been offered in sacrifice to idols, and this food and those who ate it the Jew would abhor. The Gentile converts might not be careful, when they had once come to think of the idol as nothing, and might join still in banquets with their non-Christian friends, and St Paul (1 Cor. viii. 10) supposes an extreme case, that such men might even sit down to meat in an idol-temple. If Jew and Gentile were to become one in Christ, much respect must be paid to the feelings which had been sunk deep into the minds of Israel by long years of suffering for their own idolatry.

καὶ τῆς πορνείας, *and from fornication.* This injunction must not be understood as a simple repetition of a moral law binding upon all men at all times, but must be taken in connexion with the rest of the decree, and as forbidding a sin into which converts from heathenism were most prone to fall back, and which their previous lives had taught them to regard in a very different light from that in which a Jew would see it. The Levitical law against every form of unchastity was extremely strict (Lev. xviii. and xx.), and it is probably to the observance of these ordinances that we may ascribe the persistence of the Jewish type, and the purity of their race at this day. Whereas among the heathen unchastity was a portion of many of their temple rites, and persons who gave themselves up to such impurities were even called by the names of the heathen divinities. To men educated in the constant contemplation of such a system, sins of unchastity would have far less guilt than in the eyes of those to whom the Law of Moses was read every sabbath-day.

καὶ τοῦ πνικτοῦ κ.τ.λ., *and from what is strangled and from blood.* The prohibition of blood was made as soon as animal food was given to men (Gen. ix. 4), and it was frequently enforced in the Mosaic law (Lev. iii. 17, vii. 26, xvii. 10, 14, xix. 26). To eat blood was counted a sin against the Lord in the days of Saul (1 Sam. xiv. 33), and with strict Jews it is an abomination to this day. Things strangled are not specially mentioned in the law of Moses, but that they should not be eaten follows from the larger prohibition. Lev. vii. 26 does, however, make mention of the blood of fowls, and it would be in the use of them that the eating of blood began first to be practised. And in breaking the neck of an animal the Jew held that the blood was caused to flow into the limbs in such wise that it could not be brought out even by salt. See T. B. *Chullin,* 113 a.

21. Μωϋσῆς γὰρ ἐκ γενεῶν ἀρχαίων κ.τ.λ., *for Moses of old time* (lit. from generations of old) *hath in every city,* &c. Here we have the reason why these injunctions are to be laid upon the Gentile converts. It is necessary however to take the whole verse into consideration before we can decide on the force of the reason. Laying stress chiefly on the expression 'from generations of old,' some have thought that St James's argument means that the Mosaic ritual having been preached for so long a time and found to be a load too heavy to bear, must now be given up, except in these specified points. Again, the verse has been taken to mean that there was no need for the Christian Church

to legislate about the observance of the Mosaic Law other than in these few points, because there was public teaching on the subject everywhere in the Jewish synagogues. Jewish Christians were therefore supplied with guidance, and would be so supplied until by degrees Judaism had entirely given place to Christianity. No doubt the Apostle contemplates the retention by the Jewish Christians of much of their old ritual, and that they would make no breach with the services of the synagogue. But in these enactments, which were apparently only for a time (since St Paul nowhere alludes to them in his Epistles), and to promote peace between Gentiles and Jews, we must remember that the Jews are the persons who have felt offence, and for whose quieting the decree is put forth. The argument of the council seems to be this: We, Jews, may make this concession to the Gentiles without fear. It is not probable that our feelings and prejudices will be interfered with, or the Mosaic Law in its other portions set aside; 'for Moses,' &c.

ἀναγινωσκόμενος, *being read.* On the reading of the Jewish Scriptures in the synagogues, see the Excursus at the end of chap. xiii.

22—29. ANSWER AND DEPUTATION SENT FROM JERUSALEM. THE LETTER OF THE SYNOD TO THE CHRISTIANS OF ANTIOCH.

22. τότε ἔδοξε, *then it seemed good.* The expression is one often used in the official announcements of public resolutions, or decrees made by authority. (Cf. Herod. I. 3; Thuc. IV. 118.)

σὺν ὅλῃ τῇ ἐκκλησίᾳ, *with the whole Church.* The decree was the voice of the whole Church, and the deputies sent were chosen by the whole body. So it is in the name of 'apostles, and elder brethren' that the letter runs (v. 23).

ἐκλεξαμένους ἄνδρας ἐξ αὐτῶν πέμψαι, *to choose men out of their own company and send them.* The A.V. takes ἐκλεξαμένους as if it were ἐκλεχθέντας, and renders 'chosen men'; but the middle voice implies that the council and Church, 'choosing for themselves' men, sent them forth. For the accusative participle following the dative which is required by ἔδοξε we have a parallel in Soph. *Electra,* 480, ὕπεστί μοι θράσος ἀδυπνόων κλύουσαν ἀρτίως ὀνειράτων, and see on similar constructions Elmsley on *Heracl.* 693; *Medea,* 810; cf. also Thuc. IV. 118, referred to above.

σὺν τῷ Παύλῳ καὶ Βαρνάβᾳ, *with Paul and Barnabas.* That the Church of Antioch might have the confirmation of the decree from the lips of others besides these two, for they might be supposed to favour especially all that was considerate towards Gentile converts.

Ἰούδαν τὸν καλούμενον Βαρσαββᾶν, *Judas called Barsabbas.* Of this man nothing more is known than what we learn from this chapter. But as Barsabbas is clearly a patronymic, it has been conjectured that he was the brother of Joseph, also called Barsabbas, mentioned in Acts i. 23.

Σίλαν, *Silas.* This is probably the same person who in St Paul's Epistles (2 Cor. i. 19; 1 Thess. i. 1; 2 Thess. i. 1) and by St

Peter (1 Pet. v. 12) is called Silvanus. For an account of similar contracted names cf. *Winer-Moulton*, pp. 127, 128. The mention of Silas is frequent in the Acts in this and the next three chapters. He was one of St Paul's companions in the first missionary journey into Europe.

23. γράψαντες, *having written*. From the form in which the document is here given, we should judge that the original was in Greek. A translation from a Hebrew original would hardly have begun with a greeting and ended with ἔρρωσθε. It seems likely that this was so too, because the population of Antioch, the chief town in Syria, would use Greek much more than Hebrew, at this date. The nominative case γράψαντες is a construction to accord with sense rather than strict grammar. It stands as if it had been preceded by some such words as καὶ τοῦτο ἐποίησαν.

διὰ χειρὸς αὐτῶν. Literally, 'by their hand.' This is a Hebrew form of saying, *by them*. Cf. Levit. x. 11, ἅπαντα τὰ νόμιμα ἃ ἐλάλησε κύριος πρὸς αὐτοὺς διὰ χειρὸς Μωυσῆ. So Mal. i. 1, &c. The letter was not delivered to Paul and Barnabas, but to the two ambassadors from Jerusalem. It is the oldest synodical circular letter in existence, and the only one of Apostolic times which has come down to us. Bengel suggests that it was composed by James, in the name and at the request of the assembly.

οἱ ἀπόστολοι καὶ οἱ πρεσβύτεροι ἀδελφοί, *the Apostles and elder brethren*. This reading, supported by the oldest MSS., brings the text into more complete harmony with what has gone before. Hitherto, though the whole Church came together only two sets of persons have been spoken of as to be consulted or as having authority. These are οἱ ἀπόστολοι καὶ οἱ πρεσβύτεροι (verses 2, 6 and 22). It seems most natural therefore that the decree should run in the names of these two bodies.

κατὰ τὴν Ἀντιόχειαν καὶ Συρίαν καὶ Κιλικίαν, *in Antioch and Syria and Cilicia*. As we have no mention of this decree of the synod of Jerusalem in St Paul's Epistles, we may suppose that the agitation on the subject, begun at Antioch, had spread only into Syria and Cilicia, and that the authoritative decision of the mother Church quieted the controversy there, while it did not arise in the same form in other places.

χαίρειν, *greeting*. The infinitive is dependent on λέγουσι understood, but in a formula of this kind the governing verb never appears.

24. ἐξελθόντες, *which went out*. Some ancient MSS. omit this word, but it seems to have a distinct and necessary force. The disturbing teachers had come from Jerusalem, but their want of any authority is contrasted strongly with the commission of Judas and Silas (*v.* 27). The first men *went* of themselves, the new messengers were the choice of the Church.

ἀνασκευάζοντες τὰς ψυχὰς ὑμῶν, *subverting your souls*. The verb ἀνασκευάζειν is found in N.T. only here, and not at all in the LXX. In classical Greek it is applied mostly to an entire removal of goods and chattels either by the owners or by a plundering enemy. The devastation wrought in the minds of the Gentile converts through the new teaching is compared to an utter overthrow.

οἷς οὐ διεστειλάμεθα, *to whom we gave no commandment.* The Church of Jerusalem disclaims any connexion of any kind with the disturbing teachers. The sentence becomes thus much more forcible than it is with the additions of the *Text. recept.*

25. γενομένοις ὁμοθυμαδόν, *having become of one accord.* This rendering makes some distinction between ὁμοθυμαδόν with εἰμί and with γίγνομαι. With the substantive verb this adverb stands in Acts ii. 1, iv. 24, v. 12, and may there be rendered 'being with one accord.'

ἐκλεξαμένους ἄνδρας πέμψαι πρὸς ὑμᾶς, *to choose out men and send them to you.* On the language see above on verse 22.

σὺν τοῖς ἀγαπητοῖς ἡμῶν, *with our beloved.* The intention of the whole letter is to shew the honour which the Church in Jerusalem felt was due to these missionary labourers. Hence the adjective ἀγαπητός, which in N.T. is specially applied to those who are closely united in faith and love. St Peter applies it to St Paul (2 Pet. iii. 15).

Βαρνάβᾳ καὶ Παύλῳ, *Barnabas and Paul.* The order in which the names here stand is perhaps due to the fact that Barnabas had formerly (xi. 22) been sent as the accredited messenger from Jerusalem to the Church in Antioch; while St Paul was not so well known in Jerusalem.

26. ἀνθρώποις παραδεδωκόσι τὰς ψυχὰς αὐτῶν, *men that have hazarded their lives.* This Paul and Barnabas had done on several occasions. (See xiii. 50, xiv. 2, 5, 19.)

ὑπὲρ τοῦ ὀνόματος, *for the name.* Here, as often, *name* signifies the Messianic dignity and divine authority of Jesus. They have preached everywhere Jesus as the Christ.

27. διὰ λόγου, *by word,* i.e. by word of mouth.

ἀπαγγέλλοντας, *announcing.* The present tense is however equivalent to a future. 'We have sent them announcing,' i.e. as announcers, as persons to announce. So that the A.V. 'who shall tell you' is the precise sense and excellent English. The use of this tense comes from the feeling of the senders that those whom they are despatching are as good as present at their destination.

28. ἔδοξεν γὰρ τῷ πνεύματι τῷ ἁγίῳ καὶ ἡμῖν, *for it seemed good to the Holy Ghost and to us.* A third time in this clause of the narrative from 22—29 does this official word occur, from which is derived the noun *dogma.* It had been promised that to the Apostles there should be given the Spirit of truth, who should guide them into all truth (John xvi. 13), and the historian of the Acts often speaks of them as 'filled with the Spirit.' They put forward therefore this unerring guide as the warrant for their decree. And as they at the suggestion

of the Spirit were laying aside their long-standing prejudices against intercourse with Gentiles, they claim that the Gentiles in their turn should deal tenderly with the scruples of Jews.

The co-ordination of the Divine Spirit and the human instruments in the preamble of the decree is not a little remarkable.

On this verse Chrysostom says: καὶ τίνος ἕνεκεν εἶπεν, ἔδοξε τῷ ἁγίῳ πνεύματι; ἵνα μὴ νομίσωσιν ἀνθρώπινον εἶναι· τὸ δὲ ἡμῖν ἵνα διδαχθῶσιν ὅτι καὶ αὐτοὶ ἀποδέχονται καὶ ἐν περιτομῇ ὄντες.

μηδὲν πλέον ἐπιτίθεσθαι ὑμῖν βάρος, *to lay upon you no greater burden.* The Christian-Jews could now speak thus of the load of legal observances (cf. above, verse 10). Now they had selected but a small part thereof, which the circumstances of the time made necessary to be observed.

29. εὖ πράξετε, *ye shall do well,* i.e. it shall be well with you.

ἔρρωσθε, *fare ye well.* This conclusion and the greeting at the commencement of the letter are in the style of Western, rather than Oriental, epistolary language. See above on verse 23.

30—35. RECEPTION OF THE LETTER AND MESSENGERS AT ANTIOCH.

30. κατῆλθον εἰς Ἀντιόχειαν, *came down to Antioch.* As in viii. 5, Jerusalem is regarded as the chief seat of Church-government, and the centre of authority. Throughout the Bible the chosen place is always spoken of as one to which men *go up.*

συναγαγόντες τὸ πλῆθος, *having gathered the multitude.* This expression shews of how great concern the question had become to the whole Christian body. πλῆθος is used above (v. 12) of the assembly of Christians at Jerusalem.

31. ἐχάρησαν ἐπὶ τῇ παρακλήσει, *rejoiced for the consolation.* Barnabas (υἱὸς παρακλήσεως, iv. 36) was a fit member of such an embassy. The consolation would be felt both by Jews and Gentiles, by the former because they now knew how much was to be asked of their Gentile fellow-worshippers, by the latter because they were declared free from the yoke of Jewish observances. The noun very often signifies *exhortation,* but that sense is neither so apt here, nor is it borne out by the character of the letter, which sets forth a ground of peace and comfort, but is not hortatory.

32. καὶ αὐτοὶ προφῆται ὄντες, *being prophets also themselves.* προφήτης is here used in the earlier and less special sense; not as one who foretells the future, but who, being filled with the Spirit, speaks with His authority in explanation of the will of God. Judas and Silas being thus endowed were well fitted to *exhort* and *confirm* the disciples. The exhortations would be most necessary for the Gentiles who were to consent to more strict living than in times past, while the confirmation would uphold the Jews who otherwise might feel unwilling to allow the non-observance of a part of their Law. The prophetic character of the speakers would give to their words the force of revelation. Such confirmation or strengthening of the brethren is the

special charge laid on St Peter (Luke xxii. 32), who was to be the first preacher of Christ to the Gentiles, and had first received the lesson that what God had cleansed was not to be called common.

33. μετ᾿ εἰρήνης, *in peace.* This means with a parting prayer for their peace and welfare. The expression is a rendering of a common Hebrew phrase, and is found in the LXX. of Gen. xxvi. 29; Judges viii. 9, xi. 13; 1 Macc. vii. 28, &c.

πρὸς τοὺς ἀποστείλαντας αὐτούς, *unto those that had sent them forth,* who were not only 'the Apostles' (as A.V.) but the whole synod of Jerusalem.

The oldest MSS. omit verse 34. It seems to be no more than a marginal note to explain verse 40. There Paul, who did not leave Antioch, is said to have chosen Silas for his companion in his next journey. The latter must therefore have also remained in Antioch, and such an explanation, placed by some reader on the margin, came after a time to be incorporated with the text. But there are great differences in the MSS., and also in the versions.

35. διδάσκοντες καὶ εὐαγγελιζόμενοι, *teaching and preaching.* In such a community there was need not only of setting forth Jesus as the Saviour, but of much instruction concerning the ways in which God had shewn that the Gentiles were now to be made partakers of the new covenant. So that the two verbs should not be taken one as an explanation of the other. They represent different parts of the ministerial work.

36—41. A NEW MISSION-JOURNEY PROPOSED. CONTENTION BETWEEN PAUL AND BARNABAS. THEY SEPARATE, AND PAUL WITH SILAS GOES THROUGH SYRIA AND CILICIA.

36. τοὺς ἀδελφούς, *the brethren.* Implying both their own converts and those who should have been won to the Church since Paul and Barnabas came away.

κατὰ πόλιν πᾶσαν ἐν αἷς, *in every city in which.* The plural number of the pronoun αἷς is due to the plural idea involved in the πόλις πᾶσα: 'every city' means 'all the cities.'

πῶς ἔχουσιν, *how they do.* The direct interrogative instead of the dependent. The common usage of N.T.

37. Βαρνάβας δὲ ἐβούλετο, *but Barnabas wished.* Rev. Ver. 'was minded.' The reason for Barnabas' wish was probably because Mark was his nephew (Col. iv. 10).

38. τὸν ἀποστάντα ἀπ᾿ αὐτῶν, *him who departed from them.* See above, xiii. 13. He turned back to Jerusalem from Perga.

39. ἐγένετο δὲ παροξυσμὸς κ.τ.λ., *and there arose a sharp contention, so that,* &c. παροξυσμός (from which comes our English *paroxysm*) intimates a temporary rather than a prolonged dispute, although it may for the time be severe. The result to the Church was that two missionary journeys were undertaken instead of one. Though the

Apostles might differ in their estimate of Mark, they were at one with reference to the work of the Gospel. Barnabas is mentioned no more in the Acts after this chapter. His name occurs in St Paul's Epistles, 1 Cor. ix. 6; Gal. ii. 1, 9, 13; and Col. iv. 10, in which last passage, written no doubt after the events here related, we can see that Mark had been again received as a fellow-worker by St Paul. We learn too from 2 Tim. iv. 11 and Philemon 24 that St Paul became warmly attached to him afterwards.

παροξυσμός is twice used in the LXX. (Deut. xxix. 28; Jer. xxxii. 37) of the righteous anger of God against His offending people.

Chrysostom remarks on this contention: τὸ ζητούμενον, οὐχ ὅτι διηνέχθησαν ἐν ταῖς γνώμαις, ἀλλ᾽ ὅτι συγκατέβησαν ἀλλήλοις ἰδεῖν. οὕτω μεῖζον ἀγαθὸν γέγονε τὸ χωρισθῆναι, καὶ πρόφασιν ἐκ τούτου τὸ πρᾶγμα ἔλαβε. τί οὖν; ἐχθροὶ ἀνεχώρησαν; μὴ γένοιτο. ὁρᾷς γὰρ μετὰ τοῦτο Βαρνάβαν πολλῶν ἐγκωμίων ἀπολαύοντα παρὰ Παύλου ἐν ταῖς ἐπιστολαῖς. παροξυσμός, φησίν, ἐγένετο, οὐκ ἔχθρα οὐδὲ φιλονεικία.

ἐκπλεῦσαι εἰς Κύπρον, *sailed unto Cyprus*, in which island Barnabas, and it may be Mark also, was born (iv. 36). They chose therefore for their labours a district in which they were likely to have some influence.

40. παραδοθείς, *being commended*. See above on xiv. 26.

41. τὴν Συρίαν καὶ Κιλικίαν, *Syria and Cilicia*. These were the districts in which the teaching of the Judaizers had been most active, and the presence of Paul, with Silas as a representative of the Church in Jerusalem, would allay all doubts and questionings, and lead to those results which are mentioned xvi. 5, the establishing of the Churches, and their daily increase in numbers. This duty St Paul first discharged before he went on to visit any of the Churches which himself had founded.

CHAPTER XVI.

Readings varying from the *Text. recept.*

1. τινος omitted with אABCDE. Not represented in *Vulg.*

6. διῆλθον with אABCDE. *Vulg.* 'transeuntes.'

7. εἰς before τὴν Βιθυνίαν with אABCD. *Vulg.* 'in Bithyniam.'

τὸ πνεῦμα ᾿Ιησοῦ with אABCDE. *Vulg.* 'Spiritus Jesu.'

9. τῷ Παύλῳ ὤφθη with אBDE. *Vulg.* 'Paulo ostensa est.'

ἀνὴρ Μακεδών τις ἦν ἑστὼς καὶ with אABCE. *Vulg.* 'vir Macedo quidam erat stans et deprecans.'

10. θεὸς for κύριος with אABCE. *Vulg.* 'Deus.'

13. ἔξω τῆς πύλης with אABCD. *Vulg.* 'foras portam.'

ἐνομίζομεν προσευχὴν εἶναι with אABC. *Vulg.* 'videbatur oratio esse.'

16. πνεῦμα πύθωνα with אABCD. *Vulg.* 'spiritum pythonem.'

17. ὑμῖν before ὁδὸν with אBDE. *Vulg.* 'vobis.'

31. Χριστόν omitted with אAB. Unrepresented in *Vulg.*

32. σὺν for καὶ before πᾶσιν with אABCD. *Vulg.* 'cum.'

34. αὐτοῦ omitted after οἶκον with BCP. *Vulg.* 'in domum suam.'

39. ἀπελθεῖν ἀπὸ τῆς πόλεως with אAB. *Vulg.* 'egrederentur de urbe.'

40. πρὸς τὴν Λυδίαν with אABDEHLP. *Vulg.* 'ad.'

παρεκάλεσαν τοὺς ἀδελφούς omitting αὐτούς with אAB. *Vulg.* 'visis fratribus consolati sunt eos.'

Ch. XVI. 1—12. PAUL REVISITS DERBE AND LYSTRA, CHOOSES TIMOTHY FOR A COMPANION IN HIS MISSION, AND CIRCUMCISES HIM. THEY PASS THROUGH PHRYGIA AND GALATIA, AND COME INTO MYSIA AND TO TROAS. BY A VISION PAUL IS CALLED INTO MACEDONIA. HE CROSSES THE SEA AND REMAINS SOME DAYS AT PHILIPPI.

1. κατήντησεν. The preposition in this verb seems to have little or no force. Cf. its use in 2 Macc. iv. 21, 44.

εἰς Δέρβην καὶ...Λύστραν, *to Derbe and Lystra.* This is the beginning of that revisiting spoken of in xv. 36. See notes on xiv. 6.

ἦν ἐκεῖ, *was there.* The verb does not make it certain that Lystra, to which ἐκεῖ is most naturally referred, was the birthplace of Timothy, but only his home at the date of Paul's visit. He must however have resided there a good while to have earned the favourable report of the people both of that place and Iconium.

Τιμόθεος, *Timothy.* This is the person to whom St Paul addresses two Epistles, and who was the companion of his labours in this journey until his return into Proconsular Asia (xx. 4). He was the son of a Jewish-Christian mother, and his father was a Greek, whether a proselyte of the gate or not we are not told. The mother's name was Eunice (2 Tim. i. 5) and the grandmother's Lois. Timothy is spoken of as a fellow-worker with St Paul (Rom. xvi. 21). From 1 Cor. iv. 17 we find that he was St Paul's messenger to that Church, and he is joined with that Apostle in the greeting of 2nd Corinthians. He also went to and fro between St Paul and the Church in Thessalonica (1 Thess. iii. 2, 6) and must have been at Rome with St Paul soon after the Apostle's arrival there, for he is mentioned in the Epistles, to the Philippians (i. 1, ii. 19), to the Colossians (i. 1) and to Philemon (1). An imprisonment which he underwent is alluded to (Heb. xiii. 23), but we cannot be certain when or where it was. According to tradition (Eus. *H. E.* III. 14) he was the first bishop of Ephesus, and is said to have suffered martyrdom at the hands of the populace (Niceph. *H. E.* III. 11).

υἱὸς γυναικὸς Ἰουδαίας πιστῆς, *the son of a Jewess which believed.*
Her earnest education of her son in the holy Scriptures (2 Tim. iii. 15)
from his early youth marks the character of the woman, and makes it
probable that the husband of such a woman was at least a proselyte
of the gate. Timothy's father is so little mentioned that it seems
likely he had died early.

πατρὸς δὲ Ἕλληνος, *but of a father who was a Greek.* The word
Ἕλλην was widely used by the Jews about all who were not of their own
nation. The world for them was divided into Ἰουδαῖοι καὶ Ἕλληνες.
Cf. Acts xiv. 1; Rom. i. 16, &c.

2. ὃς ἐμαρτυρεῖτο, *who was well reported of.* The same word is
used about Cornelius (x. 22), and by Paul about Ananias (xxii. 12).

ὑπὸ τῶν ἐν Λύστροις καὶ Ἰκονίῳ ἀδελφῶν, *by the brethren that were
at Lystra and Iconium.* The 'brethren' are the members of the
Christian Churches. Five or six years had elapsed since St Paul's
previous visit. In that time congregations had been gathered together
and the characters of their most earnest members were well known.
We see too that there was an interchange of kindly offices between the
neighbouring Churches.

3. περιέτεμεν αὐτόν, *he circumcised him.* It must be remembered
that the decree of the synod of Jerusalem only related to the exemp-
tion of Gentiles from circumcision. It was a very different thing for
a Jew to consent to become a fellow-worshipper in the Christian
Churches with a Gentile who remained uncircumcised, and to tolerate,
at this time, the non-observance of the rite by one who was counted
for a Jew. For by the Rabbinical code the child of a Jewish mother
was reckoned as a Jew (T. J. *Jebamoth*, II. 6). It was because of this
prejudice that Timothy was circumcised. It could be no offence to
the Gentiles, and would render the labours of Timothy more acceptable to the Jews. Because he was the child of a mixed marriage the
rite had been unobserved, and so long as he did not come forward as a
teacher there would be no need felt that it should be enforced, and
there would be doubtless many others of a like class. But when he
was to take a share in the missionary labours of St Paul all this was
altered. He would at once have been met with the objection from
the Jews, that he who had been but a bad Jew was not likely to guide
others right as a Christian teacher. That St Paul saw no inconsistency in what was done in this matter is clear, for the narrative of St
Luke tells us in the next verse that to the Churches to which they
went forth he delivered the decrees of the synod at Jerusalem.

4. παρεδίδοσαν αὐτοῖς, *they delivered to them,* i.e. to the converts
in the several cities. They gave to the Gentile-Christians the decrees
to observe, for there was nothing in them which a Jew would be likely
to disregard. All that would be needed for the Jews in such cities would
be to explain the terms on which Gentiles were to be admitted to the
Christian communion.

τὰ δόγματα τὰ κεκριμένα, *the decrees that were ordained*. The phrase of James (xv. 19) was ἐγὼ κρίνω, and the decree was in the form ἔδοξεν ἡμῖν (xv. 25).

5. ἐστερεοῦντο τῇ πίστει, *were established in the faith*. This verb is peculiar to the Acts, and is used (iii. 7, 16) of the strengthening of the limbs of the lame man at the Beautiful Gate of the Temple. So its employment here indicates that thus the Church was now prepared to make great progress. The barrier to Gentile admission was removed, and so the number of Christians multiplied daily.

στερεόω is found both in the literal and metaphorical senses in the LXX. The former is mostly concerning God, ὁ στερεώσας τὴν γῆν καὶ τὰ ἐν αὐτῇ (Is. xlii. 5). In a figurative sense (Prov. xx. 21) διαλογισμοὶ ἐν βουλῇ στερεοῦνται.

6. διῆλθον δέ, *and they passed through*. The reading διελθόντες of the *Text. recept.* is probably due to the participle which immediately follows and has no conjunction.

τὴν Φρυγίαν καὶ Γαλατικὴν χώραν, *Phrygia and the region of Galatia*. This was scarcely the direction, so far as population was concerned, which would have been chosen by them of their own accord, but the inner admonition of the Holy Ghost kept them from entering Proconsular Asia. The news of the events at Jerusalem on the Day of Pentecost were known to some in Phrygia already (ii. 10), but of Galatia the history has yet made no mention, though we know from St Paul's Epistle to that Church that he afterwards had the warmest interest in and greatest anxiety concerning the Christians there, among whom Judaizers wrought like mischief with that done in Antioch. From some expressions of St Paul (Gal. iv. 19) it seems likely that it was from his own preaching at this time that Churches in Galatia were founded.

κωλυθέντες, *having been forbidden*. As they had been forbidden the one route they went by the other. St Luke says little about the events in this part of the journey, probably because he was not of the company, for his language below (*v.* 10) seems to shew that he only joined St Paul at Troas.

Chrysostom's reflection on the hindrance here spoken of is: διατί μὲν οὖν ἐκωλύθησαν, οὐ λέγει. ὅτι δὲ ἐκωλύθησαν εἶπε, παιδεύων ἡμᾶς πείθεσθαι μόνον καὶ μὴ ζητεῖν τὰς αἰτίας.

ἐν τῇ Ἀσίᾳ, *in Asia*. See note on ii. 9.

7. ἐλθόντες δὲ κατὰ τὴν Μυσίαν, *and being come over against Mysia*. The 'to' of A.V. is incorrect. The course of the journey seems to have been through Galatia and Phrygia, until they got so far to the west as to be opposite to, and on the borders of, Mysia. From this point they were inclined to go north into Bithynia, rather than further to the west, but were again hindered of their intention.

ἐπείραζον εἰς τὴν Βιθυνίαν πορευθῆναι, *they attempted to go into Bithynia*. This was their plan and they were ready to carry it out, when they were inwardly admonished to go another way.

τὸ πνεῦμα Ἰησοῦ, *the spirit of Jesus.* In like manner (Rom. viii. 9) the 'Spirit of God' is called also the 'Spirit of Christ.' Cf. also Gal. iv. 6; Phil. i. 19; 1 Pet. i. 11.

8. παρελθόντες δὲ τὴν Μυσίαν, *and having passed by Mysia,* i.e. without preaching there. Mysia was a district of Proconsular Asia, where they were forbidden, by the Spirit, to preach.

εἰς Τρωάδα, *to Troas,* the well-known seaport on the coast of Mysia.

9. καὶ ὅραμα διὰ νυκτὸς τῷ Παύλῳ ὤφθη, *and a vision appeared to Paul by night.* That such divine communications should be made after the descent of the Holy Ghost was part of the fulfilment of the prophecy of Joel about which Peter spake on the Day of Pentecost (ii. 17). For their frequent occurrence cf. ix. 10, x. 3, 17, 19, xi. 5, xii. 9, xviii. 9.

ἀνὴρ Μακεδών, *a man of Macedonia.* His nationality was made known by the words of his request.

10. ἐζητήσαμεν, *we sought.* The steps taken would be in the way of inquiry how and when they could cross into Europe. For ζητεῖν with a verb of going, cf. LXX. 1 Kings xi. 22, ἰδοὺ σὺ ζητεῖς ἀπελθεῖν εἰς τὴν γῆν σου.

At this point the writer begins to speak in the first person as if now he became a sharer in St Paul's labours. This he continues till verse 17.

ἐξελθεῖν, *to go forth.* A word suitable for the first step in the next extension of missionary work from Asia into Europe.

συμβιβάζοντες, *assuredly gathering.* The verb has the sense of 'coming to a conclusion from putting things side by side.' So it is rendered 'proving' in ix. 22 and elsewhere. Here it means 'deeming it to be proved.'

Chrysostom explains thus: τί ἐστι συμβιβάζοντες ; στοχαζόμενοι, φησί. τῷ τε γὰρ Παῦλον ἰδεῖν καὶ μηδένα ἕτερον, καὶ τῷ κωλυθῆναι ὑπὸ τοῦ πνεύματος καὶ τῷ πρὸς τοῖς ὅροις εἶναι, ἀπὸ τούτων ἁπάντων ταῦτα συνῆγον.

11. Σαμοθρᾴκην, *Samothrace.* This island lies in the north of the Aegean Sea, opposite to that part of the Thracian coast at which the river Hebrus empties itself.

Νέαν πόλιν, *Neapolis,* the port of Philippi. This place is generally identified with the modern *Kavalla.* On the discussion about its identity see *Dictionary of the Bible* (s. v.).

12. κἀκεῖθεν εἰς Φιλίππους, *and from thence to Philippi.* As there is no change of the verb (εὐθυδρομήσαμεν) for the whole description of the journey, we may conclude that it was all made by ship.

ἥτις ἐστὶν...κολωνία, *which is a city of Macedonia,* the *first of the district, a colony.* Philippi and the country round had long been famous by reason of the neighbouring gold-mines. At the time of St Paul's visit it was held by the Romans, and a colony had been founded there by Augustus. The civil magistrates and the military authorities were Roman. Hence the fear (xvi. 38) when they heard that prisoners whom they had scourged were Roman citizens. For a history of Philippi, see *Dict. of the Bible.*

It should be borne in mind that a Roman colony was not like what we now call a colony. The inhabitants did not settle as they pleased, but were sent out by authority from Rome, marching to their destination like an army with banners, and they reproduced, where they settled, a close resemblance of Roman rule and life. They were planted on the frontiers of the empire for protection, and as a check upon the provincial magistrates. The names of those who went were still enrolled in the lists of the tribes of Rome. Latin was their language, and they used the Roman coinage, and had their chief magistrates sent out or appointed from the mother city. Thus were they very closely united with Rome, and entirely free from any intrusion on the part of the governors of the provinces.

13—34. PREACHING ON THE SABBATH AT PHILIPPI. CONVERSION AND BAPTISM OF LYDIA. A SPIRIT OF DIVINATION CAST OUT BY ST PAUL. ANGER OF THOSE WHO MADE GAIN THEREBY. PAUL AND SILAS ARE SEIZED, BROUGHT BEFORE THE AUTHORITIES, SCOURGED AND IMPRISONED, BUT THE PRISON DOORS ARE OPENED BY A MIRACLE. CONVERSION AND BAPTISM OF THE JAILOR AND HIS HOUSEHOLD.

13. τῇ τε ἡμέρᾳ τῶν σαββάτων, *and on the sabbath.* The form of the phrase is common in the LXX. Cf. Lev. xxiv. 8; Num. xxviii. 9; Jer. xvii. 21, 22. But ἡ ἡμέρα τοῦ σαββάτου is also frequent.

ἔξω τῆς πύλης, *outside the gate.* The Jews probably found that their worship was less likely to attract hostile notice and less liable to interruption there than it would have been in the city.

οὗ ἐνομίζομεν προσευχὴν εἶναι, *where we supposed there was a place of prayer.* The meaning of προσευχή here and in verse 16 is 'a place of prayer.' The Jews had such προσευχαί, sometimes in buildings, sometimes in the open air, as was the case in this instance. The word is found in this sense in Josephus, *De vita sua,* 54, συνάγονται πάντες εἰς τὴν προσευχὴν μέγιστον οἴκημα πολὺν ὄχλον ἐπιδέξασθαι δυνάμενον. They are described by Philo (ed. Mang.) II. 282. They were very numerous in Rome (see Mayor, *Juvenal,* III. 296). Because of Jewish ceremonial washings they were, when in the open air, as often as might be, near a river-side or on the sea-shore. Cf. Ezra viii. 15 and 21. And no doubt the language of Ps. cxxxvii. 1, 'By the rivers of Babylon we sat down,' applies to a similar state of things.

καὶ καθίσαντες, *and having sat down.* Sitting was the usual attitude of Jewish teachers.

ταῖς συνελθούσαις γυναιξίν, *unto the women which were come together.* The Greek refers to those gathered together on this particular occasion only. Considering the little regard which the Jews had for women as persons to be conversed with and taught, it is noteworthy how large a part women play both in the Gospel History and in the Acts. It was one effect of Christianity to place woman in her true position.

14. Λυδία, *Lydia.* This may have been the woman's proper name, or it may only have been that by which she passed among the colonists of Philippi, being from the *Lydian* town of Thyatira. From inscriptions which have been found on the site of the ancient town, it is clear that dyeing was one of the staple trades of Thyatira, and it was from thence that Lydia brought over the purple which she sold in Philippi.

πόλεως Θυατείρων, *of the city of Thyatira.* This city was on the Lydian river Lycus. There was another river Lycus in Phrygia, in the valley of which stood the cities of Laodicæa, Hierapolis and Colossæ, all afterwards the seats of Christian congregations in whose welfare St Paul was deeply interested. See Col. iv. 13.

σεβομένη τὸν θεόν, *who worshipped God,* i.e. who had become a proselyte to Judaism.

ἧς ὁ κύριος διήνοιξεν τὴν καρδίαν, *whose heart the Lord opened.* St Luke recognizes that without this the word would have made no entrance. He probably makes special mention of this here because he had previously stated that the Lord had called them to preach at Philippi. Having pointed out their work, He helps them to perform it.

For the phrase compare the prayer 2 Macc. i. 4, καὶ διανοίξαι τὴν καρδίαν ὑμῶν ἐν τῷ νόμῳ αὐτοῦ.

προσέχειν, *that she attended.* For the construction see note on viii. 6. She gave such heed that she was convinced of the truth of what was taught.

Chrysostom says here: τὸ μὲν οὖν ἀνοῖξαι, τοῦ θεοῦ, τὸ δὲ προσέχειν, αὐτῆς· ὥστε καὶ θεῖον καὶ ἀνθρώπινον ἦν.

15. καὶ ὁ οἶκος αὐτῆς, *and her household.* Of a like baptizing of a household see below (*v.* 33), and also cf. xi. 14. We are not justified in concluding from these passages that infants were baptized. 'Household' might mean slaves and freedwomen.

μένετε, *abide there.* Like the two disciples who followed Jesus (John i. 38) Lydia was anxious to have the teachers whose lessons she found so suited to the needs of her opened heart near unto her.

παρεβιάσατο ἡμᾶς, *she constrained us.* Used in N.T. only by St Luke here and Luke xxiv. 29, of the two disciples at Emmaus. In the LXX. it occurs more frequently and is used (1 Sam. xxviii. 23) of the constraint put upon Saul at Endor to make him take food, also (2 Kings ii. 17) of the urgent request made to Elisha by the prophets at Jericho. Cf. also 2 Kings v. 16.

The force used was that of a prayer which would accept no 'Nay.'

16. πορευομένων ἡμῶν εἰς τὴν προσευχήν, *as we were going to the place of prayer* (see on verse 13). This verse must refer to a different occasion from that on which Lydia was converted. In the previous παρεβιάσατο it is implied that they consented to her request. Thus they had already taken up their abode in Lydia's house.

ἔχουσαν πνεῦμα πύθωνα, *having a spirit, a Python.* According to Plutarch (*De def. Orac.* 9) those persons who practised ventriloquism, called also ἐγγαστρίμυθοι, were named *Pythons.* But the damsel in this history clearly laid claim to some prophetic power, and was used as a means of foreknowing the future. So that the word Python is better here referred to the name of Apollo, the heathen god of prophecy, and the A.V. '*spirit of divination*' gives the correct idea.

ἐργασίαν πολλήν, *much gain.* ἐργασία means first the 'work done,' and secondarily the 'profit from it.' Cf. Wisdom xiii. 19, περὶ δὲ πορισμοῦ καὶ ἐργασίας, 'and concerning gaining and getting' (A. V.).

τοῖς κυρίοις αὐτῆς, *to her masters.* Some persons who having found a strange power in the maiden made use of it, as has oft been done, for their own purposes of gain, and persuaded the people to resort unto her with their questions.

μαντευομένη, *by soothsaying.* This word is found nowhere else in N.T., and wherever it is used in the LXX. it is invariably of the words of lying prophets, or those who used arts forbidden by the Jewish Law. Thus of the witch of Endor (1 Sam. xxviii. 8) μάντευσαι δή μοι ἐν τῷ ἐγγαστριμύθῳ, and (Ezek. xiii. 6) βλέποντες ψευδῆ, μαντευόμενοι μάταια. Cf. also Deut. xviii. 10; Ezek. xii. 24, xxi. 29, xxii. 28; Mic. iii. 11. Here therefore we must take it in the bad sense, 'by pretending to foretell the future.'

17. κατακολουθοῦσα τῷ Παύλῳ καὶ ἡμῖν, *following Paul and us.* Whatever may have been the nature of the mental and spiritual malady under which this damsel suffered, it produced on her the like effect which is oft recorded of evil spirits in the history of Jesus (Mark i. 24; Luke iv. 41), and forced her to confess to the true character of the Christian teachers. The devils believe and tremble (James ii. 19).

After this verse the writer ceases for a time to indicate by his language that he was with St Paul, but in xx. 5, where the Apostle comes once again to Philippi, the first person plural appears in the narrative. It seems therefore not improbable that St Luke was left behind to labour for the spread of the Gospel in Macedonia, and only taken away again by St Paul after the work had been well established.

δοῦλοι τοῦ θεοῦ τοῦ ὑψίστου, *the servants of the Most High God.* Cf. the words of the demoniac, Mark v. 7.

οἵτινες καταγγέλλουσιν ὑμῖν, *who proclaim unto you.* This is an older reading than ἡμῖν, and it seems more like what one who had been engaged in speaking as a soothsayer to others would say.

18. τοῦτο δὲ ἐποίει ἐπὶ πολλὰς ἡμέρας, *this she did for many days.* Whether this following took place only on the sabbaths, when the Apostles were going to the place of prayer, in which case the Apostles must have remained in Philippi some weeks, or whether it was on every occasion on which they appeared in public, we are not told.

διαπονηθεὶς δὲ Παῦλος, *but Paul being grieved*. The same verb is used (iv. 2) of the annoyance of the priests and Sadducees at the teaching of the Apostles, and nowhere else in N T. (See note there.) Its sense is 'to be thoroughly worn out with vexation.'

τῷ πνεύματι εἶπεν, *said to the spirit*. As Christ had acted when on earth, so Paul now will not allow the cry of the evil spirit, even though the words proclaim that he and his companions are servants of the Most High God. So in Christ's name he bids the evil power come forth.

19. ὅτι ἐξῆλθεν ἡ ἐλπὶς τῆς ἐργασίας αὐτῶν, *that the hope of their gain was gone*. The verb ἐξῆλθεν is the same word which was used of the spirit coming out of the damsel. We cannot produce the same effect by English words. When the spirit *went out*, the hope of their gain *went out* also. What the damsel herself may have thought of her power we cannot tell. Probably, for their money-making purposes, they had persuaded her that her ravings were prophetic.

ἐπιλαβόμενοι τὸν Παῦλον καὶ τὸν Σίλαν, *having caught Paul and Silas*, as being the most prominent members of the mission party.

εἰς τὴν ἀγοράν, *into the market-place*. This was the great place of concourse and where, as in the Roman *forum*, would be the seat of the authorities.

ἄρχοντας, *rulers*. A very general term, the special members of the magistracy being indicated in the next verse.

20. προσαγαγόντες αὐτοὺς τοῖς στρατηγοῖς, *having brought them to the magistrates*. These στρατηγοί were the *duumviri*, the two *prætors* specially appointed to preside over the administration of justice, in cases where there was no appeal to Rome, in the *municipia* and *coloniæ* of the Romans. The title στρατηγοί seems to indicate somewhat of a military authority, which could administer summary punishment.

ἐκταράσσουσιν, *do exceedingly trouble*. Only used here in N.T. In the LXX. it is twice found of terror arising from visions (Wisdom xvii. 3, xviii. 17 φαντασίαι μὲν ὀνείρων δεινῶς ἐξετάραξαν αὐτούς). Also in Pss. xvii. 5, lxxxvii. 17, of the trouble caused by floods of ungodliness, and by the terrors of the Lord. The kind of trouble spoken of in the text is seen from xvii. 6. 'These that have turned the world upside down' is the description of the preachers.

Ἰουδαῖοι ὑπάρχοντες, *being Jews*. On the ways in which Roman aversion was aroused and exhibited towards the Jews, for their religious exclusiveness, see Mayor *Juvenal* xiv. 96—106 notes, with the authorities there given. Jew-baiting is no modern invention.

21. καὶ καταγγέλλουσιν ἔθη, *and set forth customs*. The verb refers to the proclamation or preaching of the Apostles.

22. καὶ συνεπέστη ὁ ὄχλος, *and the multitude rose up together*, i.e. along with the aggrieved proprietors of the damsel.

περιρήξαντες αὐτῶν τὰ ἱμάτια, *rent their* (i.e. Paul and Silas's) *clothes off them*.

ἐκέλευον ῥαβδίζειν, *they commanded to beat them.* ῥαβδίζειν, to beat with rods was the office of the Roman lictor, who carried rods for this purpose when attending on the magistrates. The use of this special word is an indication that St Luke was aware of the particular kind of beating, and perhaps beheld the infliction. This is one of the occasions, no doubt, to which St Paul alludes (2 Cor. xi. 25), 'Thrice was I beaten with rods' (ἐραβδίσθην).

On the sufferings of the Apostles at Philippi, Chrysostom says: τούτοις συνεχῶς ἀναμιμνήσκωμεν ἑαυτοὺς παρακαλῶ, ὅσα ἔπαθον, ὅσα ὑπέμειναν. πῶς οὐκ ἐθορυβοῦντο ; πῶς οὐκ ἐσκανδαλίζοντο ; τὸ τοῦ θεοῦ ἔργον ἐποίουν καὶ ταῦτα ἔπασχον, οὐκ ἔλεγον, τί τοῦτο κηρύττομεν καὶ οὐ προίσταται ἡμῖν ὁ θεός ; ἀλλὰ καὶ τοῦτο αὐτοὺς ὠφέλει, καὶ χωρὶς τῆς βοηθείας αὐτῷ τῷ πράγματι εὐτονωτέρους ἐποίει, ἰσχυροτέρους, ἀκαταπλήκτους. ἡ θλῖψις, φησίν, ὑπομονὴν κατεργάζεται.

23. ἔβαλον εἰς φυλακήν, *they cast them into prison.* So that they should have no chance of teaching any longer. They appear (see *v.* 35) to have intended to keep them one night in prison and then to turn them out of the city.

24. εἰς τὴν ἐσωτέραν φυλακήν, *into the inner prison.* Necessarily a place dark and without ventilation, and hence foul and loathsome, perhaps underground, like the Tullianum at Rome (Varr. *L. L.* v. § 161; Liv. xxix. 22).

καὶ τοὺς πόδας ἠσφαλίσατο αὐτῶν εἰς τὸ ξύλον, *and made their feet fast in the stocks.* The ξύλον (literally *wood*) was a means of additional security and additional torture. The feet passed through holes and held secure made rest almost impossible. The instrument was of early use (cf. Job xxxiii. 11 (LXX.) ἔθετο δὲ ἐν ξύλῳ μου τὸν πόδα) ; and the Greeks, as well as ourselves, had also the pillory, and had it made with five apertures for head, hands and feet (Aristoph. *Eq.* 1049).

ἀσφαλίζομαι is used (Wisdom xiii. 15) of a man making his idol firm in its place, ἐν τοίχῳ ἔθηκεν αὐτὸ ἀσφαλισάμενος σιδήρῳ.

25. κατὰ δὲ τὸ μεσονύκτιον, *and at midnight.* Sleep being out of the question they passed the night in devotion. The imperfects ὕμνουν and ἐπηκροῶντο in the verse indicate that the prayers and singing were continued ; but we have no means of adequately representing this by idiomatic English.

οἱ δέσμιοι, *the prisoners.* The inner prison appears to have held more than Paul and Silas, or it may be that bars in the inner walls allowed the sound to pass into other cells. The verb is not the common one for 'hearing,' and is rarely found anywhere. It indicates attentive hearkening.

The derived noun ἐπακρόασις is found in LXX. 1 Sam. xv. 22 ἡ ἐπακρόασις ὑπὲρ στέαρ κριῶν, 'Hearkening [i.e. obedient hearkening] is better than the fat of rams.'

26. σεισμὸς ἐγένετο μέγας, *there was a great earthquake.* Just as the place wherein the Apostles prayed (iv. 31) was shaken, so here God testifies that He is near at hand.

πάντων τὰ δεσμὰ ἀνέθη, *every one's bands were loosed.* The sense in which these words are to be taken may be gathered from the rest of the description. The chains (δεσμὰ) were made fast to the wall, and the shock which burst asunder the bolts of the doors also released the fastenings which held the chains in the masonry.

27. ἔξυπνος δὲ γενόμενος ὁ δεσμοφύλαξ, *and the jailor awaking out of his sleep.* For ἔξυπνος cf. 1 Esdras iii. 3, ὁ βασιλεὺς...ἐκοιμήθη καὶ ἔξυπνος ἐγένετο. It is only found in N.T. in this verse.

σπασάμενος μάχαιραν, *having drawn his sword.* The jailor probably slept in such a place that on rising he could observe at a glance whether the prison doors were secure, and had his weapon close at hand so that he might seize and use it on any emergency. He must also have been so near to the open doors before he manifested any design of suicide that the prisoners within could see what he was doing. St Paul out of the dark could observe him before the jailor could see farther than the opened doors.

ἤμελλεν ἑαυτὸν ἀναιρεῖν, *he was about to kill himself.* For he knew what his fate would be. See xii. 19; and compare xxvii. 42, for the way in which Roman officials must answer with their lives for the escape of prisoners. Suicide under such circumstances would to the jailor's mind present the easiest way out of his difficulties, and the teaching of even the greatest minds both of Greece and Rome was that it was justifiable and under some circumstances praiseworthy. The suicide of Cato (*Catonis nobile letum*) furnished a constant text for such teaching. (Cf. Cic. *Tusc.* I. §§ 9—119; Plat. *Apol.* 40.)

28. ἐφώνησεν δὲ φωνῇ μεγάλῃ Παῦλος, *but Paul cried with a loud voice.* The sound of even one voice would arrest the jailor's action, for at the sight of the open doors he had concluded that all had made use of the opportunity and had escaped.

29. αἰτήσας δὲ φῶτα, *and having called for lights.* He would summon all the help he could, and would wish to make an inspection of his charge as speedily as possible.

ἔντρομος γενόμενος, *being terror-stricken.* For the word see above, vii. 32. It is also found in LXX. Dan. x. 11; Wisd. xvii. 9; 1 Macc. xiii. 2 ἔντρομος καὶ ἔμφοβος; and in Pss. xvii. 8, lxxvi. 18 of the earth in an earthquake, ἐσαλεύθη καὶ ἔντρομος ἐγενήθη ἡ γῆ. The jailor connected all that had occurred with the two prisoners Paul and Silas, and as they were not fled away, a change of feeling came over him, and he at once judged them to be more than other men. Hence his attitude becomes one of supplication and worship.

30. καὶ προαγαγὼν αὐτούς, *and having brought them out.* For there could be no fear that they would flee now who had remained when the open doors made escape easy.

κύριοι, *Sirs,* literally, 'Lords.' He acknowledges by the word their great superiority.

τί με δεῖ ποιεῖν ἵνα σωθῶ; *what must I do to be saved?* He had probably heard about the testimony of the possessed damsel, that Paul and Silas shewed the way of *salvation* (verse 17), and now without knowing what it fully meant, he cries out (in his misery, when despair had prompted suicide), asking for the teaching which they had to give.

31. πίστευσον ἐπὶ τὸν κύριον Ἰησοῦν, *believe on the Lord Jesus.* The word Χριστὸς which is inserted here in the *Text. recept.* would not have the same significance for a Gentile as for a Jew, and may well have been omitted in the address to the jailor. What was asked from Gentile converts was to accept *Jesus* as their *Lord.* The men whom he had just called 'Lords' point him to the only 'Lord.'

καὶ ὁ οἶκός σου, *and thy house.* The thought is that what the head of the family did would be followed by the rest. The remark made above (verse 15) on the meaning of οἶκος is not so applicable here. The jailor was not likely to have a slave-household. But whoever the members were, we see from the next verse that they were willing hearers.

The reflection of Chrysostom is: μάλιστα τοῦτο τοὺς ἀνθρώπους ἐφέλκεται, τὸ καὶ τὸν οἶκον αὐτοῦ σωθῆναι.

32. τὸν λόγον τοῦ κυρίου, *the word of the Lord,* i.e. he preached to him the doctrine of Christ, in the only way then possible, by the narrative of His life and its purpose.

33. ἐν ἐκείνῃ τῇ ὥρᾳ τῆς νυκτός, *in that same hour of the night.* It was midnight, see verse 25. But a new day, a birthday, had already begun for him and it must be kept as a feast. So he does his utmost to shew his rejoicing by care for those who had caused it.

ἔλουσεν ἀπὸ τῶν πληγῶν, *he washed their stripes.* An act of attention which had not been bestowed before. They were thrust into the inner prison with their wounds all bleeding and uncared for. The literal sense is 'washed (them) from their wounds,' i.e. from the stains and blood which their wounds had caused. Cf. Apoc. i. 5, λούσαντι ἡμᾶς ἀπὸ τῶν ἁμαρτιῶν ἡμῶν.

Chrysostom here remarks: ἐκείνους μὲν ἀπὸ τῶν πληγῶν ἔλουσεν, αὐτὸς δὲ ἀπὸ τῶν ἁμαρτιῶν ἐλούθη, ἔθρεψε καὶ ἐτράφη.

34. παρέθηκεν τράπεζαν, *he set meat* (lit. *a table*) *before them.* He would not let them remain longer in the dungeon, but took means to testify how the dawn of faith had filled him with joy.

καὶ ἠγαλλιάσατο πανοικὶ πεπιστευκὼς τῷ θεῷ, *and rejoiced with all his house, having believed in God.* He had been taught in verse 31 'to believe on the Lord Jesus,' and we must explain this verse by that. To believe on Jesus is to believe what God has made known concerning Him. This the jailor had heard in 'the word of the Lord' (verse 32), that story which told how in Jesus all the prophecies were fulfilled, and how by His mighty works He had shewn that He was the Son of God.

It is scarcely possible to help being struck in this chapter with the account of the effect of the first preaching of the Gospel in Europe.

We see at once its universality and its power. The first notable convert is Lydia, the Asiatic settler, a woman evidently of wealth, position and refinement; then the demoniac slave-girl is made an instrument of proclaiming the presence and power of the Most High God;
and last, the Roman jailor, of a class, insensible as a rule and
hardened by habit, and also disposed to despise the Jews who were
the bearers of the message of the Gospel. The converts of Philippi
(the firstfruits of St Paul's preaching in Europe) were types and an
earnest of how Christ's cause would make its way.

**35—40. THE MAGISTRATES WOULD SEND THEM AWAY, BUT PAUL
REFUSES TO BE THUS DISMISSED. HE ANNOUNCES THAT THEY
ARE ROMANS, AND THE MAGISTRATES IN FEAR BESEECH THEM TO
DEPART. THEY TAKE LEAVE OF LYDIA AND THE BRETHREN AND
LEAVE PHILIPPI.**

35. τοὺς ῥαβδούχους, *the serjeants*. Literally, 'rodbearers.' These
were the lictors, that attended on the prætors (duumviri, στρατηγοί),
probably the same persons who on the previous day had scourged Paul
and Silas, and were now sent to see that they were got rid of.

36. ἀπήγγειλεν δὲ...τοὺς λόγους τούτους, *and he reported these
words*. No doubt he came with great joy, and it is evident that
Paul and Silas had gone back to their prison after the events at midnight.

ἐξελθόντες πορεύεσθε, *come forth and go*, i.e. out of the prison, in
which they were still remaining to abide what should befall.

37. ὁ δὲ Παῦλος ἔφη πρὸς αὐτούς, *but Paul said unto them*, i.e.
to the lictors, through the jailor. It is highly probable that the conversation of the Roman officers would be in Latin, and that the proceedings of the previous day may have been conducted in that language.
In this way, if Paul and Silas were unfamiliar with the Latin speech,
we might account for the non-mention or the disregard of their Roman
citizenship. If either the Apostle did not comprehend all that was
going on or could not, amid the confusion of such a tumultuous court,
make himself understood, the message which he now sends to the
magistrates might have had no chance of being heard before the scourging was inflicted.

δείραντες ἡμᾶς δημοσίᾳ, *having beaten us publicly*. For no doubt
they had been lashed to the *palus* or public whipping-post in sight of
all the people.

ἀκατακρίτους, *uncondemned*. There had been no reality of a trial,
no attempt to get at the truth. For all that hath been listened to was
the charge of the accusers, who, leaving out all mention of the real
reason of their charge, viz. that they had lost a source of money-
making, put forward the plea that the missionaries were disturbers of
public law and order. The crowd shouted with the accusers, and the
magistrates, forgetting their position, joined with the mob (verse 22) in
the assault on the Apostles.

ἀνθρώπους Ῥωμαίους ὑπάρχοντας, *men that are Romans.* This is in marked contrast with the charge of the accusers, which ran, 'These men, being Jews.' The laws which had been violated by this act were the *Lex Valeria* (B.C. 508) and the *Lex Porcia* (B.C. 300). On the outrage, compare Cicero's language in the Verrine orations (v. 66), 'Facinus est vinciri civem Romanum, *scelus verberari*, prope parricidium necari.'

λάθρα ἡμᾶς ἐκβάλλουσιν; *are they thrusting us out privily?* The Apostle would say, Our punishment was in public, let our dismissal be public too.

οὐ γάρ, ἀλλά. The explanation of this combination of particles appears to be to understand the previous question as a refusal to come forth = 'We will not be thrust out privily. *For* that is *not* what ought to be, *but let them come,*' &c. So that the 'Nay verily' of A.V. gives the sense very well.

38. ἐφοβήθησαν δέ, *and they were afraid,* because a Roman citizen had a right of appeal to the emperor, and outrage on such a man was visited with severe penalties.

'Ῥωμαῖοί εἰσιν, *they are Romans.* The words are reported exactly as the messengers would utter them; ὅτι is no more than a mark of quotation.

39. ἠρώτων ἀπελθεῖν ἀπὸ τῆς πόλεως, *they desired them to depart from the city.* Finding how much they had offended, they become very humble, and beg the disciples to relieve them of their anxiety by quitting Philippi. We are not told how Paul and Silas established their statement, but they must have produced satisfactory proof to inspire so much fear. We hear of Paul's claim afterwards when he appeals to Cæsar. Of Silas' right to citizenship we have no further evidence.

40. πρὸς τὴν Λυδίαν, *into the house of Lydia.* Waiting there probably till they were fit to travel farther. But in the midst of the suffering they still exhort and comfort the Christians whom in their stay they had gathered into a Church.

How deep the mutual affection was, which afterwards existed between St Paul and these Philippians, his first European converts, is manifest in every line of the Epistle which he wrote to them from Rome in his first imprisonment. They are his greatest joy, they have given him no cause for sorrow, and from first to last have ministered to his afflictions, and made manifest how they prized their 'Father in Christ.' The jubilant language of the letter is marked by the oft-repeated 'Rejoice in the Lord.'

CHAPTER XVII.

Readings varying from the *Text. recept.*

1. ἡ omitted before συναγωγὴ with אABD.

4. πλῆθος πολύ with אABDE. *Vulg.* 'multitudo magna.'

5. ἀπειθοῦντες omitted before Ἰουδαῖοι with אABE. Not represented in *Vulg.*

προαγαγεῖν with אAB. *Vulg.* 'producere.'

7. βασιλέα ἕτερον λέγοντες with אAB. *Vulg.* 'regem alium dicentes.'

13. καὶ ταράσσοντες added before τοὺς ὄχλους with אABD. *Vulg.* 'et turbantes.'

15. αὐτὸν before ἕως Ἀθηνῶν omitted with אABD. *Vulg.* has 'eum.'

18. αὐτοῖς before εὐηγγελίζετο omitted with אBLP. *Vulg.* has 'eis.'

20. τίνα θέλει with אAB. *Vulg.* 'quidnam velint.'

21. ἢ for καὶ before ἀκούειν with אABD. *Vulg.* 'aut.'

23. ὃ for ὅν, τοῦτο for τοῦτον, with אABD. *Vulg.* 'Quod...hoc.'

24. ὑπάρχων κύριος with אABE. *Vulg.* 'cum sit dominus.'

26. αἵματος omitted with אAB. Not represented in *Vulg.*

προστεταγμένους with אABDEHLP. *Vulg.* 'statuta tempora.'

27. θεόν for κύριον with אABHL. *Vulg.* 'Deum.'

30. πάντας for πᾶσι with אABD. *Vulg.* 'hominibus ut omnes.'

32. καὶ before πάλιν added with אAB. Not represented in *Vulg.*

33. καὶ before οὕτως omitted with אAB. *Vulg.* has only 'sic.'

Ch. XVII. 1—9. Paul and Silas journey trough Amphipolis and Apollonia to Thessalonica, where some of the Jews raise an Uproar against them and Jason their Host.

1. διοδεύσαντες δέ, *and when they had passed through.* This verb, of rare occurrence in classical Greek, but common in the LXX. (cf. Gen. xii. 6; Ps. lxxxviii. 40; Baruch iv. 2, &c.), is found in the N.T. only here and in Luke viii. 1. The use of the same words and phrases is a noticeable point in support of the identity of authorship of the two books.

τὴν Ἀμφίπολιν καὶ Ἀπολλωνίαν, *Amphipolis and Apollonia.* The journey is made to the south and west. *Amphipolis* was about 33 miles distant from Philippi, along the Egnatiau road. It had been a famous place in the time of the Peloponnesian war, and was in St Paul's time a great Roman military station. Its name was given to it because it was as nearly as possible enclosed by the winding stream of the river Strymon. *Apollonia* was about 30 miles farther on, in the district of Macedonia known as Mygdonia, and about 37 miles from Thessalonica. The Apostle and his companions appear not to have made any stay in these towns. Chrysostom accounts for their haste thus: πάλιν τὰς μὲν μικρὰς παρατρέχουσι πόλεις, ἐπὶ δὲ τὰς μείζους ἐπείγονται, ἐκεῖθεν καθάπερ ἔκ τινος πηγῆς μέλλοντος τοῦ λόγου διαρρέειν εἰς τὰς πλησίον.

Θεσσαλονίκην, *Thessalonica,* the modern *Saloniki,* to the Christians of which place St Paul afterwards addressed the two earliest of his extant epistles. From very early times Thessalonica had been a famous place. Its old name was Therma, and it was called Thessalonica after a sister of Alexander the Great. It is now one of the most important towns in European Turkey, and it played a great part in the history of the Middle Ages as the bulwark of Christendom in the East. It was captured by the Saracens A.D. 904, then by the Crusaders in 1184, and lastly by the Turks in 1430. Even now there is a large Christian element among its population, and a still larger number of Jews.

συναγωγὴ τῶν Ἰουδαίων, *a synagogue of the Jews.* Apparently at Philippi there had been no synagogue. But Thessalonica may have had a larger Jewish population, and numerous enough to provide and support a building for their religious services.

2. κατὰ δὲ τὸ εἰωθός, *and as his manner was.* On the Apostle's constant habit of going to the synagogues see xiii. 5, 14, xiv. 1, &c. The dative case stands after εἰωθός, instead of the genitive, because the verb ἔθω governs a dative.

εἰσῆλθεν πρὸς αὐτούς, *he went in unto them.* And he was no doubt asked (as on a former occasion xiii. 15) to offer any exhortation to the people, if he were moved so to do.

ἐπὶ σάββατα τρία, *three sabbath days.* On which days the Jews would be sure to gather in greater numbers, and for the other days of the week to be less accessible.

3. διανοίγων, *opening.* St Luke (and he only in the N.T. xxiv. 32) uses this verb of making plain what before was not understood. We may see from that passage what had been St Paul's work in Thessalonica, 'He began at Moses and all the prophets and expounded unto them in all the Scriptures the things concerning Christ.'

καὶ παρατιθέμενος, *and alleging.* The more modern use of *allege =* to assert, has somewhat obscured the older English meaning, which was merely 'to set forth.' παρατίθημι signifies primarily 'to set out food, &c. on a table,' and then figuratively 'to set out arguments,' but without the idea of assertion. St Paul reasoned but only out of the Scriptures. For the English word cf. Coverdale, *Works* (Parker Soc.), p. 14, 'We will first declare our mind out of Scripture and *allege* (i.e. *set before you*) somewhat more for the better understanding of the matter.'

ὅτι τὸν Χριστὸν ἔδει παθεῖν, *that it behoved the Christ to suffer.* The Messiah, whom the Jews expected, they looked for in New Testament days only as a mighty conqueror who should deliver them from their oppressors. Their wishes had been father to their thoughts, and they overlooked all that spake of the Messiah as the 'Man of sorrows.' This portion of the Scriptures it was which St Paul opened.

καὶ ἀναστῆναι ἐκ νεκρῶν, *and to rise from the dead.* For they, like the disciples themselves in earlier days (John xx. 9), 'understood not the Scriptures (such as Ps. xvi. 10) that He must rise again from the dead.'

καὶ ὅτι οὗτός ἐστιν Χριστὸς Ἰησοῦς ὃν ἐγὼ καταγγέλλω ὑμῖν, *and this* (said he) *is Christ Jesus whom I proclaim unto you.* There is a change in the structure of the sentence from the indirect to the direct form of expression which can be best made intelligible by the insertion of 'said he.' Cf. chap. i. 4.

Jesus has fulfilled the prophecies. He has suffered, risen from the dead and ascended into heaven. And we are witnesses to and preachers of this glad tidings.

On the brevity of St Luke's reports of the discourses which he mentions, Chrysostom notes here: τὸ κεφάλαιον εἶπε τῆς διαλέξεως· οὕτως ἀπέριττός ἐστιν, οὐ πανταχοῦ τὰς δημηγορίας αὐτοῦ λέγων.

4. καί τινες ἐξ αὐτῶν ἐπείσθησαν, *and some of them were persuaded.* For the Apostle's teaching was by arguments which they could fully appreciate.

καὶ προσεκληρώθησαν, *and consorted with.* But it should be kept in mind that the verb is passive. The literal sense is 'they were allotted to.' They joined the company of the Apostles, but there was a power which acted on them other than their mere inclination. They were inwardly moved to what they did.

τῶν τε σεβομένων Ἑλλήνων πλῆθος πολύ, *and of the devout Greeks a great multitude.* These were proselytes of the gate, heathens by birth, but having in part embraced the Jews' religion (cf. xiii. 43, 50, and verse 17 of this chapter). Such men were likely to join St Paul in greater numbers, for they had not the prejudices of the born Jew.

5. ζηλώσαντες δὲ οἱ Ἰουδαῖοι, *but the Jews being moved with envy.* This must refer to those who still clung to all the ritual and traditional exclusiveness which had grown up around the Mosaic Law. ζῆλος in its worse sense expresses their anger and dislike at seeing large numbers drawn away from their opinions.

τῶν ἀγοραίων τινὰς ἄνδρας πονηρούς, *certain vile fellows of the rabble.* ἀγοραῖος, 'of the rabble,' is properly the man who having no calling lounges about the ἀγορά, the market-place, in the hope of picking up a chance living, and who is ready for anything bad or good that may present itself. We have no English word sufficiently dignified to use for such a term in translation. 'Loafer' comes nearest, but of course is too colloquial. The word 'lewd' (A.V. for πονηρούς) meant in old English 'people,' but afterwards came to signify (1) 'the common people,' and (2) 'the ignorant and rude among the people,' which is the sense intended by the A.V. The word nearest akin to 'lewd' is the Germ. *Leute* = people.

ἐθορύβουν τὴν πόλιν, *they set the city in an uproar.* The Jews in Thessalonica were clearly numerous and influential or they would never have stirred up such a tumult. To help their case they chose (see verse 7) to raise the cry that the new teachers were enemies of the Roman power.

τῇ οἰκίᾳ Ἰάσονος, *the house of Jason.* Manifestly the host of Paul and Silas. Beyond what is said of him in the following verses (6—9) we know nothing. The name is found, Rom. xvi. 21, in a list of those whom St Paul speaks of as his 'kinsmen,' but this may be quite a different person. He is most likely to have been a Jew, whose proper name perhaps was Joseph, and Jason, which is Greek, may be only that which he used in his intercourse with Gentiles.

αὐτοὺς προαγαγεῖν εἰς τὸν δῆμον, *to bring them forth to the people.* So that the excited mob might inflict summary vengeance upon them.

6. ἔσυρον Ἰάσονα, *they dragged Jason.* σύρειν is expressive of considerable violence. It is used (viii. 3) of Saul, 'haling' men and women and committing them to prison.

On Jason's conduct, Chrysostom says: θαυμαστὸς ὁ ἀνήρ, εἰς κίνδυνον ἑαυτὸν ἐκδοὺς καὶ ἐκπέμψας αὐτούς.

καί τινας ἀδελφούς, *and certain brethren.* Hence we find that in these three weeks a Church had been formed, a Christian society established.

ἐπὶ τοὺς πολιτάρχας, *to the rulers of the city.* The title πολιτάρχης is found nowhere in literature except in this chapter. But an inscription connected with this very city of Thessalonica has been preserved on an arch which spans a street of the modern city. It contains some names which occur as the names of St Paul's converts, Sosipater, Gaius, Secundus, but the inscription is probably not earlier than the time of Vespasian (see Boeckh, *Inscr.* 2, p. 52, n. 1967). There the title of the magistrates is given in this precise form; a striking confirmation of the truthfulness of the account before us.

τὴν οἰκουμένην, *the world.* Lit. 'the inhabited earth.' A phrase used in later Greek to signify the whole Roman Empire, which then embraced a very large portion of the known world (cf. Luke ii. 1). It speaks much for the spread of Christianity and its powerful influence, that words like these should come from the lips of enemies.

ἀναστατώσαντες, *having turned upside down.* The word is very rare, used by Aquila and Symmachus, and perhaps in Ps. x. 1 (LXX.), though this is not the reading of the Vatican MS. In N.T. we have it here and xxi. 38; and Gal. v. 12.

7. οὓς ὑποδέδεκται Ἰάσων, *whom Jason hath received,* as guests into his house. Thus he would be counted for a sympathizer with their teaching, as most probably he was. For the verb cf. Tobit vii. 9; 1 Macc. xvi. 15.

οὗτοι πάντες, *these all.* Implying that Paul and Silas, whom they had not found, would be included in the accusation, if they could be caught.

βασιλέα ἕτερον λέγοντες εἶναι Ἰησοῦν, *saying that there is another king, one Jesus.* So far as this chapter gives an account of St Paul's preaching, he had only drawn the attention of the Jews to the sufferings of the Messiah, but we cannot doubt that he had also spoken of His kingdom. Such language the mob would be urged to seize on, and make it the justification for their uproar, for Thessalonica though a free city was subject to the Emperor.

8. ἐτάραξαν δὲ τὸν ὄχλον, *and they troubled the people*, with language like this, which seemed to speak of insurrection. Thus the mob would be made eager for the punishment of the Apostles.

9. καὶ λαβόντες τὸ ἱκανὸν παρὰ τοῦ Ἰάσονος, *and when they had taken security of Jason*, i.e. having made him responsible either by his finding securities to be bound with and for him, or by making him give some deposit as a pledge for his good conduct, they took measures for securing, so far as those at present in custody were concerned, that they should commit no treason.

τὸ ἱκανὸν λαβεῖν seems to be a rendering of a Latin expression *satis accipere*. The Greek phrase is not found elsewhere, but the converse ἱκανὸν ποιεῖν = *satis dare*, to give security, occurs in Diog. Laert. IV. 50.

10—15. PAUL AND SILAS SENT AWAY TO BERŒA. NOBLE CHARACTER OF THE BERŒANS. THE JEWS FROM THESSALONICA FOLLOW AFTER PAUL, AND BY REASON OF THEIR ENMITY HE IS CONDUCTED TO ATHENS.

10. διὰ νυκτός, *by night*. The preposition refers to the time within (*during*) which the action took place.

ἐξέπεμψαν τόν τε Παῦλον καὶ τὸν Σίλαν, *they sent away Paul and Silas*. The after-conduct of the Thessalonian Jews (see verse 13) shews that they were determined to bring danger on the missionaries. Feeling that this was so, their friends got them out of the way.

εἰς Βέροιαν, *unto Berœa*. Still the journey is south-west. The old name of Berœa may be recognised in the modern *Vèrria*.

εἰς τὴν συναγωγήν, *into the synagogue*. See above on verse 2.

11. εὐγενέστεροι, *more noble*. εὐγενής is applied first to nobility of birth; but its secondary sense is, as here, nobility of character. The latter ought to be a consequence of the former. Cf. 2 Macc. xiv. 42 εὐγενῶς θέλων ἀποθανεῖν, wishing to die *nobly*. Also see 2 Macc. x. 13.

ἐδέξαντο τὸν λόγον, *they received the word*, i.e. the word published to them as the word of God. It was the same teaching which had been given to the Jews in Thessalonica. This we see because the Berœans go to the O. T. Scriptures to examine into the truth of what they hear. Here we have a noteworthy instance of the right of private judgment. Even an Apostle's word is not to be taken for granted. The noble Berœans were ready to listen, and then diligent to examine into the grounds of what was said.

ἀνακρίνοντες τὰς γραφάς, *searching the Scriptures*. This is a different verb from that so rendered in John v. 39, which is ἐρευνᾶν. ἀνακρίνειν has the sense of *examining* and sifting evidence. It was used in Attic law of the steps taken by the lawyers to see whether an

action would lie. It is used by the LXX. 1 Sam. xx. 12, where our
A.V. renders 'when I have sounded [Heb. *searched*] my father,' also
in Susanna 51 of Daniel's *examination* of the elders.

εἰ ἔχοι ταῦτα οὕτως, *whether those things were so.* The optative
mood implies that they had conceived the possibility in their minds,
but still would examine before accepting what was said. Cf. *Winer-
Moulton*, p. 364.

12. τῶν Ἑλληνίδων γυναικῶν τῶν εὐσχημόνων, *of honourable women
which were Greeks.* See above on xiii. 50.

The adjective Ἑλληνίς agrees in gender with γυναικῶν because it
stands before that word in the sentence, but it probably is intended
to define ἀνδρῶν too. The Jewish population has been previously
described as ready to search the Scriptures. The men as well as the
women who are mentioned afterwards were most likely all Gentiles.

13. ὁ λόγος τοῦ θεοῦ, *the word of God.* This is the language of the
author. The Thessalonian Jews would not have called St Paul's
preaching by such a name.

σαλεύοντες καὶ ταράσσοντες τοὺς ὄχλους, *stirring up and troubling
the multitudes.* The figures in these verbs are of a storm at sea where
all is stirred up from the depth. The second verb ταράσσω has already
occurred in verse 8, and it is probable from this that the trouble in
Beroea was produced in the same way as before by the statement that
the Apostles were traitors to the Roman power. For the figurative
language cf. LXX. Ps. xvii. 8, καὶ ἐσαλεύθη καὶ ἔντρομος ἐγενήθη ἡ γῆ,
καὶ τὰ θεμέλια τῶν ὀρέων ἐταράχθησαν καὶ ἐσαλεύθησαν ὅτι ὠργίσθη αὐτοῖς
ὁ θεός. Also Pss. xlvii. 5, cvi. 27.

14. εὐθέως δέ, *and immediately.* As from Thessalonica, so from
Beroea, the departure is made with all haste. The charge of conspiring against Cæsar, which was probably put forward everywhere, had
a very dangerous effect on the popular mind.

πορεύεσθαι ἕως ἐπὶ τὴν θάλασσαν, *to go as far as to the sea.* This
is to be preferred to the *Text. recept.* for several reasons. First it has
stronger MS. support. And further it agrees better with the history.
The A.V. 'to go as it were to the sea' represents the ὡς of *Text.
recept.*, and would imply that for a while the travellers made as
though they were bound towards the sea, but then to baffle pursuit
turned and took the land road to Athens. But it is difficult to understand that St Paul would have gone on through Thessaly and all the
intervening districts which lie north of Attica, and never have sought
an opportunity of preaching the word anywhere till Athens was
reached. If however he were conveyed to the sea and took ship and
was thus brought to Athens, it is easy to understand that the next
place mentioned in the journey is Athens. It is clear too from the
whole account of St Paul's travels, that he was a person who by reason
of his infirmities could not easily travel alone. That such a person
should have been brought so long a distance by land, where the sea-
voyage was so accessible and easy, is hardly to be imagined. It may
well be that at the departure from Beroea the design was to wait at the

coast till his proper companions could come to him, but that when the sea was reached there was found a speedy opportunity of sailing into Attica, which the Apostle embraced, as his conductors were willing to go all the way with him.

ὑπέμενάν τε ὅ τε Σίλας καὶ ὁ Τιμόθεος ἐκεῖ, *but Silas and Timothy abode there still.* For they had played a less prominent part, and therefore were not in such peril as St Paul.

15. οἱ δὲ καθιστάνοντες, *and they who conducted.* This form καθιστάνω, which is found nowhere else in N.T. in this sense, is the same word as the more usual καθίστημι; and the use of this word conveys the idea that the whole care and ordering of the journey was in the hands of his conductors and not of St Paul. καθίστημι is used of the way in which the Israelites led Rahab and all that belonged to her out of Jericho (Joshua vi. 23); also see 2 Chron. xxviii. 15 of the way in which the Judæan captives were sent back, καὶ ἀνέστησαν ...καὶ πάντας τοὺς γυμνοὺς περιέβαλον ἀπὸ τῶν σκύλων καὶ ἐνέδυσαν αὐτοὺς καὶ ὑπέδησαν αὐτοὺς καὶ ἔδωκαν φαγεῖν καὶ ἀλείψασθαι...καὶ κατέστησαν αὐτοὺς εἰς Ἱεριχώ.

ἤγαγον ἕως Ἀθηνῶν, *brought him unto Athens.* And of course saw him safely settled where he could wait for his fellow-missionaries, which he seems to have designed to do, without preaching, had not his spirit been roused by the sights he saw.

ὡς τάχιστα, *with all speed.* This charge was given because Paul was now to be left alone; and would not readily set about his mission till he had some companion.

16—21. PAUL, PROVOKED BY THE PREVALENCE OF IDOLATRY AT ATHENS, FIRST ADDRESSES THE JEWS AND THEN THE GENTILES. SOME OF THE PHILOSOPHERS QUESTION HIM ON HIS TEACHING, AND BRING HIM TO THE AREOPAGUS THAT THEY MAY HEAR HIM MORE AT FULL.

16. παρωξύνετο τὸ πνεῦμα αὐτοῦ ἐν αὐτῷ, *his spirit was stirred in him.* But the stirring was of the sharpest. It was a *paroxysm.* He was provoked till he could not forbear, could not hold his peace till Timothy and Silas arrived. On this Chrysostom says, οὐκ ὀργὴν ἐνταῦθα, οὐδὲ ἀγανάκτησιν ὁ παροξυσμός, ἀλλὰ διέγερσιν καὶ ζῆλον δηλοῖ, καθάπερ καὶ ἀλλαχοῦ (xv. 39). ἐγένετο, φησί, παροξυσμὸς μεταξὺ αὐτῶν. ὅρα δε πῶς οἰκονομεῖται καὶ ἄκοντα μεῖναι ἐκεῖ ἐκδεχόμενον ἐκείνους. τί οὖν ἐστι, παρωξύνετο; ἀντὶ τοῦ διηγείρετο. ὀργῆς καὶ ἀγανακτήσεως πόρρω τὸ χάρισμα. οὐκ ἔφερεν ἀλλ' ἐτήκετο.

θεωροῦντος κ.τ.λ., *as he beheld the city full of idols.* This agrees with the facts. What St Paul beheld was the numerous statues erected, some to one god, some to another. That the city was wholly given to idolatry was the inference from this abundance of idols. The mutilation of the busts of Hermes before the Sicilian expedition in the Peloponnesian war shews how numerous were the statues erected to one divinity only. Time had added many to the number before St Paul's visit.

With κατείδωλος may be compared κατάδενδρος, κατάκαρπος, κατάκομος, κατάμπελος &c., which all have the notion of 'abounding with.'

17. διελέγετο ..τοῖς Ἰουδαίοις, *therefore he reasoned in the synagogue with the Jews.* Going to them first, as sure to find from them sympathy in his horror against idolatry.

τοῖς σεβομένοις, *with the devout persons,* the proselytes of the gate. See above on xiii. 50.

καὶ ἐν τῇ ἀγορᾷ κατὰ πᾶσαν ἡμέραν, *and in the market daily.* One cannot but be reminded of the way in which Socrates some centuries earlier had thus gone about in the same city, seizing eagerly on every one who would listen, and trying, according to his light, to shew them higher things, to open their eyes that they might discern between real knowledge and conceit without knowledge.

18. τινὲς δὲ καὶ τῶν Ἐπικουρείων καὶ Στωϊκῶν φιλοσόφων, *then certain philosophers, both of the Epicureans and of the Stoics.* In St Paul's day these two systems of philosophy were most prominent throughout the Roman world, and were regarded as conflicting, though in many points they bear a strong likeness to one another. Both were the result of a desire to find some better principle for the guidance of man's moral nature than could be found in the so-called religious systems of Greece and Rome. But before the Christian era much that was best in both schools had sadly degenerated from its pristine character.

The founder of the Stoics was Zeno of Citium in Cyprus. His precise date is uncertain, but he flourished in the century between B.C. 350—250. The first lesson of his teaching was that the highest duty of the philosopher was to practise virtue. For the doing this knowledge was necessary, and the only knowledge that could be relied on was that which was based upon sensation. Reality belonged only to material things such as the senses could appreciate. In this manner the Stoic philosophy became materialist. For though owning the existence of God and of the soul in man, Zeno and his followers spake of these as, in some sense, material. But they termed God the soul of the universe, and taught that all things are produced from him, and will at last be absorbed into him again. And then a new world-cycle will begin and be in all respects like that which went before. So the Stoics were Pantheists. They taught moreover that the universe was governed by unchanging law, that the lot of individuals, and the occurrence of particular events, were all uncertain. The care of Providence was for the fabric of the universe, and only indirectly extended to particulars or individuals whose lot was bound up with the unchanging course of fixed law. The Stoics therefore were Fatalists. The way in which the individual could make the nearest approach to happiness was by bringing himself, through knowledge, into harmony with the course of the universe. But so unimportant did the individual appear to these philosophers, that suicide was held to be lawful, and at times praiseworthy. They were conscious of both physical and moral evil in the world, and from this men might escape by self-inflicted death. They taught how-

ever that, though the virtuous might have to suffer, no real evil happens
to them, nor real good to the vicious. Fortified with this thought, the
Stoic trained himself to be proudly independent of externals, and to
bear evils, should they come, with indifference, and thus he strove to
secure undisturbed peace of mind. Materialism, Pantheism, Fatalism
and pride, were the features of one of the systems into contact with
which St Paul was brought at Athens.

The Epicureans (named from Epicurus, born at Samos B.C. 342)
agreed with the Stoics that philosophy should seek to promote the
happiness of man, but maintained that this end could be best gained
by the pursuit of pleasure. By this language they did not intend profligate pleasure, but a state wherein the body was free from pain and
the mind from disturbance. They too made the senses their means of
judging of what is pleasure, and so with them man became the measure
of all good for himself. Thus the Epicureans were materialists. But
differing from the Stoics they taught the world was formed by chance,
and that the gods had no concern in its creation. Their gods were
described as perfectly happy, dwelling apart and caring neither for the
world nor its inhabitants. Thus the Epicureans were practical atheists.
With them man might approach to a state of happiness by circum-
scribing his wants, so that life might be free from care. To restrain
the senses was the Epicurean road to happiness, to crush them as much
as possible into insensibility was the path of the Stoic. But having
such thoughts of the gods, neither system had in any way run counter
to the popular theology. By doing so the Stoic would fear lest he
should be thought to deny God altogether, while the Epicurean, though
thinking all such worship folly, yet felt it too great an interruption to
the pleasure which he sought, to become an advocate of the abolition of
idol worship. So St Paul found Athens crowded with the images and
altars of the gods.

συνέβαλλον αὐτῷ, *encountered him*, i.e. met him in disputation,
argued with him. The word is used of the Sanhedrin holding a debate
among themselves (iv. 15) on what was to be done with the Apostles.

τί ἂν θέλοι ὁ σπερμολόγος οὗτος λέγειν; *what would this babbler say?*
i.e. if we would listen to him.

σπερμολόγος is not found elsewhere in N.T. or LXX. In profane
writers it is used of birds picking up scattered grain, and then figuratively of men who pick up a living as best they may, and hence are
willing to flatter for the sake of what they can get. Men without
principle or ground in what they say.

ξένων δαιμονίων...εἶναι, *he seems to be a setter-forth of strange
gods.* δαιμόνια, from which comes the English 'demon,' was used in
classical Greek mostly to denote some inferior order among the divine
beings. In the LXX. it is always applied to false gods or evil spirits.
Cf. Tobit iii. 8, Ἀσμοδαῖος τὸ πονηρὸν δαιμόνιον. It was one of the
accusations brought against Socrates, and the charge on which he was
condemned, that he introduced new δαιμόνια (Xen. *Mem.* i. 1, 2: Plato
Apolog. 40 A &c.). It has been thought by some that the Athenians,

from using this word in the plural, fancied that 'Jesus' was one new
divinity and Ἀνάστασις another. On the latter notion Chrysostom
says, καὶ γὰρ τὴν ἀνάστασιν θεόν τινα εἶναι ἐνόμιζον, ἄτε εἰωθότες καὶ
θηλείας σέβειν.

Times seem changed at Athens since the prosecution of Socrates, for
it is not anger, but scornful curiosity, which prompts the language of
the speakers. They do not mean to assail Paul for his teaching, and
amid the abundance of idols, they perhaps now would have felt no
difficulty in allowing Jesus a place, provided he did not seek to overthrow all the rest of their divinities.

The nature of St Paul's teaching 'in the market-place' has not been
mentioned until we are told that it was of 'Jesus and the resurrection.'
We may take this as a specimen of the way in which the author of the
Acts has dealt with his materials. He has not seen it needful here to
do more than specify in half-a-dozen words what St Paul had spoken
about; and so when we have a report of a speech we need not suppose
that he has given, or intended to give, more than a summary of what
the speaker said, and, adhering to the substance, has cast his abbreviated record into such form as best fitted his narrative.

19. ἐπιλαβόμενοί τε αὐτοῦ, *and they took hold of him and,* &c.
There is no need to suppose that any violence was used or intended.
The same verb is used often of taking by the hand to aid or protect
(so Mark viii. 23; Acts xxiii. 19), and is the word by which the action
of Barnabas is described (Acts ix. 27) when 'he *took* Paul and brought
him to the Apostles.' Moreover the whole context shews that the
action of the crowd was in no sense that of an arrest, for we read
(verse 33) when his speech was done 'Paul departed from among
them,' evidently having been under no kind of restraint.

ἐπὶ τὸν Ἄρειον πάγον ἤγαγον, *they brought him unto the Areopagus.*
This was an eminence to the west of the Acropolis at Athens. It was
famous in classic literature as the meeting-place of the Athenian council of Areopagus, which took its name from the place where it met. To
this hill of Mars (Ares) the philosophers led St Paul, probably at a
time when it was unoccupied (though some suppose that the court was
sitting), that they might the better hear him away from the bustle of
the market-place, and that he might more conveniently address a
larger audience.

δυνάμεθα γνῶναι...; *may we know...?* Literally 'are we able to
know...?' But the literal sense of δύναμαι (especially when used in the
first person) was often merged in that of θέλω or βούλομαι. Cf. Luke
xi. 7, οὐ δύναμαι ἀναστὰς δοῦναί σοι, 'I *cannot* rise and give thee,' where
the sense clearly is 'I *don't want* to rise.' For after importunity the
man does rise and do all that is desired. The Stoics and Epicureans
were not the people to doubt their own power of understanding anything which St Paul might say to them.

τίς ἡ καινὴ...λαλουμένη διδαχή, *what this new doctrine is which is
spoken by thee.* The sense of λαλεῖν in N.T. is not unfrequently that
of *announcing* and *publishing.* The word is also used of messages

spoken by God or by His prophets (cf. Luke i. 45, 55, 70, xxiv. 25; Acts iii. 21, 24; James v. 10). The Apostle was not speaking to the Athenians *about* the doctrine (as A.V.), his words were the doctrine.

20. ξενίζοντα γάρ τινα, *certain strange things.* Literally 'things striking us as strange.' The word implies the effect produced on the minds of the hearers. In the middle voice the word occurs in 1 Pet. iv. 4, 12 = 'to think anything strange.' The active is found, as here, in 2 Macc. ix. 6, πολλαῖς καὶ ξενιζούσαις συμφοραῖς, 'with many and *strange* torments.'

τίνα θέλει ταῦτα εἶναι, *what these things mean*, i.e. of what nature they are. Cf. above on verse 18.

21. This verse is a parenthesis explanatory of what has gone before. The audience had been struck with the strange teaching, and that it was strange was enough. Novelty was their life's pursuit. So without having any regard for the importance of the teaching, they were ready to listen because it was new.

οἱ ἐπιδημοῦντες ξένοι, *the strangers sojourning there.* The place was famous and hunters after novelty came thither from every quarter.

ηὐκαίρουν. The verb signifies (1) to have a convenient time, and then uniquely here (2) to make leisure for, to give up time to any pursuit. The imperfect tense implies that this was their constant state of mind.

καινότερον. The comparative is noteworthy. The Athenians are by it represented as thirsting ever for something 'newer still.' What had been heard at once became stale. This character of the Athenian populace is confirmed by many statements of classical authors. In Thuc. III. 38 Cleon is represented as complaining of his countrymen that they were in the habit of playing the part of 'spectators in displays of oratory, and listeners to the stories of what others had done'; and a like charge is made more than once by Demosthenes in his speeches on the vigorous policy of Philip of Macedon, which he contrasts with the Athenian love of talk and news.

22—31. SPEECH OF ST PAUL AT ATHENS.

Taking notice of the extreme religious scrupulousness which had led the Athenians to raise an altar to an unknown God, the Apostle declares to them the God whom alone they ought to worship, and whom as yet they did not know. This God was the Maker and Preserver of all things, and the Father of all men, and He desired to bring all to a knowledge of Himself. Athenian poets had spoken of this Fatherhood of God. Such a God is not fitly represented by graven images, and He would have men cease from such ignorant worship, for he will be the Judge as well as Father of men, and has given proof of the reality of the judgment and of the world to come by the resurrection of Jesus Christ.

22. ἐν μέσῳ τοῦ Ἀρείου πάγου, *in the midst of the Areopagus.* See above on verse 19.

ἄνδρες Ἀθηναῖοι, *men of Athens.* The language of the Apostle's address takes exactly the form which it would have assumed in the mouth of one of their own orators. This may be due either to St Paul's knowledge of Greek literature, and to his desire, everywhere manifest, to find words acceptable to his audience; or it may be that St Luke, giving an abstract of the speech, has cast the initial words into a form which Demosthenes would have employed. In the latter case it is no mark of unfaithfulness in the author, who clearly in these ten verses can only mean to give a skeleton of what the Apostle really uttered. St Paul spake at length, we cannot doubt, when he stood in such a place and before such an audience. The historian in the Acts gives the barest outline of what was spoken, and cannot be thought to have meant his words to be otherwise accepted, seeing that what he has given us would hardly occupy five minutes in the utterance.

κατὰ πάντα ὡς δεισιδαιμονεστέρους ὑμᾶς θεωρῶ, *in all things I per-ceive that ye are somewhat superstitious.* δεισιδαίμων has two senses: (1) superstitious, (2) religious. The Apostle intends the word in the former sense, but by the comparative he qualifies it in some degree. He implies a degree of blame which perhaps comes nearly to ' more superstitious than you ought to be.' His desire is not to offend at first by too stern an expression of blame, but by gently pointing out a fault to lead his hearers into a more excellent way. For a description of the δεισιδαίμων, which exactly answers to our ' superstitious,' see Theophrastus, *Charact.* c. XVII.

κατὰ πάντα means 'in everything which he had noticed while wandering about their city.'

23. διερχόμενος γάρ, *for as I passed along,* through your streets and squares.

καὶ ἀναθεωρῶν τὰ σεβάσματα ὑμῶν, *and noticed the objects of your worship.* ἀναθεωρέω indicates a full observation. Paul had not only looked at the statues, but had read the inscriptions on them.

σέβασμα = *an object of worship* is found three times in the LXX. Wisdom xiv. 20, τὸν πρὸ ὀλίγου τιμηθέντα ἄνθρωπον νῦν σέβασμα ἐλογί-σαντο, 'They took him now for an object of worship (A.V. a god) which a little before was honoured as a man.' So Wisdom xv. 17 κρείτ-των γάρ ἐστι τῶν σεβασμάτων αὐτοῦ, 'himself is better than the things which he worshippeth.' Cf. also Bel 27.

εὖρον καὶ βωμόν, *I found also an altar,* i.e. in addition to the multitude of statues and altars to definite deities.

ἀγνώστῳ θεῷ, *to an unknown god.* This was an altar erected on the occasion of some visitation, the cause of which was not apparent, and which could not be ascribed to any of their existing divinities. We have abundant evidence of the existence in Athens of such altars as that to which St Paul alludes. But the words in which they are described generally run in the plural number, τοῖς ἀγνώστοις θεοῖς. Thus Pausanias (I. i. 4) describing one of the ports of Athens tells us that there were there 'altars to gods styled *unknown,*' and Philostratus

in his *Life of Apollonius* says 'at Athens there are erected altars for
unknown gods.' There is a like allusion in (pseudo) Lucian's *Philo-
patris*, but it is doubtful whether that is not drawn from this passage
of the Acts. And Jerome writing on Tit. i. 12 says 'The inscription
on the altar was not, as Paul stated, "To the unknown God" but
"To the unknown gods of Asia and Europe and Africa, to unknown
and foreign gods." But, because Paul required to speak of only one
unknown God, he used the word in the singular.' But it is better to
suppose that St Paul saw what he says he saw; and as evidence that
such an inscription was not improbable, we may quote the Latin inscription found on an altar at Ostia, now in the Vatican, representing
a sacrificial group in connexion with the worship of Mithras, the Sun-
god of the later Persian mythology (Orelli, *Inscr. Gel.* II. 5000), 'Sig-
num indeprehensibilis dei,' which is a very near approach in Latin
to what the Greek inscription to which the Apostle alludes would
mean. The word 'unknown' must not be pressed into the sense
of 'unknowable' because of what comes after. Paul says that 'he
is prepared to set forth to them that power which they were wor-
shipping in ignorance.' So though man by searching cannot find
out God, yet he would desire to teach the Athenians, what he says
elsewhere, that 'the everlasting power and divinity of God may be
clearly seen through the things that are made' (Rom. i. 20).

ὃ οὖν ἀγνοοῦντες εὐσεβεῖτε, *what therefore ye worship in ignorance.*
This brings out the Apostle's meaning. He does not intend to reflect
on the nature of their worship. But they were offering it in
ignorance. This ignorance he proposes to dispel. He accepts their
religious character, takes hold on their confession of want of knowledge, and so makes way for his proposal to teach them. They have,
he presumes, accepted what he offers, but have not understood all
that it means. On this Chrysostom says: ὅρα πῶς δείκνυσι προειλη-
φότας αὐτόν. οὐδὲν ξένον, φησί, οὐδὲν καινὸν εἰσφέρω.

τοῦτο ἐγὼ καταγγέλλω ὑμῖν, *this set I forth unto you.* In his
verb the Apostle takes up their own word καταγγελεὺς of verse 18,
where they call him 'a setter-forth of strange gods.'

24. ὁ θεὸς ὁ ποιήσας τὸν κόσμον, *the God that made the world.*
He whom the Apostle set forth was no Epicurean divinity, dwelling
apart and in constant repose. Nor was the world a thing of chance,
as those philosophers taught, but the handiwork of God, and so were
all things in it.

οὐρανοῦ καὶ γῆς ὑπάρχων κύριος, *being Lord of heaven and earth,*
and having for this reason the supreme disposal of all things.

οὐκ ἐν χειροποιήτοις ναοῖς κατοικεῖ, *dwelleth not in temples made
with hands,* of which Athens held some of the most renowned in
the world. A special interest attaches to these words as being so like
to those of Stephen (vii. 48). Paul has taken up the work of him
whose martyrdom he formerly abetted.

25. οὐδὲ ὑπὸ χειρῶν ἀνθρωπίνων θεραπεύεται, *neither is served by
men's hands.* θεραπεύειν implies the sort of service yielded by a

steward to his master, or a minister to his king, a service in which
the superior is not independent of his inferior, and could not well do
without him. This is seen in the next clause. God is not like
earthly masters and kings. He gives all, and men can only offer to
Him themselves in return. Cf. Pss. l., li. for like teaching. See
also Chrysostom on this verse, λέγων δέ, μὴ ὑπὸ χειρῶν ἀνθρώπων
θεραπεύεσθαι τὸν θεόν, αἰνίττεται ὅτι διανοίᾳ καὶ νῷ θεραπεύεται.

ζωὴν καὶ πνοὴν καὶ τὰ πάντα, *life and breath and all things.* The
Apostle in the paronomasia seems to be adapting his style somewhat to his audience. Such similarity of sound was thought to give
elegance.

26. ἐποίησέν τε ἐξ ἑνὸς πᾶν ἔθνος ἀνθρώπων, *and hath made of one
every nation of men.* Thus would he bring out most prominently the
doctrine of the common Fatherhood of God. It is not merely that
men are all of one family and so all equal in God's eyes, and ought
to be in the eyes of one another. When we read 'they are made of
One' we are carried back to the higher thought of the prophet
(Malachi ii. 10), 'Have we not all one Father?' This was a philosophy not likely to be acceptable to the Athenians, among whom the
distinction between Greeks and Barbarians was as radical as that
which has grown up in America between white man and 'nigger,' or
between Europeans and natives of India.

κατοικεῖν ἐπὶ παντὸς προσώπου τῆς γῆς, *for to dwell on all the face
of the earth.* For His children the Father has provided a home.

ὁρίσας προστεταγμένους καιρούς, *having determined their appointed
seasons.* The 'seasons' referred to are those which God has ordained for seed-time and harvest, summer and winter, day and night,
which are fixed by His decree and make the earth a fitting abode
for men.

καὶ τὰς ὁροθεσίας τῆς κατοικίας αὐτῶν, *and the bounds of their
habitation,* i.e. where they can dwell and where they cannot; or, perhaps, where each nation and tribe should dwell.

27. ζητεῖν τὸν θεόν, *that they should seek God.* This was the
lesson which God meant His creation and providence to teach. Men
were to behold Him through His works.

εἰ ἄρα γε ψηλαφήσειαν αὐτὸν καὶ εὕροιεν, *if haply they might feel
after Him and find Him.* The world was to be man's lesson-book,
open before all men. In it they could read everywhere of Almighty
power and care and love. Thus stimulated, a desire to know more
might grow; and by efforts, which the graphic word of the Apostle
compares to the exertion of one groping in the dark, more knowledge would come, and at last the full discovery would be made.
God would be found. He is the rewarder of them that diligently
seek Him.

καί γε οὐ μακρὰν ἀπὸ ἑνὸς ἑκάστου ἡμῶν ὑπάρχοντα, *though He be
not far from every one of us.* And so can reveal Himself according to
the measure of the zeal shewn by those who seek Him.

XVII. 31.]   *NOTES.*   313

28. ἐν αὐτῷ γὰρ ζῶμεν, *for in Him we live*, i.e. *through* or *by* Him. For ἐν in this sense, see below verse 31.

All our existence is through His care. He must therefore be near unto each of us.

καὶ κινούμεθα, *and move*. More literally, 'are moved.' The word does not refer to the motion of persons from place to place, but to those internal movements of the mind and spirit of which the outward actions are the effect. St Paul means that the feelings of men are acted on by God, who speaks to the heart through all nature if men will but hearken. This is the truth of which Pantheism is the caricature.

ὡς καὶ τινες τῶν καθ᾽ ὑμᾶς ποιητῶν εἰρήκασιν, *as certain of your own poets have said*. The expression τῶν καθ᾽ ὑμᾶς in place of the simpler pronoun is like νόμου τοῦ καθ᾽ ὑμᾶς in xviii. 15. Cf. also xxvi. 3. The words are found in Arātus, *Phaenomena*, 5

τοῦ γὰρ καὶ γένος ἐσμέν, ὁ δ᾽ ἤπιος ἀνθρώποισι
δεξιὰ σημαίνει.

They also occur in Cleanthes' *Hymn to Jupiter*, 5. Arātus was a native of Cilicia, and St Paul may in consequence be supposed to have known of his writings as of those of a fellow-countryman. By quoting from their own literature to the Athenians, St Paul illustrates his own declaration that in his labours 'he became all things to all men.' Such a quotation was also very well devised for arresting the attention of these cultivated hearers, and winning, it may be, some consideration for the speaker, as also being a man of culture.

τοῦ. Here the article has its original force, and is equivalent to a demonstrative pronoun. See *Winer-Moulton*, p. 129.

29. οὐκ ὀφείλομεν νομίζειν κ.τ.λ., *we ought not to think*, &c. As man is of more honour than material things, how far above these must the Godhead be. The Athenians, the Apostle would teach them, had formed not too high but too low a conception of themselves.

30. τοὺς μὲν οὖν χρόνους τῆς ἀγνοίας ὑπεριδὼν ὁ θεός, *the times of ignorance therefore God overlooked but*, &c., i.e. God has not imputed unto men the errors which they committed in ignorance. But now the case is changed. Men cannot plead ignorance who have heard of Christ. Cf. Luke xii. 48.

For the sentiment cf. also Ecclus. xxviii. 7, μνήσθητι...διαθήκην ὑψίστου καὶ πάριδε ἄγνοιαν, where the A.V. translates (as here) 'wink at ignorance,' meaning 'pass over offences committed through it,' and so imitate the Most High.

τὰ νῦν παραγγέλλει τοῖς ἀνθρώποις πάντας πανταχοῦ μετανοεῖν, *now He commandeth men that they all everywhere should repent*. 'Repentance' here means the amendment of the lives which they have been leading wrongly through ignorance.

31. καθότι ἔστησεν ἡμέραν κ.τ.λ., *because He hath appointed a day*, &c. The day of judgment had, in God's foreknowledge, been long ago appointed. But through Christ the certainty has been made clear to men. Through a knowledge of Christ, who has been raised from the dead, men have learnt that there is to be a general resurrection. Christ is the firstfruits. But Christ has taught (Matth. xxv. 32) that after resurrection judgment shall come. By the resurrection of Jesus, God has given to men assurance that what Jesus taught is true. Therefore because He foretold and revealed to men the certainty of the judgment, they ought everywhere to repent, for all men shall be judged.

It is worth while to notice how St Paul's argument advances through its various stages. He speaks first of God as the Creator of the world and of men. Then of the ordinances which He has made for man's abode on earth. Next he argues that all this should inspire men with the thought that as they are more worthy than material things, so God is far exalted above men. This ought to have led them to seek after Him, and even in the darker days those who sought could find Him. But now the days of God's revelation through nature are at an end. He has spoken through that Son of Man whom the resurrection proved to be the Son of God. Through Him will God judge the world, for which judgment men should prepare themselves by repentance.

It may be that at this point the Apostle's speech was stopped. Neither party among the hearers would have any sympathy with the doctrine of a resurrection and a final judgment. Had the address been completed, St Paul would have probably spoken in more definite language about the life and work of Jesus.

32—34. EFFECT OF ST PAUL'S SPEECH. SOME MOCKED, BUT OTHERS BELIEVED.

32. ἀνάστασιν νεκρῶν. See above on verse 18.

οἱ μὲν ἐχλεύαζον, *some mocked.* So did some (Acts ii. 13) on the day of Pentecost. But they were Jews. On Mars' Hill the mockers were heathens. To the Epicurean this life was all, and the teaching of the Stoic, that all should finally be absorbed into the Godhead, forbade the belief that the dead should rise again. So of these men the Epicureans would most likely be the mockers; the Stoics might be expected to give more heed, and theirs perhaps would be the decision to hear the Apostle again. On this mockery Chrysostom writes: ὅρα αὐτὸν μείζους ἔχοντα πειρασμοὺς παρὰ Ἰουδαίοις ἢ παρ᾽ Ἕλλησιν. ἐν γοῦν Ἀθήναις οὐδὲν πάσχει τοιοῦτον, ἀλλὰ μέχρι γέλωτος τὸ πᾶν προυχώρησε, καὶ τοί γε ἔπεισεν. ἐν δὲ Ἰουδαίοις πολλὰ τὰ δεινά. οὕτως ἦσαν ἐκπεπολεμωμένοι μᾶλλον.

ἀκουσόμεθά σου καὶ πάλιν, *we will hear thee yet again.*

33. ἐξῆλθεν ἐκ μέσου αὐτῶν, *he departed from among them.* Clearly being free to go when he pleased, though it may surprise us that he did not remain longer with those who had promised him another hearing. On this Chrysostom says: τί δή ποτε πείσαντος οὕτως αὐτοῦ ὡς καὶ εἰπεῖν Ἀθηναίους, ἀκουσόμεθά σου πάλιν περὶ τούτου, καὶ κινδύνων οὐκ ὄντων ἐπείγεται τὰς Ἀθήνας ἀφεῖναι ὁ Παῦλος; ἴσως ἤδει οὐ μέγα

ὠνήσων, ἄλλως τε καὶ ὑπὸ τοῦ πνεύματος εἰς Κόρινθον ἤγετο. And
presently afterwards he adds : οἱ γὰρ Ἀθηναῖοι καίτοι ξένης ὄντες
ἀκροάσεως ἐρασταὶ ὅμως οὐ προσεῖχον. οὐ γὰρ τοῦτο ἐσπούδαζον ἀλλ' ὥστε
ἀεί τι ἔχειν εἰπεῖν.

34. Διονύσιος ὁ Ἀρεοπαγίτης, Dionysius the Areopagite, i.e. one
of the members of the upper council of Athens. He must have been a
man of position and influence, for no one could be a member of this
council unless he had filled some high office of state, and was above
60 years of age. Tradition (Euseb. *H. E.* III. 4, IV. 23) says that
this Dionysius was the first bishop of Athens, and that he was
martyred. The works which long circulated among Christians as his
compositions, and which even at the time of the Reformation occupied
much of the thoughts and labours of such men as Dean Colet, are no
doubt forgeries of a much later date than the days of this Dionysius.

CHAPTER XVIII.

Readings varying from the *Text. recept.*

1. δὲ after μετά omitted with אAB. Not represented in *Vulg.*

ὁ Παῦλος omitted with אBD. Not represented in *Vulg.*

5. λόγῳ for πνεύματι with אABDE. *Vulg.* 'verbo.'

εἶναι added after Ἰουδαίοις with אABD. *Vulg.* 'esse.'

9. ἐν νυκτὶ δι' ὁράματος with אB. *Vulg.* 'nocte per visionem.'

12. ἀνθυπάτου ὄντος with אABD.

13. ἀναπείθει οὗτος with אAB. *Vulg.* supports the contrary order.

15. ζητήματα with אABDE. *Vulg.* 'quaestiones.'

γὰρ after κριτὴς omitted with אABD. Not represented in
Vulg.

17. οἱ Ἕλληνες omitted with אAB. Not represented in *Vulg.*

18. ἐν Κεγχρεαῖς τὴν κεφαλήν with אAB. *Vulg.* 'in Cenchreis
caput.'

19. κατήντησαν with אABE. *Vulg.* supports the singular.

20. παρ' αὐτοῖς omitted with אAB. Not represented in *Vulg.*

21. ἀποταξάμενος καὶ εἰπών with אABD. *Vulg.* 'valefaciens et
dicens.'

Δεῖ με πάντως τὴν ἑορτὴν τὴν ἐρχομένην ποιῆσαι εἰς Ἱεροσόλυμα
omitted with אABE. Not represented in *Vulg.*

The δὲ after πάλιν, and καὶ before ἀνήχθη disappear as a
consequence of the preceding omission.

25. Ἰησοῦ for Κυρίου with אABDEL. *Vulg.* 'Jesu.'

26. Πρίσκιλλα καὶ Ἀκύλας with אABE. *Vulg.* 'Priscilla et
Aquila.'

τὴν ὁδὸν τοῦ θεοῦ with אAB. *Vulg.* has 'viam Domini.'

CH. XVIII. 1—11. PAUL GOES FROM ATHENS TO CORINTH, LABOURS
THERE WITH HIS OWN HANDS FOR HIS MAINTENANCE. HE IS EN-
COURAGED IN HIS PREACHING BY A VISION OF THE LORD.

1. μετὰ ταῦτα χωρισθεὶς......ἦλθεν, *after these things he departed
and came.* The ὁ Παῦλος of *Text. recept.* is an insertion of some one
who thought to make the reference clearer. The number of similar
instances in this book is large.

εἰς Κόρινθον, *to Corinth.* As Athens was the seat of culture, so
Corinth was the seat of commerce in the south of Greece. The city, at
this time the political capital of Greece and the residence of the
Roman pro-consul, stood on the isthmus which united the Peloponnesus
to the mainland, and through it all land traffic between the peninsula
and the rest of Greece must pass, while its two harbours, one on each
side of the neck of land on which Corinth stood, made it the resort of
seafaring traders both from east and west. Of Lechæum, the western
port, on the Corinthian gulf, we have no mention in the New Testament, but Cenchreæ, the harbour on the Saronic gulf, by which
communication with the East was kept up, is mentioned in verse 18.
The city was also made famous for its connexion with the Isthmian
games, from which St Paul in his Epistles draws frequent illustrations
when writing to the Corinthian Church. (See 1 Cor. ix. 24—27, &c.)
For further particulars of the history of Corinth see *Dict. of Bible*, s.v.

2. Ἰουδαῖον ὀνόματι Ἀκύλαν, *a Jew named Aquila.* The name
Aquila is Latin, and it is not likely that this was the man's Jewish name,
but as the custom was among the Jews, he had probably assumed a
Roman name during his dwelling in Italy and in his intercourse with
the Gentiles. See above on xiii. 9. The name is identified, by the
Jews, with that of Onkelos, who wrote a Targum on the Pentateuch,
and some make that Onkelos to be the same with Aquila who
translated the Old Testament into Greek, of which translation part
is preserved to us in Origen's Hexapla.

Ποντικὸν τῷ γένει, *born in Pontus.* Literally, 'a man of Pontus by
birth.' The provinces of Asia Minor abounded with Jewish families of
the Dispersion, as we may see from the whole history in the Acts. In
Acts ii. 9—11 many of these districts are mentioned as contributing
to the number of worshippers who had come to Jerusalem for the
feast of Pentecost. Pontus came under Roman sway when its king
Mithridates was conquered by Pompey, and this connexion may have
led Aquila to leave his native country for Italy. Aquila and his wife
are mentioned Rom. xvi. 3 as though they were again in Rome, so
that probably they had formed ties there which were only temporarily
severed by the Claudian edict mentioned in this verse. (It is however
questioned whether the salutations in Rom. xvi. form part of the
Epistle as it was sent to the Romans.) They were with St Paul when
he wrote the First Epistle to the Corinthians (1 Cor. xvi. 19), and were
so far settled in Ephesus, where that Epistle was written, as to have a
house which they could place at the service of the Christians there, as
a place to worship in. And if (as is most probable) Timothy was in

Ephesus when the Second Epistle (2 Tim. iv. 19) was addressed to him, they were in that city again at this later date (for Priscilla is only the diminutive form of Prisca, as the name of the wife is there written). More than this is not known of their changes of abode.

προσφάτως, *lately.* This adverb is only found here in N.T., but is more common in the LXX. Cf. Judith iv. 3 προσφάτως ἦσαν ἀναβεβηκότες ἐκ τῆς αἰχμαλωσίας. Also Judith iv. 5; 2 Macc. xiv. 36.

Πρίσκιλλαν, *Priscilla.* This name also is Latin, being a diminutive of the adjective '*Prisca*,' which was also used as a proper name, see Rom. xvi. 3.

διὰ τὸ διατεταχέναι...ἀπὸ τῆς Ῥώμης, *because that Claudius had commanded all Jews to depart from Rome.* The Jews were often objects of persecution in Rome, but this particular occasion is probably that mentioned by Suetonius, *Claud.* 25, where we read that by reason of the Jewish tumults at the instigation of one Christus (or Chrestus) they were driven out of the city. Whether this was the name of some Jew then resident in Rome, or whether it is a reference to some disturbance that had arisen from the Jewish expectation of 'the Christ' or Messiah, and the name Christus is mistakenly used by Suetonius as though it were that of some agitator actually present, we cannot tell. Or it may have been some movement of the Jews against the Christians because they taught that the 'Christ' was already come. In that case the name 'Christus' would come into great prominence, and might give rise to the statement of Suetonius that a person of that name had been the instigator of the disturbances.

3. καὶ διὰ τὸ ὁμότεχνον εἶναι, *and because he was of the same craft.* Among the Jews every Rabbi deemed it proper to practise some handicraft, and they have a proverb about R. Isaac, who was a smith, 'Better is the sentence of the smith (R. Isaac) than that of the smith's son (R. Jochanan),' thus marking their opinion that the pursuit of a craft was no injury to the teacher's wisdom (T. B. *Sanhedrin*, 96ᵃ). Thus our Lord is spoken of (Mark vi. 3) as 'the carpenter.'

There is an interesting passage bearing on this matter in the 'Teaching of the Twelve Apostles,' chap. 12. It is concerning one who comes to a Christian congregation 'in the name of the Lord.' εἰ δὲ θέλει πρὸς ὑμᾶς καθῆσαι, τεχνίτης ὤν, ἐργαζέσθω καὶ φαγέτω. εἰ δ' οὐκ ἔχει τέχνην, κατὰ τὴν σύνεσιν ὑμῶν προνοήσατε, πῶς μὴ ἀργὸς μεθ' ὑμῶν ζήσεται Χριστιανός. εἰ δ' οὐ θέλει οὕτω ποιεῖν, χριστέμπορός ἐστι.

ἔμενεν παρ' αὐτοῖς καὶ ἠργάζετο, *he abode with them and wrought.* In a passage from T. B. *Sukkah*, 51 b, part of which has already been quoted on vi. 9, we read in a description of the Jewish synagogue at Alexandria, 'The people did not sit mixed together, but goldsmiths by themselves, and silversmiths by themselves, and ironworkers by themselves, and miners by themselves, and weavers by themselves, and when a poor man came there he recognised the members of his craft, and went there, and from thence was his support, and that of the members of his house.' This may explain how readily Paul found at Corinth some persons who were of his own craft.

ἦσαν γὰρ σκηνοποιοὶ τῇ τέχνῃ, *for by their occupation they were tentmakers.* What they made was most probably tent-cloth. This was of goats' hair, and the plaiting of it into strips and joining these together was a common employment in Cilicia, to such an extent that the district gave name to the material and the articles made of it, a soldier's and sailor's rough hair-rug being named *Cilicium.* As the trade was intended in such cases as St Paul's merely to be used as a resource under circumstances of need which were not likely to come about, we can understand that while complying with Jewish feeling in the matter, a trade would be chosen for the boy which would not consume a large part of his time in learning. Mishnah *Qiddushin* IV. 14 says 'let a person teach his son a trade both clean and easy.' The most common handicraft of Tarsus offered just such a trade in the making of this rough goats' hair-cloth.

4. ἔπειθέν τε Ἰουδαίους καὶ Ἕλληνας, *and persuaded both Jews and Greeks.* No doubt as in other Gentile cities, the religion of the Jews in Corinth gained the attention of many among the Gentiles, who as proselytes or inclining thereto might form part of the Sabbath audience in the synagogue. According to his rule St Paul addressed himself to the Jews first.

5. ὡς δὲ κατῆλθον...ὁ Τιμόθεος, *but when Silas and Timothy came down from Macedonia.* After the arrival of his companions, who had been left at Beroea (xvii. 14) there was a change in the character of St Paul's preaching. It may well be that he had encouragement by their presence in his work of preaching, and also that it was not so necessary for him to consume his whole time on his craft because the Philippians had sent a contribution for his support (Phil. iv. 15; 2 Cor. xi. 9).

συνείχετο τῷ λόγῳ ὁ Παῦλος, *was constrained by the word.* The meaning is, he was earnestly occupied in preaching the word, and felt himself more urged on, and also more able to preach, because of his freedom from the necessity of constant labour. It was apparently only on the Sabbath that he had reasoned with the people before. The *usus loquendi* favours the passive meaning. Meyer (3rd ed.) renders 'he was apprehended, seized by the word' in the sense of internal pressure of spirit. For the verb cf. Wisdom xvii. 11, πονηρία προσείληφε τὰ χαλεπὰ συνεχομένη τῇ συνειδήσει, 'being pressed with conscience' (A.V.).

διαμαρτυρόμενος...εἶναι τὸν Χριστὸν Ἰησοῦν, *testifying to the Jews that Jesus was the Christ.* We are here told of the manner in which the greater earnestness of the Apostle was exhibited. He gave in all its fulness his solemn testimony, no doubt confirmed from Scripture and by the narrative of his own miraculous conversion, that this Jesus, whom he had formerly persecuted, was the Christ, the Messiah whom the Jews had long expected.

6. ἀντιτασσομένων δὲ αὐτῶν, *but when they opposed themselves.*
The word implies a strong organized opposition. They resisted like a
force drawn up for battle.

καὶ βλασφημούντων, *and blasphemed.* The same word is used in
2 Pet. ii. 2, 'The way of truth shall be *evil spoken of.*' And the
same conduct, though the word is different, is described in the
next chapter (xix. 9), 'speaking evil of the Way before the multitude.'

ἐκτιναξάμενος τὰ ἱμάτια εἶπεν, *he shook out his raiment and said.*
Cf. LXX. Neh. v. 13, καὶ τὴν ἀναβολήν μου ἐξετίναξα καὶ εἶπα Οὕτως
ἐκτινάξαι ὁ θεὸς πάντα ἄνδρα ὃς οὐ στήσει τὸν λόγον τοῦτον ἐκ τοῦ οἴκου
αὐτοῦ καὶ ἐκ κόπου αὐτοῦ. The act is figurative of entire renuncia-
tion. Nothing which pertained to them should cling to him. In
like manner he would cast them from his thoughts. Cf. xiii. 51.

τὸ αἷμα ὑμῶν ἐπὶ τὴν κεφαλὴν ὑμῶν, *your blood be upon your own
heads.* For the phrase cf. LXX. 2 Sam. i. 16; 1 Kings ii. 37; Ezek.
xxxiii. 4. The verb to be supplied is ἔστω or ἐλθέτω. The Apostle
uses the O. T. expression 'blood' in the figurative sense of 'destruction.'

εἰς τὰ ἔθνη πορεύσομαι, *I will go unto the Gentiles,* i.e. the Gentiles
in Corinth. For in his future preaching elsewhere (see xix. 8) he
addressed the Jews and went to the synagogue, as had been his
custom from the first.

7. εἰσῆλθεν εἰς οἰκίαν τινὸς ὀνόματι Ἰούστου, *he entered into a certain man's house named Justus.* St Paul perhaps used this house for the
purposes of teaching and worship. We may suppose that for his own
lodging, he still remained with Aquila and Priscilla. Some MSS. give
the name Titus (or Titius) Justus to this man, and the double name
is adopted in the Revised Version, but there is good authority for the
Text. recept.

σεβομένου τὸν θεόν, *one that worshipped God.* He was a proselyte.
See above on xiii. 43, xvii. 4. The house of Justus wás therefore an
appropriate place in which both Jews and Gentiles might meet, and
to which Gentiles would be more ready to come than to that of a Jew
by birth.

οὗ ἡ οἰκία...τῇ συναγωγῇ, *whose house joined hard to the synagogue.*
It is likely that St Paul though he came no more to the synagogue
at Corinth, chose not to betake himself far away, because he would be
ready to receive any of his brethren who might change their feelings
and come to him. On this cf. Chrysostom's language: ὅρα πῶς πάλιν
εἰπών, ἀπὸ τοῦ νῦν, οὐδὲ οὕτως αὐτῶν ἀμελεῖ. ὥστε τοῦ διεγεῖραι ἕνεκεν
εἶπε τοῦτο. καὶ λοιπὸν ἦλθε πρὸς Ἰούστον, οὗ ἦν ἡ οἰκία ὁμοροῦσα τῇ
συναγωγῇ. ἐγειτνίαζεν ὥστε καὶ ζῆλον ἔχειν ἀπὸ τῆς γειτνιάσεως εἴπερ
ἤθελον.

But we can see how, while his near neighbourhood gave opportunity
for this, the meetings of those who came to the synagogue with those
who were going to the house of Justus, would be likely to cause bitter-

ness, especially when the number of St Paul's adherents began to increase, and a ruler of the synagogue was counted among them.

8. Κρίσπος δὲ ὁ ἀρχισυνάγωγος, *and Crispus the ruler of the synagogue.* This Crispus is alluded to, 1 Cor. i. 14, as one of the few whom St Paul himself baptized. His previous distinguished position among the Jews, and the conversion of his whole family, would make him noticeable among the Christian converts. There may have been more than one synagogue in Corinth. In verse 17 we read of Sosthenes, the ruler of the synagogue. But it is quite possible that this man may have been appointed immediately after the conversion of Crispus, and may have been desirous to shew his zeal against the Christian teachers by laying an immediate information against Paul before the proconsul.

καὶ πολλοὶ τῶν Κορινθίων...ἐβαπτίζοντο, *and many of the Corinthians...were baptized.* St Paul mentions that he himself only baptized (in addition to Crispus) Gaius and the household of Stephanas. But Silas and Timothy were now by his side and would care for the admission of the new converts to baptism.

9. εἶπεν δὲ...ἐν νυκτὶ δι' ὁράματος τ. Π., *and the Lord spake to Paul in the night by a vision.* We may infer from the language used to him that for some reason the heart of the Apostle was beginning to wax faint, and that he was in danger of bodily maltreatment. The communication was made in the same way as the call to come over into Macedonia (xvi. 9, 10). Only here the Lord appeared to his servant.

λάλει καὶ μὴ σιωπήσῃς, *speak, and hold not thy peace.* Instead of fainting, be more earnest still. Let nothing stop thy testimony.

10. διότι ἐγώ εἰμι μετὰ σοῦ, *for I am with thee.* The pronoun is emphatically expressed.

τοῦ κακῶσαί σε, *to harm thee.* There will be assailants. Christ does not promise him freedom from attack. But the enemy shall not be able to do him violence. And this appearance of Christ would give the Apostle the confidence of the prophet of old (2 Kings vi. 16), 'They that be with us are more than they that be with them.'

With this genitival infinitive of *design*, cf. Luke xxiv. 29, εἰσῆλθεν τοῦ μεῖναι σὺν αὐτοῖς, also Gen. xxiv. 21, καὶ παρεσιώπα τοῦ γνῶναι εἰ εὐώδωκε κύριος τὴν ὁδὸν αὐτοῦ ἢ οὔ.

διότι λαός...ἐν τῇ πόλει ταύτῃ, *for I have much people in this city.* How important and extensive the Christian community at Corinth became we may gather from the Epistles which St Paul wrote afterwards to the Church there. And as the city was one of the great centres of commercial activity at this period, we can see how important it was (humanly speaking) for the Church to make good its footing there from the first. The Lord mercifully by this vision gave His servant assurance that his words should be largely blessed, and rising up thus comforted, he was ready for any task.

11. ἐκάθισεν δέ, *and he dwelt there.* In this word the historian seems to intend to express the quiet and content which filled the Apostle's mind after the vision. καθίζω is generally rendered 'to sit down,' and here seems to be applied purposely to the restful state of the Apostle's mind after the comforting revelation. The same verb is used by St Luke (xxiv. 49), '*Tarry* ye in the city, until ye be clothed with power from on high,' where the admonition is of like character with the advice given here to St Paul. In no other place in the New Testament is the word similarly used.

ἐνιαυτὸν καὶ μῆνας ἕξ, *a year and six months,* and beside the teaching which he gave to the Corinthians he wrote at this time the two Epistles to the Thessalonians which are the first in order of date among the Apostolic letters, and probably the earliest part of the whole New Testament.

12—17. PAUL IS ACCUSED BEFORE GALLIO, WHO DECLINES TO CONSIDER THE CHARGE AGAINST HIM. IN CONSEQUENCE, THE POPULACE FALL AT ONCE ON SOSTHENES, A CHIEF MAN AMONG THE JEWS, BUT GALLIO LETS THEIR ASSAULT PASS UNNOTICED.

12. Γαλλίωνος δὲ ἀνθυπάτου ὄντος τῆς Ἀχαΐας, *but when Gallio was proconsul of Achaia.* We come now to an episode in marked contrast to the repose and quiet spoken of just before. St Luke here gives Gallio his correct title, which is a great mark of the fidelity of his narrative. Achaia was a Roman province. Such provinces belonged either to the Senate or to the Emperor. When they were senatorial the governor was styled Proconsul. Now Achaia had been a senatorial province under Augustus, but under Tiberius became an imperial province for a time. Subsequently after A.D. 44 under Claudius (Suet. *Claud.* xxv.), which is the reign in which these events in St Paul's life occurred, it was once more made senatorial and so had a proconsul at this period for its governor. This Gallio was the brother of the famous philosopher Seneca, who was tutor, and for a time minister, of the Emperor Nero. Originally Gallio was called Marcus Annæus Novatus, and took the name of Gallio from the orator Lucius Junius Gallio, by whom he was adopted. The character of Gallio as described by his Roman contemporaries is that of a most bright, popular and affectionate man. He is spoken of as 'sweet Gallio,' and Seneca declares that 'those who love him to the utmost, don't love him enough.'

κατεπέστησαν ὁμοθυμαδόν, *they rose up with one accord.* The Jews probably hoped to avail themselves of the inexperience of a newly arrived proconsul. For this reason they came in a body and sought to have Paul expelled from the city.

καὶ ἤγαγον αὐτὸν ἐπὶ τὸ βῆμα, *and brought him to the judgement seat.* In Gallio's eyes they would seem to be a company of Jews accusing one of their own race of some erroneous teaching. If he had only lately come from Rome, he would be likely to have heard there of the troubles about 'Christus' (see above on verse 2), and he would consider that he had come into the midst of a quarrel about the same matter.

13. παρὰ τὸν νόμον, *contrary to the law*, i.e. the Jewish law. The Jewish religion was one of those allowed throughout the Roman Empire, and their hope is to induce the proconsul to protect the Jewish law by Roman law. But the majesty of the Roman power was far too august to be invoked for settling a quarrel between the members of a merely 'tolerated' religion. He would not meddle in their matters.

14. μέλλοντος δὲ τοῦ Παύλου ἀνοίγειν τὸ στόμα, *but when Paul was about to open his mouth.* The Roman proconsul has too much contempt for the whole matter and all who are concerned in it to listen to any defence. For the law of the Jews, its breach or its observance, he has no care, and will not be used by either party. Chrysostom praises Gallio's conduct. ἐπιεικής τις ἄνθρωπος οὗτος εἶναί μοι δοκεῖ, καὶ δῆλον ἐξ ὧν ἀποκρίνεται συνετῶς.

εἶπεν ὁ Γαλλίων πρὸς τοὺς Ἰουδαίους, *Gallio said unto the Jews.* He declines to hear any argument, for he is determined to give no opinion.

εἰ μὲν ἦν ἀδίκημά τι ἢ ῥᾳδιούργημα πονηρόν, *if it had been a matter of wrong or wicked villany.* The two things of which the magistrate would take account are (1) any evil-doing (cp. xxiv. 20), an act of injustice, or (2) any unscrupulous conduct involving moral wrong. He would be, that is, a minister of law and equity, for that was his duty.

κατὰ λόγον ἂν ἀνεσχόμην ὑμῶν, *reason would that I should have borne with you.* A very happy idiomatic rendering of the Greek, like many others in the A. V. Gallio shews by his language how far he feels the Roman citizen above the tolerated Jews. But if their case had called for its exercise they should have had the benefit of toleration, and he would have inquired into matters that were the business of his office.

15. εἰ δὲ ζητήματά ἐστιν περὶ λόγου καὶ ὀνομάτων, *but if they are questions about words and names.* The use of the indicative ἐστίν shews that Gallio considers this is what they are.

There would no doubt be many points brought forward from St Paul's teaching to which the Jews would object. And whether Jesus was the Christ or not would seem to the Roman a matter entirely of definition, and on which the law had no bearing. If he had heard the name of 'Christus' at Rome (see on verse 2), it would make Gallio the more ready to imitate his royal master, and get rid of the disputants as fast and as far as possible.

καὶ νόμου τοῦ καθ' ὑμᾶς, *and of your own law.* On this circumlocution see xvii. 28 note. The accusers had without doubt been striving to make out that in teaching a different manner of worship (ver. 13) Paul was bringing forward a religion not enjoying toleration by the Roman government. But Gallio sees through their intention, and counting them all for Jews, he will not be drawn into their questions, ὄψεσθε αὐτοί, *look to it yourselves.* The pronoun is very emphatic. For the form ὄψεσθε used as an imperative, cf. LXX. Numb. xiii. 19, καὶ ὄψεσθε τὴν γῆν τίς ἐστι, καὶ τὸν λαόν. Also Judges vii. 17, xxi. 21; 1 Sam. vi. 9; &c.

κριτὴς ἐγὼ τούτων οὐ βούλομαι εἶναι, *I am not minded to be a judge of these matters.* Gallio knows his own business and will only look to that. It is not a case where his jurisdiction can interfere, and so he leaves the whole untouched. There is no question here about his own regard and disregard of enquiries about religion. He sits to administer Roman law, and this dispute among the Jews at Corinth lies outside his cognizance altogether.

16. καὶ ἀπήλασεν αὐτοὺς ἀπὸ τοῦ βήματος, *and he drave them from the judgement seat.* The description given by St Luke makes it probable that Gallio's βῆμα was in some open public place, whither all might come and bring their plaints. The proconsul would be attended by his lictors and other officials, and those he now commands to clear the place of these troublesome cavillers about words and names. The new magistrate found perhaps enough to do in matters which came within his jurisdiction in the busy mercantile life of Corinth.

17. ἐπιλαβόμενοι δὲ πάντες Σωσθένην τὸν ἀρχισυνάγωγον, *and they all laid hold on Sosthenes the ruler of the synagogue and, &c.* The verb is used (xxi. 30) of the violent action of the mob at Jerusalem, and just afterwards (xxi. 33) of the chief captain's conduct when he rescued Paul. Neither of these would be a very gentle measure. And we may understand something of the same kind here. The surrounding crowd, of whom no doubt most would be Greeks, catching the tone of the magistrate, prepared to follow up his decision by a lesson of their own, of a rather rough kind. Sosthenes had probably been the spokesman of the Jews, and Paul would not improbably have some sympathizers among the Gentiles. And 'Jew-baiting' was not unknown in those days. So with impunity the crowd could wreak their own vengeance on these interrupters of the proper business of the court, and beat Sosthenes before he was out of the magistrate's presence. The name Sosthenes was a very common one, and we need not identify this man with the Sosthenes mentioned in 1 Cor. i. 1.

καὶ οὐδὲν τούτων τῷ Γαλλίωνι ἔμελεν, *and Gallio cared for none of these things,* neither for the questions raised nor for those who raised them. How little Jewish life was regarded by the Romans is shewn in many places in their literature (see Farrar's *St Paul*, Vol. I. Exc. xiv.). Tiberius banished four thousand of them to Sardinia, saying that if the unhealthy climate killed them off 'it would be a cheap loss' (Tac. *Ann.* II. 85). Coming from Rome where such feeling was universal, the lives and limbs of a few Jews would appear of small importance, and like the Emperor just named he may have thought it mattered little what became of them.

It is best to take οὐδέν as subject of ἔμελεν, and τούτων not as governed by ἔμελεν, but by οὐδέν.

18—23. PAUL LEAVES CORINTH TO GO INTO SYRIA, HALTING A SHORT
TIME AT CENCHREÆ, AND SOMEWHAT LONGER AT EPHESUS. HE
LANDS AT CÆSAREA, GOES UP TO JERUSALEM, AND FROM THENCE TO
ANTIOCH, AND AFTER A TIME DEPARTS ON HIS THIRD MISSIONARY
JOURNEY.

18. προσμείνας ἡμέρας ἱκανάς, *having tarried many days.* This
seems to refer to the period after the appearance before Gallio. We
are told (verse 11) that he settled quietly for a year and six months.
Then came an opportunity of attacking him on Gallio's arrival. Of
this the Jews tried to avail themselves, and when their attempt was
at an end, the Apostle had another time of peace among his converts.
So that the whole stay in Corinth extended over more than a year and
a half.

ἀποταξάμενος, *having taken leave of.* A strictly N.T. use of the
word. It occurs again below in verse 21 and in Mark vi. 46; Luke ix.
61.

ἐξέπλει εἰς τὴν Συρίαν, *he sailed for Syria.* We have no motive
given why the Apostle at this time sailed back. Some have suggested
that he was carrying a contribution to the brethren in Jerusalem. It
is clear that when the return was resolved on, he wished to reach
Jerusalem as soon as possible, for he declined to tarry in Ephesus even
though his preaching was more readily received there than by the
Jews in many other places. It may have been the wish to fulfil his
vow, which could only be brought to its conclusion by a visit to the
temple in Jerusalem.

κειράμενος ἐν Κεγχρεαῖς τὴν κεφαλήν, εἶχεν γὰρ εὐχήν, *having shorn
his head in Cenchreæ, for he had a vow.* We can observe all through
the narrative of the Acts that St Paul, although the Apostle of the
Gentiles, never ceased to regard the festivals and ceremonies of the
Jews in things which did not militate against the Christian liberty.
For some reason, either during sickness or in the midst of his conflict
at Corinth, he had taken a vow upon himself of the nature of the
Nazirite vows (Numb. vi. 1—21). This could only be brought to its
fitting close by a journey to Jerusalem to offer up the hair, which it
was a part of the vow to leave uncut. At Jerusalem when the cere-
mony was completed the head was shaven (see Acts xxi. 24), but it
seems to have been allowed to persons at a distance to cut the hair
short and to bring that with them to the temple and to offer it up
when the rest was shaven. This appears to be what St Paul did at
this time, at Cenchreæ, before starting on the voyage to Syria. The
Greek word for 'having shorn' stands in the original next to Aquila.
Hence some have contended that it was he who had the vow, and who
cut his hair. They have pointed out also that the order of the
names 'Priscilla and Aquila' seems to have been adopted purposely
to make this connexion of words possible. But the name of the wife
stands before that of her husband in Rom. xvi. 3; see also 2 Tim. iv.
19 and according to the best MSS. in verse 26 below. This order of the
names may have been adopted because by her zeal she made herself a

very conspicuous member of the Church wherever she lived. But it seems very unlikely that all this detail of a vow and its observance would be so prominently mentioned in connexion with Aquila, who played but a small part in St Luke's history; while it is a most significant feature in the conduct of St Paul that he so oft conformed to Jewish observances.

19. κατήντησαν δὲ εἰς Ἔφεσον, *and they came to Ephesus.* Ephesus was the famous city, the capital of Ionia, and afterwards the scene of a large portion of St John's labours. It stood not far from the sea on some hilly ground, by a small river which flows into the sea in the district lying between the greater rivers, the Hermus and the Meander. In St Paul's day it was by far the busiest and most populous city in Proconsular Asia. For a more complete account of its inhabitants and the special worship of Artemis (Diana) for which it was celebrated, a fitting place will be found in the notes on chap. xix.

κἀκείνους κατέλιπεν αὐτοῦ, *and he left them there.* They probably had business connexions with the large city of Ephesus, which caused them to end their journey here. These people though working at their trade appear to have been above the position which would be implied by Dr Farrar's expression (*St Paul* I. 573), 'his lodging in the *squalid* shop of Aquila and Priscilla.' They travelled about and lived now at Rome, now at Ephesus, and now in Corinth (1 Cor. xvi. 19; Rom. xvi. 3; 2 Tim. iv. 19), and on their condition when in Ephesus, see above on verse 2.

εἰς τὴν συναγωγήν, *into the synagogue.* He could not give up his own people, though he was constantly exposed to hard usage by them. He seeks them out again here as soon as he arrives. In Ephesus however his message seems to have been received with less hostility, for those who heard him begged him to stay a longer time. The cosmopolitan character of the Ephesian population may have had something to do with this.

20. ἐρωτώντων δὲ αὐτῶν ἐπὶ πλείονα χρόνον μεῖναι, *and when they asked him to tarry a longer time.* We need not from this suppose that more impression had been produced on this occasion than made the Jews willing to give him a patient hearing.

21. ἀλλὰ ἀποταξάμενος καὶ εἰπών, *but bidding them farewell and saying.* The words in the *Text. recept.*, which are omitted from this verse, seem to be an addition suggested by xx. 16. The authorities for the omission are numerous, both uncials, cursives and versions.

πάλιν ἀνακάμψω πρὸς ὑμᾶς τοῦ θεοῦ θέλοντος, *I will return again to you, if God will.* Having the opportunity, he soon redeemed his promise. See xix. 1.

22. εἰς Καισάρειαν, *to Cæsarea.* This was the home of Philip the Evangelist, and we may suppose that St Paul would make the success of his distant mission known to his fellow-labourer. He made the house of Philip his home in Cæsarea on a later occasion (xxi. 8).

ἀναβάς, *having gone up,* i.e. from the coast to the city of Jerusalem καὶ ἀσπασάμενος τὴν ἐκκλησίαν, *and having saluted the Church.* This must strike every reader as a very brief notice of a visit to the centre of all Church life and action at this time. And we cannot but be surprised that there is no mention (as in xiv. 27) of a gathering of the Church, and of the report of what the great missionary had been enabled to effect. Dr Farrar (*St Paul*, II. 5) suggests that St Paul met with a cold and ungracious reception, and that the position which he assumed towards the Law in his preaching to Gentile converts raised him up adversaries among the Christians in Jerusalem, who were naturally zealous for the Law. It is certainly strange that even the name of the city is not mentioned, nor are we told a word about the fulfilment of the vow. For some reason or other, the Apostle hastened, as soon as his salutations were ended, to the more congenial society of the Christians at Antioch who had rejoiced over his success on a former visit.

23. καὶ ποιήσας χρόνον τινά, *and after he had spent some time there.* As they had experienced for themselves the troubles of the Judaizers, the people at Antioch would sympathize with the Apostle, if he were meeting with like opposition now in his own work.

For χρόνον ποιεῖν cf. xv. 33, xx. 3; 2 Cor. xi. 25; Jas. iv. 13.

ἐξῆλθεν, *he departed*, making Antioch his starting point as he had done in both his former missions.

διερχόμενος καθεξῆς…Φρυγίαν, *passing through all the region of Galatia* and *Phrygia in order.* No doubt he took the same route as before. Thus he would visit Lystra and Derbe before he came to the more northern portions of Asia Minor mentioned in this verse.

στηρίζων, *strengthening.* The return of the Apostle to the Churches which he had once visited would infuse new spirit, while his presence and words would everywhere quicken Christian activity.

24—28. Visit of Apollos to Ephesus, and his Teaching there. He is more fully instructed by Aquila and Priscilla, and afterwards passing over into Achaia, preaches Christ there with great power.

24. Ἰουδαῖος δέ τις Ἀπολλὼς ὀνόματι, *now a certain Jew named Apollos.* The five verses following are a digression to introduce the narrative of the next chapter.

The name Apollos is an abbreviation of Apollonius, which is read in one MS. (D). His influence as a Christian teacher made itself most felt in Corinth. (Cp. 1 Cor. i. 12, iii. 5, iv. 6.)

Ἀλεξανδρεὺς τῷ γένει, *an Alexandrian by birth.* On Alexandria as a place where Jews abounded, cf. vi. 9. It was in Alexandria and by Jews that the Septuagint Version was made.

ἀνὴρ λόγιος, *an eloquent man* (Rev. Ver. 'learned'). The word includes both senses. He had stores of learning, and also could use them to convince others.

κατήντησεν εἰς Ἔφεσον, δυνατὸς ὢν ἐν ταῖς γραφαῖς, *came to Ephesus, and he was mighty in the Scriptures.* The study of the Old Testament flourished greatly in Alexandria, and Apollos had great power in the exposition and application of these Scriptures. The literary activity and philosophic pursuits of the Greek population of Alexandria were not without their effect on the more conservative Jews, and we find from many sources that the Jewish writings were studied with all the literary exactness which marked the Greek scholarship of the time, and the Jews, conscious of the antiquity of their own records and yet impressed with the philosophic character of their cultured fellow-citizens, bent themselves greatly to find analogies between the Mosaic writings and the teachings of the schools. In study like this Apollos had no doubt been fully trained.

δυνατὸς ἐν is in the N. T. used only by St Luke, see Luke xxiv. 19; Acts vii. 22. It is frequent in the LXX., cf. Ecclus. xxi. 7, γνωστὸς μακρόθεν ὁ δυνατὸς ἐν γλώσσῃ.

25. οὗτος ἦν κατηχημένος τὴν ὁδὸν τοῦ κυρίου, *this man was instructed in the way of the Lord.* The verb κατηχέω (whence our 'catechize') implies a course of instruction distinct from his own study of the O. T. Scriptures. We know from Josephus (*Antiq.* xviii. 5. 2) that the teaching and baptism of John produced great effect among the Jews. We need not therefore wonder at finding among Jews in Alexandria and Ephesus men who had accepted the Baptist's teaching about Jesus. But in considering such cases we must remember where such instruction as they had received would stop short. They would know that John baptized in preparation for the coming of the kingdom, they would have heard that he pointed to Jesus as the Lamb of God, being certified thereof when He came to be baptized. But when John was dead and the life of Jesus was brought to a close on Calvary, except the few of John's disciples who had joined the followers of our Lord, none would know of the way in which the foundations of the heavenly kingdom were laid, none would understand the institution of the Sacraments, nor the sending down of the Holy Ghost, nor the teaching of repentance, and of the gift of salvation to the faithful through grace. Of these things John had known nothing, and we must not forget in our attempt to estimate his work and its effects, that there came to himself a day when he sent to Christ to ask 'Art thou He that should come?' (Matth. xi. 3.)

καὶ ζέων τῷ πνεύματι ἐλάλει καὶ ἐδίδασκεν ἀκριβῶς τὰ περὶ τοῦ Ἰησοῦ, *and being fervent in spirit he spake and taught carefully the things concerning Jesus.* By πνεῦμα is meant Apollos's own spirit and zeal. The reading of the *Text. recept.* τὰ περὶ τοῦ Κυρίου seems to have been the suggestion of some one who did not understand the plain statement of the text. In the previous expression 'the way of the Lord' we have only the Old Test. words (Is. xl. 3) quoted by the Evangelists concerning John's preaching. (Matth. iii. 3; Mark i. 3.) There may have been some timidity felt about the further statement that Apollos taught the things 'concerning Jesus,' and so the reading of the early part of the verse was brought in here also. But after what has been said above we can see how this Alexandrian Jew might publish with the utmost accuracy all that John had proclaimed about the coming of the Kingdom of Heaven, and enforce it from his own studies of the Old Testament Scriptures. He might declare how John had pointed to Jesus, and might even relate much of the works and words of Christ, as an evidence that God was sending greater prophets than they had known for long, and that therefore Christ's life was a testimony that redemption was near. All this he might know and preach most carefully, and yet lack all that further knowledge which Aquila and Priscilla imparted. Chrysostom on the contrary explains πνεῦμα of the Holy Ghost, and suggests that the case of Aquila is somewhat like that of Cornelius, where the Holy Spirit was given before baptism in the name of Christ. For ζέων τῷ πνεύματι cf. Rom. xii. 11.

ἐπιστάμενος...Ἰωάννου, *knowing only the baptism of John.* In this sentence we have the solution of any difficulty which there may seem to be in the verse. He knew nothing of that other baptism, which is the entrance into Christ's kingdom, and therefore he could merely be looking forward for the fulfilment of the prophecies, and the power of his teaching would consist in the zealous way which he published that the voice of God in His older Revelation proclaimed Messiah's advent very near.

26. οὗτός τε ἤρξατο παρρησιάζεσθαι ἐν τῇ συναγωγῇ, *and this man began to speak boldly in the synagogue.* The verb παρρησιάζεσθαι has been frequently used of the boldness of the disciples (cf. ix. 27, 29, xiv. 3, &c.). Here too was the same spirit and the same need of it. For the Jews were not all ready to listen to announcements of the approach of the Messiah. The speaker must be prepared with arguments as well as courage who dwelt on this theme, about which the Jews had been deluded by many impostors.

ἀκούσαντες δὲ αὐτοῦ Πρίσκιλλα καὶ Ἀκύλας, *but when Priscilla and Aquila heard him.* Here as in other places (see above on 18) the name of the wife precedes that of her husband. By joining her in this marked way with Aquila in the communications with Apollos, the historian indicates that she was a woman of great power and zeal among the Christians. It has been suggested that she was perhaps a born Jewess and her husband not so, which might account for the prominence given in several places to her name. It may be noted here, as so often, that Aquila and his wife, like the other Judæo-Christians, still attended the worship of the synagogue.

προσελάβοντο αὐτόν, *they took him unto them.* He would be much more in sympathy with them than with many of the Jewish congregation. He was prepared to accept the Messiah, but did not yet understand that Jesus was He. Priscilla and Aquila must have been persons of some mark to be warranted in taking Apollos thus to their company.

καὶ ἀκριβέστερον...τὴν ὁδὸν τοῦ θεοῦ, *and expounded unto him the way of God more carefully.* For the adverb cf. the previous verse.

The use of the same word in both verses seems to shew that the studies of Aquila and his wife in the Scriptures had been of the same earnest kind as those of Apollos. By the 'way of God' we must understand God's further working out of the Old Testament prediction in the closing events of the life of Jesus, and in the gift of the Holy Ghost. That Joel's prophecy, quoted by St Peter on the day of Pentecost (Acts ii. 16), had been thus fulfilled, was new learning for the eloquent Alexandrian. As also the newly-appointed means of grace in baptism and the breaking of bread, with the promise of salvation through faith in Christ. These also may be included as part of the 'way of God,' being means whereby men are brought nearer to Him.

27. βουλομένου δὲ αὐτοῦ διελθεῖν, ε. τ. Ἀ., *and when he was minded to pass over into Achaia.* We find from xix. 1 that the centre of his labours there was Corinth. Being acquainted with the philosophy and learning of Greece he was well fitted to be a preacher to the Greeks as well as to the Jews, and he may have felt that Corinth was the place where he could do most good. We are not told of any Apostolic commission to Apollos, but we know from 1 Cor. i. 12, &c. that he came to be regarded by some Corinthians as the equal of St Paul, and that there arose some strong party feeling in that Church, which is rebuked in St Paul's letter to them. We cannot suppose that this was brought about by Apollos, for St Paul speaks of him as watering what he himself had planted, and it may be that the knowledge of the existence of such a spirit accounts for the unwillingness of Apollos to come back to Corinth (1 Cor. xvi. 12) which we read of somewhat later.

προτρεψάμενοι...ἀποδέξασθαι αὐτόν, *the brethren encouraged him and wrote to the disciples to receive him.* For προτρέπομαι cf. Wisdom xiv. 18, καὶ τοὺς ἀγνοοῦντας ἡ τοῦ τεχνίτου προετρέψατο φιλοτιμία. Also 2 Macc. xi. 7, αὐτὸς δὲ πρῶτος ὁ Μακκαβαῖος ἀναλαβὼν τὰ ὅπλα προετρέψατο τοὺς ἄλλους. Here we find the first instance of letters of commendation sent from one Church to another. 'The brethren' at Ephesus were probably only a small number, but Aquila and Priscilla would be well known to the Christians in Corinth.

ὃς παραγενόμενος...διὰ τῆς χάριτος, *who when he was come helped them much which had believed through grace.* διὰ τῆς χάριτος may be joined either to συνεβάλετο or to τοῖς πεπιστευκόσιν. But as the history is occupied with the work of Apollos, it seems more natural to explain the 'grace' spoken of, as the gift which was already in Apollos, and which the more full instruction that he had just received had tended to increase. He had formerly been but partially enlightened. Now that he knows the truth in Christ, his former ability becomes more helpful still. He helps others through his grace. His work seems rightly estimated by St Paul, 'he watered' what the Apostle had 'planted' (1 Cor. iii. 6).

For συμβάλλομαι in the sense of 'helping,' cf. Wisdom v. 8, τί πλοῦτος μετὰ ἀλαζονείας συμβέβληται ἡμῖν; 'What good hath riches with our vaunting brought us?' (A.V.).

28. εὐτόνως γὰρ τοῖς Ἰουδαίοις διακατηλέγχετο, *for he mightily confuted the Jews.* The verb implies that Apollos brought the objections of the Jews to the test (ἔλεγχος) of Scripture, and shewed them to be futile. The disciples, who had already believed, appear to have been suffering from Jewish gainsayers. It was by his power in the Scriptures that Apollos was helpful against these adversaries of the faith.

For εὐτόνως, which in N.T. is found only here and in Luke xxiii. 10, cf. LXX. Josh. vi. 8, σημαινέτωσαν εὐτόνως. Also 2 Macc. xii. 23. διακατελέγχομαι occurs nowhere else.

δημοσίᾳ, *publicly.* By his discourses in the synagogue. This was an important feature in the help that Apollos gave. He was a learned Jew, able to set forth to whole Jewish congregations how their Scriptures were receiving their fulfilment. Thus they who already believed would be strengthened.

ἐπιδεικνὺς...τὸν Χριστὸν Ἰησοῦν, *shewing by the Scriptures that Jesus was the Christ.* See above on verse 5. The Jews had complained before Gallio that St Paul was teaching a religion 'contrary to the Law.' Those who heard Apollos learnt that in Jesus they were accepting the 'fulfiller of the Law.'

Chrysostom says here: ἐντεῦθεν πῶς ἦν δυνατὸς ἐν ταῖς γραφαῖς Ἀπολλὼς δείκνυσι· τοὺς μὲν γὰρ Ἰουδαίους σφόδρα ἐπεστόμιζε. τοῦτο γάρ ἐστι τὸ διακατηλέγχετο· τοὺς δὲ πιστεύοντας θαρρεῖν μᾶλλον ἐποίει, καὶ ἵστασθαι πρὸς τὴν πίστιν.

CHAPTER XIX.

Readings varying from the *Text. recept.*

1. εὑρεῖν for εὑρών with אAB. *Vulg.* supports this having 'veniret ...et inveniret.'

2. εἶπον omitted with אABDE. *Vulg.* has 'dixerunt.'

3. πρὸς αὐτούς omitted with אAE. Not represented in *Vulg.*

4. Χριστὸν omitted with אABE. Not represented in *Vulg.*

9. τινός omitted with אAB. *Vulg.* has 'cujusdam.'

10. Ἰησοῦ omitted after Κυρίου with אABDE. Not represented in *Vulg.*

12. ἐκπορεύεσθαι for ἐξέρχεσθαι ἀπ' αὐτῶν with אABDE. *Vulg.* has 'egrediebantur' only.

13. ὁρκίζω with אABDE. *Vulg.* 'abjuro.'

14. υἱοὶ after ἑπτά and omitting οἱ with אABE. *Vulg.* has 'septem filii qui hoc faciebant.'

15. αὐτοῖς added after εἶπεν with אABD. *Vulg.* has 'eis.'

16. ἀμφοτέρων for αὐτῶν with אABD. *Vu*lg. 'amborum.'

24. οὐκ ὀλίγην ἐργασίαν with אABD. *Vulg.* 'non modicum quæs-tum.'

29. ὅλη omitted with אAB. *Vulg.* does not represent it.

33. συνεβίβασαν with אABE. *Vulg.* 'detraxerunt.'

34. ἐπιγνόντες with אABDEHLP. *Vulg.* seems to support *Text. recept.*

35. ἀνθρώπων with אABE. *Vulg.* 'hominum.'
θεᾶς omitted with אABDE. Not represented in *Vulg.*

40. περὶ οὗ οὐ with אABHLP. *Vulg.* has 'de quo possumus.'

Сн. XIX. 1—7. PAUL RETURNING TO EPHESUS FINDS THERE SOME
DISCIPLES OF JOHN THE BAPTIST.

1. ἐν τῷ τὸν Ἀπολλὼ εἶναι ἐν Κορίνθῳ, *while Apollos was in Corinth.*
The digression concerning Apollos being ended, the history now re-turns to St Paul. Apollos found, no doubt, that Corinth was the most effective centre for his work in Achaia, and apparently made that his head-quarters.

Παῦλον διελθόντα τὰ ἀνωτερικὰ μέρη, *Paul having passed through the upper country.* The districts alluded to are those mentioned in xviii. 23, Galatia and Phrygia, to reach which he would also pass through Lycaonia. ἀνωτερικός signifies the upland away from the sea; here the more eastern parts of Asia Minor.

ἐλθεῖν εἰς Ἔφεσον, *came to Ephesus.* This he had promised to do if he could (xviii. 21).

καὶ εὑρεῖν τινὰς μαθητάς, *and found certain disciples.* These men are called *disciples* because they were, like Apollos, to a certain extent instructed concerning Jesus, and what they already knew drew them to listen to St Paul who could teach them more.

2. εἰ πνεῦμα ἅγιον ἐλάβετε πιστεύσαντες; *did ye receive the Holy Ghost when ye believed?* On the use of εἰ as simply the mark of an interrogation cf. i. 6.
The position of these disciples is difficult to understand. St Paul addresses them as believers. But this perhaps is only because they presented themselves among the real Christian disciples, and his recent arrival made it impossible for him to know the history of all who appeared among the members of the congregation. He presumes they are believers from the company in which he finds them.

ἀλλ' οὐδὲ εἰ πνεῦμα ἅγιόν ἐστιν ἠκούσαμεν, *nay, we did not so much as hear whether the Holy Ghost was given.* This is the sense of the verse, and not that given by the A.V. Of the existence of the Holy Ghost no disciples of John could (as might be conceived from the A.V.) be ignorant. In his preaching John had proclaimed that the baptism of Him who was to come after him should be with the Holy

Ghost and with fire. But in the Greek where, as in this verse, the expression 'Spirit' or 'Holy Spirit' is found without an article (although in English we are forced to put 'the' before it) it signifies not the personal Comforter, but an operation or gift of the Holy Spirit. Thus in John vii. 39, the A.V. rightly renders οὔπω γὰρ ἦν πνεῦμα ἅγιον 'for the Holy Ghost was not yet *given*,' although there is no verb for 'given,' because the noun is without an article in the Greek, and so signifies 'a spiritual outpouring.' These disciples at Ephesus, then, imply by their answer not that the name 'Holy Ghost' was strange, but that they were unacquainted (as was the Baptist himself) with any special bestowal of the gifts of the Spirit.

3. εἰς τί οὖν ἐβαπτίσθητε; *into what then were ye baptized?* The phrase, derived from the language of Christ (Matth. xxviii. 19), was βαπτίζειν εἰς τὸ ὄνομα. Hence the form of this question and of the answer, εἰς τὸ Ἰωάννου βάπτισμα, which means 'We were baptized into that into which John baptized.' These men may have been disciples of Apollos, and been baptized by him before his fuller instruction by Priscilla and Aquila.

4. εἶπεν δὲ Παῦλος, Ἰωάννης ἐβάπτισεν βάπτισμα μετανοίας, *and Paul said, John baptized with the baptism of repentance.* Such was John's description of his own baptism (Matth. iii. 11), but after the day of Pentecost the language of the Christian preacher (Acts ii. 38) is, 'Repent and be baptized in the name of Jesus Christ for the remission of sins, and ye shall receive the gift of the Holy Ghost.' These Ephesian disciples knew nothing of baptism for the remission of sins, or of the other sacrament of the Lord's Supper, nor of the gift of the Spirit to the Church, nor of the doctrines of faith in Christ and salvation by grace through faith.

βάπτισμα μετανοίας, found Mark i. 4; Luke iii. 3; Acts xiii. 24, is explained by βαπτίζειν εἰς μετάνοιαν of Matth. iii. 11. The baptized were pledged to amendment of life, and to a preparation for the coming Messiah.

εἰς τὸν ἐρχόμενον μετ᾽ αὐτόν, κ.τ.λ., *on Him which should come after him, that is, on Jesus.* In his preaching John had constantly used the phrase 'He that cometh after me.' This was the stage of instruction at which these disciples had arrived. They knew that John spake of one who was to come. St Paul's teaching made clear to them that this was Jesus. The closing words of the sentence (εἰς τὸν Ἰησοῦν) are a condensation of all the explanations by which the Apostle convinced them that Jesus, whom he preached, was the prophet whom John announced. St Luke does not anywhere give speeches or arguments *in extenso*, but only so much as is needed to explain the results which he describes.

5. ἀκούσαντες δέ, *and when they heard.* What they heard was not the mere statement that Jesus was the Messiah; but all the arguments with which St Paul demonstrated that this was so, and proved that in Him the Scriptures were fulfilled. The conviction need not have been sudden, though its description is brief.

εἰς τὸ ὄνομα, *into the name.* Cf. Matth. xxviii. 19 and Acts ii. 38 note. These men followed the order appointed for admission to the privileges of the Christian covenant. No argument can be drawn from this verse for a repetition of baptism. These disciples had never received such a baptism as Christ ordained. John's baptism was but a washing symbolical of the repentance which he preached; baptism into the name of Christ is the pledge of a covenant of salvation.

6. ἦλθεν τὸ πνεῦμα τ. ἅ. ἐπ' αὐτούς, *the Holy Ghost came upon them.* The gift of the Holy Ghost to these disciples appears to have been a special provision of the Spirit for the great work which was to change Ephesus, from the city wholly devoted to the goddess Diana, into the centre of Christian life throughout the west of Asia Minor for several centuries.

ἐλάλουν τε γλώσσαις, *and they spake with tongues.* A Pentecostal outpouring; for as in Jerusalem the gift wrought its effect among the Jews when gathered there from every quarter, so was the Spirit given in this great centre of Gentile activity that a like result might follow, and that the amazement and marvel at such a power might win attention to the message and gain converts to Christ.

καὶ ἐπροφήτευον, *and prophesied.* Probably in this case to be understood of the exposition of Old Testament prophecy, and of the power of preaching bestowed on them by the gift of the Holy Ghost. The foretelling of future events would be no such help to the cause of Christ as would the power of prophecy in this other sense.

7. ἦσαν δὲ οἱ πάντες ἄνδρες ὡσεὶ δώδεκα, *and they were in all about twelve men.* A new band of Apostles.

The verse has been the cause of much remark. Why the inspired historian should speak with an 'about,' has been asked by some. With that we are not concerned, only to observe that the Spirit has not prompted him to speak otherwise. Some have seen in the number and the circumstances a resemblance to the Apostles and their supernatural endowment; others have looked back as far as the Patriarchs and have made of these men the beginning of another Israel. May it not be that the 'about' was written to admonish us of the unprofitableness of such speculations? Cp. Josh. vii. 5.

Here Chrysostom asks: πῶς οἱ λαβόντες τὸ πνεῦμα οὐκ ἐδίδασκον, ἀλλ' Ἀπολλὼς μήπω τὸ πνεῦμα λαβών; ὅτι οὐκ ἦσαν οὕτω ζέοντες οὐδὲ κατηχημένοι· ἐκεῖνος δὲ καὶ κατηχημένος ἦν καὶ σφόδρα ζέων. ἐμοὶ δὲ δοκεῖ ὅτι καὶ πολλὴ ἦν ἡ παρρησία τοῦ ἀνδρός. ἀλλ' εἰ καὶ ἀκριβῶς ἐλάλει τὰ περὶ τοῦ Ἰησοῦ; ὅμως ἐδεῖτο ἔτι ἀκριβεστέρας διδασκαλίας. οὕτω καίτοι οὐκ εἰδὼς πάντα ἀπὸ τῆς προθυμίας ἐπεσπάσατο τὸ πνεῦμα τὸ ἅγιον καθάπερ οἱ περὶ Κορνήλιον.

8—20. PAUL PREACHES TO THE JEWS FIRST AND AFTERWARDS TO THE GENTILES. THE WORD OF GOD PREVAILS MIGHTILY.

8. εἰσελθὼν δὲ εἰς τὴν συναγωγήν, *and having entered into the synagogue.* As the incident of John's disciples is mentioned before anything else, it seems likely that St Paul found them among the few

Christian brethren in Ephesus, and began his teaching of them before he commenced his visits to the synagogue.

ἐπὶ μῆνας τρεῖς, *for three months.* Going there, that is, on all occasions of religious service, and so giving to his brethren of Israel a full opportunity of hearing all his reasoning, and of inquiring whether what he taught was in accordance with the Scriptures. The abiding a longer time with them, which they had asked for (xviii. 20) on his previous visit, does not seem to have gained him more adherents among the Jews. Perhaps he had noticed when the request was made that it was not with great fervour. Otherwise, it is not like the Apostle to pass by an opened door.

διαλεγόμενος, *reasoning.* The word is the same as in xvii. 2. There ἀπὸ τῶν γραφῶν is added. The same sense is no doubt intended here. It must be from their Scriptures that the congregation of the synagogue would be convinced.

9. ὡς δέ τινες ἐσκληρύνοντο καὶ ἠπείθουν, *but when divers were hardened, and believed not,* that is, refused the persuasion spoken of in the previous verse. The same two verbs are found together in Ecclus. xxx. 11 of the training of a son, θλάσον τὰς πλευρὰς αὐτοῦ ὡς ἔστι νήπιος μήποτε σκληρυνθεὶς ἀπειθήσῃ σοι.

κακολογοῦντες τὴν ὁδὸν ἐνώπιον τοῦ πλήθους, *speaking evil of the Way before the multitude.* The evil speaking is the final manifestation of the hardening. The Apostle continued his exhortations to stony-hearted hearers for three months, but when their obstinacy changed into malignity he left them. ἡ ὁδός was soon given as a distinctive name to 'the Christian religion.' See note on ix. 2 and cf. below verse 23.

It was not mere opposition to the arguments of the Apostle which these Jews employed, they took occasion to excite the crowds of the city against him. And it would seem from verse 33, where the Jews attempt to put forward a spokesman in the tumult, that they wished the heathen populace to believe that Paul was not approved of by his own nationality.

ἀποστὰς ἀπ᾽ αὐτῶν, *departing from them,* i.e. ceasing to take part any longer in the services at the synagogue, through which the evil speaking had been aroused.

ἀφώρισεν τοὺς μαθητάς, *he separated the disciples.* The Christian part of the congregation, with any of the Jews who were attracted more than the rest by his teaching.

διαλεγόμενος, *reasoning* (as in verse 8). Among these more sympathizing hearers, he would only have to set forward the arguments for the faith which he preached unto them. His teaching now could go on *constantly* (καθ᾽ ἡμέραν), and was not confined to the synagogue times of service.

ἐν τῇ σχολῇ Τυράννου, *in the school of Tyrannus.* This teacher, whether a heathen or a Jew, was a man well known. Otherwise we can conceive no reason for the mention of a proper name. As the name is Greek, some have thought that the place meant was the lecture-room of a philosophic teacher; others, thinking that St Paul would hardly have chosen such a place for his preaching, have preferred to consider it a Jewish school or *Beth-Hammidrash*, in which his Jewish hearers would be more willing to assemble. Since the listeners are described, in the next verse, as being partly Jews, and partly Greeks, it is impossible to arrive at a conclusion. No doubt the Jews in Ephesus were numerous enough to render such ' schools' necessary for their education, and in their intercourse with Gentiles they not unfrequently adopted a Gentile name in addition to their Jewish one. So Tyrannus may have been a Jew.

10. ἐπὶ ἔτη δύο, *by the space of two years.* Speaking to the Ephesian elders at Miletus the Apostle says he ceased not to admonish the Church there for ' *three* years. The two statements need not be conflicting. To the two years mentioned here when the three months of verse 8 are added, and the time which may have preceded his teaching in the synagogue (see on verse 8), the duration of the Apostle's stay in Ephesus would be described in Jewish reckoning as ' three years,' which in their mode of speech need only consist of one whole year, and parts of that which preceded, and that which followed it. Cf. the reckoning of *three* days between the Crucifixion and the Resurrection.

ὥστε πάντας...ἀκοῦσαι τὸν λόγον τοῦ κυρίου, *so that all they which dwelt in Asia heard the word of the Lord.* By *Asia* is meant ' proconsular Asia' (see note on ii. 10). The seed of the Seven Churches of the Apocalypse was sown in these two years. It is evident from the tumult described in this chapter that the Christian teaching was making as much way among the Gentiles as among the Jews. The language of St Luke here implies that the audience of St Paul was made up not of the settled inhabitants of Ephesus only, but of those who visited the city for business or pleasure, and carried news of the preacher and his message to all corners of the district. Philemon from Colossæ may have been one of St Paul's converts during this time.

11. δυνάμεις τε οὐ τὰς τυχούσας ὁ θεὸς ἐποίει διὰ τῶν χειρῶν Παύλου, *and God wrought special* (or *no common*) *powers by the hands of Paul.* The language of the historian is noteworthy. God works, Paul is the instrument. (Cp. the mighty hand of Moses, Deut. xxxiv. 12.) The imperfect tense of the verb in the Greek implies that these manifestations of God's power were continued during the Apostle's stay. This was no mere spasmodic excitement over some powerful discourse. ' By the hands' is probably only the Jewish mode of expressing ' by.' See note on v. 12.

On οὐ τὰς τυχούσας = ' not such as are usual' cf. below chap. xxviii. 2, and 2 Macc. iii. 7, καὶ οὐ τῷ τυχόντι περιῆψαν ψόγῳ, 'And they attached to them no ordinary blame.'

12. ὥστε καὶ...ἀποφέρεσθαι ἀπὸ τοῦ χρωτὸς αὐτοῦ, *so that from his body there were carried away unto the sick.* St Luke is careful to intimate that the Apostle did not of himself adopt or recommend these methods, but the faith of the converts was such that it manifested itself in this way, and God was pleased to bestow blessings because of their faith. In the city of Ephesus where, as we find from this chapter, exorcism and 'curious arts' of witchcraft and incantation were familiarly exercised, God appears to have made the cures that were wrought to be specially evidences of the power of faith. Paul does not go to the sick, and even the sons of Sceva (verse 13) recognise that it is not to Paul, but to Jesus whom he preacheth, that the 'powers' are to be ascribed. Thus was God's minister made to differ from the pretenders to miraculous power with which the Ephesian people were familiar. A specimen of these may be seen in the life of Apollonius of Tyana, IV. 3 (Kayser, p. 66).

σουδάρια ἢ σιμικίνθια, *handkerchiefs or aprons*. Some take the latter word to signify the cincture, by which the loose robes of the Orientals were gathered together round the waist. This would be expressed by 'belts' or 'girdles'. Others think they were the aprons used by the Apostle while working at his trade. The derivation of the word favours the latter sense. They seem to have been employed to cover the front half of the dress during work.

The words are both Latin, *sudarium* and *semicinctium*, and the latter is sometimes written σημικίνθιον.

καὶ ἀπαλλάσσεσθαι ἀπ' αὐτῶν...ἐκπορεύεσθαι, *and the diseases departed from them and the evil spirits went away*. These converts acted on the popular belief, that virtue proceeded from the bodies of our Lord and His Apostles. St Luke notices this belief in his Gospel (viii. 44), and St Mark says of Jesus (v. 30) 'perceiving in Himself that the power proceeding from Him had gone forth.' The words of Scripture can hardly be made to countenance, though they recognise, the popular belief. Yet, even though these men employed means which were unnecessary and superstitious to display their faith, because of the reality of this faith God did not suffer it to lose its reward.

13. ἐπεχείρησαν δέ τινες καὶ τῶν περιερχομένων Ἰουδαίων ἐξορκιστῶν, *and certain also of the Jews that went about as exorcists took upon them*. In addition to the real, though ignorant, faith of the converts alluded to in verse 12, some impostors, who had no faith, tried to win more credit for their jugglery by employing the names of Paul and Jesus. These were certain Jews who went about from place to place, professing by charms and spells to cure diseases. The A.V. 'vagabond' conveys in modern language a moral censure, which probably these men well deserved, but which is not in the Greek. The Rev. Ver. has adopted **strolling**, which gives more nearly the sense of the original but is not a very dignified word. We read in Josephus (*Ant.* VIII. 2. 5) that 'God gave Solomon skill against demons for the help and cure of men. And he arranged certain incantations whereby diseases are assuaged, and left behind him forms of *exorcism*, wherewith they so put to flight the overpowered evil spirits that they never return. And this method of curing is very prevalent among us up to the present time.' The Jews at Ephesus were professors of this pretended art of healing.

ὀνομάζειν...τοῦ κυρίου Ἰησοῦ, *to name over them which had evil spirits the name of the Lord Jesus.* From an early date the traditional literature of the Jews ascribed great effects to the utterance of the incommunicable divine name. By means of this (they say) it was that Moses slew the Egyptian, and Elisha brought destruction on the mocking children 'by the name of Jehovah.' We can understand therefore, if the fame of St Paul were become known, and the name of Jesus connected with his preaching, and with the powers vouchsafed, how these men (living among superstitious Jews) would make a pretence to the possession of the same secrets by which, as they would declare, the cures were wrought.

On these men Chrysostom remarks: τὸν Ἰησοῦν δὲ λέγουσι ἐκεῖνοι ἀπλῶς, δέον εἰπεῖν τὸν τῆς οἰκουμένης σωτῆρα, τὸν ἀναστάντα. ἀλλ' οὐκ ἤθελον ὁμολογῆσαι τὴν δόξαν αὐτοῦ. διὸ καὶ ἐλέγχει αὐτοὺς ὁ δαίμων ἐπιπηδήσας αὐτοῖς, καὶ εἰπὼν τὸν Ἰησοῦν γινώσκω καὶ τὸν Παῦλον ἐπίσταμαι. ὡσεὶ ἔλεγεν· ὑμεῖς οὐ πιστεύετε.

λέγοντες, Ὁρκίζω, *saying, I adjure.* The singular is the form which each particular pretender would use, when he was performing his exorcism.

14. ἦσαν δέ τινες...ἀρχιερέως ἑπτὰ υἱοί, *and there were seven sons of one Sceva, a Jew, a chief priest.* We cannot tell why the title 'chief priest' is given to Sceva, but it is not improbable that the name was applied to the heads of the twenty-four courses of the Levitical priesthood, who are called in the Old Testament 'heads of fathers' houses.'

τοῦτο ποιοῦντες, *who did this,* i.e. which agreed to adopt this form of words in their exorcisms. There is no need to suppose that the whole seven were present in the case about to be named, but only that they were all exorcists, and in their wish to seem the best of their class they determined to use words which should connect them with the Christian preacher through whom many miracles were known to have been wrought.

Chrysostom's comment here is: σὺ δέ μοι σκόπει τοῦ συγγραφέως ἐνταῦθα τὸ ἀνεπαχθές, καὶ πῶς ἱστορίαν μόνον γράφει, καὶ οὐ διαβάλλει. τοῦτο τοὺς ἀποστόλους ἐποίει θαυμαστούς. ἀλλὰ τίνος ἦσαν υἱοὶ τὸ ὄνομα λέγει καὶ τὸν ἀριθμόν, διδοὺς τοῖς τότε τεκμήριον ἀξιόπιστον ὧν ἔγραφε. τίνος δὲ ἕνεκεν καὶ περιήρχοντο, ἐμπορίας χάριν. οὐ γὰρ δὴ τὸν λόγον καταγγέλλοντες. πῶς γάρ; καλῶς δὲ ἔτρεχον λοιπόν, κηρύττοντες δι' ὧν ἔπασχον.

15. ἀποκριθὲν δὲ τὸ πνεῦμα τὸ πονηρὸν εἶπεν αὐτοῖς, *and the evil spirit answered and said to them.* They had taken upon them to use the name of Jesus, but the result was far contrary to their wishes and intentions. 'Evil spirit' is used for the man in whom the spirit was. Cf. Mark iii. 11.

τὸν Ἰησοῦν γινώσκω καὶ τὸν Παῦλον ἐπίσταμαι, *Jesus I know and Paul I know.* It is hardly possible in a translation to mark the difference of the two verbs. In γινώσκω there seems to be intended a recognition and admission of power, in ἐπίσταμαι a recognition of an appointed ministry thereof. The spirit speaking through the man would intimate: I recognise that Jesus has power over evil spirits, and I know that Paul is a true servant of Jesus, through whom Jesus manifests His power. The LXX. has the two verbs in the same sentence (Is. xlviii. 8) οὔτε ἔγνως, οὔτε ἠπίστω.

ὑμεῖς δὲ τίνες ἐστέ; *but who are ye?* Ye are not like Paul, devoted servants of Jesus. Ye are mere pretenders coming in His name.

16. ἐφαλόμενος, *leaping upon*, with the power, more than natural, so often displayed by madmen.

κατακυριεύσας ἀμφοτέρων, *having gained the mastery over both of them.* Here the reading ἀμφοτέρων preserves for us the information that on the occasion here spoken of only two of the family were present. This reading would never have been substituted for the simpler αὐτῶν. But how prone scribes would be to put the simple for the less obvious is easy to see. It is no objection to the recall of this old well-supported reading, that other words in the verse, referring to these brethren are plural and not dual. Plural verbs and adjectives are not unfrequently used with dual subjects. Cf. Matth. iv. 18, εἶδεν δύο ἀδελφοὺς βάλλοντας ἀμφίβληστρον εἰς τὴν θάλασσαν· ἦσαν γὰρ ἁλιεῖς. There is no instance of a dual noun in the N.T.

ἴσχυσεν κατ' αὐτῶν, *he prevailed against them.* He put them to flight, tearing their clothes to shreds, and leaving marks of his violence upon their bodies. ἰσχύω is used of a victory won by Alexander in 1 Macc. x. 49.

17. τοῦτο δὲ ἐγένετο γνωστόν, *and this became known.* The sentence refers to a gradual spreading of the story. We may be sure that 'the sons of Sceva' said as little about it as they could help.

πᾶσιν Ἰουδαίοις τε καὶ Ἕλλησιν τοῖς κατοικοῦσιν τὴν Ἔφεσον, *to all both Jews and Greeks that dwelt at Ephesus.* Exorcists were plentiful in Ephesus, and what had happened would be taken for a warning.

ἐπέπεσεν φόβος, *fear fell on.* This was the first and most prevalent result. It touched every body that heard the history.

ἐμεγαλύνετο τὸ ὄνομα τ. κ. Ἰ., *and the name of the Lord Jesus was magnified.* This was the later and no doubt less widespread effect. It was produced among those by whom Jesus was becoming known and worshipped.

18. πολλοί τε τῶν πεπιστευκότων, *and many of those who had believed*, i.e. who had made a profession of their faith. Clearly it was as yet only an imperfect belief. But the N.T. charity often names those 'saints' who are only on the way to become so.

ἤρχοντο ἐξομολογούμενοι, *came and confessed*, i.e. came before the Apostle and the Christian brethren, and acknowledged that their profession had not as yet been completely followed by their practice.

καὶ ἀναγγέλλοντες τὰς πράξεις αὐτῶν, *and published their deeds.* ἀναγγέλλω implies the 'making of a public announcement.' The πράξεις were the practices connected with witchcraft, sorcery and

after the verb, cf. LXX. Gen. viii. 10, καὶ ἐπισχὼν ἔτι ἡμέρας ἑπτὰ ἑτέρας. We may perhaps infer from the mention of Asia rather than Ephesus that St Paul did not remain constantly at Ephesus, at all events when the congregation there became firmly established, but making that city his head-quarters, went out into other districts of the province of proconsular Asia.

23—41. HEATHEN OUTBREAK AGAINST ST PAUL AND HIS TEACHING.

23. κατὰ τὸν καιρὸν ἐκεῖνον, *about that time*. This is better than A.V. 'the same time,' and there is some gain in accuracy of rendering of these connecting phrases. The literal rendering allows of the lapse of some period between the action of the converts in burning their magic books, and the uproar of the silversmiths. No doubt one movement was in part, but need not have been entirely, a consequence of the other, and the A.V. connects them more closely than is done by the original.

περὶ τῆς ὁδοῦ, *about the Way*. See above on verse 9.

24. ἀργυροκόπος is found in LXX. Judges xvii. 4; Jerem. vi. 29.

ναοὺς ἀργυροῦς Ἀρτέμιδος, *silver shrines of Diana*. These appear to have been little models either of the temple or of the shrine in which the image was preserved. We may be quite sure that the ingenuity of Greek artists devised forms enough and sizes enough to suit all needs. Smaller specimens might be carried about and worn as ornaments and amulets at the same time; the larger could be kept in the houses of their possessors, and would be a sign of wealth as well as of devotion.

The goddess worshipped at Ephesus was called Artemis, but this Ephesian Artemis was totally distinct from Artemis the Greek goddess, the sister of Apollo. It is believed that the Ephesian worship was originally Asiatic, and that when the Greeks sent colonies to Asia Minor they found it already established there, and from some resemblance which they discovered in the worship they gave the Asian divinity the name of Artemis. The Ephesian Artemis was the personification of the fruitful and nurturing powers of nature, and so the image in the temple represented her with many breasts. Her whole figure is said to have been like a mummy, standing upright and tapering downwards to a point. Her crown and girdle and the pedestal on which the figure stood had upon it engraved signs or letters, and the body was covered with figures of mystical animals. All these things would furnish abundant variety for the craft of the silversmiths.

οὐκ ὀλίγην ἐργασίαν, *no small gain*. The R.V. renders 'no little business.' The word no doubt means primarily 'employment' by which a living is made, but we have it used twice in chap. xvi. 16, 19 of the 'gain' made by the Philippian masters from the ravings of the girl who was possessed, and here too 'gain' seems the better sense. It was because their gains were going that the uproar was made, and probably Demetrius himself, the most fierce of all the

rioters, did none of the work, but through employing many workmen
had a large share of the gains. He calls the gain a business or craft
(the same word) in verse 25, that being, as has been said, the first
sense of the word, but there is no need to cast aside the other sense
which it equally bears.

25. οὓς συναθροίσας καὶ τοὺς περὶ τὰ τοιαῦτα ἐργάτας, *whom having gathered together along with the workmen of like occupation.* His
own special branch of the craft was the carving and engraving of
these shrines, as we learn from the word ἀργυροκόπος. But before the
work reached the higher stage, the materials had to pass through
many hands in preparation, and from the smelter of the metal up to
him who added the final touches of adornment and polishing all were
concerned in the threatened loss of trade.

ἐκ ταύτης τῆς ἐργασίας ἡ εὐπορία ἡμῖν ἐστιν, *from this craft we have
our wealth.* Such an appeal would go home at once. Their income
and prosperity were assailed by the new teaching.

26. καὶ θεωρεῖτε καὶ ἀκούετε, *and ye see and hear.* Of what had
happened in Ephesus they were eyewitnesses, while the falling-off in
the demand for their wares would be brought to their knowledge from
all sides. The Christian preaching and preachers did not confine
themselves to Ephesus.

οὐ μόνον Ἐφέσου ἀλλὰ σχεδὸν πάσης τῆς Ἀσίας, *not alone at
Ephesus, but almost throughout all Asia.* Beside Ephesus itself we
have only notices through St Paul's writings of Churches founded at
Colossæ, Laodicæa, and Hierapolis. But in the Apocalypse we find
beside these, Pergamus, Smyrna, Thyatira, Sardis and Philadelphia,
places whose position shews us that through about two-thirds of the
coastline of Asia important centres of Christian life were formed before
that book was written, and we cannot doubt that by St Paul and his
fellow-workers the Gospel was preached in all that district. Hence the
alarm of Demetrius.

ὁ Παῦλος οὗτος, *this Paul.* If we think of the bodily presence of
St Paul which he himself always describes as insignificant, and which
would be familiar to the hearers of Demetrius, we can fancy the scorn
which would be thrown into the words as they fell from the angry lips
of the probably stalwart craftsman.

πείσας μετέστησεν, *hath persuaded and turned away,* i.e. from their
devotion to Artemis, and so from their purchase of shrines.

27. οὐ μόνον δὲ τοῦτο κινδυνεύει ἡμῖν τὸ μέρος εἰς ἀπελεγμὸν ἐλθεῖν,
and not only is this our craft in danger to be set at nought. τὸ μέρος =
the portion or share which we make by our trade. ἀπελεγμός seems
to be found only here. The simpler form ἐλεγμός, in the sense of
rebuke, is not uncommon in the LXX.

On this Chrysostom comments thus: ὅρα παρ' ἐχθρῶν τὰς μαρτυρίας
τοῖς ἀποστόλοις γινομένας. ἐκεῖ μὲν ἔλεγον, ἰδοὺ πεπληρώκατε τὴν Ἱερουσαλὴμ τῆς διδαχῆς ὑμῶν. ἐνταῦθα ὅτι μέλλει καθαιρεῖσθαι τῆς Ἀρτέμιδος
ἡ μεγαλειότης. τότε οἱ τὴν οἰκουμένην ἀναστατώσαντες ἤκουον, ὅτι οὗτοι
καὶ ἐνθάδε πάρεισι, νῦν ὅτι κινδυνεύει ἡμῖν τοῦτο τὸ μέρος εἰς ἀπελεγμὸν

ἐλθεῖν. οὕτω καὶ Ἰουδαῖοι ἐπὶ τοῦ Χριστοῦ ἔλεγον. ὁρᾶτε ὅτι ὁ κόσμος ὀπίσω αὐτοῦ ὑπάγει.

τὸ τῆς μεγάλης θεᾶς ἱερὸν Ἀρτέμιδος, *the temple of the great goddess Diana* (Artemis). This was one of the wonders of the ancient world, and the glory and pride of all the Ephesians, and the recent explorations of Mr Wood (see Wood's *Ephesus*) have made us aware of the grandeur of the edifice and the consequent reason for this pride. Even the fragments of the architecture in the British Museum make it plain that the whole temple must have been a work of unsurpassed magnificence. No expense had been spared on its building, and the munificence of worshippers maintained it in full splendour. It was also used as a divinely-secured treasure-house, and those who made use of it in this way no doubt paid liberally for the protection. Tradition said, as it said of many another heathen idol, that the image in the shrine fell down from heaven. The description of this image (see ver. 24) is taken from coins which were current at the date when the Acts of the Apostles was written.

εἰς οὐθὲν λογισθῆναι, *should be made of no account*, as would be the case if men began to think that they were no gods which were made with hands. In his eagerness to save the trade, Demetrius forgets to put forward what the townclerk mentions afterwards (verse 35), that the image was held to have come down from heaven. He is only interested in the support of what supplied his wealth.

καὶ καθαιρεῖσθαι τῆς μεγαλειότητος αὐτῆς, *should even be deposed from her magnificence.* μεγαλειότης is sometimes used for the 'mighty power' of God, cf. Luke ix. 43, and the 'majesty' of Christ, cf. 2 Pet. i. 16.

The collocation in the same clause of τε καί here and in xxi. 28 in the sense of *and even* is very unusual, and not found in classical Greek, where these particles unite different clauses as *both...and*. See *Winer-Moulton*, p. 548.

ἣν ὅλη ἡ Ἀσία καὶ ἡ οἰκουμένη σέβεται, *whom all Asia and the world worshippeth;* for wealth from the East as well as from Greece and Rome was bestowed at this gorgeous shrine.

28. ἀκούσαντες δὲ κ.τ.λ., *and when they heard this, they became filled with wrath*, &c. Demetrius had appealed to them in such wise as to excite them more by each fresh argument. Their self-interest first, and their pride and superstition afterwards.

29. καὶ ἐπλήσθη ἡ πόλις τῆς συγχύσεως, *and the city was filled with the confusion.* The city was not so directly interested in the gains of the silversmiths, but equally with them was proud of the glory and magnificence which Ephesus had, as the seat of the worship of Artemis. So that the noise that began in the meeting which Demetrius had gathered was taken up by the Ephesian population, and they needed a wider space for the crowds now pouring together from every side. σύγχυσις intimates that the throng gathered in great excitement.

εἰς τὸ θέατρον, *into the theatre.* The theatre was the scene of all the great games and exhibitions of the city. Its ruins still remain and give evidence that when this crowd assembled there it was a building that could hold 25,000 or 30,000 people (see Wood's *Ephesus,* p. 68; Fellowes, *Asia Minor,* p. 274). As Gaius and Aristarchus were not Jews, but the former perhaps of Roman extraction, if we may judge by his name, and the latter a Greek, with rights which even the Ephesian mob would not venture to outrage, we do not read of anything more done to them, than their being dragged along with the crowd towards the place of meeting. It might be thought that they could tell how St Paul was to be found, and when they could not, they were let go.

συναρπάσαντες, *having carried off with them.* The verb implies that a search had been made wherever the preachers were likely to be found. Gaius and Aristarchus must have been seized by the crowd because they were not able to find Paul. We may see therefore that between the meeting of the craftsmen and the greater assembly in the theatre, there had been search made by the mob that they might lay hands on the Apostle. It is interesting to note that the companionship of these Macedonian converts gives evidence of the permanent effect of the labours of St Paul in that country on his previous journey. The brevity of the record in the Acts makes it important to observe such indications wherever they are given undesignedly. This Gaius is not identical with any other of the same name met with in Acts xx. 4, and Rom. xvi. 23 ; 1 Cor. i. 15. Of Aristarchus we hear again in xx. 4 and xxvii. 2, for he accompanied St Paul in his voyage to Rome, and is mentioned in the Epistles written at that time (Col. iv. 10; Philemon 24). As natives of Colossæ, and most probably Philemon himself, came to Ephesus and heard the preaching of St Paul there, Aristarchus may have been personally known to those to whom the Apostle sends his greeting in the above-named letters.

30. Παύλου δὲ βουλομένου εἰσελθεῖν εἰς τὸν δῆμον, *and when Paul was minded to enter in unto the people.* Through a strength not his own, the Apostle, feeble in frame though he seems to have been, waxed bold in danger where an opportunity appeared to be offered of testifying unto Christ.

οὐκ εἴων αὐτὸν οἱ μαθηταί, *the disciples suffered him not.* These were the brethren forming the Christian congregation, to some of whom the storm that was rising would be known much sooner than to the Apostle. They had evidently conveyed him from his usual abode, and were taking care of him until the excitement was allayed. They would tell him, of course, all that they heard of what was doing, and it was on hearing this, that he wanted to go and appear before the crowd in the theatre.

31. τινὲς δὲ καὶ τῶν Ἀσιαρχῶν, ὄντες αὐτῷ φίλοι, *and certain also of the chief officers of Asia, being his friends.* The Ἀσιάρχαι were officers in the various cities of proconsular Asia, appointed to preside over the games and religious festivals. In Ephesus these men would be of much importance, for in addition to the other games over which they would preside, the whole month of May was sacred to Artemis, being called Artemision, and was given up to festivals in honour of the city's idol. We read of an Asiarch at Smyrna in the narrative of the martyrdom of Polycarp (Euseb. *H. E.* iv. 15).

It would seem, from the fact that some of these prominent officials were friends to St Paul, that though presiding over the games and festivals for the satisfaction of the populace, they had no great care for Artemis or her worship.

πέμψαντες πρὸς αὐτὸν παρεκάλουν, *sent unto him and besought him.* παρακαλέω generally = beseech. The use of such a word indicates the personal interest these officers felt in the Apostle's safety. We also gather from the narrative that they knew where Paul was, though the mob had failed to find him.

32. ἄλλοι μὲν οὖν ἄλλο τι ἔκραζον, *some therefore cried one thing and some another.* As the craftsmen had not secured Paul, against whom Demetrius had directed their rage, there was no central object to arrest the general attention. Hence no settled cry was raised.

ἦν γὰρ ἡ ἐκκλησία συγκεχυμένη, *for the assembly was confused.* The σύγχυσις in the city (see verse 29) had become intensified by the rush into the theatre.

καὶ οἱ πλείους οὐκ ᾔδεισαν κ.τ.λ., *and the greater part did not know,* &c. All that would be heard by many would be the shouts of the mob, from which nothing could be gathered about St Paul as the offender. Amid cries of 'Artemis for ever' or 'Hurrah for Demetrius,' little would be learnt of how the tumult had begun.

33. ἐκ δὲ τοῦ ὄχλου συνεβίβασαν ᾿Αλέξανδρον, *and some of the multitude instructed Alexander.* What he seems to have been intended to do, was to explain on behalf of the Jews, that he and his fellow Jews had no more sympathy with St Paul than the heathen multitude had. It is just possible that this Alexander may be the same with him who is mentioned 2 Tim. iv. 14.

συμβιβάζω in this sense of 'to instruct' is common in the LXX., cf. Exod. iv. 12, 15; Deut. iv. 9, &c. But προεβίβασαν of the *Text. recept.* gives a very good sense, 'and out of the crowd they brought forward Alexander.'

προβαλόντων αὐτὸν τῶν ᾿Ιουδαίων, *the Jews putting him forward.* Thus it becomes clear that Alexander was no Christian, for the Jews could have had no interest in bringing forward anybody who would speak in defence of St Paul. But they were clearly concerned in hindering, if they could, this uproar, raised against one who to the heathen would be counted as a Jew, from developing into a general attack on their race. We see that this might be no unlikely result, for the crowd, recognising the Jewish face of the intending speaker, would not hear a word that he had to say.

κατασείσας τὴν χεῖρα, *having waved the hand,* i.e. so as to ensure silence. The more usual form in N. T. is κ. τῇ χειρί. Cf. Acts xii. 17, xiii. 16, xxi. 40.

ἤθελεν ἀπολογεῖσθαι τῷ δήμῳ, *would have made a defence.* There was nothing laid against him. But the Jews felt that they were all likely to be included in the vengeance to be taken on these Jews whom Demetrius had attacked. So they put forward their spokesman to disclaim all connexion with St Paul and his companions.

34. ἐπιγνόντες δέ, *but when they perceived.* The Jews would everywhere be readily known, both by their features and by their garb. We can see from the way in which the mob took fire at the sight of a Jewish speaker, that the apprehension of an attack on the Jews generally was not without grounds.

φωνὴ ἐγένετο μία ἐκ πάντων, *all with one voice.* The grammar here is disjointed. After ἐπιγνόντες we should have a verb in the plural (e.g. ἐφώνησαν). Instead of this the participle is left in suspense, and a new nominative introduced. For a participle similarly left cf. Mark ix. 20.

ὡς ἐπὶ ὥρας δύο, *for the space of two hours.* They had found a common object to cry out against. Thus they became all of one voice. They took up the cry, first started by the craftsmen, and persisted in it with all the energy which characterizes a fanatical mob.

Chrysostom's reflection is: παιδικὴ ὄντως ἡ διάνοια. καθάπερ φοβούμενοι μὴ σβεσθῇ τὸ σέβας αὐτῶν συνεχῶς ἐβόων.

35. κατασπείλας, *having quieted,* i.e. reduced them to such a degree of order that he could make himself heard. The 'appease' of A.V. is too strong. They were hardly appeased even when his speech was done. Cf. 3 Macc. vi. 1, Ἐλεάζαρος...τοὺς περὶ αὐτὸν καταστείλας πρεσβυτέρους. In the verse preceding we are told ἀνεβόησαν φωνῇ μεγάλῃ σφόδρα.

ὁ γραμματεύς, *the townclerk.* It is not easy to find an English word which comes at all near the significance of this title. 'Recorder' has been proposed, because he had charge of the city archives, and Luther calls him 'chancellor.' He was a most important personage, and his title is found at times on the coinage. He also gave name in some places to the year, like the Archon at Athens. Through him all public communications were made to the city, and in his name replies were given. It is this part of his duty which has led to the rendering 'townclerk.'

φησίν, *he says.* The speech is full of ability, and shews that the man was fitted for his eminent position. It seems to shew also that the higher classes (as has been noticed in the case of the Asiarchs) were not so devoted to the service of the goddess as were the common people.

νεωκόρον, *worshipper.* Rev. Vers. 'temple-keeper.' Lit. 'temple sweeper.' The name no doubt was first used to imply that any office in the service of so magnificent a goddess was a grand distinction; and not in Ephesus only did the worshippers of a special divinity apply this title to themselves. Thus Josephus *B. J.* v. 9 4 applies it to the Jews as worshippers of Jehovah. The word also occurs in Plato's *Laws* VI. 759.

τῆς μεγάλης Ἀρτέμιδος, *of the great Artemis (Diana).* It seems more natural in the mouth of the γραμματεύς that θεᾶς should be omitted.

τοῦ Διοπετοῦς, *of the image which fell down from Jupiter.* The adj. Διοπετές agrees with ἄγαλμα or some such word, which would be as naturally omitted in common speech as θεᾶς in the previous clause. The first part of the speech of the γραμματεύς is directed to point out how uncalled for their uproar is. There is no need for them to shout about the greatness of the Ephesian goddess. Everybody in the world is aware how devoted the city is to her worship and how glorious is her temple.

36. ἀναντιρρήτων οὖν ὄντων τούτων, *seeing then that these things cannot be gainsaid.* Even those who spoke against the worship as St Paul had done, could not dispute the facts just stated by the γραμματεύς about the devotion of the Ephesians to their goddess.

δέον ἐστὶν ὑμᾶς κατεσταλμένους ὑπάρχειν, *ye ought to be quiet,* i.e. not raising an uproar like this. See on the verb, verse 35, above.

καὶ μηδὲν προπετὲς πράσσειν, *and to do nothing rash.* προπετές describes the headstrong outrageous uproar for which there was no reason, and from which no good could come, and also their conduct in seizing two persons who were not the offenders and against whom, as it appears, they could take no proceedings.

In the LXX. the word is always used of rash talk. Cf. Prov. x. 14, xiii. 3; Ecclus. ix. 18.

37. τοὺς ἄνδρας τούτους, *these men,* Gaius and Aristarchus.

ἱεροσύλους, *robbers of temples.* As the temple at Ephesus had a great treasure-chamber, the offence might not be unknown among them. All that was placed under the guardianship of the goddess would be for the time the property of the temple, to steal which would be sacrilege.

ἱερόσυλος is applied to Lysimachus (2 Macc. iv. 42) for his plundering of the temple at Jerusalem. αὐτὸν δὲ τὸν ἱερόσυλον παρὰ τὸ γαζο-φυλάκιον ἐχειρώσαντο.

οὔτε βλασφημοῦντας τὴν θεὸν ἡμῶν, *nor blasphemers of our goddess.* In a popular address it is natural that such a speaker would identify himself with his fellow-citizens. We may gather from this verse that the language of St Paul and his companions had been measured when they had spoken about the special worship of Ephesus. They had inculcated the great principle that those were no gods which were made with hands and had allowed that to do its work. We find the same restraint put on himself by St Paul at Athens, though he was greatly moved to see the city wholly given to idolatry. Different conduct in either of these cities would most likely have deprived him of all chance of a hearing.

38. ἔχουσιν πρός τινα λόγον, *have a matter against any man,* i.e. have any charge which they wish to bring. For the concerns in

which the shrine-makers are interested must be such as the legal
tribunals can take cognizance of.

ἀγοραῖοι ἄγονται, *the law is open.* This is the general sense. With
ἀγοραῖοι we must supply ἡμέραι. The sense will then be 'court days
are appointed' i.e. there are proper times fixed when such causes can be
heard; or perhaps better, because of the verb which seems to imply
that the opportunity of legal action is even now open, 'court-*meetings*
are now going on.' In this latter sense σύνοδοι or some similar noun
must be supplied with ἀγοραῖοι.

καὶ ἀνθύπατοί εἰσιν, *and there are proconsuls.* For the word ἀνθύπατος, cf. xiii. 7, 8, 12. Asia, in which Ephesus was situated, was a
proconsular province (see Conybeare and Howson, II. 78). The difficulty in the present verse has arisen from the use of the plural number,
for there was only one proconsul over a province at the same time,
and there could only be one in Ephesus when the townclerk was
speaking. But if we consider that he is speaking merely of the provision made by the institutions of the empire for obtaining justice in
a case of wrong, we can see that his words need not occasion much
trouble. 'Proconsuls are (he says) an imperial institution. In every
province like ours there exists such a supreme magistrate, and so
there is no fear about obtaining redress for real injuries.' Another
explanation (due to Basnage, and alluded to in the notes of Conybeare
and Howson, *u. s.*) is that after the poisoning of the proconsul Silanus
(as related Tac. *An.* XIII. 1), Celer and Ælius, who governed the province of Asia as *procurators*, might be intended by this plural title.
Others have thought that there might be present in Ephesus some
other proconsul from a neighbouring province, as Cilicia, Cyprus,
Bithynia or elsewhere; but the first seems the easier explanation.

ἐγκαλείτωσαν ἀλλήλοις, *let them accuse one another.* Of course the
accusation would be one side, the defence the other. What the
γραμματεύς means is 'let them take steps to obtain a legal decision.'

39. εἰ δέ τι περὶ ἑτέρων ἐπιζητεῖτε, *but if ye seek anything about
other matters.* The 'seeking' alluded to is by a legal process. If the
matter were of such a character as to come before the proconsul, there
he was, ready to hear the cause. It was, as we might say, 'assize
time.' But if the question was of another kind, one for the jurisdiction of the ordinary city courts, then they could apply at the proper
time and place.

ἐννόμῳ ἐκκλησίᾳ, *in the regular assembly.* There were no doubt
legally fixed days and times for the city courts. To these it is that
the allusion is made.

Chrysostom explains: ἔννομον ἐκκλησίαν φησί, διότι τρεῖς ἐκκλησίαι
ἐγίνοντο κατὰ νόμον καθ' ἕκαστον μῆνα.

40. καὶ γὰρ κινδυνεύομεν ἐγκαλεῖσθαι στάσεως περὶ τῆς σήμερον,
for indeed we are in danger to be accused of a riot concerning this day.
ἐγκαλεῖν in the previous verse = to accuse, and this meaning should be
preserved here. στάσις is the name which the γραμματεύς hints, by this

sentence, that other people will give to the gathering in the theatre. He calls it by a gentler term, συστροφή.

μηδένος αἰτίου ὑπάρχοντος, *there being no cause,* i. e. why any concourse should have been gathered.

περὶ οὗ οὐ δυνησόμεθα ἀποδοῦναι λόγον τῆς συστροφῆς ταύτης, *and as touching it we shall not be able to give account of this concourse.* It seems clear that περὶ οὗ could not mean (as A. V.) *whereby.* The insertion of a second οὐ, = not, is warranted by much MS. testimony, but it is not easy to render, and Westcott and Hort think that there must still be some error in the text. The relative οὗ does not grammatically accord with any part of the sentence to which it ought to be referred. But the rendering given is perhaps the best which can be made of the word, and οὗ as a neuter must be taken to refer to the matter as a whole.

41.   **ἀπέλυσεν τὴν ἐκκλησίαν,** *he dismissed the assembly.* This he could do in his official capacity. Probably the last argument which he used would have most weight with his audience. If such riotous conduct were reported at Rome it might lead to a curtailment of the privileges of their city.

Chrysostom remarks: οὕτως ἔσβεσε τὸν θυμόν. ὥσπερ γὰρ ῥαδίως ἐξάπτεται, οὕτω καὶ ῥαδίως σβέννυται.

CHAPTER XX.

Readings varying from the *Text. recept.*

1.   **μεταπεμψάμενος** after θόρυβον with אBE, and **παρακαλέσας** before ἀσπασάμενος with AB. The *Vulg.* has 'vocatis Paulus discipulis et exhortatus eos valedixit.'

4.   **Πύρρου** after Σώπατρος with אABDE. *Vulg.* 'Sopater Pyrrhi.'

7.   **ἡμῶν** for τῶν μαθητῶν τοῦ with אABDE. *Vulg.* 'cum convenissemus.'

8.   **ἦμεν** for ἦσαν with אABDEHLP. *Vulg.* 'eramus.'

15.   **καὶ μείναντες ἐν Τρωγυλλίῳ** omitted with אABCE. Not represented in *Vulg.*

16.   **κεκρίκει** for ἔκρινε with אABCDE. *Vulg.* 'proposuerat.'

19.   **πολλῶν** before δακρύων omitted with אABDE. Not represented in *Vulg.*

24.   **ἀλλ' οὐδενὸς λόγου ποιοῦμαι τὴν ψυχὴν τιμίαν ἐμαυτῷ** with אBCD. *Vulg.* has 'Sed nihil horum vereor, nec facio animam meam pretiosiorem quam me.'

μετὰ χαρᾶς omitted with אABD. Not represented in *Vulg.*

25.   **τοῦ θεοῦ** omitted with אABC. *Vulg.* has 'Dei.'

26.   **καθαρός εἰμι** with אBCDE. *Vulg.* has 'mundus sum.'

27.   **ὑμῖν** placed after θεοῦ with אBCD. *Vulg.* 'Dei vobis.'

23. κυρίου for θεοῦ with ACDE.   *Vulg.* has 'Dei.'

29. ἐγὼ οἶδα with אABCD.   *Vulg.* 'ego scio.'

32. ἀδελφοί omitted with אABD.   Not represented in *Vulg.*

     ὑμῖν omitted with אABDE.   Not represented in *Vulg.*

CH. XX. 1—6. PAUL JOURNEYS THROUGH MACEDONIA AND GREECE, AND
              RETURNS AS FAR AS TROAS.

1. μετὰ δὲ τὸ παύσασθαι τὸν θόρυβον, *and after the uproar was
ceased.* We may suppose some little time to have passed, and public
feeling to have become calm. Then once more there could be a gathering of the Christian congregation.

μεταπεμψάμενος ὁ Παῦλος τοὺς μαθητάς, *Paul having sent for the
disciples.* Perhaps to some place where he had been staying in private. He would hardly deem it wise to leave Ephesus till he had seen
the Church in quiet again.

ἀσπασάμενος ἐξῆλθεν πορεύεσθαι εἰς Μακεδονίαν, *having taken leave
of them, departed to go into Macedonia.* For ἀσπάζομαι see below xxi.
6. Paul sets out to Macedonia in fulfilment of his intention mentioned in xix. 21. We see from 2 Cor. ii. 13 that he went first to
Troas, expecting to meet Titus there. He did not find him till he
reached Macedonia, from which country he wrote the second letter to
Corinth. We may supply what is omitted here by comparing 1 Cor.
xvi. 17, 2 Cor. i. 16, 17, ii. 12, 13, viii. 18, 19, and we may learn
something of St Paul's own feelings during this time from 2 Cor. i. 8,
iv. 10, 11, x. 10, xii. 7.

For the seeming redundancy of verbs, cf. Gen. xii. 5, καὶ ἐξῆλθοσαν
πορευθῆναι εἰς γῆν Χαναάν.

2. διελθὼν δὲ τὰ μέρη ἐκεῖνα, *and when he had gone over those parts,*
visiting especially, of course, the Churches of Philippi, Thessalonica
and Beroea, among whi h St Luke may have been left from the former
visit, and have laboured to carry on the work which St Paul had
begun. Some have judged this to be very probable, and that in this
Macedonian residence St Luke's Gospel may have been written. It
was also, as it seems, at this time that St Paul made the journey into
Illyricum alluded to in Rom. xv. 19.

λόγῳ πολλῷ, *with much exhortation.* We may form some idea of
the topics which would be embraced by such exhortation, if we read
the two Epistles to the Thessalonians which had been written to that
Church since St Paul's former visit to Macedonia. The most marked
language in the first Epistle is against sorrowing immoderately for the
dead. By the words of St Paul on this subject the Christian congregation had been much troubled concerning the nearness of the coming
of the Son of Man, and the second letter is written to bring them to
a calm and thoughtful mind. The Apostle's 'much exhortation'
would be an echo of what he had said in his letters, 'Watch and be

sober,' 'Abstain from every form of evil,' 'Be at peace among your-selves.'

The use of the masculine pronoun αὐτούς after τὰ μέρη is not un-exampled. The people are understood when the land is mentioned. See above on viii. 5.

3. ἦλθεν εἰς τὴν Ἑλλάδα, *he came into Greece.* There is nothing said of the places which St Paul visited in this journey, but as he was always anxious to strengthen any work which he had before begun we may feel sure that Athens and Corinth, on this account, as well as for their importance as centres of intellectual and commercial life, were the places in which he spent the greater part of his three months' stay. In the latter Church especially there were many things to be set in order. He had already written to the Corinthians his two Epistles. In the first, sent from Ephesus, he had found it necessary to rebuke them for the party-spirit in the Church, some calling them-selves by the name of Peter, some of Apollos, and some of Paul himself, instead of finding true unity in Christ; he had also censured the dis-orders in the Eucharistic feast, had given his judgment on a notorious offender, and on many topics raised by the difficulties of a Christian Church growing up amid heathen surroundings. These matters, and the guidance into a right channel of the exercise of those special gifts of preaching and speaking with tongues with which God endowed the Church in Corinth, would give the Apostle little rest during his brief stay, even if he bestowed his whole time on Corinth alone.

ποιήσας τε μῆνας τρεῖς, *and when he had spent three months.* On ποιέω in this sense, cf. xv. 33, xviii. 23. So also *Acta Barnabæ Apocryph.* 7, ἐλθεῖν ἐν Κύπρῳ καὶ ποιῆσαι τὸν χειμῶνα.

γενομένης ἐπιβουλῆς κ.τ.λ., *and when a plot was laid against him by the Jews.* The Jews, who had tried to engage Gallio in their matters on St Paul's last visit to Corinth, now take a secret instead of a public means of wreaking their vengeance on him. And we may judge that St Paul anticipated some trouble from the Judaizing party at Corinth by the tone of the latter portion (after chap. ix.) of his second Epistle written to them while he was on his way, but detained in Macedonia. There were persons in Corinth who spoke slightingly of the Apostle. His bodily presence was weak and his speech contemptible. And in opposition to the remarks of these opponents, the Epistle concludes with an assertion of St Paul's equality to the chiefest Apostles, a recital more full than in any other place of his sufferings for the Gospel, and an account of revelations divinely made unto him. It is clear there-fore that among those who would be counted as Christians St Paul was not everywhere accepted. The Jews under such circumstances would have some abettors in their animosity even among the Judæo-Christians, and seem to have planned some means whereby St Paul might be attacked on his sea voyage to Syria. No doubt the intention was to kill him. ἐπιβουλή is the word used (ix. 24) when the Jews watched the gates of Damascus night and day to kill him.

μέλλοντι ἀνάγεσθαι εἰς τὴν Συρίαν, *as he was about to set sail for*

Syria. He had apparently gone so far as to arrange for his passage and go on board, and was nearly departed, before he got the warning news. For ἀνάγεσθαι refers to the actual preparation for setting sail. Perhaps some heart, among the people to whom the plot was known on shore, was moved to give a hint of the great peril at the last moment. This is the more probable if we suppose some previous communications between the Jews and the Judaizers among the Christians.

ἐγένετο γνώμης κ.τ.λ., *he determined to return through Macedonia.* As the scheme for killing him had been meant to be carried out at sea, the choice of an overland journey and a prompt departure made the forming of a new plan impossible to the conspirators.

For the genitive after γίνομαι, cf. Apocal. xi. 15, ἐγένοντο αἱ βασιλεῖαι τοῦ κυρίου ἡμῶν. Also ἐλπίδος γίνεσθαι, Plutarch, *Phoc.* 23.

The grammar of the whole verse is remarkable for its freedom from rule. Beginning with ποιήσας, we come next to μέλλοντι, and presently the construction is once more changed in ἐγένετο γνώμης.

4. συνείπετο δὲ αὐτῷ ἄχρι τῆς Ἀσίας, *and there accompanied him as far as Asia.* We find (xxi. 29) that Trophimus went on to Jerusalem, and (xxvii. 2) that Aristarchus was with St Paul in the voyage to Rome.

συνείπετο standing first in the sentence is in the singular to agree with the one word to which it comes closest.

Σώπατρος Πύρρου, *Sopater the son of Pyrrhus.* A various reading here has *Sosipater,* a name found also in Rom. xvi. 21. But there is no reason why we should connect the two persons. We know nothing of Sopater beyond the mention of him in this verse, though the name occurs, with those of Gaius and Secundus, as that of one of the Politarchs of Thessalonica on an arch still existing in the modern *Saloniki.* See xvii. 6.

Θεσσαλονικέων δὲ Ἀρίσταρχος καὶ Σεκοῦνδος, *and of the Thessalonians Aristarchus and Secundus.* Aristarchus has been before mentioned (xix. 29), and in the Epistles written during the Roman imprisonment to Philemon (24) he is one of those who sends greeting, and also to the Colossians (iv. 10), in which place the Apostle calls him his fellow-prisoner, shewing that he shared in a great degree the whole hardships of St Paul's life at Rome. Secundus is only mentioned here. With this name we may compare Tertius and Quartus (Rom. xvi. 22, 23). It has been conjectured that all these persons belonged to the freedman, or slave, class and had therefore no family names.

Γάϊος Δερβαῖος καὶ Τιμόθεος, *Gaius of Derbe and Timothy.* As Timothy was probably of Lystra, these men may have been friends from an early period, and the former may have been a convert at the same time as the latter. We only know of him from this verse, and he has no connexion with any other Gaius named in the New Testament.

Ἀσιανοὶ δὲ Τυχικὸς καὶ Τρόφιμος, *and of Asia, Tychicus and Trophimus.* Of the former of these we have mention several times.

In Eph. vi. 21, he is called a beloved brother and faithful minister, and St Paul states that he is about to send him to Ephesus. To the Colossians (iv. 7) he writes, 'All my state shall Tychicus declare unto you.' From both which notices we see that Tychicus was with St Paul in his first Roman imprisonment. He was also at hand when the Apostle wrote to Titus (Tit. iii. 12), and also had been with St Paul in the later imprisonment, when the Second Epistle to Timothy was written (iv. 12), and had again been sent to Ephesus. Perhaps Tychicus like Trophimus was by birth an Ephesian. Trophimus also continued much with St Paul, for we read (2 Tim. iv. 20) that the Apostle at that time had left him detained by sickness at Miletus.

5. οὗτοι δὲ προελθόντες κ.τ.λ., *but these had gone before and were waiting for us at Troas.* What the writer wants to point out is that these men before-mentioned did not stop like St Paul at Philippi, nor indeed tarry at all in Macedonia. As in this verse the change of pronoun indicates that the writer of the narrative again becomes a fellow-traveller with St Paul, we may presume, as has before been said, that he had been left here by the Apostle, who now separated himself for a brief time from his companions that he might pick up St Luke.

6. μετὰ τὰς ἡμέρας τῶν ἀζύμων, *after the days of unleavened bread.* Another reason why St Paul tarried at Philippi seems to have been because of the Jewish feast. As there could be no sacrifice of the Passover out of Jerusalem, the Apostle would feel no difficulty about remaining at any other form of the feast, and we know how loth he was to sever himself from his people in all things which he might lawfully share with them.

εἰς τὴν Τρωάδα ἄχρι ἡμερῶν πέντε, *to Troas after five days.* Troas could not be without much interest both to St Paul and Luke and Timothy, for at least these three had been here together, on that former visit when they were called over to Macedonia by a vision. Aristarchus and Secundus represented in part the fruits which God had granted to their work.

ἄχρι represents the *terminus ad quem*, the final point of time which made up the sum of the journey. They went on *until* the time had reached five days.

7—12. PAUL PREACHES AT TROAS. EUTYCHUS IS RESTORED TO LIFE.

7. ἐν δὲ τῇ μιᾷ τῶν σαββάτων, *and upon the first day of the week,* which had now, in memory of the Resurrection, begun to be observed as a holy day by Christians. In an Epistle written before this visit to Troas (1 Cor. xvi. 2) the day is appointed by St Paul as the special time when the Christian alms should be laid aside.

For the phrase ἡ μία τῶν σαββάτων, which has come from the use of the Hebrew cardinal אֶחָד=one, for the ordinal, cf. Matth. xxviii. **1;** Mark xvi. 2; Luke xxiv. 1, &c. Also LXX. Genesis i. 5 καὶ ἐγένετο ἑσπέρα καὶ ἐγένετο πρωί, ἡμέρα μία, and Exod. xl. 2 ἐν ἡμέρᾳ μιᾷ τοῦ μηνός.

συνηγμένων ἡμῶν κ.τ.λ., *when we were gathered together to break bread.* Wherever a Christian congregation was established the first and most natural religious service was the communion of the body and blood of Christ.

ὁ Παῦλος διελέγετο αὐτοῖς, *Paul discoursed with them.* The meeting was one where reasoning and conversation were used to solve doubts and clear away difficulties which might be in the minds of the Christians at Troas. For we can perceive that there was a Church established here. Indeed wherever St Paul came he was enabled to leave that mark of his visit behind him. It is true the meeting was only still in an upper chamber, but the 'many lights' shews that it was not a mere gathering of one or two with the Apostle and his friends, but a settled Christian congregation.

μέλλων ἐξιέναι τῇ ἐπαύριον, *intending to depart on the morrow.* They had met first for an evening service, but the consolation of Christian intercourse and the additional zeal infused into the Church by the Apostle's visit caused the irregular conversational meeting to be protracted beyond the intended time. As the Jewish mode of reckoning would probably be retained, the meeting would be on what we now call Saturday evening. This would be the beginning of the first day of the week. If this be so, St Paul did not hesitate to travel on Sunday.

8. ἐν τῷ ὑπερῴῳ, *in the upper room.* Our thoughts go back to the upper room in Jerusalem where (Acts i. 13) the first preachers of Christianity waited for the promised gift of the Holy Ghost.

οὗ ἦμεν συνηγμένοι, *where we were gathered together.* The first person as in the previous verse.

9. καθεζόμενος δέ...ἐπὶ τῆς θυρίδος, *and there was sitting in the window.* The window in that climate was only an opening in the wall, and not as in our country provided with a framework, the bars of which would have prevented the accident which is here described. The young man was sitting upon (ἐπί) the sill of the opening.

καταφερόμενος ὕπνῳ βαθεῖ, *borne down with deep sleep.* He is not represented as a careless hearer. But the hour was late, and he was young, and could resist sleep no longer. Here the verb is constructed with the dative, in the next line with ἀπό and a genitive. It would be hard to make a distinction between the two.

διαλεγομένου τοῦ Παύλου ἐπὶ πλεῖον, *and as Paul discoursed yet longer.* ἐπὶ πλεῖον refers either to the expectation of this youthful hearer or to his exhausted powers. Longer than he expected or longer than he could keep awake.

ἔπεσεν ἀπὸ τοῦ τριστέγου κάτω καὶ ἤρθη νεκρός, *he fell down from the third storey and was taken up dead.* The latticework with which such windows were closed in the East would be set wide open to admit the cool air into the crowded room. The lad fell out, and down to the floor of the court-yard. There has been much debate whether the restoration of Eutychus was meant to be described as miraculous;

whether, that is, 'dead' may not be taken foɪ 'in a swoon like death.'
But St Luke's expression (ver. 12) 'They brought him alive' seems to
leave no room for question. That life was gone by reason of the fall
and was restored by the prayer of the Apostle is the natural reading
of the story, which has all the vividness that marks the narrative of
an eyewitness.

10. καταβὰς δὲ ὁ Παῦλος ἐπέπεσεν αὐτῷ, *and Paul went down and
fell on him.* The access to Eastern houses was by a staircase on the
outside, so that the way down would be at hand. The action of the
Apostle recalls that of Elijah (1 Kings xvii. 21) and of Elisha (2 Kings
iv. 34). No doubt the Apostle, like the Old Testament prophets,
accompanied his action with a cry unto the Lord.

καὶ συμπεριλαβών, *and embracing him.* The word is classical but
is only found here in N.T.

As he clasped the child in his arms, Paul would feel the returning
motion, and know that his prayer was heard. The boy seems to have
been left to the care of some members (perhaps women) of the congregation, who tended him till the service was over.

μὴ θορυβεῖσθε, *trouble not yourselves,* i.e. don't make any tumult or
distress yourselves.

11. ἀναβὰς δέ, *and when he was gone up.* The Apostle's calmness,
as well as his words, was not without effect on the congregation. He
returns to the upper room, and the unfinished act of worship is completed.

καὶ κλάσας τὸν ἄρτον, *and had broken the bread,* i.e. the bread of
the Eucharistic service. The sermon came first (verse 9) and then
the Lord's Supper.

καὶ γευσάμενος, *and eaten,* i.e. partaken of the more substantial
meal of the 'Agapè.' This in the early Church followed after the
Communion.

ἐφ' ἱκανόν τε ὁμιλήσας, *and had talked with them a long while.*
ὁμιλέω means the talking of friendly intercourse. The previous discourse had been on more solemn subjects; the spread of Christ's kingdom and the part which each of them might take in helping it forward.

For ἐφ' ἱκανόν cf. 2 Macc. viii. 25 συνδιώξαντες δὲ αὐτοὺς ἐφ' ἱκανὸν
ἀνέλυσαν.

12. ἤγαγον δὲ τὸν παῖδα ζῶντα, *and they brought the lad alive.* It
would seem as though those who had had the care of him brought
him, before the congregation broke up, perhaps even before the Apostle's departure, back again into the upper room.

13—16. PAUL GOES ON FOOT TO ASSOS, THEN BY SEA TO MILETUS.

13. ἡμεῖς δὲ προελθόντες ἐπὶ τὸ πλοῖον, *but we going before to the
ship.* St Luke now describes what he and the rest, without St Paul,
did next. They started from Troas before St Paul's departure, and
coasted along while the Apostle went by land.

ἀνήχθημεν ἐπὶ τὴν "Ασσον, *and set sail for Assos.* ἀνάγειν is the verb for 'putting out to sea.' Assos was in Mysia, on the north shore of the gulf of Adramyttium. Opposite and about seven miles out at sea lay the island of Lesbos. There was a Roman road from Troas passing through Assos. So while the ship went round the cape Lectum, the Apostle was able to come by land and be taken on board by his companions.

οὕτως γὰρ διατεταγμένος ἦν, *for so he had arranged.* This is used as a middle perfect, and intimates the personal provision of the Apostle. This is also emphasized by the αὐτός in the next clause.

πεζεύειν, *to go by land.* πεζεύω when opposed to a journey by sea need not necessarily signify a pedestrian journey, and it seems better not to press that meaning here. For although the distance between Troas and Assos is only 20 miles, yet after the labours and excitement of the past night, a walk of that length would scarcely have been contemplated by the Apostle, when his companions in the ship already had the start of him. Many reasons have been suggested why St Paul separated for a few hours from his friends: that he wished for solitude: that he would not be at sea one moment before he could help it: that there was some Christian duty which he could perform on the way: or for his health's sake. The historian, who probably knew, has not told us, and conjectures in such a case are valueless.

14. εἰς Μιτυλήνην, *to Mitylene.* The voyage was a coasting voyage, the nights being each spent in some harbour. Mitylene was the capital of Lesbos, to which place they went from Assos, probably because it had a better anchorage. There could have been little time for anything on St Paul's land journey like meeting Christian friends, since the vessel left Troas in the morning, and by an indirect course came to Mitylene before nightfall.

15. τῇ ἐπιούσῃ κατηντήσαμεν ἄντικρυς Χίου, *on the following day we came over against Chios.* The island of Chios is about five miles distant from the mainland. It was in the shelter of the roadstead that the Apostle and his companions passed the night in their vessel.

τῇ δὲ ἑτέρᾳ παρεβάλομεν εἰς Σάμον, *and the next day we touched at Samos.* For παραβάλλειν in this technical sense cf. Joseph. *Ant.* XVIII. 6. 4 Ἀγρίππας δὲ εἰς Ποτιόλους παραβαλών. The island of Samos lies off that part of the coast of Asia Minor where the ancient Ionia joined on to Caria. It has been famous both in ancient Greek and modern European history. See *Dict. of Greek and Rom. Geog.* s. v.

In the *Text. recept.* we find here καὶ μείναντες ἐν Τρωγυλλίῳ. But in the oldest MSS. there is no trace of these words. How they came to be inserted it is not easy to say. Trogyllium lay on the mainland opposite Samos, at the termination of the ridge of Mycale. It may be that some annotator noticed that the previous verb παραβάλλειν only implied the touching at Samos. If he knew the locality it is possible that on his margin he suggested Trogyllium as the night's halting-place, of which the historian had made no mention. But it is more difficult still to understand how if they had formed part of the original text they should be wanting in the earliest of all our authorities.

τῇ δὲ ἐχομένῃ κ.τ.λ., *and on the day after we came to Miletus.* Miletus had been a most famous sea-port in the earlier Greek history, but in the days of St Paul its fame was eclipsed by Ephesus. It lay on the coast of Caria, some 20 or 30 miles distant by land southward from the city of Ephesus, and one day's sail from Trogyllium. The site of the town is now some distance from the sea, and was not close to it in the Apostle's time, as we shall see below (verse 38).

16. κεκρίκει γὰρ ὁ Παῦλος, *for Paul had determined.* In the midst of a large Christian congregation, such as we know to have existed by this time in Ephesus, there would have arisen many causes of delay which the Apostle in this rapid journey desired to avoid. Perhaps too there might have been some hostility roused against him, and either from a wish not to awaken this, or from fear lest the allaying of it should consume time, he resolved to send for the heads of the Church to confer with him at Miletus.

ὅπως μὴ γένηται αὐτῷ χρονοτριβῆσαι ἐν τῇ Ἀσίᾳ, *that he might not have to spend time in Asia.* St Paul felt that he could not go to Ephesus and leave again in a day or two.

χρονοτριβέω is nowhere else in N. T. or LXX. and very rarely in any Greek authors, though χρόνον τρίβειν is common enough. See however Aristot. *Rhet.* III. 3.

ἔσπευδεν γάρ, *for he was hastening.* The verb expresses the whole character of his journey, and we can only conclude that there was some difficulty in finding a vessel at Troas, or he would not have stayed there so long as he did, and not have given a day to Ephesus, which he felt he was hardly likely to see again.

τὴν ἡμέραν τῆς Πεντηκοστῆς, *the day of Pentecost.* Pentecost at Jerusalem must have become a Christian as well as a Jewish festival. There would be at such a time an opportunity for the Apostle to meet the more prominent members of the Christian body, and, while bringing his contributions from the Churches which he had founded, he would gladden them with the news of what God had enabled him to do.

17—38. PAUL SENDS FOR THE ELDERS FROM EPHESUS, GIVES THEM HIS PARTING CHARGE, AND LEAVES MILETUS.

17. ἀπὸ δὲ τῆς Μιλήτου, *and from Miletus.* At Miletus the Apostle and his party must have tarried more than one day. It would take quite that time to send his messenger and summon those whom he wished to see. If they came to him on the next day, that would be consumed in their conference and leavetaking, and the voyage could hardly be begun again till the third day at the earliest.

μετεκαλέσατο, *he summoned to him.* This verb, found in N. T. only in the Acts (vii. 14, x. 32, xxiv. 25), is used of very earnest or authoritative invitation.

τοὺς πρεσβυτέρους τῆς ἐκκλησίας, *the elders of the Church.* These might be called 'presbyters.' In verse 28 however they are named ἐπίσκοποι, i.e. 'bishops.' It is well established that the titles πρεσβύτερος and ἐπίσκοπος were in the early ages of the Church synonymous.

It is curious to notice in connexion with the history of these words that in the recently discovered 'Teaching of the Twelve Apostles' there is no mention anywhere made of πρεσβύτεροι.

18. εἶπεν αὐτοῖς, *he said to them.* This is the only speech recorded in the Acts of the Apostles which we can be sure that the writer heard St Paul make. This is probably the reason why we have it somewhat in detail, and why it is so marked, as we shall see it is, with expressions that are to be found in the Apostle's letters. While giving other speeches in abstract St Luke employs his own diction or that of some who were his authorities.

ὑμεῖς ἐπίστασθε, *ye yourselves know.* The pronoun is expressed emphatically, and should be represented. Had St Luke been giving the speech in substance, his Greek training would have made him commence, as he so often does, Ἄνδρες ἀδελφοί. That he has not done so in the speech which he gathered from St Paul's own lips is an evidence of a faithful reporter.

ἀπὸ πρώτης ἡμέρας ἀφ᾿ ἧς, *from the first day that.* The repetition of the preposition in the relative clause is not common. The more usual form is either to omit the second preposition or to write ἀφ᾿ ἧς ἡμέρας, but when πρώτης was to be used this was not very practicable. We must understand ἡμέρας with the relative to make the grammar complete.

ἐπέβην εἰς τὴν Ἀσίαν, *I set foot in Asia.* The Apostle is appealing not only to what he had done in Ephesus itself, but to what they had heard of his labours elsewhere in Asia. Ephesus was no doubt the greatest centre of Christian life in Proconsular Asia, and all that was done elsewhere would be reported there, and the lesser Churches would seek for intercommunion with a Church in which they could learn so much of what St Paul had taught.

πῶς μεθ᾿ ὑμῶν τὸν πάντα χρόνον ἐγενόμην, *after what manner I was with you all the time,* i.e. all the time which I spent with you. The Apostle calls to their remembrance *how* he had borne himself during all the period of his ministry in Asia.

19. δουλεύων τῷ κυρίῳ μετὰ πάσης ταπεινοφροσύνης, *serving the Lord with all humility of mind.* The verb is interesting when we remember how often St Paul calls himself in his Epistles δοῦλος Ἰησοῦ Χριστοῦ. Cf. Rom. i. 1; Phil. i. 1; Tit. i. 1.

καὶ δακρύων, *and tears.* The πολλῶν of the *Text. recept.* is a comment derived from the statement in verse 31 below. In 2 Cor. ii. 4 St Paul uses διὰ πολλῶν δακρύων.

καὶ πειρασμῶν τῶν συμβάντων μοι ἐν ταῖς ἐπιβουλαῖς τῶν Ἰουδαίων, *and with trials that befell me by the plots of the Jews.* We could only see in the account of the tumult at Ephesus some indications how

anxious the Jewish population were to make it plain that they had no
sympathy with the Apostle who was so obnoxious to the Gentiles.
Here we have an express declaration made before those who knew all
the circumstances that plots had been laid against Paul's life by the
Jews. It did not fall in with St Luke's purpose to tell us of them,
but he manifestly knew about them, for he feels no difficulty in re-
cording the Apostle's own mention of them here, nor has he a thought
that his narrative will be held for other than true, though men may
point out here an allusion to events of which he had made no mention
before. We cannot too often bear in mind that the book is not meant
for a history of either one or other Apostle, but as a record of how the
course of the Gospel was guided according to Christ's injunction,
'beginning at Jerusalem' and ending when an Apostle had proclaimed
Christ in the Imperial capital.

20. ὡς οὐδὲν ὑπεστειλάμην τῶν συμφερόντων τοῦ μὴ ἀναγγεῖλαι
ὑμῖν, *how that I shrank not from declaring unto you anything that was
profitable.* For the form of the sentence, cf. verse 27 below. ὑπο-
στέλλω is applied to the wrapping up of anything to keep it out of
sight or to stow it away. For example, it is applied to the 'furling' of
sails. Hence it has the metaphorical sense of 'cloaking' what ought
to be spoken out. St Paul had never from any cause done this.
What he means by τὰ συμφέροντα we may gather from his own words,
1 Cor. x. 33, τὸ [συμφέρον] τῶν πολλῶν ἵνα σωθῶσι. The message,
which pointed men to the way of salvation would at times be couched
in terms of rebuke and reproval, and would not always be pleasant to
deliver, however necessary. From none of this had the Apostle
shrunk.

καὶ διδάξαι ὑμᾶς δημοσίᾳ καὶ κατ' οἴκους, *and from teaching you
publicly and from house to house.* Here we are afforded another
glimpse into the zealous character of St Paul's work. It was not
only in the school of Tyrannus that he waited for and taught those
who came to hear, but he also went about among the people, seeking
to impress any who would listen.

21. διαμαρτυρόμενος, *testifying*, i.e. proclaiming to them their
need of.
Here Chrysostom says: οὐχὶ πρὸς ὑμᾶς, φησί, μόνον, ἀλλὰ καὶ πρὸς
Ἕλληνας. ἐνταῦθα ἡ παρρησία. καὶ ὅτι κἂν μηδὲν ὠφελῶμεν λέγειν δεῖ.
τὸ γὰρ διαμαρτύρασθαι τοῦτό ἐστιν, ὅταν πρὸς τοὺς μὴ προσέχοντας
λέγωμεν.

22. καὶ νῦν ἰδοὺ δεδεμένος ἐγὼ κ.τ.λ., *and now, behold, I go bound in
the spirit unto Jerusalem.* In these words the Apostle refers to his
own spirit, the constraint which in his own mind was laid upon him.
Some therefore to make this plain would render 'in *my* spirit.' The
verb implies that he felt there was no freeing himself from the impulse
to go, but it has no such sense as that he already regards himself as a
prisoner, that he will be seized and deprived of his liberty when he
arrives at Jerusalem.

μὴ εἰδώς, *not knowing.* Hence we see that the Holy Ghost had not given to the Apostle more than a general sense that in all places he would be called on to suffer for Christ.

23. πλὴν ὅτι...διαμαρτύρεταί μοι, *save that the Holy Ghost witnesseth unto me in every city.* The Holy Ghost had called him to the work (xiii. 2) and moved the disciples (xxi. 4) and Agabus (xxi. 11) to warn him of the sufferings which were at hand. We may suppose too that such warnings came more frequently than St Luke has recorded them.

δεσμά καὶ θλίψεις, *bonds and afflictions.* The two nouns are combined in Phil. i. 16 θλίψιν ἐπιφέρειν τοῖς δεσμοῖς μου, where the sense is most probably 'to add mental grief to my bodily suffering in prison.' Such 'afflictions' are harder to bear than any 'bonds.'

24. ἀλλ' οὐδενὸς λόγου ποιοῦμαι τὴν ψυχὴν τιμίαν ἐμαυτῷ, *but I hold not my life of any account as dear unto myself.* This is the best rendering possible of the text for which there is most support. But it is a very feeble expression, and unlike the words of St Paul. In a very clear paper on the verse Dr Field has shewn that there is probably some omission before 'dear unto myself' of the same character, though not exactly the same, as what is supplied in the A.V., and that the reading of ℵ, B, and C, which the R.V. has tried to give in English, arose after the words, of which he suggests the loss, had fallen away from some very early exemplar. The literal English of Dr Field's suggestion would be 'Neither make I account of anything, nor think my life dear unto myself.'

ὡς τελειῶσαι, *in order to complete,* i.e. I leave everything else out of consideration, so as to finish my course. This is the single instance in N.T. of a final ὡς followed by the infinitive. Cf. 3 Macc. i. 2, Θεόδοτος δὲ...διεκομίσθη νύκτωρ ἐπὶ τὴν τοῦ Πτολεμαίου σκηνήν, ὡς μόνος κτεῖναι αὐτόν.

τὸν δρόμον μου, *my course.* The figure of the Christian life as a race is common enough in St Paul's language (cf. xiii. 25). The Apostle signifies by his words that the race will last as long as life endures, and that he must not faint in the middle, whatever suffering may be in store.

καὶ τὴν διακονίαν ἣν ἔλαβον, *and the ministry which I received.* The Apostle refers to the commission which he received at his conversion. The work and the sufferings are both foretold to Ananias from the first (Acts ix. 15, 16), and St Paul speaks of this ministry or service by the same word as here in 1 Tim. i. 12, 'I thank Him that enabled me, even Christ Jesus our Lord, for that He counted me faithful, appointing me to His *service*' (θέμενος εἰς διακονίαν).

διαμαρτύρασθαι τὸ εὐαγγέλιον τῆς χάριτος τοῦ θεοῦ, *to testify the gospel of the grace of God.* To bear witness to men of the good news that God is willing to be gracious. In the context of the passage just quoted (1 Tim. i. 14) St Paul shews how fit a person he was to bear such testimony. He had been a blasphemer, a persecutor and injurious, but had obtained mercy...and to him the *grace* of our Lord Jesus Christ *abounded exceedingly.*

25. οὐκέτι ὄψεσθε κ.τ.λ., *ye all shall no more see.* We cannot be sure that the Apostle never again came to Ephesus. For we learn from Philemon 22 that, toward the close of his imprisonment at Rome, he had hopes and the intention of visiting Philemon, who was at Colossæ, and we can hardly think that if he went to Colossæ he would fail on the way to stay at Ephesus. Some have therefore been inclined to lay a great stress on the word πάντες in this clause, as though the Apostle only meant that they were sure some of them to be dead before he paid their city another visit. It seems better to take the words as the conviction of the Apostle's mind at the moment. He was impressed with the belief that he would never come back. We have seen, however, just above that the Spirit did not give him definite knowledge of what would befall him in every place. And the sense that he was to be seized and imprisoned might make him sufficiently alive to the chances of his martyrdom for Christ to warrant the words which he here uses.

ἐν οἷς διῆλθον κηρύσσων τὴν βασιλείαν, *among whom I went about preaching the kingdom.* Though speaking to the Ephesians only, the memory of the Apostle recalls those missionary visits throughout Proconsular Asia which we may feel sure that he made during his 'three years' residence at Ephesus.'

For the use of βασιλεία alone as equivalent to ἡ βασιλεία τοῦ θεοῦ, cf. Matth. iv. 23, ix. 35, &c.

26. διὸ μαρτύρομαι ὑμῖν, *wherefore I take you to record.* St Paul testifies unto his hearers, but he also challenges them to confirm or refute what he says.

ἐν τῇ σήμερον ἡμέρᾳ, *this day.* For this redundant expression, cf. LXX. Joshua xxii. 29; 1 Sam. xxvi. 21; Jerem. i. 18, &c. Joseph. *Ant.* XIII. 2. 3.

ὅτι καθαρός εἰμι ἀπὸ τοῦ αἵματος πάντων, *that I am pure from the blood of all men.* St Paul looks upon himself as one like the watchmen of the house of Israel (Ezek. xxxiii. 8) to each of whom God says, if he warn not the wicked from his way, 'his blood will I require at thine hand.'

For the phrase καθαρὸς ἀπό cf. Tobit iii. 14, καθαρά εἰμι ἀπὸ πάσης ἁμαρτίας.

27. οὐ γὰρ ὑπεστειλάμην κ.τ.λ., *for I shrank not from declaring,* &c. See above on verse 20.

By πᾶσα ἡ βουλὴ τοῦ θεοῦ is meant the whole plan of salvation, what God offers and what he asks from men. This includes 'repentance and faith' (verse 20) as well as the 'grace and mercy' (verse 24).

28. προσέχετε ἑαυτοῖς, *take heed to yourselves.* On the construction see on chap. v. 35, viii. 6. The Apostle now resigns into their hands a charge which before had been his own, and the form of his language would remind them that the discharge of their duty after his example would be the means of saving both themselves and those over whom they were placed.

καὶ παντὶ τῷ ποιμνίῳ, *and to all the flock.* The Apostle commits to them, as Christ had at first done to St Peter, the charge to feed both lambs and sheep. This must be in the name and with the word of the 'Good Shepherd' Himself.

ἐπισκόπους, *overseers.* Above they are called πρεσβύτεροι (verse 17), and here the R.V. renders 'bishops.' We have no information how these 'elders' had been chosen or appointed, but we can see from this verse that there had been some solemn setting apart of the men for their office. The Church, as in xiii. 2, had recognised some indication that they were to be placed over the Church. By reminding them from whence their appointment came, St Paul would enforce on them the solemnity of their position. Though they be 'in the flock' they are not as others, more has been given unto them, and so more will be required. Cf. 'Teaching of the Twelve Apostles' § 15.

ποιμαίνειν τὴν ἐκκλησίαν τοῦ κυρίου, *to feed the Church of the Lord.* Perhaps no text in the N. T. has been so much discussed as this. Many ancient authorities read θεοῦ instead of κυρίου, and this has been claimed as a direct testimony to the Divinity of our Lord. That doctrine does not stand or fall by this verse. The whole subject has been discussed fully by the late Dr Ezra Abbott of Harvard University who decides in favour of κυρίου (see *Bibliotheca Sacra* for 1876). Westcott and Hort on the contrary think θεοῦ assuredly genuine. One difficulty which arises if θεοῦ be read is that from what follows there must be implied the use of some phrase like 'the blood of God' which is only found in the Epistles of Ignatius, and is unlike N. T. language. Some have found support for θεοῦ in the peculiar collocation of the words which follow, διὰ τοῦ αἵματος τοῦ ἰδίου. Some special force is thought to lie in ἰδίου thus placed, and that it must be taken in the sense of 'through the blood that was His own,' i.e. because it was His Son's. Another suggestion which would make all easy, is that after τοῦ ἰδίου the word υἱοῦ fell out in very early times anterior to all our MSS. Lachmann, Tischendorf and Tregelles declare in favour of κυρίου.

ἣν περιεποιήσατο, *which He purchased.* The verb conveys the idea of making anything peculiarly one's own.

29. μετὰ τὴν ἄφιξίν μου, *after my departing.* This noun is only found here in N. T. In classical Greek it most frequently means 'arrival,' but not always. But as the person who *arrives* at one place must have *departed* from some other, it is only a change in the point of view. Here there is no doubt of its meaning. It does not refer to St Paul's death, but to his departure from Asia, with the thought that he should return no more.

λύκοι βαρεῖς, *grievous wolves.* The Apostle seems first to refer to false teachers who should come in from without. He must have been familiar with the dangers to which the Ephesian Church was exposed, and we know from his Epistles how much harm had already been inflicted on the Christian Church by the Judaizers and Gnostics. Even when writing to so undisturbed a Church as that in Philippi, we find the Apostle giving warning against both kinds of error. And if we turn to those early parts of the Apocalypse in which the condition of the Churches of Asia is described, we can read of a crop of errors the sowers of which St Paul may have had in his mind as he spake at Miletus. 'Nicolaitans,' 'those who say they are Jews and are not, but are a synagogue of Satan,' 'those that hold the teaching of Balaam,' ' the woman Jezebel, which calleth herself a prophetess,' all these could not have risen in a moment, but must have given indications of their existence long before they became so prominent as they were when St John wrote. He must have read the New Testament with little appreciation who speaks of the words here ascribed to St Paul as a 'prophecy after the event' made by the writer of the Acts in the second century. Cf. 'Teaching of the Twelve Apostles' § 16.

30. καὶ ἐξ ὑμῶν αὐτῶν, *and from among your own selves.* This gives an idea of the greater nearness of the apostasy which the Apostle predicts. Not some who may come *of* those to whom he speaks, but even out of the present existing Christian body. We know from St Paul's own experience that he learnt (and no doubt had learnt this long before he wrote to Timothy) how out of the professedly Christian body some would go back like Demas (2 Tim. iv. 10) through love of this world's good things, and some would err concerning the truth, like Hymenæus and Philetus, and that their word would eat like a canker, and they would overthrow the faith of some. These are the speakers of perverse things, such as would twist even the Apostle's own words into a wrong sense.

τοῦ ἀποσπᾶν τοὺς μαθητὰς ὀπίσω ἑαυτῶν, *to draw away the disciples after them,* i. e. to pervert the other members of the Christian body. It is not that these men will desire and endeavour to gain disciples, but they will do their best, after their own falling-away, to drag others likewise from the true faith. This is expressed also by the verb which implies the *tearing away* from that to which they are already attached, and this more literal translation of the verb expresses the labour and exertion which these false teachers will spend to achieve their object. On the genitival infinitive τοῦ ἀποσπᾶν cf. iii. 2 note, and for an exact parallel to the instance in this verse, see 2 Chron. xx. 23 ἀνέστησαν εἰς ἀλλήλους τοῦ ἐξολοθρευθῆναι.

31. διὸ γρηγορεῖτε, *therefore watch.* And the sort of watching indicated is that unsleeping alertness which can never be taken by surprise.

μνημονεύοντες κ.τ.λ., *remembering that by the space of three years.* St Paul enforces watchfulness by appealing to his own example. Be ye watchful, bearing in mind that I was so night and day while I laboured among you. The three years may be a speaking in round numbers, but it cannot have been a much less time that St Paul spent in Ephesus. See notes on xix. 8, 10.

οὐκ ἐπαυσάμην μετὰ δακρύων νουθετῶν κ.τ.λ., *I ceased not to admonish every one with tears.* We know from his appeal to the Corinthians (2 Cor. xi. 29) and from other places, how sympathetic St Paul was in all that concerned his flock. 'Who is weak, and I am not weak? who is offended, and I burn not?' And if for weakness and offences, how much more in a city like Ephesus where idolatry was rampant everywhere! We need not confine the 'every one' to the presbyters; St Paul's labour was spent on the whole Ephesian Church.

32. καὶ τὰ νῦν παρατίθεμαι ὑμᾶς, *and now I commend you.* It is as if he said : I am to leave you, but I leave you to the care of One who will help you as He has helped me, and who will not leave you. ὁ λόγος τῆς χάριτος αὐτοῦ means the gracious promises of the Gospel, such as those which Christ gave to His disciples when He foretold the mission of the Comforter (John xvi. 7—12), and which the Christian preachers might repeat as His words to the converts who believed on His name.

τῷ δυναμένῳ, *which is able.* This must be referred to θεῷ, and not to the intervening explanatory clause. It is God who can build up His people and give them their heavenly inheritance.

τὴν κληρονομίαν, *the inheritance,* that to which, by becoming sons of God through Christ, you are made heirs. The figure is taken from the apportionment of the promised land among the Israelites. The share of each of God's servants in the heavenly Canaan is to be regarded as definitely as were the possessions of the chosen people in the earthly Canaan.

ἐν τοῖς ἡγιασμένοις πᾶσιν, *among all them which are sanctified.* More literally 'which have been sanctified.' But just as the Apostle uses 'saints' frequently in his Epistles to mean those who have been called to be such, so here his words do not indicate that those of whom he speaks have attained the perfection of holiness. When they reach their inheritance, then they will have been perfected in Christ.

33. ἱματισμοῦ, *apparel.* In which Oriental wealth largely consisted. Hence Naaman brings 'changes of raiment' as well as money among the rewards which he expects to give for his cure (2 Kings v. 5), and the value attached to changes of raiment may be noticed in many other parts of the Scripture history. Cf. Gen. xxiv. 53, xlv. 22 ; 2 Kings vii. 8, &c. Cf. 'Teaching of the Twelve Apostles' § 13.

ἱματισμός is frequent in the LXX. Cf. 1 Sam. xxvii. 9 ; 1 Kings xxii. 30 ; and in 1 Macc. xi. 24 we find λαβὼν ἀργύριον καὶ χρυσίον καὶ ἱματισμὸν ἐπορεύθη πρὸς τὸν βασιλέα, where there are put together the three classes of Eastern riches exactly as in this verse.

34. αὐτοὶ γινώσκετε, *ye yourselves know.* The working in company with Aquila and Priscilla, which the Apostle began in Corinth, was probably continued when they came together to Ephesus, and so the Apostle's trade and his steady pursuit of it would be well known to many of the listeners. It has been suggested that he was a partner in trade-matters with Philemon during this residence at Ephesus. Cf. Philemon 17.

τοῖς οὖσιν μετ᾽ ἐμοῦ, *to them that were with me.* We cannot determine under what circumstances the Apostle felt himself called upon to minister by his hand-labour to the support of his companions.

We may be sure however that the necessity was there, and that St
Paul, working himself, did not countenance indolence in others. And
when we read of Timothy's 'often infirmities' (1 Tim. v. 23) we may
conjecture that there were those among the companions of St Paul
who were less able to work with the hands than the Apostle himself.

αἱ χεῖρες αὗται, *these hands.* No doubt, he held them forth, and
they bore marks that not only while at Ephesus, but since that time
they had laboured for the means of living.

35. πάντα ὑπέδειξα ὑμῖν, *in all things I gave you an example.* Cf.
John xiii. 15, ὑπόδειγμα γὰρ ἔδωκα ὑμῖν.

ὅτι οὕτως κοπιῶντας, *how that thus labouring,* i.e. as I myself
laboured and you beheld and knew. The verb implies 'wearying toil.'
He had spared for no fatigue. He speaks of this toil (2 Cor. xi. 27)
ἐν κόπῳ καὶ μόχθῳ.

δεῖ ἀντιλαμβάνεσθαι τῶν ἀσθενούντων, *ye ought to help the weak.*
By ἀσθενοῦντες does St Paul here mean those standing in need of
material or moral help? Grimm (s. v.) takes it for the poor, those
who are in want from any cause, as those must have been who could
not support themselves, and whose wants the Apostle supplied by his
own labour. Yet this is a very rare sense, as he admits, for the verb
to have, and 'feebleness' of faith and trust is much the more common
meaning. And that sense suits well here. If among new converts
large demands should be made for the support of those who minister,
they who are weak in the faith as yet may be offended thereby, and
becoming suspicious, regard the preacher's office as a source of temporal gain. An example like St Paul's would remove the scruples of
such men, and when they became more grounded in the faith, these
matters would trouble them no more. For the use of ἀσθενής and
ἀσθενέω in the sense of moral, rather than physical, weakness, cf. Job
iv. 3, 4; Is. vii. 4; 1 Macc. xi. 49.

τῶν λόγων τοῦ κυρίου Ἰησοῦ, *the words of the Lord Jesus.* St Paul
appeals to these words as though the saying was well-known, and as
we notice this, we cannot but wonder at the scanty number of the
words which have been handed down as 'words of Jesus' beyond what
we find in the Gospel. This is the only one in the New Testament,
and from all the rest of the Christian literature we cannot gather more
than a score of sentences beside. See Westcott, *Introd. to Study of the
Gospels*, pp. 428 seqq.

ὅτι αὐτὸς εἶπεν, *how He himself said.* The emphatic pronoun should
not be overlooked.

μακάριόν ἐστιν μᾶλλον διδόναι ἢ λαμβάνειν, *it is more blessed to give
than to receive.* In support of what has just been said about strengthening the feeble in faith, these words seem as readily applicable to
that view of the Apostle's meaning, as to the sense of 'poverty.' What
would be given in this special case would be spiritual strength and
trust; what is referred to in λαμβάνειν is the temporal support of the
preacher, which St Paul refrained from claiming. We cannot doubt

that he felt how much more blessed it was to win one waverer to Christ than it would have been to be spared his toils at tent-making by the contributions of his converts.

36. θεὶς τὰ γόνατα, *having knelt down.* The kneeling posture marks the special character and solemnity of the prayer. We find the Apostle doing the same in his parting from the brethren at Tyre (xxi. 5). On the usual custom of standing in prayer, cf. Mark xi. 25 and the account of the Pharisee and publican (Luke xviii. 11—13). It has often been noticed that the historian, who gives the speech with unusual fulness, does not venture to record the prayer.

37. κατεφίλουν αὐτόν, *they kissed him.* The verb expresses earnest and sorrowful salutations.

38. ἐπὶ τῷ λόγῳ ᾧ εἰρήκει, *for the word which he had spoken.* On the attraction of the relative cf. i. 1.

τὸ πρόσωπον αὐτοῦ θεωρεῖν, *to behold his face.* The Apostle in verse 25 uses only ὁράω, the ordinary word. Here in θεωρεῖν is expressed the earnest reverent gaze, with which we can fancy those who knew the Apostle and his work would look upon him. His presence filled not only the eye, but the mind, they contemplated the scenes which the sight of him would recall.

προέπεμπον δὲ αὐτὸν εἰς τὸ πλοῖον, *and they brought him on his way to the ship.* Cf. xv. 3, xxi. 5. They would not lose a word or a look until they were forced to do so. We gather from this verse that the harbour was at some distance from the town of Miletus. See above on verses 15 and 17.

CHAPTER XXI.

Readings varying from the *Text. recept.*

3. κατήλθομεν for κατήχθημεν with אABE. *Vulg.* 'venimus.'

4. ἐπιβαίνειν for ἀναβαίνειν with אABC.

5. προσευξάμενοι ἀπησπασάμεθα ἀλλήλους καὶ with אABCE.

8. οἱ περὶ τὸν Παῦλον omitted with אABCE. Not represented in *Vulg.*

ἤλθομεν for ἦλθον with אACE. *Vulg.* 'venimus.'

10. ἡμῶν omitted with אBCH.

11. δήσας ἑαυτοῦ τοὺς πόδας καὶ τὰς χεῖρας with אBCDHLP. *Vulg.* 'alligans sibi pedes et manus.'

13. τότε before ἀπεκρίθη with אABC. *Vulg.* 'tunc respondit.'

14. τοῦ κυρίου τὸ θέλημα with אABCE. *Vulg.* 'Domini voluntas.'

20. θεόν for κύριον with אABCEL. *Vulg.* 'Deum.'

ἐν τοῖς Ἰουδαίοις with אBCE. *Vulg.* 'in Judæis.'

24. γνώσονται for γνῶσι with אABCDE. *Vulg.* 'scient.'

25. μηδὲν τοιοῦτον τηρεῖν αὐτούς, εἰ μὴ omitted with אAB. Not represented in *Vulg.*

34. ἐπεφώνουν for ἐβόων with אABDE.

μὴ δυναμένου δὲ αὐτοῦ with אABDE.

36. κράζοντες with אABE. *Vulg.* 'clamans.'

Ch. XXI. 1—6. Paul's Voyage from Miletus, and his Stay in Tyre.

1. ἀναχθῆναι ἡμᾶς ἀποσπασθέντας ἀπ' αὐτῶν, *when we were gotten from them and had set sail.* The vessel in which they sailed from Troas to Patara seems to have been under the Apostle's control, so that they could stay wherever and as long as they pleased.

The verb ἀποσπασθέντας expresses the great wrench of the separation: so Chrysostom δείκνυσι δὲ τὴν βίαν τῷ εἰπεῖν ἀποσπασθέντες.

εὐθυδρομήσαντες ἤλθομεν εἰς τὴν Κῶ, *we came with a straight course unto Cos.* Cos is a small island, now called *Stanchio*, on the coast of Asia Minor, just at the entrance of the Archipelago, and in old times was famous for its wines and some light-woven fabrics. There was also in the island a temple of Aesculapius to which was attached a medical school.

τῇ δὲ ἑξῆς εἰς τὴν Ῥόδον, *and the day following unto Rhodes.* Rhodes is the famous island at the south-west extremity of Asia Minor, off the coast of Caria and Lycia. The city of Rhodes and the island of which it is the capital were famous in the times of the Peloponnesian war. It was well supplied with timber fit for ship-building and hence became famous for its navy, and its position has caused the island to play a conspicuous part in European history from that time onward. It was celebrated for the great Temple of the Sun, whose worship in the island is marked by the head of Apollo on the coinage. With this worship was connected the great statue known as the Colossus, which was meant as a figure of the sun, and was one of the wonders of the world. In the Roman times many privileges were granted to Rhodes by the Roman emperors, while in mediæval history this was the last Christian city which resisted the advance of the Saracens.

Πάταρα, *Patara.* This was a city on the coast of Lycia. It was devoted to the worship of Apollo, who is hence sometimes called by classical writers *Patareus.* The city was not far from the river Xanthus, and Patara was the port of the city of Xanthus. We can understand, therefore, why St Paul's voyage in the coasting vessel should end here, because at such a port he would be likely to find a larger vessel to carry him to Syria.

2. πλοῖον διαπερῶν εἰς Φοινίκην, *a ship sailing over [lit. crossing] unto Phœnicia.* Phœnicia was the country on the Levant, north of Palestine. It contained the important maritime cities of Tyre and Sidon.

3. ἀναφάναντες δὲ τὴν Κύπρον, *and when we had come in sight of Cyprus.* On Cyprus, see notes on xiii. 4. The more usual construction would be ἀναφανείσης τῆς Κύπρου, but cf. with this alteration of construction Gal. ii. 7, πεπίστευμαι τὸ εὐαγγέλιον, meaning πεπιστευμένον ἔχω τὸ εὐαγγέλιον.

εἰς Συρίαν, *into Syria.* This was the general name for the whole district lying along the Mediterranean from Cilicia down to Egypt.

κατήλθομεν εἰς Τύρον, *we landed at Tyre.* Tyre was one of the chief ports of Phœnicia, and a city of very great antiquity. It was built partly on the mainland and partly on an island, and is often mentioned both in Scripture and in profane literature. It is noticed as a strongly fortified city as early as Joshua xix. 29. We read of its fame in the time of Solomon in connexion with the building of the Temple; and Jezebel, the wife of Ahab, was the daughter of Ethbaal, called King of the Sidonians in Scripture, but in Josephus (*Ant.* viii. 13. 2) King of Tyre. The city was besieged by Shalmaneser and afterwards by Nebuchadnezzar, and was captured by Alexander the Great.

Christ went on one of His journeys from Galilee into the neighbourhood of Tyre, if not to the city itself, which was about 30 miles from Nazareth, and it must have been then in much the same condition as at this visit of St Paul.

ἐκεῖσε γὰρ...ἀποφορτιζόμενον τὸν γόμον, *for there the ship was to unlade her burden.* And so in all probability the further voyage to Ptolemais was made in a different vessel, this one going no further. With regard to the exact meaning of this clause, there is no need to suppose ἐκεῖσε is the same as ἐκεῖ, though the English idiom may ask for 'there' in our rendering. The full idea of the words is, 'thither the ship was going and would there unlade &c.' The reason for the use of ἦν ἀποφορτιζόμενον is probably to be found by understanding that the ship was in the habit of sailing to Tyre with cargoes. Cf. James i. 17, πᾶν δώρημα τέλειον ἄνωθέν ἐστι καταβαῖνον.

4. ἀνευρόντες δὲ τοὺς μαθητάς, *and having found the disciples.* This means the members of the Christian Church of Tyre, not some disciples who by chance happened to be at Tyre. That there was already a Christian congregation there is probable from the account of the spread of the Gospel given in xi. 19, and as brethren in Phœnicia are spoken of in xv. 3. If there were such anywhere in that country, they would presumably be in Tyre.

It was so much the custom for Jews to seek out their fellow Jews in whatever place they came to, that it would be natural in St Paul and his companions to inquire after the Christians in every city in the same way.

ἡμέρας ἑπτά, *seven days.* It appears that the Apostle, having finished nearly all his sea voyage, found that he could easily accomplish his journey to Jerusalem in time, and so he no longer hastened as he did when all the probable mishaps of a coasting voyage were before him.

οἵτινες τῷ Παύλῳ ἔλεγον διὰ τοῦ πνεύματος, *and these said to Paul through the Spirit.* The Apostle himself was urged by some inward prompting to go on to Jerusalem 'not knowing what might befall him.' The Spirit warns these disciples of the dangers which would come upon him. We need not judge that these things are contrary one to the other. The Apostle knew that bonds and afflictions were to be his lot everywhere, and though the Spirit shewed to his friends that he would suffer, yet the impulse of the same Spirit urged him forward, because it was God's will that he should suffer thus in the cause and for the greater furtherance of the Gospel.

μὴ ἐπιβαίνειν εἰς Ἱεροσόλυμα, *that he should not set foot in Jerusalem.* After verbs of commanding, urging, directing &c. when the command is in the negative form μή is used, because in the direct sentence this would be the particle, as here μὴ ἐπίβαινε.

5. ὅτε δὲ ἐγένετο ἡμᾶς ἐξαρτίσαι τὰς ἡμέρας, *and when we had accomplished those days.* Literally, 'when it came to pass that we had &c.' For the construction in the Greek cf. above verse 1.

τὰς ἡμέρας means, of course, the seven days previously mentioned. The verb ἐξαρτίζω is very unusual in this sense, though the Vulgate explains it so (*expletis diebus*) and Chrysostom gave it that meaning (πληρῶσαι), so we may accept it. Some, keeping to a more common use of it, 'to fit out,' have proposed to understand the word 'ship' as the object of it, and to render 'when we had refitted (or fitted the ship with stores) during those days.'

προπεμπόντων ἡμᾶς πάντων σὺν γυναιξὶ καὶ τέκνοις, *while they all escorted us, with wives and children,* i.e. with their wives and children. The whole Christian community attended the Apostle to the shore. The mention of families here confirms what was said on verse 4 about 'the disciples.' They were the Church of Tyre.

ἕως ἔξω τῆς πόλεως, *till we were come outside the city.* ἕως is used in a local signification with many phrases which signify the point to which the movement or action is continued.

καὶ θέντες τὰ γόνατα κ.τ.λ., *and kneeling down on the beach.* On the action cf. xx. 36 and note there.

προσευξάμενοι ἀπησπασάμεθα ἀλλήλους, *we prayed and bade each other farewell.* The verb ἀπασπάζομαι is exceedingly rare. It occurs nowhere else in N.T. or LXX.

6. καὶ ἐνέβημεν εἰς τὸ πλοῖον, ἐκεῖνοι δὲ ὑπέστρεψαν εἰς τὰ ἴδια, *and we went on board the ship, but they returned home again.* There is nothing in the Greek to tell us whether the ship was the same in which they had come to Tyre, or not.

7—14. PAUL'S JOURNEY TO CÆSAREA, AND HIS STAY THERE.

7. τὸν πλοῦν διανύσαντες, *when we had finished the voyage.* The distance was but short, and would be accomplished in a day.

κατηντήσαμεν εἰς Πτολεμαΐδα, *we came to Ptolemais.* Ptolemais is the name which was given during Macedonian and Roman rule to the city anciently called Accho (Judges i. 31), and known in modern history as *St Jean d'Acre* or often simply *Acre*. In the earliest times it was the most important town on that portion of the coast, but at the beginning of the Christian era was far surpassed by Cæsarea, which was the residence of Herod and of the Roman governor.

καὶ ἀσπασάμενοι τοὺς ἀδελφούς, *and having saluted the brethren*. It is clear then that there was a Christian society in Ptolemais also. As the city lay on the great high-road by the coast it was certain to be visited by some of the earlier preachers, when the disciples were dispersed from Jerusalem after the death of Stephen.

8. τῇ δὲ ἐπαύριον ἐξελθόντες ἤλθομεν εἰς Καισάρειαν, *and on the morrow having departed we came to Cæsarea*. This part of the journey was made by land, though it could have been made by sea. But the road between the two places was one of the best.

εἰς τὸν οἶκον Φιλίππου τοῦ εὐαγγελιστοῦ, *into the house of Philip the evangelist*. Philip is named next after Stephen in the narrative (vi. 5) of the choosing of the seven, and though no such prominent exhibition of his zeal is narrated as of Stephen, yet we are told that he went away from Jerusalem and was the first to carry the Gospel to the Samaritans (Acts viii. 5). He also was directed by the angel of the Lord to go and baptize the Ethiopian eunuch (viii. 26—38), thus being doubly an ambassador to the Gentiles, and earning his title of 'Evangelist.' He preached afterwards at Azotus, and from the chapter before us we may conclude that he had made his home at Cæsarea. Such a situation, the meeting-place of Gentiles with Jews, was the proper scene for such a missionary to labour in, and such a labourer would rejoice greatly to welcome to his house the great apostle who had gone forth once and again unto the Gentiles and with such mighty blessing on his work.

ὄντος ἐκ τῶν ἑπτά, *who was of the seven*, i.e. those seven who were chosen (Acts vi.) to relieve the Apostles from the duty of 'serving tables.'

9. τούτῳ δὲ ἦσαν θυγατέρες τέσσαρες παρθένοι κ.τ.λ., *now this man had four daughters, virgins, which did prophesy*. The family of the Evangelist were walking in their father's steps. These daughters, instead of resting at home, took upon them the hard duty of publishing the message of the Gospel. The English word 'prophesy' has come to have, since about the beginning of the seventeenth century, only the one sense of 'to predict what is yet to come.' In the time of Queen Elizabeth 'prophesyings' meant 'preachings,' and Jeremy Taylor's famous work on the 'Liberty of Prophesying' was written to uphold the freedom of preaching. These women were, in their degree, Evangelists also.

10. ἐπιμενόντων δὲ ἡμέρας πλείους, *and as we tarried there many days*. In this phrase πλείους loses its comparative sense, and means only 'several,' 'some,' 'many.' It is frequent in the LXX. Cf. Numb. xx. 15, καὶ παρῳκήσαμεν ἐν Αἰγύπτῳ ἡμέρας πλείους. Joshua xi. 18, καὶ ἡμέρας πλείους ἐποίησεν Ἰησοῦς τὸν πόλεμον. See also Numb. ix.

19; Josh. xxiii. 1, xxiv. 7, &c. With the omission of ἡμῶν here, leaving the genitive absolute without a subject, cf. Luke xii. 36, ἐλθόντος καὶ κρούσαντος where αὐτοῦ is similarly omitted.

προφήτης ὀνόματι Ἄγαβος, *a prophet named Agabus.* Most probably the same who (xi. 28) foretold the coming famine. The prophets mentioned on that occasion had also come up from Jerusalem. And the name Agabus is not one of common occurrence.

11. καὶ ἐλθών...δήσας ἑαυτοῦ τοὺς πόδας καὶ τὰς χεῖρας, *and coming...he bound his own feet and hands.* The adoption by Agabus of this figurative action makes it almost certain that the man was a Jew. Similar actions are common in the Old Testament prophets. Thus Isaiah (xx. 3) walks naked and barefoot. Jeremiah (xiii. 5) hides his girdle by the river Euphrates, and (xix. 10, 11) breaks the potter's vessel in the Valley of Hinnom; Ezekiel (iv. 1—3) draws on a tile a picture of the siege of Jerusalem, and (v. 1—4) cuts off his hair and burns and destroys it as God commanded. So too Zedekiah the son of Chenaanah made horns of iron (1 Kings xxii. 11). With this act of Agabus may be compared our Lord's words to St Peter (John xxi. 18).

The girdle was that band with which the loose Oriental robe was drawn together at the waist. It was of considerable size, and served the purposes of a pocket, the money being carried in it. To judge from the verb (ἄρας) employed in describing the prophet's action, it seems that St Paul had laid aside his girdle and that it was taken up by Agabus from the place where it lay.

τάδε λέγει τὸ πν. τ. ἅ., *thus saith the Holy Ghost.* That we may the better note the Apostle's zeal for carrying out the Lord's will, we are once more told how the Holy Ghost made known to him through others that he was about to be made a prisoner. Still we see him go forward unmoved, because though others might know that he was to suffer, and might in their affection strive to hold him back, he was convinced that such suffering was the Lord's way for him. Therefore he went on.

12. ἡμεῖς τε καὶ οἱ ἐντόπιοι, *we and they of that place.* We (i.e. St Luke and the rest who were fellow-travellers with St Paul) and the Christian congregation of Cæsarea. The act of Agabus was in all probability done with some publicity; perhaps in some meeting where St Paul had laid aside his girdle for greater freedom while he spoke.

13. τί ποιεῖτε κλαίοντες καὶ συνθρύπτοντές μου τὴν καρδίαν; *what do ye, weeping and breaking my heart?* i.e. what are you seeking to effect thereby?

συνθρύπτειν is a very rare word; its sense is to weaken the purpose of any one. The Apostle does not mean 'break my heart' in the ordinary sense of adding to his load of sorrow so as to overpower him. The deterring from his journey by weakening his determination is what his words indicate.

ἐγὼ γὰρ κ.τ.λ., *for I,* &c. The pronoun stands emphatically, though

we cannot express its force in English.   St Paul had long ago counted
the cost of Christ's service, and had found the sufferings of the present
time not worthy to be compared with the future glory.

ἀποθανεῖν εἰς Ἱερουσαλήμ, *to die at Jerusalem.*   For εἰς following a
verb indicating rest, but implying previous motion, cf. Acts viii. 40,
Φίλιππος δὲ εὑρέθη εἰς Ἄζωτον.

14.   τοῦ κυρίου τὸ θέλημα γινέσθω, *the will of the Lord be done.*
They gathered from the Apostle's language that he had a higher leading than theirs in what he was doing, and feeling that Christ's guidance was better than any other, they quieted their minds with the
thought that the work was 'for the name of the Lord Jesus,' who
would strengthen His servant to do His will.

15, 16.   THE JOURNEY TO JERUSALEM.

15.   ἐπισκευασάμενοι, *having made ready our baggage.*   The verb is
used now and then in the LXX. of making ready the lamps &c. in the
house of the Lord.   In classical Greek it is common enough, but only
occurs here in N.T.

16.   συνῆλθον δὲ καὶ τῶν μαθητῶν, *and there went with us also some of
the disciples.*   The genitive without government in this fashion is rare,
and the more usual thing is to find ἐκ, or some other preposition to
govern it, as in John xvi. 17, εἶπον οὖν ἐκ τῶν μαθητῶν αὐτοῦ, Some
then of His disciples said.   Somewhat like the construction in this
verse is Isaeus, VII. 5, ὁ Θράσυλος τῶν ἐν Σικελίᾳ κατελέγη τριηράρχων,
and Xen. *Mem.* I. 2. 31, Κριτίας τῶν τριάκοντα ἦν.   But these are not
with an active verb like συνῆλθον.

ἀπὸ Καισαρείας, *from Cæsarea.*   The Evangelist had formed a
Church where he had settled, and the congregation were, like their
teacher, concerned at St Paul's danger, and so some went with him to
Jerusalem.   Perhaps the nucleus of the Church may be dated from
the baptism of Cornelius, and Philip settling in Cæsarea carried on
what had been begun by St Peter.

ἄγοντες παρ' ᾧ ξενισθῶμεν Μνάσονί τινι Κυπρίῳ, ἀρχαίῳ μαθητῇ,
*bringing with them one Mnason of Cyprus, an early disciple, with whom
we should lodge.*   The construction is not easy to settle.   The rendering
just given takes παρ' ᾧ ξενισθῶμεν as an inserted clause interfering with
the regular government, which would be ἄγοντες Μνάσονά τινα &c.
The antecedent however is made to correspond in case with
the intruded relative.   This appears simplest, but others suppose
the sense to be ἄγοντες (ἡμᾶς) παρὰ Μνάσονά τινα...παρ' ᾧ ξενισθῶμεν,
'leading us to the house of Mnason' &c.   It seems more natural to
suppose that for some reason or other Mnason was at this time at
Cæsarea, and that the arrangement by which the Apostle's party became his guests was made with him there, than to consider that the
disciples in Cæsarea, knowing Mnason's hospitality and that he could
receive such guests, agreed to carry them thither.

On Mnason's reception of St Paul Chrysostom reflects thus: Παῦλον
ἐξένιζεν ἐκεῖνος.   τάχα τις ὑμῶν ἐρεῖ· εἴ τις κἀμοὶ Παῦλον ἔδωκε ξενίσαι,

ἑτοίμως ἂν καὶ μετὰ πολλῆς τῆς προθυμίας τοῦτο ἐποίησα· ἰδοὺ τὸν Παύλου
δεσπότην ἔξεστί σοι ξενίσαι, καὶ οὐ βούλει. ὁ γὰρ δεχόμενος, φησίν, ἕνα
τῶν ἐλαχίστων, ἐμὲ δέχεται.

Mnason belonged to Cyprus, but had now his home in Jerusalem.
Just as Barnabas and Mary, the mother of John Mark, were also
Cypriotes, but had fixed their home in the holy City. Mnason is
called ἀρχαῖος μαθητής as having become a Christian in the *beginning*
of the Gospel preaching, soon after the day of Pentecost. At the
time of any of the great feasts it was no unnecessary precaution to
settle on a lodging beforehand, for Jerusalem was certain to be full of
people, and by this arrangement made in Cæsarea, the whole party
was saved the trouble of searching for quarters when they arrived.
To find a house in which the Apostle and those with him might all be
received would probably have been attended with much difficulty. To
be the owner of such a house Mnason must have been one of the
wealthier members of the congregation. His name is Greek, and he
was most likely one of the Hellenists, or, if he were a Jew, Mnason
was perhaps substituted for some Jewish name, e.g. *Manasseh*.

17—36.   ARRIVAL AT JERUSALEM.   PAUL'S RECEPTION BY THE CHURCH AND BY THE PEOPLE.

17.   ἀσμένως ἀπεδέξαντο ἡμᾶς οἱ ἀδελφοί, *the brethren received us
gladly.* The brethren, whose joy is here spoken of, would be those
Christians who first learnt of the arrival of Paul at Mnason's house.
It is not the public reception which is here intended, for however
welcome Paul may have been to individuals, the heads of the Church
were manifestly apprehensive of trouble which might arise from his
presence in Jerusalem.

18.   τῇ δὲ ἐπιούσῃ εἰσῄει ὁ Παῦλος σὺν ἡμῖν πρὸς Ἰάκωβον, *and the
day following Paul went in with us unto James.* This was the Church's
reception of the returned missionaries. Notice of their arrival would
soon be given, and the authorities who were at the time resident in
Jerusalem were gathered together. There was not any Apostle there or
St Luke would hardly have failed to mention the fact, as he was one
of those present. Paul took with him to this interview all who had
shared in his labours, that their work as well as his own might receive
the recognition of the mother Church of Christ. The James here
mentioned is the same who appears recognised as the head of the congregation in Jerusalem (xii. 17, xv. 13). He was most probably one
of our Lord's brethren. See note on xii. 17.

πάντες τε παρεγένοντο οἱ πρεσβύτεροι, *and all the elders were present.*
These men, with James, formed the governing body of the Church,
and were the persons to whom the Apostle would naturally desire to
give an account of his labours. In the proceedings which follow, the
narrative does not, as in the council at Jerusalem, represent James as
taking the lead, or being spokesman; he is only mentioned as the
person to whom the missionaries specially went. The advice given to
St Paul is couched in the plural number, as if the elders had jointly
tendered it.

19. καὶ ἀσπασάμενος αὐτούς, *and having saluted them.* ἀσπάζομαι
is used of the greetings both at parting and arrival. For the latter,
cf. 1 Macc. xi. 6, ἠσπάσαντο ἀλλήλους καὶ ἐκοιμήθησαν ἐκεῖ. For parting
see above, xxi. 1. Oriental greetings are of a much more formal character than is common in Western countries.

ἐξηγεῖτο καθ᾽ ἓν ἕκαστον ὧν, *he rehearsed one by one the things which.*
Such a narrative must have consumed much time, though St Luke,
having given us before a sketch of St Paul's work, omits here any
speech of the Apostle.

For the attraction of the relative into the case of its antecedent see
note on i. 1. Here however the antecedent τούτων is not expressed.

ἐποίησεν ὁ θεός...διὰ τῆς διακονίας αὐτοῦ, *God had wrought among
the Gentiles by his ministry.* We cannot doubt, from what remains
to us of St Paul's writings, that this was the tone of all that he would
say. God had been pleased to use him, and for His own glory had
made Paul's weakness effective.

20. ἐδόξαζον τὸν θεόν, *they glorified God.* They took up the strain
of thanksgiving which had run through all the Apostle's story. Nothing could show more clearly than such a result how little of himself,
and how much of God, there had been in St Paul's narrative.

εἶπάν τε αὐτῷ, *and they said unto him.* Their anxiety makes itself
apparent at once, and we come here face to face with what must have
been one of the greatest difficulties for the early Christians. Before
Jerusalem was destroyed there must ever have been at that centre a
party zealous for the Law, with whom labour among the Gentiles
would find small favour.

θεωρεῖς, ἀδελφέ, *thou seest, brother.* The use of θεωρέω seems to
imply that there had already been some opportunity for the Apostle
to behold and estimate the character of a Christian gathering in Jerusalem. At this feast of Pentecost the Christians would have as much
interest in a commemorative assembly as the Jews.

πόσαι μυριάδες, *how many thousands.* Literally 'myriads.' But the
word is used indefinitely of a large number, just like our 'thousand.'

εἰσὶν ἐν τοῖς Ἰουδαίοις τῶν πεπιστευκότων, *there are among the Jews
of them which have believed.* These were persons who, as was not
unlikely to be often the case, accepted Christianity as the supplement
of Judaism, but made no break with their old faith, of the observances of which their life-long training had made them tenacious. To
such men, as Christianity rested on the Old Testament Scripture,
there would seem little need to make a rent between their old life and
the new.

καὶ πάντες ζηλωταὶ τοῦ νόμου ὑπάρχουσιν, *and they are all zealous
for the Law,* i.e. rigorous maintainers of all the ceremonial of the
Mosaic code. Ζηλωταί was the name of a most rigid sect among the
Jews, begun in the times of the Maccabees. It is used in a bad sense,
'Teaching of the Twelve Apostles' § 3.

21. κατηχήθησαν δὲ περὶ σοῦ, *and they have been informed concerning thee.* κατηχέω is a very significant verb. It is the root of our English 'catechize.' It implies, therefore, that the process of educating public opinion in Jerusalem about St Paul had been a diligent business. The Pharisaic party had taught the lesson persistently till their hearers were fully trained in it. We can hence understand the great hostility which the Apostle experienced, and his strong language about these Judaizers. They must have had their partizans at work in preparation for his visit, and have poisoned men's minds against him.

ὅτι ἀποστασίαν...πάντας Ἰουδαίους, *that thou teachest all the Jews that are among the Gentiles to forsake Moses.* The calumniators made use of the Apostle's earnest words to Gentile converts, that they should not accept Judaism first as a door to Christianity, to bring a charge that, to Jews also, he spake of the Law as no longer to be regarded. We can see from what we know of his words and actions how false this was, but at such a time and amid such a populace the charge would rouse great animosity, and have no chance of being refuted.

ἀποστασία is found 1 Macc. ii. 15, of those who were being compelled to forsake the Law and the ordinances and to sacrifice unto idols. οἱ παρὰ τοῦ βασιλέως οἱ καταναγκάζοντες τὴν ἀποστασίαν...ἵνα θυσιάσωσι.

λέγων μὴ περιτέμνειν αὐτοὺς τὰ τέκνα, *telling them not to circumcise their children.* Circumcision had so long been the mark of the Jew, and the expression 'uncircumcised' meant something so abhorrent to his mind, that we cannot wonder that this is put in the forefront of the charge. For the sense of contempt and abomination in the name 'uncircumcised,' cf. 1 Sam. xvii. 26; Ezek. xxviii. 10, xxxii. 29, 30.

μηδὲ τοῖς ἔθεσιν περιπατεῖν, *nor to walk after the customs.* The customs are the ceremonial laws of the Jews. The recurrence of words = 'to walk after' gives quite an Old Testament ring to the language of these speeches.

22. τί οὖν ἐστιν; *what is it therefore?* i.e. How stands the matter? A question used as introductory to the consideration of what is best to be done.

πάντως δεῖ συνελθεῖν πλῆθος, *a multitude must needs come together.* These words are accepted by Lachmann and Tischendorf, but omitted by Tregelles, and also in the Rev. Vers. They appear to suit very badly with the sense. St Paul had just been addressing the conspicuous members of the Church at Jerusalem. They recommend to him a certain course by which certain Judæo-Christians might learn in their visits to the Temple that the Apostle against whom such evil reports had been circulated was taking part in the observance of the legal customs. In all this there was nothing done with special reference to a crowd, nor do we read of the gathering of any crowd till the seven days of the vow were nearly ended, and then it was the Jews of Asia who stirred up the multitude.

23. τοῦτο οὖν ποίησον, *do therefore this.* They advise St Paul to take a part in the ceremonies of a Nazirite vow. He could not go through the whole course of the observance, for these men had already for sometime had the vow upon them, but it was permitted among the Jews, to anyone who wished, to join in the final purification cere-monies of this vow; and this was the more readily permitted, if the person wishing to take a share only in this concluding portion bore the charges of the person or persons to whom he joined himself. It is significant of the intense clinging to the older ceremonial in the Jewish Church that among the Christian congregation there were men found who had taken this vow upon them. If the authorities knew of St Paul's previous observance of a like vow (xviii. 18) they would have no scruple in urging him to take part in a similar service again. For an account of the Nazirite's vow, see Numbers vi. 1—21. It is not there specified how long the observance of the vow lasted, and the time may have varied in different cases, but the final ceremonies here appear to have lasted seven days.

24. τούτους παραλαβὼν ἁγνίσθητι σὺν αὐτοῖς, *them take and purify thyself with them*, i. e. make thyself one of their company, and observe all the ordinances which they observe with regard to purification, and avoiding what is unclean.

καὶ δαπάνησον ἐπ᾿ αὐτοῖς, *and be at charges for them.* Josephus (*Ant.* xix. 6. 1) tells how Herod Agrippa took upon him the expenses of many Nazirites (ξυρᾶσθαι διέταξε μάλα συχνούς). Cf. also *Bell. Jud.* ii. 15. 1, from which passage it appears that then the whole time of a Nazirite's vow was thirty days. This latter passage relates to a vow made by Berenice.

ἵνα ξυρήσονται τὴν κεφαλήν, *that they may shave their heads.* This use of the future indicative after ἵνα is found in several places in N. T. Whether it occurs in classical Greek is very doubtful; though ὅπως is found with this construction.

The shaving of the head took place at the conclusion of the vow, and when the victims were offered, the hair was burnt in the fire which was under the sacrifice of the peace-offering. The charges which had to be borne by St Paul would be the cost of the victims and other things connected with the sacrifice.

καὶ γνώσονται πάντες, *and all shall know*, i. e. learning from what they actually behold.

κατήχηνται, *they have been informed.* See above on verse 21 for the force of the word. They had been taught this calumny about St Paul as if it were a lesson to be learnt.

οὐδέν ἐστιν, *are nothing*, i.e. have no truth in them. Cf. xxv. 11.

στοιχεῖς καὶ αὐτὸς φυλάσσων τὸν νόμον, *thou thyself also walkest orderly keeping the Law.* στοιχέω (as its derivation from στοῖχος=a row, would intimate) is always used of going by a rule or example, fol-lowing a pattern. What the pattern here is is expressed in the parti-cipial clause. Of the value which the Jew attached to such following, cf. Ecclus. xxi. 11, ὁ φυλάσσων νόμον κατακρατεῖ τοῦ ἐννοήματος αὐτοῦ. He may not understand at first, but obedience will lead him to a mastery of all that the Law means.

25. περὶ δὲ τῶν πεπιστευκότων ἐθνῶν, *but as touching the Gentiles which believe.* The elders, while urging on Paul the course they have described in consideration of Jewish prejudices, are yet careful to distinguish from this the liberty of the Gentiles, and to confirm that liberty. They make it plain to the Apostle that they are of the same mind as when the council was held (Acts xv.). They refer now to the decisions then arrived at.

ἡμεῖς ἐπεστείλαμεν, *we wrote.* This is said in reference to the time when the decrees were first published (Acts xv. 23). ἐπιστέλλω is used there (xv. 20) just as here. The proceedings of the synod are referred to in their technical language.

κρίναντες, *giving judgment.* In this word also there is a reference to the language of xv. 19 where James says ἐγὼ κρίνω. And although James is not specially mentioned here as the speaker, there must have been one who acted as the mouthpiece of the presbytery, and none was more likely to do so than he.

φυλάσσεσθαι αὐτοὺς κ.τ.λ., *that they should keep themselves from things sacrificed to idols, and from blood, and from what is strangled and from fornication.* On these prohibitions and the reasons for them see notes on xv. 20.

26. τότε ὁ Παῦλος παραλαβὼν τοὺς ἄνδρας, *then Paul having taken the men.* This consent of Paul to the advice of James and the elders has been taken by some for a contradiction of the words and character of the Apostle as represented in his own writings. But he has testified of himself (1 Cor. ix. 19—23) that for the Gospel's sake he was made all things to all men, unto the Jews becoming as a Jew that he might gain the Jews, and for the same end, to them that are without law, as himself without law. And these brethren of the Church of Jerusalem to whom St Paul joined himself were Christians, and therefore were not clinging to legal observances as of merit towards salvation, but as ordinances which were of divine origin, and which education had made them careful to observe. The same spirit had actuated the Apostle to manifest by an outward act his thankfulness for some deliverance when, on a former occasion, he took this vow on himself without the suggestion of others (xviii. 18). In the Christian services of the earliest days there was very little outlet for the expression by action of any religious emotion, and we cannot wonder that a people whose worship for a long time had been mainly in external observance should cling still to such outward acts, though they had grown to estimate them as of no saving virtue in themselves. With reference to the supposed contradiction in the two pictures of St Paul as given by St Luke and by himself, we need only compare his language about Judaizers in the Epistle to the Galatians with what he says of the preaching of the Gospel at Rome by similar adversaries, when he was writing to the Philippians, to see that the Apostle in what he said and did had ever an eye to the circumstances. To the Galatians he speaks in the strongest terms against the Judaizers because their influence was to draw away the Christians in Galatia

from the simple Gospel as offered by him in Christ's name to the
Gentiles, and to make them substitute for it the observance of the law
of Moses as a necessary door to Christianity. He has no words strong
enough to express his horror of such teachers in such a place. But the
same Paul concerning Rome, the condition of whose people may be
learnt by a perusal of the first chapter of his letter to that Church, says
(Phil. i. 15—18), 'Some preach Christ even of envy and strife, supposing to add affliction to my bonds. Notwithstanding every way,
whether in pretence or in truth, Christ is preached, and I therein do
rejoice, yea, and will rejoice.' Assuredly there is as much of so-called
contradiction between Paul as described in different places by himself,
as between his own description and what St Luke has left us of his
history.   Contradiction it is not, but only such concession as might
be expected from one strong in the faith as St Paul was when he was
dealing, as he was called upon to deal, with two classes of men who
could never be brought to the same standpoint. To observe the ceremonial law was not needful for the Gentiles, therefore the Apostle
decried its observance and opposed those who would have enforced it.
The ceremonial law was abolished for the Jew also in Christ, but
it had a divine warrant for those who had been trained in it from
their youth up, therefore all that the Apostle here desired was that
their true value only should be set on externals. He felt that time
would develop Christian worship to fill the place which the Temple
Service for a long time must hold among the Christians of Jerusalem.

τῇ ἐχομένῃ ἡμέρᾳ...εἰς τὸ ἱερόν, *the next day, having purified himself
with them, he entered into the Temple.* The regulation was that the
Nazirite should avoid all persons and things that would cause ceremonial defilement, and that this might be more thoroughly accomplished the closing days of the vow appear, at this time, to have been
passed within the Temple precincts. This, of course, must have been
a later arrangement than any which is spoken of in the institution of
the vow (Numb. vi.).

On the Apostle's action at this time Chrysostom remarks: ὅρα τὸν
Παῦλον. οὐ λέγει...καὶ μὴν δύναμαι πεῖσαι τῷ λόγῳ· ἀλλ' ἐπείσθη αὐτοῖς
καὶ πάντα ἐποίησε. καὶ γὰρ οὕτω συνέφερεν. οὐ γὰρ ἦν ἴσον εἰς ἀπολογίαν
καταστῆναι, καὶ οὐδένος εἰδότος ποιῆσαι ταῦτα. ἀνύποπτον ἦν τὸ καὶ
δαπανᾶσθαι.

διαγγέλλων τὴν ἐκπλήρωσιν τῶν ἡμερῶν τοῦ ἁγνισμοῦ, *declaring the
fulfilment of the days of purification.* The meaning is that St Paul
gave notice to the proper officials of the Temple that the completion
of the vow would be at a certain time. It would be needful for him
to do this, as otherwise they would have expected him to keep the
full number of days which the others observed. After his explanation
that he was only a sharer for a time in the vow of his companions, it
would be understood that his days of purification should terminate
when theirs did.

ἕως οὗ προσηνέχθη...ἡ προσφορά, *until the offering was offered for
every one of them.* ἕως οὗ depends on εἰσῄει, 'he entered in...(to stay)
till the offering, &c.' The words are not a part of St Paul's notice to

the priests, but of St Luke's history. The Apostle performed these observances, and intended to continue as a Nazirite till the whole ceremonial for all of them was ended.

27. ἔμελλον...συντελεῖσθαι, *were almost completed.* Seven days appear to have been the period devoted to the more secluded residence
in the Temple. For συντελεῖσθαι, of the completion of a portion of
time (which is not very common), cf. Job i. 5, καὶ ὡς ἂν συνετελέσθησαν
αἱ ἡμέραι τοῦ πότου.

οἱ ἀπὸ τῆς ᾿Ασίας ᾿Ιουδαῖοι, *the Jews from Asia.* It seems from this
that a portion of the visitors to Jerusalem had known the Apostle in
his missionary labours, and may have come after him, in their enmity,
to damage his reputation by calumnious reports of his teaching, reports which had as much ground in truth as the story about Trophimus from which the tumult arose at this time in Jerusalem.

συνέχεον πάντα τὸν ὄχλον, *stirred up all the multitude.* These Asian
Jews were coming up to the Temple for their worship, and may even
have been of the company in the ship by which the Apostle and his
companions came from Patara. They certainly had known, or found
out, that Trophimus was an Ephesian and a Gentile. If they had
seen the Apostle in familiar converse with him, this would be enough
to rouse their indignation, especially as Paul and his companion
would probably be living together in the same house and at the same
board (cf. Acts xi. 3).

28. βοηθεῖτε, *Help.* The cry is as if an outrage had been committed, and they, the strangers visiting Jerusalem, were the persons who
could afford the best testimony to what had been done. For had they
not seen and heard Paul in Ephesus and elsewhere?

οὗτός ἐστιν ὁ ἄνθρωπος ὁ κατὰ τοῦ λαοῦ κ.τ.λ., *this is the man that
teacheth all men everywhere against the people.* By their language
they would intimate that he was bringing the whole nation into contempt. The Jews no doubt were treated with contempt among the
Gentiles, and to hear that one of their own nation had helped this on
would rouse them as much as anything could.

καὶ τοῦ νόμου καὶ τοῦ τόπου τούτου, *and* [against] *the Law and this
place.* How great a change has come over the Apostle since the day
when he joined with those who charged Stephen (ch. vi. 13) with
speaking blasphemous words against this holy place (the Temple) and
the Law. Now a like multitude brings similar charges against him.

ἔτι τε καὶ ῞Ελληνας εἰσήγαγεν εἰς τὸ ἱερόν, *and moreover he has
brought Greeks also into the Temple.* On the occurrence of τε καὶ in
the same clause, cf. on xix. 27. There is no doubt a special emphasis
intended to be given to ῞Ελληνας in this clause which may explain
St Luke's irregular language.

There was in the Temple a 'court of the Gentiles,' but the accusation against St Paul was that, during his own sojourn in the sacred
precincts, he had brought his Gentile companions into places which
were forbidden to them. How unscrupulous their charge was is indi-

cated by the plural 'Greeks,' whereas the only person to whom such a
term could be applied was Trophimus.

καὶ κεκοίνωκεν κ.τ.λ., *and hath defiled this holy place.* They themselves as Jews were in the court allotted to their nation, which was
deemed more sacred than that of the Gentiles. The Greek word
κεκοίνωκεν is literally 'hath made common,' and carries the thought
back to St Peter's vision, where the Gentiles were figured by the beasts
which the Apostle deemed '*common* (κοινά) or unclean' (Acts x. 14).

29. Τρόφιμον τὸν Ἐφέσιον, *Trophimus the Ephesian.* Hence we
see that Trophimus had come with the Apostle not only 'as far as
Asia' (see note on xx. 4), but all the way to Jerusalem. His name
bespeaks the man a Greek, and, from the anger of these Asiatic Jews,
he was doubtless a convert to Christianity without having been a
proselyte of Judaism. It is noticeable that so ready were these men
to find a cause for attacking St Paul, that they began it on a mere
thought, 'They supposed Paul had brought him into the Temple.'

30. καὶ ἐγένετο συνδρομὴ τοῦ λαοῦ, *and the people ran together.*
So καὶ ἐγένετο συνδρομὴ ἐν πάσῃ τῇ παρεμβολῇ (Judith x. 18) of the
crowding around Judith as she came into the camp of Holophernes.

What occurred is a proof that the words of James and the elders
were true. The whole Jewish community had been 'catechized' on
the doings of St Paul among the Gentiles. The least spark set the
whole train on fire.

καὶ ἐπιλαβόμενοι τοῦ Παύλου εἷλκον αὐτόν, *they laid hold on Paul
and dragged him.* Their design was probably to get him out of the
Temple precincts before they proceeded to further violence. It is
clear that all the ceremonies of the Apostle's vow were not yet accomplished, and had they not laid violent hands on him he might have
fled to the altar for safety. That such a murder as they contemplated
was possible in Jerusalem at this period we have evidence in the case
of Stephen.

ἐκλείσθησαν αἱ θύραι, *the doors were shut.* We need not suppose
that any of the Levites, the gatekeepers of the Temple, were of the
same mind with the rioters. Their action in closing the gates was
only to prevent any profanation of the building by the uproar which
they saw to be beginning.

31. ζητούντων τε αὐτὸν ἀποκτεῖναι, *and as they were seeking to kill
him.*

For the omission of the pronoun, which is not rare with the genitive
absolute of the third person, see on verse 10 above and cf. 1 Chron.
xvii. 24, μεγαλυνθήτω τὸ ὄνομά σου ἕως αἰῶνος λεγόντων Κύριε, κύριε
παντοκράτωρ.

For ζητεῖν in the sense of 'wishing' as here cf. Exod. iv. 24, συνήν-
τησεν αὐτῷ ἄγγελος κυρίου, καὶ ἐζήτει αὐτὸν ἀποκτεῖναι. The desire of
the mob was clearly, now that they had the Apostle in their power,
to beat him to death in the crowd, and thus avoid a charge of murder
against any individual.

ἀνέβη φάσις τῷ χιλιάρχῳ τῆς σπείρης, *tidings came up to the chief captain of the band.* The chief military officer of the Romans in Jerusalem was stationed in the tower of Antonia, which was situate on the N.W. of the Temple on the hill Acra. This tower had been built by Herod, and was so close to the scene of the tumult that news would be brought at once. The military officer (probably a *tribune*) is called χιλίαρχος, that is, officer over a thousand men. On the word σπεῖρα for a Roman cohort, or troop of soldiers, cf. x. 1. The verb ἀνέβη 'came up to' shews that the writer was familiar with the locality and had the whole scene in his mind. On the Tower of Antonia, see Josephus, *Vita*, 5.

φάσις is used in classical Greek for a formal accusation laid before a law court. It is only found once in the LXX. where φάσις θεοῦ is the order from God given for the punishment of an offender, Susanna 55. The name of the χιλίαρχος is from the further history (xxiii. 26) found to have been *Claudius Lysias*, but nothing is known of him beyond what we read in the Acts.

συγχύννεται, *was in confusion.* Cf. the σύγχυσις at Ephesus, xix. 29. At the time of the feast religious party feeling was sure to run very high, and the multitudes of strangers visiting the city would think to shew their zeal for the Temple and the Law by their eagerness to avenge any supposed profanation.

32. στρατιώτας καὶ ἑκατοντάρχας, *soldiers and centurions.* Clearly the χιλίαρχος had charge of a considerable troop, which might perhaps just at the feast be augmented in anticipation that the incourse of so many foreigners might lead to a disturbance.

κατέδραμεν ἐπ' αὐτούς, *ran down upon them.* The tower was on the height above the Temple, so the verb is very correct.

ἐπαύσαντο τύπτοντες τὸν Παῦλον, *they left beating of Paul.* The mob probably knew that Roman law would do justice, and that if the Apostle were found by the chief captain to have been wrongfully treated they would be brought to an account.

33. ἐπελάβετο αὐτοῦ, *laid hold on him.* The verb implies a formal arrest. The chief captain did not come with a view to relieve St Paul, but to find out what was the matter, and seeing the Apostle in the hands of the mob, himself arrested him, that he might not be killed without a hearing.

ἁλύσεσι δυσί, *with two chains,* cf. xii. 6. Evidently, as appears from his language afterwards (verse 38), the χιλίαρχος regarded St Paul as some desperate criminal. He would have thought little of the matter, had it seemed merely a question about Jewish law (see xxiii. 29).

καὶ ἐπυνθάνετο, *and inquired.* From those who appeared most prominent in the crowd.

τίς εἴη καὶ τί ἐστι πεποιηκώς, *who he was, and what he had done.* The optative mood in the first half of the question shews that this was a question about the answer to which there might be uncertainty. The indicative in the latter half proclaims the conviction of the χιλίαρχος. He was quite sure some wrong had been done.

34. ἄλλοι δὲ ἄλλο τι ἐπεφώνουν, *and some shouted one thing and some another.* ἐπιφωνέω is the verb which St Luke gives for the din of the multitude which shouted against Jesus (Luke xxiii. 21), 'Crucify Him'; also for the adulatory shouting in honour of Herod Agrippa (Acts xii. 22). No other New Testament writer uses the word. It is twice found in the LXX. (1 Esd. ix. 47; 2 Macc. i. 23), both times of loud responses in prayer.

The chief captain appears to have made an effort to learn what was laid to the charge of the Apostle.

διὰ τὸν θόρυβον, *because of the uproar.* Probably, as at Ephesus (xix. 32), a large part of the shouters hardly knew themselves why the clamour was raised.

ἄγεσθαι...εἰς τὴν παρεμβολήν, *to be led into the castle.* παρεμβολή signifies 'an encampment,' but was employed to designate the barracks which the Romans had in the Tower of Antonia. The same word is rendered 'army' in Heb. xi. 34. Cf. also LXX. 1 Sam. iv. 5, 6, 7.

35. ἐπὶ τοὺς ἀναβαθμούς, *upon the stairs.* The noun is common in the LXX. (cf. 1 Kings x. 19, 20, &c.) but not in classical Greek. It occurs Herod. II. 125.

The stairs mentioned here are the flight of steps leading from the Temple area up to the tower where the soldiers were stationed. They were not covered in, for St Paul is able to address the multitude while standing on them (verse 40).

διὰ τὴν βίαν τοῦ ὄχλου, *by reason of the violence of the crowd.* The people pressed on St Paul with all the more fury because they saw that he was now to be taken out of their hands. Hence it came to pass, that some of the soldiers were obliged, in order to keep him safe, to lift him from his feet and carry him up till he was out of reach, their comrades meanwhile keeping back the people from the foot of the stairs.

36. τὸ πλῆθος...κράζοντες, *the multitude...crying.* The plural masculine participle is used, because the notion of πλῆθος is plural.

αἶρε αὐτόν, *away with him.* The same cry which (Luke xxiii. 18) was used by the Jews before Pilate in reference to Jesus.

37—40.   PAUL ASKS LEAVE TO ADDRESS THE CROWD.

37. μέλλων τε εἰσάγεσθαι, *and when he was about to be brought.* This must have been when a place on the stairs had been reached where Paul was safe out of reach of the mob, and needed no longer to be borne up by the soldiers.

εἰ ἔξεστίν μοι εἰπεῖν τι πρός σε; *may I speak to thee?* Literally 'may I say something to thee?' On εἰ as a mere mark of interrogation, cf. on i. 6.

Ἑλληνιστὶ γινώσκεις; *dost thou know Greek?* The χιλίαρχος had evidently come down with a preconceived notion who the offender was about whom the disturbance had arisen. And from some source or other he appears to have known that the Egyptian, whom he supposed St Paul to be, could not speak Greek.

38. οὐκ ἄρα σὺ εἶ, *thou art not then* (as I supposed thee to be). Probably St Paul had addressed him in Greek already.

ὁ Αἰγύπτιος, *the Egyptian.* The person to whom allusion is here made was a sufficiently formidable character, if we only reckon his followers at four thousand desperadoes. Josephus (*Ant.* xx. 8. 6; *Bell. J.* II. 13. 5) tells how he was one of many impostors of the time, and that when Felix was governor he came to Jerusalem, gave himself out as a prophet, gathered the people to the Mount of Olives in number about 30,000, telling them that at his word the walls of Jerusalem would fall down, and they could then march into the city. Felix with the Roman soldiers went out against him. The impostor and a part of his adherents fled, but a very large number were killed and others taken prisoners. The narrative of Josephus does not accord with the account of St Luke, but if the former be correct, we may well suppose that the numbers and the occasion spoken of by the chief captain relate to an event anterior to that great gathering on the Mount of Olives. The fame of the impostor may have grown; indeed, must have done so before he could collect the number of adherents of which Josephus speaks.

ἀναστατώσας καὶ ἐξαγαγών, *who stirred up to sedition and led forth.* ἀναστατόω is found, beside here, in Acts xvii. 6; Gal. v. 12, and is always active. So ἄνδρας must be governed by both these verbs, and not, as in A.V., by the latter only.

τῶν σικαρίων, *of the assassins.* σικάριοι is a word derived from the Latin *sica* = a dagger, and imported into Greek. Josephus (*B. J.* II. 13. 3) in an account of the lawless bands which infested Judæa in these times, says (after relating how a notorious robber named Eleazar had been taken with his followers and sent in chains to Rome), 'But when the country was thus cleared there sprang up another kind of plunderers in Jerusalem called Sicarii. They kill men by daylight in the midst of the city. Particularly at the feasts they mix with the crowd, carrying small daggers hid under their clothes. With these they wound their adversaries, and when they have fallen the murderers mix with the crowd and join in the outcry against the crime. Thus they passed unsuspected for a long time. One of their earliest victims was Jonathan the high priest.' For further notices of the Sicarii cf. Josephus *B. J.* II. 17. 6 and *Ant.* xx. 8. 10.

39. ἐγὼ ἄνθρωπος μέν εἰμι Ἰουδαῖος, Ταρσεύς, τῆς Κιλικίας, *I am a Jew of Tarsus in Cilicia.* See vi. 9 and notes.

οὐκ ἀσήμου πόλεως πολίτης, *a citizen of no mean city.* Tarsus was the metropolis of Cilicia, and a city remarkable for its culture, and the zeal of its inhabitants for philosophic studies.

ἐπίτρεψόν μοι λαλῆσαι πρὸς τὸν λαόν, *give me leave to speak unto the people.* An objection has been here raised that it is extremely improbable that the chief captain could have held this conversation with St Paul amid the tumult, and also that he would have granted permission to speak to a man whom he had just taken as his prisoner, and whom he afterwards arranges to examine by scourging (xxii. 24). But we have only to remember that the Apostle and his interlocutor were high up above the crowd, and so away from the noise; that the staircase crowded with soldiers, who could not rapidly be withdrawn because they were restraining the multitude, made some delay absolutely unavoidable, and that, added to this was the surprise of the chief captain that his prisoner could speak Greek, and we have enough warrant for accepting the story as it is here told. Moreover the Greek which the Apostle used was of a very polished character, shewing the education and refinement of the speaker, and making good his claim to respect.

40. ἐπιτρέψαντος δὲ αὐτοῦ, *and when he had given him leave.* As in the previous verse.

κατέσεισεν τῇ χειρί, *he beckoned with his hand.* Apparently the chief captain had also been so far impressed by the conversation of his prisoner, that he allowed at least one of his hands to be released from its chain (see above, verse 33) while he spake to the multitude, and this he waved to ask for silence.

πολλῆς δὲ σιγῆς γενομένης, *and when there was made a great silence.* The unusual circumstance, and the gesture which could be seen through the whole crowd, would gain an audience very readily. Beside which an Oriental mob is less persistent than those of the western world.

τῇ Ἑβραΐδι διαλέκτῳ, *in the Hebrew language.* This alone, as soon as it was heard, would gain the speaker an audience with many. It was their own speech, for by 'Hebrew' here is meant the Aramaic dialect of Palestine.

CHAPTER XXII.

Readings varying from the *Text. recept.*

9. καὶ ἔμφοβοι ἐγένοντο omitted with ℵABH. Not represented in *Vulg.*

16. αὐτοῦ for τοῦ κυρίου with ℵABE. *Vulg.* 'ipsius.'

20. τῇ ἀναιρέσει αὐτοῦ omitted with ℵABE. Not represented in *Vulg.*

24. ὁ χιλίαρχος εἰσάγεσθαι αὐτὸν with ℵABCDE. *Vulg.* 'tribunus induci eum.'

26 ὅρα omitted with ℵABC. Not represented in *Vulg.*

30. ἀπὸ τῶν δεσμῶν omitted with אABCE. Not represented in *Vulg.*

αὐτῶν after συνέδριον omitted with אABCE. Not represented in *Vulg.*

Ch. XXII. 1—21. St Paul's Defence.

1. ἀκούσατέ μου τῆς πρὸς ὑμᾶς νυνὶ ἀπολογίας, *hear ye my defence which I now make unto you.* With regard to the construction of the verse, it seems, as in John xii. 47, that ἀκούω is here followed by a double genitive of the person and thing, 'Hear from me the defence &c.' This is sometimes found also in classical Greek.

2. ἀκούσαντες δέ, *and when they heard.* The beckoning with the hand (xxi. 40) had procured silence enough for the Apostle's first words to be heard, and now they caught the sound of their own dialect.

μᾶλλον παρέσχον ἡσυχίαν, *they were the more quiet.* ἡσυχία is stillness as opposed to motion, while σιγή (xxi. 40) is quiet as opposed to noise. The phrase in this verse indicates that the crowd not only abstained from cries and shouts, but kept still in their places that they might hear the better. Thus a very high degree of quiet is described.

3. ἐγώ εἰμι ἀνὴρ Ἰουδαῖος, *I am a Jew.* These first words of the Apostle would correct many wrong impressions among the crowd, for we may be sure that many, beside the chief captain, had the notion that St Paul was one of those foreign desperadoes with which Judæa abounded at this time.

γεγεννημένος ἐν Ταρσῷ τῆς Κιλικίας, *born in Tarsus of Cilicia.* On Tarsus, cf. note on vi. 9.

ἀνατεθραμμένος δὲ ἐν τῇ πόλει ταύτῃ, *but brought up in this city.* St Paul means not that from his infancy he had lived in Jerusalem, but that, when he had reached an age fitted for it, he was sent from home to be educated under Gamaliel. The verb is used in this sense in classical Greek. On Gamaliel, see note on v. 34.

παρὰ τοὺς πόδας, *at the feet.* The most usual position of teacher and pupils at the time of St Paul was that both should sit, the former on a higher level than the latter. For the evidence on this matter from the Talmud, see Taylor *Pirke Aboth*, pp. 28, 29.

πεπαιδευμένος κατὰ ἀκρίβειαν τοῦ πατρῴου νόμου, ζηλωτὴς ὑπάρχων, *instructed according to the strict manner of the law of our fathers, being zealous,* &c. For an account by the Apostle himself of his Jewish birth, education, and character, cf. Phil. iii. 5, 6. He was a Hebrew of the Hebrews, and his language shews how learned he was in all that concerned his own people. He makes frequent allusions to Jewish customs, laws, and festivals, and reckons his time by the Jewish calendar. He was also a Pharisee, and none of his contemporaries surpassed him, while but few equalled him, in strictness of legal observance.

THE ACTS   BB καθὼς πάντες ὑμεῖς ἐστε, *as ye all are.* The Apostle, who never puts himself in peril when no good end is to be served by it, wishes to set himself in an acceptable light before his audience. This is his reason for explaining that he, like themselves, had been a zealous observer of the law.

4. ὃς ταύτην τὴν ὁδὸν ἐδίωξα ἄχρι θανάτου, *and I persecuted this Way unto the death.* On ἡ ὁδὸς as the designation of the Christian religion, cf. note on ix. 2. We are not told of any Christians who were put to death through Saul's zealous persecution, for in the case of Stephen he was not a very active agent, but his own statement in this verse, and the stronger expression xxvi. 10, 'when they were put to death I gave my voice against them,' make it certain that the persecutions in which he took part were carried beyond imprisonment, even to the martyrdom of the accused.

εἰς φυλακάς, *into prisons.* The plural here used is probably intended to express, what in chap. xxvi. is given in more detail, viz., the wide field over which Saul's zeal was exerted, 'being exceedingly mad against them, I persecuted them even unto strange cities.' The usual phrase has the singular. Cf. 2 Chron. xvi. 10, καὶ παρέθετο αὐτὸν εἰς φυλακήν. Also Gen. xl. 3, ἔθετο αὐτοὺς ἐν φυλακῇ.

5. ὡς καὶ ὁ ἀρχιερεὺς μαρτυρεῖ μοι, *as also the high priest doth bear me witness.* The Apostle refers not to the high priest at the time when he was speaking, but to him who had held that office when (ix. 1) in his earnestness against the Christians he had desired a commission from the authorities to carry his persecuting measures as far as Damascus. Josephus (*Ant.* xviii. 5. 3) tells us that in A.D. 37 Theophilus, son of Ananus, was made high priest in the place of his brother Jonathan. The high priest to whom St Paul here alludes was one of these two brothers, for Theophilus held office till he was removed by Agrippa and his place occupied by Simon, called Kantheras (see Jos. *Ant.* xix. 6. 2, and cf. Farrar's *St Paul,* I. 178). Ananias was high priest at the time of St Paul's arrest. See xxiii. 2.

καὶ πᾶν τὸ πρεσβυτέριον, *and all the estate of the elders.* Though it was now more than twenty years since St Paul's conversion, it was not improbable that some members of the Sanhedrin which granted him his commission were still alive, and the records of the transaction were doubtless preserved and could be appealed to.

πρεσβυτέριον is used for the position of an elder in LXX. Susanna 50.

ἐπιστολὰς δεξάμενος πρὸς τοὺς ἀδελφούς, *having received letters unto the brethren,* i.e. to the Jewish authorities in Damascus. The Jews spake of all their race as brethren from the earliest times (cf. Deut. xviii. 15). The whole family were Jacob's children.

ἄξων καὶ τοὺς ἐκεῖσε ὄντας, *to bring them also which were there,* i.e. any Christians whom I was able to find in Damascus. ἐκεῖσε has here the force of ἐκεῖ, as it sometimes has in the Greek poets.

δεδεμένους εἰς Ἰερουσαλήμ, *to Jerusalem in bonds.* Thus they were to be treated as the veriest criminals.

6. περὶ μεσημβρίαν, *about noon.* The time of the day at which the vision occurred is not noticed in chap. ix., but in chap. xxvi. the Apostle also mentions that it was 'at mid-day,' at which time the heavenly brightness must have been very overpowering to shine above the glare of an Eastern sun.

7. ἤκουσα φωνῆς, *I heard a voice.* As in chap. ix. 4 and 7, so here, and below in verse 9, the case of the noun is varied, so as to mark that the hearing in St Paul's case was different from the hearing of his companions. The verb can be connected with either a genitive or accusative case. In both the narratives a variation is made, and it was not without its significance (see notes on chap. ix.). St Paul heard intelligible words, the others heard a sound, but it was not speech to them. Cf. the narrative in Daniel x. 6—9.

8. ὁ Ναζωραῖος, *of Nazareth.* This adjective is found only in this one of the three accounts of Saul's conversion; though in some MSS. to make the one place conform more exactly to the other they have been inserted in ix. 5.

9. The words καὶ ἔμφοβοι ἐγένοντο which appear in the *Text. recept.,* but which the chief MSS. omit, are not like other words which have been inserted in various portions of this book. There is nothing like them either in chap. ix. or chap. xxvi. It is possible that they are of early authority, and may have been omitted by a scribe whose eye passed from the NTO of ἐθεάσαντο to the same letters at the end of ἐγένοντο. They are omitted from the present text according to the decision of Lachmann, Tischendorf and Tregelles, but their difference from other words similarly omitted is worthy of consideration.

τὴν δὲ φωνὴν οὐκ ἤκουσαν, *but they heard not the voice,* i.e. the words which were spoken to Saul. They were only conscious of a sound round about them. See above on verse 7.

10. ὧν τέτακταί σοι ποιῆσαι, *which are appointed for thee to do.* On the attraction of the relative into the case of its antecedent, see on i. 1.

God had explained to Ananias (see ix. 15) what Saul's future work should be: how he was a chosen vessel to bear His name before Gentiles and kings and the children of Israel; and still more about his labours was to be revealed to the new Apostle himself. According to xxvi. 16—18 the character of the work to which he was called was from the first indicated to Saul; though as no mention is made of Ananias in that passage, it may well be that the Apostle there brings into one statement both the words he heard on the way and those which were afterwards spoken to him by Ananias.

11. ὡς δὲ οὐκ ἐνέβλεπον ἀπὸ τῆς δόξης τοῦ φωτὸς ἐκείνου, *and when I could not see for the glory of that light.* This explanation of the reason of the Apostle's blindness is only given in this place.

ἐμβλέπω is found Mark viii. 25 of sight returned after blindness.

12. Ἀνανίας δέ τις, ἀνὴρ εὐλαβὴς κατὰ τὸν νόμον, *and Ananias, a devout man according to the Law.* The Apostle neglects nothing in his

address which can conciliate his audience, and so he tells them that
the messenger whom God sent to him was 'well reported of by all the
Jews that dwelt in Damascus.' (For *Ananias* see note on ix. 10.) The
hostility towards Christians, which was so strong in Jerusalem, had
not at the time of St Paul's conversion manifested itself so greatly in
Damascus, since Ananias, 'a disciple,' was still in good repute with the
Jews there.

13. καὶ ἐπιστάς, *and standing by me.* The Apostle in his blindness
was seated, no doubt, and the messenger came and stood over him.

ἀνάβλεψον...ἀνέβλεψα εἰς αὐτόν, *receive thy sight...I looked up
upon him.* For the two renderings of the verb, cf. Luke xix. 5, where
ἀναβλέψας is used of Jesus *looking up* at Zacchæus in the sycamore
tree, with John ix. 11, where ἀνέβλεψα is said by the blind man who
describes how *he received his sight.*

14. ὁ θεὸς τῶν πατέρων ἡμῶν, *the God of our fathers.* Ananias
spake naturally as one Jew to another. At the commencement of the
Christian Church there was no thought of a rupture with Judaism,
and nothing is more to be noticed in the Acts than the gradual advance made by the Apostles and their companions in apprehending
what the result of their mission would be.

προεχειρίσατό σε, *hath appointed thee.* The verb is only here and
in xxvi. 16 in N.T. In the LXX. it is found Exod. iv. 13, προχείρισαι
ἄλλον δυνάμενον ὃν ἀποστελεῖς, where Moses would excuse himself from
going unto Pharaoh; also Joshua iii. 12; 2 Macc. iii. 7, viii. 9: always
with the notion of selecting some one into whose hands an important
duty can be committed.

γνῶναι τὸ θέλημα αὐτοῦ, *to know His will.* For this reason it is
that St Paul so often in the commencement of his Epistles speaks of
himself as an Apostle according to the *will* of God. 1 Cor. i. 1; 2
Cor. i. 1; Eph. i. 1; 1 Col. i. 1, &c. The whole passage Eph. i. 1—11
forms a comment on this clause.

καὶ ἰδεῖν τὸν δίκαιον, *and to see the righteous One,* i.e. Jesus. See
note on vii. 52 above.

καὶ ἀκοῦσαι φωνὴν ἐκ τοῦ στόματος αὐτοῦ, *and to hear a voice from
His mouth.* That in this way St Paul might, even as the other Apostles, be taught of Jesus.

15. ὅτι ἔσῃ μάρτυς αὐτῷ, *for thou shalt be His witness.* Thus the
commission of the later-called Apostle was exactly in the same terms
in which Christ (Acts i. 8) had spoken to the Eleven before his Ascension.

πρὸς πάντας ἀνθρώπους, *unto all men.* Paul, with his usual discre-
tion, does not utter the word 'Gentiles' till he is forced to do so.

ὧν ἑώρακας καὶ ἤκουσας, *of what thou hast seen and heard.* For by
revelation the Apostle was made aware of the whole scope of Christian
truth, and of those doctrines which Christ during His life on earth
had communicated to the Twelve. And at a later time (see 2 Cor. xii.

2, 3) greater revelations appear to have been made to St Paul concerning the world to come than to any of the other Apostles.

16. καὶ νῦν τί μέλλεις; *and now why tarriest thou?* According to the narrative in ix. 15, the message of Ananias had already proclaimed the gift of the Holy Ghost to Saul, and the favour of God had been shewn in the recovery of his sight. So the question of Ananias becomes parallel to that of St Peter in the house of Cornelius: 'Can any man forbid water that these should not be baptized, which have received the Holy Ghost as well as we?'

ἀναστὰς βάπτισαι, *arise and be baptized.* Though the gift of the Spirit was announced yet God directs that the means of grace, the sacrament of baptism, which the Apostle must offer to others, should also be received by himself.

καὶ ἀπόλουσαι τὰς ἁμαρτίας σου, *and wash away thy sins.* The close connexion of the sacramental sign with renewing grace is spoken of in like terms by the Apostle in his Epistle to Titus (iii. 5), 'according to His mercy He saved us, by the washing of regeneration, and the renewing of the Holy Ghost.'

ἐπικαλεσάμενος τὸ ὄνομα αὐτοῦ, *calling on His name,* i.e. τοῦ δικαίου, the name of the righteous One, Jesus, mentioned in verse 14.

17. ὑποστρέψαντι εἰς Ἰερουσαλήμ, *when I had returned to Jerusalem.* This refers to that visit of the Apostle recorded in Acts ix. 26 seqq. We learn from Gal. i. 18 that three years had elapsed between the conversion of Saul and this visit to Jerusalem, which period is supposed to have been consumed in Arabia (cf. Gal. i. 17). The preaching of Saul at Jerusalem we are told in the Acts roused the anger of the Greek-speaking Jews, and that in consequence of their attempts against Saul the Christian congregation sent him away first to Cæsarea and then to Tarsus.

The double construction of the participle first in the dative after ἐγένετο and then in the genitive absolute is noteworthy. But there is a degree of difference in the sense 'after my return' and 'while I was praying.'

προσευχομένου μου ἐν τῷ ἱερῷ, *while I prayed in the Temple.* It is worthy of note how often in this address St Paul incidentally expresses himself in such wise as to conciliate the crowd. His visit to the Temple for the purpose of prayer was at once a proof that he was not likely to despise Jewish ordinances and religious observances.

γενέσθαι με ἐν ἐκστάσει, *I fell into a trance.* This was the occasion of one of those 'visions and revelations of the Lord' of which St Paul speaks to the Corinthians (2 Cor. xii. 1) and with which, from his conversion onwards, he was many times instructed and comforted.

The infinitive, as here, after ἐγένετο is common in St Luke. The present example is however more noteworthy, because it is of the form ἐγένετό μοι...γενέσθαι με.

18. καὶ ἰδεῖν αὐτὸν λέγοντά μοι, *and saw Him saying unto me.* In Acts ix. 29, 30 no mention is made that a vision had appeared to

Saul commanding him to depart from Jerusalem. It is only said that
'the disciples' sent him away. But these two statements are not
inconsistent with each other. Saul might be warned to go, and the
disciples at the same time prompted to send him. In the same way
two different causes, one natural, the other supernatural, are mentioned
Acts xiii. 2—4, viz. the prompting of the Holy Spirit, and the act of
the Church of Antioch. And still more like is the statement of St
Paul (Gal. ii. 2), that he went up to Jerusalem 'by revelation,' when
it is placed side by side with Acts xv. 2, where we are told that the
Christians of Antioch determined that Paul and Barnabas should go
up to consult the Church in Jerusalem.

ἔξελθε ἐν τάχει ἐξ Ἱερουσαλήμ, *get thee quickly out of Jerusalem.*
We know from Gal. i. 18 that the duration of the Apostle's stay was
only fifteen days.

ἐν τάχει used adverbially is common both in classical Greek and in
the LXX.

οὐ παραδέξονταί σου μαρτυρίαν περὶ ἐμοῦ, *they will not accept from
thee testimony concerning me.* The Apostle, as is clear from what follows
in the next verse, considered that he would be specially a messenger
likely to persuade and convince men in Jerusalem of the truths of the
Christian faith. God, in the vision, points out that this will not be so.

19. Κύριε, αὐτοὶ ἐπίστανται, *Lord, they know.* The effect of the
expressed pronoun is not to be reproduced in English. These are, he
thinks, the very men to whom he can best appeal. Saul is confident
that he will be known by many to whom he would speak, and that his
zealous persecution of the Christians less than four years before cannot have fallen out of men's memories.

ἐγὼ ἤμην φυλακίζων καὶ δέρων, *I imprisoned and beat.* The peculiar form, the substantive verb with the participle, implies that this
conduct was continuous. Saul was regularly engaged in the work.

φυλακίζω is a rare word, found only here in N.T., and in LXX.
Wisdom xviii. 4, ἄξιοι μὲν γὰρ ἐκεῖνοι στερηθῆναι φωτὸς καὶ φυλακισθῆναι
ἐν σκότει.

κατὰ τὰς συναγωγάς, *in the synagogues.* For the synagogues as
places where such punishment was inflicted cf. Matth. x. 17, xxiii. 34;
Mark xiii. 9; Luke xxi. 12. That they were also places in which
charges were heard is seen from Luke xii. 11.

20. Στεφάνου τοῦ μάρτυρός σου, *of Stephen, thy witness.* The Greek
word μάρτυς had not yet come to be applied, as it afterwards was, to
those Christians who *bore witness* to the truth by their death.

συνευδοκῶν, *consenting.* On the force of ἤμην with the participle,
which here implies that Saul took a share in the proceedings from first
to last, see the previous verse.

καὶ φυλάσσων τὰ ἱμάτια, *and kept the raiment.* See on vii. 58.

21. ἐγὼ εἰς ἔθνη μακρὰν ἐξαποστελῶ σε, *I will send thee forth far
hence unto the Gentiles.* We need not understand the command as

implying that the Apostle's missionary labours were to begin from that moment, but that God's work for him was now appointed, and would begin in His own time; and it would be not among Jews or Greeks at Jerusalem, but among the Gentiles in distant places.

St Paul had kept back as long as ever he could the word which he was sure would rouse the anger of his hearers, and we may well suppose from the conciliatory tone of much of his speech that the attention of the crowd had been enlisted, for the speaker was a man of culture and spoke their own tongue. But when the Gentiles are spoken of as recipients of God's message they break forth into all the excitement of an Oriental mob.

22—29. FURY OF THE JEWS. THE CHIEF CAPTAIN ORDERS PAUL TO BE SCOURGED, BUT ON HEARING THAT HE IS A ROMAN, RECALLS THE ORDER IN ALARM.

22. ἄχρι τούτου τοῦ λόγου, *unto this word*, i.e. Gentiles. It is probable that here and there in the speech the Apostle may not have entirely pleased them. Their feelings however could not be restrained when the hated name was spoken to them by one who professed to be bearing abroad the message of Jehovah.

οὐ γὰρ καθῆκεν αὐτὸν ζῆν, *for it was not fit that he should live*, i.e. he ought to have been put to death long ago. Cf. Ecclus. x. 23, οὐ καθῆ-κεν δοξάσαι ἄνδρα ἁμαρτωλόν, i.e. it neither is nor ever has been proper to magnify a sinful man. In which passage however the Vat. MS. reads καθήκει.

23. ῥιπτούντων τὰ ἱμάτια, *casting off their clothes*, i.e. the loose upper robe which could easily be laid aside, and which in such an excitement would interfere with their movements. Compare the conduct of the crowd when our Lord rode into Jerusalem, and also the behaviour of Jehu's friends, 2 Kings ix. 13. Such loose parts of the dress were rolled up for carrying and thus progress in a crowd was made more easy.

καὶ κονιορτὸν βαλλόντων εἰς τὸν ἀέρα, *and casting dust into the air*. With this compare the action of Shimei, 2 Sam. xvi. 13, where the marginal rendering shews that the dust was thrown at David. Perhaps it may have been meant in the present case to be thrown at St Paul, who was above the crowd, at the top of the stairs. The attempt to reach him with what they threw was futile, but it shewed what they would fain have done. For a like action as a sign of grief, cf. Job ii. 12.

24. ἐκέλευσεν ὁ χιλίαρχος εἰσάγεσθαι αὐτὸν κ.τ.λ., *the chief captain commanded him to be brought into the castle*. Probably the chief captain understood nothing of what St Paul had been saying, and would be surprised at the outbreak of rage on the part of the people, and conclude from it that there was some serious charge laid against him which he might best ascertain by subjecting his prisoner to torture till he should confess.

εἴπας μάστιξιν ἀνετάζεσθαι αὐτόν, *having bidden that he should be examined by scourging.* The active verb ἀνετάζειν is found LXX. Susanna 14, ἀνετάζοντες ἀλλήλους, but it is of very rare occurrence.

The mode of examination by torture among the Romans consisted in binding the limbs of the person to be tortured fast to a framework on which arms and legs were spread apart (*divaricatio*), and then the beating was inflicted by means of rods.

δι' ἣν αἰτίαν οὕτως ἐπεφώνουν αὐτῷ, *for what cause they cried so against him.* Here the antecedent has been, as is not uncommon, transferred into the relative clause.

25. ὡς δὲ προέτειναν αὐτὸν τοῖς ἱμᾶσιν, *and when they had tied him up with the thongs.* The person to be scourged was stretched forward (προτείνειν) so that he might be in a position to receive the blows. Some have translated 'for the thongs,' but ἱμάς is nearly always used for straps employed for straining or binding tight, and rarely, if ever, for the implement by which the chastisement is inflicted.

πρὸς τὸν ἑστῶτα ἑκατόνταρχον, *to the centurion that stood by.* He was superintending the tying up of the prisoner to the whipping-post, which was done by the common soldiers.

ἄνθρωπον Ῥωμαῖον, *a man that is a Roman.* It was an offence punishable with the severest penalties for a man to claim to be a Roman citizen, if he were not one. The peril of such an assertion, if it were not true, convinces the centurion at once, and though we are not told so expressly we may feel sure that the operation of 'tying up' was stopped.

26. τί μέλλεις ποιεῖν; *what art thou about to do?* It was forbidden under a heavy penalty, by the *Lex Porcia*, to scourge a Roman citizen (Liv. x. 9).

28. τὴν πολιτείαν ταύτην ἐκτησάμην, *obtained I this citizenship.* It was the Roman boast 'I am a Roman *citizen*' (Cic. *in Verr.* v. 63). The sale of the freedom of Rome was at times the perquisite of some of the Imperial parasites and favourites, who made what they could of such a privilege.

ἐγὼ δὲ καὶ γεγέννημαι, *but I am a Roman born.* How St Paul came to be a Roman citizen by birth we cannot tell; probably some ancestor for meritorious conduct had been rewarded with enfranchisement. Tarsus was a free city, and had its own laws and magistrates, but that did not constitute its inhabitants Roman citizens.

29. οἱ μέλλοντες αὐτὸν ἀνετάζειν, *those who were about to examine him.* The verb is used here euphemistically for the scourging which it had been proposed to inflict on the Apostle.

αὐτὸν ἦν δεδεκώς, *he had bound him,* i.e. bound him for the purpose of scourging. To be bound with a chain as a prisoner was not prohibited in the case of Romans. Hence we find St Paul speaking often in the Epistles, written during his imprisonment at Rome, of the bonds and the 'chain' with which he was afflicted. Cf. Phil. i. 7, 13, 14, 17; Col. iv. 18; Philem. 10, 13. Also Acts xxviii. 20, while the next verse in this chapter shews that though the Apostle was unloosed from the whipping-post, he was still kept in bonds.

30. THE CHIEF CAPTAIN BRINGS PAUL BEFORE THE SANHEDRIN.

30. βουλόμενος γνῶναι, *desiring to know.* The chief captain was anxious, as a Roman officer, that justice should be done, and this could only be by having both sides before some authoritative council.

τὸ τί κατηγορεῖται ὑπὸ τῶν Ἰουδαίων, *of what he is accused by the Jews.* In a similar way a whole sentence is treated as one nominal idea by the prefixing of the neuter article in 1 Thess. iv. 1, παρελάβετε παρ᾽ ἡμῶν τὸ πῶς δεῖ ὑμᾶς περιπατεῖν.

καὶ ἐκέλευσεν συνελθεῖν τοὺς ἀρχιερεῖς, *and commanded the chief priests to come together.* He had discovered thus much, that the offence charged against his prisoner was concerning the religion of the Jews. He therefore summons the chief religious authorities as those who were best able to decide whether any wrong had been done.

καὶ πᾶν τὸ συνέδριον, *and all the council.* By this is meant the whole Jewish Sanhedrin. They were to meet in some place to which Paul could be brought, and where the case might be fairly heard. The place where the Sanhedrin met for their own consultations was called *Lishkath-Haggazith*, and was a hall built of cut stone so situate that one half was built on holy, the other half on the profane ground, and it had two doors, one to admit to each separate section, T. B. *Joma* 25a. But whether this was the place of meeting at this time we have no means of deciding.

καὶ καταγαγὼν τὸν Παῦλον, *and having brought Paul down.* The castle was situate in the highest part of the city, above the Temple, so that wherever he had to go, the chief captain must come down.

ἔστησεν εἰς αὐτούς, *he set him before them.* The idea of εἰς is 'he brought him *in among* them.' Perhaps the phrase is purposely used, to intimate that Paul was not committed to them, nor brought into their presence as if they were to be his judges, but only that both accusers and accused might be heard on common ground.

CHAPTER XXIII.

Readings varying from the *Text. recept.*

6. Φαρισαίων for Φαρισαίου with ℵABC. *Vulg.* 'Pharisæorum.'

9. τινὲς τῶν γραμματέων with ABC. The *Vulg.* does not represent τῶν γραμματέων τοῦ μέρους, having only 'quidam Pharisæorum.'

μὴ θεομαχῶμεν omitted with ℵABCE. Not represented in *Vulg.*

10. φοβηθεὶς for εὐλαβηθεὶς with ℵABCE. *Vulg.* 'timens.'

11. Παῦλε omitted with ℵABCE. Not represented in *Vulg.*

12. οἱ Ἰουδαῖοι with ℵABCE. *Vulg.* 'quidam ex Judæis.'

15. αὔριον omitted with אABCE. Not represented in *Vulg.*

20. τὸν Παῦλον καταγάγῃς εἰς τὸ συνέδριον with אABE. *Vulg.* 'producas Paulum in concilium.'

μέλλων for μέλλοντες with אABE. *Vulg.* represents the plural.

27. αὐτόν after ἐξειλάμην omitted with אABE. Not represented in *Vulg.*

30. μέλλειν ὑπὸ τῶν Ἰουδαίων omitted with אABE. The *Vulg.* has ' quum mihi perlatum esset de insidiis quas paraverant illi.

ἔρρωσο omitted with AB. *Vulg.* 'vale.'

32. ἀπέρχεσθαι for πορεύεσθαι with אABE.

34. ὁ ἡγεμὼν omitted with אABE. Not represented in *Vulg.*

35. κελεύσας for ἐκέλευσέ τε with אABE. *Vulg.* 'jussitque.'

Ch. XXIII. 1—10. St Paul before the Sanhedrin. Disagree-
ment between the Pharisees and Sadducees.

1. ἀτενίσας δέ, *and earnestly beholding.* The verb is one which
St Luke very frequently employs to note a speaker's expression at the
commencement of a speech, and it is one of those features in the Acts
which shew us where the compiler has acted as editor to the narratives
which he used. He very generally gives some word to indicate the
gesture or look of the person who speaks.

On its use in describing St Paul's earnest look, see xiv. 9, note.

ἄνδρες ἀδελφοί. See note on i. 16.

ἐγὼ πάσῃ συνειδήσει...ἄχρι ταύτης τῆς ἡμέρας, *I have lived in all
good conscience before God until this day.* The ἐγώ is emphatic. It is
as though the Apostle would say, ' You see me before you as though I
were an offender, but personally I feel myself innocent.' πολιτεύομαι
in profane authors signifies ' to discharge the duties of a citizen.' St
Paul implies by its use that he has been obedient to God's laws, as a
good citizen would be to the laws of his country. He employs the
verb again in his epistle to the Philippians (i. 27). It is also found in
LXX. 2 Macc. vi. 1, xi. 25 πολιτεύεσθαι κατὰ τὰ ἐπὶ τῶν προγόνων
αὐτῶν ἔθη.

So far as being devoted to God's service, St Paul's whole life up to
the present moment had been of one piece, it was only that his conscience had been enlightened, and so his behaviour had changed. He
had at first lived as a conscientious and observant Jew, his conscience
now approved his conduct as a Christian.

2. ὁ δὲ ἀρχιερεὺς Ἀνανίας, *and the high priest Ananias.* This was
Ananias the son of Nebedæus (Joseph. *Ant.* xx. 5. 2). In the time
of the Emperor Claudius he had been suspended from his office for

some offence and sent to Rome (*Ant.* xx. 6. 2) but afterwards seems to have been held in great reputation in Jerusalem (*Ant.* xx. 9. 2).

τύπτειν αὐτοῦ τὸ στόμα, *to smite him on the mouth.* No doubt St Paul's address, before the high priest gave this order, had extended much beyond the single sentence which St Luke records. He only preserves for us that which appears to have moved the anger of the authorities, his claim to have led a life of which in God's sight he was not ashamed. The action was intended to put a stop to what would be counted the presumptuous language of St Paul.

For τύπτειν τὸ στόμα τινος, which is not a common form, cf. Luke xxii. 64.

3. τύπτειν σε μέλλει ὁ θεός, τοῖχε κεκονιαμένε, *God shall smite thee, thou whited wall.* Here we may see how very far even the excellence of St Paul comes short of the behaviour of the Divine Master, who when He suffered threatened not, and when reviled, reviled not again. We need not however consider that St Paul's language here was a wish for evil upon the high priest, but only an expression of confidence in God that such conduct as that of Ananias would not be allowed to go unpunished. We know from Josephus (*B. J.* ii. 17. 9) that Ananias did come to a violent end. St Paul calls him 'whited wall' because he bore the semblance of a minister of justice, but was not what he seemed. Cf. 'whited sepulchres' (τάφοι κεκονιαμένοι, Matth. xxiii. 27). κεκονιαμένοι μετὰ ἀδικίας is found in LXX. (Prov. xxi. 9).

καὶ σὺ κάθη κρίνων με, *and dost thou sit judging me.* The σὺ seems intended to refer to the epithet just applied to Ananias. Dost thou (such an one) sit, &c.

παρανομῶν, *contrary to the law.* Literally 'transgressing the Law.' For St Paul had not yet been heard to the end. Cf. John vii. 51.

4. τὸν ἀρχιερέα τοῦ θεοῦ, *God's high priest.* So styled because he sat on the judgment-seat as God's representative, cf. Deut. xvii. 8—13. In the Old Test. the priestly, and even other, judges are sometimes called by God's own name 'Elohim.' (See Exod. xxi. 6, xxii. 8, 9 and cf. Ps. lxxxii. 1.)

5. οὐκ ᾔδειν, ἀδελφοί, ὅτι ἐστὶν ἀρχιερεύς, *I knew not, brethren, that he was the high priest.* Several explanations have been given of this statement of St Paul. Some think that it may have been true that St Paul from defect of sight, with which he is supposed to have been afflicted, could not distinguish that the speaker was the high priest; others that the high priest was not in his official position as president of the court; or that owing to the troublous times, and St Paul's recent arrival in Jerusalem, he was not aware who was high priest; or that he was speaking in irony, and meant to imply that the action of the judge was of such a character that none would have supposed him to be high priest; or that he meant by οὐκ ᾔδειν that for the moment he was not thinking of what he was saying. It is most consonant with St Paul's character to believe that either his own physical deficiency, or some lack of the usual formalities or insignia,

made him unable to distinguish that he who had given the order was
really the high priest.

Chrysostom's opinion on the subject is given thus: καὶ σφόδρα πείθομαι μὴ εἰδέναι αὐτὸν ὅτι ἀρχιερεύς ἐστι· διὰ μακροῦ μὲν ἐπανελθόντα
χρόνου, μὴ συγγινόμενον δὲ συνεχῶς 'Ιουδαίοις· ὁρῶντα δὲ καὶ ἐκεῖνον ἐν τῷ
μέσῳ μετὰ πολλῶν καὶ ἑτέρων. οὐκέτι γὰρ δῆλος ἦν ὁ ἀρχιερεὺς πολλῶν
ὄντων καὶ διαφόρων.

γέγραπται γάρ, *for it is written.* The quotation is from Exod.
xxii. 28 and is another illustration of what was said above on verse 4.
The whole sentence of the O. T. is 'Thou shalt not revile the gods, nor
curse the ruler of thy people,' and the marginal note on 'gods' is '*Or,*
judges,' which margin should be in the text.

6. γνοὺς δὲ ὁ Παῦλος, *but when Paul perceived.* We are not told
in what way the knowledge which the Apostle here acted on was
gained. Perhaps the Pharisees, as in the parable of the Pharisee and
publican, kept themselves apart; or to a Jewish eye some mark of
their dress may have been enough to bespeak a difference of party. St
Paul used this party spirit in a perfectly legitimate manner. What
he did was not done merely to set them by the ears, but to secure an
opportunity for speaking on that central doctrine of Christianity, the
resurrection of the dead. (Cf. xxiv. 21.)

υἱὸς Φαρισαίων, *a son of Pharisees.* This reading has the advantage of removing St Paul's language beyond the questioning
which has sometimes been raised about it. 'I am a Pharisee,' he
says. And it has been asked, whether he had a right to describe
himself thus. When he continues 'a son of Pharisees' we see that
he is stating that by descent and birth his family had for generations been members of that party. Having said this, he then pro-
pounds that doctrine which, of all their teaching, was that which
severed them from the Sadducees. That this point also was the central
doctrine of Christianity makes St Paul's address not disingenuous, but
an appeal to those who agreed with him thus far in his belief to hear
what he had further to say which might meet with their acceptance.
And it is not as if the Apostle had raised the question in their midst
on some side-issue. The whole teaching of the Christian Church rested
on the truth of the Resurrection, and therefore with much wisdom and
without any thought of deception he cries, 'I am a Pharisee, and for
teaching the doctrine of the Resurrection (which they hold) I am now
called in question.'

On the καὶ before ἀναστάσεως which almost=*namely,* 'for the hope,
even the resurrection of the dead,' cf. *Winer-Moulton,* p. 546. See
also above on i. 25.

7. ἐγένετο στάσις, *there arose a dissension.* The two parties began
to take sides for and against the Apostle.

8. Σαδδουκαῖοι μὲν γὰρ λέγουσιν μὴ εἶναι ἀνάστασιν, *for the Sadducees say that there is no resurrection.* It is said that their teaching had
its rise in the thought that 'God's servants should not do service
with the hope of reward.' As the life to come would be a reward we

are told that their doctrine developed into the denial of the Resurrection. As we meet with them in the New Testament, they are mainly members of the priestly order, and appear to have accepted only the written Law, as distinct from tradition; yet in spite of the mention of angels in the Pentateuch they appear to have explained the language in such wise as to identify these angelic appearances with some manifestation of the divine glory, and thus to have come to deny the existence of any spiritual beings distinct from God Himself. In political matters they were on the side of Rome, and in consequence are found uniting at times with the Herodians.

μήτε ἄγγελον μήτε πνεῦμα...ἀμφότερα, *neither angel nor spirit, but the Pharisees confess both.* Here the ἄγγελος and πνεῦμα are coordinate, and must be taken as together signifying 'manifestations of a spirit world.' Then ἀνάστασις is one point, and the rest of the sentence another included under the word ἀμφότερα.

Chrysostom remarks here, καὶ μὴν τρία ἐστί· πῶς οὖν λέγει ἀμφότερα; ἢ ὅτι πνεῦμα καὶ ἄγγελος ἕν ἐστι, ἢ ὅτι οὐ μόνον ἡ λέξις περὶ δύο, ἀλλὰ καὶ περὶ τριῶν λαμβάνεται.　καταχρηστικῶς οὖν οὕτως εἶπε καὶ οὐ κυριολογῶν.

9. ἐγένετο δὲ κραυγὴ μεγάλη, *and there arose a great clamour.* The noise of an excited assembly. κραυγή is used in the Parable of the Ten Virgins (Matth. xxv. 6) to describe the shout at midnight 'the bridegroom cometh.'

τινὲς τῶν γραμματέων τοῦ μέρους τ. Φ., *and some of the Scribes that were of the Pharisees' part,* i.e. certain individuals as representatives of the whole body.

διεμάχοντο, *strove.* The verb is used of strife in words, Ecclus. viii. 3 μὴ διαμάχου μετὰ ἀνθρώπου γλωσσώδους.

εἰ δὲ πνεῦμα ἐλάλησεν αὐτῷ ἢ ἄγγελος, *and if a spirit hath spoken to him, or an angel....* St Luke appears to have left the sentence as an incomplete exclamation. This the Rev. Ver. has endeavoured to represent by rendering the clause 'And what if a spirit hath spoken to him, or an angel?' The temper of these Pharisees is so very much akin to the counsel of Gamaliel in chap. v. 39, that it is not difficult to understand how a thoughtful reader filled up on his margin the unfinished exclamation by an adaptation of Gamaliel's language (μὴ θεομαχῶμεν), and that these words found their way in a short time into the text.

10. ὁ χιλίαρχος, *the chief captain.* He must have been in some position where he could watch all the proceedings, though we can hardly think that he was presiding in the Sanhedrin.

μὴ διασπασθῇ, *lest he should be pulled in pieces.* The Pharisees had constituted themselves protectors of the Apostle, and so the possession of his person had become the object of a struggle between them and their opponents. διασπάω is frequently used in the LXX. of wild beasts tearing their prey in pieces. For the Apostle's position among the assembly cf. xxii. 30 on εἰς αὐτούς. He was evidently where the people could lay hands on him (cf. ἐκ μέσου αὐτῶν, below in this verse).

ἐκέλευσεν τὸ στράτευμα καταβὰν κ.τ.λ., *he commanded the soldiers to go down*, &c. They were in the tower of Antonia, overlooking the Temple-precincts, and so were ready to interfere in the struggle as soon as they were bidden. They were in considerable numbers, for στράτευμα is properly *an army*, as the A.V. renders in verse 27 below. Jerusalem was at this time in such an excited state that the presence of a large Roman force was necessary.

11—25. PAUL IS CHEERED BY A VISION. THE JEWS CONSPIRE TO KILL HIM.

11. τῇ δὲ ἐπιούσῃ νυκτί, *and the night following*. The Apostle was now, though not rightly a prisoner, yet kept, that he might be out of harm's way, under the charge of the Roman soldiers. The hearing of his case having been interrupted, another time was to be appointed when the examination should be completed.

ἐπιστὰς αὐτῷ ὁ κύριος, *the Lord stood by him*. Appearing in a vision as before at Corinth. Cf. on xviii. 9.

For the verb ἐπιστάς see above on xxii. 13.

θάρσει, *be of good cheer*. The Apostle could hardly be otherwise than downcast with the events of the previous day. He had entered the Temple and undertaken the Nazirite vow with a view of conciliating the Jews and he had only been saved from being torn in pieces of them through the interference of the Roman commander.

οὕτω σε δεῖ καὶ εἰς Ῥώμην μαρτυρῆσαι, *so must thou bear witness also at Rome*. St Paul had already written to the Roman Church of his 'longing to see them,' and that 'oftentimes he had purposed to come unto them' (Rom. i. 11—13), and St Luke (Acts xix. 21) records the intention in the history of St Paul's stay at Ephesus. The way to compass such a visit had not yet been found, but now it is pointed out by the Lord Himself.

The preposition εἰς implies, as in other instances, that the Apostle is to go *to* Rome, and then bear his testimony. See note on viii. 40.

In διαμαρτυρέω in this verse there seems to be an allusion to the thoroughness and zeal of St Paul's work hitherto.

12. γενομένης δὲ ἡμέρας, *and when it was day*. While Paul was receiving comfort from the Lord, the Jews were plotting to secure his destruction, and they let no time be wasted; their plans were ready by the next day, and as soon as it arrived they set about their execution.

ποιήσαντες συστροφὴν οἱ Ἰουδαῖοι, *the Jews having banded together*. To form such a compact is quite in the spirit of the time. The men who did so were probably belonging to the Zealots of whose fanaticism Josephus gives several instances.

ἀνεθεμάτισαν ἑαυτούς, *bound themselves under a curse*. Lit. 'placed themselves under an anathema.' The noun is used in very solemn language twice over by St Paul (Gal. i. 8, 9), 'Let him be accursed.' It was an invocation of God's vengeance upon themselves, if they failed to do the work which they undertook.

μήτε φαγεῖν μήτε πιεῖν, *neither to eat nor drink.* So that there was no time to be lost. Their work must be promptly executed.

13. πλείους τεσσεράκοντα, *more than forty.* Shewing the excited state of popular feeling at this moment among the Jews. They may have been prompted to this method of getting rid of the Apostle, because they had not the power of life and death any longer, and were not likely to procure Paul's death at the hands of the Roman authorities, on any accusation connected with a religious question.

οἱ ταύτην τὴν συνωμοσίαν ποιησάμενοι, *who had made this conspiracy.* The middle voice, which is the best supported reading, is the most in accordance with classical usage. The Greeks use ποιεῖν to be a cause (to others) of anything, ποιεῖσθαι to bring about for oneself. So they say ποιεῖσθαι πόλεμον, εἰρήνην, συμμαχίαν, when men procure the war, peace or alliance unto themselves.

14. τοῖς ἀρχιερεῦσιν καὶ τοῖς πρεσβυτέροις, *to the chief priests and elders.* These most likely were Sadducees, and so would have no wish that Paul should be spared.

ἀναθέματι ἀνεθεματίσαμεν ἑαυτούς, *we have bound ourselves under a great curse.* Literally, 'with a curse have we cursed ourselves.' This is a Hebrew mode of expressing the intensity and earnestness of an action. Cf. above on ch. v. 28.

μηδενὸς γεύσασθαι, *to taste nothing.* This includes both eating and drinking.

Chrysostom says on this: ἄρα διαπαντός εἰσιν ἀναθεματισμένοι ἐκεῖνοι, οὐ γὰρ ἀπέκτειναν τὸν Παῦλον.

15. νῦν οὖν ὑμεῖς...σὺν τῷ συνεδρίῳ, *now therefore do ye with the council signify,* &c. ἐμφανίζω in this sense of giving notice or information is frequent in LXX. Cf. Esther ii. 22, καὶ αὐτὴ ἐνεφάνισε τῷ βασιλεῖ τὰ τῆς ἐπιβουλῆς. See also 2 Macc. iii. 7, xi. 29. The chief priests and elders, of the Sadducees' party, were to use their influence in the council, that a request might proceed from the whole body of the Sanhedrin, for Paul to be again brought before them by the chief captain. From what we read of the Sadducees in the N.T. and Josephus, it is easy to believe that they would be in a majority.

καταγάγῃ αὐτόν, *that he bring him down,* i.e. from the tower of Antonia to the place where the Sanhedrin held its meetings. See above on verse 10.

ὡς μέλλοντας διαγινώσκειν ἀκριβέστερον τὰ περὶ αὐτοῦ, *as though ye would judge of his case more exactly.* They would profess a desire to know the whole right and wrong in the matter.

ἕτοιμοί ἐσμεν τοῦ ἀνελεῖν αὐτόν, *we are ready to kill him.* So that the suspicion of complicity in the crime would not fall upon the chief priests and elders. Their intention would appear to have been to give St Paul a fair hearing, and the murder would seem to be the work of some fanatics unconnected with the council.

For ἕτοιμος followed by the genitival infinitive, cf. LXX. 1 Sam. xiii.

21, καὶ ἦν ὁ τρυγητὸς ἕτοιμος τοῦ θερίζειν, and 1 Macc. xiii. 37, ἕτοιμοί ἐσμεν τοῦ ποιεῖν ὑμῖν εἰρήνην. Also 2 Chron. vi. 2, &c.

16. ἀκούσας δὲ ὁ υἱὸς τῆς ἀδελφῆς Παύλου, *but Paul's sister's son heard*, &c. We have no other mention of the family of St Paul anywhere in the history. It seems improbable that the sister and her son were settled inhabitants of Jerusalem, or we should have been likely to hear of them on Paul's previous visits. His imprisonment at this time was only to keep him from being killed, and so any relative or friend was permitted to come to him.

παραγενόμενος καὶ εἰσελθών, *he went and entered*, &c. Another punctuation joins παραγενόμενος with the former clause of the sentence, so that the sense is 'he heard of their lying in wait, having come in upon them.' Thus it would describe the way in which he had gained his information. But this rendering seems to press too much into this participle.

17. ἕνα τῶν ἑκατοντάρχων, *one of the centurions.* The Apostle was under the charge of a military guard, and so would have no difficulty in getting his message conveyed. And the knowledge that he was a Roman citizen, and that by birth, would have spread among the soldiery and would not be without its influence.

ἔχει γάρ τι ἀπαγγεῖλαι αὐτῷ, *for he hath something to tell him.* We have nothing to guide us to a knowledge of how Paul's nephew became acquainted with the plot to murder his uncle. As we know nothing of any kinsmen of St Paul being Christians, we may perhaps be right in supposing that the young man was a Jew, present in Jerusalem on account of the feast, and that he had heard among the Jewish population about the uproar, and the undertaking of the would-be assassins. In his interview with the chief captain it is clear that he was prepared with evidence which was convincing to that officer.

18. παραλαβὼν αὐτὸν ἤγαγεν, *he took him and brought him.* With soldier-like obedience and raising no questions.

ὁ δέσμιος Παῦλος, *Paul the prisoner*, a title which the Apostle used often afterwards to apply to himself. Cf. Eph. iii. 1, iv. 1; Philemon 1 and 9, &c.

19. ἐπιλαβόμενος δὲ τῆς χειρός, *and having taken him by the hand.* The messenger sent by a Roman citizen was entitled to some consideration, and the action of the chief captain is meant to encourage the young man. The chief captain would naturally incline after his conversation with him to favour Paul rather than his Jewish accusers. We can gather this from the tone of the letter which he subsequently sent to Cæsarea.

κατ᾽ ἰδίαν ἐπυνθάνετο, *inquired privately.* The A.V. joins the adverb with ἀναχωρήσας, but as this verb of itself implies a going aside, it is better, and more also in accordance with the order of the Greek, to join it with ἐπυνθάνετο.

20. ὡς μέλλων τι ἀκριβέστερον πυνθάνεσθαι, *as though thou wouldest enquire somewhat more accurately.* μέλλων is to be preferred to μέλλοντες, for in addressing the chief captain Paul's nephew would naturally speak as though he, who had control of the whole proceedings, was the person to enquire; while the plural in verse 15 is equally natural in the mouth of a speaker among the Zealots, who would say to the chief priests 'as though *ye* would enquire.'

21. σὺ οὖν μὴ πεισθῇς αὐτοῖς, *do not thou therefore yield to them.* The οὖν refers to the idea of a scheme in which the chief captain was to be made use of; this has only been suggested in the previous verse, not directly stated.

ἀνεθεμάτισαν ἑαυτούς, *they have bound themselves under a curse.* Cf. verse 12 above.

προσδεχόμενοι τὴν ἀπὸ σοῦ ἐπαγγελίαν, *looking for the promise from thee,* i.e. which they are coming to try and induce thee to make to them.

22. ὁ μὲν οὖν χιλίαρχος ἀπέλυσε τὸν νεανίσκον, *so the chief captain let the young man depart.* For ἀπολύειν = *to dismiss* a person, and let him go, cf. 2 Macc. xii. 25, ἀπέλυσαν αὐτὸν ἔνεκα τῆς τῶν ἀδελφῶν σωτηρίας.

ὅτι ταῦτα ἐνεφάνισας πρὸς ἐμέ, *that thou hast shewed these things to me.* Here the sentence which began in the *oratio obliqua* passes into the *oratio recta.* If the original form of the clause had been continued the close should have been = 'bidding him tell no one that he had shewed these things to him.' For a similar change though not so unmanageable to translate cf. i. 4.

23. τινὰς δύο, *two.* The effect of τινάς is to intimate that the number is not precisely given; 'two or so,' 'about two.' But this cannot be put into acceptable English.

ὅπως πορευθῶσιν ἕως Καισαρείας, *to go unto Cæsarea.* ἕως literally 'as far as.' Cæsarea was the residence of the Roman governor and the seat of the chief jurisdiction. The distance from Jerusalem to Cæsarea is about 70 miles.

δεξιολάβους, *spearmen.* The Greek word is a very unusual one, and signifies 'graspers by the right hand.' Hence it has been explained, as in the A.V., of soldiers who carried a spear in their right hand; others have thought a military guard was meant, who kept on the right hand of the prisoners of whom they had charge. Others, soldiers who were fastened to the right hand of the prisoners. This is improbable, because for such a purpose two hundred could not have been needed. The Vulgate gives *lancearii,* lancers.

ἀπὸ τρίτης ὥρας τῆς νυκτός, *at the third hour of the night.* This, according to Jewish reckoning, would be 9 P.M.

This was to be the point in time *from* which the journey was to commence. Hence ἀπό is used to define it.

24. **κτήνη τε παραστῆσαι.** Here we have the contrary change to that noted in verse 22. With ἐτοιμάσετε began a direct order, and this is continued in the *oratio recta* down to the close of verse 23. But with 24 the construction is oblique, as if some verb like ἐκέλευσεν had preceded παραστῆσαι. Consequently the Rev. Vers. has inserted in italics *he bade them.*

πρὸς Φήλικα τὸν ἡγεμόνα, *to Felix the governor.* Felix was made procurator of Judæa by Claudius in A.D. 53. He was the brother of Pallas, the favourite freedman of Claudius, and it was by the interest of his brother that Felix was advanced, and retained in his position even after the death of Claudius. The character of Felix, as gathered both from Roman and Jewish historians, is that of a mean, profligate and cruel ruler, and even the troublous times in which he lived are not sufficient to excuse the severity of his conduct. After his return to Rome, on the appointment of Festus to be governor in his stead, Felix was accused by the Jews of Cæsarea and only saved by the influence which his brother Pallas had with Nero, as he had had with his predecessor. Felix was connected with the Herodian family by his marriage with Drusilla the daughter of Herod Agrippa I. He continued to hold office at Cæsarea for two years after St Paul's coming there (xxiv. 27), and during the whole of that time the Apostle was his prisoner.

25. **ἐπιστολὴν ἔχουσαν τὸν τύπον τοῦτον,** *a letter after this form.* As both the writer and receiver of the letter were Romans, it is most likely that Latin was the language in which it was written, and that St Luke has given us a representation of the substance of the document rather than its very words.

26—30.　LETTER OF CLAUDIUS LYSIAS TO FELIX.

26. **τῷ κρατίστῳ ἡγεμόνι Φήλικι χαίρειν,** *to the most excellent governor Felix sendeth greeting.* The infinitive χαίρειν is governed by λέγει or some similar verb understood. See above, xv. 23.

The title κράτιστος 'most excellent' is that which is given by St Luke at the beginning of his Gospel to the Theophilus for whom he wrote it. Hence it is probable that Theophilus held some official position, it may be under the Romans in Macedonia, where St Luke remained for some time and where he may probably have written his gospel.

27. **τὸν ἄνδρα τοῦτον συλλημφθέντα ὑπὸ τῶν Ἰουδαίων...ἐξειλάμην.** *This man who was taken of the Jews...I rescued.* συλλαμβάνειν implies a seizure or arrest. It is used (Matth. xxvi. 55 ; Mark xiv. 48) of the party of men who came to seize our Lord, and (Acts xii. 3) of Herod Agrippa's arrest of St Peter.

It is to be noted that the chief captain is represented as employing throughout the letter ἀνήρ not ἄνθρωπος for *man.* The former implies much more respect, and was used no doubt because he was presently about to mention that he was a Roman citizen. The same distinction exists in Latin as in Greek, so that the original may have been in either language.   There can be little doubt that Roman officers at this time were familiar enough with Greek to write in it, if need were.

καὶ μέλλοντα ἀναιρεῖσθαι, *and likely to be killed.*   The chief captain does not give a very exact report of what had happened.   He says nothing about the strife between the two religious parties.   Perhaps he did not understand either its nature or cause.

ἐπιστὰς σὺν τῷ στρατεύματι, *coming upon them with the soldiers.* This must refer rather to the first rescue from the mob in the Temple-precincts (xxi. 32).   There is no word said of what happened afterwards, the binding with two chains, and the intention of scourging the prisoner.

On στράτευμα see above, verse 10 note.

μαθὼν ὅτι Ῥωμαῖός ἐστιν, *having learnt that he was a Roman.*   The chief captain puts this in such wise as to claim credit for interference on behalf of a Roman citizen, and in so doing omits to state that it was only when Paul was about to be scourged and had protested against it that he was discovered to be a citizen of Rome by birth.

28. βουλόμενός τε ἐπιγνῶναι, *and desiring to know.*   The method by which the chief captain proposed to satisfy this desire was by scourging the prisoner (cf. xxii. 24).

τὴν αἰτίαν δι᾽ ἥν, *the cause wherefore.*   For which we had in xxii. 24 the attracted form δι᾽ ἣν αἰτίαν.

29. ὃν εὗρον ἐγκαλούμενον, *whom I found to be accused.*   At first he would have discovered that the outcry against St Paul had something to do with the regulations of the Temple, then that there was a dispute about the resurrection of those who were dead, and that on this point some of the Jewish leaders sided with St Paul.   Such questions about their law would seem to the Roman officer quite as unworthy of consideration as they did to Gallio at Corinth (xviii. 15).

30. μηνυθείσης δέ μοι ἐπιβουλῆς εἰς τὸν ἄνδρα ἔσεσθαι ἐξ αὐτῶν, *and when it was shewn to me that there would be a plot against the man by them.*   The construction is very strange.   The full sentence would be grammatically μηνυθείσης μοι ἐπιβουλῆς ἐπιβουλὴν ἔσεσθαι κ.τ.λ.

ἔπεμψα πρός σε, *I sent to thee*, i.e. I sent him.   Of course Lysias implies by his language that he felt Felix to be a more fit person than himself to deal with such a case.

λέγειν αὐτοὺς ἐπὶ σοῦ, *themselves to speak before thee*, i.e. to say whatever they had to say.

31—35.   PAUL IS BROUGHT TO CÆSAREA, AND KEPT PRISONER BY FELIX.

31. οἱ μὲν οὖν στρατιῶται...ἀναλαβόντες τὸν Παῦλον, *so the soldiers...took Paul and*, &c., i. e. they formed a party for his escort and placed him in their midst.

On this escort Chrysostom remarks: καθάπερ βασιλέα τινὰ δορυφόροι παρέπεμπον μετὰ τοσούτου πλήθους καὶ ἐν νυκτὶ φοβούμενοι τοῦ δήμου τὴν

ὀργὴν τῆς ὁρμῆς· ἐπεὶ οὖν τῆς πόλεως αὐτὸν ἐξέβαλον τότε ἀφίστανται. οὐκ
ἂν δὲ ὁ χιλίαρχος μετὰ τοσαύτης αὐτὸν ἀσφαλείας ἐξέπεμψεν εἰ μὴ καὶ
αὐτὸς οὐδὲν ἦν αὐτοῦ κατεγνωκώς, καὶ ἐκείνων ᾔδει τὸ φονικόν.

ἀναλαμβάνω is thus used LXX. Gen. xxiv. 61, of the servant of
Abraham, when he escorts Rebecca to his master.

διὰ νυκτός, *by night,* i.e. that same night, starting off early in the
night and travelling during night-time, thus getting clear away from
Jerusalem before the ambush of the Jews was prepared.

εἰς τὴν Ἀντιπατρίδα, *to Antipatris.* This place was 42 miles from
Jerusalem and 26 from Cæsarea. It was in early times called Caphar-
saba, but Herod the Great rebuilt it and named it Antipatris in
memory of his father Antipater. It lay in a beautiful part of the
Vale of Sharon and was both well watered and rich in wood. The remains of a Roman road have been found close by it. For notices of
the older city, see Josephus, *Ant.* xvi. 5. 2; 1 Macc. vii. 31; of the
place as rebuilt, see Josephus, *B. J.* i. 4. 7; ii. 19. 1 and 9; iv. 8. 1.

32. τῇ δὲ ἐπαύριον, *but on the morrow.* That part of the escort
which now seemed no longer needed returned, and would get back to
Jerusalem on the day of the intended plot. Those who returned were
the στρατιῶται and the δεξιολάβοι.

ἐάσαντες τοὺς ἱππεῖς ἀπέρχεσθαι σὺν αὐτῷ, *having left the horsemen
to go on with him.* Now that they were far away from Jerusalem and
in no fear of a surprise, seventy horsemen were guard enough for the
remainder of the way. But it may give us some idea of the dangerous state of the country at the time, when we consider that the chief
captain thought it needful to send with this one prisoner a guard of
470 soldiers. We may also form some idea of what the garrison in
Jerusalem must have been when so many men could be detached at a
moment's notice.

ὑπέστρεψαν εἰς τὴν παρεμβολήν, *they returned to the castle.* Apparently coming back as quickly as it was possible for them to do so. As
the road was one much travelled they were probably able to obtain a
change of horses here and there.

33. οἵτινες, *who,* i.e. the horsemen who went on with St Paul. It
is better with Rev. Vers. to break up the relative into a conjunction
and personal pronoun. 'And they, when,' &c.

παρέστησαν καὶ τὸν Παῦλον αὐτῷ, *presented Paul also unto him.*
If the letter as given above be a rendering of the original, the prisoner
was not mentioned in it by name, but the soldiers would merely
declare that this was the man that had been committed to their
charge, and Felix would learn all the rest by questioning Paul.

34. ἐκ ποίας ἐπαρχίας ἐστίν, *of what province he was.* Cilicia had
been at one time, and perhaps still was, attached to the province of
Syria. It was so in the time of Quirinus. This will explain why at
once Felix without question decided that, at the proper time, he would
hear the cause.

35. διακούσομαί σου, *I will hear thee.* The verb implies a full and thorough hearing of a case. 'I will give thee a full hearing.' The Rev. Vers. renders 'I will hear thy cause.'

ὅταν καὶ οἱ κατήγοροί σου παραγένωνται, *when thine accusers are also come;* assuming that they would appear, since they had been bidden to do so by the chief captain, as was explained in his letter. Of course Lysias had not said a word of this to the Jews when his letter was written, but intended to do so when Paul was safely on the road to Cæsarea.

ἐν τῷ πραιτωρίῳ τοῦ Ἡρώδου φυλάσσεσθαι, *to be kept in Herod's palace.* πραιτώριον may signify either the palace of a prince, the tent of a general, or the barracks of the soldiery. Here it is probably the name of the palace which Herod had erected for himself, and which now was used as the governor's residence. It seems (from xxiv. 24— 26) that it was close to the quarters of Felix himself, and that Paul could speedily be sent for. φυλάσσεσθαι only implies that Paul was to be taken care of; he was not kept in close imprisonment. 'A Roman and uncondemned' would not be subject to needless indignities, when his accusers were Jews who could make no such claim for consideration. Cf. xxiv. 23.

CHAPTER XXIV.

Readings varying from the *Text. recept.*

1. πρεσβυτέρων τινῶν for τῶν πρεσβυτέρων with אABE. *Vulg.* 'cum senioribus quibusdam.'

5. στάσεις with אABE. *Vulg.* 'seditiones.'

7, 8. Omitted from καὶ κατὰ to ἐπὶ σέ with אABHLP. See notes.

11. ἤ before δώδεκα omitted with אABEHLP. *Vulg.* has 'quam.'

13. με after παραστῆσαι omitted with אABEL. *Vulg.* does not represent it.

σοι after δύνανται added with אABE. *Vulg.* 'tibi.'

14. τοῖς ἐν before τοῖς προφήταις added with אBE. Not added in *Vulg.*

15. νεκρῶν omitted with אABC. Not represented in *Vulg.*

20. εἰ before τί omitted with אABCEHLP. *Vulg.* 'si.'

ἐν ἐμοί omitted with אAB. *Vulg.* 'in me.'

22. ἀνεβάλετο δὲ αὐτοὺς ὁ Φῆλιξ with אABCE. *Vulg.* 'distulit autem illos Felix.'

23. αὐτὸν for τὸν Παῦλον with אABCE. *Vulg.* 'eum.'

ἤ προσέρχεσθαι omitted with אABCE. Not represented in *Vulg.*

24. τῇ ἰδίᾳ γυναικί with BC. *Vulg.* 'uxore sua.'

ʼΙησοῦν after Χριστόν added with אBEL. *Vulg.* 'Christum Jesum.'

25. ἔσεσθαι after μέλλοντος omitted with אABCE. Not represented in *Vulg.*

26. ὅπως λύσῃ αὐτόν omitted with אABCE. Not represented in *Vulg.*

27. χάριτα for χάριτας with אABC. *Vulg.* 'gratiam.'

Сн. XXIV. 1—9. ARRIVAL OF THE ACCUSERS. SPEECH OF TERTULLUS, THEIR ADVOCATE.

1. μετὰ δὲ πέντε ἡμέρας, *and after five days.* Most naturally this means after St Paul's arrival in Cæsarea, and the events narrated at the end of chap. xxiii. But it may mean five days after the departure of the Apostle from Jerusalem. The chief captain would give notice to the high priest of what he had done as soon as it was safe to do so. After learning that they must go to Cæsarea with their accusation, the enemies of St Paul would spend some little time in preparing their charge for the hearing of Felix, and in providing themselves with an advocate. And as they would not probably travel with as much haste as St Paul's convoy did, five days is not a long interval to elapse before they arrived in Cæsarea.

κατέβη ὁ ἀρχιερεὺς ʼΑνανίας, *Ananias the high priest came down.* He would be sure to be hot against St Paul after that speech about the 'whited wall.'

The verb καταβαίνω is used because the journey was from inland towards the seashore.

μετὰ πρεσβυτέρων τινῶν, *with certain elders.* It would only be a portion of the elders who came. Those of the Pharisees' party would rather have spoken in favour of the Apostle. The persons likely to take the journey to Cæsarea would be the Sadducees.

καὶ ῥήτορος Τερτύλλου τινός, *and with an orator, one Tertullus.* This man, as we may judge from his name, which is a modification of the Latin *Tertius*, was a Roman, and would be chosen because of his knowledge of Roman law, and his ability to place the case before Felix in such a light as to make it seem that Paul was dangerous to the Roman power, and not merely a turbulent and renegade Jew. We see below that he endeavoured to do this.

οἵτινες ἐνεφάνισαν, *and they informed.* On the breaking up of the relative in translation see above on xxiii. 33. If the relative rendering 'who' were kept, it might be supposed to refer only to Tertullus.

ἐμφανίζω St Luke uses in other places (Acts xxv. 2, 15) of the laying a formal information before a judge. It is also used in LXX. (Esther ii. 22) of Esther laying the information of the plot of the two chamberlains before king Ahasuerus.

2. κληθέντος δὲ αὐτοῦ, *and when he was called*, i.e. summoned by the official of the court, whose duty it was to call on the case.

ἤρξατο κατηγορεῖν ὁ Τέρτυλλος, *Tertullus began to accuse him*. St Luke has given us but the digest of the advocate's speech. The seven verses, in which it is included, and a large part of which is occupied with compliments to the judge, would not have occupied three minutes in the delivery.

3. πολλῆς εἰρήνης τυγχάνοντες διὰ σοῦ, *seeing that by thee we enjoy much peace*. The orator seizes on almost the only point in the government of Felix on which he could hang any praise. By severity he had put down false Messiahs, and the partisans of an Egyptian magician, as well as riots in Cæsarea and Jerusalem, so that the country was in a more peaceful condition than it had been for a long time past.

For εἰρήνης τυγχάνειν, cf. 2 Macc. xiv. 10, ἄχρι γὰρ Ἰούδας περίεστιν, ἀδύνατον εἰρήνης τυχεῖν τὰ πράγματα. See also the next note.

καὶ διορθωμάτων γινομένων τῷ ἔθνει τούτῳ διὰ τῆς σῆς προνοίας, *and that by thy providence evils are corrected for this nation*. The sentence, which began with a nominative case τυγχάνοντες, is now varied by the introduction of a genitive absolute. πρόνοια is found in a very parallel passage, 2 Macc. iv. 6, ἑώρα γὰρ ἄνευ βασιλικῆς προνοίας ἀδύνατον εἶναι τυχεῖν εἰρήνης, where A.V. renders ἅ. βασ. πρ. 'unless the king did look thereto,' which shews what the force of the word is here. It was by the severe looking thereto of Felix that disorders were corrected, though we learn from Tacitus (*Hist.* v. 9, *Ann.* xii. 54) that his severity in the end bore evil fruit, and it seems probable that his main motive in suppressing other plunderers was that there might be the more left for himself.

πάντῃ τε καὶ πανταχοῦ ἀποδεχόμεθα, *we accept it in all ways and in all places*, i.e. we acknowledge and are glad of it. Some would join πάντῃ τε καὶ πανταχοῦ with the previous clause, 'evils are in all ways and in all places corrected &c.' But this connexion is not favoured by the order of the Greek.

κράτιστε Φῆλιξ, *most excellent Felix*. The title is the same which was given to Felix in the letter of Claudius Lysias (xxiii. 26), and which is afterwards given to Festus by St Paul (xxvi. 25).

4. ἵνα δὲ μὴ ἐπὶ πλεῖόν σε ἐγκόπτω, *but that I be not further tedious unto thee*. The notion in the verb is that of stopping a person's way and so hindering him. Tertullus would imply that Felix was so deeply engaged in his public duties that every moment was precious.

ἐπιεικείᾳ, *clemency*. The usage of this word in the LXX. is always of the divine mercy. Cf. Baruch ii. 27; 2 Macc. ii. 22, x. 4, &c.

5. εὑρόντες γὰρ...λοιμόν, *for having found this man a pestilent fellow*. The Greek is literally 'a pestilence.' But the word is used of persons, 1 Macc. x. 61, καὶ ἐπισυνήχθησαν πρὸς αὐτὸν ἄνδρες λοιμοὶ ἐξ Ἰσραήλ, where, as here, the A.V. gives 'pestilent fellows.' In the Greek there, the phrase is further defined by ἄνδρες παράνομοι. Cf. also υἱοὶ λοιμοί, 1 Sam. ii. 12, x. 27, and λοιμή used of Hannah, 1 Sam. i. 16.

By εὑρόντες Tertullus would convey the impression that they have already spent some pains in detecting the evil ways of the accused.

καὶ κινοῦντα στάσεις, *and a mover of seditions.* The first charge made was one of general depravity. On coming to particulars Tertullus puts that first which would most touch the Roman power, and against which Felix had already shewn himself to be severe. Insurrections were of such common occurrence that one man might at this time be readily the prime mover in many.

It should be noticed that εὑρόντες in this sentence is left entirely in suspense, the construction never being completed. It should run, 'having found him &c....we &c.,' but the conclusion is forgotten in the orator's accumulation of wrongdoings.

πᾶσιν τοῖς Ἰουδαίοις τοῖς κατὰ τὴν οἰκουμένην, *among all the Jews throughout the world.* We must bear in mind that Paul had been assailed at a time when Jerusalem was full of strangers who had come to the feast. It is not improbable that from some of the Jewish visitors particulars had been gathered about the Apostle's troubles at Philippi, Corinth, Ephesus and elsewhere, which in the minds and on the lips of his accusers would be held for seditious conduct, conduct which had brought him at times under the notice of the tribunals. This Tertullus would put forward in its darkest colours. ἡ οἰκουμένη at this time meant 'the whole Roman Empire.' Cf. Cæsar's decree (Luke ii. 1) that 'all the world' should be taxed.

πρωτοστάτην τε, *and a ringleader.* The word is used in classical Greek of the front-rank men in an army. It is found in LXX. (Job xv. 24), ὥσπερ στρατηγὸς πρωτοστάτης πίπτων, where the Hebrew describes a man fitted for the battle.

τῆς τῶν Ναζωραίων αἱρέσεως, *of the sect of the Nazarenes.* The adjective is used as a term of reproach equivalent to 'the followers of Him of Nazareth,' which origin was to the mind of the Jews enough to stamp Jesus as one of the many false Messiahs. Cf. on the despised character of Nazareth, John i. 46.

6. ὃς καὶ τὸ ἱερὸν ἐπείρασεν βεβηλῶσαι, *who moreover assayed to profane the Temple.* The orator puts as a fact now, what had at first been only an opinion of the Asiatic Jews, that Paul had brought Trophimus into the Temple (xxi. 29). The mob made it as a charge in their excitement, but Tertullus speaks in cold blood.

ὃν καὶ ἐκρατήσαμεν, *whom we also took,* i.e. laid hold of by main force. The verb implies that force was needed for Paul's arrest. Here the words, which are rendered in the A.V. 'and would have judged according to our Law. But the chief captain Lysias came upon us, and with great violence took him away out of our hands, commanding his accusers to come unto thee,' are omitted in nearly all the oldest MSS., while the Greek text in those MSS. in which the passage is found exhibits many variations. Yet in spite of this it is hard to see how the advocate could have avoided some allusion to the circumstances mentioned in these words. Of course he puts the matter in a light most favourable to the Jews. 'We would have judged him according to our Law' is very different language from that in which (xxiii. 27) Lysias describes Paul as in danger to be killed by the Jews. The action of Lysias too is described by Tertullus as one of great violence. Probably the Roman soldiers would not handle the mob tenderly. But Tertullus is trying to cast blame upon the chief captain and to represent his party as doing all things according to law.

If the words be an interpolation, it is one which differs very greatly from those which are common in the Acts. In other places of the book such insertions have merely been made to bring the whole of a narrative under view at once, and there has been no variation of an account previously given elsewhere. But here we have a passage not representing the facts as stated before, but giving such a version of them as might make Lysias appear to have been in the wrong, and to have exercised his power in Jerusalem most arbitrarily against men who were only anxious to preserve the purity of their sacred temple. As both the Syriac and the Vulgate represent the passage it is not quite satisfactory to reject it.

8. παρ' οὗ δυνήσῃ αὐτὸς ἀνακρίνας, κ.τ.λ., *from whom thou wilt be able by examining him thyself to take knowledge*, &c. When the *Text. Recept.* stood, the words 'whom' and 'him' in this passage referred to Claudius Lysias, from whom Felix might naturally be expected to make enquiry; without the supposed interpolation the words apply to St Paul. Thus Tertullus suggests to Felix that the truth of the case against the Apostle would be found to be supported by an examination of the accused. This appears strange reasoning. It has therefore been suggested that the word ἀνακρίνας has regard to some process of torture by which a prisoner might be forced to confess the truth. But for this no sufficient support has been found. The noun ἀνάκρισις derived from this verb is employed (xxv. 26) for the enquiry before Agrippa. On the whole there seems quite as much to be said in favour of the *Textus Receptus* from internal evidence as can be brought against it by the evidence of MSS.

9. συνεπέθεντο δὲ καὶ οἱ Ἰουδαῖοι, *and the Jews also joined in the charge*, i.e. by language of their own reiterated the accusation. For the verb used of an attack made in common, cf. LXX. Ps. iii. 6, οἱ κύκλῳ συνεπιτιθέμενοι.

φάσκοντες ταῦτα οὕτως ἔχειν, *affirming that these things were so.* Tertullus had of course been instructed in his case by Ananias and the elders. Having supplied him with his arguments they now express their accord with what he has said.

10—21. St Paul's Answer to the Charge.

10. ἀπεκρίθη τε ὁ Παῦλος, *and Paul answered.* When the governor had given him leave to speak the Apostle addressed his defence to the points charged against him. He had not excited the people, nor been the leader of any body of Nazarenes, nor had he polluted the Temple.

ἐκ πολλῶν ἐτῶν, *for many years.* We have arrived in the history at about A.D. 58 or 59, and Felix had been made procurator in A.D. 52. So that 'many years' means about six or seven. But the governors were often recalled before they had held office so long. In verse 17 'many years' must be about four or five.

εὐθύμως τὰ περὶ ἐμαυτοῦ ἀπολογοῦμαι, *I cheerfully answer for myself.* St Paul was so far of good courage, because the experience of Felix, and his knowledge of Jewish manners and customs, would enable him to appreciate the statements which related to the Apostle's presence in Jerusalem.

11. δυναμένου σου ἐπιγνῶναι, *seeing that thou art able to take knowledge.* The Apostle refers to the acquaintance which Felix had gained of Jewish habits and customs and their festivals, and the manner of observance thereof. This knowledge would make him appreciate St Paul's statement.

οὐ πλείους εἰσίν μοι ἡμέραι δώδεκα, *it is not more than twelve days.* The time may be accounted for thus : the day of St Paul's arrival, the interview with James on the second day, five days may be given to the separate life in the Temple during the vow, then the hearing before the council, next day the conspiracy, the tenth day St Paul reached Cæsarea, and on the thirteenth day [which leaves five days (xxiv. 1), as Jews would reckon from the conspiracy to the hearing in Cæsarea] St Paul is before Felix. See Farrar's *St Paul*, II. 338 (note).

ἀφ᾽ ἧς ἀνέβην προσκυνήσων εἰς Ἱερουσαλήμ, *since I went up to Jerusalem for to worship.* The purpose of the Apostle was 'to worship.' Was it likely that he would try to profane the Temple? And προσκυνήσων expresses all the lowly adoration common among Orientals. The Apostle probably chose it for this reason. He would have Felix know that it was in a most reverent frame of mind that he came to the feast.

ἀφ᾽ ἧς (ἡμέρας) is the construction in full.

12. καὶ οὔτε ἐν τῷ ἱερῷ κ.τ.λ., *and they neither found me in the Temple disputing,* &c. The Apostle gives a flat denial to the charge of insurrection, and challenges them to prove any single point of it. He had not even entered into discussion with any man.

On St Paul's reply Chrysostom remarks: καὶ οὐδὲν εἶπεν ὧν εἶχεν εἰκότως εἰπεῖν· ὅτι ἐπεβούλευσαν· ὅτι κάτεσχον αὐτόν· ὅτι ἔνεδρον ἐποίησαν· ταῦτα γὰρ παρ᾽ ἐκείνων λέγεται γενέσθαι, παρὰ δὲ τούτου, καὶ κινδύνου ὄντος, οὐκ ἔτι· ἀλλὰ σιγᾷ καὶ μόνον ἀπολογεῖται καί τοι μυρία ἔχων εἰπεῖν.

ἢ ἐπίστασιν ποιοῦντα ὄχλου, *or causing a stir of the crowd.* Rev. Ver. 'stirring up a crowd.' The crowd had really been gathered by the Jews.

13. οὐδὲ παραστῆσαι δύνανταί σοι, *neither can they prove to thee.* The proof must be such as the Law required, not the mere multiplied assertions of the accusers. The verb παρίστημι implies a formal setting-forth of evidence, and is used by Josephus (*De vita sua* 6), of an *array of proof* which he has set forth to shew that his fellow-countrymen did not enter on a war till they were forced.

14. κατὰ τὴν ὁδὸν ἣν λέγουσιν αἵρεσιν, *after the Way which they call a sect.* So the rendering of αἵρεσις is made to correspond with verse 5 above. For 'the Way' meaning the Christian religion, see note on ix. 2.

οὕτω λατρεύω τῷ πατρῴῳ θεῷ, *so serve I the God of our fathers.* The verb λατρεύω is used of service which a man is bound to pay, and by its use, as well as by the reference to 'the God of our fathers,' the Apostle wants to shew that he has cast off no morsel of his old allegiance, has not severed himself from the ancestral faith of the Jewish nation.

πιστεύων...γεγραμμένοις, *believing all things which are according to the Law, and which are written in the Prophets.* The Apostle thus testifies to his complete acceptance of all the Jewish Scriptures. Sometimes the division is given as 'the Law, the Prophets, and the Psalms' (Luke xxiv. 44), but more frequently, as in the text, only two sections are named (cp. Matth. vii. 12, xi. 13, xxii. 40; Luke xvi. 16; John i. 45).

15. ἐλπίδα ἔχων, *having hope.* The way in which this hope is described, ἀνάστασιν μέλλειν ἔσεσθαι, explains the expression in xxiii. 6 περὶ ἐλπίδος καὶ ἀναστάσεως. The hope was *even* of the resurrection of the dead.

ἣν καὶ αὐτοὶ οὗτοι προσδέχονται, *which they themselves also look for.* Here the Apostle is of course alluding only to the Pharisees among his own people, but he puts them as representatives of the larger part of the nation. The Rev. Ver. renders 'which these also themselves look for.' If the Apostle employed the words in that sense he must have turned towards the body of Jews in the court rather than to the Sadducees and their spokesman.

ἀνάστασιν μέλλειν ἔσεσθαι, *that there shall be a resurrection.* St Paul adheres to the point which had before provoked the anger of Ananias and his party, and they must have been the more irritated because the words of the Apostle declare their opponents, the Pharisees, to be holding the true faith, and imply that such is the general belief of the Jewish people.

δικαίων τε καὶ ἀδίκων, *both of the just and unjust.* Speaking in the presence of Felix, the Apostle seems to have chosen words which might touch the conscience of the Procurator.

16. ἐν τούτῳ καὶ αὐτὸς ἀσκῶ, *herein also I exercise myself.* Herein, i.e. in the worship, faith and hope spoken of in the last two verses; while holding this belief, and because I hold it, I try to keep my conscience clear. 'I exercise myself' that I may, by constant training and striving, at length get near to what I aim after.

ἀπρόσκοπον συνείδησιν ἔχειν, *to have a conscience void of offence.* The primary meaning of ἀπρόσκοπος is found Ecclus. xxxii. (xxxv.) 21 where ὁδὸς ἀπρόσκοπος=a plain way, one where there are no stumblers nor anything to stumble at. A man of whose conscience the figure could be used was neither likely to be a profaner of the Temple nor a mover of sedition. The adverb διαπαντός has a very emphatic place as the last word in the verse.

17. δι' ἐτῶν δὲ πλειόνων, *now after many years.* St Paul had come to Jerusalem on the return from his second missionary journey in A.D. 53. It was now A.D. 58, so that his absence had lasted four or five years (see note on verse 10).

ἐλεημοσύνας ποιήσων εἰς τὸ ἔθνος μου, *to bring alms to my nation.* These consisted of the money which had been collected in the Churches of Macedonia and Achaia at St Paul's request, and which is often alluded to in his Epistles (cp. 1 Cor. xvi. 1; Rom. xv. 26; 2 Cor. viii. 4, &c.). There could be no desire to wound the feelings of the Jews in a man who had come for such a purpose. It is noticeable too that he describes the alms as not for the Christians only, but for his nation, conveying by the word the impression of his great regard for all the Jews.

St Paul can say ἐλεημοσύνας ποιεῖν, for though the gifts were not his own, he was the cause of their being sent.

καὶ προσφοράς, *and offerings.* These were the sacrifices connected with the vow which he had undertaken. They must be offered in the Temple, and the offerer was not likely to be one who thought of profaning the holy place.

18. ἐν αἷς, *amidst which,* i.e. engaged in offering these oblations.

εὑρόν με ἡγνισμένον, *they found me purified,* i.e. abstaining from all things forbidden by the Law of the Nazirites (see Num. vi. 3—8). A man who religiously purified himself could by no means be suspected as likely to defile the Temple. All things tell the same way.

οὐ μετὰ ὄχλου οὐδὲ μετὰ θορύβου, *neither with multitude nor with tumult.* The two things that would be steps towards profanity in such a place, would have been to gather a crowd and then to raise an uproar. Nothing of the sort could be laid to Paul's charge.

τινὲς δὲ ἀπὸ τῆς Ἀσίας Ἰουδαῖοι, *but there were certain Jews of Asia.* It was from the Asiatic Jews, perhaps those from Ephesus, that the uproar had at first originated. It would appear also that part of Tertullus' argument was derived from their information. Of these Asiatic Jews St Paul was now about to speak, but he checks himself, and does not say any word against them, only that they ought to have been here to explain the offence for which he had been assailed.

19. καὶ κατηγορεῖν, *and to make accusation.* They had set the cry against him, yet did not come to say what he had done wrong. They were probably on their way home, now that the feast was over.

20. ἢ αὐτοὶ οὗτοι εἰπάτωσαν, *or let these men themselves say,* i.e. Ananias and his party. The assailants of St Paul were of two classes, first the Asiatic Jews, who were furious against him because of his preaching among the Gentiles in their cities, then those in Jerusalem who hated him for preaching the resurrection. He challenges them both, and when the former do not appear, he turns to the other.

τί εὗρον ἀδίκημα, *what evildoing they found.*   Paul uses ἀδίκημα as
being the word which the Sadducees would use, not adopting it himself.

στάντος μου ἐπὶ τοῦ συνεδρίου, *when I stood before the council.*   Up
to the moment when in the presence of the council he had spoken of
the resurrection, and so produced a division in the assembly, there was
no act of St Paul which had to do with any disturbance.   The tumult
in the Temple and while he was speaking from the tower-stairs was all
caused by the Jewish mob.

21. ἢ περὶ μιᾶς ταύτης φωνῆς, *except it be for this one voice,* i.e. this
exclamation or cry.   From xxiii. 6 we can see that St Paul raised his
voice when he mentioned the resurrection.

ἤ=other than.   τί...ἤ=τί ἄλλο ἤ.

22—27. ADJOURNMENT OF THE CAUSE.   FELIX'S TREATMENT OF ST
PAUL.

22. ἀκριβέστερον εἰδὼς τὰ περὶ τῆς ὁδοῦ, *having more perfect
knowledge of the Way.*

On ἡ ὁδὸς=the Christian religion, see on ix. 2.   Felix was more
likely to understand something of the relations between Judaism and
Christianity, because he had a Jewish wife, Drusilla, daughter of
Herod Agrippa I., one who had been brought by her position into
connexion with the movements of the time.

ὅταν Λυσίας ὁ χιλίαρχος καταβῇ, *when Lysias the chief captain
shall come down.*   There had been nothing said in the letter of Lysias,
so far as we have it, about his coming to Cæsarea, but no doubt he
went often between Jerusalem and the residence of the governor.   The
language of this verse gives some support to the genuineness of verse 7.
(See note there.)

διαγνώσομαι τὰ καθ' ὑμᾶς, *I will determine your matters.*   On
διαγιγνώσκω see above, xxiii. 15.

23. διαταξάμενος τῷ ἑκατοντάρχῃ, *having commanded the centurion.*
It might perhaps be one of the two whom Lysias had put in charge
of the conveyance of Paul (xxiii. 23).   One might be appointed to go
on to Cæsarea, while the other returned with the larger part of the
convoy from Antipatris.

τηρεῖσθαι αὐτόν, *that he should be kept in charge.*   τηρεῖσθαι only
conveys the idea of safe keeping, not of severe detention, and it is
clear that for some reason Felix shewed himself well-disposed towards
the Apostle.   Either his conscience moved him or his hope of gain,
or perhaps the flattery and compliments of Tertullus had overshot
their mark.

ἔχειν τε ἄνεσιν, *and should have indulgence,* i.e. the strict prison
rules were to be relaxed in his favour.

For ἄνεσις cf. 1 Esdras iv. 62, ἔδωκεν αὐτοῖς ἄφεσιν καὶ ἄνεσιν.

καὶ μηδένα κωλύειν, *and that he should hinder no one.* Here is a change of subject in the sentence. Παῦλον was the subject to the two first infinitives, to κωλύειν the subject is τὸν ἑκατοντάρχην.

τῶν ἰδίων αὐτοῦ, *of his friends.* More literally 'of his own people.' Here from our limited knowledge we are only able to think of Philip the Evangelist, who would be particularly a friend of St Paul; but he had been more than once before in Cæsarea, and he had no doubt made himself known there as in other places. Those unnamed disciples of Cæsarea (xxi. 16) would be among the persons who had a warm interest in St Paul, and it is clear from St Luke's language that there were friends at hand and ready to visit the Apostle when they were allowed.

ὑπηρετεῖν αὐτῷ, *to minister unto him.* ὑπηρετεῖ implies the doing of those services of which a prisoner even under such liberal conditions must ever stand in need. They would be his means of communication with the outer world. And the cupidity of Felix may have suggested that through these friends the means might be supplied for purchasing the Apostle's release.

24. μετὰ δὲ ἡμέρας τινὰς κ.τ.λ., *but after certain days Felix came,* &c. Felix did not always reside in Cæsarea. After the first hearing of St Paul's cause he had gone away for a time, but on his return he sent for the Apostle to question him on his doctrine. Perhaps those words about the resurrection of the just and unjust had made him uneasy.

σὺν Δρουσίλλῃ τῇ ἰδίᾳ γυναικὶ οὔσῃ Ἰουδαίᾳ, *with Drusilla his wife who was a Jewess.* She was a daughter of Herod Agrippa I. and so sister of Agrippa II. and of Bernice. She had formerly been married to Azizus, king of Emesa, but had been induced by Felix to leave her husband and become his wife. Though she had been only six years of age when her father died (Acts xii. 23) she may have heard of the death of James the brother of John, and the marvellous delivery of St Peter from prison: for such matters would be talked of long after they had happened, and perhaps her father's sudden death may have been ascribed by some to God's vengeance for what he had done against the Christians. Her marriage with the Gentile Felix shewed that she was by no means a strict Jewess, and what she had heard of Jewish opposition to St Paul's teaching may have made her, as well as her husband, desirous to hear him.

μετεπέμψατο τὸν Παῦλον, *sent for Paul.* The Apostle was lodged in some part of the procurator's official residence (see xxiii. 35 note) and so was close at hand.

καὶ ἤκουσεν αὐτοῦ περὶ τῆς εἰς Χριστὸν Ἰησοῦν πίστεως, *and heard him concerning the faith in Christ Jesus.* The addition of Ἰησοῦν supported by the oldest MSS. gives force to the sentence. What St Paul would urge was not only a belief in the Christ, for whose coming all Jews were looking, but a belief that Jesus of Nazareth was the Messiah whom they had so long expected.

25. διαλεγομένου δὲ αὐτοῦ κ.τ.λ., *and as he reasoned of righteousness and temperance and the judgment to come.* It was no barren faith which St Paul commended, but was to have its fruits in the life. Felix perhaps expected some philosophical dissertation on the subject of the resurrection, and the life after death. His own conduct, of which Tacitus (*Ann.* XII. 54, *Hist.* v. 9) speaks as mean and cruel and profligate, would make the subjects on which St Paul addressed him peculiarly disturbing. For what if this man's teaching should be true?

ἔμφοβος γενόμενος ὁ Φῆλιξ ἀπεκρίθη, *becoming terrified Felix answered.* It can hardly be conceived that St Paul was ignorant of the character of those to whom he was speaking. Felix had been in office long enough to be well known. And the Apostle's themes were exactly those by which he could find the joints in the procurator's harness. Of 'righteousness' his life's history shews no trace, and for 'temperance,' i.e. self-control, the presence of Drusilla by his side proved that he had no regard. Well might such a man be full of fear at the thought, as St Paul would urge it home, of the judgment after death. But the influence of his terror passed away, for we do not read that the Apostle ever beheld such signs of penitence as led him to quiet the terror, by preaching Christ as the atonement for sin.

ἔμφοβος is used, 1 Macc. xiii. 2, to describe the terror of the Jews at Tryphon's invasion, εἶδε τὸν λαὸν ὅτι ἐστὶν ἔντρομος καὶ ἔμφοβος.

τὸ νῦν ἔχον, *for the present.* Cf. for the phrase Tobit vii. 11, ἀλλὰ τὸ νῦν ἔχον ἡδέως γίνου, 'Nevertheless for the present be merry' (A.V.).

καιρὸν μεταλαβὼν μετακαλέσομαί σε, *when I have a convenient season, I will call for thee.* The convenient season never arrived. Felix did not change his conduct. When two years more of his rule were ended and he was superseded by Festus, the Jews in Cæsarea brought an accusation against him before Nero, and had it not been for his brother Pallas' influence he would have been punished for his cruelty and injustice. We have no record of how long he lived after his recall from Cæsarea.

26. ἅμα καὶ ἐλπίζων κ.τ.λ., *at the same time also hoping that money would be given him by Paul.* He had heard the Apostle speak of the contributions which he had gathered for the Jews in Jerusalem. His thought would naturally be that if he could raise money for the needs of others, he could do so for his own release.

διὸ καί, *wherefore also,* i.e. this was a second reason why Paul was frequently sent for, that he might, if he were disposed, offer Felix a bribe. The first reason was to hear what the Apostle had to say about the faith in Christ.

ὡμίλει αὐτῷ, *he communed with him.* ὁμιλέω implies that he established a degree of friendly intercourse with his prisoner. Thus the way was made smooth for any proposal about the terms of release, had Paul been inclined to make one.

27. διετίας δὲ πληρωθείσης, *but when two years were fulfilled,* i.e. fully completed. It may be that St Luke intends to indicate by his

expression, that it was not a reckoning of time such as was usual
among the Jews, where portions of a year were sometimes counted for
a whole, but that the Apostle's detention endured for two years
complete.

ἔλαβεν διάδοχον ὁ Φῆλιξ Πόρκιον Φῆστον, *Porcius Festus came into
Felix' room.* Lit. 'Felix received Porcius Festus as a successor.'
Festus was made governor by Nero probably in A.D. 60 and died in
about two years. Josephus (*B. J.* II. 14. 1) gives him a far better
character than his predecessor, but he had the same kind of difficulties
to deal with in the outbreaks of the populace and the bands of
assassins with which the country was infested. (Jos. *Ant.* xx. 8. 10.)

θέλων τε χάριτα καταθέσθαι τοῖς Ἰουδαίοις ὁ Φῆλιξ, *and Felix desiring to gain* (lit. to store up) *favour with the Jews.* What Felix particularly desired at this time was to blunt the anger which the Jews
(especially those of Cæsarea) felt towards him, that they might be less
bitter in their charges against him on his recall. And so he used Paul
as his 'Mammon of unrighteousness' and left him detained that he
might make himself friends thereby.

κατέλιπε τὸν Παῦλον δεδεμένον, *left Paul bound* (R.V. *in bonds*).
This seems to indicate that before his departure Felix withdrew the
indulgence which had been previously granted to Paul, and put him in
bonds, so as to give to his successor the impression, which the Jews
desired, that he was deserving of punishment. It would be very
interesting to know what St Paul did during the two years that he
was kept at Cæsarea. Various conjectures have been ventured on, but
none with any ground of certainty. Some, accepting him as the
author of the Epistle to the Hebrews, point to this period as the time
of its composition. Others assign to this imprisonment those letters
of the Apostle which speak so much of his bonds, viz. to the Ephesians,
the Philippians, the Colossians and Philemon, but the evidence in
favour of Rome as the place whence they were written seems far to
outweigh all that can be said on behalf of Cæsarea. Our only reflection on such a gap as this in the history of St Paul's work must be
that the Acts was not intended to be a narrative of any man's labours,
but how God employed now this servant, now that, for the establish-
ment of the Kingdom of Christ. The remembrance of this will prevent
us seeking from the book what it was not meant to give.

CHAPTER XXV.

Readings varying from the *Text. recept.*

2.   οἱ ἀρχιερεῖς with אABCEL.   *Vulg.* 'principes sacerdotum.'

5.   ἄτοπον after ἀνδρὶ with אABCE.   *Vulg.* 'crimen.'

6.   ἡμέρας οὐ πλείους ὀκτὼ ἢ δέκα with אABC.   *Vulg.* 'dies non
amplius quam octo aut decem.'

7.   κατὰ τοῦ Παύλου omitted with אABC.   Not represented in
Vulg.

8. τοῦ Παύλου ἀπολογουμένου with אABC. *Vulg.* 'Paulo ratio-nem reddente.'

16. εἰς ἀπώλειαν omitted with אABCE. *Vulg.* has in some texts 'damnare,' in others 'donare' for χαρίζεσθαι.

18. πονηράν added at the end of the verse with AC. *Vulg.* 'malum.' See notes.

22. ἔφη omitted with אAB. *Vulg.* has 'dixit.'

    ὁ δὲ omitted with אAB. *Vulg.* does not represent it.

25. κατελαβόμην with אABCE. *Vulg.* 'comperi.'

    αὐτόν after πέμπειν omitted with אABC. *Vulg.* does not repre-sent it.

26. τί γράψω with אABC. *Vulg.* 'quid scribam.'

CH. XXV. 1—12. ARRIVAL OF FESTUS. PAUL'S CAUSE HEARD BEFORE HIM. PAUL APPEALS TO THE EMPEROR.

1. ἐπιβὰς τῇ ἐπαρχίᾳ, *was come into the province.* This may either mean 'when he had reached Cæsarea,' to which, as the seaport, he would naturally come first; or, with margin of the Rev. Vers., 'when he had entered upon his province.' The former seems to be the prefer-able sense because of what follows.

ἐπαρχία, which only occurs in N. T. here and in xxiii. 34, is common in the Apocryphal Acts. Cf. *Acta Petri et Pauli,* §§ 3, 5, &c.

μετὰ τρεῖς ἡμέρας ἀνέβη, *after three days he went up.* Festus took a very short time to make himself acquainted with what would be his principal residence, and then went up to visit the Capital.

2. ἐνεφάνισάν τε, *and they informed.* The verb indicates that the proceedings here assumed a legal form. It was no mere mention in any irregular way, but a definite charge was made, no doubt in the same terms which Tertullus had used before.

See on this verb above, xxiii. 15, 22, xxiv. 1.

οἱ ἀρχιερεῖς, *the chief priests.* No doubt Ananias, as before, was the leader of the accusation, but he got others of his own class to support him in Jerusalem. He was their representative when the hearing was in Cæsarea.

καὶ οἱ πρῶτοι τῶν Ἰουδαίων, *and the principal men of the Jews.* The wealthiest men of the nation belonged to the party of the Sadducees.

3. αἰτούμενοι χάριν κατ᾽ αὐτοῦ, *desiring favour against him,* i. e. they begged that their case might have some special consideration. They were many and rich; the accused man was alone and an obscure person, and it was much easier to bring one man from Cæsarea, than for their whole body to undertake a journey from Jerusalem thither. No doubt too they hoped that with a new governor their influence and good position would not be without weight.

ἐνέδραν ποιοῦντες ἀνελεῖν αὐτὸν κατὰ τὴν ὁδόν, *laying wait in the way to kill him.* They still adhered to their plan of assassination, than which no crime was more common at this time in Judæa. Perhaps too those men who had bound themselves by a vow, though they had been forced to break it, yet felt dissatisfied that Paul was still alive.

4. ἀπεκρίθη τηρεῖσθαι τὸν Παῦλον εἰς Καισάρειαν, *he answered that Paul was kept in charge at Cæsarea.* The governor's position was that the prisoner had been placed by his predecessor in a certain state of custody, and that this could not be interfered with.

ἑαυτὸν δὲ μέλλειν ἐν τάχει ἐκπορεύεσθαι, *and that he himself was about to depart thither shortly.* A governor newly arrived must move about actively, and could not remain long even in the capital. To have waited till all the arrangements, which the accusing party were supposed to be ready to make, were complete, would have consumed time, which must be occupied in learning the details of his provincial charge.

For ἐν τάχει, cf. xii. 7, xxii. 18, above.

5. οἱ οὖν ἐν ὑμῖν...δυνατοί, *let them which are of power among you.* The words of Festus do not refer to whether some of them could go to Cæsarea or not, but to the character of those who should go down, that they should be men of influence and character, such as would fitly represent the powerful body who appealed to him.

συγκαταβάντες, *going down with me.* For they were evidently wealthy persons, whose companionship on the journey might be no discredit to the governor. Festus was no doubt willing to conciliate the influential people in the nation, though he had refused to break through a regulation of his predecessor at their request.

εἴ τι ἐστὶν ἐν τῷ ἀνδρὶ ἄτοπον, *if there is anything amiss in the man.* For ἄτοπον in this sense cf. Luke xxiii. 41; also LXX. Job xxxvi. 21; Prov. xxx. 20; 2 Macc. xiv. 23, καὶ ἔπραττεν οὐθὲν ἄτοπον 'and he did no hurt' (A.V.).

6. ἡμέρας οὐ πλείους ὀκτὼ ἢ δέκα, *not more than eight or ten days.* This seems a more likely reading than that of the *Text. recept.* It is more probable that the writer would use words to mark the shortness of the stay than a form which would seem to describe ten days as a long residence at Jerusalem. Festus was evidently full of business and anxious to get it done.

For the omission of ἤ after the comparative πλείους before numerals cf. iv. 22, xxiii. 13, 21, xxiv. 11.

τῇ ἐπαύριον, *the next day.* The Jewish authorities must have accepted the governor's invitation, and have gone down along with him, so that the hearing could begin at once. Probably they would think it good policy to join the party of Festus, as they might turn their opportunities on the journey to some account against St Paul.

7. περιέστησαν αὐτὸν οἱ...κ.τ.λ., *the Jews which had come down from Jerusalem stood round about him.* They were eager to set upon him and so compassed him about on every side.

πολλὰ καὶ βαρέα αἰτιώματα καταφέροντες, *bringing against him many and grievous charges.* In the two years lapse of time they had gathered up every rumour they could collect, and these they brought forward, even though they could not support them by evidence.

For καταφέρειν of an accusation cf. LXX. Gen. xxxvii. 1 κατήνεγκαν δὲ κατὰ Ἰωσὴφ ψόγον πονηρόν.

8. τοῦ Παύλου ἀπολογουμένου, *while Paul said in his defence.* He offered an ἀπολογία for himself. He did not make a defence against the unsubstantiated charges, but alluded only to those points on which they would try to prove their case, i.e. his alleged attempt to defile the Temple, his breaches of the Jewish Law, and any insurrectionary outbreaks, in which the accusers would try to prove him a leader, and which might be construed into opposition to the Roman power. On this last his accusers would lay most stress. St Luke has only given us the three heads of St Paul's *Apologia.*

οὔτε εἰς τὸν νόμον τῶν Ἰουδαίων, κ.τ.λ., *neither against the law of the Jews...have I sinned at all.* The accusation on the former occasion had not dwelt on this point, but in the course of two years they had discovered that the Apostle had taught among the Gentiles that circumcision was no necessary door for admission to Christianity, and this they would construe into an offence against the Jewish Law.

9. ὁ Φῆστος δὲ θέλων τοῖς Ἰουδαίοις χάριν καταθέσθαι, *but Festus desiring to gain favour with the Jews.* See above, xxiv. 27. Though he had not consented to their request when in Jerusalem Festus now went some way towards doing so by his question to Paul.

θέλεις εἰς Ἱεροσόλυμα ἀναβὰς κ.τ.λ., *wilt thou go up to Jerusalem, &c.* What Festus proposed was equivalent to acquitting the Apostle of any charge which would come under Roman law. He is therefore appealed to on the other accusations. The offences against the Law of the Jews and against the Temple must be heard before the Sanhedrin. Would Paul accept an acquittal on one count and submit to a trial before his own people on the rest? And Festus would be present to see that right was done.

10. ἐπὶ τοῦ βήματος Καίσαρος ἑστώς εἰμι, *I am standing before Cæsar's judgment seat.* The Roman authorities had taken charge of him and had kept him in custody for two years. Of this he reminds the governor, and refuses to be turned over to another tribunal, where he would have for judges, if he ever were allowed to live till his trial, those persons who had been cognizant of the plot to murder him.

οὗ με δεῖ κρίνεσθαι, *where I ought to be judged,* because I am a Roman citizen.

ὡς καὶ σὺ κάλλιον ἐπιγινώσκεις, *as thou also very well knowest.* St Paul does not mean to say that Festus is to be blamed for his proposal. Probably he saw that the governor was acting with a view to

conciliate the Jews. But he intends to say that after all that the
governor has heard, any man would say at once that there was no
case against the prisoner.

The comparative force in κάλλιον may be brought out somewhat thus,
'better than from your proposal to turn me over to Jews you would
appear to know.'

11. εἰ μὲν οὖν ἀδικῶ, *if then I am a wrong-doer.* He has asserted
that he was innocent so far as the Jews are concerned. If there be
anything against him, it is for the civil jurisdiction of Rome, not for
the religious tribunal at Jerusalem, to decide upon.

εἰ δὲ οὐδέν ἐστιν ὧν, *but if there be none of these things whereof,* i.e.
if they be all nothing, all without truth; cf. on οὐδέν ἐστιν, chap. xxi.
24 above.

οὐδείς με δύναται αὐτοῖς χαρίσασθαι, *no man can deliver me unto
them,* i.e. there is no authority or power by which I may be given into
their hands.

χαρίσασθαι properly signifies 'to grant us a favour,' and the use of
it by St Paul seems to shew that he saw through all that Festus was
doing, and how he was seeking (verse 9) to ingratiate himself with the
Jews. For other instances of this verb, cf. 2 Macc. iii. 31, 33, and in
the signification of 'to make a present,' 2 Macc. iv. 32.

Καίσαρα ἐπικαλοῦμαι, *I appeal unto Cæsar,* the final tribunal for
a Roman citizen being the hearing of the Emperor himself.

On St Paul's appeal Chrysostom says: ἀλλ' εἴποι ἄν τις ἐνταῦθα· καὶ
τίνος ἕνεκεν ἀκούσας ὅτι καὶ ἐν Ῥώμῃ σε δεῖ μαρτυρῆσαι τὰ περὶ ἐμοῦ, ὡς
ἀπιστῶν ταῦτα ἐποίει; μὴ γένοιτο, ἀλλὰ καὶ σφόδρα πιστεύων. μᾶλλον
οὖν πειράζοντος ἦν τὸ θαρρεῖν ἐκείνῃ τῇ ἀποφάσει, καὶ εἰς μυρίους ἑαυτὸν
ἐμβάλλειν κινδύνους, καὶ λέγειν, ἴδωμεν εἰ δύναται ὁ θεὸς καὶ οὕτως ἐξελέσθαι με. ἀλλ' οὐ ποιεῖ τοῦτο Παῦλος ἀλλὰ τὰ καθ' ἑαυτὸν πάντα εἰσφέρει τὸ
πᾶν ἐπιτρέπων τῷ θεῷ.

12. συλλαλήσας μετὰ τοῦ συμβουλίου, *having conferred with the
council.* Having taken the opinion of those who sat as assessors with
him. Such persons would be specially needed for a new governor,
and the governors of Judæa were changed frequently. Of the existence
of such assessors in the provinces, see Suetonius *Tib.* 33; *Galba* 19.

**13—22. FESTUS CONSULTS KING AGRIPPA ABOUT HIS PRISONER.
AGRIPPA WISHES TO HEAR PAUL'S DEFENCE.**

13. ἡμερῶν δὲ διαγενομένων. For διαγίνεσθαι, of the lapse of time,
cf. Mark xvi. 1; Acts xxvii. 9.

Ἀγρίππας ὁ βασιλεύς, *king Agrippa.* This was Herod Agrippa II.,
son of Herod Agrippa I., and consequently a great-grandson of Herod
the Great. He was therefore brother of Bernice and Drusilla. On
account of his youth he was not appointed to succeed his father when
he died. But after a time the Roman emperor gave him the kingdom
of Chalcis, from which he was subsequently transferred to govern the
tetrarchies formerly held by Philip and Lysanias, and was named

king thereof. His kingdom was afterwards increased by the grant of
other cities which Nero gave him. At the fall of Jerusalem he retired
to Rome, with his sister Bernice, and there died A.D. 100. He had
sided with the Romans in the war against the Holy City. Festus was
likely to avail himself of an opportunity of consulting Agrippa, for he
would expect to be soundly advised by him on any question of Jewish
law.

καὶ Βερνίκη, *and Bernice.* She was the eldest daughter of Herod
Agrippa I. She had first been married to her uncle Herod, king of
Chalcis. Her connexion with her brother Agrippa II. was spoken of
both by Roman and Jewish writers as immoral. She was subsequently
married to Polemon, king of Cilicia, but soon left him and lived with
Agrippa II. in Rome.

κατήντησαν εἰς Καισάρειαν ἀσπασάμενοι τὸν Φῆστον, *arrived at
Cæsarea, and saluted* (lit. having saluted) *Festus.* The Greek seems
to imply that they had met and paid their salutation to Festus before
arriving at Cæsarea. If this had occurred, yet still the vassal-king
Agrippa would probably feel bound to pay a formal visit of welcome to
the representative of Rome in Cæsarea, the official residence.

15. οἱ ἀρχιερεῖς, *the chief priests.* See above on verse 2, and on
ἐμφανίζω also.

καταδίκην, *judgment,* but always with the sense of adverse judgment.
Hence Rev. Ver. 'sentence.' The word implies that those who asked
thought there could be but one opinion and that a condemnatory
sentence might be at once pronounced, even by the newly arrived
governor.

16. χαρίζεσθαί τινα ἄνθρωπον, *to give up any man.* See above,
verse 11, on the force of χαρίζεσθαι. The language throughout shews
that the Jews thought the influence of their party was enough to gain
from Festus the condemnation of this so obscure a prisoner, whatever
might be the merits of his case.

τόπον τε ἀπολογίας λάβοι, *and have had opportunity to make his
defence* (lit. 'place of defence'). On τόπος in this sense cf. Ecclus. iv.
5 μὴ δῷς τόπον ἀνθρώπῳ καταράσασθαί σε. See also Rom. xv. 23 where
'having no more place in these parts' signifies 'no further opportunity
for preaching the Gospel.'
The two verbs ἔχοι and λάβοι are the only two cases of an optative
after πρὶν ἤ in the N. T.

17. συνελθόντων οὖν αὐτῶν ἐνθάδε, *therefore when they were come
together here,* i.e. the accusers from Jerusalem and the accused who
was in custody. Then they were κατὰ πρόσωπον, as the Roman law
required.

18. περὶ οὗ σταθέντες οἱ κατήγοροι, *concerning whom the accusers
when they stood up.* Or there may be the same sense in the expression
as in περιέστησαν of verse 7, 'When they stood round about him'
eager each to give emphasis to the charge.

οὐδεμίαν αἰτίαν ἔφερον ὧν ἐγὼ ὑπενόουν πονηράν, *they brought no evil accusation of such things as I supposed.* With αἰτία πονηρά may be compared ῥαδιούργημα πονηρόν above, chap. xviii. 14.

19. περὶ τῆς ἰδίας δεισιδαιμονίας, *concerning their own religion.* Cf. St Paul's use of the cognate adjective, when he was speaking to the Athenians. The word is one which might be employed without offence by any one in speaking of a worship with which he did not agree. Addressing Agrippa, Festus would not wish to say a word that might annoy, any more than St Paul wished to irritate the Athenians by his speech.

περί τινος Ἰησοῦ, *concerning one Jesus.* Neither in the hearing of the cause before Felix nor when Festus made his inquiry, does St Luke record any mention of the name of Jesus, but it is clear from the explanation here given that not only had Paul stated the doctrine of the Resurrection generally, which the Pharisees accepted, but had also asserted in proof of it that Jesus had risen and 'become the firstfruits of them that sleep.'

20. ἀπορούμενος δὲ ἐγὼ τὴν περὶ τούτων ζήτησιν, *and I being perplexed how to inquire concerning these things.* The whole subject would be strange to Festus, and when he found that some Jews in part at least agreed with St Paul, while others of them were his bitter opponents, he could find no better plan than to turn to a Jew for an explanation. He did not himself know how to conduct an inquiry on such a subject, and yet the Jews' religion, being now allowed by the Empire, must have its causes adjudicated on.

21. τηρηθῆναι αὐτὸν εἰς τὴν τοῦ Σεβαστοῦ διάγνωσιν, *to be kept for the decision of the emperor.* τηρεῖσθαι is used above, xxiv. 23, where the centurion was commanded to 'keep' Paul. He desired to be under the care of the Roman authorities until his case could be properly heard. Σεβαστός, the title given first to Octavianus, was afterwards conferred on his successors, and so came to mean 'His Imperial Majesty,' whoever might be on the throne. The present Σεβαστός was Nero. In the noun διάγνωσις we have a word which implies 'thorough inquiry,' which a final appeal was supposed always to receive.

22. ἐβουλόμην καὶ αὐτὸς τοῦ ἀνθρώπου ἀκοῦσαι, *I was wishing* [Rev. Ver. 'could wish'] *also to hear the man myself.* Agrippa intimates that he knew something of the Apostle and his labours, as indeed was not unlikely, and that in consequence he had for some time been desirous to see and hear St Paul.

23—27. ASSEMBLY OF THE COURT, AND ADDRESS OF FESTUS.

23. μετὰ πολλῆς φαντασίας, *with great pomp.* The children follow in the steps of their father, who formerly had sat on his throne in Cæsarea arrayed in royal apparel, to listen to the flatteries of the Tyrian deputation (xii. 21).

φαντασία is found only here in N.T., and in this sense is very rare anywhere.

ἀκροατήριον, *the place of hearing.* The word is found nowhere else in N.T. It was no doubt some special room attached to the governor's palace, where causes were tried. In classical Greek it is found in the sense of 'a lecture-room.'

χιλιάρχοις, *chief captains.* The word is frequent for the 'praefectus' of a Roman cohort.

ἀνδράσιν τοῖς κατ' ἐξοχήν, *the principal men.* The word ἐξοχή is used of any thing which is prominent. Cf. LXX. Job xxxix. 28 ἐπ' ἐξοχῇ πέτρας, 'on the crag of the rock.' Hence in the text of persons who are prominent. But the phrase is not common.

24. ἐνέτυχόν μοι, *made suit to me.* In all other places of N. T. ἐντυγχάνειν is used of 'making intercession' to God. In the LXX. it is also used thus, Wisdom viii. 21 ἐνέτυχον τῷ κυρίῳ; but also very frequently of those who come before some authority with a complaint, as the Jews did against St Paul. See 1 Macc. viii. 32, x. 61, 63, 64, xi. 25; 2 Macc. iv. 36.

καὶ ἐνθάδε, *and also here.* No doubt the Sadducees from Jerusalem had been able in the course of two years to work up a great deal of feeling against Paul among their party in Cæsarea. So when Festus came he was appealed to by the great men of the residential city as well as by those from Jerusalem.

25. ἐγὼ δὲ κατελαβόμην, *but I found.* Cf. above, verses 18 and 19.

μηδὲν ἄξιον αὐτὸν θανάτου πεπραχέναι, *that he had committed nothing worthy of death.* To ask for the life of a prisoner because of some offence against the religious observances of the Jews would be absurd in the eyes of the Roman procurator, and the more so when the accused was a Roman citizen.

Σεβαστόν, *the emperor.* See on verse 21.

26. τῷ κυρίῳ, *to my lord.* Octavianus by an edict forbade the title 'Lord' to be given to him. The practice had its rise from parasites; but you find 'Dominus' often used in Pliny's letters to Trajan, so that not many emperors were like Octavian.

ἐφ' ὑμῶν, *before you.* Spoken with a glance towards the chief priests and great personages who were present on the bench.

καὶ μάλιστα ἐπὶ σοῦ, *and especially before thee,* i.e. as one most likely to be able to clear up the difficulties which I feel about the prisoner.

τῆς ἀνακρίσεως γενομένης, *the examination having been made.* The English of A.V. is very idiomatic, 'after examination had.' In classical Greek ἀνάκρισις is used of a preliminary examination of a cause before the Archon, to see whether there is ground for proceeding further. So Festus uses the technical term in its proper sense.

σχῶ τί γράψω, *I may have somewhat to write.* Lit. 'what I may write.' With this use of the interrogative τί, where in classical Greek a relative would have been used, cf. Matth. x. 19, δοθήσεται ὑμῖν...τί λαλήσετε.

27. ἄλογον, *unreasonable*. In this sense, which is quite the classical usage of the word, ἄλογος is not found again in N. T.

πέμποντα, *when sending*. This may mean 'when I am sending,' and if so taken, then the accusative participle following the dative pronoun μοι may be compared with Heb. ii. 10, ἔπρεπεν αὐτῷ...ἀγαγόντα, and the construction is not uncommon with words like ἔξεστι. But πέμποντα may be general in its application and mean 'that any one when sending, &c.,' and no doubt it would be as unreasonable in the case of any other person as of Festus.

CHAPTER XXVI.

Readings varying from the *Text. recept.*

3. σου after δέομαι omitted with אABE. Not represented in *Vulg.*

6. εἰς τοὺς πατέρας ἡμῶν with אABCE. *Vulg.* 'ad patres nostros.'

7. τῶν before Ἰουδαίων omitted with אABCEHILP.

βασιλεῦ at the end of the verse, omitting βασιλεῦ Ἀγρίππα with אBCEI. *Vulg.* puts 'rex' at the end.

12. καὶ after ἐν οἷς omitted with אABCEI. Not represented in *Vulg.*

14. λέγουσαν πρός με with אABCI omitting καὶ λέγουσαν afterwards. The *Vulg.* has only 'loquentem mihi.'

15. ὁ δὲ κύριος εἶπεν with אABCEIL. *Vulg.* 'Dominus autem dixit'

25. ὁ δὲ Παῦλος with אABE. *Vulg.* ' et Paulus.'

28. ποιῆσαι for γενέσθαι with אAB. *Vulg.* 'fieri' representing γενέσθαι.

29. εἶπεν omitted with אAB. Not represented in *Vulg.*

μεγάλῳ for πολλῷ with אAB. *Vulg.* 'magno.'

30. καὶ ταῦτα εἰπόντος αὐτοῦ omitted with אAB. Not represented in *Vulg.*

Ch. XXVI. 1—23. PAUL'S DEFENCE BEFORE AGRIPPA.

1. ἀπελογεῖτο, *made his defence*. The verb is the same as before (xix. 33, xxiv. 10, xxv. 8), and intimates that what is coming is an *apologia*. St Luke here as in other places notices the gesture of the speaker (ἐκτείνας τὴν χεῖρα).

2. ἥγημαι ἐμαυτὸν μακάριον, *I think myself happy*. Because Agrippa was sure to understand much of the feeling imported into the case which would be entirely obscure to a Roman magistrate. Paul would thus be able to make his position clear, and get it explained through Agrippa to the Roman authorities.

ἐπὶ σοῦ, *before thee.* So xxiv. 19, and frequently in N.T. ἐπί with genitive in this sense is also found in classical Greek, but not so commonly with a personal pronoun. For an example of the use, cf. *Acta Pauli et Theclæ*, 16, εἰπάτω ἐπὶ σοῦ τίνος ἕνεκεν ταῦτα διδάσκει.

3. μάλιστα γνώστην ὄντα σε, *especially because thou art expert.* Some have joined μάλιστα with γνώστην, 'because thou art especially expert.' But there is nothing to shew that this was so. He knew, as other Jews knew, the character and meaning of Jewish customs, but nothing more.

γνώστης is used most frequently in the LXX. of those diviners and dealers with familiar spirits spoken of in the historical books. Cf. 1 Sam. xxviii. 3, 9 ; 2 Kings xxi. 6, xxiii. 24. Also in Susanna, verse 42, we have ὁ θεὸς αἰώνιος ὁ τῶν κρυπτῶν γνώστης.

Here Chrysostom says: καίτοιγε εἰ συνῄδει ἑαυτῷ φοβηθῆναι ἐχρῆν παρὰ τῷ πάντα εἰδότι δικαζόμενον. ἀλλὰ καθαροῦ συνειδότος τοῦτό ἐστι, τὸ μὴ παραιτεῖσθαι δικαστὴν τὸν ἀκριβῶς εἰδότα τὰ γεγεννημένα, ἀλλὰ καὶ χαίρειν.

τῶν κατὰ Ἰουδαίους ἐθῶν, *of customs which are among the Jews.* For this adjectival use of κατὰ followed by a noun or pronoun, cf. οἱ καθ᾿ ὑμᾶς ποιηταί (Acts xvii. 28).

μακροθύμως, *patiently.* Only here in N.T., and not found in LXX. though μακρόθυμος is very common there.

4. τὴν μὲν οὖν βίωσίν μου, *now my manner of life.* βίωσις is only found here in N.T. and nowhere in profane authors. We have the word in the prologue to Ecclus., ὅπως...ἐπιπροσθῶσι διὰ τῆς ἐννόμου βιώσεως, 'that...they may profit in living according to the Law.' This is said of exactly such a life as St Paul led before his conversion.

ἀπ᾿ ἀρχῆς, *from the beginning.* The Apostle though born in Tarsus yet came early to Jerusalem for his education, and it was in the Holy City that his character was formed and his manner of life shewed itself.

ἔν τε Ἱεροσολύμοις, *and at Jerusalem.* This addition of τε implies that even before coming to Jerusalem the Apostle had always dwelt among his own people, and so was not likely to be one who would undervalue Jewish privileges or offend against Jewish prejudices.

ἴσασι πάντες οἱ Ἰουδαῖοι, *know all the Jews.* Because in the persecutions of the Christians Saul had made himself a conspicuous character, and so had been in favour with the chief priests and allowed to undertake the mission to Damascus.

5. προγινώσκοντές με ἄνωθεν, ἐὰν θέλωσι μαρτυρεῖν, *having knowledge of me from the first, if they be willing to testify.* ἄνωθεν is found Luke i. 3, where the Evangelist is describing his perfect understanding of the Gospel story 'from the very first.' When we remember that the early part of his Gospel can hardly have been gathered from anybody but the Virgin Mary, who alone could know many of the details, we may well think that the word ἄνωθεν here implies that St Paul had been known from his very childhood. The rest of the sentence seems

to intimate that there were some among those who were now his accusers who could give evidence about his previous years if they were so minded.

κατὰ τὴν ἀκριβεστάτην αἵρεσιν, *after the straitest sect.* αἵρεσις in the singular = sect, as it is rendered everywhere in the Acts (in A.V.) except xxiv. 14. In the Epistles where the plural only occurs it is ' heresies.'

τῆς ἡμετέρας θρησκείας, *of our religion.* θρησκεία refers more especially to the outward marks of religious observance or life. Thus it would describe well the ceremonial for which the Pharisees were specially distinguished. In the LXX. it is only used of the worship of idols. See Wisdom xiv. 18, 27.

6. καὶ νῦν...ἕστηκα κρινόμενος, *and now I stand here to be judged,* i.e. I am on my trial.

ἐπ' ἐλπίδι τῆς εἰς τοὺς πατέρας ἡμῶν ἐπαγγελίας κ.τ.λ., *for the hope of the promise made by God unto our fathers,* i.e. because I entertain the hope that the promise which God made to the patriarchs and to David shall be fulfilled to us. The ' promise' must be of the Messiah, and of His coming into the world as King. For this is what the ten tribes were looking for. But this in St Paul's view embraced the doctrine of the Resurrection, because that was God's assurance to the world (Acts xvii. 31) that He who was so raised up was to be the judge of quick and dead.

7. εἰς ἥν, *unto which (promise).* This makes it clear that the promise was the sending of the Messiah, that in Him all the families of the earth should be blessed.

τὸ δωδεκάφυλον ἡμῶν, *our twelve tribes.* For the word see *Protev. Jacobi* chap. i. ἀπίει εἰς τὴν δωδεκάφυλον τοῦ λαοῦ.

The Jews regarded themselves as representing the whole race, and not merely the two tribes of the kingdom of Judah, and this no doubt was true, for tribal names continued to be preserved, and with the people of Judah there came back many of the members of the previous captivity of Israel. Thus in the N.T. we find (Luke ii. 36) that Anna was of the tribe of Asher, and St James addresses his Epistle (i. 1) ' to the twelve tribes that are scattered abroad'; and Paul himself knew that he was of the tribe of Benjamin. Cf. also 2 Chron. xxxi. 1 for evidence of the existence of some of the ten tribes after the Captivity. In T. B. *Berachoth* 20 a Rabbi Jochanan says 'I am from the root of Joseph.'

ἐν ἐκτενείᾳ, *earnestly.* The expression ἐν ἐκτενείᾳ μεγάλῃ is found twice in Judith iv. 9, rendered in A.V. (1) 'with great fervency' and (2) 'with great vehemency.'

περὶ ἧς ἐλπίδος, *for which hope's sake,* i.e. because I entertain it and press it upon others.

ἐγκαλοῦμαι ὑπὸ Ἰουδαίων, *I am accused by Jews,* members of the twelve tribes to whom the promise was made. Thus Paul brings out the inconsistency of the situation.

8. τί ἄπιστον κρίνεται παρ' ὑμῖν εἰ ὁ θεὸς νεκροὺς ἐγείρει; *why is it judged incredible with you if God doth raise the dead?* The last clause is not to be understood hypothetically, but 'If God doth, as He hath done in the case of Jesus.' So that it is equivalent to 'Why should you not believe that Jesus has been raised from the dead?'

Chrysostom points out that the strange thing was that the doctrine was not believed: εἰ γὰρ μὴ τοιαύτη δόξα ἦν, εἰ γὰρ μὴ ἀνατεθραμμένοι ἦσαν ἐν τούτοις τοῖς δόγμασι, νῦν δὲ εἰσεφέρετο, ἴσως οὐκ ἂν ἐδέξατό τις τὸν λόγον.

9. πρὸς τὸ ὄνομα, *contrary to the name,* i.e. to the faith of Jesus Christ, into whose name believers were to be baptized. Cf. v. 41, note. 'Name' is constantly used in O. T. as the equivalent of 'Godhead,' and any Jew who heard the language of such a verse as this would understand that the Christians held Jesus to be a Divine Being.

Ἰησοῦ τοῦ Ναζωραίου, *of Jesus of Nazareth,* whom we proclaim now as having been raised from the dead, and as being the fulfiller of the promises which were made to our forefathers.

10. ὃ καὶ ἐποίησα ἐν Ἱεροσολύμοις, *which thing I also did in Jerusalem.* Saul must have been a most active and prominent agent in the work of persecution in Jerusalem, for we learn here that the death of Stephen was not the only one for which he had given his vote. He had also had the warrant of the chief priests for other arrests beside those he intended to make in Damascus. We can see that the slaughter of the Christians was not in all cases the result of a sudden outburst of rage at some act or speech, but that some of them were imprisoned, then subjected to a form of trial, and afterwards put to death as men condemned by law.

φυλακαῖς. On the use of this word in the plural see xxii. 4, note.

ψῆφον, *vote.* Of course the sense is the same as 'voice' in A. V., but the literal translation brings out more prominently that these proceedings were all carried on in a formal and quasi-legal manner.

11. καὶ κατὰ πάσας τὰς συναγωγὰς πολλάκις τιμωρῶν αὐτούς, *and punishing them often in all the synagogues.* This shews how zealous Saul's labours against the Way had been. Of the synagogues as places where offenders were accused and punished, cf. Matth. x. 17, xxiii. 34; Mark xiii. 9; Luke xii. 11, xxi. 12.

ἠνάγκαζον βλασφημεῖν, *I strove to make them blaspheme.* ἀναγκάζω is frequently rendered 'constrain' or 'compel,' but being here in the imperfect tense, it seems to indicate that the attempt was repeated often, and needed to be so, for it was not in some cases successful. Saul kept on with his constraint. βλασφημεῖν, i. e. the name of Jesus, into which they had been baptized. They were to be forced to renounce the belief in the divinity of Jesus. Cf. on blasphemy of the Divine Name, Lev. xxiv. 11—16.

ἕως καὶ εἰς τὰς ἔξω πόλεις, *even unto foreign cities,* that is, cities outside the country of the Jews proper. So that, as it appears,

Damascus was but one among several cities to which Saul had gone
on his errand of punishment.

Cf. ὁ ἔξω ἄνθρωπος, 2 Cor. iv. 16.

12. ἐν οἷς, *wherein*, i.e. in doing this work. The margin of Rev.
Ver. represents the sense very well, ' on which errand.'

μετ᾽ ἐξουσίας καὶ ἐπιτροπῆς τῆς τῶν ἀρχιερέων, *with the authority
and commission of the high priests.* Saul was the commissioner sent
by the Jewish magistrates, and at this particular time Damascus had
been assigned as the district where he was to search for the Christians.

13. ἡμέρας μέσης, *at midday.* There could be no question about
the supernatural character of a light which overpowered the midday
glare of an Eastern sun.

14. ἤκουσα φωνὴν λέγουσαν πρός με, *I heard a voice saying unto
me.* Saul alone gathered the import of what was said. His companions merely heard the sound, but nothing of the words. Cf.
Dan. x. 7.

τῇ Ἑβραΐδι διαλέκτῳ, *in the Hebrew language.* And this is represented in the proper name, which is not Σαῦλος as usual, but Σαούλ, a
transliteration of the Hebrew form.

σκληρόν σοι πρὸς κέντρα λακτίζειν, *it is hard for thee to kick against
the pricks* (lit. the goads). This is the only place where the oldest
MSS. give these words. See note on ix. 5. The figure is from an ox,
being driven on in his work. When restive or lazy, the driver pricks
him, and in ignorance of the consequences, he kicks back, and so gets
another wound. The words would imply that God had been guiding
Saul towards the true light for some time before, and that this zeal
for persecution was a resistance offered to the divine urging. It is not
unusual for men who are moved to break away from old traditions at
such times, by outward acts, to manifest even more zeal than before
for their old opinions, as if in fear lest they should be thought to be
falling away. This may have been Saul's case, his kicking against the
goads. The figure is very common in classical literature. Cf. Aesch.
Prom. 323 ; Eur. *Bacchæ* 791.

15. τίς εἶ, κύριε; *who art thou, Lord?* The readiness with which
' Lord,' an expression of allegiance, comes to the Apostle's lips lends
probability to the notion that God's promptings had been working in
his heart before, and that the mad rage against ' the Way' was
an attempt to stifle them.

16. προχειρίσασθαί σε ὑπηρέτην, *to appoint thee a minister.* Cf.
for the verb, xxii. 14. It implies a deliberate selection and appointment. For this reason St Paul was σκεῦος ἐκλογῆς (ix. 15).

καὶ μάρτυρα ὧν τε εἶδες, *and a witness both of those things which thou
hast seen.* The Rev. Vers. gives ' wherein thou hast seen Me,' reading
με after εἶδες. This reading gives a good sense, for St Paul dwells not
unfrequently in his Epistles on his having seen Jesus. Cf. 1 Cor. ix. 1,
xv. 8, &c., and he makes this the ground of his independence in the

Apostolic work, so that he can say he is not a whit behind any of the other Apostles.

But the *Text. recept.* is accepted by Lachmann, Tischendorf and Tregelles.

For the attraction of ὧν for ἅ see note on i. 1.

ὧν τε ὀφθήσομαί σοι, *and of those things in the which I will appear unto thee.* St Paul was more favoured than the rest of the Apostles, as far as we gather from the N.T. records, with visions from God to guide and comfort him at critical points in his work. Cf. Acts xviii. 9, xxiii. 11; and 2 Cor. xii. 2. It was specially important that Paul should have seen Jesus, so that he might bear independent witness to the truth of his Resurrection.

17. ἐξαιρούμενός σε ἐκ τοῦ λαοῦ, *delivering thee from the people.* The verb implies that the Apostle will be seized, and that the deliverance will be a rescue. From the first even in Damascus Saul found this, and he knew that in every city bonds and persecutions were to be his lot.

εἰς οὓς ἐγὼ ἀποστέλλω σε, *unto whom I send thee.* The full force of the verb = 'I make thee an Apostle.' In the oldest texts ἐγώ is emphatically expressed. 'Thou,' as well as the rest, 'art an Apostle chosen by Me, the Lord Jesus.' The mission to the Gentiles seems to have been made clear to Saul from the very first. Compare his own language, Gal. i. 16. And in Acts ix. 29 his preaching appears to have been rather directed to the Greek-Jews than to the members of the Church in Jerusalem.

18. ἀνοῖξαι ὀφθαλμοὺς αὐτῶν, τοῦ ἐπιστρέψαι, *to open their eyes that they may turn.* Here we have another shade of meaning of the genitival infinitive. By the opening of their eyes the Gentiles will be enabled to turn. Cf. LXX. 1 Kings viii. 58, ἐπικλῖναι καρδίας ἡμῶν ἐπ᾽ αὐτὸν τοῦ πορεύεσθαι ἐν πάσαις ὁδοῖς αὐτοῦ.

ἀπὸ σκότους εἰς φῶς, *from darkness to light.* So complete is the change which the Gospel knowledge works.

ἐν τοῖς ἡγιασμένοις πίστει τῇ εἰς ἐμέ, *among them which are sanctified by faith in me.* It is by their belief in Jesus that men are sanctified, and here 'sanctified,' as so often 'saint' in St Paul's Epistles, is applied to those who have been set on the way of salvation, and not to those who are perfect in holiness; to that they will be brought if they persevere.

19. οὐκ ἐγενόμην ἀπειθής, *I was not disobedient.* More literally, 'I did not become, or prove, disobedient.' The thought goes back to the 'kicking against the pricks,' the opposition of previous times. That was at an end now. Jesus was 'Lord,' and Saul's only question 'What wilt thou have me to do?'

τῇ οὐρανίῳ ὀπτασίᾳ, *to the heavenly vision.* ὀπτασία is a word of late origin. It occurs several times in N.T., Luke i. 22; 2 Cor. xii. 1; also frequently in the LXX. of Daniel.

20.   καὶ ἐν Ἱεροσολύμοις, *and at Jerusalem.* Cf. ix. 29. Here he spake boldly in the name of the Lord Jesus, and disputed against the Grecians, so that they went about to kill him.

πᾶσάν τε τὴν χώραν τῆς Ἰουδαίας, *and throughout all the country of Judæa.* This accusative of place after ἀπαγγέλλειν without a preposition is very unusual, but all the oldest authorities agree in omitting εἰς. The omission is probably due to the position of the words between the two datives Ἱεροσολύμοις and τοῖς ἔθνεσιν.

Of this ministration in Judæa we are only told, ix. 30, that the brethren finding Saul in danger in Jerusalem brought him to Cæsarea, and thence sent him to Tarsus. But as we see in the history of Felix (cf. xxiii. 34, note) that Cilicia was sometimes reckoned as a part of the province of Judæa, the preaching in Cilicia may be included in the expression 'country of Judæa.' And we may feel sure that Paul, wherever he might be, never laid aside the character which Christ's mission had imposed upon him.

ἀπήγγελλον, *I declared.* The literal sense should be kept in mind. Saul had a message given to him to deliver. He was henceforth God's *evangelist.*

ἄξια τῆς μετανοίας ἔργα πράσσοντας, *doing works worthy of their repentance.* Thus the force of the article is more nearly given, for the works were to be a sign of their repentance and turning unto God; the means whereby the reality of their sorrow and the earnestness of their desire were to be shewn.

21.   ἕνεκα τούτων, *on account of these things.* R.V. very well 'for this cause.'

Ἰουδαῖοι συλλαβόμενοι, *the Jews having seized me.* The verb implies an arrest with violence.

ἐπειρῶντο διαχειρίσασθαι, *endeavoured to kill me.* St Paul combines the riot in the Temple with the subsequent plot before he was sent to Cæsarea, or he may be alluding only to the violence by which he was nearly torn in pieces before the chief captain came to his rescue. The verb διαχειρίζομαι indicates the laying violent hands on any one, and so favours the latter view. It is found above, v. 30.

22.   ἐπικουρίας οὖν τυχὼν τῆς ἀπὸ τοῦ θεοῦ, *having therefore obtained the help that is from God.* The connexion by οὖν implies that only help divine could have saved him in such perils. ἐπικουρία means such succour as an ally gives, and recalls God's promise, ' Surely I will be with thee.'

ἄχρι τῆς ἡμέρας ταύτης ἕστηκα, *I stand unto this day.* The Apostle has in mind the many attempts to cast him down which had been made by Jews, and Gentiles too, during his missionary journeys. He has been rescued in many ways, and is still there standing safe and sound through the help which God hath sent him. He does not forget human agency, but this, whatever it was, was all sent of God.

μαρτυρόμενος μικρῷ τε καὶ μεγάλῳ, *testifying both to small and great.*
St Paul was now in the presence of two who would be named great,
and he knew that God had declared he was to testify 'before kings'
(ix. 15).

ὧν. For the government, see i. 1.

οἱ προφῆται...καὶ Μωϋσῆς, *the prophets and Moses,* i.e. the whole
Old Testament Scriptures. The form of the phrase is usually 'Moses
and the prophets,' according to the order of the O.T. books. Sometimes we have 'the Law and the prophets,' and once (Luke xxiv. 44)
'the law of Moses, the prophets and the Psalms.'

μελλόντων γίνεσθαι, *were about to come.* The attraction of μελλόντων into the case of the relative preceding is an uncommon occurrence.
The plain construction of the whole sentence would be ἐκτὸς τούτων ἃ
οἱ προφῆται ἐλάλησαν μέλλοντα, 'except those things which the prophets
spake of as about to come.' But τούτων being dropped, the relative is
attracted into the case of the lost antecedent, and draws the participle
in its train.

23. εἰ παθητὸς ὁ Χριστός, *that the Christ should suffer.* Literally 'if
the Christ be one who has to suffer.' And the Apostle having in his
mind the facts, puts the sentence as a topic on which there was debate
among the Jews, as indeed there was (see John xii. 34). And St Paul
says he answered this question out of the Scriptures. His answer of
course was a positive one; therefore what he taught is fairly represented by the English 'that the Christ' &c.; though the teaching was
a response to 'whether the Christ be one who is to suffer.' The same
remark applies to the use of εἰ in the next clause.

πρῶτος ἐξ ἀναστάσεως νεκρῶν φῶς μέλλει καταγγέλλειν, *He first by
the resurrection of the dead should proclaim light.* For Christ was the
first-fruits of them that sleep. His resurrection was an earnest of the
general resurrection. Thus life and immortality were brought to
light. The full force of μέλλει καταγγέλλειν 'is about to proclaim'
points on to the preaching of the Gospel from generation to generation. He shall enlighten believers thus through all time.

τῷ τε λαῷ καὶ τοῖς ἔθνεσιν, *both unto the people and to the Gentiles.*
By ὁ λαός the Jews are meant. So in St Matth. i. 21, 'He shall
save His people from their sins,' 'His people'=His own (cf. St John
i. 11), i.e. the Jews. Christ was spoken of in like terms by the aged
Simeon, 'A light to lighten the Gentiles and to be the glory of Thy
people Israel,' and he could say this because in Jesus he beheld God's
'salvation.' He could 'depart in peace,' being sure that 'to die'
was only the pledge of 'to rise again.'

24—32. INTERRUPTION BY FESTUS. APPEAL TO AGRIPPA. CONSULTA-
TION AND DECISION.

24. μεγάλῃ τῇ φωνῇ φησίν, *says with a loud voice.* Probably what
had last fallen from St Paul seemed to Festus little better than lunatic
ravings. The Gospel of the Cross did appear as 'foolishness' to the

Gentile world. And this Gospel he had just heard in all its fulness:
that the Christ by suffering of death and rising to life again should
be the source of true enlightenment both to Jews and Gentiles.

μαίνῃ Παῦλε, *Paul, thou art mad.* μαίνομαι occurs in the next
verse, and the two places should accord, though sentiment clings to
'Paul, thou art beside thyself.'

τὰ πολλά σε γράμματα εἰς μανίαν περιτρέπει, *much learning doth
make thee mad.* Literally, 'doth turn thee to madness.' For γράμματα
in the sense of 'learning' 'letters,' cf. John vii. 15. It may be also
that there is an allusion to the γράμματα, 'the Jewish Scriptures,' to
which the Apostle had been so largely appealing. As a religious literature no nation, not even the polished Greeks, had anything to place
in comparison with the sacred books of the Jews.

25. κράτιστε, *most excellent.* On this title cf. above, xxiii. 26,
xxiv. 3. St Chrysostom remarks here that the Apostle now answers
with gentleness, not as to the high-priest (xxiii. 3).

σωφροσύνης, *soberness.* In classical Greek the word is the exact
opposite of that μανία unto which Festus had just said St Paul was
turned.

26. λανθάνειν γὰρ αὐτόν τι τούτων οὐ πείθομαι οὐδέν, *for I am
persuaded that none of these things is hidden from him,* i.e. none of the
history of the life and works of Jesus, of His death and resurrection,
of the marvellous gifts of Pentecost, and the preaching of the Gospel
since Jesus had been crucified.

The grammar presents some anomaly from the occurrence of τι and
οὐδὲν in the same sentence. It is perhaps best to take the former
adverbially = 'in any degree.' Then οὐ before πείθομαι is only the
Greek manner of intensifying a negative idea, and need not be
noticed in the English idiom.

ἐν γωνίᾳ πεπραγμένον, *done in a corner.* That there was no lack of
knowledge about our Lord among the Jewish people we can be sure
from the excitement which during His life He caused by His mighty
works, also from the efforts put forth to stop His teaching, efforts
which culminated in a trial in which both Jewish and Roman magistrates were consulted, and by the exclamation of the Pharisees (John
xii. 19) 'The world is gone after Him,' and the declaration (Acts xvii.
6) 'These that have turned the world upside down.'

Chrysostom says: ἐνταῦθα περὶ τοῦ σταυροῦ λέγει τοῦτο, καὶ περὶ τῆς
ἀναστάσεως, καὶ ὅτι πανταχοῦ τῆς οἰκουμένης γέγονε τὸ δόγμα.

27. πιστεύεις...τοῖς προφήταις; *believest thou the prophets?* Whose
writings foretell the events about which I am speaking, and whose
predictions have had their fulfilment in the history of Jesus of Nazareth.

οἶδα ὅτι πιστεύεις, *I know that thou believest.* The Apostle answers
his own question, for he is sure that Agrippa would not have given a
different answer, seeing how anxious all his family were, in spite of
their relations with Rome, to be accepted of the Jewish nation. St

Paul does not imply by his words any conviction about the character of Agrippa's faith in the Scriptures.

28. ἐν ὀλίγῳ με πείθεις Χριστιανὸν ποιῆσαι, *with but little persuasion thou wouldest fain make me a Christian.* The literal rendering is, 'with (*or* in) little (labour *or* time) thou art persuading me so as to make me a Christian,' as if ποιῆσαι=ὥστε με ποιῆσαι. 'With little labour' or 'in a little time' implies that the king despised the attempt which had been made to convince him, and mocked at the language of St Paul in so readily taking for granted that he was in accord with him. It is as though he said, 'You are supposing that I accept these words of the prophets in the same sense as you do, and you are a fool for your pains, to think that with so little trouble and in so short a space you could win me over to your side. And such a side! To be a Christian.' The name had, no doubt, been given, when it was first applied (Acts xi. 26), to the adherents of Jesus as a term of reproach, and it is likely that it had not yet won its way to be a name of credit, at all events among such men as Agrippa and his friends. For we have no reason to suppose that the king was influenced at all by Paul's words.

29. καὶ ἐν ὀλίγῳ καὶ ἐν μεγάλῳ, *whether with little or with much.* The Apostle takes up the jeer of the king in a serious tone, and replies: 'I may have seemed to use little persuasion, and suddenly to have jumped at the conclusion that you accept the teaching of the prophets as I myself receive it; but whether it need little or much persuasion, or little or much time, my prayer to God is, for you and for all who listen to me, that they may become such as I am, save as to my bonds.'

γενέσθαι τοιούτους ὁποῖος κἀγώ εἰμι, *might become such as I am.* The Apostle does not use the word 'Christian,' which for himself he might willingly have accepted (cf. 1 Pet. iv. 16), but which was used by the king in a mocking sense, and therefore would not have made his wish seem an acceptable one. You may call me 'Christian' in mockery, my joy and hope and faith in Christ are such, that I know no better prayer for any than to wish you all the like blessings.

παρεκτὸς τῶν δεσμῶν τούτων, *except these bonds.* From this it is clear, in spite of the leniency with which Paul had been at first treated by Felix, that either because his case was deemed more serious in consequence of his being left in prison so long, or because he was just now before the court as a prisoner, the Apostle had been put in chains.

For παρεκτός, which is a rarely found preposition, cf. Matth. v. 32. Also 'Test. xii. Patr.' *Zab.* 1, παρεκτὸς ἐννοίας. See also 'Teaching of the Twelve Apostles,' 6.

30. οἱ συγκαθήμενοι αὐτοῖς, *they that sat with them,* i.e. the chief captains and the principal men of Cæsarea. (See xxv. 23.) The authorities withdrew to consult upon what they had heard.

31. ἐλάλουν πρὸς ἀλλήλους, *they spake one to another.* This literal sense brings out more clearly that they were all of one mind about the case.

32. ἀπολελύσθαι ἐδύνατο, *might have been set at liberty.* Thus Agrippa, looking at the question from the Jewish standpoint, confirms the opinion of the Roman magistrate (cf. **xxv.** 25). So that St Paul was acquitted on all hands, and Festus may rightly be deemed guilty because he had driven an innocent man to appeal to a higher court, from fear that he would be delivered into the power of his enemies. But God was using human means for bringing the Apostle to Rome, and so fulfilling his servant's great desire, and in such wise that he should be heard before kings in behalf of the Gospel.

εἰ μὴ ἐπεκέκλητο Καίσαρα, *if he had not appealed unto Cæsar.* The appeal put an end to all powers of a lower court either to condemn or absolve.

Chrysostom's comment here is ὅρα πῶς καὶ πάλιν ὑπὲρ αὐτοῦ ψηφίζονται, καὶ μετὰ τὸ εἰπεῖν μαίνῃ, ἀφίασιν αὐτόν.

CHAPTER XXVII.

Readings varying from the *Text. recept.*

2. μέλλοντι for μέλλοντες with ℵAB. *Vulg.* 'incipientes.'

14. εὐρακύλων with ℵ*AB. *Vulg.* ' Euroaquilo.'

16. Καῦδα with ℵB. *Vulg.* ' Cauda.'

19. ἔρριψαν with ℵABC. *Vulg.* 'projecerunt.'

29. ἐκπέσωμεν for ἐκπέσωσιν with ℵABCHLP. *Vulg.* 'incideremus.'

41. τῶν κυμάτων omitted with ℵAB. *Vulg.* has ' a vi maris.'

1—44. St Paul's Voyage and Shipwreck.

1. ὡς δὲ ἐκρίθη τοῦ ἀποπλεῖν ἡμᾶς, *and when it was determined that we should sail.* No other instance of this infinitive with τοῦ prefixed is found after κρίνω except in the *Text. recept.* of 1 Cor. ii. 2, where it is rejected by Lachmann, Tischendorf and Tregelles. But in the LXX. the construction is common enough after verbs of kindred signification, e.g. βουλεύομαι. Cf. 1 Macc. iii. 31, ἐβουλεύσατο τοῦ πορευθῆναι εἰς τὴν Περσίδα, 'he determined to go into Persia' (A.V.). See also 1 Macc. v. 2, ἐβουλεύσαντο τοῦ ἆραι τὸ γένος Ἰακώβ. So 1 Macc. ix. 69, xii. 35.

παρεδίδουν, *they delivered,* i.e. the soldiers who had the care of Paul did so by order of Festus.

ἑκατοντάρχῃ, *to a centurion.* This was generally the rank of the officers appointed to such a charge. Cf. xxi. 32, xxiv. 23, &c.

σπείρης Σεβαστῆς, *of the Augustan band.* The word σπεῖρα might be rendered 'cohort' as in the marg. of R.V., and it is said that in the time of Octavianus Augustus there were some legions to which the title Σεβαστός = Augustus was given, as being specially the Imperial troops, and that perhaps among the soldiers in Cæsarea there was a detachment of these legions. But as Cæsarea was itself called 'Sebaste' it seems more likely that the soldiers were Samaritan troops belonging to Cæsarea itself. And Josephus (*Wars*, II. 12. 5) makes mention of troops which had their name, Sebasteni, from this city Cæsarea Sebaste.

2. ἐπιβάντες δέ, *and embarking in.* This verb is the technical term for 'going on board ship.'

Ἀδραμυττηνῷ, *of Adramyttium.* This was a seaport on the coast of that district of Asia Minor called Mysia, and in early times Aeolis. It appears to have been in St Paul's time a place of considerable trade, and Pliny (v. 30) mentions it as an assize town. The reason why the Apostle and his companions embarked on board a vessel from this port was that it was probably the easiest way of getting into the line of vessels going from Asia to the West. The isle of Lesbos lay off the gulf on which Adramyttium was situated, and to which it gave name, and the town was in close connexion with Ephesus, Miletus, Pergamos and Troas, and so was a considerable centre of commerce.

μέλλοντι πλεῖν κ.τ.λ., *which was about to sail unto the places on the coast of Asia.* The centurion and his party when they had reached the Asiatic coast would be very likely to find in some of the ports there a vessel which would carry them across to Italy.

Ἀρίσταρχον, *Aristarchus.* Mentioned before (xix. 29) as one of those whom the mob in Ephesus seized in their fury against St Paul. He went, as it seems, with the Apostle into Europe, for he is enumerated amongst those who accompanied St Paul (xx. 4) on his return. After the present notice of him, we learn nothing more of his history except that from Col. iv. 10 and Philem. 24 we can gather that he remained with the Apostle during his first Roman imprisonment.

3. κατήχθημεν εἰς Σιδῶνα, *we touched at Sidon.* This is the well-known seaport on the coast of Phœnicia. κατάγειν here is a technical term for 'putting in a ship to shore,' as ἀνάγειν just before is for 'setting sail.'

φιλανθρώπως χρησάμενος, *treating kindly.* φιλανθρώπως is only found here in N.T., and only once in LXX. (2 Macc. ix. 27).

ἐπιμελείας τυχεῖν, *to refresh himself.* Literally, ' to receive attention.' The Apostle no doubt knew some of the residents in Sidon, and at his request the centurion allowed him, while the vessel stayed there, to enjoy their company and kind offices. Sidon was on the road between Jerusalem and Antioch, a journey which St Paul had frequently made.

4. ὑπεπλεύσαμεν τὴν Κύπρον, *we sailed under Cyprus,* i.e. between Cyprus and the mainland, so as to have the shelter of the island on their left to protect them from the contrary winds. Rev. Ver. 'under the lee of Cyprus.'

5.   τό τε πέλαγος τὸ κατὰ τὴν Κιλικίαν καὶ Παμφυλίαν, *the sea which is off Cilicia and Pamphylia.*   These two countries formed the coast of Asia Minor in that portion which is opposite to Cyprus.

εἰς Μύρρα, *to Myrrha*, which lies about 20 stadia (2½ miles) from the coast on the river Andriacus.

6.   πλοῖον Ἀλεξανδρινόν, *a ship of Alexandria.*   They found a means of transport into Italy sooner perhaps than they had expected. It may be that the same strong contrary winds from the west, which had altered already the course of their own voyage from Sidon, had carried this vessel across the Mediterranean to the Asiatic coast.   Myrrha was certainly out of the way for persons sailing from N. Africa to Italy.

7.   ἐν ἱκαναῖς δὲ ἡμέραις βραδυπλοοῦντες, *and sailing slowly for many days*, kept back by the same head-winds.

καὶ μόλις γενόμενοι κατὰ τὴν Κνίδον, *and with difficulty being come over against Cnidus.*   They had been forced to hug the coast all the way from Myrrha, and when off Cnidus they were only opposite to the S.W. extremity of Asia Minor.   Cnidus was, as its remains demonstrate, a famous seaport town in ancient times, and we find that Jews dwelt there in the days of the Maccabees (1 Macc. xv. 23).   It was a notable seat of the worship of Aphrodite.

μὴ προσεῶντος ἡμᾶς τοῦ ἀνέμου, *the wind not further suffering us*, i.e. not allowing us to make further progress.   The word προσεάω is not found elsewhere.

ὑπεπλεύσαμεν τὴν Κρήτην κατὰ Σαλμώνην, *we sailed under Crete over against Salmone.*   Rev. Ver. (as in verse 4) 'under the lee of.' Crete is the modern island of *Candia.*   Salmone was the eastern extremity of the island, off which when they came they sheltered themselves under the island, and sailed to the south of it, to avoid the wind as much as might be.

8.   μόλις τε παραλεγόμενοι αὐτήν, *and with difficulty coasting along it.*   παραλέγεσθαι describes a voyage made by keeping close to the shore of the island.   Against a wind N.W., or nearly so, the island of Crete would afford them some protection.

ἤλθομεν εἰς τόπον τινά, *we came to a place*, i.e. on the coast of Crete.

καλούμενον Καλοὺς λιμένας, *called Fair Havens.*   This place, though mentioned nowhere else in literature, is known by the same name still.   It is on the south of Crete, four or five miles east of Cape Matala, which is the largest headland on that side of the island.

Λασαία, *Lasæa.*   This city has also been identified very recently. Its ruins were discovered in 1856, a few miles east of Fair Havens. See Smith's *Voyage and Shipwreck of St Paul*, App. III. pp. 262, 263.

9.   ἱκανοῦ δὲ χρόνου διαγενομένου, *now when much time had been spent*, i.e. waiting for a change of wind, and in debating what course should next be taken.

καὶ ὄντος ἤδη ἐπισφαλοῦς τοῦ πλοός, *and when the voyage was now dangerous.*   It had come to be dangerous by the late season of the year. In St Paul's day navigation, both among the Jews and other nations, could only be attempted for a limited portion of the year, when the weather permitted the stars to be seen.

διὰ τὸ καὶ τὴν νηστείαν ἤδη παρεληλυθέναι, *because the fast was now already past.* The fast here meant is that on the great Day of Atonement. This is the Fast *par excellence* of the Jews, being the only one definitely appointed in the Old Testament. It falls on the tenth day of Tishri, the seventh month of the Jewish year. This corresponds to a part of September and October of our calendar; so that a stormy season was to be expected.

10. ἄνδρες, θεωρῶ......ζημίας, *Sirs, I perceive that the voyage will be with injury and much loss.* Evidently the character of the Apostle had won him the regard and respect of those in charge of the vessel as well as of the centurion. He must have had some experience of sailing in the Mediterranean, and so was fitted to speak on the question which was now being debated. We should bear in mind too that he had seen more of perils by sea already than we gather from the Acts; for some time before this voyage to Rome, he wrote to the Corinthians (2 Cor. xi. 25), 'Thrice I suffered shipwreck, a night and a day I have been in the deep.'

θεωρῶ implies the result of observation and does not refer to any supernatural communication which the Apostle had received. This is clear from the end of the verse, where St Paul speaks of hurt to the lives of those on board, which did not come to pass (verse 44). For ὕβρις used of material damage by a storm, cf. Joseph. *Ant.* III. 6. 4, σινδόνες...τὴν ἀπὸ τῶν ὄμβρων ὕβριν ἀπομαχόμεναι.

11. τῷ κυβερνήτῃ, *to the pilot.* By 'master' the A. V. means ' sailing master,' the officer who had charge of the vessel's navigation.

καὶ τῷ ναυκλήρῳ, *and to the owner of the ship,* who was probably owner of the cargo too, and if, as is most likely, this was corn, he would be sailing with it, that he might dispose of it to the best advantage when they reached Italy.

μᾶλλον ἐπείθετο, *gave more heed to.* As the centurion was in charge of prisoners for the Imperial tribunal, his wish would be much regarded by both owner and sailing-master; and it was natural when they recommended the attempt to proceed that he should not listen to Paul's advice and remain where they were.

12. ἀνευθέτου δὲ...πρὸς παραχειμασίαν, *and the haven not being commodious to winter in.* And to tarry through the winter was what they were most likely to have to do, wherever they stopped. The season for sailing was now nearly over.

ἀνεύθετος is found only here. But εὔθετος = *convenient* is common in classical literature and in the LXX.

παραχειμάζειν occurs in this verse and in xxviii. 11, also in 1 Cor xvi. 6; Tit. iii. 12, but the noun nowhere else in N. T.

ἔθεντο βουλήν, *advised.* For the expression cf. LXX. Judges xix. 30, θέσθε δὴ ἑαυτοῖς περὶ αὐτῆς βουλήν.

ἀναχθῆναι ἐκεῖθεν, *to put to sea from thence*. On the verb, see above, verse 3.

καταντήσαντες εἰς Φοίνικα, *having reached Phœnix*. Phœnix is no doubt the correct orthography of the name. The place is mentioned both by Strabo and Ptolemy, and has been identified with the modern port of Lutro (Spratt's *Crete* ii. 250 seqq.).

βλέποντα κατὰ λίβα καὶ κατὰ χῶρον, *looking north-east and south-east*. Literally 'looking down the south-west wind and down the north-west wind.' To look down a wind is to look in the direction in which it blows. So as a south-west wind would blow towards N.E., the Rev. Ver. appears to give the correct sense, and the haven of Lutro answers these conditions, being open towards the east.

χῶρος is a Greek representation of the Latin *Caurus*, one of the names given to the N. W. wind.

13. ὑποπνεύσαντος δὲ νότου, *and when the south wind blew softly*. The storm appeared to have in some degree abated, and the change of wind must have been very complete, for (see verses 7, 8) they had previously sailed under the lee of Crete to get shelter from the *north* wind.

For ὑπό in composition having this sense of 'slightly,' 'in a less degree,' cf. ὑποκινέω=to move slightly, ὑπόλευκος, somewhat white, &c.

ἄραντες ἄσσον παρελέγοντο τὴν Κρήτην, *having weighed anchor, they sailed along Crete, close in shore*. In this verse ἄσσον has been taken by some for a proper name, and endeavours been made to discover traces of some place so named in Crete. But though the translation 'when they had loosed from Assos' is as old as the Vulgate, there can be little doubt that the word is really the comparative degree of ἄγχι, 'near.' So it literally means 'nearer,' and is probably used to indicate that the coasting voyage now being made was one in which the coast was hugged more closely than usual. This is intended by Rev. Ver. ' close in shore.'

14. ἔβαλεν κατ' αὐτῆς, *there beat down from it*. αὐτῆς can only here refer to Κρήτη. And whatever sense is to be given to the preposition must be determined by the context. The effect of the wind described in this verse was to carry the vessel to the island of Cauda. And they were sailing on the south of and close under Crete. Therefore they were driven still more southward. This could only be by a wind from the north, a wind therefore blowing over Crete. Hence κατά must be taken=down from. Cf. such phrases as ῥίπτειν κατὰ τῆς πέτρας which are common enough.

What happened was that the wind suddenly changed from south to north, and coming over the land carried the vessel southward away from Crete. Such changes are not unusual in the Mediterranean (Smith's *Voyage of St Paul*, p. 99).

ἄνεμος τυφωνικός, *a tempestuous wind*. The adjective is not found elsewhere in this sense, but the noun τυφώς for 'a whirlwind' is frequent, and is represented in the English ' typhoon.'

εὐρακύλων, *Euraquilo.* This reading has the support of the oldest MSS., and has also the Vulgate 'Euroaquilo' in its favour, and it exactly describes the wind which would carry the vessel in the direction indicated. It is known in Greek by the name 'Coecias' and is a north-east wind. Some have thought that the reading of the A. V. Εὐροκλύδων, which has the support of many MSS., arose from a corruption in the mouths of sailors. For the word 'Euraquilo' is a hybrid, the first portion being Greek, the latter Latin. The form in the *Text. recept.* gives it a look of being all Greek, and the words ὁ καλούμενος seem to intimate that the name was one known to the sailors, rather than a word of general use, whereas 'Euraquilo' would have needed no such introductory expression, but have been understood at once by its etymology.

15.   ἀντοφθαλμεῖν τῷ ἀνέμῳ, *to face the wind.* Literally, 'to look the wind in the eye.' The verb is found Wisdom xii. 14, οὔτε βασιλεὺς ἢ τύραννος ἀντοφθαλμῆσαι δυνήσεταί σοι.

ἐπιδόντες ἐφερόμεθα, *we gave way to it and were driven.* The verb ἐπιδίδωμι has constantly the sense of yielding to a superior force. That force here is the wind. The A.V. makes the sense to be 'we yielded up the vessel,' which has not so much support, though it is not unexampled.

16.   νησίον δέ τι ὑποδραμόντες καλούμενον Καῦδα, *and running under the lee of a small island named Cauda.* For the verb cf. above on verses 4 and 7. νησίον is a rare word, found only here and in Strabo. The name 'Cauda' which has the best MS. support agrees well with the form which the name has assumed in modern times, 'Gozzo' and 'Gaudo.' But the form in A.V. is warranted by the orthography of Ptolemy (Claudos) and Pliny (Glaudos).

ἰσχύσαμεν μόλις περικρατεῖς γενέσθαι τῆς σκάφης, *we were able with difficulty to secure the boat.* The boats in old times were not as in modern ships made fast round about the vessel, but were carried on in tow. In stormy weather, there was of course much danger that the boat would be washed away. This was the case here, and as soon as ever they had gained the shelter of the island, they set about making sure of its safety by hauling it on board, but this they were not able to do without much difficulty, probably because it had been already filled with water.

For περικρατεῖς γενέσθαι, cf. Susanna 39 (*Codex Alex.*).

17.   ἣν ἄραντες, *and when they had hoisted it up,* i.e. from the sea and on board the vessel.

βοηθείαις ἐχρῶντο, *they used helps.* These were strong cables, which were drawn several times round the hulls of vessels, to help in keeping the timbers from parting. The technical term for the operation is 'to frap' a vessel, and it is only in modern times that the process has been abandoned.

μὴ εἰς τὴν σύρτιν ἐκπέσωσιν, *lest they should be cast upon the Syrtis.* The Syrtis Major and Syrtis Minor are two quicksands on the north coast of Africa, of which the Syrtis Major lies most to the east, between Tripoli and Barca, and was the shoal on to which the sailors at this time were afraid of being driven.

χαλάσαντες τὸ σκεῦος, *having lowered the gear.* The noun σκεῦος is a very general one, signifying 'tackling' or 'implements' of any kind. What was done was to lower everything from aloft that could be dispensed with. They could not have struck sail (as A.V.), because to do so would be to give up all the chance which remained of using the wind to avoid the Syrtis, which was what they desired to do.

χαλάω is used for the management of the rigging of a ship in LXX. (Is. xxxiii. 23), οὐ χαλάσει τὰ ἱστία.

18. σφοδρῶς δὲ χειμαζομένων ἡμῶν, *and as we laboured exceedingly with the storm,* i.e. because it continually increased in violence.

ἐκβολὴν ἐποιοῦντο, *they lightened the ship.* Literally 'they made a casting overboard.'

For the expression see LXX. Jonah i. 5 ἐκβολὴν ἐποιήσαντο τῶν σκευῶν τῶν ἐν τῷ πλοίῳ.

The verb ἐποιοῦντο, being imperfect, probably has the force of 'they set about lightening.' The Latin phrase for the operation is very similar, *jacturum facere.* The ship was probably carrying corn from Alexandria to Italy, and if so the load would be a heavy one and its removal a great relief to the struggling vessel. On the African supply of corn to Italy cp. Juv. *Sat.* v. 118 seqq.

19. αὐτόχειρες...ἔρριψαν, *they cast out with their own hands.* This reading, supported by the oldest MSS., is much more probable than the first person of the *Text. recept.* It is not likely that the writer of the narrative, even if he were a fellow-traveller with St Paul in this voyage, was employed in such a work, which is preeminently that which the sailors alone would undertake.

τὴν σκευήν, *the tackling.* As σκεῦος in 17 meant all that could be spared from aloft, so σκευή seems to mean all that could be removed from the deck or the hull of the vessel.

20. μήτε ἄστρων ἐπιφαινόντων ἐπὶ πλείονας ἡμέρας, *nor stars shone upon us for many days.* This does not imply a continuous darkness like night, but that the mist and spray made the whole sky obscure both by day and night. In such a state of things we can understand how hopeless seemed the case of the Apostle and his fellows. They were at the mercy of the storm, and could neither know the direction in which they were carried, nor see if they were nearing any danger.

λοιπόν, *at length.* The word thus used adverbially is common in classical Greek.

21. πολλῆς τε ἀσιτίας ὑπαρχούσης, *and when they had been long without food.* This was in consequence of the excitement which made it impossible to eat, as well as the condition of the vessel which made the preparation of food very difficult. They had been living on anything that happened to be attainable, and that had been very little.

ἀσιτία is used Joseph. *Ant.* XII. 7. 1 of the want of food which made soldiers unwilling to fight.

μὴ ἀνάγεσθαι ἀπὸ τῆς Κρήτης, *not to have set sail from Crete.* His exhortation had been that they should stay at Fair Havens, even though it was not so very commodious as a harbour.

κερδῆσαί τε τὴν ὕβριν ταύτην καὶ τὴν ζημίαν, *and to have gotten* (lit. *gained*) *this harm and loss*, i.e. and by so doing to have incurred this harm and loss. But κερδαίνειν is also used in the sense of 'avoiding' or 'saving oneself from' anything. Thus Joseph. *Ant.* II. 3. 2 says of Reuben's desire to save Joseph's life, καὶ τό γε μὴ μιανθῆναι τὰς χεῖρας αὐτοὺς κερδαίνειν = and that they would save themselves from having their hands defiled. So in this we may take κερδῆσαι, without a repetition of the μή from the previous clause, as meaning 'to have saved ourselves this harm &c.' The sense is the same in either case.

22. καὶ τὰ νῦν, *and now*, i.e. though my advice was rejected before I offer it again.

ἀποβολὴ γὰρ ψυχῆς οὐδεμία ἔσται ἐξ ὑμῶν, πλὴν τοῦ πλοίου, *for there shall be no loss of life among you, but only of the ship.* The Apostle now speaks in the confidence of a revelation. Before (verse 10) he had reasoned from the probabilities of the case.

23. τοῦ θεοῦ οὗ εἰμι ἐγώ, ᾧ καὶ λατρεύω, ἄγγελος, *an angel of the God whose I am, whom also I serve.* In speaking to heathens this would be the sense which the Apostle designed to convey. They had their own gods. But St Paul stood in a different relation to his God from any which they would acknowledge towards their divinities. To him God was a Father, and therefore all obedience and service were His due. Cf. the language of Jonah when he was among the heathen sailors (Jonah i. 9).

24. Καίσαρί σε δεῖ παραστῆναι, *thou must stand before Cæsar*, and that this may come to pass thou shalt be saved from the present danger.

For παρίστημι with a dative, in this sense, cf. LXX. Prov. xxii. 29, ὁρατικὸν ἄνδρα καὶ ὀξὺν ἐν τοῖς ἔργοις αὐτοῦ βασιλεῦσι δεῖ παρεστάναι, καὶ μὴ παρεστάναι ἀνδράσι νωθροῖς.

κεχάρισταί σοι ὁ θεός, *God hath granted thee.* This must be understood as in answer to prayer on the part of St Paul. In the midst of such peril, though no mention is made of the fact, we cannot doubt that the Apostle cried unto the Lord in his distress, and the gracious answer was vouchsafed that all should be preserved. It is not with any thought of boastfulness that he speaks thus to the heathen captain and centurion. All the praise is ascribed to God, and thus the heathen would learn that St Paul had God very near unto him.

25. πιστεύω γὰρ τῷ θεῷ, *for I believe God.* And he implies 'I would have you do so too, that you may be of good cheer.' In the midst of danger, few things could be more inspiriting than such an address. And by this time all in the ship must have learnt that they had no common prisoner in the Jew who had appealed from his own people to the Roman emperor.

26. εἰς νῆσον δέ τινα δεῖ ἡμᾶς ἐκπεσεῖν, *but we must be cast upon a certain island.* Hence it appears that in the vision some details of the manner of their preservation had been made known to St Paul by the divine messenger; and more evidence of this is seen in the remainder of the narrative.

27. τεσσαρεσκαιδεκάτη νύξ, *the fourteenth night,* i.e. from the time when they set sail from Fair Havens. Since that time they had been constantly driven to and fro.

ἐν τῷ 'Αδρίᾳ, *in the sea of Adria.* That part of the Mediterranean which lies between Greece, Italy and Africa is so called. The name embraced a much wider extent of sea than the present Gulf of Venice, which is called 'the Adriatic.' Cf. Strabo, II. 123. See also *Josephi Vita* 3, for an account of a voyage made in the same sea about the same period.

ὑπενόουν οἱ ναῦται, *the shipmen surmised.* Their knowledge of the sea would enable them to form an opinion from things which others would hardly notice. It may be they observed some alteration in the currents, or a different character or sound of the waves, dashed against the land as they would be, if land were near.

28. βολίσαντες, *having sounded.* In ancient times this must have been the only means of feeling their way in dark and stormy weather. The lead must have been in constant use.

εὗρον ὀργυιὰς εἴκοσι, *they found it twenty fathoms.* Literally 'they found twenty fathoms,' i.e. depth of water.

βραχὺ δὲ διαστήσαντες, *and after a little space.* The verb may apply either to lapse of time or progress in space. As here the ship was at the mercy of the waves it is better to take the phrase in reference to time. Cf. Luke xxii. 59. The movement of the vessel meanwhile is understood.

ὀργυιὰς δεκαπέντε, *fifteen fathoms.* Such a rapid decrease in the depth of the water shewed that they would soon be aground.

29. φοβούμενοί τε μήπου κατὰ τραχεῖς τόπους ἐκπέσωμεν, *and fearing lest we should be cast ashore somewhere on rocky ground.* That rocks were near was evident from the dashing of the waves. But the morning, even with the faint light which appeared through the dark clouds, might enable them to make for a part where the coast was not so full of danger.

ἐκ πρύμνης ῥίψαντες ἀγκύρας τέσσαρας, *having cast four anchors out of the stern,* thus trying as best they might to keep the head of the vessel towards the land and yet let her come no nearer to it, until they could make out what it was like.

εὔχοντο ἡμέραν γενέσθαι, *they wished* [or *prayed*] *for the day.* If 'prayed' be taken as the rendering, the similarity of the circumstances to those in Jonah's voyage would be made still greater, for then the heathen sailors prayed to their own gods.

30. τῶν δὲ ναυτῶν ζητούντων φυγεῖν, *and when the shipmen were seeking to flee*. They had hit upon a device which they thought would enable them to have the first chance for safety, and now they set about to carry it out. Everybody would agree that it was the most important matter at the moment to hold the ship in her position. So they professed to be anxious to make her secure fore as well as aft, and to lay out anchors from the foreship. For doing this they made out that the boat must be lowered from the deck, and that having been done, they intended to avail themselves of it and to row towards the shore. Paul's interference stopped them.

31. εἶπεν ὁ Παῦλος τῷ ἑκατοντάρχῃ καὶ τοῖς στρατιώταις, *Paul said to the centurion and to the soldiers*. These would probably be able to stop the intended desertion better than the captain of the vessel. At all events they were strong enough in numbers to take the matter into their own hands, and cut the boat adrift. It seems too (from verse 11) that the centurion had much to do with the direction of the ship. Probably he had chartered her for the conveyance of his prisoners and so had the right to be consulted on all that was done.

ἐὰν μὴ οὗτοι μείνωσιν ἐν τῷ πλοίῳ, *except these abide in the ship*. We see from this that every human effort was still to be made, although God had revealed to Paul that they should all be saved. If the sailors had left, the ignorance of the soldiers and other passengers would not have availed to save them at such a time. The skill of the sailors was to be exerted to carry out what God had promised.

32. τότε ἀπέκοψαν οἱ στρατιῶται τὰ σχοινία τῆς σκάφης, *then the soldiers cut away the ropes of the boat*, i.e. cut asunder the ropes which attached the boat to the ship. Thus the boat was cast away.

33. ἄχρι δὲ οὗ ἡμέρα ἤμελλεν γίνεσθαι, *and while the day was coming on*, i.e. before it was light enough to see what had best be done. Here again we may notice how every means was to be employed for safety. Paul urges them to take now a proper meal that when the time for work arrives they may be in a condition to undertake it. The remaining clauses of the verse are not to be understood as implying that the fast had been entire for so long a time. Such a thing is impossible. But what the Apostle means is that the crew and passengers had taken during all that time no regular food, only snatching a morsel now and then when they were able, and that of something which had not been prepared.

34. τοῦτο γὰρ πρὸς τῆς ὑμετέρας σωτηρίας ὑπάρχει, *for this is for your safety;* because the men when they had been strengthened by a proper meal would be able to do more towards their own preservation.

For πρός with a genitive, meaning 'in the interest of,' 'to the advantage of,' cf. Thuc. II. 86, ἡ ἐν στενῷ ναυμαχία πρὸς Λακεδαιμονίων ἐστίν.

οὐδενὸς γὰρ ὑμῶν θρὶξ ἀπὸ τῆς κεφαλῆς ἀπολεῖται, *for there shall not a hair perish from the head of any of you*. The phrase (with a variation between πεσεῖται and ἀπολεῖται) is a proverbial one to express complete deliverance. See LXX. 1 Sam. xiv. 45, ζῇ κύριος, εἰ πεσεῖται

τριχὸς τῆς κεφαλῆς αὐτοῦ ἐπὶ τὴν γῆν.　So 2 Sam. xiv. 11; 1 Kings i.
52; and Luke xxi. 18.

35. εὐχαρίστησεν τῷ θεῷ, *he gave thanks to God.* As he had
advised, so he set the example of taking food. But he did more than
this. He made an Eucharist of this meal. In the sight of the heathen
soldiers and sailors, he brake the bread in solemn thanksgiving, and
thus converted the whole into a religious act, which can hardly have
been without its influence on the minds of some, at all events, of
those who had heard St Paul's previous words about the revelation
which God had made to him.

36. εὔθυμοι δὲ γενόμενοι πάντες, *and all becoming of good cheer.*
Paul's hopeful spirit had breathed hope into the whole company, and
doubtless the religious character infused into the meal was not without
a calming influence.

προσελάβοντο τροφῆς, *took some food.* The 'some' is due to the
partitive genitive.

37. διακόσιαι ἑβδομήκοντα ἕξ, *two hundred threescore and sixteen.*
As we do not know the number of prisoners and soldiers, it is impossible to form any conclusion about the manning of such a ship as this.
The number here mentioned is very large, and we cannot suppose that
a merchantman from Alexandria to Rome would carry a very large
crew. But to accept the reading (supported by very little authority)
which makes the whole company 'about threescore and sixteen' has
equal difficulty on the other side, and the way in which it arose can be
easily explained from the use of letters for numerals among the Greeks.
A vessel which could have four anchors cast from the stern, and still
have more to spare for the foreship, must have been of large size and
have needed many hands. The occasion of the numbering was probably the near expectation of coming ashore, and so it was needful to
have all told, for the captain, in respect of the crew, and for the centurion, that of his prisoners and soldiers none might be allowed
to escape or be missing. The mention of the number at this point of
the history is one of the many very natural features of the narrative.

38. κορεσθέντες δὲ τροφῆς, *and when they had eaten enough.*
Literally 'having been satisfied with food.' When they had satisfied
their present need, there was no use in trying to save more of the food
which they had. So they set about lightening the ship. This is
implied by the tense of the verb (ἐκούφιζον), and the next clause tells
us the way they did it. They cast into the sea the corn which had
been the first cargo of the vessel from Alexandria. No doubt this was
the heaviest part of the freight, and would relieve the vessel greatly.

39. τὴν γῆν οὐκ ἐπεγίνωσκον, *they knew not the land.* We need not
from this suppose that none of the sailors were acquainted with the
island of Malta, but that the point of the land, close to which they
were, was unrecognised by them. When they were close in shore, and
amid stormy weather, this could very well happen, as they were a long
way distant from the usual harbour.

κόλπον δέ τινα κατενόουν ἔχοντα αἰγιαλόν, *but they perceived a certain bay with a beach.* αἰγιαλός is used to signify such a sandy beach as might allow a ship to be run aground upon it without the danger of her immediately coming to pieces.

εἰς ὃν ἐβουλεύοντο εἰ δύναιντο ἐξῶσαι τὸ πλοῖον, *and they took counsel whether they could drive the ship upon it,* i.e. they saw the beach to be such that they had a chance of landing there. They therefore discussed the best way of doing so in their present maimed condition.

40. καὶ τὰς ἀγκύρας περιελόντες, *and casting off the anchors.* περι- αιρέω indicates that they now cast loose all the anchors round about the stern of the vessel, where they had before laid them out. When they had thrown overboard a load of corn, there was no likelihood that they would trouble themselves with the weight of four anchors and the labour of hauling them up. So 'taken up' (of A.V.) gives a wrong idea.

εἴων εἰς τὴν θάλασσαν, *they left them in the sea,* i.e. the anchors. They had now no use for them, so they let them go.

ἅμα ἀνέντες τὰς ζευκτηρίας τῶν πηδαλίων, *at the same time loosing the rudder bands.* ζευκτηρία is found nowhere else but in this place. The rudders, of which the ancient ships had two (thus accounting for the plural number, πηδαλίων), had at first been made fast and raised out of the water, when the anchors were laid out in the stern. Now that an attempt is to be made to steer the ship toward the beach they are let down again into the sea.

καὶ ἐπάραντες τὸν ἀρτέμωνα, *and having hoisted the foresail.* ἀρτέμων was in old times the name given to the *foresail.* Cognate words are now employed as names of the larger sails of vessels in the Mediterranean. But here the foresail was all they had left. Cf. Smith's *Voyage and Shipwreck of St Paul,* pp. 102, 153, seqq.

τῇ πνεούσῃ, *to the wind.* The noun to be supplied is αὔρᾳ.

εἰς τὸν αἰγιαλόν, *towards the beach,* where they had resolved after consultation to try to land.

41. περιπεσόντες δὲ εἰς τόπον διθάλασσον, *but lighting upon a place where two seas met.* This is one of the features of the narrative by which the locality can almost certainly be identified. The little island of Salmonetta forms with the Maltese coast near St Paul's Bay exactly such a position as is here described. From the sea at a little distance it appears as though the land were all continuous, and the current between the island and the mainland is only discovered on a nearer approach. This current by its deposits has raised a mudbank where its force is broken by the opposing sea, and into this bank, just at the place where the current meets the sea-waves, was the ship driven, the force of the water preventing the vessel from reaching the beach just beyond. So it came to pass that though they got much nearer to the shore than at first, yet after all they had to swim for their lives.

ἐπέκειλαν τὴν ναῦν, *they ran the ship aground.* ἐπικέλλω is found in Homer and Apoll. Rhodius, but ἐποκέλλω is a more common word, and so in time came to be substituted for the text of the oldest MSS.

ἡ δὲ πρύμνα ἐλύετο, *but the stern began to break up.* This is the force of the imperfect tense. When the foreship was immoveable, the stern would also be held fast, and so be acted on by the waves with great violence and begin to go to pieces.

42. ἵνα τοὺς δεσμώτας ἀποκτείνωσιν, *that they should kill the prisoners.* This advice was given because, by the Roman law, the soldiers were answerable with their own lives for the prisoners placed under their charge.

For ἵνα after a word or phrase signifying 'to counsel' or 'decree' cf. John ix. 22. Also Ecclus. xliv. 18, διαθῆκαι αἰῶνος ἐτέθησαν πρὸς αὐτὸν ἵνα μὴ ἐξαλειφθῇ κατακλυσμῷ πᾶσα σάρξ.

43. ὁ δὲ ἑκατοντάρχης βουλόμενος διασῶσαι, *but the centurion, desiring to save.* The centurion could not fail to see that it was to the Apostle that the safety of the whole party was due, and he could hardly help feeling admiration for the prisoner, after all he had seen of him. From the first (see verse 3) he had been well disposed toward Paul, and the after events would not have lessened his regard. So, to save him, he stops the design of his men, and saves the whole number of the prisoners.

ἐκώλυσεν αὐτούς, *hindered them* (Rev. Vers. *stayed them*). The verb is a forcible word, and shews that the centurion was in full command of his men, and had not in the confusion lost his thought-fulness and presence of mind.

τοὺς δυναμένους κολυμβᾶν, *those who could swim.* This was the wisest course to adopt. Thus there would be a body ready on the shore to help those who only could float thither by the aid of some-thing to which they were clinging. As St Paul had already been thrice shipwrecked and had been in the deep a night and a day (2 Cor. xi. 25) we may be sure that he was among those who were told off to swim ashore.

ἀπορρίψαντας πρώτους ἐπὶ τὴν γῆν ἐξιέναι, *should cast themselves overboard* [lit. *off*] *and get first to land.* The swimmers were to get into safety first of all, that then they might be in readiness to succour those who drifted to the land on the floating spars and planks.

For the active participle in this reflexive sense cf. Arrian *Exped. Alex.* lib. II. 4. 7, οἱ δὲ εἰς τὸν Κύδνον ποταμὸν λέγουσι ῥίψαντα νήξασθαι.

44. καὶ τοὺς λοιπούς, *and that the rest.* The case is left pendent, because of the long apposition which immediately follows. Some need-ful words = 'should get to the land' are readily supplied in thought.

οὓς μὲν ἐπὶ σανίσιν, οὓς δὲ ἐπί τινων τῶν ἀπὸ τοῦ πλοίου, *some on planks, some on broken pieces of the ship.* The last clause is literally 'on some of the parts of the ship.' The things on which they were saved were pieces which on the stranding of the vessel would be broken away from the main timbers. Everything that was needless to be kept on board they had already thrown over, and so we cannot think here of loose furniture of the vessel, but only of the framework itself.

There seems in this verse to be no appreciable difference of sense between ἐπί with a dative and with a genitive. Krüger (p. 340) is quoted in a note to *Winer-Moulton* (p. 488) to the effect that ἐπί with a genitive denotes a merely accidental, free connexion; ἐπί with the dative denotes rather *belonging to*. There is no trace of such distinction here.

πάντας διασωθῆναι, *all escaped safe.* This is better than A.V.; for 'all safe' may mean no more than 'quite safe.'

CHAPTER XXVIII.

Readings varying from the *Text. recept.*

1. ἐπέγνωμεν for ἐπέγνωσαν with ℵABC.   *Vulg.* 'cognovimus.'

10. πρὸς τὰς χρείας with ℵABI.   *Vulg.* 'quae necessaria erant.'

16. ὁ ἑκατόνταρχος παρέδωκε τοὺς δεσμίους τῷ στρατοπεδάρχῃ omitted with ℵABI.   Not represented in *Vulg.*

17. αὐτόν for τὸν Παῦλον with ℵABI.   *Vulg.* has not the proper name.

25. ὑμῶν for ἡμῶν with ℵAB.   *Vulg.* 'nostros.'

26. λέγων with ℵBLP.

28. τοῦτο added before τὸ σωτήριον with ℵAB.   *Vulg.* 'hoc salutare.'

29. Omitted with ℵABE.   *Vulg.* represents it, having 'et cum hæc dixisset, exierunt ab eo Judæi, multam habentes inter se quæstionem.'

30. ὁ Παῦλος omitted with ℵABE.   Not represented in *Vulg.*

Ch. XXVIII. 1—10. The shipwrecked Company hospitably entertained in Malta. Paul, bitten by a Viper, feels no Hurt. Cure of the Father of the chief Magistrate.

1. διασωθέντες τότε ἐπέγνωμεν, *when we were escaped, then we knew,* i.e. we found out from the natives who were on the shore.

Μελίτη, *Melita.* They would at once learn what the land was from the natives whom they found on the shore. Tradition has from the earliest times identified Melita with the modern Malta. But Constantine Porphyrogenitus (*de Adm. Imp.* p. 36) and others after him have attempted to shew that *Meleda,* a small island in the Adriatic Sea, not far from the coast of Illyria, was the scene of the shipwreck. They have supported this opinion by confining the sense of Adria (xxvii. 27) to the modern Adriatic Sea, by their explanation of 'barbarians' in the next verse of this chapter, and by the absence of vipers at the

present time from the island of Malta. But the latter circumstance is
not without a parallel. The advance of cultivation and alteration of
temperature have destroyed poisonous beasts out of other districts
besides Malta, and the two first arguments are founded on mistakes.
Moreover it is hardly possible to conceive that a ship should be driven
for fourteen days in the Adriatic without going ashore, and the direction in which they sailed after finding a fresh vessel (xxviii. 11, 12) is
also completely opposed to the idea that they were wrecked in the Gulf
of Venice.

2.   οἵ τε βάρβαροι, *and the barbarians.* The word is used in the original as it was used by the ancient Greeks and Romans. Those who did
not speak their language were to them always ' barbarians,' not necessarily in our modern sense, but as strange and foreign folks. The
language spoken in Malta was probably a Phœnician dialect, as the
island had received most of its inhabitants from Carthage, but had
come under Roman rule in the Second Punic War (Livy, xxi. 51).

βάρβαρος is used 2 Macc. x. 4, by Judas Maccabeus and the Jews
with him, to describe the Greek enemy under Antiochus, who certainly
would not be ' barbarians' in the modern sense.

οὐ τὴν τυχοῦσαν φιλανθρωπίαν, *especial kindness.* Cf. above, xix. 11,
note.

προσελάβοντο πάντας ἡμᾶς, *they received us all,* i.e. took us under
their care. At first of course the hospitality would be shewn by kind
treatment on the beach, evidenced by their lighting a fire. Afterwards,
as the stay was of three months' duration, the sailors and prisoners
would find quarters in the dwellings of the natives. Paul, the centurion, and some others were received into the house of the chief magistrate. The rain continued after they had got ashore, and the storm
had so lowered the temperature that the first thing to be done was to
make a large fire.

For the verb used in this sense of hospitable entertainment, cf.
Philemon 17. Also 2 Macc. x. 15, τοὺς φυγαδευθέντας ἀπὸ Ἱεροσολύμων
προσλαβόμενοι.

3.   συστρέψαντος δὲ τοῦ Παύλου, *but when Paul had gathered.*
This is only another sign of the active spirit of the Apostle. Whatever was to be done, if he were able to take a part in it, he was never
wanting, whether it was in counselling about a difficulty, in comforting under danger, or helping by bodily labour to relieve the general
distress.

The verb is used of gathering men together, 2 Macc. xiv. 30.

φρυγάνων τι πλῆθος, *a bundle of sticks.* φρύγανα applies very fitly
to the brushwood and furze which is said to be the only material
growing near St Paul's Bay of which a fire could be made.

Chrysostom exclaims : ὅρα αὐτὸν ἐνεργοῦντα καὶ οὐδαμοῦ θαυματουρ-
γοῦντα ἁπλῶς ἀλλ' ἀπὸ χρείας· καὶ ἐν τῷ χειμῶνι γὰρ αἰτίας οὔσης προεφή-
τευσεν, ἀλλ' οὐχ ἁπλῶς, καὶ ἐνταῦθα πάλιν φρύγανα συλλέγει καὶ ἐπι-
τίθησιν.

ἔχιδνα ἀπὸ τῆς θέρμης ἐξελθοῦσα, *a viper coming out by reason of the heat.* Dr Farrar (*Life of St Paul*, II. 384 note) has remarked that the viper has disappeared from the isle of Arran, as it is now said to have done from Malta.

The viper in this case had been numbed by the cold, and on feeling the sudden heat woke up and sprang away from it.

In καθῆψεν we have an instance of the active voice used for the middle, which became not uncommon in later Greek. Cf. xxvii. 43, note.

4.   τὸ θηρίον, *the beast.* There is nothing in the Greek to represent ' venomous ' (as given in the A.V.), though it was because the inhabitants knew that such was its character that they were so astonished at what happened.

But θηρίον must have been very frequently applied to venomous creatures; for ἡ θηριακή (its derivative) is the name for an antidote against poisonous bites.

ἡ δίκη ζῆν οὐκ εἴασεν, *Justice suffereth not to live,* i.e. She is, as is her wont, finding out the wrongdoer.

5.   ὁ μὲν οὖν ἀποτινάξας τὸ θηρίον, *howbeit having shaken off the beast.* The verb is used (Luke ix. 5) of shaking off dust from the feet. The idea conveyed is that St Paul was quite composed in what he did, and that the beast was no cause of alarm to him.

6.   οἱ δὲ προσεδόκων αὐτὸν μέλλειν πίμπρασθαι, *but they expected that he would have swollen.* Such being the usual effect of the viper's bite, and making itself apparent in a very short time.

The verb πίμπρημι in classical Greek means ' to burn,' ' to burn up,' and in the passive ' to be inflamed,' but in the LXX. we have the verb used in the sense of ' to swell ' in Numb. v. 21, 23, 27, καὶ πρηθήσεται τὴν κοιλίαν.

ἐπὶ πολὺ δὲ αὐτῶν προσδοκώντων, *but when they had been long in expectation.* Keeping the same rendering for προσδοκέω in both places in the verse. The people had seen cases of viper-bite before, and they had no doubt about what was going to happen.

καὶ θεωρούντων μηδὲν ἄτοπον εἰς αὐτὸν γινόμενον, *and beheld nothing amiss come to him.* For the word cf. Luke xxiii. 41; Acts xxv. 5. It can be applied to anything abnormal whether it be a breach of the law or a change of bodily condition. For the latter sense, see Joseph. *Ant.* XI. 5. 2 ὅπως εὐχὰς ποιήσωνται τοῦ μηδὲν κατὰ τὴν ὁδὸν παθεῖν ἄτοπον.

μεταβαλλόμενοι, *changing their minds.* For the word cf. Test. XII. Patr. *Dan* 4, καὶ ἐάν τις ἐπαινῇ ὑμᾶς ὡς ἀγαθοὺς μὴ ἐπαίρεσθε μηδὲ μεταβάλλεσθε. The previous clause speaks of anger, and the last verb indicates the change to the contrary.

ἔλεγον αὐτὸν εἶναι θεόν, *they said that he was a god.* Compare the conduct of the Lycaonians in Lystra (xiv. 11 seqq.), whose behaviour afterwards shews that the opinion quickly formed was unstable, and liable to change as suddenly as it came.

Chrysostom's comment here is: ἄρα καὶ τὸν περὶ προνοίας λόγον εἶχον καὶ πολλῷ τῶν φιλοσόφων οὗτοι οἱ βάρβαροι φιλοσοφώτεροι ἐτύγχανον.

αὐτοὶ μὲν γὰρ οὐκ ἀφίασι προνοίας ἀπολαύειν τὰ ὑπὸ σελήνην· οἱ δὲ πανταχοῦ νομίζουσι παρεῖναι τὸν θεόν.

7. ἐν δὲ τοῖς περὶ τὸν τόπον ἐκεῖνον ὑπῆρχεν χωρία, *now in the
neighbourhood of that place were lands belonging*, &c. The nearest
place to what is believed to have been the scene of the wreck is the
town now called *Alta Vecchia*.

τῷ πρώτῳ τῆς νήσου, *to the chief man of the island.* Πρῶτος is known
from inscriptions (see Bochart, *Geogr.* II. 1. 26) to have been the
official title of the governor of Melita. The island of Melita belonged
to the province of the Sicilian Prætor (Cicero, *Verr.* IV. 18), whose
legate Publius probably was. Tradition makes him become bishop of
Malta.

For πρῶτος used in this way, cf. *Acta Pauli et Theclæ* 11, where
Thamyris supports his promises by saying, εἰμὶ γὰρ πρῶτος τῆς πόλεως.

ὃς ἀναδεξάμενος ἡμᾶς, *who having received us.* This was only natural in the Roman official, for Paul was under the charge of a Roman
officer, and had appealed for hearing to the Roman emperor.

τρεῖς ἡμέρας φιλοφρόνως ἐξένισεν, *entertained us courteously three
days.* This was until arrangements could be made for a more permanent dwelling-place. As they must remain in the island through the
stormy weather of winter, before they could start again, it would be
needful to provide them with settled quarters. They could not be
guests for the whole three months.

8. ἐγένετο δέ, *and it was so, that,* &c. The words do not mean as
might be thought from A. V. 'and it came to pass, that,' &c., that
the father of Publius fell ill after St Paul's arrival, but that he was ill
before.

πυρετοῖς καὶ δυσεντερίῳ, *of fever and dysentery.* The words are
technical, such as a physician, as St Luke is reputed to have been,
would be likely to use in describing the disease. πυρετοί, in the plural
number, implies the *fits of fever* which occur at intervals in such diseases as ague.

9. καὶ οἱ λοιποί, *the rest also.* It was not a few who came, but
during the three months of their stay all the others who were in sickness and heard of what had been done for the father of the chief magistrate (and it was sure to be widely noised abroad) came to be cured.

10. πολλαῖς τιμαῖς, *with many honours.* No doubt these included
gifts of money and such things as would be needed by travellers who
had lost everything in the shipwreck : but to restrict the word to the
sense of 'honorarium' or fee, such as might be paid to a physician, is
to narrow the meaning needlessly, and to put a construction on the
proceeding which it cannot bear. The Apostle who prayed and laid
his hands on the sick and healed them was not the sort of person to
whom men would offer money as a fee.

ἐτίμησαν ἡμᾶς, *they honoured us,* i. e. not only St Paul, but for his
sake the rest of the party were honoured by the people of the island.

καὶ ἀναγομένοις, *and when we sailed.* See above on xxvii. 3.

ἐπέθεντο τὰ πρὸς τὰς χρείας, *they put on board such things as we needed.* The bounty must have been large if we consider the number of those for whom it was given. But Publius would set the example, and others would not be slow to follow it.

11—16. THE VOYAGE FROM MALTA, AND THE ARRIVAL IN ROME.

11. μετὰ δὲ τρεῖς μῆνας, *and after three months.* The proper season for sailing having again come round, now that winter was over.

ἀνήχθημεν, *we set sail.* See on xxvii. 3.

ἐν πλοίῳ...'Αλεξανδρινῷ, *in a ship of Alexandria which had wintered in the island.* This was another vessel employed probably in the same corn-carrying trade as that other in which (xxviii. 6) they had embarked at Myrrha, and suffered so many perils. This vessel had got as far as Melita, on its way to Italy, before the stormy weather came on. As the harbour was then where it now is, the ship had wintered in what is now Valetta.

παρασήμῳ Διοσκούροις, *whose sign was the Twin brothers.* Διοσκοῦροι is the name given in mythological story to Jupiter's two sons (Castor and Pollux) born of Leda, who, when they were translated to the sky, became a constellation of special favour towards sailors. Horace speaks of them as 'lucida sidera' (*Od.* I. 3. 2), where he describes their beneficent influence on the ocean. By παράσημον πλοῖον is meant a boat with what we should now call a *figure-head.* But the ancient ships had such signs both at stem and stern, and often the figure was that of some divinity.

If for no other reason than the description of the vessel in which the further journey was performed we cannot accept the theory that the wreck took place in the Adriatic Sea. It would be hard to conceive of a vessel from Alexandria, which had stopped on its voyage to Italy to avoid the storms of winter, being found so far out of its course as Meleda in the Adriatic.

12. καὶ καταχθέντες εἰς Συρακούσας, *and touching at Syracuse.* The vessel takes the regular route, sailing north from Valetta to Sicily. Syracuse was one of the chief towns of Sicily lying on the south-eastern extremity, and was famous in classical history as the scene of many of the disasters of the Athenian fleet and army in their expedition to Sicily during the Peloponnesian war.

13. περιελθόντες, *having made a circuit.* They made this winding course because the favourable wind, for which they had probably been waiting during the three days' stay at Syracuse, did not come.

κατηντήσαμεν εἰς Ῥήγιον, *we arrived at Rhegium.* The modern *Reggio,* situated at the southern point of Italy, on the straits of Messina. At this place Caligula designed to construct a harbour for these corn ships coming from Egypt to Italy, but his intention was never carried out.

ἐπιγενομένου νότου, *when a south wind sprang up.* Thus by a change of wind they were able to go speedily forward, instead of tacking as they had been obliged to do from Syracuse to Rhegium.

εἰς Ποτιόλους, *to Puteoli.* This is the modern *Pozzuoli*, near Naples. In St Paul's day it was a principal port of Rome, and to it came most of the corn supply from Egypt.

A Greek name of Puteoli was Δικαιαρχία. Philo *in Flaccum* 521. Josephus, *Vita* 3.

14. οὗ εὑρόντες ἀδελφούς, *where having found brethren.* There was, we see from this, a Christian Church already established in Puteoli, and it was to such a degree well known, that the Apostle on his arrival at once learnt of its existence. From this we may gather that the Christians in Italy had already spread to a considerable extent, and hence it seems very probable that Christianity had been carried into that country from Jerusalem soon after the first Pentecostal preaching, at which time Roman visitors were present in the Holy City. Of course in such a place as Puteoli the Jews were likely to congregate, for the sake of trade, more than in many other places of Italy, and from their body the earliest converts to Christianity must have been made. But that, without any previous recorded visit of an Apostle, there should already be in Puteoli a numerous band of Christians is evidence of the zeal with which the new faith was being propagated. For it was now only about 28 years since the death of Jesus.

παρεκλήθημεν, *we were intreated.* It has generally been thought that the duration of this stay (seven days) was arranged so that the Apostle might be present with the Church in Puteoli at least over one Lord's day. Thus the Christian congregation would be able to gather in its entirety, and to hear from the lips of the great Apostle of the Gentiles, the Gospel for which he was now 'an ambassador in bonds.' We do not know whether any circumstances occurred to detain Julius in Puteoli, but if it were not so, it is a token of the great influence which St Paul had obtained over the centurion, that he was permitted to stay such a long time with his Christian friends, when the capital was so near at hand.

καὶ οὕτως εἰς τὴν Ῥώμην ἤλθαμεν, *and so we came to Rome.* The narrative at first speaks of the completed voyage, and then in verse 15 mention is made of some details which relate to the short land journey from Puteoli to the capital.

15. οἱ ἀδελφοὶ ἀκούσαντες τὰ περὶ ἡμῶν, *the brethren having heard of us.* Between Puteoli and Rome there was constant communication, and the seven days of the Apostle's sojourn in the port were amply sufficient to make the whole Christian body in Rome aware of his arrival in Italy and of the time when he would set out towards the city.

ἦλθαν εἰς ἀπάντησιν ἡμῖν, *they came to meet us.* Because the verb ἀπαντάω takes a dative after it, the same case stands after the noun. For examples cf. LXX. 2 Chron. xv. 2, καὶ ἐξῆλθεν εἰς ἀπάντησιν τῷ

'Ασậ. Also 2 Chron. xx. 18; Judges vi. 35, xx. 25; 1 Sam. xiii. 10, &c. If it were quite certain that the sixteenth chapter of the Epistle to the Romans was part of the letter which was sent to that Church we might make sure of the names of some who would be of the party which started from Rome to welcome St Paul on his arrival in Italy. Aquila and Priscilla, Epænetus; Andronicus and Junias, who are both spoken of as having been formerly fellow-prisoners with the Apostle; Rufus, Herodion and Apelles, who are mentioned there in terms of the greatest affection, could hardly have failed to be among the company at Appii Forum. But the whole closing chapter of the Epistle to the Romans appears to apply better to some Asiatic Church, probably Ephesus, than to Rome, and so it is unsafe to conclude that the Christians there mentioned were those who now met St Paul and cheered him on his way.

Perhaps however when we remember the Greek influence which prevailed in the early centuries of the Christian era at Rome we need not marvel at the Greek names we meet with in this xvith chapter. The first Bishops of Rome have nearly all Greek names, and even Clemens Romanus wrote in Greek, and not in Latin.

ἄχρι 'Αππίου φόρου, *as far as Appii Forum*, i.e. the Market of Appius. The name 'Forum' seems to have been given by the Romans to places such as we should now call borough-towns. The town here mentioned was situated on the Appian Way, the great road from Rome to Brundusium. Both road and town owed their name to the famous Appius Claudius, the Roman Censor, and this town is mentioned by Horace as crowded with sailors, and abounding in tavern-keepers of bad character (*Sat.* I. 5. 4). It was distant rather more than forty miles from Rome, and as the Appian Way was only one of two ways by which travellers could go from Appii Forum to the Imperial City, it was natural that the deputation from Rome should halt here and wait for the Apostle's arrival.

καὶ Τριῶν ταβερνῶν, *and the three Taverns*. The name '*Tabernæ*' had in Latin a much wider signification than the English 'Taverns' and was applied to any shop whatever, not as the English word to one where refreshments are sold. The site of this place has not been identified, but it is said to have been about ten miles nearer to Rome than Appii Forum: and the body of Christians who came as far as this had perhaps set out from Rome later than their brethren. The whole distance from Puteoli to Rome was about 140 miles. 'Tres Tabernæ' is placed 33 miles from Rome.

εὐχαριστήσας τῷ θεῷ ἔλαβε θάρσος, *he thanked God and took courage*. When thinking and writing about his coming to Rome, Paul had never thought that his first visit to it would be as a prisoner. He had hoped (Rom. i. 11—12) to come as the bearer of some spiritual blessing, and to be comforted himself by the faith of the Roman brethren. How different were the event from what he had pictured. But yet here were some of the brethren, and their faith and love were made manifest by their journey to meet the Apostle, and no doubt they brought with them the salutations of all the Church. This was somewhat to

be thankful for. The prisoner would not be without sympathy, and
the spiritual gift might be imparted even though Paul was no longer
free. The cause of Christ was advancing; and cheered by the evidence
of this the Apostle's heart revived.

16. ὅτε δὲ εἰσήλθομεν εἰς Ῥώμην, *and when we came to Rome.* There
was much that might have been said of this land journey from Puteoli
to Rome, and the writer of the Acts was one of the fellow-travellers.
But it is foreign to his purpose to dwell on anything which does not
concern the spread of the Gospel according to the command of Jesus
(Acts i. 8), and so he leaves all the glorious sights and scenery unmentioned, and tells us no word of the many monuments which stood
along the Appian Way, only noticing, what his history required, the
two little bands, that represented Christ's cause and the work of the
Gospel, in the great city to which they were approaching.

Here in some MSS. there is an addition, see above on the various
readings of the chapter. These additional words, not given in the
oldest MSS., are yet not of the same character as many of the sentences which seem introduced into the text of the Acts by later hands.
They are entirely independent of anything either in the Acts or the
Epistles of St Paul, and it is not easy to understand why they should
have been added to the original text. There is moreover such similarity between the ending of the first and last words in the clause,
that the eye of an early scribe may have passed over from the one to
the other, and thus omitted the clause, and in this way may have
originated the text of the MSS. which leave the passage out.

ἐπετράπη τῷ Παύλῳ μένειν καθ' ἑαυτόν, *Paul was suffered to abide
by himself.* This lenity was probably due to the commendation of
the centurion Julius, who cannot but have found that in St Paul he
had charge of no ordinary prisoner, and having been saved and aided
by the Apostle's advice would naturally wish to do something in
return.

Here Chrysostom says, οὐ μικρὸν καὶ τοῦτο τεκμήριον τοῦ πάνυ θαυμασ-
θῆναι αὐτόν· οὐ γὰρ δὴ μετὰ τῶν ἄλλων ἠρίθμουν αὐτόν.

σὺν τῷ φυλάσσοντι αὐτὸν στρατιώτῃ, *with the soldier that guarded
him.* The custom was that the prisoner should be chained by one
hand to the soldier while he was on guard. And to this chain the
Apostle often makes allusion in the Epistles (Ephesians, Philippians,
Colossians and Philemon) written during this imprisonment. See
also below, verse 20. The frequent change of the person who guarded
him would give the Apostle an opportunity of spreading the knowledge of his cause, and the message of the Gospel, very widely among
the Prætorian guards who had him in charge, and many things would
have been heard by them from the soldiers who had sailed with St
Paul, which would make them ready to attend to the narrative of their
prisoner.

17—28.   St Paul's Interview with the Jews in Rome.

17. μετὰ ἡμέρας τρεῖς, *after three days.* At first the Apostle would
naturally desire to learn all he could of the Christian congregations at

Rome from those who had been the first to welcome him on his approach to that city. But for this, three days sufficed. Then he set about explaining his position to those of his fellow-countrymen, not Christians, who were of most importance in Rome. For to them would most probably be forwarded an account of the charges to be laid against the Apostle, and of the evidence by which they were to be supported.

συγκαλέσασθαι αὐτὸν τοὺς ὄντας τῶν Ἰουδαίων πρώτους, *that he called together the chief of the Jews.* Keeping still to the rule that the Gospel should be offered first to the Jews, even here in Rome, where he had good reason to think that his message would not be received. The decree by which in the reign of Claudius all the Jews had been banished from Rome (xviii. 2) was evidently no longer in force. For clearly there was an important body of them resident in the city.

ἄνδρες ἀδελφοί. See note on i. 16.

οὐδὲν ἐναντίον ποιήσας τῷ λαῷ κ.τ.λ., *though I had done nothing against the people or the customs of our forefathers.* For everywhere he had shewn himself desirous that his own people should hear the message of the Gospel first, and for Jews he had never forbidden circumcision, only insisting that Gentile converts should not be forced to submit to the Jewish law before they were received into the Christian Church.

δέσμιος ἐξ Ἱεροσολύμων παρεδόθην, *I was delivered a prisoner from Jerusalem.* The Apostle describes the result, rather than the steps by which it was brought about. The chief captain had rescued him from the violence of the Jewish mob, and he had never since been out of the care of the Roman authorities. Yet but for the Jews he never would have been a Roman prisoner, and when the Sadducees in Jerusalem found that he was not to be given up to them, they made themselves his accusers before Felix and Festus.

18. ἀνακρίναντές με ἐβούλοντο ἀπολῦσαι, *having examined me, they desired to set me at liberty.* Alluding most probably to Agrippa's remark (xxvi. 32) and the statement of Festus (xxv. 25). It seems probable that Felix would have found means to set Paul free had the requisite bribe been offered to him (xxiv. 26). All were convinced of his innocence.

19. οὐχ ὡς τοῦ ἔθνους μου ἔχων τι κατηγορεῖν, *not that I had ought to accuse my nation of.* St Paul shews himself the patriotic Jew. He knew how many things his fellow-countrymen had suffered at the hands of the Roman power, and he did not wish in any way to bring on them more trouble. He therefore explains that he had taken the course of appealing to Cæsar only because he saw no other means of obtaining his release. If that were secured he wished to lay no charge at the door of his accusers or their brethren in Rome.

20. διὰ ταύτην οὖν τὴν αἰτίαν παρεκάλεσα ὑμᾶς ἰδεῖν καὶ προσλαλῆσαι, *for this cause therefore have I called for you to see and to speak with you.* It is possible in this sentence either to take ὑμᾶς as the object of ἰδεῖν and προσλαλῆσαι, or to understand με, and render (as in

Rev. Vers.) 'did I entreat you to see and to speak with me.' As it seems more probable that Paul would say he wished to speak to the Jews than that he wished them to come and speak with him, the A.V. which the Rev. Vers. gives on the margin appears the preferable rendering. It is quite true that παρακαλέω is generally rendered by 'beseech' 'desire' or 'entreat,' but there is no doubt that St Paul's message would be an earnest request, and we might render here 'have I desired.'

ἕνεκεν γὰρ τῆς ἐλπίδος τοῦ Ἰσραήλ, *because that for the hope of Israel.* The 'hope of Israel' is the general expectation of Messiah. In Jesus Paul believed that the expected Saviour had appeared, and for preaching this he had been attacked and made a prisoner. He held the same faith as all the Jews, only going in this matter farther than they in that he believed the ancient promise was now fulfilled. We can see from the reply of the Jews that they understood his position exactly.

τὴν ἅλυσιν ταύτην περίκειμαι, *I am bound with this chain.* περίκειμαι has a construction like that of passive verbs of which the active governs a dative of the person with the accusative of the thing, e.g. πιστεύω τινί τι of which the passive form becomes (Gal. ii. 7) πεπίστευμαι τὸ εὐαγγέλιον. Since περίκειμαι has to serve for both active and passive we cannot have the form equivalent to πιστεύω τινί τι, but in its passive sense περίκειμαι follows the same form of construction as πεπίστευμαι.

21. οὔτε γράμματα περὶ σοῦ ἐδεξάμεθα ἀπὸ τῆς Ἰουδαίας, *neither letters from Judæa concerning thee.* This may easily be understood. For no ship starting later than that in which St Paul sailed was likely to have arrived in Rome before he reached that city, and the Jews who conducted the accusation would take a little time for drawing up all the details which they desired to lay before the court of appeal, so that their despatch would be sent later than the time of Paul's sailing. And before it was determined that he should be sent to Rome they would see no necessity for informing the Jews there concerning his case.

οὔτε παραγενόμενός τις τῶν ἀδελφῶν ἀπήγγειλεν ἢ ἐλάλησέν τι περὶ σοῦ πονηρόν, *nor did any of the brethren come hither and report or speak any harm of thee.* It is very conceivable that during the time between Paul's first arrest and his arrival in Rome (a period of more than two years) many opportunities might have arisen for news about the prisoner to have been sent to Rome. But apparently the speakers here wish merely to say that no news has come to them in connexion with this trial and appeal. They seem not to have been at all anxious to move in the matter. At whatever time the edict of Claudius was withdrawn it could only be within the last few years (ten at the most) that the Jewish population had been again permitted to come to Rome. They were probably loath therefore to call public attention again to their nation by appearing before the court of appeal in a cause connected with their religion.

On the use of ἀδελφοί by the Jews in speaking of their fellow-countrymen, cf. on xxii. 5.

22. ἀξιοῦμεν δὲ παρὰ σοῦ ἀκοῦσαι, *but we desire to hear of thee.* He was a Jew, one of their own nation, and was likely to be able to put his belief before them in its true light. They professed to be open to reason, but this may have been only because they knew not what else to do.

περὶ μὲν γὰρ τῆς αἱρέσεως ταύτης, *for as concerning this sect.* It is clear from this expression that they had learnt from St Paul's speech, though St Luke does not record the words, that he was an adherent of Jesus of Nazareth, and held that in Him 'the hope of Israel' had been fulfilled.

γνωστὸν ἡμῖν ἐστίν, *we know.* Literally 'it is known to us.' Perhaps the speakers intended by this circumlocution to distinguish what they knew by report from a personal knowledge.

ὅτι πανταχοῦ ἀντιλέγεται, *that everywhere it is spoken against.* They were doubtless aware of many of the attacks which had been made by their countrymen on the Christians both in the cities of Asia and Europe, and would have heard them spoken of as the men who were turning the world upside down. The result of the conference was that a day was fixed, on which the Apostle should set forth to them his opinions, so that, as they had no other means for deciding on their course of action, they might discover for themselves what would be the best course to take.

23. εἰς τὴν ξενίαν, *into his lodging.* From this word ξενία, implying hospitable entertainment, it would seem that for the first portion of the time that Paul was in Rome, he was allowed to accept the hospitality of the Christian body, and though chained to his guard, yet to be resident in a house which his friends had provided for him, and where he was, as far as he could be under the circumstances, treated as their guest.

πλείονες, *many.* πλείων often loses its strictly comparative sense, though generally that sense may be observed in the context, though it be not capable of representation in a translation. Here, for instance, the first deputation who came to see the Apostle was a limited number, but on the day appointed for a meeting they came πλείονες, 'in greater numbers.' Cf. Luke xi. 53; Acts ii. 40, xiii. 31, xxi. 10, xxiv. 17, xxv. 14, xxvii. 20; 1 Cor. x. 5; 2 Cor. ii. 6, iv. 15; &c.

οἷς ἐξετίθετο, *to whom he expounded.* The R.V. adds in italics 'the matter' and something of this kind is required for the sense. What he expounded is declared in the succeeding words 'bearing witness of the Kingdom of God.' That is, he testified that the Messianic hope, which all Jews spake of as the Kingdom of God, or the Kingdom of Heaven, had now been revealed in Jesus of Nazareth. This was 'the matter' of the Apostle's exhortation.

ἀπὸ πρωὶ ἕως ἑσπέρας, *from morning till evening.* It is clear from what follows that as in Jerusalem so here, there were some to whom the Apostle's words were not all unwelcome. This accounts for their staying to hear him the whole day through. For the Greek, cf. LXX. Ruth ii. 7, ἀπὸ πρωίθεν καὶ ἕως ἑσπέρας.

24. οἱ δὲ ἠπίστουν, *and some believed not.* No doubt Pharisees and Sadducees had their representatives in Rome as elsewhere among the Jewish population.

25. ἀσύμφωνοι δὲ ὄντες πρὸς ἀλλήλους, *and when they agreed not among themselves.* This may have been the real cause of their inaction in the matter of the Apostle's trial. He would not have been without a party of supporters among their own body.

For ἀσύμφωνος, cf. Wisdom xviii. 10, ἀσύμφωνος βοή, 'an ill-according cry' (A.V.).

πρὸς τοὺς πατέρας ὑμῶν, *unto your fathers.* 'Your' rather than 'our' of *Text. recept.* is in accord with the spirit in which St Paul is speaking. He would wish to distinguish these obstinate Jews from himself and others who received the words of the Old Testament as fulfilled in Jesus.

26. λέγων, *saying.* The passage which the Apostle quotes is from Isaiah vi. 9, and had already been quoted by our Lord Himself against the Jews (Matt. xiii. 14; Mark iv. 12; Luke viii. 10; see also John xii. 40) when He was explaining why all His teaching was given in parables. He spake in this wise first because had He said openly all that He wished to teach He would have had far less chance of acceptance than when His message was veiled under a parable; and next He so spake that those only who cared to manifest a desire to know the deeper meaning of His words might be able to do so. His words were for those who had ears to hear. But most of those to whom he spake had not.

λέγων is masculine, though τὸ πνεῦμα is the noun to which it refers, because of the personality of the speaker.

ἀκοῇ, *by hearing,* i.e. with the outward organs ye shall catch what is said, but since ye have no heart for the message, ye shall not understand.

27. καὶ ἐπιστρέψωσιν, *and should turn again.* This rendering is to be preferred on account of the restricted meaning which in modern speech has become attached to the word 'convert' of the A.V. In the older language it signified 'to turn round and go back again.'

28. τοῦτο τὸ σωτήριον τοῦ θεοῦ, *this salvation of God.* St Paul would be very anxious to press on them that the doctrine which he was preaching and they were rejecting, that *this,* was the very message of God's way of salvation.

αὐτοὶ καὶ ἀκούσονται, *they will also hear.* The Apostle does not wish to convey, as the A.V. does, a taunt to the Jews that they come behind the Gentiles. What he wants to express is, that the message has been given according to Christ's command to the Jews everywhere, for Rome may be regarded as the centre of the then known world, and now the time has come when the Gentiles should in their turn be privileged to have everywhere the offers of the Gospel. They also will now hear (as well as you), though they have been looked upon by strict Jews as beyond the pale of salvation.

29. For the authorities which warrant the omission of this verse, see notes on various readings.

30. St Paul's Preaching and Notice of his Release.

30. ἐνέμεινεν δέ, *and he remained.* The non-insertion of the proper name by the oldest MSS. here comes about because they had nothing of verse 29. It is only the addition of that verse which rendered Παῦλος here needful to the sense.

διετίαν ὅλην, *two whole years.* Of these years we have no history, except such as we can gather from the four Epistles which were written from Rome during the time (see above on verse 16). We know that from first to last the chain galled both his body and mind (Eph. iii. 1, iv. 1; Phil. i. 13, 16; Col. iv. 18; Philem. verses 1, 9, 10), and that his case was at times an object of much anxiety (Phil. ii. 23, 24). We also learn from the same letters that beside Luke and Aristarchus (Acts xxvii. 27), he had also the fellowship, for some time at least, of Tychicus, who (Eph. vi. 21) was the bearer of his letter to Ephesus ; of Timothy, whom (Phil. i. 1 ; Col. i. 1 ; Philem. 1) he joins with himself in the greeting to the Churches of Philippi and Colossæ and also in that to Philemon. In the former of these Churches Timothy had been a fellow-labourer with the Apostle. Epaphroditus came with the Philippian contributions to the need of the imprisoned Apostle (Phil. iv. 18). Onesimus found out St Paul when in flight from his master he made his way to Rome (Col. iv. 9 ; Philem. 10). Mark, the cousin of Barnabas, was also there, and another Jewish convert, Jesus, called Justus, of whom we only know that the Apostle considered him worthy to be called a fellow-worker unto the kingdom of God (Col. iv. 10, 11). Epaphras, from the churches in Laodicea and Hierapolis, had come to visit Paul, and to bring him the greetings doubtless of the Christians there, and carry back some words of earnest counsel and advice from the Roman prisoner (Col. iv. 12). Last of all Demas was there, soon after to be mentioned as having forsaken the good way through love of this present world (Col. iv. 14 ; 2 Tim. iv. 10). More than this and the few words in this verse we do not know of this first imprisonment.

ἐν ἰδίῳ μισθώματι, *in his own hired house.* This was probably a later arrangement than the ξενία spoken of in verse 23. The means for such hiring were provided by the liberality of the Philippians and others, for the Apostle could no longer with his own hands minister even to his own wants.

πάντας τοὺς εἰσπορευομένους πρὸς αὐτόν, *all that went unto him.* For the fulness of Gospel freedom had now been reached, and the word of God and the kingdom of God were open to all who sought unto them.

31. μετὰ πάσης παρρησίας ἀκωλύτως, *with all confidence* (Rev. Vers. 'boldness'), *no man forbidding him.* παρρησία implies that 'freedom of speech' which was looked upon by the Athenians as the great mark of their liberty. For ἀκωλύτως cf. Josephus, *Ant.* xii. 1. 12.

For Englishmen there must arise the thought that perhaps from some of those Roman soldiers who heard Paul in his prison the message of the Gospel came first to our island.

The historian had now reached the end of his work, and does not even tell the manner of the Apostle's release, though as he mentions the duration of the imprisonment, he must have known how he came to be liberated. But that concerned not the purpose of his record, and so he has no word more. " *Victoria Verbi Dei. Paulus Romæ. Apex Evangelii. Actorum Finis* " (Bengel).

GENERAL INDEX.

INDEX OF GREEK WORDS.

THE PITT PRESS SERIES

AND THE

CAMBRIDGE SERIES FOR SCHOOLS AND TRAINING COLLEGES.

Volumes of the latter series are marked by a **dagger** †.

COMPLETE LIST

GREEK

Author	Work	Editor	Price
Aeschylus	Prometheus Vinctus	Rackham	2/6
Aristophanes	Aves—Plutus—Ranae	Green	3/6 *each*
,,	Nubes, Vespae	Graves	3/6 *each*
,,	Acharnians	,,	3/-
Demosthenes	Olynthiacs	Glover	2/6
,,	Philippics I, II, III	G. A. Davies	2/6
Euripides	Alcestis	Hadley	2/6
,,	Hecuba	Hadley	2/6
,,	Helena	Pearson	3/6
,,	Heraclidae	Pearson	3/6
,,	Hercules Furens	Gray & Hutchinson	2/-
,,	Hippolytus	Hadley	2/-
,,	Iphigeneia in Aulis	Headlam	2/6
,,	Medea	,,	2/6
,,	Orestes	Wedd	4/6
,,	Phoenissae	Pearson	4/-
Herodotus	Book V	Shuckburgh	3/-
,,	,, IV, VI, VIII, IX	,,	4/- *each*
,,	,, IX 1—89	,,	2/6
Homer	Odyssey IX, X	Edwards	2/6 *each*
,,	,, XXI	,,	2/-
,,	,, XI	Nairn	2/-
,,	Iliad VI, XXII, XXIII, XXIV	Edwards	**2/-** *each*
,,	Iliad IX and X	Lawson	2/6
Lucian	Somnium, Charon, etc.	Heitland	3/6
,,	Menippus and Timon	Mackie	3/6
Plato	Apologia Socratis	Adam	3/6
,,	Crito, Euthyphro	,,	2/6 *each*
,,	Protagoras	J. & A. M. Adam	4/6
Plutarch	Demosthenes	Holden	4/6
,,	Gracchi	,,	6/-
,,	Nicias	,,	5/-
,,	Sulla	,,	6/-
,,	Timoleon	,,	6/-

30000
8/9/09

GREEK continued

Author	Work	Editor	Price
Sophocles	Oedipus Tyrannus	Jebb	4/-
Thucydides	Book III	Spratt	5/-
,,	Book VI	,,	6/-
,,	Book VII	Holden	5/-
Xenophon	Agesilaus	Hailstone	2/6
,,	Anabasis I, II	Pretor	4/-
,,	,, I, III, IV, V	,,	2/- each
,,	,, II, VI, VII	,,	2/6 each
† ,,	,, I, II, III, IV, V, VI	Edwards	1/6 each
	(With complete Vocabularies)		
,,	Hellenics I, II		3/6
,,	Cyropaedeia I	Shuckburgh	2/6
,,	,, II	,,	2/-
,,	,, III, IV, V	Holden	5/-
,,	,, VI, VII, VIII	,,	5/-
,,	Memorabilia I, II	Edwards	2/6 each

LATIN

The volumes marked * contain Vocabulary

Author	Work	Editor	Price
Bede	Eccl. History III, IV	Mayor & Lumby	7/6
Caesar	De Bello Gallico		
	Com. I, III, VI, VIII	Peskett	1/6 each
,,	,, II–III, and VII	,,	2/- each
,,	,, I–III	,,	3/-
,,	,, IV–V	,,	1/6
*† ,,	,, I, II, III, IV, V, VI, VII	Shuckburgh	1/6 each
,,	De Bello Gallico. Bk I	,,	-/9
	(With Vocabulary only: no notes)		
,,	De Bello Gallico. Bk VII		-/8
	(Text only)		
,,	De Bello Civili. Com. I	Peskett	3/-
,,	,, ,, Com. III	,,	2/6
Cicero	Actio Prima in C. Verrem	Cowie	1/6
,,	De Amicitia, De Senectute	Reid	3/6 each
,,	De Officiis. Bk III	Holden	2/-
,,	Pro Lege Manilia	Nicol	1/6
,,	Div. in Q. Caec. et Actio Prima in C. Verrem	Heitland & Cowie	3/-
,,	Ep. ad Atticum. Lib. II	Pretor	3/-
,,	Orations against Catiline	Nicol	2/6
*† ,,	In Catilinam I	Flather	1/6
,,	Philippica Secunda	Peskett	3/6
,,	Pro Archia Poeta	Reid	2/-
,,	,, Balbo	,,	1/6
,,	,, Milone	Reid	2/6
,,	,, Murena	Heitland	3/-
,,	,, Plancio	Holden	4/6
,,	,, Roscio	J. C. Nicol	2/6
,,	,, Sulla	Reid	3/6
,,	Somnium Scipionis	Pearman	2/-

LATIN *continued*

Author	Work	Editor	Price
*Cornelius Nepos	Four parts	Shuckburgh	1/6 each
*Erasmus	Colloquia Latina	G. M. Edwards	1/6
,,	Colloquia Latina	,,	-/9
	(*With Vocabulary only: no notes*)		
* ,,	Altera Colloquia Latina	,,	1/6
Horace	Epistles. Bk I	Shuckburgh	2/6
,,	Odes and Epodes	Gow	5/-
,,	Odes. Books I, III	,,	2/- each
,,	,, Books II, IV; Epodes	,,	1/6 each
,,	Satires. Book I	,,	2/-
Juvenal	Satires	Duff	5/-
Livy	Book I	H. J. Edwards	*In the Press*
,,	,, II	Conway	2/6
,,	,, IV, XXVII	Stephenson	2/6 each
,,	,, V	Whibley	2/6
,,	,, VI	Marshall	2/6
,,	,, IX	Anderson	2/6
,,	,, XXI, XXII	Dimsdale	2/6 each
* ,, (adapted from)	Story of the Kings of Rome	G. M. Edwards	1/6
* ,, ,,	Horatius and other Stories	,,	1/6
,,	,, ,, ,,	,,	-/9
	(*With ,, ,, only: no notes*)		
Lucan	Pharsalia. Bk I	Heitland & Haskins	1/6
,,	De Bello Civili. Bk VII	Postgate	2/-
Lucretius	Books III and V	Duff	2/- each
Ovid	Fasti. Book VI	Sidgwick	1/6
,,	Metamorphoses, Bk I	Dowdall	1/6
,,	,, Bk VIII	Summers	1/6
* ,,	Phaethon and other stories	G. M. Edwards	1/6
*† ,,	Selections from the Tristia	Simpson	1/6
*†Phaedrus	Fables. Bks I and II	Flather	1/6
Plautus	Epidicus	Gray	3/-
,,	Stichus	Fennell	2/6
,,	Trinummus	Gray	3/6
Pliny	Letters. Book VI	Duff	2/6
Quintus Curtius	Alexander in India	Heitland & Raven	3/6
Sallust	Catiline	Summers	2/-
,,	Jugurtha	,,	2/6
Tacitus	Agricola and Germania	Stephenson	3/-
,,	Hist. Bk I	Davies	2/6
,,	,, Bk III	Summers	2/6
Terence	Hautontimorumenos	Gray	3/-
Vergil	Aeneid I to XII	Sidgwick	1/6 each
*† ,,	,, I, II, III, V, VI, IX, X, XI, XII	,,	1/6 each
,,	Bucolics	,,	1/6
,,	Georgics I, II, and III, IV	,,	2/- each
,,	Complete Works, Vol. I, Text	,,	3/6
,,	,, ,, Vol. II, Notes	,,	4/6
,,	Opera Omnia	B. H. Kennedy	3/6

FRENCH

*The volumes marked * contain Vocabulary*

Author	Work	Editor	Price
About	Le Roi des Montagnes	Ropes	2/-
Balzac	Le Médecin de Campagne	Payen Payne	3/-
*Biart	Quand j'étais petit, Pts I, II	Boïelle	2/- each
Boileau	L'Art Poétique	Nichol Smith	2/6
Corneille	Polyeucte	Braunholtz	2/-
,,	Le Cid	Eve	2/-
De Bonnechose	Lazare Hoche	Colbeck	2/-
* ,,	Bertrand du Guesclin	Leathes	2/-
* ,,	,, Part II	,,	1/6
D'Harleville	Le Vieux Célibataire	G. Masson	2/-
Delavigne	Louis XI	Eve	2/-
,,	Les Enfants d'Edouard	,,	2/-
De Lamartine	Jeanne d'Arc	Clapin & Ropes	1/6
De Vigny	La Canne de Jonc	Eve	1/6
*Dumas	La Fortune de D'Artagnan	Ropes	2/-
*Enault	Le Chien du Capitaine	Verrall	2/-
Erckmann-Chatrian	La Guerre	Clapin	3/-
,,	Waterloo, Le Blocus	Ropes	3/- each
,,	Madame Thérèse	,,	3/-
,,	Histoire d'un Conscrit	,,	3/-
Gautier	Voyage en Italie (Selections)	Payen Payne	3/-
Guizot	Discours sur l'Histoire de la		
	Révolution d'Angleterre	Eve	2/6
Hugo	Les Burgraves	,,	2/6
,,	Selected Poems	,,	
Lemercier	Frédégonde et Brunehaut	G. Masson	2/-
*Malot	Remi et ses Amis	Verrall	2/-
* ,,	Remi en Angleterre	,,	2/-
Merimée	Colomba (*Abridged*)	Ropes	2/-
Michelet	Louis XI & Charles the Bold	,,	2/6
Molière	Le Bourgeois Gentilhomme	Clapin	1/6
,,	L'École des Femmes	Saintsbury	2/6
,,	Les Précieuses ridicules	Braunholtz	2/-
,,	,, (*Abridged Edition*)	,,	1/-
,,	Le Misanthrope	,,	2/6
,,	L'Avare	,,	2/6
*Perrault	Fairy Tales	Rippmann	1/6
,,	,,	,,	-/9
	(*With Vocabulary only: no notes*)		
Piron	La Métromanie	Masson	2/-
Ponsard	Charlotte Corday	Ropes	2/-
Racine	Les Plaideurs	Braunholtz	2/-
,,	,, (*Abridged Edition*)	,,	1/-
,,	Athalie	Eve	2/-
Saintine	Picciola	Ropes	2/-
Sandeau	Mdlle de la Seiglière	,,	2/-
Scribe & Legouvé	Bataille de Dames	Bull	2/-
Scribe	Le Verre d'Eau	Colbeck	2/-
Sédaine	Le Philosophe sans le savoir	Bull	2/-

FRENCH *continued*

Author	Work	Editor	Price
Souvestre	Un Philosophe sous les Toits	Eve	2/-
,,	Le Serf & Le Chevrier de Lorraine	Ropes	2/-
*Souvestre	Le Serf	Ropes	1/6
,,		,,	-/9
	(*With Vocabulary only: no notes*)		
Spencer	A Primer of French Verse		3/-
Staël, Mme de	Le Directoire	Masson & Prothero	2/-
,,	Dix Années d'Exil (Book II chapters 1—8)	,,	2/-
Thierry	Lettres sur l'histoire de France (XIII—XXIV)	,,	2/6
,,	Récits des Temps Mérovingiens, 1—III	Masson & Ropes	3/-
Voltaire	Histoire du Siècle de Louis XIV, in three parts	Masson & Prothero	2/6 *each*
Xavier de Maistre	{ La Jeune Sibérienne. Le Lépreux de la Cité d'Aoste }	Masson	1/6

GERMAN

*The volumes marked * contain Vocabulary*

*Andersen	Eight Stories	Rippmann	2/6
Benedix	Dr Wespe	Breul	3/-
Freytag	Der Staat Friedrichs des Grossen	Wagner	2/-
,,	Die Journalisten	Eve	2/6
Goethe	Knabenjahre (1749—1761)	Wagner & Cartmell	2/-
,,	Hermann und Dorothea	,, ,,	3/6
,,	Iphigenie auf Tauris	Breul	3/6
*Grimm	Twenty Stories	Rippmann	3/-
Gutzkow	Zopf und Schwert	Wolstenholme	3/6
Hackländer	Der geheime Agent	E. L. Milner Barry	3/-
Hauff	Das Bild des Kaisers	Breul	3/-
,,	Das Wirthshaus im Spessart	Schlottmann & Cartmell	3/-
,,	Die Karavane	Schlottmann	3/-
*,,	Der Scheik von Alessandria	Rippmann	2/6
Immermann	Der Oberhof	Wagner	3/-
*Klee	Die deutschen Heldensagen	Wolstenholme	3/-
Kohlrausch	Das Jahr 1813	Cartmell	2/-
Lessing	Minna von Barnhelm	Wolstenholme	3/-
Lessing & Gellert	Selected Fables	Breul	3/-
Raumer	Der erste Kreuzzug	Wagner	2/-
Riehl	Culturgeschichtliche Novellen	Wolstenholme	3/-
*,,	Die Ganerben & Die Gerechtigkeit Gottes	,,	3/-
Schiller	Wilhelm Tell	Breul	2/6
,,	,, (*Abridged Edition*)	,,	1/6

GERMAN *continued*

Author	Work	Editor	Price
Schiller	Geschichte des dreissigjäh-rigen Kriegs. Book III.	Breul	3/-
,,	Maria Stuart	,,	3/6
,,	Wallenstein I.	,,	3/6
,,	Wallenstein II.	,,	3/6
Sybel	Prinz Eugen von Savoyen	Quiggin	2/6
Uhland	Ernst, Herzog von Schwaben	Wolstenholme	3/6
	German Dactylic Poetry	Wagner	3/-
	Ballads on German History	,,	2/-

SPANISH

Le Sage & Isla	Los Ladrones de Asturias	Kirkpatrick	3/-
Galdós	Trafalgar	,,	4/-

ENGLISH

	Historical Ballads	Sidgwick	1/6
	Old Ballads	,,	1/6
Bacon	History of the Reign of King Henry VII	Lumby	3/-
,,	Essays	West	3/6
,,	New Atlantis	G. C. M. Smith	1/6
Burke	American Speeches	Innes	3/-
Chaucer	Prologue and Knight's Tale	M. Bentinck-Smith	2/6
,,	Clerkes Tale and Squires Tale	Winstanley	2/6
Cowley	Prose Works	Lumby	4/-
Defoe	Robinson Crusoe, Part I	Masterman	2/-
Earle	Microcosmography	West	3/- & 4/-
Goldsmith	Traveller and Deserted Village	Murison	1/6
Gray	Poems	Tovey	4/-
† ,,	Ode on the Spring and The Bard	,,	8d.
† ,,	Ode on the Spring and The Elegy	,,	8d.
Kingsley	The Heroes	E. A. Gardner	1/6
Lamb	Tales from Shakespeare. 2 Series	Flather	1/6 each
Macaulay	Lord Clive	Innes	1/6
,,	Warren Hastings	,,	1/6
,,	William Pitt and Earl of Chatham	,,	2/6
† ,,	John Bunyan	,,	1/-
† ,,	John Milton	Flather	1/6
,,	Lays and other Poems	,,	1/6
,,	History of England Chaps. I—III	Reddaway	2/-
Mayor	A Sketch of Ancient Philosophy from Thales to Cicero		3/6
,,	Handbook of English Metre		2/-
Milton	Arcades	Verity	1/6
,,	Ode on the Nativity, L'Alle-gro, Il Penseroso & Lycidas	,,	2/6
† ,,	Comus & Lycidas	,,	2/-
,,	Samson Agonistes	,,	2/6
,,	Sonnets	,,	1/6
,,	Paradise Lost, six parts	,,	2/- each
More	History of King Richard III	Lumby	3/6

ENGLISH *continued*

Author	Work	Editor	Price
More	Utopia	Lumby	2/-
Pope	Essay on Criticism	West	2/-
Scott	Marmion	Masterman	2/6
,,	Lady of the Lake	,,	2/6
,,	Lay of the last Minstrel	Flather	2/-
,,	Legend of Montrose	Simpson	2/6
,,	Lord of the Isles	Flather	2/-
,,	Old Mortality	Nicklin	2/6
,,	Kenilworth	Flather	2/6
,,	The Talisman	A. S. Gaye	2/-
,,	Quentin Durward	Murison	2/-
Shakespeare	A Midsummer-Night's Dream	Verity	1/6
,,	Twelfth Night	,,	1/6
,,	Julius Caesar	,,	1/6
,,	The Tempest	,,	1/6
,,	King Lear	,,	1/6
,,	Merchant of Venice	,,	1/6
,,	King Richard II	,,	1/6
,,	As You Like It	,,	1/6
,,	King Henry V	,,	1/6
,,	Macbeth	,,	1/6
Shakespeare & Fletcher	Two Noble Kinsmen	Skeat	3/6
Sidney	An Apologie for Poetrie	Shuckburgh	3/-
Spenser	Fowre Hymnes	Miss Winstanley	2/-
Wordsworth	Selected Poems	Miss Thomson	1/6

West	Elements of English Grammar		2/6
,,	English Grammar for Beginners		1/-
,,	Key to English Grammars		3/6 *net*
Carlos	Short History of British India		1/-
Mill	Elementary Commercial Geography		1/6
Bartholomew	Atlas of Commercial Geography		3/-
Robinson	Church Catechism Explained		2/-
Jackson	The Prayer Book Explained. Part I		2/6

MATHEMATICS

Ball	Elementary Algebra		4/6
†Blythe	Geometrical Drawing		
	Part I		2/6
	Part II		2/-
Euclid	Books I—VI, XI, XII	H. M. Taylor	5/-
,,	Books I—VI	,,	4/-
,,	Books I—IV	,,	3/-
	Also separately		
,,	Books I, & II; III, & IV; V, & VI; XI, & XII 1/6 *each*		
,,	Solutions to Exercises in Taylor's		
	Euclid	W. W. Taylor	10/6
	And separately		
,,	Solutions to Bks I—IV	,,	6/-
,,	Solutions to Books VI. XI	,,	6/-

7

MATHEMATICS *continued*

Author	Work	Editor	Price
Hobson & Jessop	Elementary Plane Trigonometry		4/6
Loney	Elements of Statics and Dynamics		7/6
	Part I. Elements of Statics		4/6
	„ II. Elements of Dynamics		3/6
„	Elements of Hydrostatics		4/6
,,	Solutions to Examples, Hydrostatics		5/-
,,	Solutions of Examples, Statics and Dynamics		7/6
,,	Mechanics and Hydrostatics		4/6
Smith, C.	Arithmetic for Schools, with or without answers		3/6
,,	Part I. Chapters I—VIII. Elementary, with or without answers		2/-
,,	Part II. Chapters IX—XX, with or without answers		2/-
Hale, G.	Key to Smith's Arithmetic		7/6

EDUCATIONAL SCIENCE

†Bidder & Baddeley	Domestic Economy		4/6
†Bosanquet	{The Education of the Young from the *Republic* of Plato}		2/6
†Burnet	Aristotle on Education		2/6
Comenius	Life and Educational Works	S. S. Laurie	3/6
Farrar	General Aims of the Teacher } 1 vol.		1/6
Poole	Form Management }		
†Hope & Browne	A Manual of School Hygiene		3/6
Locke	Thoughts on Education	R. H. Quick	3/6
†MacCunn	The Making of Character		2/6
Milton	Tractate on Education	O. Browning	2/-
Sidgwick	On Stimulus		1/-
Thring	Theory and Practice of Teaching		4/6

†Woodward	A Short History of the Expansion of the British Empire (1500—1902)		4/-
† „	An Outline History of the British Empire (1500—1902)		1/6 *net*

CAMBRIDGE UNIVERSITY PRESS

London: FETTER LANE, E.C.

C. F. CLAY, Manager

Edinburgh: 100, PRINCES STREET